With Faith in God and Heart and Mind

With Faith in God and Heart and Mind

A History of Omega Psi Phi Fraternity

MAURICE J. HOBSON
EDDIE R. COLE
JIM C. HARPER II
DERRICK P. ALRIDGE

The University of North Carolina Press
Chapel Hill

This book was published with the assistance of the John Hope Franklin Fund of the University of North Carolina Press.

© 2025 Maurice J. Hobson, Eddie R. Cole, Jim C. Harper II, and Derrick P. Alridge
All rights reserved

Set in Minion Pro by Westchester Publishing Services
Manufactured in the United States of America

Library of Congress Cataloging-in-Publication Data
Names: Hobson, Maurice J., author. | Cole, Eddie Rice, II, author. |
   Harper, Jim C., author. | Alridge, Derrick P., author.
Title: With faith in God and heart and mind : a history of Omega Psi Phi
   Fraternity / Brothers Maurice J. Hobson, Eddie R. Cole, Jim C. Harper,
   and Derrick Alridge.
Description: Chapel Hill : The University of North Carolina Press, 2025. |
   Includes bibliographical references and index.
Identifiers: LCCN 2022053974 | ISBN 9781469673196 (cloth ; alk. paper) |
   ISBN 9781469673202 (ebook)
Subjects: LCSH: Omega Psi Phi Fraternity–History. | African American Greek
   letter societies. | African American college students–Political activity. |
   Civil rights movements–United States–History—20th century.
Classification: LCC LJ75.O55 H63 2023 | DDC 371.8/550973–dc23/eng/20221123
LC record available at https://lccn.loc.gov/2022053974

Cover art: (*top*) From Omega Psi Phi Fraternity, Inc., Alpha Chapter, *The Oracle*,
May 1924, 28; (*bottom*) photo of October 22, 2022, Howard University Homecoming
by Maurice J. Hobson; thanks to Michael Fair for design advice on including the
fraternity shield.

For product safety concerns under the European Union's General Product
Safety Regulation (EU GPSR), please contact gpsr@mare-nostrum.co.uk or
write to the University of North Carolina Press and Mare Nostrum Group B.V.,
Mauritskade 21D, 1091 GC Amsterdam, The Netherlands.

Contents

Introduction, 1

Chapter 1 We Will Build a Fraternity, 11
   Intellectual Foundations, 1909–1920

Chapter 2 An Unusual Emphasis on Scholarship, 44
   The Success and Challenge of Expanding Black Educational Opportunity, 1920–1929

Chapter 3 Through Days of Joy or Years of Pain, 92
   Omega Psi Phi Fraternity Responds during the Great Depression and World War II, 1930–1945

Chapter 4 Safeguarding Civil Rights, 127
   Omega Men and the Postwar Fight for Racial Equality, 1946–1959

Chapter 5 Bloody, but Unbowed, 175
   Omega Psi Phi Fraternity during the Modern Civil Rights Movement, 1960–1969

Chapter 6 Keeping Our Lamps Trimmed and Burning, 204
   Critical Crossroads in Omega Psi Phi Fraternity, 1970–1989

Chapter 7 Holding Aloft Vistas of Purple and Gold, 248
   Omega Psi Phi Fraternity, 1990 to the Present

Conclusion, 275

Acknowledgments, 281
Notes, 283
Index, 357

A gallery of images begins on page 167.

With Faith in God and Heart and Mind

Introduction

The history of the Omega Psi Phi Fraternity is African American history. From the period of the organization's founding in 1911 to the present, Omega Psi Phi members have engaged in the mission of Black uplift. Omega men have served as presidents, professors, and in various other capacities at colleges and universities. They closed ranks as soldiers and officers in the armed forces during numerous wars, and they excelled as prominent intellectuals in the Negro Literary Movement after World War I. Omega men have been pioneers in science and medicine. Robert Henry Lawrence Jr. was the first Black astronaut; Ronald McNair was the second Black American astronaut to be sent to space; Charles Bolden was a prominent astronaut and administrator at the National Aeronautics and Space Administration; and Frederick Gregory was the first Black astronaut to fly a space shuttle.[1] The Fraternity's membership also has noted scholars. They include historians Luther P. Jackson, Earl E. Thorpe and James D. Anderson, poets and literary scholars Langston Hughes and Sterling A. Brown, and college presidents Benjamin E. Mays, James M. Nabrit Jr., and Walter N. Ridley. In addition to those roles, Omega men have been civil rights leaders and elected officials. One Omega man, Jesse L. Jackson Sr., was even a serious candidate for the US presidency. The Fraternity also has produced numerous entertainers, athletes, musicians, and artists who have made innumerable accomplishments in education and civic society.

Three Howard University undergraduates—Edgar Amos Love, Oscar James Cooper, and Frank Coleman—and their faculty adviser, Ernest Everett Just, an associate professor of biology, founded the Omega Psi Phi Fraternity on November 17, 1911. At the time, they could not have known the impact the Fraternity would have in the United States, nor could they have foreseen the organization's expansion around the world. Despite Omega Psi Phi's noteworthy achievements, the breadth of the Fraternity's contributions is largely unknown among the American populace. Countless members of mainstream society recognize the Fraternity primarily for its celebrity sports and entertainer figures and unofficial image, the "Que Dog." To be clear, Omega men have embraced various aspects of those popular representations of the Fraternity; however, they also have made significant contributions to humanity in a wide array of fields that impact every sector of American life. In chronicling such contributions, *With Faith in God and Heart and Mind: A History of Omega Psi Phi Fraternity* offers readers an opportunity to gain valuable insight into this collegiate Fraternity's storied history of assisting the long struggle for Black freedom in the United States and abroad.

Edgar A. Love, Oscar J. Cooper, Frank Coleman, and Ernest E. Just established the Fraternity's Alpha chapter at Howard University on December 15, 1911. Coleman served as Basileus, Love as Keeper of Records, and Cooper as Keeper of Seals. The organization held its first Grand Conclave, or national meeting, in 1912. Two years later, on the eve of World War I, Omega Psi Phi established Beta chapter at Lincoln University near Oxford, Pennsylvania. In 1916, the Fraternity established Gamma chapter in Boston, Massachusetts. During the next two years, after the United States entered the war officially, Omega men also trained to become officers at the Fort Des Moines Army Base in Iowa—the War chapter—as well as at Camp Howard on the campus of Howard University. In 1919, as world powers convened in Paris, France, to negotiate a formal end to war, Omega Psi Phi established three more chapters: Delta at Meharry Medical College in Nashville, Tennessee; Epsilon in New York, New York; and Zeta at Virginia Union University in Richmond.[2]

Omega Psi Phi's first decade coincided with an era of race uplift. Proponents called on Black people with formal education, among other means, to lift other Black people as they themselves climbed to greater heights than preceding generations. Omega men who answered the call included Charles Young, who as a colonel was the highest ranking Black American in the US Army, and historian Carter G. Woodson, who established the Association for the Study of Negro Life and History in 1915 and the *Journal of Negro History* in 1916. Notably, in 1926, Woodson began Negro History Week, which subsequently became Black History Month.

In the spring of 1919, as Young and Woodson made great strides in their respective fields, Omega Psi Phi launched *The Oracle*, a publication that ultimately became the official organ of the Fraternity. Stanley Moreland Douglas (who later served as assistant attorney general in New York from 1944 to 1971) was *The Oracle*'s first editor. Under his leadership, the publication highlighted various accomplishments of the Fraternity and its members while expressing support for racial uplift consistent with other Black publications of the early twentieth century.

The academic literature on Omega Psi Phi is sparse but growing. Two major book-length texts exist: Herman Dreer's *The History of Omega Psi Phi Fraternity: A Brotherhood of Negro College Men, 1911 to 1939* (1940) and Robert L. Gill's *The Omega Psi Phi Fraternity and the Men Who Made Its History: A Concise History* (1963).[3] Dreer's institutional history chronicled the Fraternity's first twenty-eight years, offering a detailed history of major events, members, and challenges. He utilized numerous primary sources, including the original minutes from the Fraternity's founding, membership certificates, correspondences, and conversations with members to recount its establishment, policy, and practices. Published in 1963, a pivotal year in the civil rights movement, Gill's book complemented other texts released as scholars and scholar-activists planted the seeds of Black studies programs at colleges and universities. Gill presented the Fraternity within that historical context and identified Omega men who impacted American society at the time. His book also provided a litany of data, notably as an appendix, including lists of chapters and charter years, lists of national officers, and Grand Conclave locations between 1911 and 1961. Both Dreer and Gill provide some valuable information about the early years, such as details about Alpha, Beta, and Gamma chapters, that we do not attempt to fully rehash in this book.

The Dreer and Gill texts are important annals of the Fraternity, but, more recently, Kyle Yeldell's *The Soul of Omega: A History of Psi Chapter of Omega Psi Phi Fraternity, Inc. at Morehouse College* (2022) is a noteworthy book that appeared during the writing of *With Faith in God and Heart and Mind*.[4] Yeldell's work illuminated vital roles that Omega men initiated at Psi chapter performed in politics, industry, education, and the sciences during the first century of that chapter's existence. Besides such national and local chapter histories, rarer but notable shorter academic articles about Omega Psi Phi are also insightful. Scholars, both members and nonmembers, have taken keen interest in the Fraternity and its role in the Black freedom movement. For example, in 2016, Wendy M. Laybourn and Gregory S. Parks published an article titled "Omega Psi Phi Fraternity and the Fight for Civil Rights" in the *Wake Forest Journal of Law and Policy*.[5] Their eighty-eight-page account of Omega challenged legal scholars to rethink the history of struggles for Black freedom that long centered on formal civil rights organizations. Laybourn and Parks contended that Black fraternities and sororities were key networks that helped propel the civil rights campaigns of the mid-twentieth century. Omega Psi Phi was a leader among those Black Greek-letter organizations. In 2020, Judson L. Jeffries published "Malcolm X, the Omega Psi Phi Fraternity, Inc., and Morgan State College" in *Spectrum: A Journal on Black Men*.[6] Jeffries focused on Pi chapter during the 1960s, emphasizing its hosting famed Black Islamic leader Malcolm X in 1962. Although primarily about one event in that chapter's history, Jeffries invited readers to reconsider Omega Psi Phi within the context of the broader fight for racial equality. Paired alongside the occasional dissertation or thesis about the Fraternity, such academic articles are important, albeit brief, historical accounts of Omega men and their activities.

Despite the dearth of major books and the relative sparsity of academic articles that deal singularly with Omega Psi Phi, scholars have written much about Black Greek-letter organizations. Susan L. Smith's 1995 prize-winning book, *Sick and Tired of Being Sick and Tired*, discussed, among other things, how Alpha Kappa Alpha's Mississippi Health Project was a critical point in Black health activism before World War II.[7] Treva B. Lindsey, in a 2017 book titled *Colored No More*, highlighted the efforts of Black sorority women in relation to voting.[8] Those are only two exceptional books that demonstrate how Black sororities have been productive social engines.

Black fraternities have been equally as productive as Black sororities; however, not all fraternities update their official history books regularly. For several decades, many Omega men have expressed the need for a new fraternity book, particularly considering how much has occurred within the Fraternity in the sixty years since the publication of *The Omega Psi Phi Fraternity and the Men Who Made Its History* by Gill. Since his book's release in 1963, Omega men have captured national and international attention for leadership in a variety of fields. In the 1970s, Earl Graves Sr. launched *Black Enterprise* magazine, which became one of the world's most prominent Black business publications. In the 1980s, Jesse L. Jackson Sr. ran a prominent race for the US presidency. In the 1990s, Vernon Jordan Jr. became one of the most powerful political figures in US history when he served as an adviser for US president William (Bill) Clinton. At the same time, professional basketball player Michael Jordan solidified himself as one of the greatest athletes in sports history.

Graves, Jackson, both Jordans, and the previously mentioned McNair are considered prominent political, scientific, business, and sports pioneers; however, thousands of lesser-known members of the Fraternity have played comparably important roles in society from the late twentieth century through the early twenty-first century. Unfortunately, the contributions of the latter group of Omega men and the plethora of societal changes attributable to the Fraternity's programs during recent decades remain largely unknown due to the absence of an updated organizational history. *With Faith in God and Heart and Mind* helps fill that gap by extending the book-length scholarship of Dreer and Gill to include the more recent study of the history of Omega Psi Phi and its members' work in civil rights, education, science, and civic life.

It is important to note that Omega Psi Phi did not develop in a vacuum. Instead, the organization evolved alongside other Black Greek-letter collegiate fraternities and sororities founded during the twentieth century: Alpha Phi Alpha Fraternity (Cornell University, 1906), Alpha Kappa Alpha Sorority (Howard University, 1908), Kappa Alpha Psi Fraternity (Indiana University, 1911), Delta Sigma Theta Sorority (Howard University, 1913), Phi Beta Sigma Fraternity (Howard University, 1914), Zeta Phi Beta Sorority (Howard University, 1920), Sigma Gamma Rho Sorority (Butler University, 1922), and Iota Phi Theta Fraternity (Morgan State University, 1963). Known as the Divine Nine, those organizations were preceded by Sigma Pi Phi, a fraternity of professional Black men, founded in Philadelphia, Pennsylvania, in 1904. Each one of the abovementioned fraternities and sororities has produced several of the most prominent leaders in American history. Collectively, their organizational histories reveal the vital role Black fraternities and sororities have performed in laying a foundation for Black achievement throughout the country and the world.[9]

Of all the Black Greek-letter histories we read while writing *With Faith in God and Heart and Mind*, historian Paula J. Giddings's *In Search of Sisterhood: Delta Sigma Theta and the Challenge of the Black Sorority Movement* (1988) most influenced our methodological approach.[10] Giddings not only provided a detailed account of Delta's founding, evolution, and leadership, but she also situated Delta within Black history in general and twentieth-century Black women's history. Similarly, our book is both a history of Omega Psi Phi and a history of the Black experience in the United States primarily during the twentieth century that parallels, intersects, and interacts with what historian Vincent G. Harding helped popularize as the "Black freedom struggle."[11] We were guided by questions about what intellectual foundations undergird the Fraternity's mission. We also sought to learn what contributions the Fraternity and its members made in the sciences and the arts as well as in business and civic life. Finally, more generally, we sought to identify what overall role the Fraternity performed in the struggle for Black freedom and equality.

In responding to those questions, we examine the official activities and initiatives of Omega Psi Phi as well as the work of individual Omega men. From the onset of writing this book, we recognized that trying to cover all events, accomplishments, and other transactions of the Fraternity and its members would be futile. Our decisions regarding the scope, focus, and chronology of the book were based on available sources and page-length limitations established by the publisher. Despite such factors, it is our hope that *With Faith in God and Heart and Mind*—which draws its title from the second stanza of the

Fraternity's hymn—will motivate Omega men, entire Omega chapters, and fellow historians to write similar books on Black organizing.

Authoring a book about an organization as old as Omega Psi Phi can be a daunting task. Extant archival data are sparse and scattered. Some data are no longer available. Knowledgeable people have passed away. Hence, the archival work of Omega Psi Phi History and Archives Committee members made *With Faith in God and Heart and Mind* possible.[12] The most valuable single written source for Omega Psi Phi's history is its official organ, *The Oracle*. Since 1919, *The Oracle* has functioned as a repository documenting the institutional history of the Fraternity, various accomplishments of its members, member biographies, updates on policies and procedures of the Fraternity, and accounts of its national and district meetings. *The Oracle* also has been an outlet for engaging issues confronting the Black community. For instance, in 1937, *The Oracle* took up the issue of Black leadership. In a piece titled "Wanted: A New Negro Leadership," Omega man Melvin Beaunorus Tolson, a Beta chapter initiate, wrote: "The Negro is at the bottom of the economic ladder. The Negro is facing the most tremendous issues in his racial life since the Emancipation Proclamation made him a half-free man. Even our mossbacked Negro leaders and misleaders admit this jarring fact as they pronounce their meaningless platitudes in the White Man's Wilderness."[13] Wondering why Black people had not produced another leader comparable to famed Black abolitionist Frederick Douglass, Tolson criticized Black intellectuals, such as William Edward Burghardt Du Bois, Kelly Miller, and James Weldon Johnson for living privileged lives that, Tolson believed, made them unable to provide leadership to the Black masses. While Tolson spoke for himself, his essay was one of many such writings that revealed the intellectual debates that Omega men engaged among themselves. Indeed, *The Oracle* was not simply for celebratory stories and kudos among Omega men. Articles such as Tolson's "Wanted" provided a snapshot of broader societal issues on the minds of Omega men and reflected conversations within the greater Black body politic of the time. The caliber of articles in *The Oracle* matched those in *Crisis, Opportunity, Messenger*, and other respected Black literary publications.

In researching *With Faith in God and Heart and Mind*, we learned about a fugitive manuscript about the Fraternity written by Robert L. Gill, author of *The Omega Psi Phi Fraternity and the Men Who Made Its History*. In a letter dated November 20, 1961, Gill informed Grand Basileus Cary D. Jacobs that his original manuscript was 1,400 pages "exclusive of the *Appendix*."[14] Gill noted further that he had received no critical feedback from Richard

Kenneth Barksdale, an English professor at Morehouse College, who also served on the Fraternity's History Evaluation Committee. Gill's brief reference to a lengthy manuscript intrigued us as well as current members of the Fraternity's History and Archives Committee. We hope the publication of our book will help initiate a search among Omega men and nonmember historians to locate and acquire the manuscript. Its length alone suggests that valuable, detailed information about critical moments in the Fraternity and Black America's history may have been discussed, especially considering three of the Fraternity's four founders were still living at the time Gill prepared the 1,400-page manuscript.

Chapter 1 of *With Faith in God and Heart and Mind* opens with Howard University's incoming class in 1909 and proceeds to examine the relationship of the Fraternity's young founders, their coursework and extracurricular activities, engagement with Howard's faculty, and the Fraternity's founding itself. The chapter reveals the intellectual foundation of the Fraternity by examining the founders and other early members' participation in activities, such as the Howard Dramatics Club, the National Association for the Advancement of Colored People (NAACP), and the military officers training corps in Des Moines, Iowa, as well as at Howard during World War I. The founders' commitment to uplifting Black people is a core idea in the chapter.

Chapter 2 presents an overview of the 1920s, one of the Fraternity's most significant decades. In a careful analysis of Omega men's efforts to expand the Fraternity, the chapter explores the ideological compass that guided the establishment of chapters across the United States and into Canada. Adhering to Carter G. Woodson's forceful charge in 1920 to focus on Black history and literature, the Fraternity's leadership initiated an ambitious campaign to expand educational opportunities for Black Americans. Fraternity chapter expansion was intricately linked to that effort, which ultimately became the Fraternity's first national program. However, the rapid expansion and proliferation of individual chapters' educational programs soon challenged the young collegiate organization. Omega quickly became overwhelmed by too many programs with limited coordination. That occurrence forced the Fraternity's leaders to pause and reconsider their organization's growth in terms of members, chapters, and programs. Consequently, the latter half of the 1920s witnessed a more focused agenda for Omega than during preceding years, and the need for Black leadership in Black schools, especially institutions of higher learning, was a primary focus. The Fraternity executed its influence in assessing the curricular offerings at Black colleges and universities in alignment with the establishment of Omega chapters. In slowing its chapter expansion, the Fraternity took time to help standardize curricular offerings at aspiring Black institutions of higher education.

Chapter 3 addresses the role Omega Psi Phi and various undergraduate and graduate members played during the Great Depression and World War II. The Fraternity and its membership responded to the financial crisis of the depression and to the call to serve in the armed forces. In so doing, Omega men proved to be leaders of business and financial institutions as well as men of honor and valor during military combat. They developed strategies to inform members of the Fraternity of employment opportunities, while a smaller number of Omega men became members of US president Franklin Delano Roosevelt's Federal Council of Negro Affairs, familiarly known as the Black Brain Trust or the Black Cabinet. Yet, other Omega men won appointment to federal, state, or public offices that afforded them the ability to provide sundry valuable opportunities to their fellow Black citizens. All the while, the Fraternity itself needed to maintain a strong fiscal standing as members volunteered or were conscripted into military service, causing local and national membership numbers to fluctuate. Hundreds of Omega men served gallantly in segregated units, including the Tuskegee Airmen and the Montford Point Marines. Concurrently, the Fraternity formed alliances with the NAACP, among other organizations, that later proved to be crucial to addressing the needs of Black Americans as they fought legal battles to end Jim Crow segregation in the 1930s through World War II.

Chapter 4 demonstrates how Omega Psi Phi, immediately following World War II, launched its National Social Action program. Its first years focused on ensuring Black veterans had access to resources that they were entitled to earn for serving. Shortly after that, the Fraternity supported Omega men attorneys in the legal battles to desegregate public transportation and higher education. The National Social Action program also addressed the needs of Black Americans in the areas of public health, housing, civil rights, and education. Among these noteworthy national activities, the chapter illustrates how other Omega men worked to uplift their communities across the nation and abroad, especially in Africa, following the war and during the 1950s.

Chapter 5 opens in 1960 on the eve of the Fraternity's fiftieth anniversary. As Omega men looked forward to celebrating in 1961, the student civil rights uprising shifted much of the focus of the Fraternity and its leadership base in civil rights from older members to younger activist members still enrolled in college. That set the context for the fraternity's role in the development of the Freedom Rides of 1961, the enactment of the Civil Rights Act of 1964 and Voting Rights Act of 1965, and similar legislation that facilitated increased Black agency by, among other acts, encouraging Black citizens to assert themselves by voting in their own interests. Omega's leadership and response to Jim Crow by way of traditional civil rights efforts and the growing Black Power ethos during the 1960s is crucial to understanding the larger and longer struggle for Black liberation in the United States.

Chapter 6 details how Omega Psi Phi navigated the 1970s and 1980s. While Black American citizens enjoyed the previous decades' political, judicial, educational, and other related civil rights victories, the ability to sustain those advances required new leadership. In the early 1970s, new Omega men ascended to leadership roles in civil rights organizations, such as the NAACP and the National Urban League, while later in the decade other Omega men celebrated US president Gerald Rudolph Ford Jr.'s formal recognition of Black History Month—the fruition of Omega man Carter G. Woodson's mission to promote Black American history and culture. By the 1980s, however, issues exacerbated by the conservative US presidential administrations of Richard Nixon and Ronald Reagan were met by the Fraternity's effort to register Black people to vote. The peak of Omega Psi Phi's political organizing was seen when Omega man Jesse L. Jackson Sr. ran for president of the United States. Those moments in Omega history occurred alongside efforts to address national crises around cocaine or crack drug use, the HIV and AIDS epidemic, and militarization of local police departments in the late 1980s.

Chapter 7 pivots from the day-to-day contributions of Omega men to provide a macro-level appraisal of the Fraternity's contributions since 1990. Whereas the 1990s witnessed continued traditions, such as an Omega man becoming the first Black governor in the United States since the Reconstruction Era, that decade also noted significant internal changes. The Fraternity relocated its international headquarters away from Washington, DC, and Omega men turned their attention to literacy issues domestically and aid to African nations abroad. In the new millennium, the Fraternity's Public Policy Forum was a signature event followed by Omega men working closely with the nation's first Black president—Barack Obama—and leading the national fight for justice after state-sanctioned violence against Black people in the 2010s. The chapter demonstrates how Omega men have continued a long-standing tradition of advocating for civil rights.

―――

The development of Omega Psi Phi since 1911 is a byproduct of its founders—three undergraduate students at Howard University and their faculty adviser. Edgar Amos Love, Oscar James Cooper, Frank Coleman, and Ernest Everett Just committed the Fraternity to academic excellence, racial advancement, and cognate ideals that comprise an important through-line to assess the value of Omega's fight for social change since the organization's inception. *With Faith in God and Heart and Mind: A History of Omega Psi Phi Fraternity* provides a historical account of that fight and other notable activities that must be reckoned with, particularly when the most pressing contemporary societal issues are best understood and addressed with critical reflection on the past.

Chapter 1

We Will Build a Fraternity

Intellectual Foundations, 1909–1920

> We sing, And wing, Our thoughts with tongue and pen,
> To mould the Greatest group of thinking men.
>
> —Herman Dreer, "Omega Calls Her Sons of Light"

Friday, November 17, 1911, was cold in Washington, DC. Rain fell most of the day. The weather was inauspicious, but something historic was underway. During that evening, three Howard University undergraduates—Edgar Amos Love, Oscar James Cooper, and Frank Coleman—trekked across campus and through a gate that served as the entryway to Science Hall, a building that housed the office of a twenty-eight-year-old biology professor named Ernest Everett Just. Their subsequent meeting culminated work they began weeks earlier: founding a new fraternity, Omega Psi Phi.[1]

The early history of Omega—the first fraternity founded at a Black college or university—does not simply chronicle the formation of the Fraternity. The history entails a group of young Black men at a Black university in the nation's capital who sought to build an organization whose members were committed to advancing the fight for freedom and equality in which millions of older Black people had fought for decades. Love, Cooper, Coleman, and Just were cognizant of that fight because they were intellectuals who drew extensively from their scholarly pursuits as well as from their personal experiences at Howard University and other educational institutions. In constructing Omega, they represented a vanguard of twentieth-century race men devoted not only to academic excellence but also to societal progress. As this chapter will show, the Fraternity that Love, Cooper, Coleman, and Just birthed in 1911 continued to develop in that socially conscious milieu through 1920. In those nine years, Omega men helped lead the ongoing struggle for first-class citizenship, foreshadowing the organization's involvement in the more familiar civil rights movement of future decades.

Howard University, 1909

Love, Cooper, Coleman, and Just founded Omega Psi Phi fewer than fifty years after the official end of the American Civil War in 1865 and the subsequent enactment of the Thirteenth Amendment, abolishing legal slavery in the United States, during the same year. The Fraternity emerged as many White people continued to ponder, debate, or experiment with ways to solve the so-called Negro problem. In sum, they wanted to do something about Black people who, according to such White people, were inherently inferior and hence incapable of achieving a level of sophistication on par with White people.[2]

Steeped in pseudoscience, numerous Americans—from academicians to politicians—professed the inherent and immutable weaknesses of Black people throughout the world and not simply in the United States. According to such White Americans, their non-White contemporaries were incapable of government, political participation, familial stability, and other embodiments of civilized people. The pseudoscientific movement was as old as the country itself, but it sped during the antebellum period, intensified during the Civil War, and reached a new height during postwar Reconstruction. In 1891, after socially, politically, and culturally conservative White Americans reeled in Reconstruction and rolled out a series of unjust laws to hinder Black advancement, a Virginia-born White author, lawyer, and politician named William Cabell Bruce argued that Black people benefited from being enslaved by White people. He was not alone. Countless Whites of that time—an era that Black historian and Washington, DC, native Rayford Whittingham Logan termed the nadir of postwar Black existence in the United States—claimed that Black people never would be the equals of Whites. Furthermore, human inequality, Bruce and many other White people believed, was God's plan. Unable to adapt to industrialization and to other changing conditions because of divine will, Black people would become extinct in the near future according to some Whites, including some self-described progressives.[3]

During the 1890s and into the 1900s, activist Black Americans created or were instrumental in the creation of several organizations to counter White bias. The American Negro Academy (1897), the National Business League (1900), the Niagara Movement (1905), and the National Association for the Advancement of Colored People (NAACP, 1909) were foremost. Collectively, those organizations and a plethora of smaller, less known organizations challenged White supremacy through rigorous scholarship, the promotion of Black business acumen, and civil rights agitation. As the century progressed, Black fraternities and sororities became valuable contributors to the foregoing efforts. Comprising a significant number of collegiate undergraduates and graduates who epitomized the "talented tenth," fraternity and sorority members performed central roles in achieving racial uplift.[4] Coined by White Baptist minister and missionary Henry Lyman Morehouse, namesake of the Black all-male college in Atlanta, Georgia, and popularized by W. E. B. Du

Bois, the term *talented tenth* described the notion that a small group of extraordinary Black Americans was capable of and indeed responsible for elevating the Black masses.[5]

Black colleges and universities such as Howard and Morehouse were incubators for intellectual development. Among other matters, Black students, professors, and other people at those institutions debated and devised strategies for present and future Black leaders to execute. In the fall of 1909, Booker Taliaferro Washington visited Howard to deliver a talk at the annual opening of the university's medical school. Washington, a Howard trustee who served as president of the Tuskegee Institute, encouraged the Black physicians and aspiring physicians who attended his talk to contribute to racial uplift by improving Black people's health conditions and by expanding their knowledge of proper health care, among other useful practices.[6]

W. E. B. Du Bois, a member of Alpha Phi Alpha, was one of numerous Black educators who agreed with Washington regarding the need for well-educated and caring Black physicians; however, Du Bois also believed Black colleges and universities should focus on fostering a "college-bred community" headed by lawyers, businessmen, ministers, politicians, and scholars in addition to physicians and other health-care professionals.[7] Toward achieving that goal, some of the most respected Black educational institutions in the country offered classical education, which also focused on the sciences. Howard, Morehouse, Atlanta University in Georgia, and Fisk University in Nashville, Tennessee, headed the list of such institutions. Students at those schools tended to predominate in the arts and sciences. Completing general courses in English, Latin, Greek, mathematics, philosophy, history, and the sciences helped prepare those students to become race men and race women or to succeed at whichever endeavor they chose to pursue.[8]

Howard University was the central location for the talented tenth of the early twentieth century. Founded by an act of Congress in 1867, Howard was a bastion of Black scholarship. The university's faculty included a who's who of Black intellectuals. Ernest E. Just, an eminent biologist who helped found Omega Psi Phi in 1911; mathematician, sociologist, and writer Kelly Miller; philosopher and editor Alain Locke; and biblical scholar Sterling Nelson Brown were microcosms of the faculty's intelligentsia.[9]

In 1909, two years before Omega's founding and the same year as Booker T. Washington's visit to Howard University, the institution's administrators admitted the largest freshman class to date, forty-one male students and twelve female students. The former group included future Omega founders Frank Coleman and Oscar J. Cooper of Washington, DC, and Edgar A. Love of Baltimore, Maryland. Two other freshmen at Howard would later transfer to Indiana University in Bloomington and found Kappa Alpha Psi Fraternity in 1911. The women in Howard's 1909 freshman class included Mary Brown, who usually went by her middle name, Edna. She was the daughter of university professor Sterling N. Brown and while at Howard became the girlfriend (and later wife) of Coleman. In 1913, several months before finishing at the top of that school year's graduating class, Edna and twenty-one additional forward-looking women founded Delta Sigma Theta Sorority.[10]

Howard University had a unique relationship with the Black community of Washington, DC. The nation's capital had a sizable Black population, 28.5 percent in 1910 by one calculation, and Howard was a central feature of the city.[11] In 1911, the year of Omega's founding, the university's official quarterly publication, the *Howard University Record*, noted: "Howard is a well-equipped modern university in a city where there are nearly one hundred thousand colored people, for whose equipment and uplift it specially stands. It is peculiarly related to the growing colored population of the great cities north and south. More and more it should be vitally related to their great problems. As Hampton and Tuskegee are especially related to the rural life of the Negro, so Howard is related to his city life as well as to every aspect of his life as a citizen."[12]

Similar to students before and after them, Coleman, Cooper, Love, Edna Brown, and others in Howard University's 1909 freshman class engaged in curricular and extracurricular activities that enabled them to serve as honorable leaders as opposed to blind followers. Pursuant to becoming ethical race men and women, they completed liberal arts coursework that facilitated their being competent professionals once they finished Howard. First-year students majoring in the arts took mandatory courses in English, mathematics, the Bible, and Latin or Greek, with elective courses in physics, chemistry, biology, and history, among other courses. Mandatory courses for first-year science majors included mathematics, English, German or French, and the Bible, with electives in chemistry, biology, and physics, among other elective courses. Regardless of an individual's primary scholarly pursuit or desired profession, Howard's faculty endeavored to ensure the individual received a well-rounded education that would help produce a refined man or woman with excellent preparation to work as a race leader.[13]

Howard's liberal arts curriculum, together with the university's deep connection to the Black community of Washington, DC, influenced Omega Psi Phi's founding tremendously.[14] During their first year at Howard, future Omega founders Coleman, Cooper, and Love took a mandatory course in composition and rhetoric. Future Omega founder Ernest E. Just instructed the course, whose description stated: "History and Biography, Shakespearian drama, and fiction make up the reading matter. In building up his narrative composition the student must pursue the several steps from preparation of the reader's mind to climax of the story,—whether it be a life, an historical event or bit of fiction. Observation of the student of all that occurs around him, sympathetic interpretation of character and motive, and the forming of the product into a well-proportioned whole are parts of the work to be emphasized; note books, sketch books, pictures and newspaper cuttings [are primary] materials of the course."[15]

In addition to a rigorous arts and sciences curriculum, Howard University sponsored on-campus organizations (clubs, associations) that enabled students to hone their intellectual skills as race men and women. Just helped start and advised a dramatics club in 1909. Richard Brinsley Sheridan's *The Rivals*, set in England, was one of the first plays club members performed. Other plays included *She Stoops to Conquer* and *The Merry Wives of Windsor*, with Love, Cooper, and other future Omega men cast to play major roles.[16] Such theatrical activities sharpened their elocution skills and refined their public personas as not only race men but also as student representatives of the talented tenth. The same skills proved useful when Love and Cooper united with Just and Frank Coleman to found Omega Psi Phi in 1911.[17]

The founders usually looked at the bigger picture, as it were. For example, in a trigonometry notebook kept for a mathematics course Kelly Miller instructed, Cooper reflected on the problem of student infighting between the academic classes at Howard University and how such infighting distracted students from their coursework. At the same time, however, Cooper appreciated the possibility that conflict could heighten students' intellectual abilities. In his words, "the predominating influence of class rushes should be looked at as being the instrument through which a student is reminded . . . that he is at a college. They also arouse his enthusiasm, the thing which is life to a college, and make him feel at home by being thrown in closer contact with the rest of the students, that is if he is the right kind of person."[18] Cooper, not unlike Love and Coleman, believed in making the most of his collegiate experience. They realized their undergraduate tenure at Howard was pivotal to preparing them to be leaders and therefore spent much time developing their intellectual prowess instead of engaging in tomfoolery. Just set an example for them to follow.

As with the mathematics courses Miller instructed, Cooper kept a notebook for a zoology course instructed by Just. Cooper's scribblings revealed a college man who was cognizant of the strong relationship between academic achievement and physical activity. He committed himself to developing both mind and body, and he stressed the importance of both exercises to his peers. "The greatest needs of the University," Cooper averred, "are a gymnasium, larger and better equipped classrooms, and some kind of accommodations for students between their classes."[19] Given Cooper's familiarity with the classics, that the gymnasium in Greek culture "may have evolved from the necessity for a dedicated space where young Greek men (*ephebeia*) could train and improve their fitness to make them ready for warfare" was an idea that was not lost on him.[20]

Associating the Greek gymnasium with ideals of manhood, Cooper recognized the gym's dual role as a site of both athletic training and intellectual activity. The gym was a place where men listened to lectures and debated the topics of the day. In many ways, the gymnasiums of classical Greece and the early twentieth-century United States functioned as secondary schools and universities, all the while retaining their focuses on physical activity and training. Cooper saw a good gym (in the modern sense of the word) as essential to the development of a learned person.[21] Already primed to take full advantage of Howard's vigorous intellectual milieu before enrolling in the university, its curricular and extracurricular programs were useful in training both minds and bodies. Accordingly, Howard proved to be an ideal place for Cooper, Love, Coleman, and Just to found Omega Psi Phi.

The Founding

Cooper, Love, Coleman, and Just conceptualized and then discussed organizing a fraternity at length prior to its official founding on November 17, 1911. Fraternity historian Herman Dreer noted that, shortly after returning to Howard University for the beginning of the 1911–12 school year, Love and Cooper "looked West, North and East. They observed Clarke Hall, Miner Hall, the new Hall of Manual Arts, Science Hall, and Carnegie Library. They left the main building and walked towards Rankin Memorial Chapel. At once they saw before them Washington, District of Columbia, and almost straight before them they saw reaching skyward the domes of the Capitol and the Library of Congress. They were inspired."[22]

When Cooper walked from his apartment toward the Sixth Street gate that led onto Howard University's campus, he routinely passed the home of his classmate, Love. In time, they began to strike up conversations and became good friends. They frequently discussed the state of the world and the role they hoped to play in it, among other weighty topics. During one conversation, Cooper and Love decided boldly: "WE WILL BUILD A FRATERNITY."[23] They subsequently asked Just, for whom Cooper worked as a research assistant, to serve as the organization's faculty adviser when they established it. After further conversation, Cooper, Love, and Just agreed to add Frank Coleman to their group.[24] Love developed a close friendship with Cooper, Coleman, and Just, but his relationship with Coleman was closest. Years later, Love recollected fondly Coleman telling him "the things that he told no other living soul" while the two men served together in the US Army.[25]

In the fall of 1911, a member of Alpha Phi Alpha Fraternity invited Love and Cooper to submit letters "seeking membership."[26] Founded at Cornell University on December 4, 1906, Alpha was the oldest Black intercollegiate Greek-letter fraternity. Members established its second chapter, Beta, at Howard University on December 20, 1907.[27] Love and Cooper appreciated the invitation but declined it. The exercise of true leadership, they decided, required establishing their own fraternity. Additionally, Love and Cooper were concerned about potential consequences of Howard having a single fraternity, Alpha. They reasoned the existence of parallel fraternities at the university would provide a system of checks and balances that would benefit both fraternities. Love, reflecting further years hence, also noted that Alpha Phi Alpha seemed to be reserved for "men who had money to spend, or who had great family backings, or even color conscience."[28] Love and Cooper had something different in mind for the fraternity they envisioned creating.

Financial status and skin color were ever-present dividers among certain Black elites of the early 1900s.[29] Despite Love's concern about Alpha Phi Alpha's ostensible affluence, Omega Psi Phi's initial membership consisted of numerous men with light complexions who hailed from families of means. Those occurrences epitomized the complicatedness and frequency of colorism within and across Black organizations at the outset of the twentieth century and beyond. At Howard, colorism was a regular topic of debate. For example, in 1929—eighteen years into Omega Psi Phi's existence and long after Love, Cooper, and Coleman had graduated from Howard—a student asked, "Are fraternities and sororities the cause of color segregation?" on campus.[30] The questioner believed Howard students tended to organize themselves along class lines when they enrolled at the university.

How fraternity members at Howard University handled divisive matters related to skin color from the 1900s through the 1920s varied. All seemed to have members of various skin complexions, but all fraternities made racial uplift and self-determination a cornerstone of their foundations. The latter fact was on full display when Love, Cooper, and Coleman met at 9:00 P.M. in Just's office in Science Hall on Wednesday, November 15, 1911. They decided that establishing a new fraternity on campus was "favorable" and thereupon committed themselves to reconvening another time in Just's office on Friday, November 17.[31] In the interim, Love, Cooper, and Coleman worked diligently, studying the history of existing fraternities and poring over scholarship supporting and opposing those fraternities. Between classes on November 17, Love, Cooper, and Coleman discussed their research findings in preparation for the meeting with Just later that day. The exact length of the meeting remains unknown but, according to the minutes the men kept, they named the fraternity Omega Psi Phi, created a motto, devised four cardinal principles, and concurred on a motif for the pin and escutcheon. As Cooper would reflect years later, the principles were "not drawn out of a hat or selected by some haphazard method"; instead, his fellow founders and he debated thoroughly and purposefully. He further noted, "To finally decide on the Four Principles, required much thought and time to find the words to characterize and encompass just what we had in mind. This done we continually sought to find any other words to supplant the four words with no success: Therefore we decided upon the four words—but not just the four words, for they were selected in chronological order and in order of their importance and the sequence followed in that order."[32]

Manhood was the first principle. Without it, Love, Cooper, Coleman, and Just reasoned, the remaining three principles would have no basis for their survival.[33] In effect, manhood would unify the other principles. Such notions reflected a general infatuation with manliness that predominated in the United States from the late nineteenth century through early twentieth century.[34] During the former period, many American men began to embrace or perpetuate Victorian ideals of manhood that extolled strength, culture, masculinity, and chivalry. Some Black men adopted those ideals readily because they or their male forebears had endured White assaults on their manliness since the founding of the country. The same tragic truth applied to Black women of course.

As for Love, Cooper, Coleman, and Just specifically, they identified manhood as a guiding principle that would be essential to the empowerment of Black men. Decades after they founded Omega Psi Phi, Cooper in a letter dated November 4, 1962, listed the cardinal principles of the Fraternity: manhood, scholarship, perseverance, and uplift. He noted, "We [Omega founders] felt that Manhood was primarily the quality to be first sought as a basis for all other qualifications without which the other principles would have no foundation for their existence."[35] Scholarship, the second principle, by Cooper's enumeration, identified the type of man Love, Coleman, Just, and he believed should join the Fraternity: the ideal Omega candidate was intellectual, and he had scholarly ambition. Scholarship, not unlike manhood, was a keystone for building a "strong and [virile] organization."[36]

Perseverance, a third cardinal principle of Omega Psi Phi, was action based. The founders anticipated future struggles for Black men and therefore recognized the importance of Omega men being resilient. Uplift, a fourth principle of the Fraternity, was rooted in the progressive movement, whose participants tended to emphasize the need to reform American society through science and efficiency.[37] Progressives likewise thought academically educated and socioeconomically privileged citizens were responsible for elevating the masses.³⁸

Uplift was a salient concept in the Black community, particularly among race men and race women such as Anna Julia Haywood Cooper, Mary Church Terrell, Alexander Crummell, W. E. B. Du Bois, and Carter G. Woodson, an Omega man. Anna Julia Cooper provided uplift strategies in *A Voice from the South* (1892), among other works.³⁹ Du Bois's *The Souls of Black Folk* (1903) and Woodson's *The Education of the Negro Prior to 1861* (1915) were equally influential racial uplift treatises of the period.⁴⁰ Omega founder Cooper was explicit in identifying uplift as "service to others" and in articulating the Fraternity's commitment to engaging in uplift "beyond the narrow confines of the person or the organization represented by the person."⁴¹

In selecting Omega Psi Phi's motto in 1911, the founders sought to highlight the friendship they had forged since 1909. The motto, *Ophelema Philia Psukis*, was a Greek phrase meaning "friendship is essential to the soul."⁴² Love later recounted that Cooper, Coleman, Just, and he translated "the 'soul' freely to say 'life,'" resulting in "Friendship is Essential to Life."⁴³ The letters of Omega, ΩΨΦ, Love elaborated, "are the first ones taken from this motto."⁴⁴ The accompanying rites and rituals Cooper, Coleman, Just, and Love drafted reflected their understanding of biblical texts and familiarity with classical Greek culture and mythology as well as their knowledge of ancient African traditions.⁴⁵

Establishing an officer corps and a governing structure for Omega Psi Phi was the next major task the founders undertook. During a meeting at Howard University held on November 23, 1911, they elected Love as Grand Basileus, Cooper as Grand Keeper of Records, and Coleman as Grand Keeper of Seals. They also selected charter members for the first new members of the Fraternity, Howard's Alpha chapter. Charterers include William Gilbert, Frank H. Wimberley, Charles Y. Harris, Julius H. Love, Benjamin H. Jones, Clarence O. Lewis, William H. Pleasants, Charles B. Washington, Edgar P. Westmoreland, Clarence A. Hayes, and William A. Love.⁴⁶ Next, chapter officers Love, Cooper, and Coleman constituted a committee of themselves for the important task of writing a constitution and ritual. Fifteen days later, on December 8, the committee presented a report to the Fraternity's Grand chapter comprising Love (Grand Basileus), Cooper (Grand Keeper of Records), and Coleman (Grand Keeper of Seals).⁴⁷

In settling on an escutcheon design for the Fraternity, founders Love, Cooper, Coleman, and Just drew on their knowledge of ancient iconography and symbolism to ensure everything about the design would have meaning.⁴⁸ Omega man Herman Dreer, in his history of the Fraternity, described the original escutcheon as including Omega's "Greek letters ΩΨΦ, a star above the letters and a Greek lamp below them. Below the shield there were to be a helmet and a gauntlet; and behind the shield two unsheathed swords, the whole surrounded by a wreath of laurel."[49] Each item on the escutcheon reflected an aspect of the Fraternity's mission and offered guidance for how its members should live their lives.

As stated earlier in this chapter, scholarship informed Love, Cooper, Coleman, and Just's ideas regarding the organizational structure, rituals, and procedures of Omega Psi Phi. *Baird's Manual of American College Fraternities: A Descriptive Analysis of the Fraternity System in the Colleges of the United States*, which William Raimond Baird had edited since 1879, was a principal volume that the founders consulted.[50] Baird's descriptions of fraternities' construction of nomenclature, design of insignia, selection of honorary members, and ideas regarding grand chapters, grand conclaves, supreme councils, and district systems for dividing fraternities especially influenced Love, Cooper, Coleman, and Just. Love discussed such matters in a 1973 interview with fellow Omega man Mark Hyman: "[Just] knew [Greek] and he got a book in which there was listed all the known incorporated fraternities in America so we wouldn't take a name which was already incorporated."[51] Other matters about which Just and his fellow Omega founders Love, Cooper, and Coleman read included insignia: "The distinctive badges of the fraternities are of three kinds. First, a shield or plate of gold, displaying upon it the fraternity's name, together with symbols of peculiar significance. This is worn as a pin, as a pendant from the watch chain, or as a watch key. Secondly, a monogram of letters composing the name; these are the handsomest of all badges, and are usually jeweled. Thirdly, some symbol representing the name of the society or some of its degrees, as a skull, a harp, a key."[52] While Love did not mention *Baird's Manual of American College Fraternities* by name during his interview with Hyman, the characteristics of Omega Psi Phi's escutcheon resembled many of the characteristics adopted by earlier fraternities and discussed by Baird.

Resistance and Perseverance

Founding Omega Psi Phi was a bold enterprise, and several faculty members, administrators, and other Howard University employees opposed Love, Cooper, Coleman, and Just doing so. Some employees stonewalled the effort. Others simply ignored it. "Time after time," Love, Cooper, and Coleman "asked for a hearing before the faculty committee indicating what was our objective, and each time we were rebuffed," Love recollected decades into Omega's existence.[53] After becoming frustrated one morning in 1911,

Love recollected further, Cooper, Coleman, and he distributed flyers and placards across campus listing the names of the charter members of Omega Psi Phi. In response to Love, Cooper, and Coleman's efforts to publicize Omega Psi Phi, the name they used in their advertising campaign, Howard president Wilbur Patterson Thirkield, speaking in Rankin Chapel, declared that "no such organization" existed at the university. After meeting with Thirkield—a White educator and Methodist clergyman originally from Franklin, Ohio—Love, Cooper, and Coleman agreed to remove the advertisements.[54]

The source of the Thirkield administration's resistance to Omega's founding at Howard University remains a topic of great speculation, as no one in the administration or anyone in a successive presidential administration gave a reason for Thirkield's opposition. Possibilities abounded, however. His fear of a Black fraternity being founded at a Black institution he headed was foremost. In the first decade of the twentieth century, Black citizens across the United States established organizations and began initiatives devoted to racial uplift. Many White citizens and some non-White citizens considered a number of those organizations and initiatives to be radical— the Niagara Movement, established in 1905 on the Canadian side of the Niagara Falls by W. E. B. Du Bois, Garnett Russell Waller, a future Omega man, and others, was at the top of the radical list.[55] Insofar as Howard was a somewhat conservative university headed by a White president and a predominantly White board of directors, Thirkield and other university decision makers perhaps feared Omega men would become political and openly voice demands for greater civil rights. Besides that possibility, a Black fraternity, Alpha Phi Alpha, already chartered an undergraduate chapter at Howard. The Alphas, moreover, had a strong campus presence. Additionally, the specter of occasionally raucous Greek-letter life at White universities may have made Thirkield and his administrative team leery about the establishment of another Black fraternity at Howard. Even though American collegiate fraternities' stated purposes often were noble, many unaffiliated citizens viewed the organizations as social clubs characterized by boyish shenanigans. Thirkield and others at Howard valued the university's reputation as a serious academic institution and therefore might have sought to prevent Howard from experiencing the sorts of wild activities that took place on White campuses.[56]

Objections notwithstanding, Love, Cooper, Coleman, and Just helped establish the Alpha chapter of Omega Psi Phi at Howard University on December 15, 1911. As with Grand chapter elections for the entire Fraternity on November 23, Coleman emerged as Alpha chapter's Basileus, or president, and Love's and Cooper's roles reversed. Whereas Love was Grand chapter's Basileus, he became Alpha chapter's Keeper of Records. Cooper was Grand chapter's Keeper of Records; he became the Keeper of Seals for Alpha chapter.[57]

Cooper, Love, Coleman, and eleven additional Howard collegians—the aforementioned William Gilbert, Charles Harris, Clarence Hayes, Benjamin Jones, Clarence Lewis, Julius Love, William Love, William Pleasants, Charles Washington, Edgar Westmoreland, and Frank Wimberley—were founding members of Alpha chapter of Omega Psi Phi.[58] Thirkield and certain other Howard University employees continued to oppose the Fraternity, but its members persisted in their efforts to legitimize their organization. On one occasion, esteemed professor Kelly Miller asked Edgar Love, "Why don't you join the fraternity that's already here?" meaning Alpha Phi Alpha.[59] Miller apparently was concerned about Howard's association with Omega if the Fraternity was unsuccessful. Insofar as Cornell University was Alpha Phi Alpha's birthplace, Miller noted, "we're not responsible at Howard University for its being, but this fraternity you project [Omega Psi Phi] will be spawned on our campus and we will be the mother chapter and we will be more or less responsible for what it may become."[60] Later, Miller asked Love and other Omegas: "How do we know that this fraternity will continue to be the kind of fraternity that you men represent here?"[61] In time, however, Miller became impressed with several Omegas, whom he recognized as "gentlemen," and therefore backed some of their activities.[62]

In a fall 1929 issue of *The Oracle*, Walter H. Mazyck informed readers that during the early spring semester of 1912, while Howard University faculty considered recognizing the Alpha chapter of Omega Psi Phi as an official campus fraternity, Omega's membership assembled on February 21, 1912, to ballot for new members. A week later, on February 28, James R. Johnson, William B. Jason, Moses Clayborne, and Christopher C. Cooke became the first initiates of Alpha chapter. Even though the Thirkield administration still did not recognize Omega as a university organization and the faculty council had not yet endorsed such recognition, the Omegas elected Edgar Westmoreland as Basileus, Cooke as Keeper of Records, and Frank Wimberley as Keeper of Seals of Alpha chapter. They and other members later received further news: the Howard University Council recommended establishing Omega as a local fraternity.[63]

Alpha chapter held a banquet on March 10, 1912, to celebrate their progress with the University Council. Members enjoyed fine cuisine and displayed much cheerfulness. They ate a six-course meal and toasted one another for their hard work. Despite significant obstacles, they had remained optimistic about establishing the Fraternity at Howard University and, as a testament to one cardinal principle, they persevered. Edgar Love recapped, "Omega Psi Phi was not a spontaneous impulse or desire on the part of a few fellows for such an organization, but rather the result of several years of intimate and constant friendship on the part of many fellows in the University of like attainments and temperaments."[64] Though pleased with Omega's growth at Howard, particularly the willingness of the University Council to recognize the Fraternity as a local organization, Love and other Omega men deliberated whether to accept the council's favorable recommendation for more than a week after the March 10 banquet. They tendered their decision on March 19: because Omega Psi Phi would be a national fraternity, its members had to reject the council's recommendation for only local status.[65]

Conditions improved for Omega Psi Phi during the fall semester of 1912. According to a December 6 issue of the *Howard University Journal*, the Fraternity, on November 22 of that year, held a housewarming at 1907 Third Street Northwest: "from the parlor to the mysterious 'goat room' on the third floor were thrown open with a wide welcome to visiting friends for their inspection. This opportunity of going through a house furnished, decorated and kept by men was readily embraced by between fifty and two hundred, representing the elite of Washington society, principally women, and students of the university."[66] By highlighting the upkeep of the house and the congeniality that Omegas exhibited during the November 22 event, the *Journal* seemed to make a case for university recognition of the Fraternity as a national organization. The *Journal* declared the housewarming "should be sufficient evidence to convince those in authority who have been averse to the idea of the frat houses of its wholesomeness. Many members of the faculty were there and all seemed favorably impressed with the showing."[67] In his interview with Cooper, William Jason noted: "A softening up of the opposition did take place. As more and more faculty members became [favorably] impressed the fraternity witnessed the relevance and the meaning of perseverance."[68]

In 1913, a year before Congress incorporated Omega Psi Phi, Howard University professor Kelly Miller offered a fifty-dollar prize for the best essay on "The Effect of Emancipation Upon the Physical Condition of the Negro."[69] The topic of Miller's essay contest, which he sponsored during the spring of 1913, was appropriate given his interest in slavery's impact on both past and present Black people worldwide. In 1914, the year of Omega's congressional incorporation, Miller published *Out of the House of Bondage*, a book in which he explored slavery in the United States.[70] A year earlier, as he anticipated the book's publication, his students typewrote essays not to exceed 4,000 words. Omegas Edgar Love, Chauncey Mitchell Depew Harllee, and Frank Wimberley each submitted letters placing themselves in the competition. Not one of the three Omegas won the essay prize, but the participation of all three Omegas was a fine representation of the general commitment they and other members of the Fraternity had to the cardinal principle of scholarship.[71]

During the same semester as Miller's essay contest (spring 1913), White educator and civil rights activist Joel Elias Spingarn, one of the NAACP's most prominent members, gave a speech at Howard University about the struggle for equality. His words inspired students to found the NAACP's first collegiate branch. Viewing that organization's work as complementary to their own fraternity work, Omegas helped lead the charge to establish the branch. In 1913, Omegas Samuel A. Allen and George Edward Brice served as president and treasurer, respectively. Their positions embodied the leadership that Omegas exhibited at Howard.[72] They were representative of leading students at Black colleges and universities elsewhere in the United States.

Desiring to unite with young men of like mind, Omega men Oscar J. Cooper, William Griffith Brannon, and John H. McMorries accepted the task of establishing the second chapter of the Fraternity. Lincoln University near Oxford, Pennsylvania, was the site. Beta was the name, and February 6, 1914, was its charter date.[73] According to several accounts, the chartering ceremony for Beta chapter took place in the home of Mrs. Charlotte (Lottie) Wilson, a caterer at Lincoln University who regularly donated food to financially strapped students. Other times, Wilson used money she generated from selling food to help students pay for their books, tuition, and other necessities. When students could not afford room and board, Wilson opened her home to them. If they became ill, she nursed them back to good health.[74]

The establishment of Beta chapter at Lincoln was not a smooth one. At Lincoln, the faculty opposed the establishment of fraternities. One student, however, spoke with Mrs. Wilson about faculty resistance to Omega at Lincoln. During the conversation, Mrs. Wilson offered her home for the establishment of Beta chapter. During a banquet following the establishment of Beta chapter, Mrs. Wilson stated "I dedicate my life to Omega."[75]

Decades later, on February 15, 1967, after her recent death, Lincoln University's student paper, the *Lincolnian*, paid tribute to the woman thousands of Omegas came to know and to love simply as Lottie B.:

> In 1914, [Mrs.] Wilson's heart reached out . . . to the Omega Psi Phi Fraternity. Coming to the aid of several ambitious but beleaguered students, she opened her door to let Beta chapter of the fraternity be founded in her home. From that time on she became an integral part of the Omega life. For the first few years of Beta's history, her parlor served as the meeting place, of Lincoln's Omegas. She was present even at the pledge meetings. This was the beginning of her role as "sister" Wilson.
>
> Charlotte married Alfonso Wilson, a Lincoln graduate, in 1918. Together they continued on contributing to the university community in their own very warm and wonderful way. By no means was their help

limited to the Omegas alone, but to all fraternity men, and many nonfraternity men found a haven in their home and hearts.[76]

The twenty men first initiated at Beta chapter included a cadre of promising young race men.[77] Among the earliest members of Beta chapter, one, Charles Talmage Kimbrough of Winston-Salem, North Carolina, was a salutatorian in 1918. That same year, Kimbrough won the Bradley Medal, an honor Lincoln University bestowed on a graduating senior for maintaining the highest grade point average in selected branches of the natural sciences. Kimbrough took home that medal, which was colored gold, one year after winning a Rodman Wanamaker Prize in the English Bible.[78] Woodbury, New Jersey, native Norman Alonzo Holmes, a second Bradley Medal winner, was valedictorian of the 1915 class at Lincoln; "The Prime Importance of Secondary Education" was the title of his valedictory.[79] James Crawford McMorries and Charles Reed Saulter also were valedictorians.[80] Lincoln conferred a medal on McMorries, an eloquent orator, for his performance in the Obdyke Prize Debate.[81] In addition to that medal, he was the recipient of the Class of 1900 Prize in Debate.[82] Saulter, a comparably eloquent orator and a fine writer who enjoyed literary classics, enjoyed a Wanamaker Prize, a Moore Sophomore Prize in English, and a Miss Lafie Reid Prize in Sacred Geography, among other academic honors, before joining the Lincoln faculty as an instructor of New Testament Greek.[83]

Not unlike other middle-class, educated Black Americans of the early twentieth century, the founders of Omega Psi Phi understood the power of projecting excellence and respectability. They and countless other Black citizens believed that displaying those two ideas was foundational to a pragmatic strategy to attain equality.[84] The Omegas' work was effective: on October 28, 1914, the United States Congress incorporated the Fraternity, under the laws of the District of Columbia, as a national organization.[85]

In 1915, as the members of Beta chapter of Omega Psi Phi excelled in Lincoln University classrooms, Alpha chapter member George E. Hall extolled the virtues of the NAACP in the pages of the *Howard University Journal*. After pointing out various challenges Black people in the United States confronted, Hall posed a question to his fellow race men and to race women: "Who is to lead the American Negro to the larger freedom which by all justice is his?"[86] Identifying White leaders Abraham Lincoln, William Lloyd Garrison, and Charles Sumner as helping to lead battles for Black equality during times of yore, Hall called on his fellow Black youth to serve as twentieth-century commanders of the freedom fight. Hall was confident the NAACP and Omega Psi Phi were two organizations that could help propel racial uplift during the coming decades.

By year's end in 1916, following the founding of Beta chapter at Lincoln University in 1914, the Fraternity's undergraduate membership had reached approximately 135 members. The Fraternity's total membership was higher than 135, however. On December 13, 1916, Grand Basileus George E. Hall authorized the chartering of Gamma. As a citywide chapter located in Boston, Massachusetts, Gamma had a membership composed of undergraduates and graduates from institutions such as Boston College, Boston University, Emerson College, Harvard University, Massachusetts Institute of Technology, Northeastern University, Tufts University, and the University of Massachusetts Boston.[87]

Omegas belonging to the Alpha chapter at Howard University celebrated the national expansion of the Fraternity, which they monitored closely, but chapter members also concentrated on expanding their own local agenda. Cultivating a tradition of weekly lectures patterned after Greek lyceums was a foremost local activity. Members decided to hold the lectures on Sundays to increase the chance of having "prominent and eminent . . . men of worth and accomplishment" as lecturers.[88] In January 1917, Roscoe Conkling Bruce Sr., assistant superintendent of schools for Washington, DC, spoke about the degrading nature of segregation. James Adlai Cobb, a Howard alumnus and lawyer who formerly served as special assistant to the attorney general for District of Colombia, lectured on the importance of accomplishing small tasks that led to big accomplishments. Howard professor and chair of the English department Gordon David Houston delivered another significant talk at an Omega Sunday lecture. Titled "The Manly Elements in the Christian Religion," his talk identified unselfishness, patience, forgiveness, and love as qualities all Christian men should strive to obtain.[89]

Yet another January 1917 lecture sponsored by the Alpha chapter of Omega Psi Phi featured Carter G. Woodson, founder of the Association for the Study of Negro Life and History and editor of the *Journal of Negro History*. The national Democratic Party's dominance in the South and the West was his topic. Contending that northerners continued to abandon Black people in those regions, especially the South, from which the second Ku Klux Klan arose in November 1915, Woodson asserted: "I do not believe that the Negro question will ever become a national issue again. The North is satisfied to leave that question entirely in the hands of the South."[90]

Woodson did not provide an explication, but he perhaps referred to the federal government's purported abandonment of Black southerners following the Bargain, or Compromise, of 1877 that removed military troops from the centers of major southern cities and towns, relocating those troops to more remote areas in southern states. Signaling the effective end to the first Reconstruction, the Compromise emboldened unreconstructed White lawmakers in the South to enact additional Jim Crow laws. Concurrently, a similarly unreconstructed set of their White constituents inflicted physical terror on Black southerners. Woodson, in his 1917 Omega lecture, urged each male listener to "make himself felt in American politics" and to not wait on others, such as politicians or statesmen, to provide political power, as that wait could be long.[91] Invigorated by Woodson's imploration to be politically knowledgeable, persistently active, and personally responsible—three ideals that aligned perfectly with two Omega cardinal principles, perseverance and uplift—members of the Fraternity made Woodson one of the first honorary members of Omega Psi Phi on February 10, 1917.[92]

Writing and submitting articles for publication in the *Howard University Journal* was another regular activity in which Alpha chapter members engaged. Many submissions dealt with intellectual matters. In "America: Her Attitude Toward the Negro," Jesse Solomon Heslip discussed the hypocrisy of Americans who alleged the country was democratic. He pointed out that most Black people did not come to the United State as voluntary immigrants; instead, they were subjects "bound in chains" and susceptible to nearly every, if not every, "command and will of the white man."[93] According to Heslip, bigoted White Americans tried to enslave Black Americans a second time through Jim Crow laws even though Black people had been patriotic citizens who had served in virtually all types of skilled and unskilled capacities imaginable, from common laborers to professionally trained architects. Most Black people, moreover, were law abiding and peaceful. Even so, "white supremacists" enacted property laws excluding non-White people from living in the same communities whose houses Black people helped design or build.[94]

With ample external and internal motivations to succeed, members of Alpha chapter worked hard to maintain the high standard their four cardinal principles—manhood, scholarship, perseverance, and uplift—demanded. For example, during the fall semester of the academic year 1914–15, Omegas reported an aggregate 73.37 grade point average. Their collective performance ranked second, behind the Alphas, for all fraternities at Howard University. During the spring semester, the Omegas improved to 75.22. That score was first among fraternities. Altogether, sixteen Omegas earned academic honors during the school year. Sixteen was more than any other fraternity at the university.[95]

Published years after Omega's founding, "Omega Calls Her Sons of Light" by Herman Dreer provided insight into the Fraternity's commitment to the four cardinal principles—manhood, scholarship, perseverance, and uplift—devised in 1911:

Omega call her Sons of Light, her newborn blazing glory
Her Older heroes, honor dight, and her Immortals hoary
To meet, To greet, To chase all gloom away,
And thinking bring the everlasting day.[96]

Dreer's identifying Omega men as sons of light corresponded particularly well with the cardinal principles, especially uplift. Members emphasized illuminating the value of each other and others, especially Black people, through the acquisition and the dissemination of knowledge: "As we rise to the skies that we prize, ending wrong that has long crushed the throng, wrapped in mantles of fame for Omega's dear name."[97] Another verse offered an even more poignant description of Omega race men and their mission of racial uplift:

We are scions of black slaves whose backs were lashed to bleeding,
They rise and speak from honorable graves, encourage sons, be heeding,
Now we the free, Do proudly keep the pace,
Marching to God his brave triumphant race.[98]

As a testament to Alpha chapter's devotion to Black collective uplift, chapter members such as John G. Dingle envisioned an alliance of all Black fraternities at Howard University. Dingle articulated his vision to other members during a chapter meeting held on February 7, 1914. The members tabled the matter, but Lucius H. Brown raised it again during a meeting on February 24. He "outlined the formation of an interfraternal committee composed of representatives of the fraternities at Howard . . . to control their affairs at the university."[99] As with Dingle's item, Alpha chapter's members decided to table the matter "until the next regular meeting."[100]

Eventually, the members of Alpha chapter voted to approve the interfraternal committee about which Dingle and Brown spoke. On March 7, 1914, those making up the committee requested Howard University fraternities to form temporary committees to consider establishing a university-wide interfraternal alliance. Brown, Wimberley, and Alan L. Dingle, John's sibling, comprised Alpha chapter's temporary committee. For more than a year, they weighed the pros and cons of an alliance until on March 16, 1915, Omega founder Frank Coleman took five minutes to discuss the necessity for the alliance. Alabamian Charles Vergne Hendley, then Basileus of Alpha chapter, agreed with Coleman; nevertheless, an official alliance did not materialize until the academic year 1918–19.[101] Called interfraternity, not interfraternal when established, the alliance met for the first time on January 25, 1919. W. Spurgeon Burke, George E. Brice, and Luther O. Baumgardner represented Alpha chapter. The spirit of unity displayed at the January 1919 meeting and later gatherings of Black Greek-letter organizations undergirded the development of the National Pan-Hellenic Council that the Black Greek-letter organizations founded on May 10, 1930.[102]

The Making of Race Men

With regard to early twentieth-century Black people, race men were the quintessential representatives of the talented tenth: they were educated, refined, had sharp intellects, pragmatic objectives, and selfless commitments to uplifting Black people to the highest levels of civilization. Some people viewed race men as messianic saviors.[103] African American history is replete with examples of race men, and Omega Psi Phi contributed its fair share to the early twentieth-century list of such men. Edgar A. Love is a representative.

Love was born on September 10, 1891, in Harrisonburg, Virginia, to the reverend Julius C. Love and Susie Love (née Carr) of Lynchburg, about one hundred miles southwest of Harrisonburg. Reverend and Mrs. Love wed on February 23, 1881, having first met each other while matriculating though the Centenary Biblical Institute (known later as Morgan College and now called Morgan State University) in Baltimore, Maryland. Susie became the first woman to graduate from the institute in 1887. Three years later, her husband, Julius, earned a degree from the Howard University Theological School in Washington, DC. Both ministers, Julius and Susie, became respected leaders in the Methodist Episcopal Church.[104]

Edgar Love ultimately followed the ministerial paths of his parents. First, however, he had to journey through primary schools in Virginia and Maryland, changing residences because of the church assignments of his parents. In 1905, a fourteen-year-old Edgar secured a slot at the Normal and Industrial Academy at Morgan College in Baltimore. The institution was a good fit for an intelligent, disciplined, and idealistic teenager such as Love. The challenging curriculum was instrumental in developing his academic skills. While at the academy, he was outspoken and expressed his awareness of the various problems confronting Black people. A 1909 graduate of the academy, his sermon "Christianity as a National Safeguard" won a "Baldwin Gold Medal for the best declamation of a sermonette."[105]

Edgar Love's time at the Normal and Industrial Academy at Morgan College cultivated his interest in the social gospel theology of the late nineteenth century and into the early twentieth century. Proponents of the social gospel focused on the application of Christianity to reform society by, among other acts, calling for justice and equality. The social gospel reflected the progressivist philosophy of the period and proved ideal for a young aspiring theologian such as Love. He was especially interested in applying social gospel reforms to assist Black people. At Howard University, where Love enrolled in

1909 to study theology, he increased his appreciation of the social gospel in ways unimaginable to him before that year.[106] Howard was an overall paradise to Love. As a freshman, he quickly immersed himself in the intellectual and social cultures of the university by earning solid grades and by playing both football and croquet. Love also became a prolific public speaker, serving as president of the Kappa Sigma Debating Society.[107]

Oscar J. Cooper was born on May 20, 1888, in Washington, DC, to James B. Cooper and Mary M. Cooper. The couple had previously lived in Virginia, but moved to Washington, DC. As a young man, Cooper was measured and thoughtful. His parents seemed to be training him for a life of racial uplift. They schooled him in strenuous work, instilled in him self-control, taught him to be punctual, encouraged him to learn the art of being a gentleman, and taught him to dress impeccably.[108] Cooper attended public schools in his natal city before enrolling in Howard Academy from 1905 to 1909. His next educational endeavor would be Howard University in the fall of 1909.[109]

Not unlike Love, Oscar Cooper was a gifted student at Howard. His keen interest in biology resulted in his seeking to spend much time with Ernest Just, an English professor who eventually became chair of the biology department. Just saw great potential in Cooper and hired him as an assistant in the science laboratory he operated. They developed a friendship that paved the way for both young men becoming founders of Omega Psi Phi in 1911. At Howard, Cooper adhered to his parents wishes to control himself and "master the arts of the fine gentleman." In his class notes from 1913, Cooper editorialized in the margins revealing a young man of intellectual curiosity and dexterity, skills that would be useful in writing the Fraternity's ritual. In 1913, upon graduating from Howard University, Cooper entered its medical school. While in medical school, he took three weeks off to focus on and complete the Fraternity's ritual. In his class lecture notes from 1913, William Jason reports that Cooper sketched a vision of the ritual, which the Fraternity approved on February 4, 1914. Jason noted that the Fraternity accepted Cooper's version of the ritual with no changes.[110]

Frank Coleman, a third Omega Psi Phi founder, was born to Benjamin and Frances Coleman in Washington, DC, on July 11, 1890. He attended the academically challenging M Street High School and, similar to Cooper, was enthusiastic about science. Whereas biology was Cooper's specialty, Coleman preferred physics. Both young men enrolled at Howard University in 1909, with Coleman selecting to major in physics. They blossomed intellectually, coming in contact with other studious individuals, among them Edgar Love. Coleman finished his undergraduate work in 1913. Afterwards, he took a teaching and chair position at Bricks Agriculture and Normal School in

Enfield, North Carolina. As with his formative years and at Howard, Coleman exhibited a stellar work ethic: T. S. Inborden, the principal of Bricks, noted: "I think he [Coleman] is going to make an excellent helper. He has started off in a very pleasing manner. He comes in my office almost daily to tell me that he is here to be used and to ask if I would like to have him do anything in the office or outside. He is a real help to me."[111] Such a disposition was helpful to Coleman as he pursued further education and service to his country.

Coleman earned a master of science degree from the University of Chicago. He completed additional course work for a PhD degree at the University of Pennsylvania but did not write a dissertation. During World War I, Coleman underwent officer training at Fort Des Moines in Iowa and then served as a first lieutenant in the US Army. Coleman later worked as a physics professor and periodically as head of the physics department at his alma mater, Howard.[112]

On May 25, 1918, as World War I entered its final official months, First Lieutenant Frank Coleman of the 368th US Infantry experienced another turning point in his life: he wed Mary E. Brown, a Washington, DC, native, Howard University alumna, and Delta Sigma Theta Sorority founder who went on to earn a master of arts degree from Oberlin College in Ohio. Brown's father, Sterling N. Brown, a Howard professor, performed the wedding ceremony. Sadly, Mary died whilst giving birth to a premature daughter on September 25, 1919. The baby passed away hours later. Those unfortunate incidents took the lives of two of Frank's most beloved family members, but, fortunately, his fellow Omega Psi Phi founders, Oscar J. Cooper, Edgar A. Love, and Ernest E. Just, were willing to provide as much support as they could muster.[113]

The eldest Omega founder, Just, was born in Charleston, South Carolina, on August 14, 1883. His parents, Mary Mathews Cooper Just and Charles Fraser (or Frazier) Just Jr., were a schoolteacher and a wharf builder, respectively. Mary also labored in the various phosphate fields and mines on James Island near Charleston. Her workload increased when Charles Jr. died. Their son, Ernest, was nearly four years old. Eventually leaving the phosphate fields, Mary founded the Frederick Deming Jr. Industrial School in an unincorporated area (eventually called Maryville) she helped found near West Ashley, approximately five miles northwest of Charleston. Frederick Deming Industrial School not only provided secular learning opportunities to Black students, including Ernest, but it also had a church where they could increase their knowledge about Judeo-Christianity.[114]

Ernest Just attended Frederick Deming Industrial School until age twelve, whereupon he headed to Orangeburg, South Carolina, to attend the laboratory, or high, school associated with the Colored Normal Industrial and Agricultural and Mechanical College (now called South Carolina State

University). A prodigy, Just studied in the classical preparatory department for the teaching profession and in 1899 earned a teaching license. He was fifteen years old at the time and could teach Black South Carolina students who were older than he was. After returning to Maryville, the small town named after his mother, Just took a job with the Clyde-Line Railroad, intending to make his way to the North. He eventually made his way to New York City, New York, and thence to Meriden, New Hampshire, where he enrolled in Kimball Union Academy.[115] Just was its only Black student. He selected a classical course of study but, realizing multiple deficiencies, despite his God-given ability, enrolled in remedial courses for English grammar, American history, spelling, and penmanship. Just also took courses in Latin, English, and algebra; and he read Caesar, Cicero, Napos, Ovid, and Virgil, mastering *The Iliad*, *The Odyssey*, and *The Anabasis*.[116] His learnedness enabled him to win posts as editor-in-chief of Kimball Union's student newspaper and as "President of the Philadelphian Society, one of the oldest debating clubs in New England."[117] Just engaged in debating, rhetoric, and oratory, and Kimball Union awarded him the Francis E. Clark Prize for Extemporaneous Speaking.[118] Bestowed the honor of delivering one of the commencement addresses in 1903, he titled his delivery "Government Ownership of Monopolies."[119]

In 1903, the same year Ernest Just graduated from Kimball Union at the top of his class and with a host of commendations and awards, he enrolled at Dartmouth College in Hanover, New Hampshire.[120] The freshman class numbered 287, and Just was its only Black member. Given his classical education at Kimball, a fine academic institution, Just was prepared for the academic work at Dartmouth. He made passing grades in oratory and mathematics; very good grades in English, Latin, and French; and secured the highest grade ever in Greek among Dartmouth freshmen. Just was not a perfect student, he performed well enough to become a Rufus Choate Scholar, a designation Dartmouth awarded to a student who amassed an average score of ninety-two in all courses. Just finished the college in 1907, graduated magna cum laude in biology with a minor in history and wearing a Phi Beta Kappa pin.[121]

Just's first job after graduating from Dartmouth was at Howard University. He joined Howard's English department in 1907, organizing a drama club in 1909, but switched departments in 1910 when the university's president, Wilbur P. Thirkield, asked him to become a member of the biology faculty. Just's ability to navigate swimmingly across disciplines and fields was a testament to his grounding in both the sciences and the humanities.[122]

In 1909, while instructing English courses at Howard University, Just began graduate studies at the Marine Biological Laboratory in Woods Hole, Massachusetts. His White mentor at the laboratory, Frank Rattray Lillie, chaired the University of Chicago's zoology department and was a pioneering embryologist. In 1912, the year after Just assisted Edgar A. Love, Oscar J. Cooper, and Frank Coleman to found Omega Psi Phi at Howard, Just rose to the rank of professor of physiology in the medical school at the university. He also taught courses in its medical school and, above all else, reflected constantly on the duties and obligations of being a race man.[123] Writing about Just in 1946, acclaimed marine biologist, Morehouse College professor and department chair and Omega man Samuel Milton Nabrit—a Morehouse alumnus and the first Black man to earn a PhD degree from Brown University—recalled Just being "unusually sensitive about race not because he was a Negro, but because of the stigma that [W]hite Americans, scientists included, applied to Negroes."[124] According to Nabrit, who served as president of the National Institute of Science in 1945, when White people told so-called Negro jokes or were guilty of other racial indiscretions in Just's presence, he removed himself from the perpetrators immediately and then stayed away from them for days.[125] As Nabrit's recollections about Just illustrated, not even a renowned Black scientist was immune to White bias, but both renowned Black scientists, Just and Nabrit, were unswervingly committed to challenging such bias through their own admirable words and deeds.

Early twentieth-century race men such as Just, Cooper, Coleman, and Love believed mastery of the sciences and the humanities would help liberate Black people. That belief undergirded Just, Cooper, Coleman, and Love's decision in 1911 to make scholarship a cardinal principle of Omega Psi Phi. They presumed the rest of the twentieth century would present challenges of mammoth proportions to Black people in the United States and abroad. Even so, Omega's founders were confident the other three cardinal principles of the Fraternity—manhood, perseverance, and uplift—would help Black people meet and, moreover, overcome those challenges. Just, Cooper, Coleman, and Love also were confident that Omega men would join their male and female comrades who belonged to other Black Greek-letter fraternities and sororities in leading the charge for equality.

Omegas and the Great War

For millions of people, their worlds changed dramatically on June 28, 1914. On that date, a Bosnian Serb student named Gavrilo Princip assassinated Archduke Franz Ferdinand (né Franz Ferdinand Carl Ludwig Joseph Maria), presumptive heir to the Austro-Hungarian throne, in Sarajevo. Within five weeks, countries around the globe had aligned formally into opposing sides in a global war. Germany, Austria-Hungary, Bulgaria, and Turkey led the Central powers. Great Britain, France, and Russia headed up the Allied powers.

US president Thomas Woodrow Wilson issued a neutrality proclamation supporting many of his constituents' belief regarding the war in Europe being of no direct concern to them.[126] Unbeknownst to scores of those and other American citizens, their government was supporting the Allied powers clandestinely to protect the country's growing position as a world leader, among other reasons. All the same, the Wilson administration pledged neutrality, operating officially under an isolationist policy. The administration continued to operate in that manner after no fewer than one hundred American citizens aboard a British ocean liner called *Lusitania* lost their lives when a German *Unterseeboot*, or U-boat (submarine), sank *Lusitania* on May 7, 1915. Almost two years later, on April 6, 1917, after Germany sank additional vessels and Wilson had secured reelection on November 7, 1916, the US Congress voted affirmatively to declare war on Germany.[127]

When the United States entered World War I officially in April 1917, Black American leaders and intellectuals were aware of the evolving geopolitics of the time and therefore situated the so-called Negro problem, the Black freedom struggle, and related matters in a global context. Scholars such as Carter G. Woodson, a newly selected honorary member of Omega, and W. E. B. Du Bois contended that wartime apartheid and poverty of Black people in the United States reflected similar conditions of African peoples throughout the world. In February 1919, as global leaders assembled for the Paris Peace Conference, Du Bois helped organize the Pan-African Congress, also held in Paris, to discuss ways to ensure Africana people across the diaspora had a place in the postwar order. Black leaders, such as Du Bois, organized a similar Pan-African Conference in London, England, in July 1900. That conference served as a basis for the February 1919 Pan-African Congress in Paris that Omega Psi Phi members supported as well as for Pan-African congresses held in London in August 1921 and in Brussels, Belgium, in September 1921.[128]

As regards to American involvement in World War I, when congressmen voted to declare war against Germany in April 1917, they pledged American troops would fight for the foundations of political liberty. Although Black Americans continued to experience the disenfranchisement of Jim Crow, many Black Americans rallied to the war cause. Army lieutenant colonel Charles Young, elected an honorary member of Omega on March 8, 1912, called on Black Americans to fight for freedom abroad in the US militaries and to resume the fight for freedom at home once the Great War ended. Other Black leaders, including Du Bois, also encouraged Black Americans to "close ranks" with White Americans and volunteer to serve the United States militarily, among other ways, during the war.[129]

Several Black college presidents and Du Bois's fellow NAACP leader, Joel Spingarn, called for the establishment of an officer training corps for Black citizens. On February 15, 1917, a few weeks before President Wilson's second inauguration on March 5, Spingarn informed Black-operated newspapers, universities, and colleges that Wilson's administration soon would establish a Black officer training corps. Omega men rose to the occasion.[130] Jesse S. Heslip, an Omega man who edited the *Howard University Journal*, wrote an op-ed and published a letter by Spingarn supporting the Black officer training corps. Heslip's fellow Omega man and student NAACP leader, George Brice, lent his support as well. Heslip noted, "there is much good for us to derive out of military training, and much service that we can render to our country and ourselves as a result of it."[131]

On May 1, 1917, Howard University administrators, faculty members, staffers, and students created the Central Committee of Negro College Men (CCNCM) to support the establishing of a training corps for Black officers. The committee consisted of the university's president, Stephen Morrell Newman, a White veteran education administrator and minister from Falmouth, Maine. Before succeeding Thirkiled in 1912, Newman's previous stints as president included tenures at Eastern College in Front Royal, Virginia, and at the Kee Mar College for Women in Hagerstown, Maryland. Newman also pastored the First Congregational Church in Washington, DC, before accepting the Howard presidency. Besides him, the university's deans and thirty-two students served on the CCNCM. Two Omegas, founder Frank Coleman, who was pursuing a master's degree at the University of Chicago, and Winston Douglas, a 1914 Beta initiate, were institutional members of the CCNCM. Their fellow members and they left Howard and traveled to a sundry of other Black colleges and universities to encourage support for a corps at Howard and to gather contact information for prospective trainees, among other things. Resulting in part from Coleman, Douglas, and other committee members' advocacy, more than 1,500 individuals applied to participate in the corps if the US Department of War established the corps. Department personnel did not do so until the summer of 1918, or a year after they formed the Seventeenth Provisional Training Regiment for Black officer candidates at the Fort Des Moines Army Base in Iowa.[132]

Howard University and Omega Psi Phi were involved with the Seventeenth Provisional Training Regiment from its outset. In 1917, the CCNCM recommended honorary Omega man and army lieutenant colonel Charles Young command the regiment. An 1889 graduate of West Point, Young had spent most of his military career with Black regiments such as the Ninth and Tenth Cavalries in the Philippines. He also assisted General John Joseph (Black Jack) Pershing in his attempt to capture Francisco (Pancho) Villa in Mexico. Young likewise taught military courses at Wilberforce University in Ohio, was the first Black national park superintendent, and, among other notable activities, worked as a presidentially appointed military attaché in the Dominican Republic, Haiti, and Liberia. Such credentials, which melded intellect and manhood, made him an exemplar of the talented tenth, a consummate scholar-soldier, and an ideal Omega.[133]

Even though Young was brilliant, courageous, and accomplished, the possibility of his commanding the Seventeenth Provisional Training Regiment was short lived. In a handwritten letter to W. E. B. Du Bois dated June 20, 1917, Young explained how his active military career was being cut short: "I went for my Examination for promotion to my Colonelcy. The surgeons claimed that as a result of finding 'high blood-pressure' and 'albumin in urine' that [they] could not recommend that I be continued in active service with troops as it was 'liable to endanger my life.'"[134] Young protested the army's decision to medically retire him and, in a show of his fitness, rode a horse approximately 500 miles from his home in Wilberforce, Ohio, to Washington, DC.[135] Although Young did not have the opportunity to serve as commander of the Provisional Regiment, he further solidified his position as a revered figure in Omega Psi Phi and Black America by epitomizing the cardinal principles of the Fraternity: manhood, scholarship, perseverance, and uplift.

Black Greek-letter fraternities were represented well when officer training commenced at the Fort Des Moines Army Base in June 1917. According to one report, 250 noncommissioned officers and 1,000 civilians submitted their names into candidacy for officer training. Two hundred acceptable candidates had Howard University affiliations. Omega Psi Phi provided a much smaller, though comparably impressive, showing. Founder Frank Coleman, one of two Omegas on the CCNCM who recommended Young command the Seventeenth Provisional Training Regiment, underwent training at Fort Des Moines. Eventually, fifteen other Omega men, including another founder (Edgar Love), Jesse Heslip, and Thomas Marshall Dent Jr., a 1916 initiate of the Alpha chapter at Howard University, trained alongside Coleman. They were joined by thirty members of Alpha Phi Alpha and by twelve members of Kappa Alpha Psi. As trainees learned strategies, tactics, and other valuable leadership items, Omegas chartered a temporary chapter at the fort. Christened the War chapter, with Heslip as its Basileus, the chapter's July 1917 initiates included Dent's brother, Francis Morse Dent. He and other Omegas initiated two more classes by the end of the camp.[136]

Omega men were invaluable to another military training operation during World War I. From August 1 to September 16, 1918, 456 students and professors representing seventy institutions participated in the Student Army Training Camp at Howard University. Developing competent military instructors for Black colleges and universities was a primary aim of the camp. During their training cycle, a group of Omegas used the success of the War chapter to advocate for a similar chapter at Howard. Their effort was successful. With Grand chapter approval, a group of Omega men assembled on September 1 inside the Alpha chapter house at 322 T Street Northwest and inducted twenty-eight men into the Fraternity. The undergraduate inductees and graduate inductees represented the following Black colleges and universities: Fisk University in Nashville, Tennessee, Talladega College in Alabama, Shaw University in Raleigh, North Carolina, Virginia Union University in Richmond, West Virginia Collegiate Institute, Atlanta University in Georgia, Biddle (now called Johnson C. Smith) University in Charlotte, North Carolina, Morehouse College in Atlanta, Georgia, and the Meharry Medical College in Nashville, Tennessee.[137]

Members of the Camp Howard chapter of Omega Psi Phi convened their first meeting on September 9, 1918. Grand Basileus Clarence F. Holmes Jr. presided. Chapter members elected Julius A. Thomas Jr. as Basileus, Louis Gans as Keeper of Records, and Jasper Alston Atkins as Keeper of Seals. The chapter was short lived, but its varied Black colleges and universities membership united students and graduates of institutions whose academic, athletic, and related rivalries occasionally resulted in heated competitions. According to Omega man Julius A. Thomas Jr., the Omega men who belonged to the Camp Howard chapter had similar aspirations, so they developed an intrafraternity bond that transcended their interinstitutional differences. That bond facilitated a sense of "moral, mental, and physical elements of life" within the Camp Howard chapter.[138]

On December 28, 1919, Omega man and US army officer Charles Young gave the keynote speech at the Eighth Grand Conclave at Tremont Temple in Boston, Massachusetts. "America's Expectations from the Negro" was his theme.[139] Similar in some ways to the address Booker T. Washington gave at the opening of the Cotton States and International Exposition in Atlanta, Georgia, on September 18, 1895, Young in his Grand Conclave speech twenty-four years later sought to convince listeners of the importance of White Americans recognizing their Black contemporaries as full citizens who had contributed immensely to the artistic, scientific, economic, and spiritual ethos of the United States.[140] But Young sought to convince his fellow Omegas attending the Boston Conclave in December 1919 that Black Americans had to remain lawful and nonviolent even as the problematically divisive color line about which such people as W. E. B. Du Bois spoke and wrote frequently thickened across the country.[141] Young, in one part of his conclave speech, declared: "The black quota, which we as a group must add to American life will include the spiritual and cultural things.... But you must have no more bloodshed, no more race riots."[142] Black Americans would continue to contribute to American history and culture but would not die for causes beyond family and achieving full citizenship. Full equality would come, Young posited, through groups like the American Legion and by obtaining the right to vote.[143]

Omega's Growth and the Fraternity's "Powerful Right Arm"

Julius Thomas—the Omega who provided information about the mental, moral, and physical strength that members of Camp Howard chapter built during wartime—believed other members could replicate that chapter's strength as the Fraternity expanded into the South. Thomas rejoiced that Omega was becoming a real national organization, but he cautioned other Omegas that such expansion presented the Fraternity with major obligations as well as opportunities. He wrote, "Omega will be first to place her banner there and her sons will strive harder to maintain the high ideals upon which it is constructed. May the day soon come when this will be possible and the name of Omega stands as an incentive to inspire her sons to higher ideals and greater accomplishments."[144]

As Omega Psi Phi grew in both number and geography during and after World War I, perceptive and visionary members such as Thomas recognized the need for an official organ, or periodical, to communicate the fraternal vision of Omega to the world. In the spring of 1919, the Fraternity published the first issue of *The Oracle*. Grand Keeper of Seals Stanley M. Douglas, first editor of *The Oracle*, had a keen sense of history and understood the periodical could help chronicle the Fraternity as well as communicate information about chapters. Omegas in one place, Douglas surmised, wanted to know what Omegas in other places were doing. Douglas believed *The Oracle* would serve that purpose while simultaneously promoting racial uplift and related ideals of the Fraternity. The periodical, he proposed in the summer of 1919, was the fraternity's "powerful right arm."[145]

June 1919 was the release date of the inaugural issue of *The Oracle*. Douglas and his fellow editors provided a retrospective on the first eight years of the Fraternity. Douglas's editorial team included statements about the founders and a reexamination of Omega's four cardinal principles: manhood, scholarship, perseverance, and uplift. In reminding readers about the perennial need to sacrifice certain desires for the common good, *The Oracle* encouraged them not to demonstrate "selfishness in dealing with their fellowmen."[146] Those types of appeals were common among many well-educated Black Americans who appreciated being the beneficiaries of formal learning opportunities of which millions of their ancestors were unable to advantage due to slavery, neo-slavery, and other societal injustices. Such Black Americans, whom some people alleged comprised a talented tenth, believed they should attempt to help their less fortunate contemporaries rise to the same or similarly high levels in society as they themselves enjoyed.

Many articles in *The Oracle* dealt with general matters of racial uplift, but more articles focused on matters specific to Omega Psi Phi. For example, the 1919 inaugural issue of *The Oracle* contained an article by Lloyd H. Newman outlining the purpose of the Grand chapter. According to him, coordinating subordinate chapters and ensuring members of the subordinate chapter relayed uniformly positive messages regarding the Fraternity were two primary tasks of the Grand chapter. Recounting four conclaves of the Grand chapter from 1915 to 1918, Newman noted the first was at the Beta chapter at Lincoln University. The next three rotated between Lincoln and Howard University. Newman's report about the conclave, held in 1918 at Howard University, was of great significance to many readers because it revealed the serious work Omegas performed as well as the establishment of their Grand chapter. He wrote, "The first day was given to very inspiring addresses pertaining to fraternity life. The outgoing Grand Basileus, Dr. [Clarence] F. Holmes, despite his great illness[,] opened the session, outlining to the new delegates in a masterly way the purpose."[147]

1919 to 1920 Expansion and Elected (Honorary) Members

Between January 1919 and September 1920, Omega Psi Phi chartered seven chapters, the first four in 1919: Delta at the Meharry Medical College in Nashville, Tennessee, on January 27, 1919; Epsilon in New York City, New York, on April 18, 1919; Zeta at Virginia Union University in Richmond on October 30, 1919; Eta in Atlanta, Georgia, on December 27, 1919. The chapters that Omegas chartered in 1920 included but were not limited to: Iota in Atlantic City, New Jersey; Kappa at West Virginia Collegiate Institute; and Lambda in Norfolk, Virginia. The designation of Kappa was later transferred to Syracuse University and Theta Psi became the chapter name for West Virginia Collegiate Institute, and Lambda was later designated Lambda Omega.[148]

Besides chartering chapters in 1919 to 1920, Omegas created a status, or designation, called elective active (hereafter honorary member). In a 1919 issue of *The Oracle*, Sumter, South Carolina, native, Howard University alumnus, and Alpha chapter initiate Robert McCants Andrews provided a few principal reasons for the designation: "Solid achievement in life counts. Ultimate worth and valuation depend on substantial doing. What a man *does* makes him who he *is* and why he will be remembered."[149] Honorary members, Andrews expounded, would be "men of solid achievement, of substance, of worth" who succeeded in life despite the obstacles they confronted.[150]

Honorary members of Omega Psi Phi included its founder, Ernest E. Just, and Carter G. Woodson. William Pickens was another honorary designee. He was an author, multilingual and multisubject college professor and administrator, NAACP official, W. E. B. Du Bois supporter, and Marcus Mosiah Garvey Jr. critic who served as a dean at Morgan College (now Morgan State University). Yet another multilingual Black American, Colonel Charles Young, and Howard University English professor and department chair Gordon D. Houston were two additional honorary designees. The June 1919 issue of *The Oracle* also listed the other honorary members. Among them were Charles Victor Roman, a leading physician; James Carroll Napier, an administrator at the federal treasury; and Garnet Wilkinson, a prominent Washington, DC, educator.[151] Bestowing honorary status on deserving men not only was a way to recognize some of the most accomplished Black Americans of the early twentieth century, but the bestowal also provided a means for Omegas to establish additional chapters throughout the country.

The honorary members were an elite class of the Black intelligentsia in the early twentieth century. Their contributions to Black race uplift traversed academia, business, education, medicine, science, and other fields held by few Black Americans. A little known, but internationally acclaimed, honorary member was Roland Wiltse Hayes who was born on June 3, 1887, in Curryville, Georgia, in the Flatwoods area of Gordon County, Georgia. His parents, William and Fannie Hayes, had constructed a log cabin with a wood-burning fireplace, chimney, and kitchen—extraordinary accruements for a Black family in the post-Reconstruction south.[152] A central part of Hayes's upbringing was going to church with his brothers and sister exposing him to the Negro spirituals, which had evolved from slavery just a few decades earlier. As a young boy, Hayes was fascinated by his father's tenor voice and ability to mimic sounds in nature, which the elder Hayes used to effectively call his hogs. Hayes's father informed him that all humans had the ability to imitate sounds in the environment if they reached into their souls. Hayes later noted his father's voice influenced him, and Hayes tried to reach the souls of many through his singing.[153]

When Roland Hayes became an honorary member of Gamma chapter of Omega in 1919, he was thirty-two years old. By then, he had attended Fisk University where he sang with the Fisk Jubilee singers, performed offstage in a silent movie theater in Louisville, Kentucky, and performed by himself and with the Fisk Jubilee Singers in Boston on the east coast.[154] Although his career in the following decades would take him to international heights, Omega viewed him as a man capable of bridging the tensions between the Black and White worlds while elevating Black artistic culture. Writing in *The Oracle* in 1923, Howard Kennedy identified Hayes as the right Omega for the times:

> Probably you have never heard of Schubert, Franck, or the old Italian masters. Hayes sings their airs, their gentle, simple, love songs with a naturalness that is surprising. We know our own songs, the Spirituals, with their deep pathos and yearning. Roland Hayes gives them the plaintiveness and wistfulness which belongs to them as the echoes of days that are past.... A man is judged by his works, and so Roland Hayes has achieved. Year after year, he has achieved, until now he is nearing the height of a brilliant career. And he does not share his success alone; millions of people of a dark skinned race share it with him.[155]

A detailed description of how honorary Omegas were selected is elusive. However, Kennedy's description of Hayes and the attributes of other honorary men reflect the four cardinal principles as criteria. Hayes personified the cardinal principles and would be revered among Omegas for decades to come.

The Ninth Grand Conclave, Carter G. Woodson, and "Democracy and the Man Far Down"

Nashville, Tennessee, was the site of the Ninth Grand Conclave from December 27 to 30, 1920. Newspapers across the country began reporting about the scheduled conclave and its slogan, "On to Nashville," weeks before those dates.[156] On December 4, the *Chicago Defender* broadcast that Woodson, then dean of the West Virginia Collegiate Institute, would be the main speaker at the opening session of the Nashville Conclave.[157] On December 11, the *Philadelphia Tribune* not only advertised the conclave but also mentioned the fall 1920 organizing of Mu chapter at the University of Pennsylvania.[158] A second December item in the *Chicago Defender*, published on Christmas day, provided details about the format of the Ninth Grand Conclave: there would be two executive sessions during the day and two sessions at night, except for the first night, which organizers reserved for social activities. The *Defender*, in its December 25 issue, projected: "These distinguished representatives of Negro college life will assemble and outline a constructive program for the Negro of this country and delineate the larger opportunities and responsibilities in this new era of reconstruction, following in the aftermath of the great world conflict."[159] Concluding, the *Chicago Defender* stated that the

Fraternity's four cardinal principles—manhood, scholarship, perserverance, and uplift—"will serve as the groundwork for a proposed national policy."[160]

During the Nashville Conclave, Omega men made a fundamental shift toward becoming more assertive about education, so Woodson was an ideal member to deliver an opening-day speech at the conclave. By 1920, he was fast becoming one of the most prominent members of Omega Psi Phi. The second Black person to complete a PhD degree from Harvard University (W. E. B. Du Bois was the first), Woodson's 1912 dissertation, "The Disruption of Virginia," explored the state's 1861 secession from the Union and its subsequent role in the four-year Civil War.[161] As mentioned earlier in this chapter, Woodson founded the Association for the Study of Negro Life and History in 1915. During the same year, the association published his book, *The Education of the Negro Prior to 1861*.[162] During the next year, he established and began editing the *Journal of Negro History*.

Woodson's scholarly development paralleled and intersected with the early history of Omega Psi Phi. As much a race man as any other member of the Fraternity, his December 27, 1920, speech at the Nashville Conclave, "Democracy and the Man Far Down," focused on the need for Black people to learn about Black history and to develop an autonomous economic base by establishing businesses that employed Black people.[163] The Omegas who heard him admired his speech, which was arguably a foundation stone for his most far-reaching and widely read book, *The Mis-Education of the Negro* (1933).[164]

Woodson's December 1920 speech at the Nashville Conclave helped place Omega Psi Phi at the forefront of what certain scholars today refer to as the early Black history movement.[165] Participants helped challenge historical inaccuracies about Black people worldwide. Such occurrences would happen in time. The *Atlanta Independent* newspaper in January 1921 summarized the immediate reaction to Woodson's speech among objective people who heard or learned about it. According to the *Independent*, "unprejudiced critics" proclaimed Woodson's delivery "as the most constructive and scholarly address of his career. Woodson's extensive research work in the economical and historical field causes him to rank as one of the foremost exponents on the American platform in his respective field," the *Independent* concluded.[166]

Owing to speeches delivered by a dynamic lineup, headed by Woodson, and to numerous other scholarly, uplifting, and festive activities at the Nashville Conclave in December 1920, *The Oracle* declared: "beyond doubt [the conclave was] the most significant convention held in the history of the National Chapter."[167] Nearly every aspect of the Nashville Conclave was fine, but Woodson's words were superb. In a single narrative, he illuminated not only the struggle of Black people, but he also forecast various challenges that lay ahead for the Fraternity. In retrospect, "Democracy and the Man Far Down" was an appropriate bookend to the first decade of Omega Psi Phi and was foundational for the Negro History and Literature Week celebrations that Omegas began sponsoring one week per year after the Nashville Conclave.[168] Though unacknowledged by Woodson, those celebrations preceded the Negro History Week he launched formally in February 1926.[169]

The origin and early development of Omega Psi Phi were influenced tremendously by its birth in the days of the so-called Negro problem, by Black people's pursuits for racial uplift, and by the Great War (World War I). As the first fraternity founded at a Black college or university, Omega occupied a unique space among Black Greek-letter organizations. Omega's seeding and germination at Howard University in Washington, DC, a center of Black activity during the early twentieth century, shaped the Fraternity to emerge full blown out of the Black experience. The challenges that lay ahead for Omega harkened back to the founding years of the Fraternity and the shared commitments of its members to always remember the unique, Black-centered genesis of the organization.

As the end of Omega Psi Phi's first decade approached, Ernest E. Just spoke to the spirit of the present and to the future of Omega: "These times demand clean men, of clear vision, of straight thinking, of unselfish doing. And every Omega man must accept this challenge," he proclaimed.[170] More vigorously, Just said: "Out of groups like ours, men who know and feel *to the utmost* Fidelity, Liberty, and Fraternity, must come to the world absolution. Only by the bonds of brotherhood, stronger than life or death, which shall grip harder and more securely as ever greater numbers feel the tie," Just concluded, "shall the world at last stand unfettered of evil, because chained in real fraternity."[171]

Chapter 2

An Unusual Emphasis on Scholarship

The Success and Challenge of Expanding Black Educational Opportunity, 1920–1929

Omega men entered the 1920s with vigor, ready to build up the Fraternity as it approached its ten-year anniversary. As the decade began, there were just more than 1,000 members spread across fifteen chapters, and most of those chapters were chartered in 1919 or 1920. Over the next ten years, however, the Fraternity's growth accelerated and, by 1930, there were more than 3,000 Omega men and eighty-two chapters. Chapters spanned the Atlantic to Pacific coasts of the United States and across the Canadian border into Quebec. But the second decade of the Fraternity was not solely devoted to organizational expansion. Inspired by the Ninth Grand Conclave message of Carter G. Woodson, Omega men committed themselves more robustly to racial advancement.[1]

From 1920 to 1929, Omega men worked collectively toward a specific goal: to expand formal and informal educational opportunities for Black Americans. The urgency of that mission became clear when Woodson drew a clear connection between the dismal state of American democracy and Black Americans' second-class citizenship. He stressed the importance of racial pride, which derived from knowledge of one's own history of triumph and liberation beyond the narrative of slavery and oppression. Following Woodson's directive, Omega men committed themselves to addressing the pressing issue of Black education. Teachers, college presidents, school principals, professors, superintendents, and others in academia who belonged to the Fraternity took up its emphasis on scholarship and applied it to their local communities. In turn, the Fraternity and its chapters launched a series of annual programs to provide information about Black history and literature. The programs included scholarships and other formal educational opportunities that enabled beneficiaries to study abroad and informal events such as public debates over current events. Even Omega men with careers in fields seemingly unrelated to academia committed themselves to the foregoing efforts because of education's significance to Black Americans' lives and livelihoods.[2]

The pages that follow will show the wide range of educational programs in which Omega men engaged during the early 1920s. Though generally successful, some initiatives revealed the Fraternity's growing pains. Rapid expansion and the proliferation of programs at times blunted the efficacy of

Omega's educational initiatives, to the point the Fraternity was forced to pause and recalibrate by 1925. In the latter half of the decade, Omega men refocused their attention toward two systemic issues: the lack of Black leaders at Black educational institutions and standardizing curricula at those institutions. Members of the Fraternity became critical actors in shaping educational policies and practices, consequently molding public discourse around the governance of Black institutions. Omega Psi Phi's educational efforts ultimately helped set standards for curricular quality and define what it meant to qualify as a bona fide institution of higher education.

The Ideological Compass Guiding Fraternity Expansion

Battling lynching was a major undertaking for many Black Americans during the 1920s. In 1920 alone, there were at least sixty-one deaths by lynching in the United States, and most people executed in these violent acts were Black. Those tragic occurrences were so prevalent that newspapers across the country created lynching-record columns to update their readers. The frequency of lynching grew to a point that one newspaper declared, "This blot on the American nation must be removed, as well as railroading a man to prison or the gallows through the guise of lawful procedure."[3]

The deeply engrained racism of the early twentieth century was part of the reason that Meharry Medical College in Nashville was important to the 1920 Conclave. A decade earlier, there had been seven Black medical schools in the United States, including: Flint Medical College in New Orleans; the Howard University Medical Department in Washington, DC; Knoxville Medical College in Tennessee; Leonard Medical School in Raleigh, North Carolina; the Medical Department of the University of West Tennessee in Memphis; and the National Medical College in Louisville, Kentucky. In 1910, the Carnegie Foundation commissioned a White education researcher named Abraham Flexner to evaluate the effectiveness of medical training facilities in the United States and Canada. He concluded many facilities did not offer appropriate training. Released in 1910, the Flexner Report, as it was called, resulted in the number of US medical schools dwindling from 155 to 81 and the number of medical school graduates decreasing by half, from around 5,000 to about 2,500 per year. The Flexner report had a devasting impact on the training for Black health-care professionals because it labeled only Howard and Meharry as acceptable programs. Owning to that determination, the number of accredited medical institutions dedicated to serving the physical well-being of Black people decreased to two, Howard and Meharry.[4]

In deciding who besides Carter G. Woodson would deliver major addresses at the Nashville Conclave from December 27 to 30, 1920, members of the host chapter, Delta, selected one of their own, Charles Victor Roman. As a physician and medical historian, Roman was familiar with the dire issues of race and medical education. Schooled at the Hamilton Collegiate Institute in Canada, from which he was graduated with high honors, and later at Meharry, Roman published widely as a scholar and eventually became the head of the Meharry Department of Ophthalmology and Otolaryngology. The *Nashville Globe* newspaper considered him an "eminent and successful Negro specialist of diseases of eye, ear, nose, and throat" despite the fact he "met the same barrier that confronts so many young men as they emerge from college—race prejudice."[5]

Roman was a race man who revered Omega Psi Phi's four cardinal principles—manhood, scholarship, perseverance, and uplift—as much as he enjoyed instructing and practicing medicine. During his 1920 address at the Nashville Conclave, he discussed the Fraternity's principles "in their philosophical phases" and emphasized the need for Omega men to help expand educational opportunities for the broader Black citizenry. Two other Delta chapter members, James Carroll Napier and William Jasper Hale, spoke and delivered more general remarks than Roman. Napier, a Nashville businessman, civil rights activist, lawyer, and former register of the Treasury, "stressed the significance of the Omega spirit." Hale, the president of Tennessee Agricultural and Industrial (A&I) State Normal School for Negroes (now Tennessee State University) in Nashville, delivered a short address.[6]

Of all the speeches Omega men heard during the Nashville Conclave, Woodson's address, with its focus on Black history and education, was most central to guiding successive initiatives. Over the course of the four-day conclave, delegates agreed to endorse "the study of the stock market," "reading of the financial review," and "the supporting of Negro schools by Negro wealth."[7] The delegates' most notable decision, however, was "to designate a week for a campaign for the study of Negro Literature and History."[8] The campaign ultimately became the Fraternity's first national program.[9] Adhering to Woodson's charge, the Fraternity's new campaign encouraged chapters to bring the study of Black history to their local communities.

The call for the widespread study of Black history and literature was a reminder that Howard University was the seedbed for the Fraternity, but it was not reflective of the country as a whole. Howard was a hub of Black intelligentsia, but the university was inaccessible to most Black Americans because they resided outside of Washington, DC, and did not have sufficient means to travel to or reside in the nation's capital. Federal censuses were illustrative. In 1920, there were 10.4 million Black people living in the United States, with most of them residing in southern states. Georgia (1,689,114), Mississippi (935,184), and Alabama (900,652) each tallied about 1 million Black residents.

South Carolina (864,719), North Carolina (763,407), Texas (741,694), Louisiana (700,257), and Virginia (690,017) each had hundreds of thousands. Fewer Black people lived in Arkansas (472,220), Tennessee (451,758), and Florida (329,487), but their numbers were sizable. Each of the foregoing eleven states—located along the Atlantic Ocean, the Gulf of Mexico, or the Mississippi River—had long-sustained economies built on slavery. Decades after the Thirteenth Amendment to the US Constitution abolished legalized slavery in 1865, many Black citizens remained largely disenfranchised because of Jim Crow laws and extralegal violence, among other unjust means. The limitations millions of Black Americans faced in the early twentieth century became further evident to Omega men as they acquired more data about educational attainment.[10]

By the time Edgar Amos Love, Oscar James Cooper, Frank Coleman, and Ernest Everett Just founded Omega Psi Phi at Howard University in 1911, researchers had begun to take stock of Black higher education. For instance, in 1910, scholar W. E. B. Du Bois and Augustus Granville Dill assessed thirty-two Black colleges in the United States. Historian James D. Anderson, author of *The Education of Blacks in the South* and a 1963 initiate of the Rho Gamma chapter, noted, this was a "careful evaluation." Du Bois and Dill reported that eleven "First-Grade Colored Colleges"—institutions with collegiate-level curricula—they evaluated included Atlanta and Morehouse in Georgia, Fisk in Tennessee, Howard in Washington, DC, and Virginia Union. They listed Lincoln in Pennsylvania, Wilberforce in Ohio, and Talladega in Alabama as "Second-Grade Colored Colleges."[11] In 1917, Thomas Jesse Jones, a White researcher and director of the educational survey of Black schools, released a two-volume study of Black colleges and universities. Not unlike Abraham Flexner's 1910 report on medical training facilities, Jones's 1917 study, which the US Department of Education supported, reflected a Progressive Era campaign to reform politics and to eliminate social excess. Though seemingly noble, the campaign further stigmatized Black education. For example, Jones's survey indicated that only one out of the sixteen Black land-grant colleges or universities, meaning institutions founded under the 1890 Morrill Land Grant Act, offered collegiate-level coursework. Florida Agricultural and Mechanical (A&M) College (now University) was that institution but, even there, according to Jones, a mere twelve students were earning a collegiate level. All other students were earning a secondary education.[12]

The Du Bois and Jones reports captured the attention of Omega men, but most of the Fraternity's members knew that assessments of Black education warranted caution. In the early twentieth century, researchers often had personal or political agendas when they evaluated Black schools. For instance, all institutions Du Bois and Dill termed first or second grade were private. Moreover, each institution tended to offer a classical liberal arts curriculum. In contrast, Jones used a narrow view of industrial and vocational education as his standard for evaluation. Omega man Carter G. Woodson later said Jones used "the well established and amply resourced Hampton Institute as his criterion" for what was a bona fide Black school.[13] Woodson and many other Omega men were critical of White officials' opinions on Black education, but the Fraternity would soon address the differences in private and public Black college curricula offerings. This would prove essential to the Fraternity's effort around education.

As stated earlier in this chapter, increasing the Fraternity's capacity to provide educational opportunities for Black Americans was a main desire of the Omega men who attended the Nashville Conclave in 1920, but, first, the campaign required logistical support. Therefore, they elected outgoing Grand Basileus Raymond G. Robinson as the Fraternity's first Field Secretary. A charter member of Beta chapter at Lincoln University in Pennsylvania, Robinson as Grand Basileus since 1918 helped the Fraternity expand from three chapters to ten, including Delta chapter which hosted the Nashville Conclave in 1920. Organizing those chapters as the Fraternity's organizational and ideological expansion took root was his primary responsibility as Field Secretary. Conclave delegates also elected William Stuart Nelson to a recently created post called Director of Publicity. A 1916 initiate of Alpha chapter, Nelson in 1920 was a first-year student at Union Theological Seminary in New York City. On New Year's Eve, having solidified the Fraternity's education mission and selected a staff to lead its execution, Robinson, Nelson, and their fellow delegates adjourned the conclave and returned to their homes, *The Oracle* reported, with "resolutions made that the year before us should be one of our best effort, of genuine sacrifice for Omega."[14]

The spirit of sacrifice among Omega men would be vital, which *The Oracle* reported was important to Omega men as they faced a difficult political environment in the United States in 1921. For example, on August 18, 1920, approximately four months before the Nashville Conclave opened, Congress ratified the Nineteenth Amendment prohibiting voting discrimination on the basis of sex and giving Congress the ability to enforce the amendment; however, White lawmakers in the South passed Jim Crow legislation that essentially nullified the chances that millions of Black women in the South would wield the ballot. Another example, in Huntsville, Alabama, roughly 110 miles south of Nashville, Black women comprised only six of the 1,445 women who registered to vote in the 1920 federal elections before the registration period ended on October 26. According to several newspapers, the reason for the dearth of Black registrants was simple: White local and state election officials applied citizenship, dictation, and literacy tests; poll taxes; and other disenfranchisement measures to both "colored men [and] colored women."[15]

Harold Hillyer Thomas, an Atlanta, Georgia, native whom Omegas elected as Grand Basileus during the Nashville Conclave, understood the precarious status of Black Americans. Born in 1895 and initiated into the Beta chapter while he attended Lincoln University in Pennsylvania from 1917 to 1919, the twenty-five-year-old Thomas used his first annual message as Grand Basileus, published in a 1921 issue of *The Oracle*, to issue a charge to all Omega men. From the Fraternity's highest office, Thomas declared: "Let us fraternity men not waste our time in dissipations, but let us accept the ideals of Omega Psi Phi as real and vital." With those words, Thomas set forth a vision for how the Fraternity should best accomplish the goals on which its members voted a few weeks earlier in Nashville. Also in his annual message, Thomas implored his fellow Omegas to "live up to [the ideals the founders established] and leave our college and our fraternity better for our having been in them."[16]

Besides voting, the expanding reach of lynching and other forms of violence targeted at Black people was a key impetus for Omega's urgent turn toward education. At the time of Thomas's election to Grand Basileus, he lived in Atlanta, his birthplace and Georgia's capital city. According to investigations conducted by employees of Tuskegee Institute, Georgia was second only to Texas in the total deaths caused by lynching in 1920.[17] Lynchers killed nine people in Georgia and ten people in Texas during that year.[18] The seven lynch killings in Alabama, where Tuskegee was located, tied Florida and Mississippi for third place among the deadliest "lynching states" in the country.[19] Many lynching deaths went unreported, however, and most informed Black people—regardless of their places of residence—were familiar with more violent encounters than newspapers, academic institutions, and other sources publicized. Years later, a study by the Equal Justice Initiative titled, *Lynching in America*, found that 589 Black people were lynched in Georgia between 1877 and 1950.[20] Those lynchings constituted the second most in the country during that period; Mississippi was first with 654.[21]

As Omega Psi Phi continued its countrywide expansion from 1920 to 1921, members reckoned with the fact that White mob violence was not limited to southern states, nor was such violence lessening.[22] As per one report, the number of lynching deaths from January through June of 1921 outpaced such deaths during the timespan in 1920.[23] Moreover, verified lynchings in California, Illinois, Minnesota, Ohio, and elsewhere in the country, the *Atlanta Constitution* newspaper declared in 1921, "shows that the evil of mob lawlessness is becoming more general; that it is no longer even measurably confined to the South." The *Constitution* went on, "lynching is no longer a sectional vice, but is rapidly becoming nation-wide."[24]

Implicitly criticizing bigoted White educators for planting and then cultivating tainted seeds of racial bias and violence in the heads of impressionable youth, Carter G. Woodson later professed "there would be no lynching if it did not start in the schoolroom. Why not exploit, enslave, or exterminate a class that everybody is taught to regard as inferior?"[25]

Informed by these ideas, Grand Basileus Harold H. Thomas's annual message in 1921 explained how education would be the cornerstone of the Fraternity going forward. "I further hold the opinion that the fraternity is a powerful influence in our educational institutions, working toward an enlightened democracy," he said. "We are striving for the control of our colleges and our country thru intelligence rather than by irrational force of ignorant numbers." Thomas also said chapter expansion should be intertwined with attention toward education. "The Omega Psi Phi Fraternity has ever placed an unusual emphasis on scholarship," he added. "Unless, as a fraternity, we can show that, in the various institutions in which our chapters are located, the scholarship of our brethren is as high as the general college average and even higher, we cannot justify our existence."[26]

In the coming months, Thomas, alongside the Fraternity's newly appointed publicist William Stuart Nelson, helped coordinate an ambitious public relations operation to draw attention to the Fraternity's Campaign for the Study of Negro Literature and History. In Georgia, the *Atlanta Independent*, a Black-owned and -operated newspaper, ensured that its readers knew details of the campaign: "In the early spring, the Fraternity will conduct a campaign to encourage the study of Negro literature and history in the various high schools, colleges, and homes throughout the land, or, in other words, to introduce the world to the Negro and, at the same time, introduce the Negro to himself." The newspaper also explained how Omega "is universally recognized among college men as having the highest and most rigid standards for membership requirements," and "its honorary rolls contain the names of men of national reputation who have brought glory upon their race and their Fraternity in the realms of politics, science, music, literature, and art."[27]

The *Atlanta Independent* was not the only Black newspaper in the United States that provided information about Omega's work in 1921. During the spring months, after the Fraternity launched its new educational campaign, several papers ran a wire story by the Associated Negro Press that elaborated on such work. The Fraternity offered a Black history manual for people that featured a series of "Do You Know?" questions. As the *Baltimore Afro-American* reported: "The Omega Psi Phi Fraternity has recently issued a folder which, among other things, presents the following facts of Negro history: Do you know the world is indebted to the Negro for the discovery of iron? Do you know the facts in the Dred Scott decision? Do you know the provisions of the Thirteenth, Fourteenth, and Fifteenth Amendments? Do you know the following men were of Negro descent: Terence in Rome, Pushkin in Russia, Dumas in France, Toussaint L'Ouverture in Haiti, Coleridge-Taylor of England?"[28] These and related questions set the tone for the campaign.

In April and May 1921, chapters conducted the first programs focused on enlightening the broader public about Black life and history. In Chester County, Pennsylvania, where Lincoln University was located, Beta chapter held several educational exercises and a public mass meeting, submitted articles to local newspapers, and distributed literature. Beta chapter editor Thomas B. Hargrave, a Lincoln theological seminarian, confirmed the "campaign has been a shining success here. Every morning, the entire student body looked forward with keen interest."[29] In Boston, Gamma chapter Basileus George C. Brouche assessed "the campaign has been quite a success in Boston. And even now the whole of Boston seems awakened to a new realization of what racial achievement and solidarity mean." Writing from Atlanta, Georgia, Grand Basileus Harold H. Thomas indicated, "the campaign has been a howling success all over the country, and more than a success in Atlanta." Omega men representing Atlanta's Eta and Omicron chapters spoke at "every institution of learning in the city, including colleges, grammar schools, and private schools." Ervie W. Greene, Basileus of Zeta chapter at Virginia Union in Richmond, requested 300 additional circulars for the chapter to share, and George D. Brooks, Basileus of Nu chapter at Pennsylvania State University, reported similar public interest, so the chapter shared articles with newspapers.[30]

Omega founder Frank Coleman celebrated the Campaign for the Study of Negro Literature and History as a noble endeavor. "Active service must be the slogan of every National Negro Greek Letter Fraternity," he said. Then, addressing fraternity men specifically, Coleman suggested they "encourage everyone with whom he comes in contact to become a regular subscriber to some good Negro newspaper."[31] Former Grand Basileus George E. Hall, a 1914 initiate of Alpha chapter, also praised the Fraternity's literature and history campaign for its practical benefits. Hall, who was instrumental in publishing the first issues of *The Oracle*, said "It is quite fair to say that a child or an adult who has never studied whatever history and literature his own race has produced should be considered ignorant." Therefore, Hall added, "The campaign for the Study of Negro History and Literature conducted by the Omega Psi Phi Fraternity should meet the approval and secure the co-operation of all Negro men and women who are interested in the intellectual growth of the race and its future achievements."[32]

While chapters executed their first Black history and literature programs, Omega Psi Phi organized new chapters as additional outposts to expand the

Fraternity's educational efforts. Pi chapter (now Pi Omega chapter), organized on April 21, 1921, was one of those chapters. A combination of new initiates and transfer brothers quickly made Pi Omega a graduate chapter of distinction whose membership included "a number of prominent citizens," the *Baltimore Afro-American* noted. Among its respected roster, clergymen Omega founder Edgar Amos Love of the Methodist Church and John Hurst of the African Methodist Church were exemplars. Pi Omega's roster also included William T. Carr, a physician who spearheaded the chapter's local education program. He led a fundraising campaign to help Morgan College (now Morgan State University) equip its science labs. Pi Omega's editor, Harry F. Pratt, indicated that Carr "conceived the idea of concentrating our concrete endeavors in the interest of Morgan College," as the "institution occupies a strategic position in the field of educational opportunity for our youth in Maryland."[33]

At the undergraduate level, numerous members of new chapters played an active role in education. Those belonging to Phi chapter at the University of Michigan were representative. Within the first year of the chapter, organized on May 2, 1921, by Raymond G. Robinson, former Grand Basileus and present Field Secretary, Phi cosponsored a program with the Ann Arbor branch of the National Association for the Advancement of Colored People (NAACP). John R. Cottin, a charter member of Phi chapter, was the only Black student in the University of Michigan Educational Club. Cottin also was appointed to the university's student advisory committee. On May 8, 1921, only six days after Phi was established, the Fraternity organized Xi chapter at the University of Minnesota with Earle F. Kyle as the chapter's Basileus.[34]

Omega's expansion unfolded as the broader struggle for Black freedom ebbed and flowed. There was Black joy and comradery. For instance, on May 27, 1921, Eta chapter in Atlanta hosted a member-only reception. Grand Basileus Harold H. Thomas read telegrams about Fraternity business and other events sponsored by Black citizens although everyone present knew future safe and joyous fellowship among friends and associates was not a guarantee, as violent White supremacists could lash out with impunity. Proof of that unfortunate fact came soon. On May 30, three days after Eta chapter's reception, White mobs targeted the heavily Black Greenwood District of Tulsa, Oklahoma. On May 31 and June 1, the mobs destroyed Black homes and businesses and killed innocent Black citizens.[35]

For years after the Tulsa massacre in 1921, estimates of Black deaths resulting from the tragedies of May 30 and 31 ranged from about three dozen to as many as 300. Scores more Black citizens suffered injuries. No different than lynching deaths, many White newspaper reports fluctuated in terms of accounting for Black death and, regrettably, the Tulsa massacre was only one of many such deadly outbreaks of ethnic violence that followed World War I. The problem was not solely about well-to-do Black families; the majority of those impacted—even in Tulsa—were working-class Black families who did not enjoy the fruits of the Black Wall Street narrative. The impact of the violence on the racial advancement efforts of Omega men, particularly young brothers, was tremendous. Decades later, Roy Wilkins, a member of Xi chapter at the University of Minnesota (and future NAACP executive director), lamented: "The Tulsa riot illustrates the classic lie of criminal assault which was used for decades to justify lynching and assaults upon Negroes in both the South and the North. . . . If young black people will study the history of their people in America," Wilkins added, "the race can go far."[36]

Wilkins's comment about the importance of learning history reflected the Omega program's intent to reach a broader segment of the citizenry than the Fraternity's membership despite staunch racism by countless White Americans. To that end, Omega chapters engaged in a hodgepodge of events around the axis of Black history and literature throughout the remainder of 1921. Mu chapter hosted an August banquet at Hotel Dale in Philadelphia, Pennsylvania. Omega founder and local physician Oscar James Cooper presided over the banquet. Omega men from Beta chapter at Lincoln University not far from Philadelphia were among the attendees. They were joined by members from Epsilon chapter in New York City, from Eta chapter in Atlanta (now at Alcorn State University), from Iota chapter in Atlantic City (now in Chicago), and from Nu chapter at Pennsylvania State University. Frank Wimberley, a charter member of Alpha chapter, delivered the keynote address. The Fraternity's future was his subject. To provide context, Wimberley, who was an attorney in Atlantic City, discussed Omega's history before outlining what the Fraternity sought to accomplish going forward.[37]

While Wimberley was the keynote speaker at the August 1921 banquet at Hotel Dale, other Omega men also gave informative talks. Julius S. McClain of Beta chapter made a "timely and spirited address on the 'International Aspects of the Fraternity.'"[38] Indeed, his topic and timing were excellent, since William Stuart Nelson was scheduled to represent the Fraternity at the Pan-African Congress in Brussels, Belgium, in September 1921. Nelson's attendance was a nod to the Fraternity's awareness of, and some brothers' interest in, the Universal Negro Improvement Association, the Black nationalist organization founded by Pan-Africanist Marcus Garvey.[39] Not long after the Pan-African Congress, Omega men in Atlanta, Georgia, hosted a grand musical and literary concert. They held the event on September 12 inside the historic Big Bethel AME Church.[40] In November, Carter G. Woodson visited the brothers of Lambda chapter (now Lambda Omega) in Norfolk, Virginia, to discuss Black history.[41]

An Unusual Emphasis on Scholarship

This range of activities the Fraternity chapters and individual brothers sponsored or participated in set the stage for the Tenth Grand Conclave that the Eta and Omicron chapters hosted in Atlanta from December 27 to 31, 1921. Notices about the conclave appeared widely in both Black- and White-owned newspapers, such as the *Chicago Defender* and the *Atlanta Constitution*, respectively, and the publicity delighted Omegas. They decided to hold the Grand Conclave in Atlanta because the city had become a premier southern destination for inward migration among Black people leaving rural areas for the growing urban space. Between 1900 and 1920, Atlanta's Black population nearly doubled from 35,727 to 67,796, and Atlanta University became a center for the study of Black life during that same period.[42]

Considering that Atlanta was an economic and educational engine among Black people by 1921, to hold that year's conclave in the city was a prudent decision. The YMCA building on Butler Street was the Atlanta Conclave headquarters. That branch of the YMCA had serviced the Black Auburn Avenue district, known affectionately as "Sweet Auburn," since 1894.[43] The 1921 Grand Conclave furthermore aligned with a Fraternity cardinal principle, uplift, by contributing to the financial well-being of a southern city with a sizable Black population. Atlanta hosted 321 conventions in 1921, and the Omegas' conclave was penultimate. It and other meetings brought approximately 100,000 attendees to the city, and they spent more than $3 million in total. Their dollars helped contribute to the livelihoods of the working-class Black people who worked in sundry capacities before, during, and even after the meetings.[44]

The Atlanta Conclave opened on December 27, 1921, with the largest attendance in the Fraternity's history. Delegates represented many colleges and universities from across the United States. Biddle (now Johnson C. Smith University), Harvard, Howard, Lincoln (Pennsylvania), Northwestern, Michigan, Meharry, Pennsylvania State, the University of Chicago, and Yale were in that number. Atlanta residents described the public ceremonies the Omegas held at the First Congregational Church as inspirational.[45]

William Pickens, a professor and dean at Morgan College in Baltimore, was the principal speaker for the Atlanta Conclave's session open to the public. According to the *Atlanta Constitution*, Pickens was an honor graduate of Yale who had great oratorical skills. He was known for his 1905 role as a founding member of the Niagara Movement, a precursor to the NAACP, and for writing multiple books. *The Heir of Slaves* (1911), the first volume of his eventually two-volume autobiography (with *Bursting Bonds*, 1923), emphasized racial tensions in the country and drew much acclaim. Omega men elected Pickens to the Fraternity on March 4, 1916, and five years later, he titled his Atlanta Conclave speech, "The Value of Group Self-Respect." After hearing it, one knowledgeable observer confirmed Pickens as "one of the leading orators of the race."⁴⁶

All other notable Omega men speakers at the Tenth Grand Conclave were from Atlanta. One speaker, William Fletcher Penn, was a prominent doctor who welcomed attendees to the city and the state. John Wesley Edward Bowen was the first Black person to earn a PhD degree from Boston University. As a professor and an administrator at the Gammon Theological Seminary in Atlanta, Bowen brought greetings on behalf of southern colleges and universities, but an address about "the kind of education necessary for the Negro's highest development" was his main speaking endeavor. William Johnson Trent Sr., executive secretary of the Butler Street YMCA, engaged conclave delegates about the Fraternity's four cardinal principles: manhood, scholarship, perseverance, and uplift.⁴⁷

Omegas held the closing sessions of the Atlanta Conclave at the Butler Street YMCA. Delegates condemned state-sanctioned physical violence and agreed to send telegrams urging members of Congress to pass the antilynching bill proposed by Missouri representative Leonidas Carstarphen Dyer. Delegates also agreed that April 2 to 8, 1922, would be the period during which chapters observed the second Campaign for the Study of Negro History and Literature. Ensuring that "all schools and colleges of the country [were] devoted to the training of Negro youth will be called upon to celebrate this week with appropriate exercises" was a main goal of the campaign. To accomplish it and allied goals of the education program, new Fraternity officers elected during the conclave knew they had to preserve or devise innovative organizational mechanisms to help guarantee efficiency and growth.⁴⁸

Delegates to the Atlanta Conclave elected Jasper Alston Atkins as Grand Basileus. Atkins, who usually went by J. Alston or Jack, was born on August 8, 1898, in Winston-Salem, North Carolina. He began his undergraduate studies at Fisk University in Nashville, but when World War I broke out, he joined the special officer training camp for Black college students that the US War Department established at Howard University. On September 9, 1918, members of the Fraternity's Camp Howard chapter elected Atkins as its Keeper of Seals during their first meeting. A week later, students finished their training at Camp Howard and, after his return to Nashville that fall, he soon joined Delta chapter when it was organized on January 22, 1919, and became Keeper of Seals there as well. Atkins graduated magna cum laude from Fisk on May 28, 1919. Afterwards, he moved to New England and joined the Gamma chapter in Boston. Next, he enrolled in the Yale Law School where, in time, he became the first Black man to serve on the editorial board of the *Yale Law Journal*, of which Atkins eventually served as editor. All the while, Atkins remained active in the growing Fraternity and joined Chi chapter when it was organized on June 11, 1921, in New Haven, Connecticut, where Yale is located. Those professional and Omega achievements were major, but one of his greatest accomplishments was when delegates elected him Grand Basileus when he was a twenty-three-year-old law student.[49]

Atkins's wide-ranging, transient, and character-building life experiences made him the archetypal Omega man to lead the ideological and organizational expansion of the Fraternity. Delegates to the Atlanta Conclave also elected other accomplished Omega men to serve as national officers: Benjamin W. Clayton, a Chicago attorney, became Grand Keeper of Records; George I. Lythcott, from Boston, Grand Keeper of Seals; and Tennessee A&I professor William Gilbert editor of *The Oracle*.[50] In his first annual message as Grand Basileus, Atkins emphasized the need for uniform bookkeeping among the chapters—a testament to his leadership in the Camp Howard, Delta, Gamma, and Chi chapters. He considered keeping accurate records as "the first thing to be done in the management of any organization is to take stock of what the organization has, discarding that which has no value, and retaining that which will promote the development and solidity of the organization."[51] Atkins also sought "to institute a system of bookkeeping and uniform records and forms by which [the Fraternity's] forces can always be marshalled."[52] In support of systematic records, Atkins also sought for *The Oracle* issues to be published on a regular quarterly schedule. Then, he turned his attention to the Fraternity's growth in 1922. "We are hoping by the end of this year to set up at least ten strong graduate chapters in strategic points throughout the country," Atkins explained.[53]

"It is hoped that we shall be able so to correlate the graduate and undergraduate chapters that there will be complete harmony and cooperation throughout the entire fraternity."[54] In support of this plan, Lythcott, the new Grand Keeper of Seals, said all of Atkins's proposed efforts together would help to "carry on properly the drive for the study of Negro history."[55]

Moving forward, Atkins, Lythcott, and other decision-making Omega men intended for chapters to be established in alignment with the goal of expanding educational opportunities to more Black Americans; therefore, the 1922 Campaign for the Study of Negro History and Literature—with the slogan "Know Thyself"—was more ambitious than the initial campaign in 1921.[56] The February 1922 issue of *The Oracle* referred to the campaign simply as "Negro Week," indicating the week "was planned to invite all Negro institutions of learning and other Negro institutions, wherever possible, to join with us in one week of intensive study of the Negro as a race." The Fraternity invited more than one hundred schools—most of which did not have an Omega chapter—to participate. "We are asking that every Omega man in the country, both graduate and undergraduate, exert every possible effort toward seeing that this campaign is made a success this year," *The Oracle* stated, adding: "See to it that notices of the campaign appear in your local dailies and weekly papers, see that your school officials are interviewed and influenced to observe" Negro Week. "Let us press toward the mark which all loyal Omega men expect of us and which is in keeping with our opportunities and capabilities," Atkins advised, expounding: "This mark is the making of the Omega Psi Phi Fraternity the greatest group of thinking Negroes in America."[57]

Before Atkins could begin implementing his plan in earnest, tragedy struck the Fraternity: on January 8, 1922, a week after the Atlanta Conclave ended, Omega man Charles Young, a US Army colonel, died while on military assignment in Lagos, Nigeria. Young was fifty-seven years old, but still accepted the assignment despite his failing health. The *Chicago Defender* correctly referred to Young as a perfect officer and, as one of the first elected (honorary) members into Omega, his death spurred an abrupt shift in the Campaign for the Study of Negro History and Literature. Originally, Atkins and other national Fraternity officers planned to continue the campaign throughout the United States. Young embodied Black history, however, so Atkins and his colleagues who made up the Fraternity's national office decided to have subordinate chapters host local memorial services in tribute to Young on March 12, his birthday. The gesture was appropriate, as Young was the quintessential Omega man, but trying to organize and execute a unified tribute countrywide foreshadowed a problem: too many initiatives for an eleven-year-old fraternity.[58]

The Fraternity's Problem of Too Many Programs

Omega Psi Phi continued to grow as its national officers—or Supreme Council—attempted to execute the Fraternity's educational campaign and to observe Young's passing. On February 18, 1922, Omega men organized Kappa chapter at Syracuse University in New York. For a brief period, the chapter was at West Virginia Collegiate Institute (now called West Virginia State University), where Omega men had established the chapter in 1920. The eighteen members of the subsequent Kappa chapter at Syracuse also comprised students from nearby Colgate University, Hamilton College, and the University of Rochester. Charles T. Kimbrough, a Beta chapter initiate who was attending Syracuse for medical school in February 1922, was the first Basileus of the northern-based Kappa chapter. Though hurt by Young's death, the Fraternity's expanded physical and intellectual presence inspired Grand Basileus Atkins. "The Supreme Council has a big program in regard to the establishment of new chapters and the development of the Fraternity generally," he stated notably.[59]

Regrettably, much of the uniformity Atkins desired among chapters in relation to programming was lost. As the Fraternity chartered additional chapters, Atkins and other national officers had to deal with mounting, and often varying, approaches to educating the public. Atkins's own agenda exacerbated issues. In addition to spreading Black history and literature in schools and communities, he issued a memorial service mandate to honor Young. The emergence of Omega men in the performing arts to demonstrate Black history and culture was an additional effort the Fraternity had to consider. The growing anti-lynching campaign, led largely by undergraduate Omegas, was a third important effort; and ever-present accolades for individual Omegas, both living and deceased, was a fourth important effort.

To the point of the memorial services, in May 1922, W. E. Hill, a member of Rho chapter chartered in December 1921 at Biddle University (now Johnson C. Smith University) in Charlotte, reported: "Our first public appearance was made on the afternoon of March 12, [1922, at] Colonel Young's memorial, and the impression made has found expression in generous commendation."[60] In Atlanta, Omega men and members of the local branch of the NAACP held a memorial service for Young at Big Bethel AME Church. There, John Wesley Edward Bowen, representing the Fraternity, said Young's "fight against poverty, tradition, and prejudice was much harder to win than facing shot and shell."[61] Although not a member of the Fraternity, John Hope, president of Morehouse College, also spoke of how education persuaded Young to attend West Point.[62] Elsewhere in the country, Omega chapters answered Grand Basileus Atkins's call to honor Young on his birthday and held similar memorial services in March 1922.

As many Omegas paid tribute to Young, some participated in the burgeoning movement in the arts on colleges and universities across the United States. It was reported in May 1922, several members of the Alpha chapter at Howard University earned lead roles in campus theater productions. One member, Thomas J. Hopkins, served as both business manager and technical director of the Howard Players. Farther south, at Morehouse College, an impressive group of young intellectuals and artists included James Madison Nabrit Jr. In addition to being the first Keeper of Seals for Psi chapter (which was approved during the Atlanta Conclave and chartered at Morehouse in April 1922), he managed the production for a campus play. In 1922, immediate past Grand Basileus Harold H. Thomas led a combined music and literature program at Ebenezer Baptist Church in Atlanta. Considered together, his and other Omega men's involvement in extracurricular programs while prioritizing their curricula obligations was a testament to the Harlem Renaissance as a growing intellectual revival of the Black arts movement and foretold other Omegas' involvement in related activities later during the 1920s.[63]

While some Omega men creatively depicted Black life and history through arts, others took part in the humanities and social sciences. Also in May 1922, members of Alpha chapter reported that Zephaniah Alexander Looby, an Alpha chapter member originally from Antigua in the British West Indies, was student council president at Howard University. About the same time, Arthur Daniel Williams, a Beta chapter initiate from Abingdon, Virginia, organized the National Student Anti-Lynching League. Its roster contained representatives of numerous Black colleges and universities from across the United States. An accomplished writer and committed activist, Williams in 1920 won a national essay contest sponsored by the NAACP for his analysis of lynching. By the time he established the anti-lynching league on March 29, 1922, three months after the Atlanta Conclave, he had dedicated himself to eradicating lynching. Of no surprise, then, Williams, an honor student who earned an undergraduate degree from Lincoln University (Pennsylvania) in June 1918, rejoiced when the US House of Representatives voted to pass the Dyer Anti-Lynching Bill in January 1922. His excitement in the seeming progressiveness of federal lawmaking had lessened significantly by May 1922, however. The US Senate was a major part of Williams's change of mind. Bigoted senators in the Democratic Party effectively blocked passage of the anti-lynching bill via a series of filibusters.[64]

The Dyer Anti-Lynching Bill's failure in the US Senate motivated Williams to accelerate his anti-lynching activism in 1922. Among other endeavors, he increased the amount of time he spent encouraging undergraduate and graduate students to demand the federal government enact an anti-lynching law. In June, newspapers like the *Norfolk Journal and Guide* in Virginia announced an Inter-Fraternal Council—comprising the Omega Psi Phi, Alpha Phi Alpha, Kappa Alpha Psi, and Phi Beta Sigma fraternities, and the Alpha Kappa Alpha, Delta Sigma Theta, and Zeta Phi Beta sororities—would hold an Anti-Lynching Day.[65] Together, the *Norfolk Journal and Guide* stated, those Black Greek-letter organizations "will seek to have a message on anti-lynching given from every pulpit in every city and town in the United States on that day."[66]

On June 30, 1922, Williams led a delegation from the National Student Anti-Lynching League to meet with US president Warren Gamaliel Harding. Williams and other anti-lynching activists, such as Maryland native Lilla L. Martin, a Black student at Howard University, already captured Harding's attention through spirited talks before churches and other organizations along the eastern seaboard.[67] At the meeting with Harding, Williams explained to the president that lynching deaths disgraced the country and presented him with a fourteen-page pamphlet titled "Lynching, Its Causes and Cures."[68] Harding, claiming to support the anti-lynching bill, predicted "everything will come out all right, for the current is flowing in that direction."[69]

For the rest of 1922 and into 1923 and onward, bigoted White US senators repeatedly caused the current about which Harding spoke optimistically to flow in reverse, meaning against passage of a federal anti-lynching law. Therefore, Williams's ability to secure a meeting with Harding was a personal achievement for Williams. In the wake of the meeting, the Fraternity continued its tradition of celebrating such achievements. In some respects, the lives Williams and other activist members of the Fraternity modeled were as great of an exhibition of the four cardinal principles—manhood, scholarship, perseverance, and uplift—as any fraternity program. The September 1922 issue of *The Oracle*, however, concentrated on one cardinal principle: scholarship. Deemed the "Educational Number," the issue highlighted Omega men's scholarly attainments.[70]

Grand Basileus J. Alston Atkins and Carter Walker Wesley were two standout class of 1922 graduates the September issue of *The Oracle* featured. While serving as Grand Basileus, Atkins completed Yale Law School and, after a brief stay in New Haven, relocated to Muskogee, Oklahoma, and joined a firm with offices in Muskogee and Tulsa. As discussed earlier in this chapter, Atkins's decision to perform legal services in those Oklahoma localities spoke to his awareness of the 1921 Tulsa massacre. Wesley was an equally accomplished young legal mind. Born in Houston, Texas, Wesley studied at Fisk University. In fact, for a brief moment, his time overlapped with Atkins as a student at the university from which Wesley graduated magma cum laude as his class's top student in 1917. Later during that year, while undergoing officer training in Des Moines, Iowa, Wesley joined the War chapter. In 1919, after commanding infantry troops overseas, he enrolled in law school at Northwestern University in Illinois. Three years later, Wesley became the first Black student to earn a juris doctorate from Northwestern. Wesley then joined Atkins in Oklahoma, where they formed the Saddler, Atkins, & Wesley law offices in Tulsa and Muskogee.[71]

The Oracle of September 1922 also highlighted Omega man Percy Lavon Julian, a chemistry instructor at Fisk University known for his dynamic lectures. Born in Montgomery, Alabama, in 1899, Julian completed undergraduate studies at DePauw University in Greencastle, Indiana, in 1920. He obviously was not a member of any graduating class in 1922, but *The Oracle* featured him because of the "numerous honors to which he has been elected by some of the leading universities of the country."[72] For instance, at DePauw, Julian became a member of Phi Beta Kappa, the historically White academic honor society founded in 1776 that did not accept its first Black member until 1877.[73] Julian later excelled at instructing chemistry at Fisk, receiving a letter of recommendation from the university's president, Fayette Avery McKenzie, to attend Harvard for graduate-level study in chemistry. McKenzie, a White educator from Pennsylvania who earned a doctorate from the University of Pennsylvania, wrote of Julian: "Fisk owes him recognition for the improvements he made in our laboratory arrangements, organization, and methods, as well as for the standard requirements of quantity and quality of work which he set for his students in chemistry. We anticipate a fine record for him in his graduate studies at Harvard."[74]

This scholarly height to which Julian rose was the standard expected of Omega men since the Fraternity's founding. Even if an Omega man fell short of reaching that standard, that he would try hard to reach that standard was the expectation. The September 1922 issue of *The Oracle* declared: "Education is the nation's greatest asset, and the annual augmentation of the numbers engaged in academic pursuits furnishes an unfailing sign of progress. Of students, there are many, but scholars remain few."[75]

Scholarly attainment was part and parcel of Omega Psi Phi's commitment to uplift, especially for Black people. Indeed, achieving racial progress was one of the Fraternity's ultimate goals. Individual Omega men's accomplishments were essential to the Fraternity, just as the Fraternity was essential to shaping individual members' impact on their respective communities. But the individual and chapters' varied efforts—memorial services, arts initiatives, and anti-lynching efforts—had grown too numerous to manage. At the start of 1922, Grand Basileus Atkins shared his goal for efficiency, but that goal had not yet been accomplished a year later. As Omega men made their way to Philadelphia for the Eleventh Grand Conclave, a series of internal changes were about to culminate.

The Great Reorganization and Growth of Omega Psi Phi

Atkins set the tone for the Eleventh Grand Conclave on December 26–30, 1922, by making a bold statement about the Fraternity. "We shall gather to take counsel of the greatest Negro Greek Letter Society in the world," he said. "Let us bring there all the brains that the Fraternity affords." The Black press also took interest in the upcoming gathering, as it was reported that "Beta chapter of Lincoln University and Mu chapter of Philadelphia plan to make this the banner conclave in the history of the fraternity."[76]

Philadelphia, like Nashville and Atlanta, was an important location for the Grand Conclave in 1922. Among other things, Philadelphia was a crucial city for abolitionist efforts prior to the Civil War. *The Philadelphia Negro* (1899) by W. E. B. Du Bois brought more attention to questions of race, education, and Black liberation.[77] One Omega man, Garnet C. Wilkinson, who served as assistant superintendent in charge of Black schools in Washington, DC, delivered the principal address, which focused on group leadership.[78] Speaking before delegates and their guests inside Allen AME Church, Wilkinson emphasized the need for well-prepared lawyers, physicians, preachers, and, of course, teachers. William Pickens, field secretary of the NAACP and the principal speaker during the Atlanta Conclave, also spoke during the Philadelphia Conclave. He, even more than Wilkinson, stressed education, particularly the need to study Black history and White discrimination. Pickens later contended that knowing one's history and the myriad damages that racism in the United States had caused for generations was essential for true racial advancement and White atonement, as there could "be no such thing as segregated equality."[79]

During the closed members-only sessions, the delegates unanimously voted to send telegrams to the governors of Kansas, Louisiana, New York, and Massachusetts urging them to condemn Ku Klux Klan activity in those states. Communicating with governors in the Midwest and Northeast was especially important to the Fraternity because the Klan was not an organization relegated to the South. While Atkins was a member of the Gamma chapter in Boston, White students at Harvard had an active student chapter of the Ku Klux Klan.[80] Collectively, the foregoing occurrences confirmed what Omega men and other informed people, regardless of skin color, already knew: racism had no regional boundaries, and college campuses were not immune. The *New York Amsterdam News* was in simpatico with the Philadelphia Conclave when it declared that "all sections of the country seemed to be of one mind regarding the fact that the race had entered upon a new era where there was a demand for educated leaders" who were not afraid to challenge racism and other forms of discrimination openly and often.[81]

For as much as the Philadelphia Conclave was about external issues like the Fraternity's education campaign and condemning Klan activity, the conclave also cumulated the Fraternity's great reorganization of 1922. Atkins stated his plans for internal efficiency after being elected during the Atlanta Conclave, and several decisions reflected those plans during his first year as Grand Basileus. For example, the Fraternity established a Vice Grand Basileus position that delegated the responsibility of expansion away from the Grand Basileus, and individual chapters of the Fraternity voted to ratify the new position in 1923. Also, the Grand Keeper of Records and Seal position was created, thus ending the Fraternity's use of the Grand Keeper of Records title. Additionally, the former Grand Keeper of Seals position was renamed to Grand Keeper of Finance. The Fraternity created another position, District

Representative, to further streamline Omega's growth, starting in 1923. The District Representative would be under the supervision of the Vice Grand Basileus and maintain contact with existing chapters and scout potential outposts for new chapters across five districts clustered together by region: the New England states, the mid-Atlantic states, the southern states, the central states, and the western states.[82]

Besides those changes, Omega men agreed to continue redesignating some chapters to make a clearer distinction between undergraduate and graduate chapters. Lambda, previously mentioned as a graduate chapter chartered in Norfolk in 1920, became Lambda Omega (the Fraternity later assigned Lambda chapter to Los Angeles), and Pi, previously mentioned as a graduate chapter chartered in Baltimore in 1921, became Pi Omega (the Fraternity later assigned Pi chapter for undergraduates at Morgan College in Baltimore). Soon, Upsilon in St. Louis became Upsilon Omega. The Fraternity also reassigned Iota chapter from Atlantic City to Chicago, and Eta chapter from Atlanta to Harvard University, while the former Eta became Eta Omega. Other chapters experienced similar changes while Atkins was Grand Basileus.[83]

The significance of these changes should not be understated. Therefore, Fraternity records and the Black press used varying officer titles and chapter names during a period of readjustment in 1923 and 1924. Those and other decisions under the Atkins leadership meant, in many ways, the officers elected during the Philadelphia Conclave would be leading a slightly different Fraternity than their predecessors. Delegates at the conclave voted to reelect Atkins as Grand Basileus, and they elected John W. Love as Vice Grand Basileus, William Gilbert (the editor of *The Oracle*) as Grand Keeper of Finance, and Campbell C. Johnson as Grand Keeper of Records and Seal. The Fraternity also created a position called Grand Marshal, to be held by a member who resided in the city of the next conclave. John H. Purnell of St. Louis was appointed to the position.[84]

A military man and 1913 initiate of Alpha chapter, Purnell rose in rank to captain following his role as a training officer during World War I. In 1919, he taught at West Virginia Collegiate Institute, but, by 1922, he was established at the Sumner Normal School, an institution to train Black teachers, in St. Louis. Purnell helped charter Upsilon Omega (then Upsilon) in that city. At the Philadelphia Conclave in 1922, he presented delegates with an outline of a plan he hatched to expand the Fraternity. His ideas focused on mentoring high school juniors and seniors, circulating literature about accomplished Omega men, and establishing a scholarship medal. Purnell explained, "The medal should be to the high school world what the Phi Beta Kappa key is to the college world."[85] Determining the best methods to achieve those goals, however, was the challenge before the Fraternity.

The quagmire resulting from not having a concrete program or programs to mentor advanced high school students, disseminate information about successful Omegas (aside from *The Oracle*), and establish a scholarship medal reflected years-long issues. After the Nashville Conclave in 1920, the Fraternity proceeded largely upon the idea that each chapter should take on Black history and literature. At the Philadelphia Conclave in 1922, however, the Fraternity discussed creating universal guidelines. From those discussions came a committee "to develop definite plans for fostering the study of Negro History in the schools and colleges of the country."[86] The need to coordinate the program was the driving force of the committee, which William Pickens chaired, and Carter G. Woodson and Stephen J. Lewis also served as leaders. Other Omega men who served as committee members included: William Gilbert and Charles Victor Roman of Nashville, Tennessee; Garnet Wilkinson of Washington, DC; Charles W. White of Boston; George Hall of New York City; and Purnell, who resided in St. Louis.[87]

Educating Black people about Black history remained on the minds of Omega men continuously, even as they organized new chapters or increased the memberships and activities of existing chapters. In the spring of 1923, Pi chapter at Morgan College in Baltimore initiated nine students.[88] Concurrently, the Eta Omega chapter (formerly Eta chapter) in Atlanta proceeded to do its part in the campaign to promote Black history. "This is an annual program promoted by the national Omega Psi Phi fraternity," reported the *Atlanta Constitution*. "Committees have been formed and a thorough canvass of the city will be made in the promotion of this worthy effort."[89] About the same time, the Tau Omega chapter in Greensboro, North Carolina, congratulated members who were "leaders in the educational and professional life in western North Carolina. Tau Omega is doing much in the state to raise the social and educational opportunities of the race." Omega men who heard, read, or otherwise learned about such reports were glad to receive such good news about the chapter, as it was not organized until April 7 of the same year. John P. Murchison, an Alpha chapter initiate and Howard University class of 1920, and Francis L. Atkins, a Beta chapter initiate (and brother of Grand Basileus J. Alston Atkins) and Lincoln University class of 1920, helped organize Tau Omega.[90]

Beyond the undergraduate chapters on Black college campuses or graduate chapters in the South, chapters like Xi chapter at the University of Minnesota, a predominately White institution, continued to establish themselves in 1923. During the summer, a standalone photograph of Xi members was published in the *Pittsburgh Courier* beneath the caption: "Among the chapters at the leading schools of the country are those at Howard University, Meharry Medical College, Columbia and New York Universities, University of Michigan, University of Pittsburgh, Tufts Medical College, Boston University, Harvard and Yale Universities."[91] During the fall, Fred D. Johnson of Epsilon chapter in New York, delivered a lecture at Liberty Hall in Harlem on "The Larger Education" as part of a series of lectures held in November.[92]

Grand Basileus Atkins envisioned Black people in general, and Omega men in particular, playing a larger formal role in education than they had done. He especially wanted more Black people leading the Black schools entrusted with Black education. In the December 1923 issue of *The Oracle*, Atkins wrote a lengthy appraisal in defense of Black youth and critiqued the shortcomings of Black schools for not teaching Black students "in the slightest [about] the grim realities of life." Instead, schools taught "idealistic dreams," he declared.[93] His was a somewhat unfair critique considering many Black teachers secretly taught school lessons that liberated Black youth with honest accounts of Black achievement and White racism despite White people's control of formal curricula decisions in public schools and budgetary allocations.[94] Even so, Atkins's point summarized the impetus behind Omega's education program that emerged from the Nashville Conclave in 1920. "The fact that other groups are largely in control of Negro education, coupled with ignorance and racial prejudice in our schools, is largely responsible for this situation," Atkins surmised.[95]

In the same December 1923 issue of *The Oracle* as Atkins's critique appeared, John H. Purnell offered a more nuanced examination of Black education in the United States. Their professions affected the lenses through which they viewed the subject. Atkins was an attorney, whereas Purnell was a teacher with a day-to-day understanding of issues facing Black education. Purnell called for a complete overhaul of how Black history is taught to Black students. "There are opportunities a plenty for acquainting Negro youth with the achievements of their forbears," he argued, adding "There are still too many teachers of Negro children who are unacquainted with the history of this important racial group."[96] The "sources of the material used" were largely from White perspectives that did not capture the depth of Black history. Purnell asked, "Why not take some of this illustrative material from such works as those of Du Bois, Washington, Douglass, Dunbar, Pushkin, Kelly Miller, and others?"[97] This was important because White scholars had strategically used history to maintain racist ideas. Therefore, Purnell and Atkins captured a turning point in the Fraternity: prioritizing Blackness—by administrators, by teachers, and regarding curricula decisions—was of utmost importance to the Fraternity's education program.

At the end of December 1923, Atkins, Purnell, and hundreds of other Omega men assembled in St. Louis for the Twelfth Grand Conclave. As Grand Marshal, Purnell coordinated local venues that reflected his earlier statements about supporting Black ideas and businesses. A reception for the conclave was hosted at Poro College, a beauty school founded by Annie Minerva Malone. A Black woman, Malone developed hair products and a mail-order business to deliver the products. Her acumen ultimately resulted in her becoming one of the first Black millionaires in the United States. Devoted to the collective-uplift ideal common to every Black Greek-letter organization (Zeta Phi Beta made Malone an honorary member), Malone established Poro College. Its aim, according to the Annie Malone Historical Society, was "to contribute to the economic betterment of 'Race Women.'"[98] Poro, at which Omega man Herman Dreer once taught, was equipped with classrooms, laboratories, dining halls, and more and was valued at more than $1 million.[99] The "gathering place" also hosted numerous Black groups, as White-owned facilities in St. Louis were segregated.[100]

The 1923 Conclave in St. Louis followed a similar format as previous conclaves. There was an opening meeting at the Union Memorial Church followed by other public gatherings. Omega men and their invited guests also journeyed across the Mississippi River toward Alton, Illinois, to visit the burial site of Elijah Parish Lovejoy, a White abolitionist. Once in Alton, a group of Omegas laid a wreath at his gravesite. In closed sessions, conclave delegates voted to elect Atkins for a third term as Grand Basileus. Other national officers elected or reelected at the St. Louis Conclave were: John W. Love, Vice Grand Basileus; William Gilbert, Grand Keeper of Finance; Campbell C. Johnson, Grand Keeper of Records and Seal; and Charles Herbert Marshall, Grand Marshal. Marshall resided in Washington, DC, the city the St. Louis delegation selected for the next conclave. The delegation likewise voted to establish an international scholarship to be awarded annually to cover the expenses for an individual to study abroad for one academic year.[101]

Atkins did not complete his third term as Grand Basileus. On January 5, 1924, a mere week after the St. Louis Conclave, he resigned from the office, attributing his resignation to "the increased duties resulting from the adoption into an already busy office of an enlarged program for 1924, and the consequent removal of one member of the [law] firm of which I am also a member." As a result of those occurrences, Atkins explained, "I find that I cannot properly function during this year as Grand Basileus. I have, therefore, resigned."[102] Atkins did not lie: he and his law partner, Carter Walker Wesley, an Omega man, were increasingly busy; and they were about to get even busier, taking on two notable legal cases, *Ingram v. Wesley* and *Grovey v. Townsend*.[103] In *Ingram*, the lawyering skills of Atkins and Wesley helped enable a "Creek freedman" (citizen with Native American and African American ancestry) retain 160 acres of oil-rich property in Oklahoma after White state officials tried to seize the property.[104] *Grovey*, a case that challenged

Whites-only election primaries in Texas, ended years later when the US Supreme Court ruled it unconstitutional to ban Black voters.[105]

As a result of Atkins's resignation in 1924, John W. Love became Grand Basileus. Up to that time, Love had overseen the District Representative position. Suddenly, he was responsible for guiding the Fraternity's forty-seven active chapters. "Omega must live and grow," said Love, he appointed Sterling A. Brown as Vice Grand Basileus.[106]

Brown was a highbrow. Minister and professor Sterling Nelson Brown of Howard University was his father. Grace Adelaide Brown, a schoolteacher in Washington, DC, who was valedictorian of her graduating class at Fisk University was Sterling A.'s mother. His sister, Mary E. Brown, who usually went by her middle name, Edna, was valedictorian of her graduating class at Howard and later wed Omega Psi Phi founder Frank Coleman. Born, literally, on Howard's campus in 1901, Sterling A. was also an excellent student who completed M Street High School. He then matriculated through Williams College in Williamstown, Massachusetts, where he was elected to Phi Beta Kappa prior to graduating in 1922. During the next year, Sterling A. earned a graduate degree in English from Harvard and later began instructing courses at the Virginia Seminary and College in Lynchburg.[107]

Love and Sterling A. Brown were gifted and talented men. However, with Atkins's resignation, his busy lawyering schedule, and no fully articulated "campaign of expansion" for 1924, Herman Dreer recalled in his 1940 book, *The History of Omega Psi Phi*, Love and Brown basically were left to their own devices to execute Atkins's known visions for academic education and membership growth.[108] The Fraternity continued to grow in both number and territory, but the Fraternity also expanded its cultural and academic programming to include stronger public stances about the need to erase the color line. For instance, on February 13, 1924, the *Daily Worker*, the newspaper of the Communist Party USA, published a lengthy report about the Negro Sanhedrin, an "all-race" conference held in Chicago.[109] Howard University professor Kelly Miller was a key organizer of the four-day event, which started in February. Miller and other conference attendees intertwined race, gender, and class issues to call for a unified effort to condemn racism and to promote organized labor. The success of that effort, and the conference itself, the *Daily Worker* asserted, would "be judged by the working class of the Negro and white races." Attendees proposed resolutions calling "for aggressive action against lynching, disfranchisement, peonage, segregation, and Jim Crowism," and they deemed the Ku Klux Klan a "common enemy" of all people. Omega Psi Phi was one among dozens of organizations, including the Associated Negro Press, NAACP, and numerous church denominations that sent delegates to participate in the Negro Sanhedrin.[110]

On March 6, 1924, the foreign study committee of Omega Psi Phi met at the 135th Street Branch of the YMCA in New York City. William Stuart Nelson chaired the committee due to his extensive international experiences, which included representing the Fraternity three years earlier at the Pan-African Congress in Brussels. During the New York meeting in March 1924, the committee conducted a comprehensive review of "the conditions in Europe as they affect the field of foreign study at the present time." Nelson and his fellow committee members also discussed details of the scholarship—named the Young Scholarship for Foreign Study—that the Fraternity approved during the St. Louis Conclave in December 1923.[111]

The committee Nelson chaired in March 1924 ultimately decided the scholarship would be worth $1,000 to cover ten months of study in Germany or France—that is, one of the two countries whose universities he had previously visited. Whether Nelson's discussions about those visits influenced any committee decisions remains unknown, but known decisions include the Fraternity creating the scholarship "to encourage advanced study and research, also to create a breadth of vision in the recipient and to better acquaint the European with the American man of color."[112] Available to any man regardless of fraternal affiliation, the requirements were: "the recipient must hold a college degree from an accredited college and must have shown extraordinary ability in some particular field of study. His general personality must be such as will be compatible with the aim of the scholarship."[113]

The *Philadelphia Tribune* assessed "the action of the Omega Psi Phi Fraternity is establishing this scholarship is looked upon as the forerunner of more scholarships of this nature which will lead to an increasingly large number of men entering the field of foreign study." In the May 1924 issue of *The Oracle*, Nelson explained the international scholarship "places the Fraternity's interests in the higher reaches of education and racial devotion."[114] The Fraternity's development of the foreign study committee was also a reminder that Black Americans were global in their thinking and understood the international struggle for human rights.

In addition to the growing number of Grand chapter initiatives, more chapters were hosting public debates over contemporary topics. In May 1924, the men of Zeta chapter were key figures at Virginia Union University when the campus hosted debaters from Lincoln (Pennsylvania) University. It was common for undergraduate students to debate pressing global topics. For instance, whether the United States should join the World Court, as stipulated by President Warren G. Harding, was one debate subject. In Richmond, the *Norfolk Journal and Guide* reported, "Union's home team was too much for Lincoln whom she gave a crushing defeat in grand style before one of the largest and most enthusiastic audience that ever filled the chapel of the university."

Virginia Union won because its team's "grasp of the subject and . . . knowledge of the whole question of internationalism was broader than that of" Lincoln's team, but members of Zeta chapter helped ease the loss: after the debate, they entertained both teams.[115]

Zeta was not the only chapter whose members participated in debates in May 1924. Members of Epsilon chapter in New York City debated local members of the Kappa Alpha Psi Fraternity. The Imperial Elks Auditorium in Harlem was the venue, and the Volstead Act banning the production or sale of wine and beer was the subject. The Omega debate team included Z. Alexander Looby, George Reed, and Fred D. Johnson. Although the Kappa team won the debate, Omega men—like the members in Richmond—helped host a social for the many "prominent Harlemites" who attended the debate.[116]

Besides advancing the foreign study campaign and participating in public academic debates in the spring of 1924, Fraternity chapters hosted annual memorial services for Charles Young as a tribute to Black history. Kappa chapter at Syracuse University was one of several chapters that held an individual memorial. In Georgia, Morehouse student and Psi chapter member Albert W. Dent advertised that five Atlanta chapters—Eta Omega, a graduate chapter; Psi at Morehouse College; Omicron at Gammon Theological Seminary; Tau at Atlanta University; and Beta Psi at Clark University (later renamed Clark College)—sponsored a joint memorial program. At Howard University, the memorial service that Alpha chapter put together was "one of the most impressive services ever held in Washington," according to the *Baltimore Afro-American*. More than 1,000 Omega men and their friends "paid tribute to the memory of the late Col. Charles Young," the same newspaper added.[117]

Discussing the control of Black schools was another important matter Omega men engaged in, in the spring of 1924. In May, John Prescott Murchison, soon-to-be editor-in-chief of *The Oracle*, argued the "education and the agents of education for the Negro today are far too inadequate. In the South, where the bulk of Negroes are to be found, the far too few public schools that are provided are poorly equipped and poorly manned." Education, "in the broadest sense," Murchison went on, "means the attempt to guide life so as to enhance its value."[118] Herman Dreer, writing from Sumner Normal School in St. Louis, added to the discussion by offering his opinion about certain types of Black education leaders. For him, simply having someone who was Black leading a school did not mean the person in the leadership position was the best person for the job. Dreer identified Booker T. Washington and his successor at Tuskegee Institute in Alabama, Robert Russa Moton, as "a conservative Negro," recalling: "When a certain Russian statesman, according to Professor Kelly Miller, heard of there being conservative Negroes, he asked, 'What do they have to conserve?'"[119] Dreer's notion of the conservative Black person as perpetually deferential to a White person was common; however, scholars later added more nuance to understanding Black college leaders like Washington and Moton.[120] Nonetheless, in 1924, Dreer's assertiveness about education was prominent among other Omega men. This included several members of Gamma chapter in Boston. They held two meetings per month: one was for Fraternity business, and one "of an educational and cultural nature."[121]

By this point in 1924, the threads in the educational fabrics of Omega Psi Phi's national education and social action programs stretched in many directions. Members held large-scale debates about important topics, alongside the campaign for Black history and literature, foreign study preparations, antilynching efforts, and memorial services. Substantively varying opinions about the foregoing and comparably important topics demonstrated the vision of the Nashville Conclave in December 1920 had not matched the actual execution; however, talk about Omega men's individual accomplishments drowned out some of the loud, divisive arguments about other subjects.

In 1924, Omega founder and associate professor of physics Frank Coleman delivered the first academic presentation in the Howard University lecture series about radio. Coleman designed his lecture "primarily for the citizen who has little knowledge of modern science in the field of radiotelegraphy," according to the *Washington Post*, and his expertise modeled the professional excellence the Fraternity wanted exhibited.[122] Coleman's activity caught local headlines, but Omega man William Justin Carter Jr. made national headlines when he joined his father's law firm in Harrisburg, Pennsylvania, in 1924. The younger Carter graduated from Howard University in 1920 and the Dickinson School of Law in Pennsylvania in 1923. Active in Omega, he had served as Keeper of Records (Keeper of Records and Seal by 1924) for the Kappa Omega chapter in Harrisburg.[123] Paul Revere Williams of Lambda chapter was yet another Omega man on whom the national spotlight shone in 1924. One of the most accomplished architects of the early twentieth century, Williams was selected by decision makers in his hometown, Los Angeles, California, to design local public schools. City officials also contracted with him in 1924 to construct a building valued at $84,000.[124]

Meanwhile, undergraduate members of the Fraternity continued to make newsworthy strides. Eugene Ellis Alston, William Boyd Allison Davis, and William Henry Hastie Jr. were exemplars. Alston was a Wilmington, North Carolina, native who completed the Gregory Normal Institute in 1916 and then enrolled at Lincoln University in Pennsylvania. A Beta chapter initiate in 1917, US military officials compounded his workload by inducting him into the student army training corps at Lincoln in 1918. His training period was brief, however. Military officials granted him an honorable discharge approximately two months after his induction. Without haste, Alston refocused his attention squarely on academics, finishing Lincoln in 1920. Desirous of becoming a physician, Alston applied and was accepted to the University of Michigan in Ann Arbor. He earned his medical doctorate from the university in 1924. Of the 2,000 students who were graduated from Michigan during that year, only Alston and thirteen other graduates were Black, according to an announcement in the *Pittsburgh Courier*.[125]

Davis, one of Eugene Ellis Alston's fellow Omega men, was a son of the nation's capital. He attended Paul Laurence Dunbar (whose name officials changed from M Street in 1916) High School, graduating as valedictorian in 1920. At the time, Dunbar had an agreement with Williams College, a predominately White campus, that permitted any Dunbar valedictorian to attend Williams via a merit-based scholarship. Davis began college in 1920 and excelled, as reflected in his election to Phi Beta Kappa. In 1924, he graduated summa cum laude with a degree in English. Davis replicated his success at Dunbar by being class valedictorian.[126]

Hastie Jr. earned a comparably sterling reputation for his academic success. A valedictorian of the 1921 class at Dunbar, Hastie displayed a particularly keen interest in mathematics, physics, and poetry. After White staffers at Amherst College recruited him to Massachusetts, he excelled in the foregoing subjects—and all others. Hastie's general demeanor and erudition were testaments to his parents, especially his mother, Roberta Childs Hastie. She was an academically educated race woman from Marion, Alabama, the county seat of Perry, whose father helped incorporate the Lincoln School in 1867 (today that school is Alabama State University in Montgomery). Hastie was born in 1904 in Knoxville, Tennessee, before Roberta and Hastie Sr. relocated to Washington after Hastie Sr. accepted a federal government position in the nation's capital. Roberta made their only son walk or ride a bicycle to school instead of allowing him to travel on an racially segregated streetcar. Hastie Jr. maintained that strong sense of racial awareness and pride, and, while amassing an excellent record at Amherst, Hastie Jr. was elected to Phi Beta Kappa in 1924 on his way to earning valedictory honors at the college in 1925.[127]

The accomplishments of undergraduate and graduate Omega men were good for the Fraternity, and the Fraternity's well-being amplified individual brothers' achievements, but a question remained: How could personal and fraternal achievements be brought into alignment? The lack of an answer brought an urgency to the Thirteenth Grand Conclave in Washington, DC, in 1924. The Fraternity had not held its annual conclave in the nation's capital since 1918, when only three chapters existed. By the end of 1924, however, there were fifty chapters across the United States and in Canada. The return to Howard University presented an opportunity to reflect on the Fraternity's founding, but this return also presented a familiar dilemma in relation to Howard: a Black campus with White leadership—a phenomenon with which Omega founders became familiar with thirteen years earlier.

Black Leaders of Black Institutions

The Washington Conclave of December 27–31, 1924, received more fanfare than any conclave to date.[128] On November 29, nearly a month before Omega men gathered in the nation's capital, the *Chicago Defender* announced the Fraternity, "with the results of its great expansion drive of the past four years, will hold forth again on native shores in a monster grand session."[129] That Omegas planned to honor prominent members of their Fraternity with whom nonmembers around the country were familiar heightened anticipation. Honorees included: Ernest Everett Just, Omega founder and "scientist of international note"; Roland Wiltse Hayes, world renowned concert tenor; Carter G. Woodson, editor of the *Journal of Negro History*; James C. Napier, a lawyer and former register of the Treasury; Nahum D. Brascher, cofounder of the Associated Negro Press; and John W. E. Bowen, president of the Gammon Theological Seminary, among other members.[130] The *Washington Post* noted the 1924 Conclave was significant because "the fraternity will be guests of trustees of Howard University, which institution gave it birth thirteen years ago as the first Negro Greek-letter fraternity founded at a colored institution."[131] Additionally, the conclave was "in the nature of a homecoming," the *Washington Post* added, as Grand Marshal Charles H. Marshall presided over welcoming delegates to Washington.[132]

On Sunday, December 28, Marshall and approximately 500 other delegates held the public meeting for the Washington Conclave in the Andrew Rankin Memorial Chapel at Howard University. In greeting the delegates and their guests, Howard president James Stanley Durkee, a White Baptist minister originally from Carleton, Nova Scotia, said he had "occasion to speak many words of welcome for those who gather within the influence of the university, but I am frank to say that the welcome today of such a group of forward-looking, far-visioned young men is a privilege that challenges any president or executive of a university."[133] Durkee continued a tradition in the fifty-seven-year history of the university having a White president.[134]

He nonetheless used his greetings to Omega men in 1924 to comment on race in the United States. The "way to future racial progress," the *Washington Post* reported that Durkee declared, "was through the development of the mental and spiritual life of the Negro."[135]

After Durkee finished greeting Omega men, William Stuart Nelson, head of the Fraternity's foreign scholarship committee and one of Howard University's theology professors, delivered a speech titled "The Negro and the World Vision." Nelson emphasized the critical importance of Black Americans staying abreast of social issues beyond the United States because "not that we loved the race less but that we loved humanity more."[136] Nelson said his recent travels to Europe proved it was necessary to broadcast the truths about Black people to challenge false narratives about the majority being unintelligent, among other things. Misinformation about Black Americans having no interest in "art and science," Nelson said, "moved unchecked over racial and national boundaries. It is only by depth of training and by extraordinary achievement in these fields that the Negro is to prove equality with the higher forces of mankind."[137]

Nelson's remarks set the stage for the principal speaker, John W. E. Bowen, who frequently delivered addresses at the Fraternity's national meetings. For the Washington Conclave, he chose the topic, "Young Men of Brain and Conscience to the Fore."[138] Bowen spoke on December 28. He emphasized education, telling his listeners, "Mind rules this world, not sentiment. That race with a conscience, dominated by mind, will succeed and conquer in the struggle of life."[139] Bowen elaborated: "At present, the black man is handicapped, but he must have faith and a knowledge of the past, and a knowledge of the constituent elements that triumph, in order to rise above his prejudices. I come to life this shibboleth before you—brain conquers everything."[140] Bowen concluded, "It is manhood rather than color that counts for the future."[141]

The December 29 session opened at 9:00 A.M. and continued until its leaders halted chapter reports at 11:30 A.M. to allow some delegates to commute to the White House for a 12:30 P.M. meeting with President Calvin Coolidge. The *Washington Post* reported, "It will be the first time a President has greeted a body of colored university men."[142] In and of itself, the meeting was an important moment in American history, but the meeting was also of importance to the Coolidge presidency. Coolidge previously endorsed the Go-to-High-School, Go-to-College campaign that Alpha Phi Alpha established in 1922, but he had not yet taken a meeting with a Black fraternity or sorority.[143] Omega delegates to the 1924 Conclave visiting Coolidge at the White House afforded him an opportunity to demonstrate his actual support of "the program of higher education for the Colored race."[144]

Upon leaving the White House on December 29, Omega men visited Arlington National Cemetery. They paid their respects and laid a wreath at the Tomb of the Unknown Soldier. They replicated those acts at the gravesite of Omega man Charles Young. The tribute to Young was fitting considering the Fraternity's chapters across the country organized annual memorial services but laying the wreath at the Tomb of the Unknown Soldier was a testament to the hundreds of other Omega men who had served in the military. During

World War I, the *Baltimore Afro-American* avowed, some 560 Omega men served, so the wreath was an especially heartfelt "tribute to Omega men who made the Supreme Sacrifice."[145]

The idea of sacrifice continued to resonate among Omega men during the closed business sessions of the Washington Conclave on December 30 and 31. Delegates voted on issues aimed at streamlining Fraternity initiatives, hence sacrificing some programs to become more efficient in the execution of others. For example, delegates voted to table—and thus postpone—graduate chapters moving forward with the foreign study scholarship. Delegates also voted to suspend the Black history and literature campaign in 1925.[146] Those two decisions alleviated a sizable burden and the disjointedness in chapters' programming efforts. As Herman Dreer would assess in *The History of Omega Psi Phi*, published in 1940, the "unparalleled expansion of the Fraternity had resulted in a loosely-knit organization incapable of maximum united effort. That Conclave enunciated the policy of internal organization and consolidation and decided to suspend the pursuit of activities demanding for their successful operation a strong organization."[147] Furthermore, by 1924, Carter G. Woodson desired the campaign for Black history and literature to expand under the umbrella of the organization he led, the Association for the Study of Negro Life and History.[148]

Having resolved the issues with foreign study scholarship and the education campaign, delegates to the Washington Conclave voted on a third: whether the Fraternity should stop covering the expenses of delegates to the Negro Sanhedrin, the all-race conference. Omega men voted to continue sending delegates to the conference even though participation would entail another sacrifice, money. But, after assessing other programs and commitments of the Fraternity, the Washington delegation decided the monetary sacrifice to continue being represented at the Negro Sanhedrin was justifiable.[149]

Chapter expansion and education were two of the most notable agendas items of the Washington Conclave in 1924. Before former Grand Basileus J. Alston Atkins resigned, Omega men started debating educational quality on a regular basis. Whereas those debates were general, the debate at the Washington Conclave involved a specific subject, Tennessee A&I. Founded in 1912, Omega man William Jasper Hale of Delta chapter was its first president. He composed the inaugural faculty by hand-selecting graduates of Atlanta, Fisk, and Howard universities. Denied adequate funding by the state government, whose White officials later redirected federal funds the normal school should have received via the Morrill Land Grant to the predominately White University of Tennessee, Hale raised enough money, elevated the curriculum, and recruited enough students to secure redesignation of the normal school to a college in 1922. The college graduated its first class in 1924, but Omega men raised concern over the fact that Tennessee A&I and many other Black colleges and universities primarily offered secondary-level curricula that seemed to emphasize agriculture, industry, or vocation more than liberal arts. Curricular levels and types constituted a problem for Omega, a collegiate fraternity, because a Black campus having men interested in establishing a chapter of the Fraternity did not mean that campus was appropriate to have a chapter. Aware of those facts, the Omega Psi Phi Committee on Recommendations suggested "a list of approved colleges and universities be drawn up by the Supreme Council and a copy of such a list be sent to each chapter."[150]

Delegates to the Washington Conclave in 1924 heeded the suggestion of the Committee on Recommendations. The delegates agreed the list of approved institutions was needed to ensure any campus with a chapter of Omega Psi Phi promoted the ideals of the Fraternity. Moreover, the list would help guarantee the expansion process of the Fraternity operated with consistency from chapter to chapter. The need for the aforementioned list also demonstrated that White people still controlled many Black colleges and universities, whether public or private, and majority White-led or White-funded Black schools continued to suffer woeful neglect and had not fully developed into genuine institutions of higher learning by 1924. White administrators at private Black colleges were notorious for their paternalistic leadership of Black students and Black faculty. The problems at Tennessee A&I under control of White elected state officials were not different from the obstacles that Howard University's White administrators, trustees, and even faculty had set before the Fraternity's founders in 1911. Hence, the Washington Conclave in 1924 was pivotal in recalibrating the Fraternity's mission. In its wake, Omega men worked together more deliberately to achieve a common goal: helping develop Black-run institutions.[151]

The Fraternity's new officers had a charge ahead of them. George L. Vaughn, an attorney in St. Louis, Missouri, was elected Grand Basileus. The other elected officers were: Julius S. McClain of Philadelphia, Pennsylvania, Vice Grand Basileus; Walter H. Mazyck of Washington, DC, Grand Keeper of Records and Seal; Daniel B. Taylor of Greensboro, North Carolina, Grand Keeper of Finance; and John P. Murchison of Atlanta, Georgia, editor-in-chief of *The Oracle*. John B. Garrett of Tuskegee, Alabama, was Grand Marshal.[152]

The election of Garrett was important to the commitment the Washington Conclave's delegation made in 1924 to support Black colleges and universities, but delegates electing him also helped ensure the Black population of Tuskegee would support the 1925 Conclave in their hometown. He was born in Laurens, South Carolina, and finished the Colored Normal Industrial and Agricultural and Mechanical College (now called South Carolina State University) in Orangeburg. In 1918, Garrett then graduated from

Amherst College, where he was the first Black vice president of an Amherst senior class, and later the Massachusetts Institute of Technology (MIT) in Cambridge before instructing bacteriology at MIT. Next, Garrett accepted a position as a bacteriologist for the US Veterans Bureau Hospital No. 91 in Tuskegee.[153]

Every delegate to the Washington Conclave in 1924 voted to select Iota Omega, a graduate chapter in Tuskegee, to host the Grand Conclave of 1925. The delegates' unanimous vote came after Iota Omega presented written invitations from Robert R. Moton, principal of Tuskegee Institute, and Joseph H. Ward, surgeon and chief medical officer for the hospital. Moton and Ward were two of the most influential Black men in Alabama.[154] Both Moton and Ward, in their 1924 invitations to Omega men, promised to be gracious hosts and to "lend every aid" at their disposals to make sure the 1925 Grand Conclave was successful.[155] Such promises extended a tradition for which Moton's predecessor at Tuskegee Institute, Booker T. Washington, was known. Washington, historian Crystal R. Sanders explained, "often invited Black people from various walks of life to campus and gave them red-carpet treatment."[156] Besides having confidence that Moton and Ward would deliver on that tradition of courteousness in 1925, Omega men knew several members of Iota Omega were instructors at Tuskegee or staff at the Veterans Hospital. Additionally, the *Chicago Defender* considered the college and hospital that Moton and Ward headed, respectively, were "two of the greatest institutions ever manned and operated by the American Negro."[157]

Omega men recognized the importance of having more members of their Fraternity ascend into leadership at Black institutions; therefore, Omega men continued to develop "a national program to bring about a sane and intelligent race leadership of the colored people of America through the organization of its college-trained men and women."[158] The educational and professional journeys of John Wesley Work Jr., an elected member to the Fraternity, provided a blueprint for college-trained leadership.[159] Work was born and raised in Nashville where his father directed several members of the original Jubilee Singers at Fisk University. Work Jr. graduated from Fisk in 1895 and began instructing history and Latin courses at the university in 1904.[160] As a poet, musician, and philosopher, Work Jr. was known for leading the ultimately famous Fisk Jubilee Singers, who toured the world raising funds for their campus since the 1870s. In 1915, Work Jr. published a compilation of Negro spirituals for present and, moreover, future generations titled, *Folk Songs of the American Negro*.[161] In 1923, he began a brief tenure as president of Roger Williams University, a private Black college in Nashville initially supported by the American Baptist Home Mission Society.[162]

In 1924, Lee Marcus McCoy began what became a thirty-three-year tenure as president of Rust College, a private Black institution in Holly Springs, Mississippi. A 1905 graduate of Rust, McCoy joined the Fraternity through the Pi Omega chapter while he worked at Morgan College in Baltimore. Upon his return to Mississippi, according to *The Oracle*, "never in the history of Rust College did any president receive a more sincere and rousing welcome than was extended to Brother McCoy by the citizens of Holly Springs, and the trustees and students of Rust College."[163] The same year, David Henry Sims started as president of Allen University in Columbia, South Carolina. During his eight-year presidency, he played other important roles in education as a member of the executive committee of the State Teachers' Association and, among other activities, as director of the Colored State Fair of South Carolina. An active member of the Epsilon Omega chapter, *The Oracle* characterized Sims as having "always been a 100 percent Omega man."[164] The hires of Work, McCoy, and Sims enabled them to join other Omega men leading Black institutions, including Robert Clisson Woods at Virginia Theological Seminary and College (now Virginia University of Lynchburg), William Jasper Hale at Tennessee A&I, and Charles Henry Parrish Sr. at Simmons College in Kentucky.[165]

The matter of Black leaders of Black schools was not just of interest to Omega men during the 1920s. There was also widespread Black student activism against the racial behaviors of White administrators and faculty on some Black campuses. For instance, in 1924, Hampton Institute (now named Hampton University) students charged that one White instructor was so underqualified that he should not be allowed to teach. They also complained that White instructors, in general, were more concerned with teaching Black students etiquette instead of academic content. Furthermore, White instructors operated a segregated club on campus and opposed hiring Black faculty. Eventually, "in response to Hampton's low academic standards and repressive racial policies, the students went on strike," historian James D. Anderson explained.[166] Similar concerns about White leaders emerged on other Black campuses. Carter G. Woodson offered a broader critique of the harm caused by White academic leaders in his book, *The Mis-Education of the Negro*. "Negro schools cannot go forward with such a load of inefficiency," he wrote, "and especially when the white presidents of these institutions are often less scholarly than Negroes who have to serve under them."[167]

Black college students' unrest on Black campuses against White administrators' Jim Crow practices reflected a new ideology spreading across Black America. In 1925, Alain Locke, a Howard University professor and leading figure in the Harlem Renaissance, published *The New Negro: An Interpretation*.[168]

Locke's seminal anthology of literature and its compilation of other authors' poems and essays was transformative. The anthology served as a nod to younger thinkers in the Black arts and literature movement, such as Langston Hughes, who was initiated at Beta chapter in 1926. Other members of that chapter nicknamed him "Boy poet," and with good reason.[169] During the same year of his initiation, Hughes—while still a student at Lincoln University in Pennsylvania—published a now-famous poem titled, "The Negro Artist and the Racial Mountain."[170] As suggested by the title, Hughes addressed the challenges of being Black and an artist, capturing the energy of the New Negro movement. While Hughes's future popularity made him a key personality in the movement, he was not the only Omega man involved in or inspired by the movement. Omega men conveyed their inspiration throughout the pages of *The Oracle*, while others submitted reports of expressive activities in their cities.[171]

In 1925, as Omega men in Tuskegee continued their preparations to host the Grand Conclave in December, and other Omega men embraced the New Negro attitude and engaged in the broader freedom struggles of activists, the Fraternity continued to devise internal ways to expand more strategically. That year, the Fraternity organized ten new chapters, but the need for a list of approved colleges limited expansion for undergraduates as Omega streamlined its foci. A single chapter, Epsilon Psi at the University of California, Berkeley, was for undergraduates. The other nine chapters chartered in 1925 were for graduates.[172]

Meanwhile, existing chapters continued to pursue programs and initiatives that delegates did not postpone during the Washington Conclave in December 1914. In March 1925, chapters hosted memorial services for Colonel Charles Young and participated in public debates about social issues. That month, Omega men belonging to Epsilon chapter in New York City debated local members of Kappa Alpha Psi. Child labor was their debate topic. In May, the Lambda Omega chapter in Norfolk, Virginia, launched "an extensive cultural programme for service."[173]

Aside from chapter activities, individual Omega men earned recognition during the first half of 1925. William Mercer Cook represented that group. After graduating from Paul Laurence Dunbar High School in Washington, DC, Cook enrolled at Amherst College, where he was a standout member of the school choir. He studied French and Greek at Amherst, and earned the Phi Beta Kappa key during his senior year at Amherst College in 1925. Cook also won the Kellogg Prize for declamation as well as the $1,500 Simpson Fellowship to study French at the Sorbonne in Paris. He was the first Black person at Amherst to win the latter award.[174] Another Dunbar High alumnus, John

Preston Davis, made history when he and his debate teammates from Bates College in Maine set sail for England in May 1925. Davis became the first Black member of an international debate team from the United States, and he was also renowned stateside at Bates and elsewhere for becoming the first Black student elected to serve as editor-in-chief of a student newspaper for a predominately White college or university. Initiated into the Fraternity through the Alpha Psi chapter, chartered at Amherst College in 1922, Davis ranked eighth in the 1926 graduating class at Bates.[175]

As regards to Omega men in graduate chapters who made noteworthy contributions to the Fraternity and to Black people in general, Leander Raymond Hill, William Johnson Trent Sr., and Lee M. McCoy were fine representatives. Hill received his dental training at Meharry Medical College in Nashville, Tennessee, in 1920. There, he served as Basileus of Delta chapter. Upon graduation, he returned to his hometown of St. Paul, Minnesota, to take and pass the state board examination, and started to practice dentistry. Hill was also instrumental in helping establish the Xi chapter at the University of Minnesota in 1921 and, in 1923, served as one of the Fraternity's first District Representatives. He was the contributing editor in multiple weekly publications, often writing to educate Minnesotans on racial topics.[176]

William J. Trent Sr. was a Charlotte, North Carolina, native who in 1898 earned valedictory honors at Livingstone College in Salisbury, about forty-three miles northeast of Charlotte. During the same year, he served with the Third North Carolina Regiment amid the Spanish-American War. In 1900, Trent began a career that spanned the next twenty-five years. In Asheville, North Carolina, west of both Charlotte and Salisbury, he worked with the YMCA, which was combined with the Young Men's Institute. From Asheville, Trent went to Atlanta, Georgia, to direct the Butler Street YMCA. He remained in Atlanta from 1911 until accepting the presidency of his alma mater, Livingstone College, in 1925, thereby adding to the list of Omega men leading colleges.[177]

Meanwhile, in Memphis, Tennessee, Rust College president Lee M. McCoy helped organize the Epsilon Phi chapter in 1925 in between his time traveling across Mississippi, Arkansas, and Tennessee recruiting and fundraising on behalf of the college. His and other Omega men college presidents' efforts were important, according to William Stuart Nelson, who, while implicitly advocating for people worldwide to know about the presidents' and other Black college employees' invaluable work to uplift their students, also championed the international scholarship: "In the sheer interest of justice, as well as in the interest of the race, the forces of education must be organized and sent bearing the banners of truth into every quarter pleading the cause of the colored American before the bar of world opinion."[178]

Taken together, the chapter activities and the accumulating individual accolades all spoke to the Fraternity's larger vision for education. Omega's goals remained steadfast, as made plain by an editorial in the June 1925 issue of *The Oracle*:

> It is the aim of the Omega Psi Phi Fraternity to develop self-confidence and self-respect in the Negro by unfolding these facts and annals through its program for the study of Negro history and literature. Through this program, the Omega Psi Phi Fraternity hopes to inject race pride and patriotism into the Negro by convincing him that no race is brighter with honest, worthy glory than his own, that slavery was not peculiar to the Negro, that he has held and has been held in bondage as other races have held and have been held, and that he should be proud to wear the name of a race that preceded the Egyptians and built cities at the same time China was laying the foundation for her civilization.[179]

Racial pride was of utmost importance but, as always in the United States, Black pride and progress was met by White resistance. For instance, in March 1925, approximately three months before the editorial appeared in *The Oracle*, White officials in Hart County, Georgia, accused a Black man named Lincoln Johnson of murder. A while later, a second Black man named Murray Bonner "was arrested for stealing a ride" aboard a Baltimore and Ohio Railroad freight car. While serving a fourteen-day sentence, a White officer for the railroad misidentified Bonner as Johnson. Bonner maintained his innocence, avowing he was working in Logan County, West Virginia, at the time of the murder. The NAACP soon came to Bonner's aid and prevented him from being unjustly extradited back to Georgia.[180] In August 1925, now two months after the editorial appeared in *The Oracle*, and as Omega men worked in their hometowns and traveled elsewhere around various states and regions to advance the Fraternity, approximately 30,000 unmasked Ku Klux Klan members punctuated the Klan's early twentieth-century resurgence by marching on Washington, DC.[181] Such vile activities proved that, as Omega men aimed to "inject race pride and patriotism" in Black Americans, as *The Oracle* editorial stated, safety from racial violence was not guaranteed. Indeed, in some ways, White people continued to treat Black people as fugitives from enslavement when they moved about. Despite that fact, Omega proceeded with its Fourteenth Grand Conclave on December 27–31, 1925, in Tuskegee, Alabama, a state where Bibb Graves, a popular candidate in the governor's race, was a Klan leader.[182]

National officers of the Fraternity took seriously the possibility of racist violence while Omega men traveled to Tuskegee to attend the Grand Conclave.

Therefore, officers coordinated special Pullman cars to transport the members at a reduced rate from Cincinnati, Ohio, or Washington, DC, to the Alabama Black Belt where Tuskegee was located. The Pullman cars departed Cincinnati and Washington on December 26, one day before the Grand Conclave opened. Protecting members was important because national officers wanted the conclave to be a success, and a single member falling victim to White terror would have ruined that chance. Reminded frequently by Robert R. Moton, Joseph H. Ward, and other Black leaders in Tuskegee about the importance of the Grand Conclave, more ordinary Black residents considered the conclave a stunning opportunity for them as well as for visiting Omega men and their guests. The *Chicago Defender* announced, "Schoolteachers and physicians in large numbers throughout the country are embracing this exceptional opportunity to visit the school established by Booker T. Washington and the Veterans Bureau hospital."[183]

Omega men held the opening public meeting of the Tuskegee Conclave inside the chapel on the Tuskegee Institute campus. Moton was unable to attend because of illness. Hence, vice principal and professor Robert Robinson Taylor welcomed conclave delegates on behalf of Moton. When he took a seat, Ward rose from his to extend greetings. Afterward, Grand Basileus George L. Vaughn offered the official response of the Fraternity.[184]

Matthew Washington Bullock, assistant to the attorney general of Massachusetts, served as the principal speaker. As a longtime member of Gamma chapter before becoming a charter member of Eta Phi chapter in Boston, Bullock first gave a brief tribute to Booker T. Washington, who had died a decade earlier in 1915.[185] Bullock then emphasized the long legacy of Black contributions to the United States. "From the time that Alonzo Pietro landed with Columbus," Bullock professed before presenting a list of notable Black people and their achievements, "we have been doing our part in contributing to America's greatness."[186] Next, the *Chicago Defender* reported, Bullock "stressed the value of obtaining full knowledge of the accomplishments of our race in the past in order to stimulate pride and ambition and achievement in the future, and urged the cooperation of members of all races in order to establish a true democracy and bring to a realization the ideals upon which the American government was founded."[187] Bullock furthermore said that Black people, despite 250 years of slavery, "did not seek aid from our former masters or ask to be supported at the government's expense." Instead, Black people "through our industry and thrift" had managed to purchase homes, operate farms, and own businesses.[188] Of course, Bullock recognized the challenges still facing Black Americans—and no amount of homeownership, farm profit, or business acumen overshadowed the realities of oppression—but he found promise in Alabama. "Our friends in the South who love justice and fair play are beginning to speak out in no uncertain terms," Bullock said, noting that was "one of the most hopeful signs of the ultimate triumph of justice."[189]

Bullock's personal experiences gave him a sensitivity to the regional similarities and differences that a national organization would face. Born in Dabney, North Carolina, in 1881, Bullock was a brilliant youth. His grades earned him admittance to Dartmouth College in Hanover, New Hampshire. While at Dartmouth, Bullock sang in the glee club and was a standout football and track-and-field athlete. After finishing Dartmouth in 1904, he earned a law degree from Harvard in 1907. Bullock then served as head football coach at Massachusetts Agricultural and Mechanical College. Now called the University of Massachusetts Amherst, its Office of Equity and Inclusion notes that Bullock was perhaps the first Black man in the United States to head coach a predominantly White institution high school, college, or university team. After his time in Amherst, he began coaching football at Morehouse College in Atlanta, Georgia. He also practiced law in the growing southern city. Bullock later returned to Boston where he was executive secretary of the Boston Urban League before accepting a position with the Massachusetts attorney general. He still held the latter position at the time of the Tuskegee Conclave.[190]

Bullock's opening address set the stage for the delegate decisions at the conclave. According to one news report, "Not only were the internal affairs of Omega thoroughly considered and plans for their progressive development outlined, but the Fraternity gave sincere thought and attention to matters of vital importance affecting the race in America."[191] The same report labeled the Tuskegee Conclave as "one of the most constructive conclaves in the history of the fraternity."[192] The delegates committed the Fraternity's "united support" of the NAACP with a $200 donation to the Legal Defense Fund (the precursor to the present-day fund started in the 1930s).[193] The Fraternity also "pledged itself to work for the passage of a law which would make lynching a federal crime" and endorsed telegrams to President Calvin Coolidge—who met with Omega delegates one year prior—to urge him to abolish "segregation and discriminatory practices in the federal civil service."[194] This was followed by delegates' demand that Congress ensure "that effective measures be adopted to restore the suffrage in the South."[195]

Finally, the Fraternity committed twenty-five dollars toward life membership in the Association for the Study of Negro Life and History and voted to reinstate its Black history and literature campaign as Achievement Week. Inasmuch as Carter G. Woodson's Negro History Week was set to commence formally in February 1926, the Fraternity's campaign was renamed Achievement Week and moved to November (as it remains today). Delegate Ulysses S.

Donaldson said of the Tuskegee Conclave decisions: "By these acts, the Fraternity went on record as a supporter of any organize [sic] movement designed to promote the welfare and uphold the rights of citizens, Negro citizens in particular."[196]

In making these decisions at the Tuskegee Conclave, individual delegates and the Fraternity as a collective affirmed a commitment to racial advancement and even seemed to have settled on a strategy for achieving real impact. The inputs of both undergraduate and graduates were principal reasons for that achievement. Key undergraduates included Earl Wilkins at the University of Minnesota, where he became the first Black student selected to the editorial board of the *Minnesota Daily* student newspaper, and Albert W. Dent at Morehouse College, where he served as Psi chapter Basileus and the business manager for *The Oracle*, the Fraternity's official journal. Key graduate members included Solomon Carter Fuller, who worked at Boston University as the nation's first Black psychiatrist, and Paul R. Williams, the accomplished Los Angeles architect and first Black person admitted into the American Architects Association. However, perhaps no Fraternity chapter or individual Omega man's efforts to advance the Black educational success in the 1920s was more impactful than those of Theophilus E. McKinney.[197]

Omega Sets the Standard for Black Education

On March 26, 1926, only three months after the Tuskegee Conclave, more than forty Black college deans and registrars assembled at the Negro Agricultural and Technical College of North Carolina (now called North Carolina Agricultural and Technical [A&T] State University) in Greensboro. The gathering kicked off the first meeting of the National Association of Collegiate Deans and Registrars in Negro Schools (NACDR), founded by McKinney, dean at North Carolina A&T. A range of institutions were represented—some private and others public, some fewer than twenty years old and others founded more than fifty years earlier immediately following the Civil War—but all representatives had a single aim: "smoothing out the various difficulties and problems with which deans and registrars are confronted."[198]

In time, the NACDR meeting fundamentally transformed Black higher education in the United States. McKinney's idea for the association, however, grew immediately following the Washington, DC, Conclave in December 1924, when the Fraternity agreed upon the need for an approved college list. McKinney and other Omega men understood that the issue of varied educational offerings at Black colleges and universities was more significant than the Fraternity's desire for systemic chapter expansion. The issue of varied offerings exemplified what Omega men had been trying to attain since

1920—namely, improved educational opportunities for Black people in the United States. According to Virginia's *Norfolk Journal and Guide* newspaper, McKinney's new association and its first conference put Black school leadership into Black administrators' hands "for the purpose of spreading information of common interest to those who are charged with the responsibility of recording the standing of students and passing on entrance conditions of Negro institutions."[199]

McKinney was positioned uniquely for the mission the *Norfolk Journal and Guide* described. A native of Live Oak, Florida, he graduated from Morehouse College in Atlanta in 1921. McKinney was initiated into Omega Psi Phi through Eta chapter when it comprised Morehouse, Atlanta University, and Clark University (renamed Clark College in 1940). After graduating from Morehouse, he moved to Boston, joining Gamma chapter while enrolled at Boston University. McKinney served as Keeper of Records for Gamma chapter for two years as he pursued his MA degree in history, government, and economics. McKinney was a methodical record keeper—a skill that foreshadowed his future role as a dean—but he also had a friendly demeanor. When he finished Boston University in 1924, others in Gamma chapter described McKinney as "an Omega man of the highest type. His place in Gamma will be hard to fill."[200]

McKinney's decision to organize the NACDR aligned well with his Fraternity work. In Boston, he became friends with J. Alston Atkins, former Grand Basileus, and Matthew W. Bullock, the assistant to the attorney general of Massachusetts (and the Tuskegee Conclave's principal speaker in 1925). McKinney, Atkins, and Bullock even appeared side by side in a Gamma chapter photograph in 1924. McKinney's tight-knit relationship and contributions to Gamma chapter earned him praise when he was hired at North Carolina A&T in 1925. Speaking for numerous others, J. Clyde Coates of Gamma chapter said: "We are especially glad to note this honor."[201]

McKinney's hire was viewed with approval within Black educational circles. Any time a Black administrator was hired to lead a Black school, that accomplishment was noteworthy, particularly considering how commonplace White surveillance and malicious funding practices were during the 1920s. One month prior to the NACDR in Greensboro meeting in 1926, Omega Psi Phi Grand Keeper of Records and Seal Walter H. Mazyck averred the "white system of education is detrimental to the Negro," adding that "one of the virulent factors in strengthening the grip of racial prejudice against the Negro in North America is its system of education."[202]

In such a troubled racial environment, McKinney's two-day gathering in Greensboro benefited from buy-in from Black educators near and far. North Carolina A&T covered a sizable portion of expenses for all visiting deans and registrars. They represented: Johnson C. Smith University in Charlotte, North Carolina; Kittrell College (now defunct) in North Carolina; Fisk University in Nashville, Tennessee; Paine College in Augusta, Georgia; Florida A&M in Tallahassee; and Tuskegee Institute in Alabama; and more than twenty other Black colleges for a total of thirty represented. Omega college presidents William Jasper Hale and William Johnson Trent Sr. also sent their deans and registrars from Tennessee A&I and Livingstone College, respectively.[203]

Omega men were also taking leadership of primary and secondary schools. In early 1926, Garnet C. Wilkinson, the Omega man who also served as assistant superintendent in charge of Black schools in Washington, DC, announced the hire of another Omega man, Gordon David Houston, as the principal of Armstrong Technical High School in Washington, DC. City officials named yet another Omega man, Eugene Clark of the Alpha Omega chapter, assistant superintendent of public schools. They offered him the superintendent position after he completed a master's degree from Teachers College, Columbia University. In accepting the position, Clark took charge of fifty-two elementary school buildings. Meanwhile, as McKinney led the effort toward curricula standardization at Black colleges, similar important leadership changes occurred at the higher education level.[204]

By the summer of 1926, word spread that Mordecai Wyatt Johnson was poised to become the next president of Howard University. If his presidency realized, he would be the first Black person in that role. Many, if not most, Omega men eagerly anticipated the possibility, but perhaps no more Omega men than those affiliated with Alpha chapter at Howard. The president of the university where Omega was birthed would finally look like its student body.[205]

Johnson was not an Omega man, but his hire in 1926 stirred praise from Omega men, nonetheless. "If, then, we waive the arithmetical method of measuring achievement, we may point to the happy demise of the old 'conflict' between industrial training and higher education, the election of Mordecai W. Johnson as president of Howard University . . . as among the most significant recent achievements of the Negro in education," wrote one member in *The Oracle*. Another Omega man, William Stuart Nelson, eventually became assistant to president Johnson at Howard, and Nelson's position provided him with valuable insights upon becoming president of Shaw University in Raleigh, North Carolina, in 1931.[206]

Johnson's hire at Howard University ultimately added another person to the roll of Black presidents. By the opening of the fall semester of 1926, there were 13,860 Black college students in the United States, with about 75 percent of them enrolled at private colleges. Those facts demonstrated progress, albeit slow, as a larger percentage of Black college students were enrolled at public Black colleges and universities. The percentage of private versus public students further highlighted the challenge before Omega college presidents, such as John W. Work Jr. at Roger Williams University in Tennessee (now defunct), Lee Marcus McCoy at Rust College in Mississippi, Robert Clisson Woods at the Virginia Theological Seminary and College (now Virginia University of Lynchburg), William Jasper Hale at Tennessee A&I, David Henry Sims at Allen University in South Carolina, William Johnson Trent Sr. at Livingstone College in North Carolina, and Charles Henry Parrish Sr. at Simmons College in Kentucky. "All members of the Omega Psi Phi Fraternity," *The Oracle* explained in 1926, "all of these brothers, despite the difficulty of enforcing a universal standard and program of education, are indeed heightening the general appreciation of values in society."[207]

Though applauded by numerous Omega men, the increased Black control of Black institutions during the mid-1920s had an adverse effect on funding. White philanthropists and missionaries who founded or funded many of these Black institutions following the Civil War reversed course, so their streams of income were no longer robust by 1926. "Now that they will not have full control of it, no longer will northern philanthropists give bountifully from their coffers for the support of Negro education," said John H. Purnell, an educator in the Upsilon Omega chapter in St. Louis, Missouri, in a candid assessment of so-called White liberals. "If more of the large sums collected by these and similar organizations can somehow be spent for higher academic and professional education, and if the bequests to education of well-to-do Negroes already so well begun can be further stimulated," Purnell pondered, "who will need to regret the shift of control in Negro education?"[208]

This question Purnell asked loomed large as Omega men descended upon Chicago, Illinois, for the Fifteenth Grand Conclave, from December 26 to 30, 1926. The Iota and Sigma Omega chapters hosted the conclave. As usual, the Black press previewed the upcoming gathering.[209] The *New York Amsterdam News* noted the "rolls of the organization contain the names of leading members of the race. Four of its members have been awarded the Spingarn Medal," the NAACP's highest honor given to a person of African descent for distinguished accomplishment.[210] The YMCA branch located on South Wabash Avenue served as the headquarters for the conclave, but delegates held the public meeting at Grace Presbyterian Church.[211] Former Grand Basileus J. Alston Atkins delivered the principal address, titled "Some Observations on the Functions and Possibilities of Negro Collegiate Fraternities and Sororities."[212] In it, he emphasized unity across all organizations. He argued that every Black Greek-letter organization had the same goals and, according to the *Chicago Defender*, were "working toward the same end."[213] Delegates praised Atkins's address. "It is needless to say that the address was that of a student and scholar," said Aaron H. Payne of the Sigma Omega chapter.[214] Also, James M. Nabrit Jr., who was initiated at Eta chapter while at Morehouse before becoming Psi chapter's first Keeper of Seals, but who eventually became a member of Iota chapter in Chicago while he studied law at Northwestern University, observed "the true purpose of fraternalism was eloquently portrayed by Brother J. A. Atkins."[215]

Atkins's address at the Chicago Conclave extended a hand to other fraternal organizations, but the business of Omega captured the attention of Black Americans across the country. "Discussions of world problems, scholarships, study of Race history, and the subject of race relationships feature the 15th annual conclave of the Omega Psi Phi Fraternity, which is now in session in this city," reported the *Chicago Defender*.[216] The same newspaper also added, "This Greek letter fraternity, the first to be established in a Race institution of learning, is carrying on a constructive program of bettering the youth of the Race."[217] Most important, as one journalist reported, was how "discussions of the internal policy of the fraternity required most of the Wednesday session when it was brought out that with 70 chapters scattered throughout the United States, Canada, and Africa, the future policy will be that of concentration as against that of expansion."[218]

In the Grand Basileus's report, George L. Vaughn discussed his having "given much thought to the question of compiling a list of colleges and universities whose standards are sufficiently high to make them eligible for chapters of the fraternity." The issue, as Vaughn saw it, was that "a number of institutions are headed by members of this fraternity. In others, members of the fraternity are on the faculty." "[However] I would not sanction the establishment of a chapter at an institution which did not come up to the requirements, even though that institution was headed by my own brother in flesh." Vaughn deferred to the rating system used at the time by the General Board of Education, Carnegie Foundation, Rockefeller Foundation, or any other educational association that was founded prior to 1926 and whose assessment jurisdiction reached beyond one state.[219]

Walter H. Mazyck, in his report of the Grand Keeper of Records and Seal for 1926, provided more details about the specific issue Vaughn had in mind. The Fraternity issued charters for nine new chapters. Six were graduate chapters: Lambda Phi (Macon, Georgia), Mu Phi (Savannah, Georgia), Nu Phi (Houston, Texas), Xi Phi (New York City), Omicron Phi (Columbia, South Carolina), and Kappa Psi (serving the Howard University professional schools). Three were undergraduate chapters: Eta Psi (Fisk University), Theta Psi (West Virginia Collegiate Institute), and Iota Psi (Ohio State University). There was no question of the caliber of education at Fisk and Ohio State; however, West Virginia Collegiate (now named West Virginia State University) chapter charter was a rarity as a public Black college or university. In 1920, that campus was briefly designated home to Kappa chapter as previously mentioned, but Kappa chapter was soon reassigned to Syracuse University. Therefore, the charter for the Theta Psi chapter was significant for a public Black campus. Howard University (Alpha chapter) in the District of Columbia considered itself a private, federally chartered institution. Also, Morgan College in Maryland (Pi chapter) and Lincoln University in Pennsylvania (Beta chapter) were not designated public institutions until 1939 and 1972, respectively. Therefore, before Theta Psi at West Virginia Collegiate, there had been much debate about what public Black campuses were developed enough to be considered a "college" in terms of curricula offerings. Some White-run associations had rated Fisk, Morehouse, Atlanta, Virginia Union, and a few other private Black colleges with Omega Psi Phi chapters as having developed college-rated curricula; however, those Black campuses were not the norm. In 1926, the Fraternity denied charter applications for chapters at Paine College in Georgia, Rust College in Mississippi, and Livingstone College in North Carolina even though the presidents of Rust and Livingstone were Omega men.[220]

Mazyck's detailed report at the Chicago Conclave also captured another issue with which the Fraternity had to deal: Omega Psi Phi's reputation was so positive and several of the Fraternity's members were so influential that Black collegians sought out membership beyond their campuses despite not having a chapter. For example, Mazyck discussed "delinquent chapters"— those "whose local inactivity or failure to maintain contact with and support the national organization." He considered those chapters "liabilities to the fraternity." By his calculation, there were twelve chapters among the Fraternity's seventy total chapters that were delinquent. He scrutinized one chapter, Delta Psi chapter at Shaw University in Raleigh, North Carolina, for its intake practices: "I have learned that some students at A&T College of Greensboro, N.C., have been taken into this chapter," Mazyck stated, adding: "A. and T. has not been recognized as a college at which to establish a chapter."[221]

Fittingly, McKinney's new association for deans and registrars addressed the problem of curricula offerings and recognizable campuses, and that became clearer as other committee chairmen presented their reports. Atkins, McKinney's friend from Boston and past Grand Basileus, chaired the Omega Psi Phi Committee on Recommendations. His report recommended that Tennessee A&I, Livingstone, and North Carolina A&T be considered for the approved college list "if rating warrants," and the Supreme Council proceeded to modify its list with an eye toward the future—and an ear toward McKinney.[222]

At the Chicago Conclave, delegates elected Julius S. McClain of Philadelphia, Pennsylvania, as Grand Basileus—Vaughn decided not to run for a third term. Delegates also elected J. D. Stewart of Greensboro, North Carolina, as Vice Grand Basileus, and delegates reelected Daniel B. Taylor as Grand Keeper of Finance and Mazyck as Grand Keeper of Records and Seal. McClain, Stewart, Taylor, and Mazyck assumed the task of ensuring the Fraternity expanded systemically because, as Mazyck stated in his thorough report, "we have passed our period of feverish expansion. New chapters are now chartered only after thorough consideration."[223]

Heeding the advice of Mazyck, among other leading Omega men, the Fraternity began a process to slow chapter expansion in 1927 not long after the Chicago Conclave ended. Concurrently, the Fraternity's efforts to expand and help facilitate meaningful educational opportunities for Black people—particularly at the Black colleges and universities, which educated most Black people—began to bear fruit. In Greensboro, where McKinney was a member of the Tau Omega chapter, he and many of members the chapter worked at North Carolina A&T. They included Warmoth T. Gibbs, who earned a master's degree at Harvard University, Mortimer G. Weaver, a Phi Beta Kappa at Williams College who also earned a master's degree at Harvard, and their fellow Tau Omega chapter member, W. Mercer Cook, a Phi Beta Kappa from Amherst College who studied abroad at the Sorbonne in Paris. Cyril F. Atkins completed a bachelor's degree at Tufts University and a master's at the University of Iowa. Paul V. Jewell finished his undergraduate studies at MIT. Each of those men previously belonged to Gamma chapter in Boston or Alpha Psi in Amherst, and all those men were aware of the resources the country's wealthiest White institutions of higher education had to educate White students.[224]

In Greensboro, Omega men such as McKinney turned their attention toward Black colleges and universities in 1927. In April, *The Oracle* stated that "the rating board visited A&T College early in the year and, as a result, has rated it as an 'A' grade college. The addition of these brothers has meant much to the chapter."[225] That rating rise was a testament to the efforts of McKinney, whom his colleagues in the NACDR reelected as president in March 1927.[226] The association soon earned national attention for its assessment of Black colleges' curricula. Under his leadership, the association also paid special attention to the different types of Black colleges. Members of the association standardized which topics were taught at Black liberal arts colleges, junior colleges, normal schools, and agricultural and technical institutions. All Black colleges had different needs, and McKinney's analysis provided data for questions the Fraternity had spent years attempting to answer about those needs. "The organization of this conference is one of the most outstanding achievements [in the] higher education for Negroes during the present century," the *Norfolk Journal and Guide* declared, "and is perhaps the only organization which really represents the higher education of Negroes in America."[227]

Omega Psi Phi chartered several chapters in 1927. Besides Mu Psi chapter at North Carolina A&T where McKinney was dean, the Fraternity chartered two other chapters at Black colleges whose presidents were Omega men: Lambda Psi at Livingstone College and Xi Psi at South Carolina State. William Johnson Trent Sr. was president of Livingstone, and Robert Shaw Wilkinson was president at South Carolina State. Xi Psi was the first Greek-letter organization on that campus, and Wilkinson enthusiastically supported its establishment. The Fraternity also chartered Nu Psi at Virginia State College. Meanwhile, in Jefferson City, Missouri, hundreds of miles west of Virginia State College, Omega man William Barrington Jason started as president of Lincoln University.[228] But even as he and other Omega men accepted or retained positions of leadership at Black colleges and universities, the Fraternity did not seize the opportunity to expand. By 1928, Grand Basileus Julius S. McClain honored the wishes of his predecessor, George L. Vaughn, and slowed the expansion of the Fraternity, even for campuses led by Omega men. When asked to share his vision for Omega, McClain stated: "First—build Omega for the benefit of Omega men—make the Fraternity worth something to itself. Then, use its influence and resources to help humanity, not one week, but 52 weeks in each year."[229]

Expansion slowed its pace under Grand Basileus McClain in 1928. The Fraternity chartered only two chapters during that year. Chi Phi in Denver, Colorado, was for graduates, and Omicron Psi at the University of Pittsburgh was for undergraduates. The next year, during McClain's third year as Grand Basileus, the Fraternity chartered a single chapter, Pi Psi at the University of Illinois. But the priorities of Black higher education and McKinney's standardization functioned in many ways like a Black-run academic accreditation association. His efforts proved more valuable than the rapid and often sporadic expansion of the Fraternity that marked the early 1920s.[230]

Education was a foremost issue for the Fraternity during its second decade. To combat the economic displacement and racial violence against Black people of the time, the Fraternity adopted a far-reaching vision to launch chapters, programs, and initiatives across the United States and into Canada. The rapidity of those efforts, however, soon outpaced the Fraternity's ability to streamline its efforts and maximize its impact. An abrupt, yet intentional, pause in the middle of the decade allowed for national officers to conduct an internal assessment. The Fraternity had expanded its presence in a manner that established chapters for students at various institutions, ranging from small private campuses like Biddle University (now Johnson C. Smith University) to larger campuses like the University of Minnesota.

The various efforts to aid Black education raised questions about the role of the Fraternity and its commitment to Black campuses, especially public Black colleges. A June 1927 editorial in *The Oracle* even questioned whether the Fraternity should focus its expansion efforts on predominately White college and university campuses with only a few Black students. The Omega man who wrote the editorial answered his own question: "Our expansion in the North and West should continue," he declared, "but not at the expense of those Negro colleges in the South that are fulfilling the requirements as approved by the American Council on Education for standardized colleges."[231] In November, another Omega editorialist in *The Oracle* wrote about the worsening disagreement between Fraternity officers and Carter G. Woodson about the study of Black history: "We are sorry that the director of the Association for the Study of Negro Life and History has proved himself small enough to consistently find opposition or competition in our Achievement Project."[232] The editorial responded to Woodson's earlier letter to Herman Dreer. Woodson was terse: "Because your Negro Achievement Project interferes with the national celebration of Negro History Week, the Association for the Study of Negro Life and History will have nothing to do with it."[233]

The internal debates among Omega men regarding Black education reflected a larger split among older and younger Black Americans and demonstrated how chapter expansion remained tied to the Fraternity's goal to influence and expand the educational opportunities for Black Americans. By the close of the decade, Theophilus E. McKinney's NACDR proved to be the most worthwhile response to the Fraternity's internal debates. The next decade would eventually see more Black college and universities earn higher curricula ratings, and more chapters would be chartered.[234]

Together with other Black Greek-letter fraternities and sororities, the new Omega Psi Phi chapters at Black colleges and universities established after the NACDR was founded were testaments to the standardization processes that Omega endorsed regarding college ratings. The Fraternity refined a model for how to adopt a race-forward agenda, and that effort gained the attention of many citizens, including sitting presidents of the United States of America. Consequently, Omega men fundamentally expanded the imagination of what Black education should be and become in the United States.

The abovementioned strides the Fraternity made during the 1920s were tremendous but, on the verge of the Great Depression, the Fraternity stood at a crossroads. What would become of its program as more educational opportunities and, in turn, more ideological conflict emerged as the Great Depression loomed and potentially exacerbated racial discrimination, unemployment, and various other issues and problems facing Black Americans?

Chapter 3

Through Days of Joy or Years of Pain

Omega Psi Phi Fraternity Responds during the Great Depression and World War II, 1930–1945

Omega Psi Phi and its members experienced the Great Depression in much the same fashion as most Black Americans. It was a period of great suffering that was exacerbated by the entrenchment of systematic racism and Jim Crow. Yet, at the same time, the Depression years were marked by profound political changes, demographic shifts, and social activism that charted a path toward progress in the decades to follow.

At the outset of the crash of the stock market in 1929, worsening economic conditions forced numerous Black Americans to remain in sharecropping agreements in rural areas or to work in low-wage jobs in urban cities. Many Black families barely made ends meet. Omega men were left in a similar situation upon graduating from college or being forced to halt their studies until the economy stabilized. Despite this, many members of the Fraternity stayed true to their commitment to racial advancement. That commitment was the same when the Fraternity dedicated its focus to expanding Black educational opportunity in the 1920s; however, the conditions of the 1930s prompted Omega men to pivot and play significant roles in helping the Black community survive, and in some cases thrive, during the Depression.

This chapter builds upon Omega men's work in education during the 1920s by demonstrating how the Great Depression shifted the Fraternity's focus. Omega men turned their attention toward Black economic advancement. The Fraternity's reach extended from the White House to the communities across the United States. For example, after Franklin Delano Roosevelt's presidential inauguration in 1933, he established the Federal Council on Negro Affairs (informally called the Black Cabinet or Black Brain Trust). Comprising select Black leaders, including some Omega men, the council informed Roosevelt about the state of Black America. While many of the New Deal programs that the Roosevelt administration developed from 1933 to 1939 expressly assisted Whites, some programs did help Black people. Meanwhile, Black voters in the Northeast, Midwest, and West emerged as a political force, while civil rights organizing gathered momentum in the South. The challenges of the 1930s soon gave way to World War II in the early 1940s. In both Depression and war, Omega Psi Phi actively launched programs to support efforts to assist Black communities across the United States. Omega men were leaders in business, military, politics, education, and law, thus making good on the motto *lifting as we climb*. Coined in 1902 by Mary Church Terrell, cofounder of the National Association of Colored Women, the motto embodied the Fraternity's various efforts during the 1930s and early 1940s to improve the moral, spiritual, and living conditions of Black America.[1]

The Fraternity and the Great Depression

The Wall Street stock market crashed on Tuesday, October 29, 1929. It was a defining moment in US history as millions of citizens were impacted, but Fraternity officers appeared undaunted in the immediate aftermath of the crash. For example, the Eighteenth Grand Conclave was held in Baltimore, Maryland, December 27–31, 1929, to handle the usual Fraternity business. Delegates elected or reelected members to the Supreme Council: Matthew Washington Bullock as Grand Basileus, Ira De Augustine Reid as Vice Grand Basileus, Walter H. Mazyck as Grand Keeper of Records and Seal, Daniel B. Taylor as Grand Keeper of Finance, and S. Malcolm Dodson as editor-in-chief of *The Oracle*.[2] Delegates unanimously voted to support Omega Psi Phi becoming a charter member of the National Pan-Hellenic Council, and they also agreed to provide scholarships to students.[3]

Delegates to the Baltimore Conclave also adopted a housing policy for Fraternity chapters that sought to purchase a house. The Fraternity agreed to issue a loan matching the amount that chapter was able to raise for the house, and it was reported in Baltimore that the Fraternity had more than $5,000 available for the home program.[4] Aside from the business meetings, on Sunday, December 29, Omega men attending the Baltimore Conclave repeated a gesture from the Thirteenth Grand Conclave in Washington, DC, in 1924, when they visited Arlington National Cemetery. Like five years earlier, Omega men laid wreaths at the Tomb of the Unknown Soldier and the gravesite of Omega man Charles Young. Afterward, members attended a show at the Lincoln Theatre in Washington, DC, followed by a dinner. The shows and dinners, alongside the commitment to help purchase chapter houses, exhibit the Fraternity's actions remained the same immediately after the stock market crash.[5]

For example, in April 1930, Grand Basileus Matthew W. Bullock celebrated the eighteenth anniversary of the Fraternity and trumpeted its success: "Eighteen years ago we had one chapter; today we have 82 chapters and more than 3,000 members. Well may we feel proud of the accomplishments of those who have directed our steps during all these years."[6] Bullock continued to praise the Fraternity in its eighteenth year and turned his attention toward a thriving future. "We must not forget that our organization is composed of graduate and undergraduate members." He added, "Each group is indispensable in the advancement of Omega. The graduates may supply the National Officers, but the life and future of the Fraternity depend entirely upon the character and scholarship of our undergraduate members."[7]

Like former Grand Basileus Julius S. McClain, who led the Fraternity from 1926 to 1929, Bullock did not focus on chapter expansion. In April 1930, the Rho Psi chapter was chartered at Tennessee Agricultural and Industrial (A&I) State Normal School for Negroes, and it would be the only chapter chartered during Bullock's first year as Grand Basileus. William Jasper Hale, the president of Tennessee A&I and a member of Delta chapter, had attempted to get the campus a Fraternity chapter as early as 1924.[8] Beyond that, Bullock focused primary on reclamation. The tone of the Baltimore Conclave in December 1929 was "harmonious," Bullock said, but by April 1930, the effects of the Great Depression were felt by the Fraternity.[9] Most Black people could not escape the perils of the Great Depression. White employers often laid off or fired Black people first, and those financial perils impacted many Omega men. The Supreme Council pondered "what should be done with our unfinancial members."[10] Bullock did not acknowledge the Depression itself but, instead, said "some of our Brothers have forgotten the obligation which they took when they were initiated and have gone so far as to withhold their financial support from the Fraternity."[11]

The growing number of Omega men not paying annual membership dues was a precursor to the Fraternity as an organization eventually being affected by the Depression. As Bullock moved deeper into his first year as Grand Basileus, the October 1930 issue of *The Oracle* published an editorial about the importance of conclaves. It was an effort to stir engagement among more Omega men during the financial downturn and reclaim members who had become unfinancial. "There will be many questions of vital importance to be decided by the Detroit Conclave: the ultimate disposition of unfinancial members, the perennial problem of a National Program, the housing situation, the future nature of The Oracle itself and a number of others," the editorial read. "If your chapter wants a voice in these affairs, it should prepare to send a delegate to Detroit."[12]

That assessment going into Detroit for the Nineteenth Grand Conclave made sense. Throughout 1930, the Supreme Council weighed important decisions that had financial implications. At the Baltimore Conclave, delegates deferred to Bullock and other national officers to determine how often *The Oracle* should be published.[13] The publication was critical to communicating updates to financial and unfinancial members, but two issues per year instead of four certain would save the Fraternity money. No decision was made to reduce the issues from four to two, but the consideration demonstrated how the Depression impacted Bullock's first year as Grand Basileus.

Bullock attempted to lead the Fraternity forward with its usual programs despite the challenges. In November 1930, Omega men held Achievement Week programs across the United States.[14] The national Achievement Week essay contest offered first, second, and third place winners prizes of $50, $35, and $15 or $25, $15, and $10 in the undergraduate and high school categories, respectively.[15] Achievement Week—no different than its first iteration in 1921—aimed to "present to our group the facts concerning the achievements of their great men and women."[16] *The Oracle* explained, "It is becoming increasingly evident that the Negro must pay closer attention to his own history, if he is to have a clear perspective of the group's achievements and a deeper appreciation of them."[17] The Fraternity remained committed to the study of Black history, and that commitment took on new meaning during the Depression. The next month, in December 1930, only weeks before the Detroit Conclave, Bullock acknowledged, "This past year has been a very difficult one for many of us. It has been hard, and money has been 'tight.'" However, he added, "many of the chapters have 'carried on' as though times were normal."[18]

The "normal" activities were evident from Achievement Week programs a month earlier. But the model for success, Bullock noted, was getting all Omega men to reinvest in the Fraternity going into the Detroit Conclave held December 27–30, 1930. But before arriving in Detroit, Bullock issued a challenge to every chapter: "Each and every chapter officer is requested to assist the Basileus in his drive to make the chapter 100% financial. The coming Conclave is destined to be the most important ever held. Questions of tremendous importance to the Fraternity are to be discussed and settled. Every chapter should be represented."[19]

Omega men's journey to Michigan was accompanied by fanfare from the Black press, much like the news coverage that accompanied conclaves during the 1920s. For instance, the *Chicago Defender* anticipated the gathering in Detroit—an important city to Black life in America—would be "the greatest conclave in the history of the organization."[20] If not the greatest, it was perhaps the most important thus far in the Fraternity's existence. In Detroit, delegates reelected each member of the Supreme Council.[21] Following the Detroit Conclave, *The Oracle* launched a campaign for advertisements. That decision exhibited the need for additional revenue at a time of financial uncertainty. "Banks, hotels, restaurants, haberdasheries, newspapers, institutions of learning, or any other concern from which ads are even remotely possible are acceptable," said Robert Grayson McGuire Jr., an Alpha Psi initiate who was studying journalism at Dartmouth College while serving as *The Oracle*'s advertising manager.[22]

Delegates also heard provisions pertaining to reinstating unfinancial members and the housing program, and Houston, Texas, was voted to host the next conclave in 1931.[23] Leaving Michigan, Omega men sang praises for the Detroit Conclave. After hearing of business and social sessions, graduate members of Nu Phi chapter felt "new life, new enthusiasm, new hope."[24] Similarly, Fred C. Cade, Basileus of Sigma Omega chapter, said, "I can visualize on the horizon of the not distant future, Omega standing out as one of the greatest Greek Letter Fraternities, owning and operating Fraternity Houses at all of the great seats of learning where the number of students of our group justify it."[25] Undergraduates at Pi chapter said the Detroit Conclave was "good both intellectually and socially," while those at Xi chapter assessed that "if each succeeding year shall be marked by such celerity and efficiency, the fraternity shall find itself farther in the front ranks of the progressive organizations of its kind."[26]

The Fraternity secured great momentum after the Detroit Conclave; however, worse news was not long in coming. The Great Depression tightened its grip on the United States, and Black people felt the strangle more than White people. By the spring of 1931, Omega man Carlyle M. Tucker published an editorial titled, "Our Economic Problem." He wrote, "This general condition of depression which has had so marked an effect upon the Caucasian, has doubly affected the Negro in all walks of life."[27] The effects of the Depression reached all Black people: no profession or level of education made one immune. "While it is true that the poorer classes have been hit the hardest," Tucker added, "the college-bred Negro is seeing some of his ambitions thwarted."[28] Tucker encouraged other Omega men to remain optimistic, however.

The Great Depression caused many Black Americans, regardless of educational attainment, to become unemployed. Aware that Black people were always challenged by job discrimination, Omega's leadership had launched the Fraternity Employment Committee as early as 1927 to keep its members advised of employment opportunities for professional and white-collar positions.[29] But the work to aid Black employment became more urgent after the Depression. In 1930 and 1931, Vice Grand Basileus Ira De Augustine Reid, then director of research for the National Urban League, maintained an effective employment information service, publishing a pamphlet titled "After College What?" that described permanent and temporary job opportunities for both graduates and undergraduate members of the Fraternity.[30] A prolific researcher, Reid conduced five studies in 1930 alone. For example, one study focused on the economic status of Black people in New York, New Jersey, and Pennsylvania. He published widely in academic journals like the *Annals of the American Academy of Political and Social Sciences* and in newspapers like the *New York Amsterdam News*, and he delivered seventeen public addresses from Ohio to Virginia, and from New York to Illinois.[31]

Reid's pamphlet, which *The Oracle* published in 1931, was described as "an authoritative analysis of the post-college problem together with some helpful suggestions."[32] The Depression limited job opportunities but, among Omega men, the challenge was also more college graduates. At the start of Bullock's tenure as Grand Basileus, there were 2,071 Black graduates who earned a bachelor's degree in the 1929–30 academic year.[33] Those graduates were met by the Depression. Noting this, Reid outlined which professional fields had demand but needed more college-trained employees. Teachers in physics, rural economics, political science, and social work were in demand. Omega men with inquiry skills were encouraged to pursue topics in social research, and those looking to be practitioners were directed toward careers in social work, business, and vocational guidance counselling. On the other hand, Reid warned the overcrowded professions included ministers, teachers, lawyers, and medical professions like nurses, dentists, and physicians. "The concentration of medical and legal practitioners in large, urban centers is one of the anomalies of Negro life, particularly so when one considers that such a large percentage of the population is rural and semi-urban."[34]

Although published in *The Oracle*, Reid did not limit his analysis to Omega men. His research on employment opportunities benefited all Black college students. Reid's intent was clear: "We hope it means something to you because we intend to keep work on the establishment of a technique that will serve the 19,000 Negro youth, who each year, are receiving college training."[35]

Reid understood Black struggle, and Omega Psi Phi's surviving and, moreover, thriving through the Great Depression required membership reclamation, employment programs, and cohesion between Fraternity members. In 1931, the Fraternity adopted its official hymn, "Omega Dear," written by Omega men Charles Richard Drew and William Mercer Cook.[36] Cook wrote the music and first stanza; Drew wrote the final two stanzas. Their song was a reminder to members that there was strength in unity and that faith was necessary to make it through both "days of joy or years of pain."[37]

Joy and pain captured the essence of the Fraternity's start to its decade. Omega men had recently rejoiced in fellowship during the Detroit Conclave in December 1930, but, as Black professionals, they were also impacted greatly by the Depression. Grand Basileus Matthew W. Bullock called it "a period of reconstruction."[38] Lives were altered. "Thousands of men are out of employment, including many of our brothers in Omega," he said. "It is for the welfare of these men that I beg your consideration."³⁹ Bullock urged Omega men, those "in a position to hire or recommend appointment," to consider their fellow Omega men for employment, even if that effort meant "lowering the standard" for work required.⁴⁰

By 1931, Samuel Wilson Rutherford was one Omega man in a position to answer Bullock's call to hire other Omega men. A member of the charter line of Alpha Omega chapter in 1923, Rutherford served on the Fraternity's Employment Committee.⁴¹ Born September 15, 1866, in rural Georgia, he started his first business—a grocery store—in Rome, Georgia, before a brief stint in business, in Lynchburg, Virginia. Rutherford's most successful venture, however, came after he moved to Washington, DC, and founded the National Benefit Life Insurance Company in 1898.⁴² The business was groundbreaking and, in January 1929, the Harmon Foundation bestowed him with its gold award for outstanding work in business. The *New York Times* noted that Rutherford "developed his company from a small sick benefit association with a capital stock in 1898 of $3,000 into a legal reserve life insurance company with $75,000,000 in policies in force, owned and operated exclusively by negroes and employing more than 1,500 field workers in addition to 300 men and women in its home offices."⁴³ The *Washington Post* added that award was "only for nationally outstanding achievement."⁴⁴ Rutherford's ability to employ Black people exemplified what Bullock and other Fraternity leaders sought from its members in business.⁴⁵

Lawrence A. Oxley was another Omega man working to improve Black economic status. In 1931, he served as North Carolina's director of the Division of Negro Welfare. Born in Boston, Massachusetts, Oxley attended public schools in Boston before enrolling at and graduating from the Prospect Union Preparatory School in nearby Cambridge. A group of Harvard University instructors tutored him privately, but he did not earn a degree from the university. Next, Oxley served in World War I, rising in rank to first lieutenant, and he was the only Black officer affiliated with the US Army's Morale Program. After the war, Oxley worked as a field director of Negro Work for Community Service across four states: Ohio, Indiana, West Virginia, and Kentucky. He then made his way to Raleigh, North Carolina, where he taught in the social sciences at St. Augustine's College for three years before, in 1925, he accepted his position as state director of the Division of Negro Welfare.⁴⁶ Furthermore, members of the Beta Phi chapter in Durham, North Carolina, found Oxley to be "a staunch support of all that means progress to Omega."⁴⁷

In June 1931, Oxley informed Omega men about the work his office was leading in North Carolina. He explained that Black well-being was essential to the well-being of society at large. Oxley clearly connected Omega's work in education during the 1920s to the Fraternity's urgent economic initiatives during the early 1930s. "Educational opportunity for the Negro child has been a goal of the state for many years," Oxley said. "It is only within the past six years that a definite public welfare program with a view to aiding the Negro has been begun."[48] At a time when the Fraternity sought models for Black economic success, Oxley's work in North Carolina was a model.

The efforts of Oxley and Rutherford were promising, but similar endeavors were not limited to Omega men in business. In 1931, William Stuart Nelson was named president of Shaw University, also in Raleigh. He was the first Black president of Shaw, a private Black institution, which was home of the Delta Psi chapter.[49] As previously mentioned, Nelson spent the early 1920s leading the publicity for the Fraternity's Campaign for the Study of Negro Literature and History, and its international scholarship committee. Since then, he earned a bachelor's degree in divinity from Yale University in 1924. Nelson's appointment was cause for celebration, as Omega men remembered their call for Black leaders of Black institutions. In fact, prior to his appointment at Shaw, Nelson worked as assistant to Mordecai Wyatt Johnson, the first Black president of Howard University.[50] Johnson was not an Omega man, but that did not stop Alpha chapter's Dutton Ferguson from dedicating a poem to Johnson published in the June 1931 issue of *The Oracle*. Ferguson's poem was titled "To an African Mask: A New Negro Litany."[51]

The same issue also published information about the upcoming conclave planned for Houston in December 1931. Omega men were made abreast of specific travel accommodations made by the Fraternity to have special Pullman cars transport them to Texas.[52] In summary, despite the broader economic conditions, Fraternity leaders felt good. They acknowledged the financial hardships, but they called on Omega men to continue the work of uplift. Rutherford and Oxley were examples in business. Nelson was another leader in education. And undergraduate members like Ferguson remained involved in the New Negro movement. But the latter half of 1931 turned quickly as financial institutions collapsed during the Depression.

On July 19, 1931, Daniel B. Taylor, Grand Keeper of Finance, informed the Supreme Council that the Northwestern Trust Company in Philadelphia, Pennsylvania, closed suddenly.[53] That year, bank suspensions occurred in major cities across the United States.[54] The suspensions were an effort to prevent massive withdrawals, but the damage the stock market crash of 1929 caused was still unfolding. Social displacements caused by the Great Depression were challenging, but the collapse of financial institutions left many organizations without what limited money they did have. Omega Psi Phi was no different.

Bullock later shared with Omega men that the Northwestern Trust Company held "a little more than one-half of our funds" when the bank collapsed.[55] Taylor was more specific in his letter to the Supreme Council, who he informed that $2,650 was on deposit with Northwestern Trust at the time of its 1931 closure.[56] "This is a very serious matter which calls for your immediate and most brilliant action," Taylor informed the Supreme Council.[57] The loss of funds meant Taylor would not pay any bill until further direction from the Supreme Council, and Fraternity leaders sought immediate solutions to regain financial stability.

First, Grand Basileus Matthew W. Bullock and other Fraternity leaders decided to cancel the Houston Conclave. It would have been the first Grand Conclave in the southwest, but financial collapse made hosting the annual meeting nearly impossible. The Supreme Council recommended cancellation, and most Omega men agreed with the recommendation. As a result, Bullock said, "the Conclave was postponed, and the financial interest of the fraternity safeguarded."[58] Bullock also saw that *The Oracle* suspend its publications to limit printing. Bullock also stopped salary payment for the Fraternity's national officers. The most notable expense that the Fraternity did proceed with was its loan to the Washington, DC, chapters for a chapter house, but all other expenses were "cut to the bone."[59] This series of cost-cutting measures helped preserve the Fraternity after losing a significant portion of its cash assets. With such sacrifice among national officers, once again, Bullock called on unfinancial Omega men to meet their obligations to the Fraternity. "If every man will put his shoulder to the wheel and do his level best toward the payment of Grand Chapter dues," Bullock professed, "it will not be long before our financial condition will be as sound as it was prior to the closing of the bank."[60]

That plea marked Bullock's entire tenure as Grand Basileus. External circumstances limited Fraternity activities, especially for the remainder of 1931 and early 1932. Sigma Psi at Samuel Huston College (later merged with Tillotson College) and Tau Psi at North Carolina College (now named North Carolina Central University) were the only chapters chartered in 1931.[61] Bullock remained focused on reclamation instead of expansion for two reasons. First, Omega men struggled to pay dues during the Depression. Second, older Omega men died.

On March 13, 1932, Robert Shaw Wilkinson passed. He was president of South Carolina State College (now named South Carolina State University) in Orangeburg. Born on February 18, 1865, in Charleston, South Carolina, where Wilkinson completed high school at the Avery Institute, he excelled as a student. Wilkinson was admitted to the US Military Academy in West Point, New York. His health forced him to withdraw, and he continued his undergraduate education at Oberlin College in Ohio. There, Wilkinson earned bachelor's and master's degrees before he became a professor of Greek and Latin at Simmons College, a private Black institution at Louisville, Kentucky. In 1896, after four years in Kentucky, he returned to his home state to join the faculty when South Carolina State was founded. In 1911, the same year Omega Psi Phi was founded, Wilkinson was named president of the college. The loss of Wilkinson sent sorrow throughout the Fraternity as he was a model Omega man, having served as Basileus of the Epsilon Omega chapter in Orangeburg. "His achievements and contributions to Negro education are worthy of emulation by every Omega man," one report read. "Omega has lost her greatest son in South Carolina. The Negroes of the State have lost a great champion. The State has lost a loyal citizen and a great leader has fallen from the ranks of educational leadership of the country."[62]

The Oracle returned to publication a month after Wilkinson's death with its April 1932 issue dedicated to the Great Depression. Regarding Northwestern Trust Company, Bullock informed Omega men that "at the present time, it is impossible to determine what our losses will be."[63] Richard York Nelson, Basileus of Mu chapter and law student at Temple University, published an essay titled, "The Negro and the Depression."[64] Langston Hughes, Omega's most famous poet by that point, also published three poems in the Great Depression issue. One poem, titled "Negro Ghetto," captured Hughes' descriptive look at Black life during the Depression.[65] The twenty-page issue was shorter than *The Oracle*'s previous issues, but it signaled Omega men's embodiment of the cardinal principle, perseverance.

The summer of 1932 looked much like previous summers. The Fraternity celebrated Omega men's scholarly attainments. Percy Lavon Julian was championed as an example of Omega excellence—just as he had featured in *The Oracle* featured in 1922 at the start of his career. A decade later, Julian had his PhD degree in chemistry from the University of Vienna in Austria and returned to the United States to head the chemistry department at Howard University.[66] A younger Omega man, Walter Nathaniel Ridley was also featured. He completed his bachelor's and master's degrees in education at Howard in 1931 and 1932, respectively. As of summer of 1932, Ridley planned to attend Harvard University or the University of Chicago for his doctorate.[67] Soon, as many individual Omega men moved forward, Grand Basileus Bullock was also ready to resume a productive program for the Fraternity.

In September 1932, Bullock announced plans for the Twentieth Grand Conclave in Richmond, Virginia. "Two years have passed since we last met in Grand Conclave," he said. "They have been momentous years, many things have happened."[68] Bullock added, "In a period such as this, it was not at all surprising that our organization should have suffered with the rest."[69] He said he believed the Depression had passed, but Omega men were the determining factor in Omega Psi Phi's future success. Bullock called on members to pay their dues or Omega would fail to rebuild. He stated plainly: "If you love the Fraternity, now is the time to show it."[70]

In Richmond, Omega men would have two years' worth of business to handle. Much had happened since the Detroit Conclave in December 1930. Financial challenges aside, the Fraternity still had its programs geared toward Black advancement. Achievement Week and Black voter legislation were among them. Therefore, the Richmond Conclave came with a sense of urgency. An editorial in the October 1932 issue of *The Oracle* read, "This means that, depression notwithstanding, more than ever before there is the need for the greatest representation on the conclave floor we have had in the history of the fraternity."[71]

The Black press also took note of the upcoming conclave, from December 27 to 30, 1932. The *Norfolk Journal and Guide* reported that Richmond "intends to surpass all its former hospitality in greeting the brothers."[72] The *Chicago Defender* and *Philadelphia Tribune* also offered preview news coverage for Black Americans following Omega men's collective action.[73]

Once in Richmond, delegates were hosted by members of Zeta chapter and Phi Phi chapter, and they immediately went about addressing matters that culminated over the previous two years. Walter H. Mazyck, Grand Keeper of Records and Seal, announced that delegates would consider whether a biennial conclave should be adopted. He also noted that scholarships and essay contests would likely become something led by the Fraternity's chapters instead of the national officers. "The conclave will undoubtedly stress as its program, the strengthening of the internal organization of the fraternity," Mazyck said. "The fraternity has suffered heavy financial losses due to the failure of a bank in which some of its funds were kept, and the general economic condition has contributed to prevent the recouping of the treasure to the extent which would enable the fraternity to resume its altruistic activities."[74] The economy was the primary issue considered by delegates as they voted. For instance, delegates decided to continue the Fraternity's housing program and Achievement Week activities. "While many constructive plans for economies were adopted, affecting all items of the budget," one news report stated, "none will essentially lower the efficiency of the administration or discontinue any part of the Omegas' annual program."[75]

Delegates also voted on new national officers for the first time in two years: Lawrence A. Oxley was elected Grand Basileus, alongside William E. Baugh as Vice Grand Basileus and Jesse B. Blayton as Grand Keeper of Finance. Mazyck was reelected as Grand Keeper of Records and Seal—a position he had held since 1924—and S. Malcolm Dodson was reelected as editor-in-chief of *The Oracle*.[76] Bullock did not to run for a fourth term as Grand Basileus.[77] The decision closed his three-year stint as Grand Basileus, with three chapters—Upsilon Psi at Florida Agricultural and Mechanical College (now University), Alpha Alpha in Hampton, Virginia, and Psi Phi in Winston-

Salem, North Carolina—being chartered in 1932, and a total of only six chapters organized under his leadership.⁷⁸

The Fraternity slowed its program in reaction to the Great Depression, focusing on reclamation more than expansion, but the fellowship in Richmond after a two-year hiatus was considered one of the Fraternity's "best and most enthusiastic conclaves in its history."⁷⁹ Delegates took that enthusiasm and looked south toward Durham, North Carolina—selecting it as host city of the next conclave. Durham was a thriving Black economic center despite the ill effects of the Depression and, as previously mentioned, Oxley (the incoming Grand Basileus) was North Carolina's director of the Division of Negro Welfare.⁸⁰ Oxley and Durham's George W. Cox, selected as Grand Marshal, were ready to take the Fraternity's economic program forward.⁸¹ However, as Fraternity officers looked ahead to address the woes of Black Americans, in 1933 even more opportunities would open for Omega men to lead the nation.

Black Brain Trust: Intellectual and Economic Justice

On January 24, 1933, less than one month after the Richmond Conclave, the Virginia Mutual Benefit Life Insurance Company was chartered.⁸² Its founding would not have been possible, however, if Omega man Samuel Wilson Rutherford's National Benefit Life Insurance Company had not dissolved in 1931. Rutherford's business had thrived entering the 1930s, but it suffered during the Depression and amid some controversial legal issues.⁸³ Sudden dissolvement aside, Rutherford's business made way for Virginia Mutual to be founded as a model Black insurance business. Black insurance companies were a leading employer during the Depression, and several former National Benefit field workers joined the newly formed Virginia Mutual in Richmond.⁸⁴ It was evidence that Omega men were, directly and indirectly, influencing a new phase of intellectual and economic justice.

Grand Basileus Lawrence A. Oxley also wasted no time starting his work leading the Fraternity. On February 4, 1933, he joined other members of the Supreme Council in Washington, DC Oxley visited from Raleigh, North Carolina, while Baugh, the new Vice Grand Basileus, traveled from Indianapolis, Indiana. Blayton, the new Grand Keeper of Finance, came from Atlanta, Georgia. All were met by Mazyck—the then longest-serving member of the Supreme Council—who resided in Washington, DC, as Grand Keeper of Records and Seal. They met at the new chapter house in Washington, where the Supreme Council "outlined a sane and progressive program and defined some major policies for the guidance of Omega in 1933."⁸⁵

The Fraternity's new leaders had their work cut out for them, however. By this point, Omega Psi Phi had chartered ninety chapters, and there were about

4,000 members. That was promising in terms of reach and scope for the Fraternity's programs to aid Black Americans. But the problem was nearly half of those chapters were inactive and, among those, several chapters had been noncontributors for at least three years—a testament to the effects of the Great Depression. The Supreme Council needed to revive those inactive chapters.[86]

The fight for racial justice meant Oxley, like his predecessor Matthew W. Bullock, would have to focus on reclamation. Therefore, Oxley explained, "a major policy of the present administration relates to a concerted movement to bring back within the fold of Omega every worthy unfinancial Omega man."[87] An example of that policy was seen across the United States on March 12, 1933, when the Fraternity observed Colonel Charles Young Memorial Sunday. As it had been done in the past, Omega men reflected on Young's historic life. This was important while working to shape a better Black future. Then, after the day of observation, Omega men spent the following week reclaiming unfinancial Omega men in their respective communities. Oxley wanted a "healthy revival" of inactive chapters and reinstatement of members by getting them to pay dues.[88] "The cooperation of every loyal Omega man is expected," Oxley said, while adding: "No organization can long exist without a strong and active membership—Omega is no exception to this rule."[89]

Oxley made reclamation a national priority, while promising to execute other programs on a "strict economy."[90] He vowed to keep Omega men informed about the Fraternity's financial status. This was a sound approach since every corner of the nation felt, or was at least keenly aware of, the Depression. An economic activist himself, Oxley championed a program that would help the Fraternity grow in its efforts to positively impact local communities across the United States. But while Oxley worked on the Fraternity's national programs, individual Omega men were doing their share of racial justice work in their neighborhoods, towns, and cities.

In Decatur, Alabama, Frank Jehoy Sykes, a 1914 initiate at Alpha chapter, was one Omega man who worked for justice in his local community. In March 1933, the criminal trials of nine Black children captured national attention. Two years earlier, in 1931, the Black group, ranging between thirteen and twenty years old, were riding a freight train between Chattanooga and Memphis. It was common for people to ride trains looking for work, town to town, and the Black boys were no different. But along the way, in rural Alabama, they got into an altercation with a White group. The Black boys were apprehended by a White posse and accused of raping two White women. Then, in a hasty trial held in Scottsboro, Alabama, all but one was found guilty and sentenced to death.[91] They became known as the Scottsboro Boys, and news of the verdict and lack of evidence brought them legal representation from the Communist Party USA and the National Association for the Advancement of Colored People (NAACP), and, over the next two years, legal appeals and retrials were held to determine the boys' guilt or innocence.[92]

By 1933, a change of venue request for the retrial landed the Scottsboro Boys in a courtroom in Decatur, Alabama, the hometown of Sykes, known as "Doc," because he was a dentist. Sykes testified in March 1933 and early April 1933. He was a professional and one of a few Black people registered to vote in the county. Black people were never selected as jurors in Morgan County. In fact, no Black people had been considered among the 2,500 people called before various cases over the previous four years.[93] That lack of Black jurors existed despite having residents like Sykes registered to vote and, thus, eligible for the juror pool. He was the first Black person called by the defense to testify when the question of Black jurors was raised before the court. Sykes presented a list of more than 120 names of Black people qualified to serve as jurors in the county and, as he sat before the court, twenty-four other Black people also appeared in the courtroom prepared to testify.[94] The White press used its usual racist tropes to describe Sykes as "unusually intelligent in appearance and employed good English."[95] White shock aside, Sykes's intellectual range was no surprise to many Black people. After joining Omega Psi Phi during his undergraduate studies, he eventually completed dental school at Howard in 1918. For years, Sykes played professional baseball in the Negro leagues. He pitched for various professional teams, notably with the Baltimore Black Sox from 1919 until 1925. Sykes left baseball behind when he left Baltimore.[96]

But Sykes returned home to Decatur and handled the prosecution's courtroom fastballs better than the batters he faced on the field. His actions were bold, but they came with consequences. Ku Klux Klansmen burned crosses in front of homes and businesses owned by Black people who testified. Also, a residence that housed Black out-of-town journalists, such as one from the *Baltimore Afro-American*, was targeted. The Klan intimidation was part of their attempt to strike terror in Black residents and maintain the status quo. Rumors even swirled that some White residents would "take care of" any other Black people who stood before the courts like Sykes, and the death threats ultimately forced Sykes to move back to Baltimore.[97]

Omega men's influence in the fight for justice—as seen with Sykes in Alabama—also received a boost at the national level. The previous fall, Americans elected Franklin Delano Roosevelt president of the United States on his promise to develop programs to aid citizens and businesses a top priority. By April 1933, after Roosevelt was inaugurated, his New Deal programs were launched. Scholars later summarized the programs as providing relief, recovery, and reform.[98] Those programs were geared toward addressing the needs of citizens whom the Great Depression left impoverished and devastated by implementing financial, infrastructural, and regulatory reforms—all of which had implications for Black Americans.[99]

In turn, Roosevelt formed the Federal Council on Negro Affairs, sometimes referred to as the Black Cabinet or the Black Brain Trust. Its members served as public policy advisers for Roosevelt and his wife, Eleanor Roosevelt. This was an informal group, not officially part of Roosevelt's cabinet, but it included many of the nation's most influential Black leaders. That included some Omega men: Grand Basileus Lawrence A. Oxley, alongside William Henry Hastie Jr., and Robert Clifton Weaver.[100] Over the course of the Roosevelt administration, dozens of Black leaders served on the Black Cabinet led by Mary McLeod Bethune, a member of Delta Sigma Theta. Omega men served in various capacities as advisers to Roosevelt or in other federal capacities. While being Grand Basileus, Oxley was chief adviser in the Department of Labor.[101] Hastie worked in the Department of the Interior while Weaver served as adviser to Secretary of the Interior Harold L. Ickes. Weaver's associates, John Prescott Murchison and Dewey R. Jones, were also Omega men and worked with him on federal matters. Omega man Alfred E. Smith was chief adviser for the Public Works Administration. Meanwhile, Omega man Roy Ellis was a clerk in the Department of Commerce. "Omega men in Washington have a keen appreciation of the obligations and responsibilities that are theirs in the important positions they hold," *The Oracle* reported, "and at the same time, they are ever aware of the pleasure and honors that belong to them as Omega men."[102]

Six months earlier, in December 1932, Omega men met in Virginia for the Richmond Conclave and focused on economic initiatives, internally and externally. Omega men adhered to the Fraternity's emphasis on justice—intellectual and economic—through their work at the local and federal level. As a result, some Omega men answered Franklin Delano Roosevelt's call for Black advisers as he entered the White House and signed the first New Deal programs into law in 1933. That captured the first half of 1933 for Omega Psi Phi. But as national officers sought to help the Fraternity and the nation recover during the Depression, news of one of Omega's most loyal members unexpectedly sent another form of depression through the Omega men.

Walter H. Mazyck: An Institution

On August 7, 1933, Walter Herbert Mazyck died in Washington, DC[103] At the Washington Conclave in 1924, he was elected Grand Keeper of Records and Seal. For nearly ten years, Grand Conclave delegates repeatedly reelected Mazyck who worked diligently to develop and maintain a thorough record-keeping system for the Fraternity. By 1933, at a time when the Fraternity actively sought to reclaim hundreds of unfinancial members, Mazyck was one of the most dedicated Omega men until he passed from a rare autoimmune, neuromuscular disease called myasthenia gravis. He was thirty-seven years old.[104]

In the spirit of friendship, Omega men had always paid tribute to its members who had passed. The annual Charles Young memorial services were a required program and, as previously mentioned, *The Oracle* offered occasional short articles about Omega men who had entered Omega chapter—the chapter designation for deceased members—such as Robert Shaw Wilkinson.[105] However, Mazyck's death was different and, in 1933, the Fraternity dedicated an issue of *The Oracle* to being the "Mazyck Memorial Number."

Mazyck was born on December 14, 1895, in Charleston, South Carolina. There, he attended Winslow's Private School before completing his secondary education at the Avery Institute in 1914. Mazyck then left his hometown and traveled north to Washington, DC, where he enrolled at Howard University. There, Mazyck became friends with Campbell C. Johnson, and both were initiated at Alpha chapter in 1916. Johnson later recalled that Mazyck "made an enviable scholastic record at Howard."[106] That assessment held true. Mazyck wrote essays and brief literary sketches, although he kept most of his writing private during college.[107]

Mazyck soon turned his attention away from his studies and toward service to the nation. As noted in Chapter 1, Fort Des Moines Army Base was organized after the United States officially entered World War I in April 1917. Mazyck volunteered his services and made his way to Des Moines, Iowa. He served there until October 15, 1917, when he was commissioned as a first lieutenant of infantry. Afterward, Mazyck was assigned to Camp Meade, Maryland, but after several months in camp, he fell ill. He was recovering at a US Army hospital in New Haven, Connecticut, when his unit from Camp Meade deployed to France. Once recovered, he was assigned to Marshall, Texas, where he worked at Wiley University (renamed Wiley College in 1929)—home of Theta chapter—with the Students Army Training Corps Unit.[108]

In 1919, Mazyck returned to Washington, DC, after being honorably discharged from the army at the rank of first lieutenant. By day, he worked as a clerk in the Navy Department, where he helped develop a process for paying thousands of people enlisted in the Navy Reserves. Mazyck earned promotions along the way as the department grew: first clerk, then technical adviser. It was an early indicator of his aptitude as a record keeper and stickler for precision. His rise in the Navy Department accompanied his top-notch performance as a student. Once back in Washington, DC, he reenrolled at Howard and attended its law school in the evening. Mazyck was his class's top student each of his three years enrolled and eventually found himself using his law school lessons when he started advising the Navy Department on legal matters for the Retainer Pay Section in the Division of Supplies and Accounts.[109]

In 1922, Mazyck graduated from the Howard University Law School magna cum laude. He was noted to have won first place in every academic prize offered. Shortly after commencement, he passed the bar exam for admittance to practice law in Washington, DC. Mazyck was admitted to practice law before the Supreme Court and the Court of Appeals of Washington, DC. Ultimately, he became law partners with Campbell C. Johnson and John W. Love.[110] The three Omega men were old friends. Johnson was Mazyck's predecessor as Grand Keeper of Records and Seal, and Love was a 1914 initiate of Alpha chapter and a former Grand Basileus. In 1929, Mazyck was promoted to the rank of captain all while serving for multiple years as Grand Keeper of Records and Seal.[111] Mazyck's remarkable professional accomplishments were notable, but Omega men's tributes to him focused on personal attributes: his thirst to document history, the love of his life, and his love for Omega Psi Phi—all three of which were captured in the last year of his life.

In 1932, Mazyck published his book, *George Washington and the Negro*. His 180-page history of the relationship between the first president of the United States and Black people was published on the bicentennial of Washington's birth in 1732. Mazyck's book received favorable reviews from periodicals and academic journals. The *Journal of Negro History*, founded by Omega man Carter G. Woodson, called the book "true to history," adding that "the author has presented the facts as they are, believing that facts properly set forth will speak for themselves."[112] Meanwhile, the White-run *Mississippi Valley Historical Review* called it a "clear account of the views of Washington and is the fullest treatment of the subject."[113] Fanfare for Mazyck's book made its way through literary circles in 1932, but even that feat was topped by his marriage.

On December 22, 1932, Mazyck married Naomi Grant—a childhood friend. The two had known each other since growing up together in Charleston, South Carolina. Their families were long-time friends. Equally brilliant, Grant attended Morris Brown College in Atlanta, and she was considered "well known, admired, and liked in the social circles" in Charleston and Washington, DC.[114] As Mazyck said to friends prior to falling ill, "These last seven months have been the happiest of my entire life and no one can take them from me."[115] Mazyck passed happy with his life, but Omega men expressed great sorrow.

Grand Basileus Lawrence A. Oxley assessed, "Much of the modern structure of Omega was built by Walter Mazyck."[116] Oxley also credited Mazyck with the efficiency of the Fraternity's programs on racial advancement: "To him, the welfare of Omega, the widening of its influence, and the extending of the service which the Fraternity could render to our racial group were of the greatest importance."[117] Oxley reflected in awe at Mazyck's attention to details. He said no task was too small for Mazyck to address with extreme care, even duties that seemed trivial to other Omega men. "All Omega mourns the loss of a great man and brother."[118]

Campbell, Mazyck's friend and former law partner, said other lawyers wished Mazyck would "throw himself fully into the practice."[119] But Campbell understood that Mazyck was never considered a lawyer. He was more than that. Campbell said the legal cases that Mazyck did handle at the firm "subsequently showed him to be possessed of more than ordinary ability," but his reach went beyond the law practice and the Fraternity.[120] This was evident from Mazyck's supervisor at the Navy Department: "It is foolish to say we are going to replace Mr. Mazyck. His place just cannot be filled. It will take years to train a man who will be half as good."[121]

Aside from the written tributes, the special issue of *The Oracle* dedicated to Mazyck published photographs from the funeral procession.[122] The issue also featured two poems, "The Two Roses" and "Lincoln Memorial Bridge," written by Mazyck. Also, editor-in-chief of *The Oracle*, S. Malcolm Dodson, published his sketch of Mazyck.[123] Additionally, it was mentioned that Mazyck had finished archival research for a book he planned to write on Abraham Lincoln and Black people, and he was twenty-five pages from finishing a manuscript on Omega man Charles Young. Finally, there was an editorial titled, "They Say He's Dead," which perhaps best captured the breadth of Mazyck's works. Mazyck was the person who delegates turned to during Grand Conclaves when business sessions stalled due to questions about Fraternity policies. The same occurred during Supreme Council meetings when other national officers were confused on how to proceed. The editorial stated that asking Mazyck a question was more efficient than spending hours reading the Fraternity's constitution and bylaws. "To Omega men, Mazyck was more than a name or a person, he was an institution."[124]

Mazyck had articulated the Fraternity's goals in words and procedures that other Omega men were unable to convey. Among his writings, he presented the Fraternity with "Members versus Men." Mazyck wrote, "The value of our Fraternity is not in numbers, but in men, in real brotherhood. Eight men thoroughly immersed in the true Omega Spirit are far greater assets than eighty with lukewarm enthusiasm." It was not long before various Fraternity chapters adopted said slogan.[125] In an era where intellectual and economic justice was the Fraternity's focus, Omega men offered fitting tributes to Mazyck. His life was dedicated to the Fraternity and its struggles toward Black freedom. This was ever more pressing during the Great Depression. But Mazyck's passing also inspired Omega men. In the last quarter of 1933, the Fraternity prepared for its Twenty-First Grand Conclave in Durham, North Carolina, where Omega men would gather to try to replicate Mazyck's spirit and determination toward racial justice.

On to Durham . . . and Beyond

Grand Basileus Lawrence A. Oxley and the Supreme Council adopted a slogan: "Five Hundred Omega Men Reinstated Before the Durham Conclave."[126] The Great Depression presented financial limitations, but the national officers found ways to engage Omega men. Vice Grand Basileus William E. Baugh led that effort. In 1933, Baugh wrote more than 1,000 letters to leaders in Fraternity chapters and District Representatives to reclaim unfinancial members and to encourage financial members to maintain their status. From his home in Indianapolis, Indiana, Baugh traveled across the Midwest to visit numerous Omega outposts: Upsilon chapter and Delta Alpha chapter in Ohio; Iota chapter, Pi Psi chapter, and Sigma Omega chapter in Illinois; Nu Omega chapter in Michigan; and Upsilon Omega in Missouri.[127]

Aside from Baugh's personal touch, coupled with the legacy of Mazyck, Durham was a fine city to entice Omega men to become financial. The Supreme Council understood that a dear friend always made the Grand Conclave special because Omega men could reconnect and reflect. Additionally, Durham was a thriving Black city. If seeing old friends was not enough on its own, the chance to see Black people thriving despite the Depression was another reason to attend.

George W. Cox, Grand Marshal for the Durham Conclave, made the latter clear. He explained that the city was home to North Carolina Mutual Life Insurance Company, Mechanics and Farmers Bank, Durham Mortgage Company, and Dunbar Realty Company, among other Black-owned and -operated businesses. The city's large tobacco companies employed about 10,000 Black people. Furthermore, when it came to education, Durham stood among the strongest Black educational centers. North Carolina College (now named North Carolina Central University) was described as "having beautiful grounds, lovely spacious buildings, splendidly equipped, and a carefully selected faculty."[128] Hillside High School was equally impressive, Cox said, making the city "heralded around the world."[129]

Omega men played a significant role in helping make Durham a thriving business and education center for Black people. In 1933, Omega man Asa Timothy Spaulding joined North Carolina Mutual Life Insurance as its actuary. Spaulding was a North Carolina native. He attended Howard University in Washington, DC, prior to earning a bachelor's degree in accounting from New York University in 1930. Two years later, he earned a master's degree in actuarial science from the University of Michigan in Ann Arbor.[130] John Hervey Wheeler, an Omega man, was also a North Carolina native who, in 1929, moved to Durham after graduating from Morehouse College in Atlanta to work at the Mechanics and Farmers Bank.[131] Other Omega men in Durham business circles included Richard Lewis McDougald, who was simultaneously vice president and cashier of the Mechanics and Farmers Bank, vice president of the North Carolina Mutual Life Insurance Company, and secretary of the Mutual Building and Loan Association. North Carolina Mutual Life Insurance Company also employed William D. Hill as its assistant secretary and auditor, David Crockett Deans Jr. and John L. Wheeler as assistant agency directors, Aaron Day Jr. as supervisor of sales training, and Martin A. Goins in the investment department. John S. Stewart and Frank L. McCoy worked for the Building and Loan Association as assistant secretary and retiring secretary, respectively, and Rencher N. Harris, was secretary and manager of the Bankers Fire Insurance Company.[132]

Omega men were among Durham's most prominent business leaders, and their arrival excited other local Black leaders. James E. Shepherd, the founder and president of North Carolina College, welcomed Omega men, stating "the college believes that the principles of your Fraternity are sound and will aid much in the forward progress of the race if they are carried out."[133] Likewise, Charles Clinton Spaulding, president of North Carolina Mutual Life Insurance, extended "a most cordial welcome" to Omega men.[134] He added that his company and Omega Psi Phi, "two organizations—dissimilar in purpose, yet endowed with similar objectives. That measure of success achieved may be attributed to moral fitness, sincerity of purpose, and strict adherence to the underlying motive that actuated their founders."[135] The two greetings—on education and business—reflected the Fraternity's focus in a grand welcome to the "Negro Wall Street."[136]

Hosted by the Beta Phi chapter, the Durham Conclave was held December 26–30, 1933, and it followed a similar format as previous conclaves. There was a formal opening and events that welcomed the public. There were also committee and chapter reports. Updates on Achievement Week were also made. Among the speakers was Harold H. Thomas, former Grand Basileus. The only notable change in the four-day agenda compared to prior conclaves was the Durham Conclave held a memorial service specifically for Walter H. Mazyck.[137]

The 216 delegates reelected all national officers. That included James Arthur Weiseger, who replaced Mazyck as Keeper of Records and Seal in August 1933. They also voted to petition Congress to pass an anti-lynching law—something Omega men had agreed upon since the early 1920s. In terms of economic recovery, delegates voted to assess each of the Fraternity's ninety-two chapters $1.50 toward Omega Psi Phi's membership on the Joint Committee on National Recovery. The committee, whose executive secretary was John Preston Davis, an initiate of the Alpha Psi chapter when he attended Bates College in Maine, was "a coalition of twenty-two major Negro organizations which sought to secure nondiscriminatory treatment for Negroes under New Deal programs." As Omega men left Durham, Oxley informed the membership that the Fraternity had more than $2,600 on hand, and that recovery nearly three years after the Northwestern Trust Company collapse was largely due to a new rule that required Omega men to present financial cards to enter all business and social events.[138]

For the next two years, 1934 and 1935, Omega men moved forward on the winds of momentum from Durham. Work toward Black economic advancement and the Fraternity's financial stability continued. A select group of Omega men continued to work in federal capacities. That included Grand Basileus Lawrence A. Oxley, a member of President Franklin Delano Roosevelt's Black Cabinet. Meanwhile, Omega men read articles about Black people and the economy. In April 1934, *The Oracle* published an article titled "Economic Status of the Negro."[139] And Omega men in New York City were working to address that status. Like President Roosevelt's Black Cabinet in Washington, DC, members of Epsilon, Zeta Psi, Upsilon Phi, and Xi Phi chapters formed their own cabinet. "The functions of the inter-chapter cabinet," Donald D. Adams of Epsilon explained, "are to coordinate the activities of the chapters and to cooperate with the Supreme Council in matters of national concern."[140]

By June 1934, Omega men were reading about Omega man John Prescott Murchison's accession into federal politics after he was appointed assistant supervisor in the Subsistence Homesteads Division of the Department of Interior. Murchison, the former editor-in-chief of *The Oracle*, was responsible for "integrating the colored population into the subsistence homesteads benefits."[141] His work was another instance where Omega men extended the Fraternity's emphasis on Black economic advancement into practice. By the fall, however, internal discussion questioned the effectiveness of the Black Cabinet.

In September 1934, *The Oracle* published an article titled "The Negro in the American Chaos." The article acknowledged the New Deal investments being made at the federal level and the role Black leaders, including some Omega men, played in earmarking said investments. "But above all this social, economic, and political unrest," the article read, "we see the towering figure of Frank Roosevelt, supplemented by the Brain Trust and inflated dollars, marching with measured military strides to a better day in America."[142] It questioned, however, if "The Negro, the forgotten man, where will he be when the storm is over?"[143] It was a provocative question but, in 1934, it was one of the utmost importance to Omega men. Throughout the year, Omega men at the national and local level worked to implement the Fraternity's agreed-upon programs aimed at Black economic recovery. That set the stage for the next Grand Conclave at the end of the year.

In December 1934, Omega men made their way to the Twenty-Second Grand Conclave in St. Louis, Missouri. This made St. Louis the first city to repeat as Grand Conclave, besides when Alpha chapter and Beta chapter alternated hosting conclaves between 1914 and 1918, and John H. Purnell of Upsilon Omega served as Grand Marshal in 1934 just as he had done when the city hosted in 1923.[144]

On December 27, at 11:05 A.M., the Grand Conclave was called to order by Grand Basileus Lawrence A. Oxley. Immediately, Omega business was streamlined to aid the financial standing of the Fraternity. For instance, a year earlier, members were required to be financial to attend all business meetings and social events. Similarly, after Oxley's opening and roll call, Albert Walter Dent of the Rho Phi chapter in New Orleans suggested the delegates be fined $0.50 for being late and $1.00 for being absent from sessions. The motion carried, and it was a decision related to the Oxley administration's focus on cutting cost and generating revenue.[145]

In the Grand Basileus's report, Oxley provided updates on Fraternity expansion. He informed delegates about some recently chartered during his administration. Among undergraduate chapters, he named Chi Psi at LeMoyne College (now named LeMoyne-Owen College) in Memphis, Tennessee, and Psi Psi at Kentucky State College (now named Kentucky State University) in Frankfort—both Black colleges. Among graduate chapters, there were: Delta Alpha in Dayton, Ohio; Epsilon Alpha in Fort Worth, Texas; Zeta Alpha in Henderson, North Carolina; and Eta Alpha in Jefferson City, Missouri. The growth was a net positive, Oxley said, and so were the financial conditions of the Fraternity itself. He informed delegates that the Fraternity's cash was insured and there were deposits in Citizens Trust Company in Atlanta, Georgia, and Mechanics and Farmers Bank in Durham, North Carolina.[146] Both were Black-owned banks unlike the Northwestern Trust Company in Philadelphia that collapsed in 1931.

Aside from internal matters like Fraternity finances, Omega men weighed their efforts around Black people's economic status. Vice Grand Basileus William E. Baugh reported on the employment project, something the Fraternity had engaged in throughout the Great Depression. It was common for the Fraternity to issue updates on job opportunities. Baugh presented two examples. Herman Dreer requested two classroom teachers at the secondary school level, and Percy L. Julian looked for a school principal. Both Dreer and

Julian sought any available Omega men for the positions.¹⁴⁷ Baugh offered the lengthiest report just before delegates voted.

Delegates voted to have the Supreme Council petition against lynching to the president, vice president, and both houses of Congress.¹⁴⁸ "We go on record as vigorously condemning mob violence and lynching in America," read part of the Fraternity's resolution.¹⁴⁹ Delegates—like their fellow Omega man Frank "Doc" Jehoy Sykes—also publicly supported the Black boys on trial, stating "To the nine innocent Scottsboro Boys, and to the International Labor Defense defending them, we pledge our support."¹⁵⁰ Delegates also voted in favor of $300 of the Fraternity's funds be given to the Joint Committee on National Recovery—breaking down the contribution to $25 per month.¹⁵¹ "We cannot close this Conclave without expressing the hope of Omega Psi Phi Fraternity that the present Federal Administration will equitably integrate Negro Workers and Farmers into the recovery program it has designed," read the Fraternity's final resolutions.¹⁵² It continued: "Any action indicative of discrimination based on race, creed, or color meets our hearty disapproval."¹⁵³

Delegates' adopted resolutions made clear that Omega men agreed with the Oxley administration's progress. Their commitment to racial justice through Fraternity programs earned universal support at the St. Louis Conclave. Like in Durham, delegates tendered unanimous votes to reelect all national officers except one, noting S. Malcolm Dodson did not seek reelection after being editor-in-chief of *The Oracle* since 1928. In that case, delegates voted Herman Dreer as the next editor-in-chief.¹⁵⁴ Finally, by a vote of thirty-five to twenty-eight, delegates selected Atlanta over New Orleans as the next conclave location, and Jesse O. Thomas was elected Grand Marshal.¹⁵⁵

The Fraternity's national programs, particularly those focused on economic recovery, maintained their success in 1935. Those efforts paired with President Roosevelt's additional reforms. The next wave of federal policies and programs, often referred to as the Second New Deal, offered more legislative reforms and, in so doing, helped establish the foundation for the modern social welfare system in the United States. Notable programs included the Social Security Act of 1935, the National Labor Relations Act of 1935, and the Banking Act of 1935.¹⁵⁶

Aside from federal-level influence, Omega men also focused on economic recovery and leadership at the local level. They discussed various aspects of Black life and how the Fraternity programs could be deployed by individual members. For example, the September 1935 issue of *The Oracle* featured several essays on the topic. Herman Dreer, the new editor-in-chief, wrote "How the Negro Must Do Business."¹⁵⁷ Meanwhile, Emmett J. Marshall of Xi chapter at the University of Minnesota added to the conversation by considering a Black internationalist perspective. Understanding the global struggle for Black freedom, Marshall wrote an essay titled, "Cuba and the Color Question—Is it Economic or Racial?"[158] Robert N. Owens of the Upsilon Omega chapter in St. Louis, Missouri, penned another essay titled, "The Negro Faces the Future," which posed the question "is it not the question of individualism vs. collectivism that is paramount in the minds of mankind throughout the civilized world?"[159]

The matter of individualism versus collectivism had captured the essence of Omega Psi Phi since its rapid expansion of the early 1920s. That said, while Omega men's written analyses of Black people and economic programs captured the Fraternity leaders' collective focus, individual Omega men also made strides in 1935. Among undergraduate members, William Martin, who was initiated at the Pi Psi chapter at the University of Illinois, remained at the university for law school. In 1935, he became the first Black law student at Illinois to make the honor roll.[160] In Memphis, three Chi Psi chapter members— Oscar E. Knight, Jackson (Jack) Townsend, and Edward Ateman—led the LeMoyne College (now named LeMoyne-Owen College) debate team. The undergraduate Omega men were skilled orators who had recently competed in a debate tournament in Des Moines, Iowa, where they represented LeMoyne as the only Black college to participate.[161] Graduate members also represented the Fraternity's commitment to excellence. By 1935, Albert Walter Dent, a 1926 graduate of Morehouse College where he was initiated at Psi chapter, was superintendent of the Flint–Goodridge Hospital in New Orleans, Louisiana. The hospital had a formal relationship with Dillard University, a Black college.[162] The same year, Asa T. Spaulding, previously mentioned as working for the North Carolina Mutual Life Insurance Company in Durham, assumed the role as assistant secretary for the famed Black insurance company.[163]

Those accomplishments—both individual and collective—set the stage for the Fraternity's next four Grand Conclaves: the Twenty-Third Grand Conclave in Atlanta, Georgia; the Twenty-Fourth Grand Conclave in Philadelphia, Pennsylvania, in 1936; the Twenty-Fifth Grand Conclave in Cleveland, Ohio, in 1937; and the Twenty-Sixth Grand Conclave in Chicago, Illinois in 1938. A series of important decisions were made over this four-year stretch.

In 1935, as customary during the last week of December, Omega men gathered for the Grand Conclave. That year, in Atlanta—the first conclave in that city since 1921—seventy-two delegates voted to adopt recommendations made by the Fraternity's Committee on Rethinking the Program of Omega. Delegates also heard J. Arthur Weiseger, Grand Keeper of Records and Seal, report that the reclamation program had reinstated eighty-eight Omega men in 1935. There were also 338 new members being initiated that year.[164]

Additionally, with Lawrence A. Oxley not seeking reelection, delegates elected a new Grand Basileus for the first time since the Richmond Conclave in 1932. William E. Baugh, who served under Oxley as Vice Grand Basileus from 1932 to 1935, was elected to the Fraternity's top office. Other elected or reelected officers were Weiseger as Grand Keeper of Records and Seal, Jesse O. Thomas as Vice Grand Basileus, Jesse B. Blayton as Grand Keeper of Finance, and Herman Dreer as editor-in-chief of *The Oracle*. And with Philadelphia selected as the next conclave location, William C. Paul was elected Grand Marshal. Two of the Fraternity's founders—Oscar James Cooper and Edgar Amos Love—were in attendance and conducted the installation ceremony for the new officers. Notably, Omega men found it "most encouraging" that Paris V. Sterrett of Upsilon chapter at Wilberforce University challenged Thomas for the seat of Vice Grand Basileus. Albeit unsuccessful, Sterrett's attempt was considered the first time an undergraduate had campaigned for a Grand office since the Fraternity's initial years.[165]

As for the new Grand Basileus, Baugh was tasked with leading the Fraternity into its twenty-fifth year of existence. Baugh was born in Tuscaloosa, Alabama. A child of the South, Baugh attended public schools throughout his childhood in Alabama. He continued his studies at Tuskegee Institute but for only one year. Afterward, Baugh followed a path like many talented southern Black youth who sought a more traditional collegiate education. Therefore, he entered the college preparatory school at Howard University in Washington, DC, in 1895. Baugh completed the prep program in 1898 and went on to earn a bachelor's degree from Howard in 1902. A year and a half later, after being "a special student" at Cornell University, Baugh moved to Indiana where he started his career in the Indianapolis public schools, where he quickly excelled from teacher to principal.[166] There, he was also initiated by the Zeta Phi chapter in 1925. Baugh immediately had a significant impact on the Fraternity. In 1925, he served as a delegate to the Tuskegee Conclave, and only missed the Detroit Conclave in December 1930.[167] Baugh, who earned the nickname "the biggest man in the Fraternity," was celebrated not only for his physical stature but even more so for his tremendous impact.[168]

As previously mentioned, he personally financed his own travel as Vice Grand Basileus to numerous chapters to revive Omega outposts during the Great Depression. Entering 1936, he was the Grand Basileus—a fitting position considering his dedicated work in the field of education and Omega. In Philadelphia, Baugh led the Twenty-Fourth Grand Conclave, dubbed the Silver Jubilee Conclave, at the close of December 1936. It had been fourteen years since Philadelphia hosted a conclave, and the hosts were the Mu and Mu Omega chapters, the latter led by Oscar James Cooper as chapter Basileus.[169]

On December 27, 1936, Baugh and other out-of-town Omega men opened the conclave in the City of Brotherly Love.[170] The twenty-fifth anniversary of the Fraternity was a moment of pause and reflection. In memoriam, stalwarts like Walter H. Mazyck, longtime Grand Keeper of Records and Seal, were recognized alongside younger Omega men like Don Carlos Parker, who died on September 30, 1936, only months after becoming a charter member of the Gamma Sigma chapter established at Alabama State College on April 1, 1936.[171] Gamma Sigma was one of nine chapters (most at Black colleges and universities) chartered in 1936 during Baugh's first year as Grand Basileus.[172] Among the living Omega men, national officers celebrated who they called the "Makers of Omega."[173] This included some of the most influential Black leaders whose work helped advance Black America. Among the key Omega men of its first twenty-five years, former Grand Basileus Lawrence A. Oxley, two-time Grand Marshal John H. Purnell, and ten-year District Representative S. Herbert Adams were listed.[174]

Reflecting on the past with eyes toward the future, delegates heard founder Edgar Amos Love deliver before the Philadelphia Conclave a stirring address on Sunday, December 27. His speech was described as "a challenge to leadership. Do we, the men of Omega, accept the challenge?"[175] It was a fitting challenge for the Philadelphia Conclave, which was described as "the most elaborate and biggest convention in the history of Race Greek letter fraternities."[176]

Over the next three days, the Black-centered agenda of the Fraternity was on display. From what started as a collegiate fraternity, over its twenty-five years Omega men had since served in World War I, strategized to expand Black educational opportunity, and advised federal officials on issues of Black economic recovery. Baugh's leadership sought to ensure that the Fraternity's agenda strengthened over the next twenty-five years. The *Philadelphia Tribune* reported that the eighty delegates voted on the following: "The advocacy of a 'finish fight' for anti-lynching legislation, abolishment of the peonage system, a square deal for the sharecroppers, and better employment conditions for the Negroes, was the unanimous decision reached at the conclave sessions of the Omega Psi Phi fraternity held Monday, Tuesday, and Wednesday at Houston Hall, University of Pennsylvania. The conclave sessions, presided over by William E. Baugh of Indianapolis [Grand Basileus], further went on record as supporting the NAACP scholarship fund, the national Omega scholarship funds, and a 'war' on discrimination and race prejudices."[177]

The focus on Black advancement and ending all forms of racism resonated with the founders of Omega Psi Phi. Edgar Amos Love, who opened the conclave with a challenge for leadership, was satisfied by the closing session. Afterward, Love said of the Philadelphia Conclave: "This is one of the greatest conclaves in the history of Omega."[178]

The fanfare and straightforwardness of the Fraternity program captured an important moment for Omega men. Like its education program of the

1920s, the Fraternity's agenda for the 1930s had come into focus by the latter half of the decade. As the nation's economy slowly crawled out of the looming Great Depression, Omega men were also fighting the many racist barriers that confronted Black Americans. In Philadelphia, William E. Baugh was reelected Grand Basileus for another year until the Twenty-Fifth Grand Conclave in Cleveland, Ohio, in 1937. There, delegates offered Baugh a standing ovation that lasted half an hour.[179] Baugh was then succeeded in 1937 by Albert Walter Dent as Grand Basileus, and delegates voted to authorize a committee on the history of Omega Psi Phi to prepare the Fraternity's first history.[180] The Fraternity's program appeared to move along smoothly as similar decisions in support of racial justice were made during the Twenty-Sixth Grand Conclave in Chicago, Illinois, in 1938. Yet, no different than how the Depression interrupted the Fraternity's programs entering the 1930s, another global event at the end of the 1930s began: World War II.

Omega Men Prepare for World War II

Just before World War II, as Americans eased out of the Great Depression, the Fraternity also reembraced growth. In 1938, the first year of the Dent administration, six chapters were chartered. Four were undergraduate chapters—Lambda Sigma at Claflin University, Mu Sigma at Allen University, Nu Sigma at Wayne State University, Xi Sigma at Xavier University of Louisiana—and two were graduate chapters—Pi Alpha in Princess Anne, Maryland, and Rho Alpha in Mobile, Alabama.[181] Fittingly, among the six 1938 chapters, Xi Sigma at Xavier was in New Orleans, where Dent resided. In New Orleans, Dent was a member of the Rho Phi chapter, superintendent of the Flint–Goodridge Hospital, and business manager of Dillard University, whose president was Omega man William Stuart Nelson.[182] In 1939, four more chapters—Sigma Alpha in Miami, Florida; Tau Alpha in Salisbury, North Carolina; Chi Alpha in Bluefield, West Virginia; Upsilon Alpha in Atlantic City, New Jersey—were chartered.[183] Therefore, growth and prosperity, two things desolate for many Omega men during the Great Depression, seemed promising as Dent prepared to lead the Fraternity's Twenty-Seventh Grand Conclave in New York City, cohosted by the Epsilon, Zeta Psi, and Xi Phi chapters.[184]

But, before delegates reached the New York City Conclave held December 27–30, 1939, Germany invaded Poland on September 1, 1939, officially marking the start of World War II.[185] Omega men long had an eye on international affairs and global human rights struggles. Their participation in Fort Des Moines in Iowa in 1917 and Camp Howard in Washington, DC, in 1918 were early examples. In 1921, William Stuart Nelson's work in Europe and attendance at the Pan-African Congress with the support of the Fraternity was another example. Therefore, as the 1930s concluded, it was no surprise that Omega men immediately turned their attention abroad.

The war would prove to be significant to the Fraternity but, in June 1940, less than a year into the start of World War II, Herman Dreer, former editor-in-chief of *The Oracle*, published the Fraternity's first history book.[186] The book was in production by the time key events took place, such as Omega man Benjamin Elijah Mays being appointed president of Morehouse College in 1940. Yet, by October 1940, the pages of the Fraternity's other publications, such as *The Oracle* and *Omega Bulletin*, featured essays and reprints of articles pertaining to Black people and military service. For example, one essay titled "Our Status in National Defense . . ." provided Omega men with a historical overview of the discrimination Black people had faced when enlisting for military service. There was discussion of "colored units" of the army, but also how racial discrimination had been struck down by the Selective Service and Training Act of 1940—passed September 16, 1940. The act banned such discrimination and allowed anyone to serve "regardless of race or color."[187] Omega men's special consideration of Black people's history in the US military was important, and the topic emerged as they prepared for their next Grand Conclave.

It was fitting that Omega men were engrossed in questions of history as delegates gathered for the Twenty-Eighth Grand Conclave held in Nashville, Tennessee, on December 27 to 30, 1940.[188] It was the first conclave held in Nashville since December 1920 when Carter G. Woodson called on fellow Omega men to carry the study of Black history into their communities. Then, Delta chapter was the only chapter of the Fraternity in the city. Twenty years later, Nashville had grown into an important Omega hub, and the Nashville Conclave of 1940 was cohosted by Omega men in Delta, Gamma Phi, Eta Psi, and Rho Psi chapters—the first time a Grand Conclave had four chapters serve as host.[189] Nonetheless, Omega men descended upon Tennessee's capital city in 1940 with the same mission as twenty years earlier: recognizing Black history as part of their commitment to improve Black life in America.

In Nashville, Grand Basileus Albert W. Dent bestowed a special medal of recognition from the Fraternity upon his longtime friend, William Boyd Allison Davis—known as W. Allison or simply Allison.[190] Previously, in chapter 2, Davis was mentioned as a star undergraduate Omega man at Williams College, where he became a member of Phi Beta Kappa and graduated as class valedictorian in 1924. Following his undergraduate studies, Davis did not slow his intellectual pursuits. He earned a fellowship to Harvard University and completed a one-year master's degree in English and began teaching English at Hampton Institute in 1925, published the acclaimed Harlem Renaissance-era essay, "In Glorious Company," in 1927, and completed additional graduate-level study in anthropology at Harvard and the London School of Economics in the early 1930s.[191] In 1935, Davis joined the faculty at Dillard University in New Orleans.[192] There, he and Dent—who were both actively involved Omega undergraduates in the early 1920s—reconnected while Dent served as superintendent of the Flint–Goodridge Hospital, which was affiliated with Dillard. By 1940, Davis was at the University of Chicago pursuing his PhD in anthropology, and published the coauthored book, *Children of Bondage: The Personality Development of Negro Youth in the Urban South*, the same year. Davis's groundbreaking anthropological research on race in the US South led the Supreme Council to recognize Davis as "a person who has achieved merit in his field, and at the same time contributed to the onward march of his race."[193]

In addition to recognizing Davis, Nashville Conclave delegates also focused on internal affairs. They officially adopted the "Sweetheart Song," composed by Don Q. Pullen of the Rho Psi chapter.[194] Delegates also voted to continue a $500 fellowship offered by the Fraternity to support "advanced study or creative work in any field of letters, art, or science."[195]

Understanding that the Great Depression negatively impacted Black people more than other races, delegates authorized an Employment Placement Bureau to help undergraduate members secure summer employment and, like the Nashville Conclave in 1920, delegates started a national book club among Omega men to "encourage more widespread interest in the good books produced by Negro authors."[196]

Internal matters aside, Omega men were most focused on national security. Omega men who were members of the Black Cabinet—the Black advisers to the Roosevelt administration—organized a conclave forum on "the Negro in the national defense."[197] Panelists included Robert C. Weaver, Campbell C. Johnson, Lawrence A. Oxley, Frank S. Horne, and William Johnson Trent Jr.[198] William H. Hastie Jr. was also scheduled to participate, but travel delays led him to arrival after the panel, which was held at the Fisk University Chapel and open to the public.[199]

Regarding the election of new national officers, delegates to the Nashville Conclave elected Zephaniah Alexander Looby—known as Z. Alexander or simply Looby—as Grand Basileus. Looby succeeded Dent who had served in that role since 1937. Delegates reelected each Omega man currently serving in other national officer roles: Mifflin T. Gibbs as Vice Grand Basileus, George A. Isabel as Grand Keeper of Records and Seal, Jesse B. Blayton as Grand Keeper of Finance, and Frederick S. Weaver as editor-in-chief of *The Oracle*. And with Indianapolis, Indiana, selected as the host city for the Twenty-Ninth Grand Conclave, Emory A. James of Indianapolis was selected as Grand Marshal.[200]

Looby was poised to lead this group of national officers through domestic and international conflict. As previously noted, he was student council president and member of Alpha chapter while he was an undergraduate at Howard University in the early 1920s. A native of Antigua in the British West Indies, Looby completed his undergraduate studies at Howard in 1922. He then enrolled at Columbia University, where he earned his law degree in 1925. He remained in New York City and, in 1926, earned a doctor of juridical science from the New York University School of Law—a doctorate rarely conferred to anyone at the time. After graduation, Looby's legal career brought him to Nashville to join the Fisk University faculty in 1926. Two years later, he was admitted to the Tennessee bar, opened a legal practice, and took up civil rights within his industry like many Omega men did. He assisted the NAACP in various legal battles in the South. Noticing a dearth of Black southern lawyers, Looby founded the Kent College of Law in Nashville in 1932. Looby served as its dean, and the school earned approval from the American Bar Association.[201]

Looby vowed to create more opportunities for Black people to earn legal training in the South where most White law schools remained segregated and most Black colleges did not offer graduate or professional programs. Therefore, as delegates left the Nashville Conclave in December 1940, the Fraternity was led by Looby whose entire career was dedicated to racial equality, and he did so from an international perspective. But Omega men did not know that events over the next year would severely alter the Fraternity before they were able to assemble in Indianapolis in December 1941.

Ernest Everett Just and the War Effort

On October 27, 1941, a fall Monday in Washington, DC, Omega Psi Phi founder Ernest Everett Just died. He passed at his sister Inez Just's home on Third Street in Northwest DC, near Howard University. He had been ill for weeks as Inez cared for her brother until his death. The cause of death was pancreatic cancer. He was fifty-eight years old.[202]

Just had long been an inspiration to Omega men. It was Just's office where the three young undergraduate founders—Edgar Amos Love, Frank Coleman, and Oscar James Cooper—founded Omega Psi Phi on November 17, 1911, and he continued to be a model race man for the next thirty years. An internationally recognized scientist, Just received the first Spingarn Medal—the NAACP's highest honor given to a person of African descent for distinguished accomplishment—in 1915. The next year, in 1916, he earned his PhD from the University of Chicago. All the while, he spent summers conducting research at the Marine Biological Laboratory in Woods Hole, Massachusetts.[203] By 1930,

Just conducted research and trained graduate students with the support of $80,000 per year from the Julius Rosenwald Fund.[204]

A prolific scholar, he published more than fifty scholarly papers during his career, including two books—*Basic Methods for Experiments on Eggs of Marine Animals* and *The Biology of the Cell Surface*—both published in 1939.[205] Just's breakthrough scientific research earned him membership in numerous national or international societies, such as the American Society of Zoologists, American Association of Naturalists, Washington Academy of Science, and American Society of Ecologists. Just was also a member of Phi Beta Kappa (earned as an undergraduate at Dartmouth) and Sigma Xi honorary societies.[206]

Nonetheless, Black achievement never protected an individual from racism, and Just's life was no different than other Black Americans. He was stifled in science because of his race, and he found more receptive scientists abroad. In fact, leading German biologists selected Just to write an in-depth analysis on fertilization. Just would work in laboratories in Germany, Italy, and France. The latter soon extended membership to Just to enter the Mathematical and Natural Science Society of France.[207] He resided in France when his books were published, but by mid-1940, German soldiers invaded France. As later explained in Just's biography, *Black Apollo of Science*, "he was forced out of his laboratory room at Roscoff Station in Finistère, France. The Nazis had taken over, and the station closed its doors to all foreign scientists." The war halted Just's success and life in Europe, and he was detained and imprisoned by Nazis before he could escape France. Upon his release, Just returned to Washington, DC, living only a year longer before his death.[208]

After he died, Just was buried the next day, October 28, 1941, at Lincoln Cemetery outside of Washington, DC. The date—October 28—of his funeral service was the twenty-seventh anniversary of the Fraternity being incorporated in Washington, DC. Perhaps apropos, that date would serve as a reminder of the day that Omega men first had to bury a founder. Just's death was a tremendous loss for Americans, even if Black Americans were the only citizens to recognize it. Alpha Phi Alpha general president Charles H. Wesley, who was also dean of the Howard Graduate School, eulogized Just, his longtime colleague. Omega men Percy Lavon Julian, Sterling A. Brown, and Abram L. Harris served as pallbearers, while Frederick S. Weaver, editor-in-chief of *The Oracle*, was designated by Grand Basileus Z. Alexander Looby in Nashville, Tennessee, to represent the Fraternity during the homegoing services. Frank Coleman represented the other founders, Edmund Wyatt Gordon represented Alpha chapter, and Tecumseh Bradshaw and Alfred Neal represented Alpha Omega chapter.[209]

A native of South Carolina, Just had survived Jim Crow limitations on education and excelled in science. He had also survived being a prisoner of war in the growing world war that, at the time of his death in October 1941, the United States had not formally entered combat. Yet, that changed only weeks after he passed. On December 7, 1941, the Empire of Japan's naval air service attacked Pearl Harbor in the territory of Hawaii. Roughly 2,500 people were killed, the bulk of whom were members of the US military.[210] Afterward, US president Franklin Delano Roosevelt declared war officially entering the nation into World War II.

Omega men intended to continue their annual Grand Conclaves after the Indianapolis Conclave in December 1941, but the world war disrupted plans. There were no Grand Conclaves held again until December 1944, as Omega men played various roles during World War II in service to the nation and their race, domestically and abroad. For example, Paul Revere Williams, the famed Los Angeles architect, and longtime Lambda chapter member, wrote an essay in the March 1942 issue of *The Oracle* about national defense regarding architecture.[211] Following the attack on US territory at Pearl Harbor, Roosevelt signed off Executive Order 9066, which relocated away from the west coast thousands of Japanese Americans and imprisoned them at internment camps.[212] The fear of another Japanese attack prompted such a drastic, racist move by federal officials. Meanwhile, Williams was called upon positively to aid national security—causing him to miss the Indianapolis Conclave. Williams was busy on the West Coast of the United States constructing air raid shelters. He was an expert on material, informing Omega men that "magnesium will be a new metal" used by architects when "our defense program is completed" and "industries return to peacetime production."[213]

Similarly, although not serving in the military, the war called upon the expertise of Charles Richard Drew. In 1931, the Fraternity adopted its official hymn, "Omega Dear," which Drew helped prepare. Since then, he earned a doctor of medicine from McGill University in Montreal, Canada, in 1933. The next year, he served as a diplomate of the National Board of Medical Examiners. Starting in 1935, he had on and off leave from faculty appointments at Howard while he completed a residency in surgery at both the Freedmen's Hospital in Washington, DC, and Presbyterian Hospital in New York City. Keen on having an eye for medical research, in 1940, Drew earned a second doctorate, a doctor of medical science, from Columbia University.[214] He titled his dissertation "Banked Blood: A Study in Blood Preservation."[215] Immediately, Drew's work in blood plasma and blood banking was called upon abroad to aid war-torn Britain. Called the Blood for Britain project, Drew was selected by the Blood Transfusion Association as the "best qualified of anyone we know to act in this important development."²¹⁶ Drew's leadership in creating the blood bank was another example of civilian Omega men serving during World War II; however, most other Omega men were more directly engaged in challenging racial barriers during wartime training and combat, and undergraduate and graduate members alike served.

From 1941 to 1945, there were few aspects of the military that did not have Omega men in key roles despite racial policies that segregated or minimized their service. David A. Lane served at the US Army Headquarters in Heidelberg, Germany. At the time, Lane was dean at Louisville Municipal College for Negroes (now defunct) and was called to work in the army's Historical Division helping manage manuscripts for high-ranking military officials.²¹⁷ S. Randolph Edmonds, professor at Dillard University, served as morale services officer at Fort Huachuca in Arizona, and at least five other Omega men—Prince A. Barker, George C. Branche, Richard Allen, William H. Waddell, and J. A. Kennedy—served in the Medical Corps during World War II.²¹⁸ In the navy, Dennis D. Nelson and Reginald Goodwin served among the first Black commissioned officers. They served in the Pacific sailing between the Caroline Islands, Marshall Islands, and Okinawa, Japan.²¹⁹ In the US Marine Corps, starting in 1942, at Montford Point near Jacksonville, North Carolina, Omega men were also among the first Black enlistees at the training site for the first Black Marine recruits since the Corps remained segregated at the time.²²⁰ Yet, as servicemen sailed the seas, and others served in ground forces, perhaps the largest cluster of Omega men protected the skies.

More than eighty Omega men trained as pilots or worked in administration at the Tuskegee Army Air Field in Alabama.²²¹ The airfield opened in July 1941, and it was located about twelve miles away from Tuskegee Institute. The field was an extensive military operation with hundreds of engineers, mechanics, and other technical specialists based there to aid the pilots. It was stated that, "not only is the Tuskegee Army Air Field pinning wings on Negro pilots, but it is steadily producing skilled technicians, air mechanics, photographers, radio operators, weather men, and many other technicians essential to the Army Air Forces."²²²

Many of the Omega men at Tuskegee had recently graduated from college or postponed their studies when called to serve. For instance, George Spencer Roberts was a graduate of West Virginia State College (now named West Virginia State University) and earned the rank of major during the war. Roberts commanded an air squadron that shot down several planes during the Battle of Anzio, off the coast of Italy. Lee Rayford was a graduate of Lincoln University in Pennsylvania who earned the rank of captain during the war. Rayford commanded the 332nd Fighter Group and was among the first members of the Ninety-Ninth Fighter Squadron to encounter enemy forces on foreign soil.²²³ Richard H. Harris, who was the former Basileus at Eta Psi chapter at Fisk University, also served as a fighter pilot overseas. Meanwhile, Orville Maurice Lewis, formerly of Alpha chapter, had also graduated from the Yale University Engineering School, and served in Tuskegee on the staff. Both Harris and Lewis had earned the ranked of second lieutenant at the time.²²⁴ Summarizing the many contributions of Omega men, *The Oracle* read, "Here at the Tuskegee Army Air Field, Omega men have played a dominant role in helping to win a place in the history of the Army Air Forces in World War II."²²⁵

World war was another way that Omega men pushed for racial advancement and demanded equal opportunity. Yet, Black contributions to the war effort were often dismissed.²²⁶ Despite the racial segregation that persisted, Omega men still served, and some gave their lives in the process, such as Wilmeth W. Sidat-Singh of Syracuse University and Cornelius May of Fisk University who were killed during fighter training. *The Oracle* in December 1944 read: "Many brothers have fallen in the line of duty in the present war in their pursuits to give their all to their nation."²²⁷

World War II officially ended on September 2, 1945. The conclusion of the war also marked the conclusion of a fifteen-year period of sacrifice made by Omega men and other Black Americans. The Fraternity entered the 1930s with great promise. National officers' focus on education during the 1920s looked to bear fruits of their labor as the Fraternity entered the next decade; however, the Great Depression's impact on Americans' economic well-being halted much of the Fraternity's momentum.

During the Depression, Omega men were forced to alter the vision of Black progress. The 1930s brought Omega men to the forefront of the economic recovery at the local, state, and federal levels. Omega men were called upon to advise the US president as members of his Black Cabinet. Others led local businesses like Black insurance companies and banks that sustained Black communities across the nation. All the while, the Fraternity cut its costs and operated on a lean budget, as national officers refused salaries while never disinvesting in Black advancement. Omega men also remained involved in the day-to-day battles for racial justice—even as some fought until their death.

Despite the nation's racism, Omega men did not hesitate to serve the nation or work in their communities. The period could be marked by fellowship or sorrow and by joy or pain. As civilian and military servants, the Fraternity halted its annual fellowship at Grand Conclaves during the peak war years. Omega men served on the home front and abroad engaging in battle by land, sea, and air. Many made the ultimate sacrifice giving their lives for the United States. Yet, as the war concluded, Black veterans returned home from a war over democracy to find themselves even more isolated due to racism. This captured the essence of the Double V (Double Victory) campaign that, as one *Pittsburgh Courier* editorial explained in 1942: "The first V [is] for victory over our enemies from without, the second V [is] for victory over our enemies from within. For surely those who perpetrate these ugly prejudices here are seeking to destroy our democratic form of government just as surely as the Axis forces."[228] As the Fraternity looked toward the future, and Black Americans demanded an end to second-class citizenship, new battles were about to unfold for Omega men. The same spirit that carried Omega men in all branches of the military would soon carry the Fraternity and its members in the next battle: civil rights.

Chapter 4

Safeguarding Civil Rights

*Omega Men and the Postwar Fight for
Racial Equality, 1946–1959*

After World War II, Omega men—like many other Black Americans—were further infuriated by the blatant contradictions of American society. Hundreds of Omega men and other Black people served the United States in a war fought in the name of democracy. Many of those Omega men left stable employment to fight for the nation. They risked their lives in military combat only to return home and have their sacrifices met by a long-standing enemy: racism. The United States had never delivered on its promise of democracy, freedom, and equal opportunity, but the culmination of suffering during the Great Depression and wartime service stirred a more forceful determination among Black Americans to rid the nation of racial discrimination. Furthermore, the grip of racism was not limited to the Jim Crow South. Racism spanned regional boundaries, and Omega men across the nation accelerated their work to end inequality.

In 1946, the Fraternity launched a civil rights program that would guide Omega men for the next two decades. This program was different than previous decades where the Fraternity's efforts revolved around a singular focus, such as education in the 1920s or equitable economic recovery in the 1930s; however, the new program launched after World War II was all-encompassing and sought racial equality in the military, education, housing, and employment. Omega men were focused on securing aid for Black veterans returning from the war. It was an important step toward ensuring equality in access to government programs for veterans. Regardless of race, veterans soon sought formal higher education by way of the Servicemen's Readjustment Act of 1944—known informally as the G.I. Bill. In turn, the Fraternity's decades-long work in education took on new meaning. A new wave of Omega men ascended to the college presidency and served on federal education commissions. All the while, Omega men with legal training—many of whom were attorneys for the National Association for the Advancement of Colored People (NAACP)—joined the all-out assault on unjust laws in the late 1940s and 1950s across the United States.

During this period, Omega men were among the most active leaders in civil rights activism in various communities, states, and the nation. The Fraternity pooled resources to aid the NAACP, condemned segregation in higher education, and strategized to support boycott efforts. Internally, the postwar period renewed long-standing conversations about membership and scholarship requirements, saw the creation of an undergraduate Supreme Council position and Fraternity executive secretary, and engaged in the global human rights efforts. Combined, the middle years of the twentieth century were significant as Omega Psi Phi's social action campaign challenged racism, inspired legal agitation in the courts, and stirred direct confrontation in local communities. Those efforts would demonstrate how Omega Psi Phi, in collaboration with other organizations, closed its first fifty years safeguarding civil rights.

Social Action: Omega and American Democracy

Robert L. Gill understood that history provided insight into the present. An Omega man and professor of history and government at Morgan State College, Gill knew that change was coming. The past was his guide to the future. Gill had an eye for making sense of White people's attempts to maintain school segregation, deny Black citizens the right to vote, lay off or underpay Black workers, and block Black applicants' admission to some colleges and universities. Just as World War II was a series of military moves and countermoves, Gill saw a clear connection to another war unfolding domestically. In December 1945, only three months after the end of World War II, he assessed: "History reveals that after every war, a period of reaction sets in."[1]

It was a poignant analysis of how the past met present, and Omega men were poised to play a significant role in the reaction to the war against their basic civil rights. Earlier in 1945, New York became the first state to pass an antidiscrimination law.[2] But Omega men desired national change, not piecemeal legislation gradually passed state by state. Therefore, Gill's words reached his Fraternity brothers just before delegates and their guests made their way to the Thirty-First Grand Conclave in Washington, DC. Held December 27–30, 1945, Omega men met in the nation's capital ready to act on, and not just react to, the issue of racial discrimination.

Grand Basileus Z. Alexander Looby presided over the four-day meeting, which featured public addresses from two non-Omega speakers: Howard president Mordecai W. Johnson and US secretary of commerce Henry A. Wallace.[3] The presence of Johnson and Wallace demonstrated that federal officials and Black academics acknowledged the social impact of the Fraternity and its members. Yet, aside from the public meeting, the business of Omega—and that of American society—occupied most of the Omega men's time in Washington.

Looby presented his Grand Basileus report, which recapped the challenges of World War II and internal adjustments made during his administration.[4] Additionally, Vice Grand Basileus John H. Calhoun Jr. reported that a year earlier the Fraternity's finances were depleted to about half of the total assets available in 1941 and 1942. For example, in 1944, roughly half of the Fraternity's chapters were financial, and Omega men were hardly able to secure a quorum for national meetings and some district meetings were not held.[5] Thus, entering the Washington Conclave, the Fraternity had a little more than $27,000 in total assets.[6] The financial struggles, however, had turned for the better in 1945, and Omega men reengaged the Fraternity following the war and turned an eye toward growth and service.

In terms of growth, five chapters were chartered in 1945. Those new Omega outposts grew the Fraternity to 138 total chapters.[7] That growth also stirred an internal debate among Omega men about a "return" to an emphasis on the undergraduate members.[8] Therefore, a new position—Second Vice Grand Basileus—was created to be held by an undergraduate. Dexter Eure of Theta Psi at West Virginia State would first hold this position, and it brought undergraduate representation back to the Supreme Council for the first time since the Fraternity's first decade.[9]

In terms of service, among the decisions delegates made, their agreement to form a National Social Action Committee was most impactful. The goal was for the Fraternity to "occupy a progressive and constructive place in the civil life of the nation."[10] That was an ambitious goal that required every Omega man's commitment. "Busy prominent brothers as well as the rank and file should assume responsibility for the program," Calhoun said. "We cannot expect success unless each of us does his part."[11] Furthermore, the Fraternity informed Omega men that: "such fields as public education, housing, health, full and fair employment, civil rights, the franchise and social security are among matters appropriate for inclusion in this program."[12] With all Omega men working together, the rationale for the all-out attack on discrimination was simple: "Omega stands on the threshold of a new era."[13]

In concluding the Washington Conclave, delegates elected or reelected officers to the Supreme Council. Looby closed his five-year, war-torn administration and was succeeded by Campbell C. Johnson as Grand Basileus. Other new officers included: John H. Calhoun Jr. as First Vice Grand Basileus; Eure—the previously mentioned undergraduate—as the Fraternity's first-ever Second Vice Grand Basileus; C. R. Alexander as Grand Keeper of Records and Seal; Jesse B. Blayton as Grand Keeper of Finance; and Nathaniel D. Williams as editor-in-chief of *The Oracle*. Finally, in choosing Fort Worth, Texas, as the next conclave location, Kay W. McMillian was elected as Grand Marshal.[14] Johnson was well equipped to lead this group. As previously mentioned,

Johnson was a 1916 initiate of Alpha chapter at Howard University and, in 1917, attended the Officers Training Camp at Fort Des Moines Army Base. But, since then, he had led a distinguished career in law, civic leadership, and the military.

Born in 1895, Campbell Carrington Johnson grew up in Washington, DC. As a teenager, he graduated from M Street High School (later renamed Paul Laurence Dunbar High) in 1913. In 1920, following his hiatus from his studies at Howard to serve during World War I, Johnson earned a bachelor of science degree. Two years later, he earned a second degree from Howard—a bachelor of laws degree—and was admitted to the bar to practice law in Washington, DC, and North Carolina. Professionally, he held several jobs between graduating from Howard and becoming Grand Basileus. From 1922 to 1926, he was a partner in a law practice with fellow Omega men Walter H. Mazyck and John W. Love while serving as the Fraternity's Grand Keeper of Records and Seal. Johnson was also executive secretary of a YMCA branch in Washington, DC, from 1923 to 1940. When elected Grand Basileus, he had taught at Howard, something Johnson had done occasionally since 1919, in the School of Religion since 1931. As a career military man, in 1940, US president Franklin Delano Roosevelt appointed him to the Selective Service National Headquarters. It was a fitting role since Johnson was an active-duty service member during World Wars I and II, ultimately earning the rank of colonel on September 21, 1943.[15]

On February 23, 1946, the National Social Action Committee met for the first time after it was assembled during the Washington Conclave. It was a significant gathering, as nineteen of the twenty-five-person committee attended—a who's who among Omega men. It included Johnson and many of the Fraternity's District Representatives. Also present were Looby, the former Grand Basileus, and Edgar Amos Love and Frank Coleman, two of the three living Omega founders. They were joined by other prominent Omega men: Frank S. Horne, assistant director of the United States Housing Authority; James M. Nabrit Jr., civil rights attorney and Howard University law professor; and Albert W. Dent, former Grand Basileus and current president of Dillard University in New Orleans.[16] Ira De Augustine Reid chaired the committee.

Among the first orders of business, Reid advised Fraternity chapters to write a letter to Georgia governor Ellis G. Arnall thanking him for a recent stand he had taken that was favorable for Black voters in Georgia. Omega men were urged to write a similar letter to the National Board of the Young Women's Christian Association because that organization had at its recent national convention outlawed discrimination within the YWCA. The flood of support from Omega men across the nation were important. Reid said: "The first step in action is education, thought, and consciousness."[17] Additionally, Reid sent instructions on studying housing discrimination in local communities and advised Fraternity chapter officers to send their findings to Frank S. Horne, a member of the National Social Action Committee who also served as a race relations adviser to the commissioner of the US Housing Authority.[18] It was not long before the Fraternity's request for local Omega men to take up active roles in civil rights came into fruition.

On February 25, 1946, only two days after the first National Social Action Committee meeting, racial tensions escalated in Maury County, Tennessee. That morning, a Black woman named Gladys Stephenson visited a local shop in the town Columbia to have her radio repaired. William Fleming, a White repairman, did not fix the device, but the store still charged Stephenson. That sort of racist slight toward Black people was common. Yet, many of these encounters ended without violence. But, in this small Tennessee town, Fleming also slapped Stephenson after she confronted him about being charged. In response, James Stephenson, her son and a navy veteran, pushed Fleming through the store's glass window. The scuffle led to the Stephensons being charged with assault. A White lynch mob soon assembled in town with intent to take justice into their own hands, but local police had already moved the Stephensons to a safer location. The mob turned its attention toward Mink Slide, a Black residential and business district in town; however, Black residents fought back against the mob—thus starting what was considered the first race riot in the United States after World War II.[19]

In the aftermath, many of the Black men in town—estimated at more than one hundred—were arrested compared to only two White men. Among them, twenty-five of the Black men were charged with attempted murder when the two White men were soon released. The riot captured the urgency of the Fraternity's plan to help confront racial injustice. Therefore, when the NAACP sent defense attorneys to defend the accused men, immediate past Grand Basileus Z. Alexander Looby was among the civil rights attorneys who answered the call.[20]

As Looby began preparations to defend justice in rural Tennessee, William H. Hastie, another Omega man, was deeply engrossed in another civil rights case that originated in Virginia. As mentioned earlier, Hastie was educated at Amherst College and Harvard University, and he had played pivotal roles in the federal government during the 1930s. He also taught at Howard University Law School from 1930 to 1937. By 1943, however, he resigned from his federally appointed role as Civilian Aid to the Secretary of War in protest over policies of the War Department and its treatment of Black soldiers.[21] It was also announced on January 5, 1946, that Hastie would be appointed governor of the US Virgin Islands.[22] As he awaited the US Senate's confirmation, Hastie was headed to the US Supreme Court to fight for civil rights.

Two years earlier, in July 1944, Irene Morgan—a Black woman—boarded a Greyhound bus in Gloucester County, Virginia, headed for Baltimore, Maryland. Morgan began the bus ride from rural Virginia with ease. She initially occupied the five-person bench at the rear of the bus alone. As the bus proceeded, and more passengers boarded, Morgan moved to a two-person vacant seat just ahead of the rear bench; however, when a White couple boarded the bus, the White bus driver asked Morgan to move. Morgan replied that she would if there were another empty seat, but since the bus was full at that point, she refused to move. Morgan was arrested in Middlesex County, Virginia, where she was found guilty in a brief trial later in 1944.[23]

On March 27, 1946, arguments began in *Morgan v. Virginia*. Hastie led a team of NAACP attorneys who, through a series of appeals, eventually brought the case before the Supreme Court. The *Morgan* case was considered the first to challenge segregation statutes in interstate travel since *Hall v. DeCuir* in 1877.[24] Hastie argued before the Supreme Court alongside his former law student, Thurgood Marshall, who graduated from Howard's law school in 1933.[25] The legal strategy was to contest whether segregation alongside interstate highways violated the Fourteenth Amendment's Equal Protection Clause. On June 3, 1946, nearly three months later, the High Court ruled in Morgan's favor. Citing the Commerce Clause of the US Constitution, most of the justices ruled "the Virginia statute in controversy invalid."[26] Hastie and Marshall were successful in validating Morgan's rights as a Black passenger. The court did not, however, rule that Virginia violated the Fourteenth Amendment.[27] The Supreme Court's ruling was important, but it did not completely dismantle segregation in public transportation. This led the Fraternity to do what it had done since the 1920s: advertise special Pullman cars arranged to transport Omega men to Fort Worth, Texas, for its next conclave to be held in December 1946.[28]

In October 1946, between Hastie's case before the Supreme Court and the December conclave, Looby and the NAACP team of attorneys made arguments in the Mink Slide riot trial in Tennessee. Afterward, twenty-three of the twenty-five Black men charged with attempted murder were acquitted.[29] Looby's efforts reflected a goal of the Fraternity's National Social Action program: "justice under the law and equal enforcement."[30] But equal justice was not as simple as Black attorneys fighting in courtrooms. Those court arguments came with dangers. There was great risk going to and from small towns in the Jim Crow South, as evident in the Mink Slide trials. The next month, after the trial to appeal the two remaining Black men, Thurgood Marshall had joined Looby and other NAACP attorneys in Tennessee. After getting one of the two men acquitted, the attorneys departed town but were followed by local White police officers. Looby, Marshall, and others were stopped and questioned three times. On the third time, Marshall was accused of drunk driving and apprehended, and Looby and colleagues were directed to continue out of town. Yet, Looby followed the officers, noticing that they were not returning to town to arrest Marshall but, instead, to where White men had assembled by a nearby river. Looby closely trailed the police, which prompted the police to instead take Marshall into town. He was later released safely avoiding what, years later, Marshall recalled as a lynch mob. Less than a year removed from his role as Grand Basileus, Looby helped save Marshall's life.[31]

The actions of Looby and Hastie were two examples of how Omega men took up a commitment to civil rights, but discussions at the Thirty-Second Grand Conclave in Fort Worth focused on planning to have the Fraternity-wide National Social Action program be more impactful. For instance, on December 27, 1946, Grand Basileus Campbell C. Johnson formally opened the four-day conclave. As always, delegates were presented information about Fraternity business, such as matters of the constitution and bylaws, budget, and proposed new chapters. Ira De Augustine Reid, chair of the National Social Action Committee, presented on the progress of the Fraternity's program. He assessed that "the social action program was set-up for functioning but was able to do very little during the year."[32] Reid concluded his report stating the National Social Action Committee's subcommittees were given full autonomy to implement programs in the upcoming year; Johnson, as the Grand Basileus, would become chair of the overall committee while Reid served as a consultant, and Fraternity chapters would receive new materials related to social action by March 1, 1947.[33]

Reid's report followed the report from First Vice Grand Basileus John H. Calhoun Jr., who further captured the essence of the Fort Worth Conclave's focus on civil rights. He said the Fraternity's strides in 1946 had "placed us upon the threshold of the greatest opportunity that ever faced such an organization. We are on the move, but so are the forces of reaction."[34] The emphasis on the reaction in the form of counter movements was a similar statement to what Robert L. Gill had stated a year earlier. As a result, Calhoun called out the "devil of a decadent society—white supremacy."[35] Calhoun added, "Day to day, we note international actions to the end that minority peoples all over the world are denied the benefits of Democracy that our brothers have fought and died for."[36] Calhoun knew it would require a collaborative effort to challenge the global denial of equal rights: "Therefore, we are in a position to work with other Greek letter organizations in forming the most effective group of trained men and women in the Negro race. We must, however, develop our own Program first."³⁷

Regarding the Omega program, delegates also heard Frank S. Horne speak. He sat on the National Social Action Committee while he worked for the US Housing Authority. In Fort Worth, Horne's conclave address presented an overview of the Fraternity's work. His address also explained how the work of the Fraternity was related to his work at the federal level.³⁸ Earlier in 1946, the committee called on Omega men to document local housing discrimination, and Horne was their point of contact. It was a useful strategy. Horne was born in New York City on August 18, 1899. He completed a bachelor's degree from City College of New York in 1921, and later earned a master's degree from the University of Southern California in 1932. The next year, in 1933, he started a role with the National Youth Administration. Over time, he worked with the likes of famed Black educator and activist Mary McLeod Bethune and fellow Omega man Robert C. Weaver.³⁹ By the time he spoke at the Fort Worth Conclave, the forty-nine-year-old Horne noted that "practically every recent racial conflict in cities like Chicago, Atlanta, and Detroit has arisen out of the tensions created by the lack of housing for all people and all the sharp dividing lines created by covenants and other racial restrictions."⁴⁰

Horne's analysis was direct. The issue of housing impacted other aspects of American life. Neighborhoods determined school options. School options impacted professional opportunities. Those opportunities were intricately linked to an individual's net income. Altogether, housing was the culprit of many racial tensions in American cities, and the Fraternity aimed to further implement its National Social Action program to address housing and other issues. Thus, Omega men left Fort Worth ready to advance civil rights over the next year.

On March 16, 1947, W. Montague Cobb, longtime chairman of the Fraternity's Scholarship Commission, delivered an address for the annual memorial service program hosted by the Theta Psi and Xi Alpha chapters. The joint program was held on the campus of West Virginia State College (now University). Cobb's speech, titled "Strictly on Our Own," paid tribute Charles Young, the famed Omega man and military leader who passed in 1922. Cobb professed that "the status of the Negro was raised by Charles Young."⁴¹ That achievement occurred despite the racism that Young faced. For example, Cobb said Young had forty-four classmates from the US Military Academy earn "promotion to brigadier," but Young "was retired as physically unfit."⁴² Young did not reap the benefits of his military service, but Cobb said he paved the way for Black veterans who were recognized during World War II. "Charles Young was on his own all the way, and his career is a glorious inspiration for all Americans."⁴³ In conclusion, the past—Cobb argued—was critical to the Omega men and their guests gathered on the West Virginia State campus. "Our historians, educators, and press have taught us well to look behind, and to high and useful purposes," Cobb said. "I have thought it fitting and wise, this evening, to direct your attention ahead."⁴⁴

It did not take long for Omega men to heed Cobb's advice. On April 9, 1947, less than a month after Cobb's speech, which was also reprinted in *The Oracle*, Omega men looked ahead.

That day, Bayard Rustin, an Upsilon chapter initiate in the 1930s at Wilberforce University, led a group of activists in testing if states were adhering to the previous summer's Supreme Court ruling in *Morgan v. Virginia*. It was the beginning of a two-week civil rights exercise called the Journey of Reconciliation, sponsored by the Congress of Racial Equality (CORE) and the Fellowship of Reconciliation. Notably, James Leonard Farmer Jr., a 1936 initiate of Theta chapter at Wiley College in Texas, cofounded CORE in 1942, and members from both groups formed a collection of Black and White people who took various bus trips throughout the Upper South. Starting in Washington, DC, and then traveling through Virginia, North Carolina, Tennessee, Kentucky, and Virginia, before returning to Washington on April 23.⁴⁵

Rustin's involvement was indicative of how Omega men often challenged segregation from various directions. The *Morgan* case was one example. In 1946, Hastie, as an older Omega man and civil rights attorney, argued against segregation in bus travel before the Supreme Court. A year later, Rustin, a younger Omega man, put the court's ruling to test along the highways. Rustin later coauthored a report with George M. Houser, a non-Omega man, as both reflected on their two-week journey. The two found that, in many instances, local police, bus drivers, and passengers "did not know of the *Morgan* decision or, if they did, possessed no clear understanding of it."⁴⁶ As a result, Rustin and colleagues called on people to take direct action. "It is our belief that without action on the part of groups and individuals, the Jim Crow pattern in the South can not be taken down."⁴⁷

By the end of the summer, Omega men were reading even more analyses of civil rights in the pages of *The Oracle*. In September 1947, a four-page essay, titled "Safeguarding Civil Liberties," was published detailing "methods of protecting these liberties."⁴⁸ Those methods included exercising and demanding the right to vote, organizing and supporting local civil rights groups, writing elected officials, and not voting based on political party but instead for candidates whose past actions warranted support.⁴⁹ To that final point, Omega men were adamant that their Black political support was to be earned, not given, and Grant Reynolds embodied that belief.

Born in 1908 in Florida, Reynolds, a 1931 initiate of Epsilon chapter, was in his late thirties by 1947. He was a trailblazer from an early age. In 1938, he became the first Black person to earn a bachelor of divinity degree from Eden Theological Seminary in Missouri. During the same year, he accepted the pastorate of Mount Zion Congregational Temple in Cleveland, Ohio, though his ministerial ordination did not take place until 1939. In Cleveland, he later served as president of the local NAACP prior to taking on chaplaincy duties in the US Army in 1941. Three years later, in 1944, Reynolds resigned from the military post due to racism. This spurred Reynolds to seek change through public office. In 1946, Reynolds, a Republican, attempted to represent the twenty-second congressional district made up by Harlem, New York, but his attempt was unsuccessful. Incumbent congressman Adam Clayton Powell Jr., a notable Black minister and civil rights activist originally defeated Reynolds 32,722 to 19,513 according to a report by the National Newspaper Publishers Association.[50]

The political defeat, however, did not halt Reynolds's desire to defeat racial discrimination. On October 10, 1947, Reynolds and A. Philip Randolph formed the Committee Against Jim Crow in Military Service and Training, or simply the Committee Against Jim Crow. The committee's goal was simply: "the abolition of Jim Crow in military service and in proposals for peacetime conscription."[51] Reynolds chaired the committee while Randolph—a labor organizer in the Brotherhood of Sleeping Car Porters, American Federation of Labor and Congress of Industrial Organizations—served as treasurer. The committee's legal committee comprised seven civil rights attorneys. Two were Omega men—James M. Nabrit Jr. and Matthew Washington Bullock Jr. (son of the former Grand Basileus). The other five noteworthy attorneys were the husband–wife duo of Raymond Pace Alexander and Sadie Tanner Alexander (née Mossell), Robert Lee Carter, Charles Hamilton Houston, and Belford Vance Lawson Jr. Reynolds and Randolph saw the committee as integral to the fight against Jim Crow and it was "formed to dramatize the fight."[52]

As Reynolds organized that fight at the federal level, that fight was unfolding across the nation in various locales. In October 1947, in the nation's heartland, Omega men in Indiana were one standout example of the Fraternity's National Social Action program's impact on local fights for democracy. Indianapolis was described as "the capital of Northern bigotry," but that did not stop Omega men from expanding their program.[53] For example, members of the Zeta Phi chapter—chartered in 1925—had been busy helping organize and establish undergraduate chapters across the state. In Indiana, where racial segregation remained common, establishing new chapters of Omega Psi Phi on predominately white campuses was not an easy task, but there had been recent progress. The Rho Sigma at Purdue University was chartered in 1942, and Chi Sigma at Indiana State Teachers College was chartered in 1946.[54] However, in 1947, Indiana University—where another Black fraternity, Kappa Alpha Psi, was founded in 1911—was older than Purdue and Indiana State, and, arguably, the state's flagship university.

Omega men in Zeta Phi understood the value of having undergraduate men implement the Fraternity's National Social Action program on a campus like Indiana. Upon their insistence, Tenth District Representative Chester Smith investigated the Bloomington campus. He noted that the university was accredited by the North Central Association of Colleges and Universities, and it was a "member of the Big Nine, which includes University of Chicago, Northwestern University and University of Michigan."[55] After his evaluation of the university and the students listed as interested, Smith stated that "because the university is an A-1 institution" and "because thorough investigation has been made of all the above names and others and they have been found to be A-1 material," he approved establishing the Zeta Epsilon chapter—chartered October 20, 1947.[56]

The chartering of Rho Sigma, Chi Sigma, and Zeta Epsilon was strategic. Members of Zeta Phi in Indianapolis agreed that education was a critical space to desegregate, and they challenged limits on Black educational opportunity in secondary education and higher education. In November 1947, less than a month after the charter of Zeta Epsilon, the Zeta Phi chapter expanded its Achievement Week activities to confront segregation in Indianapolis's public schools. Omega men in Indianapolis demanded the city's school system open the Fraternity's essay competition to all students—not only students at Crispus Attucks High, the city's Black high school. The move hearkened back to the origins of Achievement Week in the 1920s when Omega challenged how Black history had been taught in America. All students could benefit from knowing the full history of Black achievement, and Zeta Phi members aimed to "serve as a wedge to the democratization of the Indianapolis schools."[57] News of Omega men's actions in Indiana set the stage to welcome other members of the Fraternity to the Midwest, where Detroit, Michigan, held the Thirty-Third Grand Conclave on December 27–30, 1947.

Just before the Detroit Conclave, earlier in December, Charles W. Collins, editor-in-chief to *The Oracle*, published a ten-page editorial titled "Civil Rights."[58] It was a far-reaching statement that reflected on past and future struggles. "My primary purpose in writing this piece, however, is to call your attention to the honor roll—the roll of noble ones who have carried the torch when the hour was darkest, who have not feared to stand up and be counted on the side of decency in affairs among men."[59] Collins's editorial was a call to action. A similar call that Omega men had made and answered over previous decades. In the same issue, Harry T. Penn, Third District Representative, summarized what the Fraternity had done so far: "Consequently, on a national basis, this fraternity has given moral and financial support to the NAACP, The Association for the Study of Negro Life and History, the Urban League, scientific research by Negroes, scholarships to Negro graduate students, and to the Mississippi Health Project sponsored by the Alpha Kappa Alpha Sorority."[60] Omega men had engaged in ambitious efforts over the decades, but how the National Social Action program would build upon that earlier organizing would be discussed in Detroit.

On the afternoon of December 27, the Detroit Conclave was called to order with Grand Basileus Campbell C. Johnson presiding as more than 500 Omega men from thirty-five states, Washington DC, and the Virgin Islands made their way to Detroit.[61] The large turnout reflected the rapid expansion of Johnson's tenure as Grand Basileus. In the previous two years, thirty-nine chapters had been chartered, sixteen of which since the previous year's conclave in Fort Worth, Texas.[62] After being stalled during World War II, the late 1940s became a second period of rapid expansion for Omega Psi Phi.

The next day, December 28, Johnson presided over a panel discussion sponsored by the National Social Action Committee. Panelists included Reynolds, cofounder of the Committee Against Jim Crow, and Isabel Chisholm, director of publicity for the National Urban League. The conversation discussed discrimination in the Veterans Administration. More than two years after the war, Black veterans were still struggling to access benefits. In some cases, the widows of World War I veterans were also unaware that they were entitled to a pension. Meanwhile, conclave attendees learned about the Urban League's efforts to aid social workers in cities across the Midwest, West, and South. Additionally, Reynolds discussed his fight to end discrimination in the military and called for financial support to help carry on his program. As Grand Basileus, Johnson endorsed Reynolds's plea and asked every chapter of the Fraternity to support it.[63]

Discussing and acting on initiatives to confront racism was a theme throughout the conclave. It was not confined to the National Social Action Committee. Speakers reiterated that agenda from the first to last day of the meetings. William H. Hastie, the civil rights attorney who argued the *Morgan v. Virginia* case, spoke in the afternoon following the panel discussion. His speech title was "Reacting to Racism."[64] The Detroit Conclave did not lead to any delegate decisions that shifted the Fraternity's focus. Instead, delegates largely confirmed their continued belief in the National Social Action program, which launched two years earlier when Johnson was elected Grand Basileus, and a fitting tribute to breaking racial barriers: the Fraternity honored Jackie Robinson, the first Black player in Major League Baseball, with its Outstanding Citizen Award. Robinson, who was not a member of the Fraternity, was unable to be Omega men's guest and was not on hand to receive the honor.[65]

Nonetheless, before leaving Detroit, delegates elected the next round of national officers. Harry T. Penn, the previously mentioned Third District Representative, was elected Grand Basileus, and Thomas A. Lassiter, an undergraduate student at Johnson C. Smith University, was elected Second Vice Grand Basileus. Reelected officers included First Vice Grand Basileus John H. Calhoun Jr., Grand Keeper of Records and Seal J. Arthur Weiseger, Grand Keeper of Finance Jesse B. Blayton, and editor-in-chief of *The Oracle* Charles W. Collins. The Supreme Council was set just in time for the next prominent racial battle to start a week after the Detroit Conclave.

Black Progress and White Resistance

On January 7, 1948, the lifelong work of Oklahoma civil rights attorney Amos T. Hall culminated before the US Supreme Court. It had been a long time coming. Hall was born October 2, 1896, in Bastrop, Louisiana. It was a small town in the center of the triangle formed between three slightly larger towns: Ruston, Louisiana; Vicksburg, Mississippi; and Hamburg, Arkansas. Later in his youth, Hall left Bastrop to attend Rust College in Holly Springs, Mississippi. He graduated from Rust and eventually returned to his hometown to teach but, in 1921, Hall moved to Tulsa, Oklahoma. The next four years were a distinct example of Black persistence and ingenuity. Hall worked a custodial job at a Tulsa church. There, he stumbled across an old, dated collection of law books. Soon, his desire to learn the law occupied his spare time. Hall became a justice of the peace in the process and, in 1925, Hall, who self-taught himself Oklahoma law, passed the state bar and was admitted to practice.[66]

More than twenty years later, the *Sipuel v. Board of Regents of the University of Oklahoma* case was before the Supreme Court. Hall represented Ada Lois Sipuel, a Black woman, in her fight to be admitted to the University of Oklahoma Law School. She was an undeniably qualified student. Sipuel was an honors graduate of Langston University in 1945, and she wanted to become an attorney. Therefore, she applied to the state's only public law school—the University of Oklahoma. Skilled in every measure, but denied because of her race, Hall led Sipuel's charge against educational segregation all the way to Washington, DC.[67]

At the Supreme Court, Hall represented Sipuel alongside the NAACP's Thurgood Marshall.[68] Marshall was the former Howard law student of Omega man William H. Hastie and, in 1946, former Grand Basileus Z. Alexander Looby helped save Marshall from a potential lynching. Now, in January 1948,

Alpha Phi Alpha member Marshall stood alongside Hall, another Omega man. A member of the Xi Omega chapter in Tulsa, Hall led what was considered one of the most important challenges to the "separate but equal" doctrine.[69] Represented by Hall and Marshall, Sipuel's case was successful after, on January 12, 1948, the Supreme Court ruled in her favor. The court decided, "the petitioner is entitled to secure legal education afforded by a state institution," adding that "to this time, it has been denied her although, during the same period, many white applicants have been afforded legal education by the State."[70]

Omega men rejoiced following the decision. It was a fitting follow-up to a related older Supreme Court ruling in *Missouri ex rel. Gaines v. Canada* on December 12, 1938, after Lloyd Gaines, a Black student, applied to study law at the University of Missouri.[71] Hall had represented Sipuel through the appeals in Oklahoma courts and the Supreme Court, and his efforts had ramifications beyond Oklahoma. "As a result of the recent decision by the United States Supreme Court in this case, the educational set-up of every state below the 36 degree-30-minute parallel have really been upset," read *The Oracle*.[72] *Sipuel v. Board of Regents* was a stirring moment of Black progress but, in America, that progress was always met by White resistance. Oklahoma legislators quickly passed laws that allowed its formerly all-White universities to segregate Black students. The Black students were directed toward separate seating and restrooms, special library tables, and other restrictions. Therefore, Sipuel's admission hardly meant integration into the law school.[73] This reality—progress then resistance—would epitomize the coming years as Omega men and the Fraternity's National Social Action program sought to secure equal rights.

For example, in March 1948, sixty members of Pi chapter at Morgan State College in Baltimore, Maryland, picketed the segregated Ford's Theater.[74] The dozens of undergraduate Omega men joined members of the Baltimore NAACP and the Non-Segregation Theater Committee.[75] "These men of Pi Chapter have made up their minds that their place is on the line—the line of battle," read one report.[76] "The realization that Greek-letter men must be instrumental in forging the instrument that will deal the death blow to segregation and discrimination is foremost in their minds as they trudge before the theater."[77] Meanwhile, southern segregationist governors and state legislators were proposing a workaround to resist the Supreme Court's *Sipuel v. Board of Regents* ruling that states must admit Black students to graduate programs not offered at Black colleges or universities. Racists did not spare any expense when it came to maintaining segregation. Therefore, their proposal was to set up and establish Black-only graduate and professional schools across the South. These new institutions would open instead of desegregating their states' White universities.[78]

In April 1948, Ira De A. Reid, consultant to the National Social Action Committee, called the regional education proposal states' attempt to "perpetuate educational segregation and discrimination with the express approval of Congress."[79] It was a perverse plan. In many instances, as explained earlier, Black colleges and universities were woefully underfunded and underdeveloped across the South. Omega men had spent much of the 1920s wondering how to address that issue in higher education. Therefore, by 1948, Reid and others had grown tired of southern states' legislators continuously avoiding court rulings. This time, fourteen southern governors agreed that states should take over some existing Black colleges. In Nashville, Meharry Medical College—home of the Delta chapter—was identified as part of the southern governors' regional education program. "The dilemma," Reid said, "seems to be this: how can the South extend a just measure of its education to all of its citizens without violating the spirit and letter of the nation's law, and while maintaining its own conception of separate facilities for Negroes and whites?"[80]

Reid's question was important as Omega men pushed back on White resistance. In May 1948, John Wesley Dobbs, an Omega man and prominent Atlanta civic leader, started a multistate journey with a White reporter for the *Pittsburgh-Post Gazette*. The reporter disguised himself, making his skin darker and using an alias name, as Dobbs escorted him across the South. It was a bold endeavor as the reporter went undercover to report on racism in the South. The reporter later documented the journey in a book.[81] The next month, May 1948, while Thurgood Marshall was at Virginia State College to receive an honorary degree, the men of the Delta Omega chapter in Petersburg hosted a special event to honor Marshall.[82]

The activities of Omega men over the first half of 1948 were a strong indicator of the broader participation in the Fraternity's National Social Action program. Individual Omega men like Amos T. Hall fought legal battles for racial equality while others like John Wesley Dobbs risked his life to expose southern racism to the rest of the nation. Meanwhile, collective chapters like the undergraduate men of Pi chapter participated in demonstrations against segregated businesses as the men of Delta Omega chapter publicly praised Thurgood Marshall. Those actions at the individual and chapter level were paired with Fraternity leaders, such as Ira De A. Reid, condemning racist proposals to maintain segregation in southern higher education; however, those actions would need to be amplified as White resistance expanded that summer.

On July 14, 1948, during the Democratic National Convention in Philadelphia, Pennsylvania, a subset of members of the Democratic Party walked out of the convention. The broader party decided to adopt a stronger civil rights platform, but southern segregationists disagreed. The White resistance that led to the political split within the party would have broader ramifications as the group that separated—known as Dixiecrats—led the charge over states' rights.[83] The events in Philadelphia were part of the reason a special meeting was called for the National Social Action Committee on July 25 in Washington, DC. The abrupt shift in national politics meant the Fraternity had to act decisively to advance its program. Therefore, the purpose of the urgent meeting was "to formulate presentations to be made before several committees of Congress on legislation covered by the National Social Action program."[84]

The next day, on July 26, 1948, US president Harry S. Truman signed Executive Order 9981, which banned segregation in the armed forces.[85] It was welcomed news for Omega men, especially Grant Reynolds who led the Committee Against Jim Crow and lobbied to federal officials. The decision immediately impacted millions of Black Americans. For example, roughly 2.5 million Black people registered for military draft before the end of 1945 and, among them, a million were selected to serve in the armed forces.[86] The momentum from Truman's executive order led the National Social Action Committee to affirm that it would maintain its "same outline" moving forward.[87] In summary, Omega men felt their efforts were creating positive change, and as one quote in the *Omega Bulletin* stated, "Progress in every field of endeavor in the United States has been influenced by the American Negro."[88]

It was an eventful year fighting for Black progress, and Omega men gathered for the Thirty-Fourth Grand Conclave in Columbus, Ohio, ready to end the year as strong as it started. On December 27, 1948, Grand Basileus Harry T. Penn presided after the conclave was called to order. Penn was direct in making recommendations during his Grand Basileus report. First, he felt the Fraternity should join other Black Greek-letter organizations "in a unified program of action as outlined by the American Council on Human Rights."[89] He also suggested the Fraternity make annual contributions to the NAACP, National Urban League, and the United Negro College Fund.[90] Delegates also considered other recommendations made during the conclave, including the creation of an Executive Director position. The position was designed to maintain a full-time Fraternity employee to avoid having "the constant removal of the administrative offices" every time a new Grand Keeper of Records and Seal was elected.[91] This was important to sustaining an efficient internal- and external-facing program, and delegates agreed and voted in favor of the new position but under the title Executive Secretary instead of Executive Director.[92]

Delegates also voted in favor of series of resolutions that would aid the National Social Action Committee's plan to present to Congress over the course of 1949. Omega men condemned international tensions that threatened the stability of the United Nations "by laying the foundations for World War III."[93] It was another reminder that Omega men, like many Black Americans, understood Black internationalism and the global struggle for human rights. For example, in 1948, William Stuart Nelson returned to the United States after a year of traveling and lecturing in India on "interracial understanding," while at least six other Omega men were working in Liberia to help modernize the western African nation shortly after it joined the United Nations.[94] Delegates also agreed to call for a stronger labor law that did not support unions who discriminated, to demand any federal loyalty oaths did not violate citizens' "basic civil and constitutional rights," to stress stronger civil rights legislation, and to condemn southern governors' regional schools proposal.[95]

The Columbus Conclave featured an avalanche of decisions that accelerated the Fraternity's fight for racial justice. Omega men looked toward 1949 with intent to foster change in labor rights, education, international affairs, public health, and other areas. Harry T. Penn was reelected Grand Basileus by unanimous ballot. He would carry forward the Fraternity's program alongside other national officers, including: Milo C. Murray as First Vice Grand Basileus; Malcolm Corrin, an undergraduate of Psi chapter at Morehouse College, as Second Vice Grand Basileus; William R. Maynard as Grand Keeper of Records and Seal; and Jesse B. Blayton as Grand Keeper of Finance.[96] In the face of White resistance, this slate of leaders was tasked with leading the Fraternity's bolder and more robust goals forward.

Penn started 1949 by instructing Omega men that, first, "our new program should be designed to meet the complex problems of the day," and many members answered his call.[97] For example, in March 1949, Omega men were informed that one of their own, Robert W. Gray, an attorney in Jacksonville, Florida, co-led a successful challenge to segregation in that state. In Florida, any graduate of a law school chartered in that state was automatically admitted to the bar and could practice law in that state; however, Gray was a Black attorney who, due to segregation, was forced to attend law school out of state. Gray challenged the provision, and it ended up at the Florida State Supreme Court in Tallahassee. That court ruled in his favor and, as a result, "Negro law graduates, who are residents of Florida, under the present law, may be admitted to the bar without submitting to examination by the bar examiners."[98]

About 200 miles north, in Montgomery, Alabama, Robert Clinton Hatch of the Sigma Phi chapter was appointed to a state committee to study Black higher education in the state. Hatch was a part-time instructor at Alabama State Teachers College and supervisor of instruction for the state's Department of Education.[99] Two years earlier, Hatch was a delegate for the Gamma Sigma chapter at the Detroit Conclave.[100] Now, he was positioned to help implement the Fraternity's National Social Action program in education across his entire state.

Meanwhile, as the work of Gray in Florida and Hatch in Alabama focused primarily on equality in public higher education in the South, a month later, on April 11, US president Harry S. Truman called for support of the United Negro College Fund. Founded in 1944 in order to fundraise for private Black colleges and universities, Truman urged the broader American public to also support these institutions through a fundraising drive set to launch on April 19, 1949. The formal launch of the campaign was to be held at the Rockefeller Center where John D. Rockefeller Jr. would speak. Additionally, the campaign chair was John R. Suman, vice president of the Standard Oil Company.[101] White philanthropists, as Omega men knew well from the longtime White leadership of Howard University prior to 1926, were interwoven with private Black higher education and Black education more generally.[102] "For many thousands of Negro youth, local, private Negro colleges offer the best opportunity for education and advancement," Truman said. "These colleges have their origins deep in the roots of America." He added, "Their continued growth and improvement should be a source of pride to all Americans, for they represent the sincere efforts of people who have banned together in the American way—to help themselves by helping one another."[103]

In 1949, helping one another—or uplift, one of the Fraternity's cardinal principles—was important to several Omega men who were presidents of private Black colleges and universities. When Truman called for support of the United Negro College Fund, Omega men who led those colleges included William Johnson Trent Sr. at Livingstone College in North Carolina, former Grand Basileus Albert W. Dent at Dillard University in Louisiana, Lee Marcus McCoy at Rust College in Mississippi, Leland Stanford Cozart at Barber-Scotia College in North Carolina, and Benjamin Elijah Mays at Morehouse College in Georgia. At the same time, Omega men Egbert Chappelle McLeod was the outgoing president of Wiley College in Texas and Earl Hampton McClenny Sr. was the incoming president of Saint Paul's College in Virginia.[104]

Meanwhile, as Omega college presidents worked in higher education leadership, other milestones were unfolding. On July 1, 1949, H. Carl Moultrie started his role as the Fraternity's first executive secretary—the position created during the Columbus Conclave. Before moving to Washington, DC, to work at the Fraternity's headquarters, Moultrie lived in Wilmington, North Carolina, and managed the Hillcrest Housing projects. A former Sixth District Representative, he was an active member of the Omicron Alpha chapter and Wilmington's NAACP chapter.[105]

Later that summer, speculation swirled in the Black press that William H. Hastie, the civil rights attorney and current governor of the US Virgin Islands, could become the first Black person appointed to the US Supreme Court. The national optimism swirled after President Truman appointed Hastie in 1947 to the US Circuit Court of Appeals, Third Circuit, making him the first Black person to ever preside over a federal court.[106] He had certainly made his mark. The successful arguments before the Supreme Court in *Morgan v. Virginia* demonstrated his mastery of the law. Furthermore, no one could deny his belief in American democracy. Hastie held various government positions before his current role as a governor. Therefore, Omega man Paul R. Williams, the famed architect, hosted a gala for Hastie at Williams's Los Angeles home. The guest list was impressive as many visited from across the United States. Non-Omega guests included diplomat Ralph J. Bunche, former heavyweight boxer champion Jack Dempsey, California assemblyman Augustus F. Hawkins, and Howard University professor Rayford W. Logan. Nearly twenty Omega men were also present, including Twelfth District Representative Thomas M. Dent and others from as far away as Chicago, Illinois, and New York City.[107]

On September 14, 1949, shortly after Omega men welcomed Moultrie as Executive Secretary and celebrated Hastie as a national leader, William K. Payne was named interim president of Georgia State College (now named Savannah State University). A member of the Mu Phi chapter in Savannah, Payne was an experienced educator and college administrator. He graduated from Morehouse College and Columbia University earning his bachelor of arts and master of arts degrees, respectively, in 1923 and 1927. Payne had also done additional graduate study in administrative finance at Columbia and the University of Minnesota during summers. Therefore, he was "equipped to handle problems pertaining to administration—both educational and financial."[108] A month later, on October 3, Grand Keeper of Finance Jesse B. Blayton officially went on air in Atlanta with the first Black-owned radio station in the United States. A member of the Supreme Council since 1932, Blayton saw the station as a tremendous business opportunity. He was a certified public accountant, vice president of Citizens Trust Company, president of Brown Boy Bottling Company, and president and owner of Midway Television Institute of Georgia.[109] When the former owners of the station, WERD, sought to transfer control, Blayton was "unwilling to risk the loss of this opportunity to aid the advancement of the Negro in the South by further delay" and "he immediately undertook the problem of acquisition."[110]

The local achievements in Georgia toward Black advancement were noteworthy. Payne as a college president and Blayton as owner of a Black radio station in a city with nearly 250,000 Black residents were examples of Black progress. Paired with the national achievements of other Omega men, the year 1949 demonstrated numerous benefits of the Fraternity's more robust National Social Action program adopted during the Columbus Conclave. Yet, Grand Basileus Harry T. Penn did not want to feel Omega men could rest on a bed of progress. White resistance was still prominent and, in response, Penn said Omega Psi Phi could be "a purely social organization," or it could "become considerably more than that and provide a campus and post-graduate leadership that will fully merit the lofty ideals of our founders."[111] In turn, the charge entering the next Grand Conclave was for the Fraternity to "adopt a program befitting our fraternity—a program which will be of service to mankind."[112]

On December 28, 1949, Omega men returned to the Midwest for the Thirty-Fifth Grand Conclave in Chicago, Illinois.[113] There, Penn presided as Grand Basileus while delegates weighed important issues of White resistance, especially issues faced by undergraduate chapters of the Fraternity located on predominately White campuses. This was a challenge for the Fraternity's Housing Authority, which was chaired by Asa T. Spaulding of Durham. The Fraternity had attempted to support the purpose of chapter houses since the start of the Great Depression but, nearly twenty years into the program, some Omega men offered criticism of the program. There continued to be confusion among Omega men over the role, scope, and even purpose of the housing program.[114] Despite this, delegates agreed that the housing program had a specific purpose in the case of some chapters.

During the Chicago Conclave, the Zeta Epsilon chapter at Indiana University was the topic of discussion.[115] The chapter had been chartered in 1947 but, for more than two years, the university's Interfraternity Council did not recognize Omega men. The lack of recognition as an official student organization meant Zeta Epsilon could not use Indiana University facilities for its meetings or social functions. Omega men were also denied access to university funds for programming. Zeta Epsilon was also not listed among student organizations. The circumstances "entailed considerable difficulty for the brothers of Zeta Epsilon."[116] To support the thirteen members of the chapter, Penn and members of other graduate chapters personally sent letters of protest to the university's White administrators. In response, administrators informed Omega men that fraternities required having a chapter house to earn university recognition.[117]

The stipulation brought a proposal before delegates to help Zeta Epsilon purchase a home and, during the Chicago Conclave, the Housing Authority recommended that funds—up to $5,000—be offered to aid the undergraduate brothers. Delegates approved.[118] The issue of Black fraternities not being recognized was not limited to Indiana University, however. At Ohio State University, the Iota Psi chapter was chartered in 1926, but the university's council of presidents did not allow Omega Psi Phi into its membership as of December 1949. The reasoning for denial captured the challenge of being a Black fraternity on a predominately White campus. This was a period when the national offices of some White fraternities and sororities were removing constitutional clauses that banned Black students from membership. In turn, Iota Psi was denied recognition on the Fraternity council because it was perceived to bar White students from membership into Omega Psi Phi.[119]

That context explains why six months earlier—on June 4, 1949—the Upsilon Phi chapter in Newark, New Jersey, initiated three White and six Black undergraduate students enrolled at nearby Rutgers University in New Brunswick. That graduate chapter initiating those nine undergraduates, according to Fraternity records, made it the "first interracial chapter" of Omega Psi Phi.[120] At Rutgers, university officials banned any new groups "whose membership requirements are restrictive."[121] Therefore, as Omega men sought inclusion on predominately White campuses, delegates formally voted to adopt a resolution stating the Fraternity commended "the recent trend of Greek Letter organizations to admit all qualified persons regardless of race, creed, or color."[122]

The resolution was notable in that it confirmed Omega men's desire to end segregation. Throughout the latter half of the 1940s, Omega men sought to defend American democracy and attain equal rights for Black Americans but, with a new decade approaching, the Fraternity was set to adopt an even more forceful role in challenging segregation. The tenor of the Chicago Conclave dictated such future action, and delegates elected a new Grand Basileus to lead them into the next decade as Milo C. Murray of Gary, Indiana, the First Vice Grand Basileus, defeated Harry T. Penn by a sizable margin. With Murray as the new Grand Basileus, the new Supreme Council was Grant Reynolds as First Vice Grand Basileus; Malcolm Corrine, an undergraduate of Psi chapter at Morehouse College, as Second Vice Grand Basileus; William R. Maynard as Grand Keeper of Records and Seal; Jesse B. Blayton as Grand Keeper of Finance; Herbert E. Tucker as Grand Counselor; and Ellis F. Corbett as editor-in-chief of *The Oracle*.[123] It was this group led by Murray, not Penn, that was tasked with leading the Fraternity into the 1950s.

Paving the Road to Desegregation

In April 1950, a resounding reminder of the perils of racial segregation echoed through the Fraternity. On April 1, Charles Richard Drew died in an automobile accident while driving through North Carolina. He was forty-five years old and internationally recognized for his breakthrough research in blood plasma as his blood banking techniques saved thousands of lives during and after World War II.[124] Since then, Drew was awarded the 1944 Spingarn Medal, the NAACP's highest honor given to a person of African descent for distinguished accomplishment, and served as a professor in the Howard University School of Medicine and chief of staff at the Freedmen's Hospital in Washington, DC. Multiple accomplishments aside, it was well known among "his brothers in Omega that Charles Drew wore his honors lightly."[125] For twenty-five years as a member the Fraternity, "Brother Drew maintained his loyalty."[126] There was no better example of his loyalty than the fact that he cowrote the Fraternity's hymn, "Omega Dear."[127]

Two days following Drew's death, on April 3, 1950, Carter G. Woodson died in Washington, DC, of a sudden heart attack. He was seventy-four years old. Omega men celebrated his many contributions, among them his initiation of Negro History Week, which had its origins at the Nashville Conclave in 1920. "Every year, thousands of public and private schools and colleges participate in this observance," read *The Oracle*.[128] As a result, Woodson received the 1926 Spingarn Medal.[129] For the next three decades, Woodson and Omega Psi Phi were interwoven, and the fight to teach Black history to Black people—aside from White control—marked his legacy as tributes poured in from Omega men across the nation.

Then, on April 13, 1950, Luther Porter Jackson died suddenly at his Petersburg, Virginia, home. Jackson was a professor and chair of the history department at Virginia State College. A native of Lexington, Kentucky, he earned degrees from Fisk University, Columbia University, and the University of Chicago—earning his PhD at the latter institution. Jackson and Woodson were personal friends as both were members of the Association for the Study of Negro Life and History. Jackson had published several books on the history of Black teachers, Black labor, and Black elected officials in Virginia, and less than an hour before his death, Jackson had been working on his latest Black history project. He also only recently brought some of his students to Washington, DC, to witness court arguments against segregation at the Supreme Court. Like Woodson, Jackson's professional work of Black history and Omega were linked. *The Oracle* read, "Brother Jackson, always an inspiring member of Omega Psi Phi, was actively affiliated with Delta Omega chapter of Petersburg. Just a few days before he succumbed, he was host to members in a chapter meeting."[130]

All three Omega men—Drew, Woodson, and Jackson—were revered for their distinct contributions to Black life, but their deaths stood as a reminder of how racism benefited no American. Omega men rightfully reflected on how many more lives could have been saved if Drew had not been limited in medical research if not for race. The same questions loomed over whether Woodson's keen understanding of history could have reached more Americans if his findings were not dismissed because he was a Black historian. Additionally, as members of the Delta Omega and Nu Psi chapters gathered for Jackson's funeral on the Virginia State campus, it was only fair for the hundreds of mourners in attendance to ponder if Jackson's recent testimony in favor of the bill against segregation at the State House in Richmond was fully appreciated.[131]

If there were to be a path toward ending segregation, thus ceasing such limits of Black achievement, Omega men saw that road would be paved through education. In May 1950, Omega men learned that Oscar James Chapman joined the ranks of Omega college presidents when he was named head of Delaware State College (now University) in Dover. Born October 1, 1908, Chapman was a native of Stockton, Maryland, a small community in Worcester County on the Atlantic Ocean nestled between Delaware and Virginia. Therefore, it was somewhat logical for him to attend the high school department of Hampton Institute in Virginia. He finished his secondary studies there in 1928 before proceeding to earn a bachelor of arts degree from Lincoln University in Pennsylvania in 1932, a master of arts from the University of Michigan in 1936, and a PhD from Ohio State University in 1940.[132]

Chapman's promotion was paired with news that Walter Strother Davis was steadily growing the faculty of Tennessee Agricultural and Industrial (A&I) State College (now named Tennessee State University) in Nashville. Davis was a Mississippian born just west of Jackson in Canton on August 9, 1905. He completed his elementary school studies at nearby Tougaloo College before completing the high school department of Alcorn Agricultural and Mechanical (A&M) College (now named Alcorn State University). Davis remained there for two years of collegiate instruction before transferring to Tennessee A&I. There, he became a 1931 graduate of the college before earning his master of science and PhD from Cornell University in 1933 and 1941, respectively. As president of his alma mater, he had launched the first school of engineering for Black students south of Washington, DC. The size of the Tennessee A&I faculty had grown to about 200, with twenty-three of them holding a PhD degree, and the physical value of the campus was $6 million. The growth was significant since Davis's predecessor, Omega man William Jasper Hale, served as Tennessee A&I's first president.[133]

In May 1950, in North Carolina, Francis Loguen Atkins, president of Winston-Salem Teachers College (now named Winston-Salem State University), had recently been named the city of Winston-Salem's Outstanding Negro Citizen of the Year. The award was presented by the Junior Chamber of Commerce.[134] Born December 6, 1896, Atkins was from a prominent Winston-Salem family.[135] His father founded Winston-Salem Teacher College in 1892 as a local industrial school for Black children. Atkins and his siblings took pride in carrying on as leaders of the college after their father's death, and they led it to tremendous growth. Therefore, Atkins's award from the city was for "his accomplishment in securing a record-breaking capital outlay appropriation from the last session of the North Carolina General Assembly."[136] Atkins's brother, former Grand Basileus J. Alston Atkins, served as the college's executive secretary.[137]

The leadership and growth of Black colleges and universities was important to Omega men and the collective of Black Americans; however, on June 5, 1950, two Supreme Court decisions in *Sweatt v. Painter* and *McLaurin v. Oklahoma State Regents* impacted Black people's ability to attend segregated White universities in the South.[138] In Texas, state officials attempted to hurriedly open a law school at Texas State University for Negroes (now named Texas Southern University) in Houston after a Black man, Heman Marion Sweatt, applied to the University of Texas School of Law. The Supreme Court ruled that separate educational facilities must also be equal in terms in facilities and faculty, not just in name.[139] Similarly, the court ruled that states could not separate students by race as dictated by state laws following the Supreme Court's *Sipuel v. Board of Regents* ruling in 1948.[140]

The two higher education desegregation cases were brought before the Supreme Court by the NAACP that, by mid-1950, had several Omega men among its leadership. That included Roy Wilkins who, as mentioned in chapter 2, was an initiate of Xi chapter at the University of Minnesota in the early 1920s when the racial massacre in Tulsa, Oklahoma, shaped how he saw society. Now, nearly thirty years later, Wilkins served as administrator of the NAACP. Other Omega men who led the NAACP included: Madison S. Jones Jr., administrative assistant of the NAACP; James W. Ivey, editor of the *Crisis*—the official magazine of the NAACP; and Henry Lee Moon, director of public relations. For Omega men, it was fitting that so many members of the Fraternity held high-ranking positions. *The Oracle* stated, "It is universally conceded that the one organization in the United States which speaks with authority for the millions of Negro citizens is the National Association for the Advancement of Colored People, and it is to be expected that representatives of the Omega Psi Phi Fraternity are to be found in the vanguard opposing anti-democratic practices."[141]

As NAACP officials and attorneys challenged segregated student bodies, other Omega men paved the way toward desegregation in other ways through education. By the end of 1950, as the year closed, several Omega men were the first, only, or one of the few Black professors on many predominately White campuses. At Michigan State University in East Lansing, David Wilson Daly Dickson was an assistant professor of English. At the University of Chicago,

William Boyd Allison Davis—known simply as W. Allison Davis—was the first Black person to serve as a full-time professor at a predominately White university since the Reconstruction era.[142] He earned tenure in 1947 and was promoted to full professor in 1948.[143] There was also Abram Harris, an economics professor the University of Chicago, and William T. Fontaine, a philosophy professor at the University of Pennsylvania. Percy L. Julian had also briefly taught at his undergraduate alma mater, DePauw University, in the 1930s before his current role as director of research at the Glidden Laboratories in Chicago. In many cases, the Omega professors had full-time appointments at Black colleges and universities but were on leave to accept visiting professorships. In total, Omega men had full-time or visiting professor positions at New York University, the University of Wisconsin, Western Michigan State College, Syracuse University, Vassar College, and the University of Minnesota. "The Negro college professors in mixed universities are no longer guinea pigs. They have proven themselves," wrote then-Omega Grand Historian Robert L. Gill. "True to the principles of Omega's social action program and America's democratic process ... they are serving as a great cementing force for national integration."[144]

The road toward "integration," however, would raise important questions for Omega men over the next year or so. Omega men were among the NAACP leaders helping the NAACP's legal efforts to challenge segregation in all forms, but especially in education, while other Omega men were breaking barriers on predominately White college campuses. Yet, over the next year or so, many people pondered what desegregation would mean for Black education. For instance, Grand Basileus Milo C. Murray presented the United Negro College Fund with a $500 check from the Fraternity.[145] Meanwhile, Omega man William Johnson Trent Jr.—whose father was president of Livingstone College—served as executive of the United Negro College Fund.[146] The Fraternity leaders campaigned and fundraised for Black colleges and universities as other Omega men called for higher education desegregation. It was a reminder that ending racial segregation was a unifying goal, but not everyone agreed with how or its implications.

During the Thirty-Sixth Grand Conclave in Boston, Massachusetts, held December 28–30, 1950, the 308 delegates reelected Murray as Grand Basileus alongside few other changes among the Supreme Council.[147] Yet, Omega milestones and broader societal changes throughout 1951 only amplified the question about desegregation and the future of Black institutions. There were experienced Omega men leading Black colleges, such as Thomas B. Jones, president of Harbison Junior College (now defunct) in Irmo, South Carolina, since 1943, and James Ward Seabrook, president of Fayetteville State Teachers College (now named Fayetteville State University) in North Carolina since

1933.[148] Fittingly, it was during Seabrook's tenure as president that the Delta Gamma chapter was chartered in 1951 and became the first Greek-letter organization on the Fayetteville State campus.[149] Yet, about seventy miles north of Fayetteville, the aftermath of the Supreme Court cases were materializing in Chapel Hill when two younger Omega men enrolled at the University of North Carolina School of Law. William A. Marsh and Harvey Beech left the North Carolina College School of Law in Durham to be among the first Black students at the formerly segregated university. For their undergraduate studies, Marsh attended North Carolina College (now named North Carolina Central University) and Beech attended Morehouse College.[150]

The duality of the desegregation set the tone for the Thirty-Seventh Grand Conclave in Miami, Florida, on December 27–30, 1951. Leading up to the Miami Conclave, Fraternity leaders readied Omega men for a visit to "the New South."[151] It was the Fraternity's first conclave in the heart of the Southeast since the Nashville Conclave in 1940. Since then, the closest annual meetings were in Little Rock, Arkansas, or Fort Worth, Texas, but the Miami Conclave would bring Omega men through the soul of the Jim Crow South as the Sigma Alpha chapter served as host. Also, with questions of education and segregation looming over Fraternity leaders, it was appropriate that Benjamin Elijah Mays served as the principal speaker to keynote the Miami Conclave's public meeting.[152]

Among the dozens of Omega college presidents, Mays, the president of Morehouse College since 1940, was arguably the most famous. In fact, six months earlier in June 1951, Mays was the featured speaker at the NAACP's National Convention in Atlanta. There, Mays spoke on the New South, stating "This emerging new south is pictured most dramatically in the area of education where staggering sums are being spent to improve the segregated Negro schools and where Negroes are now enrolled in several State universities in the south."[153] The nuance across the South was notable as Mays articulated the differences within the South and the thin line between being lynched or surviving simply based on location. In Miami, Mays brought a similar message to the estimated 1,000 Omega men in attendance alongside their guests.[154]

It was not lost on attendees that the forceful message from Mays on December 28 came only days after the Christmas Day bombing of the Mims, Florida, home of husband-and-wife Harry T. Moore and Harriette Moore. The Moores were heavily involved in the Brevard County branch of the NAACP. Harry was also a state-level NAACP leader and challenged racism throughout the state. He died shortly after the bombing as Harriette fought for her life in a hospital as Omega men met in Miami.[155] Delegates agreed to contribute $1,000 from the Fraternity as part of the reward for arresting and sentencing the responsible parties.[156] In passing a resolution condemning the murder, Omega men stated, "To the task of making America free and strong, this Grand Conclave re-dedicates itself and pledges resources and leadership in every town and hamlet of this country."[157]

The commitment to race leadership was clear as delegates concluded the Miami Conclave. The Fraternity bestowed the NAACP's Thurgood Marshall, who was a member of Alpha Phi Alpha, with its Citizen of the Year award. Delegates also elected First Vice Grand Basileus Grant Reynolds to the position of Grand Basileus. Reynolds led the Committee Against Jim Crow, founded in 1947, in its successful effort to end segregation in the military, and his election was notable nationally as the Black press described him as a "militant civic leader."[158] Over the years, Omega men had elected dynamic professionals and incredibly accomplished leaders as Grand Basileis, but, in Miami, a new type of leader was selected. Reynolds had largely worked in local contexts, but as Robert L. Gill later explained, Reynolds "was one of the new and bright stars of Omega to appear on the national scene during the post-World War II years."[159] Under his leadership, starting 1952, Omega men would witness more direct confrontations over old ways as a new society emerged during the remainder of the 1950s.

Direct Action: Omega Men Lead, Strategize

For three days, April 16–18, 1952, more than 300 people gathered in Washington, DC, for what was described as "one of the most significant conferences ever held at Howard University."[160] The attendees represented forty-eight national organizations, and they arrived from twenty-seven states, from Texas and Florida in the South to California in the West. Held in the Andrew Rankin Memorial Chapel, this conference focused on "The Courts and Racial Integration in Education," and the prominent group of speakers included Omega men.[161]

The timing of the conference was important as the NAACP was simultaneously sponsoring individual school desegregation cases in South Carolina, Virginia, Kansas, Washington, DC, and Delaware. Furthermore, Supreme Court rulings on higher education cases originating in Missouri, Oklahoma, and Texas suggested that legalized racial segregation was proving more difficult for segregationists to uphold.[162] Therefore, the moment warranted the participation of many Black leaders in education, law, journalism, and other professional fields. Many of the leaders present were non-Omegas, but Omega men had long celebrated them nonetheless, such as Howard president Mordecai Wyatt Johnson, who brought the greetings and welcomed attendees, and Thurgood Marshall, who had just received Omega Psi Phi's Citizen of the Year award four months earlier during the Miami Conclave.[163] Both men spoke on Thursday, April 17, but on the conference's final day, Omega men Benjamin E. Mays and James M. Nabrit Jr. delivered two sophisticated analyses on education and current court proceedings.

As president of Morehouse College, Mays was the first speaker during the Friday morning session on "Problems Incident to Racial Integration in Higher Education." Mays discussed the status and future of desegregation at private White colleges in the South, and he was personally and professionally equipped to discuss matters pertaining to *all* higher education, not only Black colleges and universities.[164] He spoke across the nation, as evident in his address during the Miami Conclave. In fact, a day before his arrival in Washington, Mays delivered the Yale University's Henry J. Wright Lecture—a series of lectures on "The Christian Way of Life in a Democracy"—and he was the first Black person to ever deliver a "major lecture series" at the university.[165] But his rise to national prominence started from modest beginnings.

Benjamin Elijah Mays was born August 1, 1894, in rural South Carolina to Hezekiah Mays and Louvenia Carter Mays—both born into slavery.[166] Some accounts state 1895, but Mays frequently referred to the 1900 US Census and stated his birth year was 1894.[167] His birthplace was so isolated in upstate South Carolina that Mays himself described his Greenwood County home by the small communities and towns of Greenwood, Ninety-Six, and Epworth.[168] As a teenager, Mays attended the high school department of South Carolina State College (now University) in Orangeburg, where he graduated as valedictorian in 1916.[169] In a fairly common move, Mays did like many talented Black youth in the South and pursued higher education in the Northeast or Midwest. In his case, after one year at Virginia Union University in Richmond, Mays moved to Lewiston, Maine, to enroll at Bates College in 1917.[170] At Bates, he had a distinguished student career despite being among the few Black students on campus. Mays was an honors student, president of the Debating Council, and won first prize in the Sophomore Declamation Contest.[171] He was also a student assistant in mathematics on campus.[172] Mays was initiated at Gamma chapter in Boston in 1919.[173]

Mays graduated from Bates in 1920 and spent most of his time after Bates working in higher education or organizing. For example, he taught mathematics at Morehouse College from 1921 to 1924 while also serving as pastor of Shiloh Baptist Church in Atlanta. Next, he earned his master of arts from the University of Chicago in 1925 before he returned to Orangeburg to teach English at South Carolina State College for the 1925–26 academic year. Between 1926 and 1930, Mays worked for two years as the executive secretary of the Tampa Urban League in Florida and then national student secretary of the YMCA. A serious classroom teacher and theologian, Mays directed a two-year study of Black churches from 1930 to 1932 before ultimately being named dean of the Howard University School of Religion in 1934. While dean at Howard, he earned his PhD from the University of Chicago in 1935, and he returned to Morehouse, where he started his career, when he was named president in 1940.[174] Therefore, by the time Mays stood before conference attendees in Washington, DC, the fifty-seven-year-old college president was one of the most prolific academic leaders of his era. He had published multiple books, dozens of academic articles, and reviewed several books.[175]

Mays spoke at length about a study of more than 200 Black and White colleges. The evaluation assessed enrollments, student demographics, and campus administrators' intentions on desegregating. It was a far-reaching study, and Mays assessed that "it seems clear too that the decisions of the Federal courts have not challenged the church-related colleges, Negro or white, to accept Negroes or whites as students."[176] Furthermore, the study unveiled that international students were more likely to be enrolled than Black people. "That data also shows that education follows the pattern of segregation in American life generally," said Mays, who was one of twenty-five educators serving on the US Department of Education's Educational Council. "All other minority groups are welcomed before the Negro is welcomed."[177]

Following the straightforward speech by Mays, conference attendees reassembled later that day for the evening session on "The Courts and Racial Integration in Education" as Omega man James M. Nabrit Jr. made it his way to the lectern. Earlier in this book, Nabrit was an undergraduate Omega man in the early 1920s at Morehouse College before he joined Iota chapter in Chicago while he studied law at Northwestern University in nearby Evanston. But in the thirty years since then, Nabrit had established himself as one of the nation's most prominent civil rights attorneys. Nabrit joined the faculty of the Howard University School of Law in 1936 and worked with Thurgood Marshall and Charles Hamilton Houston, both members of Alpha Phi Alpha, on civil rights cases for the NAACP.[178]

"Law and government must change as society and philosophies change," Nabrit told the conference attendees.[179] He then offered the legal history behind the "separate but equal" doctrine as he taught the audience about the evolution of law. Nabrit's point was especially relevant as society was about to see its own evolution in terms of Black tolerance of racism. A series of direct-action protests and boycotts were about to unfold across the United States, especially in the South. Therefore, Nabrit's remarks at the end of the conference were timely and captured a new energy emerging among Omega men and dozens of other Black organizations. "Successful court action alone will not *ipso facto* achieve racial integration in education," Nabrit said, adding that "I do not agree with any of the reasons given for avoiding a direct attack on segregation.... The attack should be waged with the most devastating forces at hand."¹⁸⁰

Less than a month later, the new "militant" Grand Basileus Grant Reynolds concluded his spring speaking tour on May 10, 1952, in Evanston, Illinois, as he led the attack being waged by the Fraternity across the country. Before his final stop, Reynolds had carried the word on confronting segregation across the United States with speeches in Charleston, West Virginia; Cheyney, Pennsylvania; Youngstown, Ohio; New Haven, Connecticut; and Bloomington, Indiana. Specifically, in Charleston and Youngstown, Reynolds launched local campaigns for the NAACP. Furthermore, he spoke at the meeting of the Ninth District (at the time, Louisiana, Oklahoma, Texas) held in Houston, Texas, surely carrying his same message to Omega men in that portion of the country.¹⁸¹ Reynolds made clear that Black people should demand equality.

Omega men were shining examples of this throughout the summer of 1952. For instance, John S. Chase of the Epsilon Iota chapter in Austin, Texas, graduated from the University of Texas. He was the first Black person to earn an architecture degree from the university. His degree was a clear benefit of the *Sweatt v. Painter* decision in 1950. A graduate of Hampton Institute (now University), Chase was a construction supervisor for a Black-owned lumber company in Austin.¹⁸² Also, Charles A. Ray, a professor of English and director of the news bureau at North Carolina College in Durham, earned his PhD from the University of Southern California. Ray was the first Black person to earn a doctorate in English from the university.¹⁸³

At the chapter level, Omega men in the Xi Omega chapter in Tulsa, Oklahoma, arranged a meeting with a hiring director for Douglas Aircraft Company's facility in that state and demanded the advancement of Black workers within the company.¹⁸⁴ Reynolds was certainly pleased with such direct efforts to confront social norms. Omega men were breaking educational barriers entering academic programs that had long dismissed Black applicants, and they were putting the Fraternity's National Social Action program into action at the local level.

Meanwhile, on September 25, 1952, Reynolds himself appeared on national television. His appearance on the DuMont Television Network, one of the nation's commercial networks, was a model of direct action as Reynolds was a guest of the popular show *The Author Meets the Critics*. Reynolds discussed Black journalist Carl T. Rowan's new book, *South to Freedom*. Before a nationally televised audience, Reynolds discussed the merits of the book as an opportunity to have a broader conversation about Black freedom in the United States.¹⁸⁵

Reynolds's appearance on national television was momentum in pushing the Fraternity forward entering Achievement Week. Held November 9–15, 1952, the theme was "Democracy: Now or Never" as Omega men were adamant about more direct action.[186] Shortly after Achievement Week, on November 24, a group of Omega men visited the White House to present US president Harry S. Truman an award "for his outspoken stand on civil rights."[187] The scroll presented to Truman by members of the Alpha, Alpha Omega, and Kappa Psi chapters in Washington, DC, was for the president's "unswerving stand on the issue of civil rights."[188]

The next Grand Conclave certainly reflected Omega's own stand on civil rights, and human rights globally, under Reynolds as Grand Basileus. In 1952, as customary during the last days of December, Omega men gathered for the Thirty-Eighth Grand Conclave in Philadelphia, Pennsylvania. There, delegates approved a resolution that expressed their faith in the United Nations as Omega men "urged a reconciling of the theories of capitalism and communism," and supported "the efforts of people to attain their independence with colonialism."[189] Omega men understood how global capitalism and colonialization harmed Black people, and the anti-communist sentiment was often used to cease civil rights efforts. Therefore, delegates at the Philadelphia Conclave also condemned the Immigration and Nationality Act of 1952, known as the McCarran–Walter Act, because it upheld the use of quotas to limit immigration totals by certain nations, particularly from Asian and African nations.[190]

It was an important stance for the Fraternity to take as Dwight Eisenhower was inaugurated as president of the United States on January 20, 1953. As the Fraternity took its stand, some districts of the Fraternity also took stands to amplify the efforts of Omega men. For example, in April 1953, the seventy-five delegates attending the meeting of the Seventh District (Alabama, Florida, Georgia, Mississippi) pledged to "continue our cooperation with the NAACP and assert our support of this association in its all-out efforts to legally abolish the segregated public school system."[191] The Fraternity's Seventh District was most impacted by the Fraternity's National Social Action program, especially as it pertained to education. As mentioned during the meeting, "the doors of the state universities are still tightly closed to Negroes" in the four states comprising the district.[192] The Fraternity's Sixth District (North Carolina, South Carolina) would eventually see its delegates take a similar stand against segregation.[193]

Omega men were willing to engage in and support a growing number of direct-action efforts to challenge segregation across the South. For example, there were the increasingly common instances of Black students breaking racial barriers, such as Walter Nathaniel Ridley, an Alpha chapter initiate, who, in 1953, earned a doctorate at the University of Virginia—the first Black person to achieve that degree at formerly segregated White universities in the South.[194] Another example, in June 1953, occurred when thousands of Black residents in Baton Rouge, Louisiana—home of the Beta Sigma chapter at Southern A&M University and Lambda Alpha chapter—boycotted the city's public buses over segregated seating policies.[195] Such efforts were emerging across the nation with the support of Omega Psi Phi, NAACP, CORE, and other organizations whose memberships regularly included Omega men: and this moment in history defined the Fraternity while Reynolds served as Grand Basileus.

Entering the Thirty-Ninth Grand Conclave, held in Cincinnati, Ohio, Reynolds stood as one of the most accomplished Omega men to serve as Grand Basileus until that point. In addition to being an activist himself, he was a sound administrator of the Fraternity. Highlights from the Reynolds administration included an overhaul of the Fraternity's financial system, a new report structure from District Representatives to aid with assessment, a new emphasis on "fraternity–community relations" instead of "purely social undertakings," and he founded the Century Club for members who donated $100.[196] Omega men recognized that Reynolds did not "come up through the ranks" serving in various chapter, district, and then Supreme Council roles.[197] Instead, Reynolds was an organizer whose work directly confronting segregation captured his Fraternity brothers' attention as he quickly ascended to Grand Basileus. Therefore, as Omega men reflected on his leadership, *The Oracle* surmised that "Grant Reynolds was a surprise to a few, but a disappointment to none."[198]

During the Cincinnati Conclave, on December 29, 1953, Reynolds announced that he would not seek reelection. Some Omega men speculated that he desired a third term, but he honored an unofficial agreement in the Fraternity that a Grand Basileus only serve two one-year terms.[199] His decision ultimately led to delegates representing 234 chapters electing John F. Potts to succeed Reynolds as Grand Basileus. Grand Counselor Herbert E. Tucker was elected to the First Vice Grand Basileus position while Howard C. Davis, a Howard University student and Alpha chapter member, was elected to the Second Vice Grand Basileus position.[200] Cary D. Jacobs succeeded Tucker as Grand Counselor while Jesse B. Blayton and Ellis F. Corbett were reelected to their roles Grand Keeper of Finance and as editor-in-chief of *The Oracle*, respectively. Meanwhile, Walter H. Riddick was not up for reelection since the Cincinnati Conclave marked the halfway point of his two-year term as Grand Keeper of Records and Seal.[201] In leaving office, Reynolds delivered a forceful farewell address to Omega men: "Return to your communities with full determination to remove every semblance of segregation on account of race, creed, and color to make democracy in America reach its fullest potential."[202]

Reynolds delivered the charge, but it was Potts who would be responsible for *how* the Fraternity accepted the charge. As an educator, however, it was natural for Potts to emphasize scholarship.

John Foster Potts Sr. was born on April 18, 1908, in Hot Springs, Arkansas, but his parents moved back to their home of East Flat Rock, North Carolina, when Potts was still a child. The young Potts eventually attended Lincoln Academy in Kings Mountain, North Carolina, about seventy miles east of East Flat Rock. Afterward, the promising student moved to Columbia, South Carolina, where he attended the high school department of Benedict College and eventually earned a degree from the institution in 1930. With a college degree in hand, Potts initially stayed local to teach before being promoted to assistant principal at Booker T. Washington High School in Columbia. In 1936, Potts briefly taught at Roosevelt High School in Gary, Indiana. The next year, he earned a master's degree from Cornell University. He returned to Columbia and, in 1939, was named principal of Waverley Elementary School, and during World War II, he served in the US Naval Reserve. Following the war, he spent his longest professional stint as director of the Avery Institute in Charleston, South Carolina, the same school that educated earlier Omega men Walter Herbert Mazyck and Robert Shaw Wilkinson.[203]

Potts directed the Avery Institute when he was elected Grand Basileus, and one of his first tasks was to make sense of a major conversation that occurred during the Cincinnati Conclave. The Fraternity's Scholarship Commission hosted a panel that left some questions unanswered as Omega men entered 1954. The panel of commission members included some notable Omega educators: Mays, president of Morehouse; Matthew T. Whitehead, president of Miner Teachers College; George H. Spaulding, chair of chemistry at Morgan State College; Arnette G. Macklin, director of education at Virginia State; and Arthur P. Davis, professor of English at Howard, who chaired the committee. As the Potts administration began, the commission members pondered why the grade average of Fraternity chapters had declined and made suggestions for how to improve those averages. "High scholarship is a tradition which must be respected in Omega," was one reported statement from the panelist. "During the 'twenties,' this high scholarship was obvious by the large number of Omega men who had won Phi Beta Kappa and other honors on the great campuses of the nation."[204]

The commission members' statement about the 1920s, however, was missing important context, and it was not a completely fair assessment of undergraduate Omega men. There had been significant changes internal and external to the Fraternity in the thirty years since the 1920s when Omega men strategized around education. For instance, during the 1920s, there were fewer chapters of the Fraternity and Black college students in general. That earlier period in history posed a challenge for Omega men as few Black students were enrolled on campuses that offered collegiate-level curricula or a chapter of the Phi Beta Kappa honor society. Yet, after World War II, there was a dramatic increase in college enrollments after the launch of the Servicemen's Readjustment Act of 1944, known as the G.I. Bill, which financially supported veterans seeking higher education.[205] In turn, by the mid-1950s when the Fraternity had 240 chapters, Omega men were further disbursed across the vast chasm of American higher education, spanning from a few of the wealthiest White campuses to several of the long-underfunded Black campuses.[206]

Therefore, the question of scholarship standards was really an outgrowth of educational segregation and varied resources by campus. As Omega men discussed that question and others in early 1954, five individual school desegregation cases—originating in South Carolina, Virginia, Kansas, Washington, DC, and Delaware—had come together into a single Supreme Court case. In December 1953, the *Brown v. Board of Education* case had been reargued before the High Court and, on May 17, 1954, the justices issued a unanimous decision that the "separate but equal" doctrine governing education was unconstitutional.[207] Thurgood Marshall was considered the lead strategist for the case, but a team of NAACP attorneys played a role in the *Brown* case. The NAACP credited at least eight legal minds, many of which either worked at or attended the Howard University School of Law. Three of the attorneys were Omega men: James M. Nabrit Jr., Oliver Hill, and Spottswood Robinson III. In addition to Marshall, some other non-Omega attorneys involved with the *Brown* case were Jack Greenberg, Constance Baker Motley, Robert Carter, and Charles Hamilton Houston.[208] The landmark Supreme Court decision had significant implications for American society and an immediate personal impact on Potts.

Less than two months after *Brown*, Potts officially became president of Voorhees School and Junior College (now named Voorhees University) in Denmark, South Carolina, on July 1, 1954.[209] He became the first Omega man to simultaneously serve as a college president and Grand Basileus. Furthermore, the historic Avery Institute in Charleston, which was founded by the American Missionary Association, closed in 1954, citing financial struggles—a decision that ran parallel to *Brown*.[210] Therefore, it is unsurprising that Omega men during the Potts administration revamped education as the Fraternity's leading area for direct action.

This was evident when Woodrow H. Jones, an initiate of the Phi Psi chapter at Langston University, graduated in the summer of 1954 as the first Black person to earn a PhD from the University of Oklahoma.[211] Similarly, in the fall, Omega men learned that members of the Iota Psi chapter at Ohio State University secured the fourth highest grade average among fifty-two fraternities on campus.[212] Also in the fall of 1954, James Phillip Holland, Keeper of Finance in the Psi Psi chapter at Kentucky State, was nominated by US senator John Sherman Cooper (R-KY) to attend the US Military Academy in West Point, New York, due to him having the highest grade average among all men on campus. Holland was the state's first Black nominee; however, he declined and remained a student at Kentucky State.[213] The individual accomplishments—from Jones in Oklahoma, the Iota Psi members in Ohio, and Holland in Kentucky—directly challenged segregated higher education by breaking racial barriers.

As a collective, delegate decisions at the Fortieth Grand Conclave in Atlanta, on December 27–30, 1954, and Forty-First Grand Conclave in Los Angeles on August 18–23, 1955—both of which Potts presided—captured Omega men's renewed internal and external interest in education. In Atlanta, delegates passed a resolution calling for "full integration of education in all areas."[214] Less than a year later, in Los Angeles, delegates heard NAACP administrator Roy O. Wilkins speak during a session titled, "Desegregation, a Way-Station; Integration, Our Destination."[215] He also led a workshop strategizing against segregation.[216] Delegates voted to accept the Scholarship Commission's recommendation to increase the grade average requirement for Fraternity membership, and with Potts's second term ending after the Los Angeles Conclave, they elected Herbert E. Tucker to succeed Potts as Grand Basileus.[217]

Yet, less than a week in office, Tucker's tenure as Grand Basileus was marked by one of the most gruesome moments in American history when, on August 28, 1955, fourteen-year-old Emmett Till, while visiting Mississippi with family from Illinois, was kidnapped, tortured, and murdered by two White men. It was a defining moment amid the realities of hate, racism, and bigotry.[218] Mamie Elizabeth Till-Mobley (née Bradley) insisted a coroner not touch her son, Emmett, whose casket she demanded be left open so "'all the world' [could] witness the atrocity."[219] Till-Mobley's funeral, according to the *New York Amsterdam News*, among other publications, drew approximately 50,000 people to line the streets in Chicago, Illinois, on the first night Emmett's mutilated body lay in state, to see him before his funeral on September 3, 1955.[220] The published photographs of young Emmett stirred direct action on an unprecedented scale.

In North Carolina, regarding the *Brown* decision, Omega man John Hervey Wheeler stood before Governor Luther H. Hodges in a public meeting and condemned "the deliberate attempt on part of the state of North Carolina to bypass the May 17 decision of the U.S. Supreme Court."[221] From there, the echoes of Wheeler's plea reverberated to Omega men in Alabama where, on December 1, 1955, a White bus driver in Montgomery accused Black seamstress, NAACP official, and veteran civil rights activist Rosa Louise Parks (née McCauley) of violating a municipal ordinance that segregated passengers by race. The driver summoned police officers, who subsequently arrested Parks for refusing to yield to a White passenger and move farther back in the colored section. Four days later, on December 5, thousands of Black residents and others agreeing that "it would be more honorable to walk in dignity than ride in humiliation," initiated a citywide bus boycott.[222]

As with past challenges to segregation, Omega men volunteered for frontline duty in the campaign against segregated seating on city buses in Montgomery. Parks's lawyer, Fred David Gray, was an exemplar. He was a Montgomery native who attended the Alabama State College for Negroes (now called Alabama State University), where he was a 1949 initiate of the Gamma Sigma chapter. After graduating from the college in 1951, Gray enrolled in the Western Reserve University (now named Case Western Reserve University) School of Law in Cleveland, Ohio, since legal training was not provided for Black people in Alabama. Gray's educational journey to the Midwest was not uncommon, as several southern Omega men sought graduate or professional training outside of the segregated South. Yet, Gray was committed to complete Western Reserve and return to Montgomery to execute his years-long plan to "destroy . . . everything segregated [he] could find."[223] As a lawyer, Gray provided services for not only Parks but also for many other activists including Martin Luther King Jr., pastor of the Dexter Avenue Baptist Church in Montgomery, one of the leaders of the boycott. The twenty-seven-year-old King was an Atlanta native who earned a bachelor's degree from Morehouse College in 1948 and a PhD from Boston University in 1955. King was a member of Alpha Phi Alpha, but he often called Omega man Benjamin E. Mays, president of Morehouse, his "spiritual mentor."[224]

While the boycott continued into 1956, Omega men continued to work or support others in education. That year, Omega founder Edgar Amos Love attended the inauguration of Willa Beatrice Player as president of Bennett College in Greensboro, North Carolina.[225] The event was significant as Player became the first Black woman president of a four-year college in the United States, and Love served on Bennett's board of trustees.[226] Less than a mile away, North Carolina A&T also inaugurated a new president in 1956, and it was longtime college administrator and Omega man Warmoth Thomas Gibbs.[227] As mentioned in chapter 2, Gibbs had worked at the college since the 1920s and was a member of the Tau Omega chapter when the Fraternity sought to standardize Black college curricula. Now, thirty years later, he was president of the college he had served for most of his life. Also in 1956, Omega man Samuel Milton Nabrit was inaugurated as president of Texas Southern University in Houston. Nabrit was the younger brother to James M. Nabrit Jr., the Howard law professor and NAACP attorney, and other Omega presidents traveled to Houston to witness his inauguration, including former Grand Basileus and Dillard University president Albert W. Dent and Arkansas A&M (now named the University of Arkansas at Pine Bluff) president Lawrence A. Davis.[228]

Outside of academic leadership, Omega men were also leaders in civil rights protests and boycotts. In 1956, Tallahassee residents also boycotted city buses, and Omega man Millard Curtis Williams, a local dentist known as M. C., was among its most recognized leaders. Williams graduated from the Howard University School of Dentistry in 1952 and had also helped fight for equal pay for Black teachers in Florida.[229] Meanwhile, in 1956, Omega man and Mississippi physician Theodore Roosevelt Mason Howard—known as T. R. M. Howard—continued his national speaking tour advocating for civil rights. Howard was a well-known civil rights leader and had also spoken at the Los Angeles Conclave, but he had since moved away from Mississippi due to death threats.[230] Furthermore, in 1956, Autherine Lucy became the first Black person to enroll at the University of Alabama in Tuscaloosa. Her education at the once-segregated university was financed, in part, thanks to a $400 contribution from the Sigma Phi chapter in Montgomery. A race riot among a White mob unfolded shortly thereafter and trustees expelled Lucy but, beforehand, she thanked "progressive organizations like the Omega Psi Phi Fraternity which have so graciously expressed their encouragement in terms of financial contributions."[231]

The range of direct-action involvement in 1956 among Omega men, from Williams and Howard as street-level activists to the new Omega college presidents, inspired Grand Basileus Herbert E. Tucker. So, too, was the ruling from the three-judge panel at the US District Court for the Middle District of Alabama in *Browder v. Gayle* case, which Gray helped lead, that bus segregation was unconstitutional.[232] The Supreme Court upheld the ruling. Therefore, as Omega men gathered in late 1956 for the Forty-Second Grand Conclave in Baltimore, Maryland, Tucker said, "Omega can hold its head high—proud of the fact that it has been a factor which contributed to the well-being of America without resorting to violence or bloodshed."[233]

On December 27, a light snow welcomed Omega men to Baltimore— "Monumental City"—the nation's sixth largest city at the time.[234] Morgan State College, home of the Pi chapter, served as conclave headquarters, and among the campus's facilities, the Edward P. Hurt Gymnasium was most impressive. Hurt was an Omega man and longtime, multisport coach of the several championship football, basketball, and track teams at the college.[235] Several other Omega men served on the Morgan State faculty, including Grand Historian Robert L. Gill and Scholarship Commission member George H. Spaulding. It was a fitting location with two of the oldest graduate and undergraduate chapters in Baltimore and leading Omega men on campus. It was also the first conclave in Baltimore since December 1929, and the first since Los Angeles in August 1955. The longer-than-usual break between annual conclaves brought a warmed-up spirit to Baltimore despite the chilly weather.

The fiery desire to fight segregation made the Baltimore Conclave more civil rights convening than its usual mix of Fraternity business and social action. The conclave theme was "Wanted: Techniques for Strengthening and Furthering Our Democratic and Christian Heritage."[236] Each of the principal speakers were Omega men involved in civil rights in the areas of law or education. On December 28, Warmoth T. Gibbs, the new president at North Carolina A&T, spoke on "How to Improve Relations between College and Fraternity," and Walter N. Ridley, dean at Saint Paul's College in Virginia, discussed "Manners and Morals in Fraternities." On December 29, James M. Nabrit Jr., Howard law professor and NAACP attorney, spoke on "The Northern Viewpoint on Segregation," while Fred D. Gray, the Montgomery attorney, explained "The Southern Viewpoint on Segregation." Finally, in tying those topics in education and law together, on December 30, Omega founder Edgar Amos Love, a bishop in the Methodist Church, discussed "The Friendship of Omega."[237]

Exhibiting their commitment to and support of civil rights, Omega men bestowed Martin Luther King Jr. its Citizen of the Year award for his leadership in the Montgomery bus boycott. King was present to accept the award, and he was joined in Baltimore by Coretta Scott King, his dynamic and talented activist wife. She sang during the conclave's Talent Hunt program—a performance arts competition for youth that originated in North Carolina but became an annual conclave event during the Cincinnati Conclave in December 1953.[238]

In closing the Baltimore Conclave, Omega man Roy Wilkins stood before delegates in the same vein as he had done during the Los Angeles Conclave in August 1955. Since then, Wilkins had been promoted from NAACP administrator to executive secretary as he reported to the Baltimore delegates that Fraternity chapters and individual Omega men had contributed nearly $11,000 toward NAACP life memberships. "I am pleased, indeed, to have my own fraternity as a solid support in the great crusade of the Association for first class citizenship," Wilkins said.[239] "As every Brother knows, the battle for equality is waging," he added, while explaining how "Certain southern states are doing everything in their power to halt the drive for desegregation and to maintain the Jim Crow system. They have used bombs and guns against our people in the South and their state legislatures are trying to drive the NAACP out of business."[240]

In concluding his report, despite the moments of racial progress, Wilkins succinctly summarized why the Fraternity and its National Social Action program remained necessary. Omega men were needed to support the civil rights effort as on-the-ground activists, legal strategists, and institutional leaders. No role was too large or too minor for Omega men. It was dangerous work. But it was also expensive work, and the financial contributions mattered. "You can't fight a war for free, and we are in a war," Wilkins declared. "I am confident Omega will do its part."[241]

The Baltimore Conclave in 1956 presented perhaps the most accurate snapshot of the Fraternity in the years immediately following World War II. In 1946, the Fraternity launched its National Social Action program. It was an initiative developed with the intent of dismantling racial segregation as Black veterans returned to the United States from war in the name of democracy only to find antidemocratic, second-class treatment awaiting them. Omega men implemented their national program at the local, district, and national level but, for every step forward, they were often met by White resistance. Despite pushback from segregationists and their White supremacist beliefs, the Fraternity and its members still found success in paving a road toward segregation through educational leadership, federal court battles, and other direct-action efforts.

By the mid-1950s, as civil rights activism increased in scope and size, the Fraternity's three living founders—Edgar Amos Love, Oscar James Cooper, and Frank Coleman—regularly attended Grand Conclaves to witness their Fraternity brothers debate civil rights matters and approve resolutions and programs aimed at dismantling White supremacy.[242] Those actions materialized in various ways after the Baltimore Conclave. For example, the Southern Christian Leadership Conference was formed January 10, 1957, as one of the most important civil rights organizations of the period, and historians have noted that Omega man Bayard Rustin "helped to place [Martin Luther] King at the head of a new organization of black Southerners."[243] By the spring of that year, undergraduate members in the Theta Sigma chapter at Dillard University decided to donate chapter funds to the New Orleans Improvement Association to aid the local civil rights efforts instead of using the budget to host their annual Omega–Delta dance with members of Delta Sigma Theta Sorority.[244] And, in September 1957, as Arkansas segregationist governor Orval Faubus denied nine Black students the right to enroll at Little Rock Central

High School, Wiley Austin Branton, former Basileus of the Tau Phi chapter, represented them.[245]

Omega Psi Phi ended the 1950s—and its fifth decade—with a clear focus on civil rights. The efforts of individual Omega men and the Fraternity had grown in alignment over the years. The growing pains of the 1920s and turmoil of the Great Depression 1930s and World War II in the early 1940s appeared to be healing as Omega Psi Phi expressed great clarity in its goals and ambitions following war. The National Social Action program had become the anchor that held Omega men's varying interests in place. Omega men were poised to witness even greater accomplishments as the Fraternity celebrated its Golden Anniversary in 1961. Yet, on the eve of that significant fifty-year milestone, a new era of social change—and protest—emerged.

Omega man Carter G. Woodson, Ph.D. Source: Scurlock Studio Records, circa 1905–94, Archives Center, National Museum of American History, Smithsonian Institution.

Omega man John H. Wheeler, a noted Black business leader in North Carolina. Source: Dr. James E. Shepard Memorial Library, North Carolina Central University Faculty and Staff Photographic Collection, University Archives, Records and History Center, North Carolina Central University.

Omega man Asa Spaulding, a key leader of North Carolina Mutual Life Insurance Company. Source: Dr. James E. Shepard Memorial Library, North Carolina Central University Faculty and Staff Photographic Collection, University Archives, Records and History Center, North Carolina Central University.

Italy, circa 1945: Omega man George Spencer "Spanky" Roberts (*second from right*) stands alongside his fellow Tuskegee Airman. *Left to right:* Marcellus G. Smith; James A. Walker; unknown airman; Roberts; and Benjamin O. Davis. Colonel Davis is seen presenting Omega man Roberts and others war bond for best kept A/C (Active Component of the military). Source: Toni Frissell/Buyenlarge via Getty Images, Library of Congress, www.loc.gov/item/2007675061/.

ROSTER

of

Class SE 42-C

Lemuel Rodney Custis

Charles Henry De Bow

Mac Ross

George Spencer Roberts

Captain Benjamin O. Davis, Jr.

PROGRAM

Invocation
Post Chaplain

Address
and presentation of
commissions and diplomas
Major General George E. Stratemeyer

Presentation
of
Wings
Colonel Frederick V. H. Kimble

Benediction
Reverend Harry V. Richardson

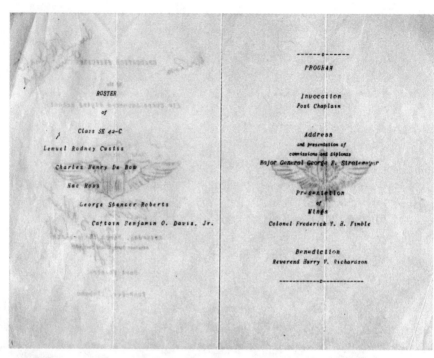

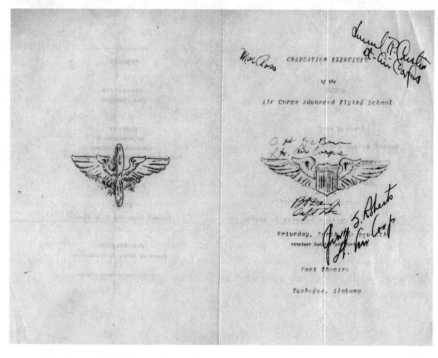

GRADUATION EXERCISES

of the

Air Corps Advanced Flying School

Saturday, March the seventh
nineteen hundred and forty-two

Post Theatre

Tuskegee, Alabama

Form 348
Rev. 1-1-40

UNITED STATES OF AMERICA
CIVIL AERONAUTICS AUTHORITY
WASHINGTON, D. C.

C-6/14/40

AIRMAN CERTIFICATE NO. 16292-40

This certifies that **GEORGE SPENCER ROBERTS** is properly qualified and is physically able to perform the duties of **PRIVATE PILOT**

Address **317 QUARRY AVE., FAIRMONT, W. VA.**

DATE OF BIRTH	WEIGHT	HEIGHT	HAIR	EYES	SEX
9/24/18	$152\frac{1}{2}$	5' $8\frac{1}{2}$"	BROWN	BROWN	M

THIS CERTIFICATE is of 60 days' duration and, unless the holder hereof is otherwise notified by the Authority within such period, shall continue in effect indefinitely thereafter, unless suspended or revoked by the Authority, except that it shall immediately expire (1) at the end of each **TWELVE** months' period after the date of issuance hereof if the holder of this certificate fails to secure an endorsement by an authorized Inspector of the Authority within the last 45 days of each such period, or (2) at any time an authorized Inspector of the Authority shall refuse to endorse this certificate after inspection or examination.

Endorsement Refused:
Date:_____

Date of Issuance **SEPTEMBER 23/1940**
By direction of the Authority:
Signature _NELSON W. BROWN_
Inspector, Civil Aeronautics Authority Title: **ASSO. AERONAUTICAL INSPECTOR**

This certificate is not valid unless there is attached hereto the appropriate Rating Record bearing the above number. Any alteration of this certificate is punishable by a fine of not exceeding $1,000 or imprisonment not exceeding three years, or both.
(Over) Signature of Holder: _George Spencer Roberts_

Copy of Omega man George Spencer "Spanky" Roberts's original Tuskegee Airman induction program (on previous page) and pilot's license (above). Courtesy of Lanell Roberts Brent.

Omega man Howard M. Fitts Jr. (*left*) pictured with an unknown Army serviceman. Courtesy of Howard M. Fitts Jr.

Omega man John H. Lucas of North Carolina, influential in the state's Black and White teacher associations. Source: Book 1 Board of Directors Roll 17, October 17, 1964, Board of Directors [1/2], 1965, series 8, box 3258, folder 13, National Education Association-Photographs, NEA1009-RG, Special Collections Research Center, George Washington University.

Omega man Hobart Kornegay of Mississippi, a noted dentist in Meridian and the first Black elected official in Lauderdale County. Courtesy of Patricia Smith.

United States, July 29, 1964. Omega men were three of nine civil rights leaders photographed at a "summit meeting." *Left to right:* Omega man Bayard Rustin; Jack Greenberg; Whitney Young Jr.; Omega man James L. Farmer; Omega man Roy Wilkins; Martin Luther King Jr.; John Lewis; A. Philip Randolph; and Courtland Cox. Source: Arthur Buckley/NY Daily News Archive via Getty Images.

Chapter 5

Bloody, but Unbowed

*Omega Psi Phi Fraternity during the
Modern Civil Rights Movement, 1960–1969*

Entering 1960, Omega Psi Phi was widely regarded as a leading organization inspiring social change, and Omega men expressed excitement about celebrating the Fraternity's upcoming golden anniversary. It would be an occasion to reflect on the past and an opportunity to look ahead another fifty years. The previous decades had exhibited how Omega Psi Phi and its members impacted many areas of American life through efforts to protect Black veterans, secure fair housing, desegregate education, and expand equal employment opportunities, among other initiatives. In the legal realm, Omega men filed, served as plaintiffs, or helped to underwrite lawsuits, litigate cases, or write amici curiae briefs. In education, several college presidents, deans, professors, school principals, teachers, and rigorous education researchers were Omega men. In government, Fraternity members advised state and federal officials on policies that would impact millions of Black Americans.

The year 1960, however, brought abrupt change to the struggles for racial equality. Soon, direct-action protests grew in scope and size as more boycotts and sit-in demonstrations were launched in departure from methods long used by older Omega men. It became clearer that undergraduate and graduate Omega men understood the fight for first-class citizenship in the country was not only in the courts, formal government roles, or academic leadership. There also had to be more resistance and agency on the streets.[1]

As the Fraternity moved into its next fifty years, traditional civil rights efforts received their fair share of critique in the United States. Some observers described the movement as a predominantly Black middle- or upper-class phenomenon grounded in the politics of respectability. Omega Psi Phi, however, contributed participants from all echelons, and their reach was worldwide. Omega men fought to dismantle White supremacist strongholds not only in the United States, but also in Africa, Asia, the Caribbean, and South America.

With social unrest increasing, the Fraternity entered new territory. The maturation of Black activism called for not only civil rights, but cries of

Black Power, which hoisted an expressive arm known as the Black Arts Movement and rallied Black communities. While this movement demonstrated diverse perspectives of political activism among Black Americans, the relevance and quest for civil rights remained front and center.

At Fifty, Omega Enters a New Era

On February 1, 1960, Warmoth Thomas Gibbs had called the campus of North Carolina Agricultural and Technical (A&T) home since 1926. A 1917 Gamma chapter initiate, the sixty-seven-year-old Gibbs carried a heavy load of life experiences. In 1917, he helped Omega founder Edgar Amos Love establish the Fraternity's War chapter at Fort Des Moines in Iowa before he went on to serve during World War I. That experience led him to arrive in Greensboro as dean of men and an instructor of military science at the then-named Negro Agricultural and Technical College of North Carolina. Gibbs was an effective leader and, in 1929, he was promoted to dean of the college. He remained dean until he was appointed president in 1956 and, one year later, the formal name of the college changed to Agricultural and Technical College of North Carolina.[2]

Gibbs knew the college as well as any administrator in its history up until that point. He had witnessed students matriculate through its halls for decades. Yet, on that Monday in 1960, Gibbs faced a new challenge, one that even he considered "unusual."[3] This new challenge was the student-led sit-in demonstrations. That day, four freshman North Carolina A&T students held a peaceful demonstration at a Whites-only lunch counter inside the Greensboro Woolworth's store. They requested service but were denied because of their race. The four Black students' demonstration, however, initiated similar student-led lunch counter sit-ins as a student civil rights uprising spread across the South and solidarity demonstrations were launched across the nation. For Gibbs, a long-standing Omega man, his administration were mere novices facing a new phenomenon that seemingly appeared out of nowhere. Yet, when local White leaders demanded he put an end to the sit-ins by reprimanding student protestors, Gibbs refused.[4]

Omega men and other Black people who had long been considered leaders in civil rights efforts abruptly adopted supporting roles. For instance, in North Carolina, Ella Baker—the forceful Black woman activist—helped organize the national movement as students from across the South met for a conference on April 15–17, 1960, at Shaw University in Raleigh. She worked for the Southern Christian Leadership Conference (SCLC), of which Omega man Bayard Rustin helped position Martin Luther King as its leader, but Baker remained adamant that the students remain in control of the sit-in movement.[5] Two days later, on April 19, in Nashville, Tennessee, the home of former Grand Basileus Z. Alexander Looby was bombed. Student demonstrations in that city had led to hundreds of arrests over the previous weeks, but Looby, the acclaimed civil rights attorney, had provided legal counsel on behalf of 153 of the arrested students. Looby and Grafta Mosby Looby, his wife, escaped the bombed home without injury despite its blast so powerful that it shattered 147 windows at Meharry Medical College across the street. Afterward, Looby said the assassination attempt was "very definitely connected" to the sit-in movement.[6]

The bombing also shook Omega men. In May 1960, the cover of *The Oracle* was a photograph of Looby's bombed home. It was 85 percent destroyed, and an editorial beneath the headline "The Price of Freedom" read the cover image was "an illustration of the awful price which many have paid and are paying for the cause of freedom in the world."[7] Grand Basileus Isham Gregory Newton, who succeeded Herbert E. Tucker, however, did not want the violent undertakings to distract from the unprecedented activism led by Black college students. Aware of earlier sit-ins and boycotts involving Black students, such as the previously mentioned Morgan State College demonstrations in the 1940s and 1950s, Newton still observed differences in the 1960 demonstrations, noting that he could not "recall any modern national social movement of this stature being organized and participated in by American college students."[8] His observations accurate, Newton assessed that, "The successful or failure of this social phenomenon may well forecast future actions of American college students."[9]

Meanwhile, by the time Omega men read Newton's sit-in observations in May 1960, delegates to the Fraternity's Sixth District meeting had already voted to contribute $500 to aid arrested students.[10] Delegates at the Third District meeting also endorsed the sit-in demonstrations and urged support.[11] The resolutions and donations made sense considering Omega men were among the sit-in demonstrators. For example, Charles Sherrod and Frank G. Pinkston, both Zeta chapter initiates, led the student sit-in demonstrations in Richmond, Virginia. Both graduated from Virginia Union University with bachelor's degrees in 1958, but they remained at the university pursuing graduate degrees in the School of Religion. In leading the sit-ins, Sherrod and Pinkston received legal counsel from Clarence Newsome, an Omega man and Richmond attorney.[12] The sit-ins in 1960 heightened attention and urgency about civil rights in the United States. That pressure was felt at the federal level as US senator John F. Kennedy (D-MA) campaigned for US president using a platform promising stronger civil rights legislation and, on

November 8, 1960, he was elected after defeating US vice president Richard Nixon (R-CA).

The sit-ins, which involved many younger Omega men, and the election of a pro-civil rights presidential candidate set the stage for the Forty-Sixth Grand Conclave held in San Antonio, Texas, in late December 1960. The conclave agenda featured sessions that unpacked the sit-ins and strategized how the Fraternity could aid the students. For example, the San Antonio Conclave's theme was "Youth of the World: Accelerators of Progress and Change."[13] Sessions included a December 29, panel discussion featuring four Omega college presidents: Benjamin E. Mays, Morehouse; Samuel M. Nabrit, Texas Southern; Walter S. Davis, Tennessee A&I State; and former Grand Basileus John F. Potts, Voorhees Junior College.[14] Delegates voted to contribute $250 to a family in New Orleans, Louisiana, after the parents refused to withdraw their child from a segregated White school. The father—James Cabrielle—lost his city job as a water meter reader and later moved to Providence, Rhode Island, after receiving death threats.[15] The delegates also reelected Grand Basileus Isham Gregory Newton—known as Gregory Newton—and voted to emphasize "academic excellence and social action" at the Golden Anniversary Grand Conclave in August 1961 in Washington, DC.[16]

Entering the year of the Fraternity's fiftieth anniversary, the need for the National Social Action program was immediately clear less than two weeks after the San Antonio Conclave. On January 9, 1961, two Black students—Charlayne Hunter and Hamilton Holmes—enrolled at and desegregated the University of Georgia campus. Two days later, a White mob overran the campus in protest over the federal court order that allowed the two Black students to enroll.[17] Later that month, on January 20, John F. Kennedy was inaugurated as president of the United States; however, by May 1961, freedom riders tested Kennedy's promise on civil rights when they challenged whether prior Supreme Court rulings that banned highway segregation were being implemented by traveling along southern highways.[18]

The first of the Freedom Rides that year was led by Omega man James Leonard Farmer, cofounder of the Congress of Racial Equality (CORE) and a 1936 initiate of Theta chapter. It began in Washington, DC, and made its way through the Upper South and into the Deep South. The number of riders increased over time, but most jarring to the civil rights movement was the violence geared toward freedom riders when they arrived in Alabama a little over a week later. In Anniston, Alabama, the bus was burned while a White mob attempted to trap the riders inside the burning vehicle.[19] Similar violence met freedom riders in other Alabama cities. President Kennedy and his brother, Attorney General Robert Kennedy, remained lukewarm about the Freedom Rides, but the Kennedys knew inactivity would not bode well for their political futures outside the South and doubtless would result in greater bloodshed inside the region. On May 24, Robert Kennedy issued a statement: "In this confused situation, there is increasing possibility that innocent persons may be injured. A mob asks no questions. The Alabama and Mississippi law enforcement officials are meeting the test today, but their job is becoming increasingly difficult. A cooling off period is needed." Robert Kennedy then closed: "It would be wise for those traveling through these two States to delay their trips until the recent state of confusion and danger has passed and an atmosphere of reason and normalcy has been restored."[20]

Alabama governor John M. Patterson, speaking from the state capital of Montgomery, said the May 24 statement by Robert Kennedy about a cooling-off period reflected "the first time the federal government... displayed any common sense in some days."[21] Farmer displayed a different reaction about the suggested period. Epitomizing three of the four Omega Psi Phi cardinal principles—manhood, perseverance, and uplift—Farmer instructed Martin Luther King Jr.: "Please tell the attorney general that we've been cooling off for 350 years. If we cool off any more, we will be in a deep freeze."[22]

The stern directive from Farmer was a message directly from an Omega man committed to civil rights, and that message carried over as other Omega men made their way to Washington, DC, for the Forty-Seventh Grand Conclave—also called the Golden Anniversary Grand Conclave. The Fraternity's national officers had planned a significant celebration starting August 13 in the nation's capital, but they could not dismiss what the first eighteen months of the 1960s had presented to the world. A new form of activism had emerged among a subset of Omega men who were tired of the slow pace of multiyear court proceedings, advisement to federal officials, or annual pleas for equitable funding of Black schools and institutions of higher education. Omega men like Farmer were not going to take it slow any more, and that dilemma hovered over the Golden Anniversary Grand Conclave and delegates' decisions pertaining to the National Social Action program.

More than 900 Omega men registered for the conclave held at the Sheraton Park Hotel in Washington, DC. The six-day gathering was considered the largest delegation in the history of the Fraternity and speakers included some of the most prominent Americans. For example, Attorney General Robert Kennedy, who months earlier Omega man James L. Farmer had vehemently disagreed with, addressed Omega men and their guests.[23] It was not surprising that Kennedy visited the conclave considering his brother—US president John F. Kennedy—had recently appointed Omega man Robert

Clifton Weaver to his cabinet. An economist who earned a PhD in economics from Harvard University, Weaver's appointment as head of the US Housing and Home Finance Agency made him the first Black man to hold a presidential cabinet position.[24] During his remarks, Robert Kennedy stated that Weaver was "typical of the quality of men that our administration is proud to appoint to high office."[25] Kennedy then promised he would work to ensure equal opportunity for all Americans. "This is what I believe the vast majority of Americans want for everyone, regardless of the color of his skin."[26]

Aside from Kennedy's address, there were other sessions based on the Fraternity's cardinal principles. For example, in a discussion on scholarship, Weaver addressed the conclave on the topic of "the creative value of academic scholarship in solving daily problems," and called on Americans to be attentive to the recruitment of students who can pursue advanced research study.[27] In the manhood session, Ohio State University head football coach Woody Hayes joined a panel conversation with Omega men Walter N. Ridley, president of Elizabeth City Teachers College (now Elizabeth City State University) and former Grand Basileus Herbert E. Tucker. During the closing session, on the topic perseverance, Omega men again made time to welcome a global perspective to their fight for racial equality when they heard from Richard Edmund Kelfa-Caulker, ambassador to Sierra Leone; Ebenezer Moses Debrah, who represented the Ghana ambassador; and Francis John Ellah representing Nigeria. Their appearance was timely considering many African nations were finally coming from under colonial rule. Other sessions featured notable Omega attorneys Oliver Hill, who worked for the Federal Housing Authority, and Spottswood Robinson III, dean of the Howard University School of Law. Both men were involved with the *Brown v. Board of Education* case in 1954.[28] Regarding Robinson's deanship, he succeeded Omega man James M. Nabrit Jr. who, in 1960, became president of Howard University.

The week-long gathering was not limited to civil rights discussion. Omega men also paid homage to the founders of Omega Psi Phi. In attendance were longtime friends Edgar Amos Love, Oscar James Cooper, and Frank Coleman, and delegates also held a memorial service for deceased founder Ernest Everett Just. The Golden Anniversary Grand Conclave was a tribute to their vision fifty years earlier. In their earlier lives, they were young race men committed to creating a more equitable society and, fifty years later, nearly 1,000 Omega men gathered in special honor of what the Fraternity had achieved; however, Omega men could not dwell on the past with rapid social changes unfolding domestically and abroad.[29]

At fifty years old, Omega Psi Phi boasted more than 22,000 members located around the world but, looking ahead, delegates voted to use their collective voices to continue its efforts toward equality. In Washington, delegates passed a resolution that called on President John F. Kennedy to extend the federal government's Commission on Civil Rights for five more years. Omega men also voted to join several other national organizations in helping raise $1 million to construct a medical research facility in West Africa.[30] The latter decision made sense since several Omega men worked in Africa throughout the 1950s, such as Kermit Clifford King, a 1934 initiate via Epsilon chapter who was appointed president of the University of Liberia in 1954, and the Fraternity chartered the Tau Chi chapter in Liberia—the second international chapter and first chapter chartered on another continent—in 1955.[31]

With an agenda set entering the next fifty years, the new Supreme Council tasked with leading Omega forward included: Cary D. Jacobs, Grand Basileus; George E. Meares, First Vice Grand Basileus; Robert H. Tucker, Second Vice Grand Basileus; Jesse B. Blayton, Grand Keeper of Finance; Walter H. Riddick, Grand Keeper of Records and Seal; Ellis F. Corbett, editor-in-chief of *The Oracle*; and Jeff Greenup, Grand Counselor. Those seven men would be joined by H. Carl Moultrie, who continued in his full-time role as Executive Secretary.[32]

Nonetheless, even with new officers in place, undergraduate members coordinated more direct action and dialogue around racial justice over the next two years, and there was perhaps no better example than on the campus of Morgan State College in Baltimore, Maryland. As mentioned in chapter 4, sixty members of the Pi chapter at Morgan State picketed Ford's Theater in 1948. Therefore, the student activism of the early 1960s was not new to anyone familiar with the history of Black students on that northeast Baltimore campus. In 2020, political scientist and Omega man Judson L. Jeffries wrote at length about Pi chapter and broader student activism of Morgan State students starting in the mid-1950s and into the 1960s.[33]

Leaving the Golden Anniversary Grand Conclave, Omega men vowed to continue their "crusade for freedom and equality," and Pi chapter was a leading fraternal crusader in 1962.[34] Members of the chapter invited Nation of Islam eminence and "oratorical wizard" Malcolm X to speak at Morgan State.[35] In Jeffries's research, Pi members Oliver Jackson and Samuel McNeil drove from the campus to Mosque No. 7 in the Harlem community of New York City, a journey of more than 200 miles, to personally invite Malcolm X.[36]

Both Jackson and McNeil were reared in New York City and attended some of Malcolm X's soap-box speeches, but they did not know him personally.[37] All the same, Malcolm X accepted their invite, and debated August A. Meier, a White history professor at Morgan State, on March 28, 1962.[38]

Malcolm X appearing at Morgan State was a milestone in the history of Omega Psi Phi and, as Jeffries noted, some Black presidents of Black colleges were conservative and did not welcome controversial figures like Malcolm X because consenting might impact campus funding from White-controlled state legislators and private businesses.[39] Nonetheless, Pi members were allowed to host Malcolm X, who had previously debated Omega man Bayard Rustin in October 1961 and twice debated Omega man James L. Farmer Jr. in January and March 1961.[40]

The remainder of 1962 featured other key moments on college campuses within the broader debate around racial equality. As Pi members witnessed Malcolm X spar against the history professor, two other Omega men—Walter Thaniel Johnson Jr. and David Robinson—were concluding their first academic year as the first Black students enrolled at the Duke University School of Law in Durham, North Carolina.[41] But not all southern White universities were ready for Black students to cross the campus color line. In September 1962, the nation watched a race riot unfold at the University of Mississippi after a federal court order mandated that James Meredith—a military veteran—be admitted as that campus's first Black student with the help of Omega man Thomas Covington Dent.[42] For Omega men, undergraduate and graduate members alike, social change had made an abrupt appearance in 1960 and shaped the Fraternity's golden anniversary. Yet, for as unprecedented as the student activism was in 1960 alongside the gruesome White violence, the year of 1963 would become one of the most violent and significant for Omega Psi Phi and American society.

Omega and the Bloody Year of 1963

There were a series of events in the first half of 1963 that Omega men paid close attention to, and Martin Luther King Jr., the mentee of Omega man and Morehouse president Benjamin E. Mays, was front and center at many watershed moments in the quest for full equality. In April 1963, he was arrested during the Birmingham campaign in Alabama. It was a nonviolent movement led by King and the SCLC.[43] While in police custody, on April 16, King penned his now-famous "Letter from Birmingham Jail"—critiquing White moderates who were more concerned with gradual equality instead of immediate change. Roughly two weeks later, on May 3, 1963, Americans watched Birmingham law enforcement officers use police dogs and high-powered water hoses on children participating in a peaceful civil rights march. The images soon circulated around the world.[44]

The next month in nearby Tuscaloosa, just fifty-five miles southwest of Birmingham, Alabama segregationist Governor George Wallace brought more international attention to the segregation question in the United States. Wallace vowed to keep Alabama higher education segregated—making the state the last holdout after South Carolina desegregated Clemson College (now University) and the University of South Carolina enrolled Black students in January 1963. Therefore, on June 11, Wallace took his infamous "stand in the schoolhouse door" to deny the enrollment of two Black students—Vivian Malone and James Hood—on the university's Tuscaloosa campus.[45] Then, early the morning of June 12, Medgar Evers, a National Association for the Advancement of Colored People (NAACP) leader in Mississippi, was assassinated in his driveway.[46] The violence and staunch resistance to Black equality set the stage for one of the modern civil rights movement's largest events: the March on Washington for Jobs and Freedom.

In August 1963, two months after Evers was murdered, the event, which countless people have referred to simply as the March on Washington, was the culmination of organizing efforts by persons, such as A. Philip Randolph and Bayard Rustin, who began planning for the march in December 1961. Randolph was a member of the Phi Beta Sigma Fraternity, but he had collaborated with former Grand Basileus Grant Reynolds in the late 1940s to form the Committee Against Jim Crow. Prior to that, Randolph called for a 10,000-person march on Washington in January 1941, but he rescinded his call after US president Franklin Delano Roosevelt issued Executive Order 8802 in June, prohibiting racial discrimination in defense industries and, among other acts, establishing the Committee on Fair Employment Practice, also called the Fair Employment Practice Committee. Other eventual organizers or key participants in the actualized March on Washington on August 28, 1963, included Thomas Kilgore Jr., Martin Luther King Jr., James L. Farmer Jr., John Lewis, Roy Wilkins, and Whitney M. Young Jr.[47]

As made plain earlier in this book, Rustin, Farmer, and Wilkins were Omega men. Kilgore, a Baptist minister and Morehouse college alumnus from Woodruff, South Carolina, was also an Omega man. Hundreds of other Omega men joined Kilgore, Rustin, Farmer, and Wilkins in the nation's capital on August 28. They were joined by an estimated 250,000 other participants, a considerable number of whom gathered at or as close as they could get to the Lincoln Memorial to hear Randolph, Lewis, Farmer, Young, and other speakers. However, King delivering his now-famous "I Have a Dream" speech was the highlight of the day.[48]

Afterward, *The Oracle* editor Ellis F. Corbett titled the September 1963 issue of the publication "Omegas 'March' Too."[49] Its cover featured photographs that First Vice Grand Basileus George Meares, a 1938 Epsilon chapter initiate, snapped of fellow Omega men who participated in the March on Washington. They included Second Vice Grand Basileus Jesse Louis Jackson;

Twelfth District Representative J. Quintin Mason; Executive Secretary H. Carl Moultrie; and Third District Representative Hiram F. Jones. Meares also photographed former Grand Basileus Herbert E. Tucker Jr. and Omega man and Morehouse president Benjamin E. Mays. A Baptist minister and frequent speaker, Mays was one of the most respected Black men in the United States and spoke, delivering the benediction, at the March on Washington. Omega men helped organize and spoke at the march, while hundreds of other Omega men assembled at the house of the Alpha and Alpha Omega chapters at 1231 Harvard Street Northwest during the morning hours to march under a large Fraternity banner. After the march, the Omegas, their wives, other family members, and guests enjoyed a "period of relaxation and refreshment" at the house.[50]

Regrettably, the hundreds of thousands of people who attended the March on Washington in August 1963 did not see many women in leading roles. The dearth of women was not unique. Black women, including "young crusaders," to quote historian and author V. P. Franklin, were exceptionally active in the movement, but they rarely had visible leadership roles: the spotlight usually shown on men.[51] While girls and women faced unjust White police officers, vicious beatings by cruel White segregationists, dog bites, fire hoses, and all other violent aspects of the movement on local levels, when it came time for national events, they tended to be singers, marchers, or behind-the-scenes organizers. The March on Washington was no exception.

One woman, Dorothy I. Height, held the position as team member alongside the Big Six—A. Philip Randolph, Martin Luther King Jr., James L. Farmer Jr., John Lewis, Roy Wilkins, and Whitney Young—after they, on July 2, 1963, made a public announcement regarding the March on Washington. At the time, Height was president of the National Council of Negro Women, and she formerly served as national president of the Delta Sigma Theta Sorority. Educator, journalist, and politician Anna Arnold Hedgeman was the sole woman on the administrative committee for the March on Washington. Her many professional duties before the march included serving as executive director for the National Council for a Permanent Fair Employment Practices Commission and as assistant dean of women at Howard University. For the march, leaders of the National Council of Churches hired Hedgeman to coordinate its participation. She and Height were acclaimed civil rights leaders on whose organizational skills men such as the Big Six and Bayard Rustin relied heavily; however, the Big Six, Rustin, and their male counterparts initially rejected most of Height's and Hedgeman's advice relative to women speaking at the march.[52]

Less than a week before the march, Omega man Wilkins was the first to voice support for Hedgeman's recommendation, to which others ultimately agreed. Therefore, the official program featured some Black women: vocalist

Marian Anderson to lead the national anthem, conductor Eva Jessye to guide a choral selection, and Anderson's fellow vocalist, Mahalia Jackson, to sing.[53] Several other women had onstage roles, but not one of those women was a scheduled speaker. All the same, Hedgeman pronounced: "Men may have called the march . . . , but women are a major force behind it. Women usually lead any crusade. They don't always get front-line notice, but they're there, and their force is felt."[54]

This is important context for understanding Omega Psi Phi's role in the struggle to advance civil rights protections as Hedgeman, Omega men, and several other participants in the March on Washington called on Congress to pass a pending civil rights bill. President John F. Kennedy, who seemed to disfavor the march, supported passage of the bill. A vocal bloc of members of Congress stanchly opposed the bill and cited the activities of Hedgeman and other march participants, especially leaders such as King, to help justify its opposition. As per one of the congressmen's most hackneyed arguments, most supporters of the bill were communists.[55]

Kennedy believed American citizens, federal officials included, needed to address racial problems in the country peacefully. Observers worldwide, he noted, saw televised coverage, or listened to radio broadcasts of clashes in Birmingham, Alabama, and elsewhere in the United States between nonviolent protesters and violent counterprotesters including law enforcement personnel. That the US government continued to send military troops to Vietnam ostensibly pursuant to promoting democracy and stopping the spread of communism made domestic chaos in the United States even more troubling for the Kennedy administration.

Omega Psi Phi Grand Basileus Cary D. Jacobs endorsed Kennedy's call for peaceful solutions to the nation's racial problems, but he disapproved of Kennedy's reservations about the utility of the March on Washington and other forms of nonviolent mass resistance. Jacobs, in a commentary featured in the September 1963 issue of *The Oracle*, conveyed delight that Omega men were at the fore of freedom fighting in "every Community, City, Town, and Hamlet" in the country.[56] Jacobs acknowledged the "courageous leadership" that Second Vice Grand Basileus Jesse L. Jackson was providing in the movement generally and in North Carolina specifically.[57] "Brothers, the Battle for Freedom and Jobs, NOW, is on," Jacobs proposed. "We have given our time, money and energy in this movement. [We] cannot afford to rest on our record, good as it is. We must gird our loins, grit our teeth and strain our purse, and thus, continue to do our part in helping those who are bearing the burden in the heat of the day to carry the load, so that when the battle has been fought and the victory has been won, we can then look back over a well spent life."[58]

Although the March on Washington was successful and Grand Basileus Jacobs's post-march exhortation was moving, it did not take long for White terrorists to make clear that Jacobs was correct about the marchers, Omega men, and other citizens who desired justice and equality not being able to rest on their records. On Sunday, September 15, 1963, at least four members of the Ku Klux Klan bombed the Sixteenth Street Baptist Church in Birmingham, Alabama. They used no fewer than fifteen sticks of dynamite. Four Black girls—Addie Mae Collins, Carol Denise McNair, Carole Rosamond Robertson, and Cynthia Dionne Wesley—who ranged in age from eleven to fourteen years old died because of the bombing. The Klansmen chose Sixteenth Street Baptist because, owing to its long history of civil rights activity and downtown location, the church often was a starting point for protest marches and other demonstrations. Sixteenth Street Baptist also served as a training facility for students engaged in civil disobedience activities—even the events months earlier in Birmingham. The Klansmen's murdering of the aforementioned "four beautiful and innocent little girls" as they fellowshipped inside the church heightened international attention to the demoniac depths to which certain bigoted White Americans would stoop to prevent equality in the United States, especially its southern region.[59]

Omega man Emory Overton Jackson, long-time editor of the *Birmingham World* newspaper and an ardent civil rights proponent, was appalled but not surprised by Klansmen bombing the Sixteenth Street Baptist Church. Though born in Buena Vista, Georgia, Jackson was reared in Birmingham, which many people referred to as "Bombingham" by the early 1960s because of violent White supremacists' decades-long use of bombs against Black and other non-White citizens, particularly freedom fighters.[60] Jackson earned a bachelor of arts degree from Morehouse College in Atlanta, Georgia, in 1932 and then returned to Alabama, where he taught school in Dothan and later in Birmingham before accepting a staff position at the *Birmingham World*. He became editor of the paper in 1941. A devoted member of the Alpha Phi chapter and the NAACP, Jackson questioned the use of mass direct action, even if it were nonviolent, to produce long-term positive societal change. Accordingly, he had begun to distance himself from civil rights leaders, such as King, by the time Klansmen dynamited the Sixteenth Street Baptist in 1963. In the wake of the deadly act, which Jackson covered thoroughly, he telegrammed the parents of Collins, McNair, Robertson, and Wesley. Jackson printed the telegrams in the *Birmingham World*. As noted by his autobiographer, Kimberley Mangun, he assured the parents "that he and the newspaper's staff would do their part to ensure that the girls had not died in vain[, and one] important way to honor their memory was to continue the fight for suffrage."[61]

A second personal tragedy with civil rights and federal policy implications that Jackson covered in the *Birmingham World* occurred on November 22, 1963. While greeting the public from the backseat of a 1961 open-top Lincoln Continental in Dallas, Texas, three bullets were shot at US president John F. Kennedy.[62] The first bullet entered and exited Kennedy's neck but was not fatal.[63] The second bullet, which entered his head, was fatal, and the third bullet missed him.[64] Authorities soon arrested and arraigned Lee Harvey Oswald for assassinating Kennedy. Two days later, on November 24, Jack Ruby shot and killed Oswald at the local police department.[65]

Jackson, writing about Kennedy in one 1963 editorial, described him as a "man of courage and a 'symbol of freedom for all liberty-loving persons.'"[66] Jackson nonetheless "wondered how historians would assess [Kennedy's] legacy and place among other presidents, especially because he didn't have an opportunity to finish his term in office."[67] Another editorial Jackson wrote after Kennedy's assassination emphasized the necessity to sustain the fight for equality. "The struggle for civil rights must go on and be won," Jackson proposed, "for the good of our nation and for the benefit of" humankind.[68] But *The Oracle* published an editorial about Kennedy that was more somber: "At long last, the Black man of this nation and in the world had now a friend in high places, at last the cause had a champion, and at last the Negro in America was on his way toward complete emancipation. His death was a great loss to them. His appearance at this time brought new hope, new vision and new 'vigor' to this nation, let us pray that he has not died in vain."[69]

Surviving the Squalling Sixties

Omega Psi Phi's national leaders were quite vocal about civil rights matters during the first fifty years of the Fraternity's existence from 1911 to 1961. During the next few years, however, the leaders were noticeably quiet about the murders of civil rights icons. For example, not a single 1964 issue of *The Oracle* referenced Mississippian Medgar Evers. *The Oracle* was comparably silent about New York based Malcolm X in 1965, and made only a vague reference to James Chaney, an implied murder victim in "the Mississippi murder of three," in 1964.[70]

Omega's national leadership reacted much differently to the assassinations of other civil rights dignitaries than to Evers, Malcolm X, and Chaney. When US president John Fitzgerald Kennedy was gunned down in Dallas, Texas, in 1963, an *Oracle* editorial remembered him as a "real friend" and a "young man [who] brought to his office boundless energy and with it . . . new hope and aspirations to other young men."[71] According to the editorial, Kennedy served as a "champion" for Black people who, with the help of his administration, were on their way "to complete emancipation."[72] Continuing to honor the slain president, the editorial deemed his "death ... a great loss," as Kennedy "brought new hope, new vision, and new 'vigor' to this nation," and asserted, "let us pray that he has not died in vain."[73] Honoring Kennedy openly with little acknowledgment of Evers or Malcolm X, and only referencing Chaney inexplicitly, suggested the Fraternity's conservative leadership during the early to mid-1960s perceived the latter martyrs as controversial.

While Omega's national leaders were reserved about certain civil rights icons during the mid- to late 1960s, the Fraternity's leaders were enthusiastic about the continued renaissance of Black expressive culture, which echoed cultural, economic, financial, and political activities of the period. Omega men in all districts assisted in developing the talents of youth as a major venture in the Fraternity's social action program, and such mentorship hardly was new. Since 1946, when the Sixth District initiated the talent hunt, the Fraternity had supported established and experimental artists to help make their creations accessible to society.[74] As stated in a 1963 issue of *The Oracle*, Omega's national talent hunt committee encouraged all members of the Fraternity to contact "public school and private music teachers, soliciting their aid to secure the best musical talents available."[75] With a large trend of the Black Arts Movement witnessed through the efforts of activist LeRoi Jones, born in Newark, New Jersey (né Everett Leroy Jones [known later as Imamu Ameer Baraka and later still as Amiri Baraka]), among other Black nationalist personalities, Omega's national officers furthered this trend through the Fraternity's talent hunt committee to demonstrate that expressive culture often resulted from social, political, economic, and cultural movements such as civil rights and Black Power.

By 1964, a new energy was building in the streets as well as in the Fraternity. Omega men remained energized into 1965. In May, a White minister named Samuel Sharpp gave a plenary address titled "The Responsibility of the Negro College Man in Today's Civil Rights Struggle" during the Fourth District's twenty-fifth annual meeting in Youngstown, Ohio.[76] Considering that Black people in the United States had been legally free for fewer than one hundred years, Sharpp declared, Black men attending colleges and universities had very demanding obligations in the struggle for equality.[77] Perhaps Sharpp knew that the White America, from whence he hailed, would never be assuaged by nonviolent action and demanded more, which was a stark departure from the nonviolent direct action preferred by his ministerial contemporary, Martin L. King Jr., and implemented by Omega man Bayard Rustin, among numberless other civil rights activists. Whether this was the case or not, the coming wave, Black Power, was complimented by Malcolm X, motivated by the defiant southern manhood of Muhammad Ali, who exemplified courage and pride, and flanked by student activity and the rise of revolutionary organizations such as the Lowndes County Freedom Organization, in Alabama, and the Black Panther Party for Self-Defense.[78]

In 1964, a year before the Lowndes County Freedom Organization popularized the slogan "Black Power for Black People," Omega men held their Forty-Ninth Grand Conclave in Denver, Colorado with a theme of "Human Dignity, Ballots, and Freedom."[79] They met from August 16 to 20. During a plenary session on August 18, Fraternity founder and Methodist bishop Edgar Amos Love delivered an address he titled "Human Dignity, Ballots and Freedom," which adhered to the theme of the Forty-Ninth Grand Conclave.[80] Here, George E. Meares, Grand Basileus, Ellis F. Corbett, First Vice Grand Basileus, Dorsey C. Miller, Second Vice Grand Basileus, Walter H. Riddick, Grand Keeper of Records and Seal, Jesse B. Blayton, Grand Keeper of Finance, Audrey Pruitt, editor-in-chief of *The Oracle*, and Marion W. Garnett, Grand Counselor, were elected.[81] Among other acts, Love tied ongoing Black political changes to the actual core values of his three Omega Psi Phi founders and him as well as to the purported core values of the White men who founded the United States. Love not only illustrated how his personal views on dignity were rooted in his understanding of faith, but he also threaded definitions of Omega's four cardinal principles—manhood, scholarship, perseverance, and uplift—with the altruism of American representative government and the necessity of Black citizens to be active political participants. In one particularly rousing segment of his address, Love challenged his fellow Omega men to use their influence to encourage participation in American democracy:

> When we speak of ballots, we visualize the opportunity, responsibility, and duty to vote. In voting, we make an assertion, an affirmation and a declaration of approval or protest. This is a legal right of every American citizen. However, too many of our citizens are denied this right which is equivalent to the negation of freedom.
>
> When we speak of freedom, we visualize liberty as the right to make a choice, the right to vote and the right to exercise discretion. Thomas Jefferson said, "the God who gave us life gave us liberty at the same time." This brief analytical statement of the four cardinal principles of the Omega Psi Phi Fraternity and the theme for this year, involve many challenges which we face and must, with courage, stand our ground. America and the world, torn and divided by opposing ideologies, face a great challenge.[82]

While Love delivered those words at Colorado in the Mountain West, a voter registration campaign known popularly as Freedom Summer was underway at Mississippi in the Deep South. Aaron Edd Henry and other campaign leaders who belonged to Omega Psi Phi validated the Fraternity's resolve to increase Black political strength. Insofar as registering Black Mississippians to vote required the bravery of manhood, the discretion of scholarship, the grit of perseverance, and the compassion of uplift, Love's venerating the vote complemented the mass struggle that Omega men such as Henry led during Freedom Summer. Concurrently, the Fraternity's undertaking of cultivating leaders and building schools aligned calculated efforts for similar resources to those in need while Freedom Summer organizers pushed the envelope through voter registration. Though the passage of the Voting Rights Act of 1965 was universal, Congress embedded certain terms in the act to deal with states where it specifically eliminated literacy tests and other devices in areas where less than 50 percent of the adults were able to vote previously, Black and other multiracial people registered to vote and began to assert their political might within a few years of the act becoming law.[83] Mississippi had 28,500 Black registered voters in 1965 and 406,000 in 1968, an increase from 6.7 percent of voting-eligible Black Mississippians to 59.4 percent.[84]

While the world watched Americans being beaten in Selma, Alabama, voting was not the only major issue for civil rights. During this same period, Omega men in that state and elsewhere in the country made improving healthcare availability for elderly and other vulnerable American citizens a central feature in their social action programs. In 1966, US vice-president Hubert Horatio Humphrey Jr. congratulated former Omega Psi Phi Grand Basileus Lawrence August Oxley on his vital role in the campaign to secure passage of Medicare and Medicaid legislations, formally the Social Security Amendments of 1965.[85] For years, Oxley had been director of special programs for the National Council of Senior Citizens and, as per one source, his family friend and US attorney general Robert Francis Kennedy asked him to lobby Congress to pass the Medicare legislation, which White physicians in the American Medical Association (AMA) described as "socialized medicine."[86]

In 1965, Oxley and a second Omega man, William Montague Cobb, flew with President Lyndon Baines Johnson to the Medicare and Medicaid law signing ceremony in Independence, Missouri, hometown of former American president Harry S. Truman.[87] Oxley and Cobb's flying with Johnson was doubly important to those Omega men. In addition to Oxley's aforementioned lobbying efforts, Cobb, as president of the predominately Black National Medical Association (NMA), for eight years tried to get AMA officers and regular members to discuss the color line during various conferences the NMA sponsored or cosponsored, but his attempts were unsuccessful. The AMA sent representatives to the Imhotep National Conference on Hospital Integration the NMA cosponsored with the NAACP and the Medico-Chirurgical Society of the District of Columbia on May 8 and 9, 1957; however, AMA officers rejected future invitations from the NMA to participate in its conferences, and they refused to allow non-White physicians to participate in AMA conferences and related AMA events before Johnson's signing of the Civil Rights Act of 1964 into law on July 2 forced the AMA to break its color line.[88] A year later, during the July 30 Medicare and Medicaid law signing ceremony, at which Oxley and Cobb sat next to Truman, Cobb praised Johnson for his continued commitment to health-care expansion as well as to "ending racial discrimination from American life."[89] In scholar Beatrix Hoffman's judgment, Johnson clearly believed the Social Security Amendments of 1965 would not have become law without the unceasing advocacy of Omega men such as Oxley and Cobb.[90]

More than 690 Omega men journeyed to Detroit, Michigan, in December 1965 for the Fiftieth Grand Conclave held at the Sheraton-Cadillac Hotel, welcomed by addresses from Fraternity founder Edgar Amos Love, Grand Marshal Wendell F. Cox of the Nu Omega chapter, and a host of other speakers. Here, delegates reelected George E. Meares as Grand Basileus, Ellis F. Corbett as First Vice Grand Basileus, Walter H. Riddick as Grand Keeper of Records and Seal, Jesse B. Blayton as Grand Keeper of Finance, Audrey Pruitt as editor-in-chief of *The Oracle*, and Marion W. Garnett as Grand Counselor. The only change in the grand officers was the election of Harold D. Thompson as Second Vice Grand Basileus.[91]

Black Power

On July 5, 1966, nearly a year after Johnson's signature effectuated the Social Security Amendments on July 30,[92] James Meredith, a Black US Air Force veteran from Kosciusko, Mississippi, set out on a 210-mile "march against fear" from Memphis, Tennessee, to Jackson, Mississippi, about seventy-one miles southwest of Kosciusko.[93] His march made headlines, as he was shot by Aubrey James Norvell, an unemployed White gunman who shot Meredith three times while hiding in the bushes. But Meredith was no stranger to media publicity; as previously mentioned, he became the first known Black person to be graduated from the University of Mississippi in Oxford on August 18, 1963.

Even though Omega Psi Phi Grand Basileus and 1938 Epsilon chapter initiate George E. Meares was a well-educated man and an educator with myriad experiences dealing with all sorts of personalities, he did not attempt to psychoanalyze Aubrey James Norvell while drafting a line about the Meredith shooting for the fall 1966 issue of *The Oracle*.[94] Instead, Meares—who attended Johnson C. Smith University, completed his undergraduate studies at New York University, performed graduate work in the Atlanta University School of Social Work, and served Omega Psi Phi in numerous capacities including First Vice Grand Basileus—predicted the shooting and similarly cruel "acts are certain to add additional laws to our statutes whose ultimate goal is to end discrimination in theory as well as in practice; to close the gap between the ideals we have professed in American life and the unsatisfactory reality in which we live."[95] Meares revisited the shooting in an article featured in the winter 1966 issue of *The Oracle*. Aware that undergraduate members of the Fraternity were front and center in a postshooting protest march during which non-member Stokely Carmichael of the Student Nonviolent Coordinating Committee (SNCC) reiterated the need for Black Power, Meares warned Omega men about "the great 'backlash' [the] cries for 'Black Power' set into motion."[96] Meares believed those cries, made loudest by students, inflamed White voters who, in turn, supported White supremacist office seekers like Georgia gubernatorial candidate Lester Garfield Maddox Sr.[97] "It is worth noting," Meares wrote, "that Carmichael and his ilk did a great disservice in fostering Black Power and the Black Panther Party in Lowndes County, Alabama. In that County, where the Negro is 80% of the population and the entire slate of Negro candidates was offered the people—not one was elected."[98]

Meares's remarks in the winter 1966 *Oracle* reflected a growing conservatism among many Black leaders as freedom protests grew more assertive than numerous earlier protests. Meares granted that unrest in places such as Oakland, California, Cleveland, Ohio, Chicago, Illinois, and Atlanta, Georgia, was warranted. At the same time, he thought national guardsmen suppressing the unruly behavior of "Negro snipers, rioters, arsonists, looters and brick throwers" also was warranted.[99] Focusing on the South, where the 1965 federal voting rights law caused the number of Black people registered to vote to increase exponentially, Meares worried that, even in places with large Black voting populations, "a candidate too thoroughly identified with a Negro movement" did not stand a reasonable chance of winning a popular election, particularly against "a white man's candidate."[100] In essence, Black Power, in Meares's estimation, was a "kiss of death" that, besides killing any opportunity for a candidate associated with that principle to hold public office, "gave Congress the strength to kill the 1966 Civil Rights Bill."[101] Meares therefore gave full-throated support to the notion that "the Negro revolution is moving 'too fast.'"[102]

Meares understood the vicious cycle of second-class citizenship for Black Americans. As access to public accommodations, educational opportunities, voting privileges, and related staples of citizenship expanded, Black Americans set their eyes on securing even more fundamental liberties. When the latter occurrence proved to be a "dream deferred," to borrow language from Omega man and brilliant writer Langston Hughes, Black Americans experienced resentment compounded by the "frustrations and indignities" of previous generations, Meares suggested.[103] But, inasmuch as "too fast in the Senate is too slow in the ghetto," Meares placed blame on certain Black people themselves—singularly, lower socioeconomic lawbreakers—for not achieving first-class citizenship.[104]

In Meares's opinion, Black Americans' twentieth-century struggle for human and civil rights developed in three phases, though not entirely linear. Legal, or constitutional, was phase one. It encompassed the formation of the NAACP in 1909, the US Supreme Court *Brown v. Board of Education of Topeka* rulings in 1954 and 1955, and unnamed rulings by the same court in the 1960s.[105] Congressional passage of civil rights bills in 1957, 1960, and 1964, the Twenty-Fourth Amendment abolishing poll taxes in 1964, and the 1965 Voting Rights Act marked phase two, which also was legislative.[106] Implying the Black Power movement was phase three, Meares described it as "rioting and street fighting in the great cities, not only in the North but in the South as well."[107] Meares elaborated, "The first two phases were necessary, meaningful and productive. The third was not helpful but rather destructive and our [Black Americans'] only defense comes from an explanation—it is in part the outcome of mass grievances and of combustible social conditions."[108]

Meares's arguments were provocative. Had not Black Americans been constructive, intelligent, responsible citizens before members of the Lowndes County Freedom Organization, Stokely Carmichael, and others in SNCC, among other individuals, began employing the phrase *Black Power*? Had Black Americans not been brave, noble, and patriotic officers, soldiers, and support personnel in wars, believing the US Constitution one day would safeguard their present and future lives and livelihoods? Meares, looking through a Black middle- to upper-class lens, placed blame on lower-class Black Americans, blaming them for their plight and acting as if he knew what was best for the Black masses.[109] Moreover, those masses included many undergraduates and some graduates in Omega Psi Phi who were drawn to Black Power through student activism and who were unwilling to wait for positive societal change, as had their foreparents. Ignoring those facts, Meares contended the "crisis of this third phase of the civil rights revolution is really a crisis inside the Negro leadership. It must be resolved by them."[110] Though news media elevated Martin King Jr. and later Carmichael to a position of *the* leader of the civil rights movement, the movement actually had thousands of leaders. In relation to Omega Psi Phi, numerous members of the Fraternity who embraced

Black Power strategies and tactics balanced Meares's distaste for Black Power (i.e., the movement), but they and he continued to fight for positive change.

Great Migrations of a Different Kind

For very simple reasons, many Black students in the South who sought to pursue certain graduate or professional study for much of the early twentieth century had to attend institutions outside that region to do so.[111] Segregationist White state officials in the South often partnered with northern and midwestern colleges and universities to offer out-of-state scholarship programs for Black students, reimbursing the students for travel, tuition, and select other fees. Such programs ensured graduate and professional schools in the South would remain segregated, while the northern and midwestern colleges and universities accepting Black students from the South enjoyed revenues generated from double tuitions.[112] The US Supreme Court declared such programs unconstitutional in 1950 but, even after the court ended de jure segregation, countless Black Americans were skeptical about enrolling in or engaging with southern predominantly White schools.[113] Thus, Omega Psi Phi partnered with northeastern and midwestern colleges and universities to continue pipelining Black students who sought quality graduate and professional educations in desegregated environments. This model, proving to be effective, opened doors for all college programs of equal significance. According to *The Oracle*, citing the *Wall Street Journal*, the number of Black students who enrolled in desegregated colleges or universities was 70 percent higher in the fall of 1965 than the fall of 1964.[114]

Even though there were good reasons for aspiring Black graduate and professional students in the South to attend predominantly White colleges and universities in their home states after court-ordered desegregation in 1950 and onward, their attending those colleges and universities marked serious challenges to the enrollments of historically Black colleges and universities (HBCUs), of which most were in the southern region. Known today as the "Black brain drain," the phrase describes familiar attendance and employment patterns in education prior to, during, and following desegregation.[115] Omega man and scholar Maurice Hobson explained, "Before Blacks were allowed to attend or be employed at state-supported and traditionally white institutions of higher learning, large northern universities hired away top faculty from southern universities. . . . Because good black professors attracted good black students," some students went to White colleges and universities to study under those professors.[116] Omega man James Phillip Holland, a 1953 Psi Psi initiate, was one such professor.

Holland was born in Bowling Green, Kentucky, in 1934. He attended a local high school called State Street, earning valedictory honors in 1952. He then enrolled at Kentucky State College (now University). As mentioned in chapter 4, US senator John Sherman Cooper nominated him to the US Military Academy at West Point during his sophomore year. Despite being the first Black student to win a nomination from anyone representing Kentucky in Congress, Holland remained at Kentucky State, finishing magna cum laude in 1956. He then earned a master of science and PhD degree in endocrinology from Indiana University at Bloomington in 1958 and 1961, respectively. He earned a postdoctoral research fellowship from the University of Wisconsin system and instructed science courses at Howard University in Washington, DC, before joining the faculty at his alma mater, Indiana. A brilliant instructor who promoted the value of ethnic diversity, Holland started the Ernest Everett Just Organization in Biology at the latter university. Named after an Omega Psi Phi founder, Dartmouth alumnus, and Howard professor who became the first Black man in the country to earn a doctorate in both zoology and physiology, the organization that Holland began at Indiana extended educational opportunities for Black students at that university.[117]

In 1966, as Holland conducted breakthrough scientific research, advanced his career in the academy, and mentored students, another Omega Psi Phi founder whom Holland revered, Edgar A. Love, continued to demonstrate his commitment to the Fraternity. In an April letter to the membership, Love mentioned delegates to the Detroit Conclave authorizing the formation of a committee to examine the "internal structure of the Fraternity, including a complete study of the ritual, constitution, by-laws, operating structure and current programs of the Fraternity."[118] Grand Basileus George Meares appointed the committee and named Love, a two-time Grand Basileus, as chairman. Love celebrated Omega's fifty-four-year existence but, considering its duration, suggested a review of the Fraternity's "whole machinery" to determine if other items might need revamping or overhauling to prepare to help ensure the future success of the Fraternity.[119]

Love's letter to his fellow Omega men appeared in the May issue of *The Oracle*. In that same issue, other challenges faced by the Fraternity's national leaders were addressed. Monetary concerns were foremost. According to Harold D. Thompson, Second Vice Grand Basileus, 80 percent of the men who pledged Omega Psi Phi were unfinancial. A lack of undergraduate fraternity houses, weak relationships between undergraduates and graduates, and more effective recruitment mechanisms were three matters plaguing the Fraternity in Thompson's judgment. Additionally, he explained, "Omega Psi Phi is entering a period of great fraternal and social uncertainty in which external pressures, such as academic and political institutions, as well as other Greek organizations, are seeking to crush us."[120] Though unmentioned by Thompson, the worsening conflict in Vietnam was an additional external pressure that bore on the Fraternity. Excepting Vietnam, a military issue that could have a direct effect on large numbers of draft-eligible Omega men but whose resolution principally was beyond their control, Thompson believed many of the foregoing challenges, uncertainties, and pressures seemed irreconcilable, "but they seem this way only because we make them so," he concluded.[121]

As the committee Love chaired investigated the need to overhaul the machinery of Omega Psi Phi, and as Thompson requested all members do their respective parts to secure a strong future for the Fraternity, a sobering set of events unfolded that paralleled the significance of those worthy efforts. On February 24, 1967, founder Frank Coleman died at Freedmen's Hospital in Washington, DC, after a lengthy illness. His death left another void in the Fraternity, as founder Ernest Everett Just transitioned on October 27, 1941. Similar to Just, the passing of Coleman impacted the entire community where he resided as well as Howard University. As an editorial in the spring 1967 issue of *The Oracle* recognized, Coleman identified with Howard for more than fifty years. The quintessential race man, Coleman was active in public affairs but had affinity for civic organizations devoted to guiding youth and encouraging positive community relations. A devoted member of the Calvary Episcopal Church, he worked tirelessly to assist any sick or shut-in member, among other godly deeds.[122] As a student, an alumnus, and a professor for more than forty years, Frank Coleman had committed his best talents to Howard University and was remembered as one of the university's most loyal sons.

As regards to Omega Psi Phi, Coleman saw the Fraternity as a powerful institution whose members could help Americans citizens of all backgrounds and complexions enjoy freedom and equality. Evidence of his humanitarian worldview was plentiful. During the academic year 1913–14, he worked at the Joseph Keasley Brick Agricultural, Industrial, and Normal School in Enfield, North Carolina. Coleman's patriotism and interest in military affairs did not wane during peacetime. Eventually, he cofounded the James E. Walker Post 26 of American Legion in Washington, DC, and he worked both as a member of the Area Boards and as a member of the appeals with the Selective Service boards in Washington, DC. Coleman's civic engagement was equally as notable as his military engagement. Among other activities, he worked with the District of Columbia Board of Public Welfare, the District of Columbia Motor Vehicle Parking Agency, as well as the Board of Directors of the Twelfth Street YMCA and the Saint Anna's Home for the Aged. Coleman exemplified the true essence of an Omega man and, for that reason, Omega men, chapters, and districts from across the United States paid their respects at his memorial service inside Rankin Chapel at Howard University on February 28, 1967. Clergyman James O. West officiated, and Grand Chaplain H. Albion Ferrell assisted. Ferrell along with founders Edgar Love and Oscar James Cooper, Grand Basileus George Meares, Executive Secretary H. Carl Moultrie, and Grand Keepers of Records and Seal Walter H. Riddick represented the Fraternity officially.[123]

Not long after Coleman's homegoing, his widow, Mabel Raymond Coleman, penned a note to Ferrell, stating the "conventional little cards which I shall be mailing very soon cannot sufficiently express my gratitude to you for the rites you conducted as Chaplain of the great Omega Psi Phi Fraternity, Inc."[124] She continued, "I am deeply grateful for everything everyone has done to help me bear the terrible loss of a wonderful husband."[125] Omega men appreciated the gesture and, as a suitable testament to their second departed founder, recommitted themselves to the Fraternity and its four cardinal principles: manhood, scholarship, perseverance, and uplift. Omega men embodied those principles when they met in Boston, Massachusetts, from August 12 to 17 for the Fifty-First Grand Conclave hosted by Gamma, Eta Phi, and Iota Chi chapters. The theme for this conclave was "Opportunities for Fraternities in a Changing Educational World." Here, Omega delegates elected Ellis Franklin Corbett as Grand Basileus.[126] Corbett stressed the need for Omega Psi Phi to extend its history of strong leadership in American society. Problems stemming from or associated with crime, health and health care, inadequate housing, poverty, quality education, a dearth of recreational outlets, and unemployment were the main areas on which Corbett called on Omega men to lead.[127]

In the wake of the Boston Conclave, Robert L. Gill, author of *The Omega Psi Phi Fraternity and the Men Who Made Its History: A Concise History*, offered additional encouragement for Omega men to be community leaders.[128] In an article featured in the winter 1967 issue of *The Oracle*, he inquired:

> What do we want Omega to be? We want our Fraternity to represent unity, loyalty, and discipline from every one of its sons. . . . What do we want Omega to be? A civil rights organization? (NAACP, CORE, SNCC, SCLC) A political party? (Democrat, Republican, Liberal, Conservative) An alumni association? . . . A neighborhood club? . . . No—your historian does not want his Fraternity to become either one of those [organizations]. But he wants to see Omega men involved in all of them. . . .
>
> The burdens upon a son of Omega in an open society are heavy. The pitfalls in community action are many if we are to help educate, elevate, and ennoble the less fortunate in the inner city and the rural areas: Our actions will be misinterpreted by others and efforts will be made no

doubt by selfish interests to mislead those whom we are trying to help and to misrepresent their best interests, when what we are doing was our sole aim.[129]

Gill presented a series of questions and answers that fell squarely between civil rights and Black Power. The turbulence of the 1960s had shaken American society to its core and, if Omega Psi Phi was to be at the fore of Black freedom, Gill, in 1967, proposed he and his fellow Omega men had much to consider. Understanding that government entities had few programs that addressed the specific needs of Black communities, Omega Psi Phi recalibrated old programs and created new ones that national officials, such as Corbett and Gill, mandated all individual members and chapters carry out. Of these programs, the memorials, achievement, scholarship, and social action were foremost. In establishing those initiatives, Corbett, Gill, and others in the national officer corps gave new meaning to the Fraternity's raison d'être—specifically, that Omega should aid in the elevation, education, and ennoblement of those less fortunate in urban and rural areas. They called on every son of Omega, to quote Gill, to reexamine his individual contribution to the Fraternity.[130]

As Gill queried Omega men implicitly about their commitment to the Fraternity's cardinal principles, other Omegas explored the Fraternity's National Achievement Week theme, "Wanted: Solutions to the Problems of America's Urban Society."[131] Members throughout the country held private or public programs from November 5 to 12 featuring local or national eminences. As Omega men and their guests attended those programs, the tempest between certain White and non-White Americans that accounted for many problems in urban society continued to brew. A few months earlier, on July 28, US president Lyndon Johnson assembled an eleven-member National Advisory Commission on Civil Disorders and tasked its members with investigating the causes of the oftentimes destructive and nearly always costly mass demonstrations (rebellions, revolts, riots, uprisings) that had taken place in majority Black or Latino neighborhoods in places such as Watts in Los Angeles, California, from August 11 to 16, 1965; along Division Street in Chicago, Illinois, from June 12 to 14, 1966; in Newark, New Jersey, from July 12 to 17, 1967; and along Twelfth Street in Detroit, Michigan, from July 23 to 28, 1967. Nicknamed the Kerner Commission after its chairman, Illinois governor Otto Kerner Jr., the commission had a second task: recommending ways the federal government could help prevent the types of demonstrations Omega Psi Phi Grand Basileus George Meares chided certain Black Americans for carrying out.[132] While the commission was formed in July 1967, the final report from Kerner and his committee peers was released on February 29, 1968.

They concluded that White racism—not anarchistic, lawbreaking, uncivilized, low-class street fighters, and looters, to paraphrase Meares—was the primary cause of demonstrations.[133]

The Kerner Commission prescribed creating jobs, constructing new housing units, dismantling de facto segregation, and ending poverty as principal means to prevent demonstrations in the future.[134] A month after the commission released its report in February 1968, and civil unrest in certain areas of the United States continued to swell, members of the Beta chapter of Omega Psi Phi at Lincoln University in Pennsylvania, led by chapter Basileus Cordell Richardson, hosted a day-long Black Identity Conference inside the Mary Dodd Memorial Chapel on March 30.[135] Because Beta chapter wanted to be at the fore of the Black Arts Movement, as the university held a strong fine arts department, the conference celebrated the Black Arts Movement, the expressive arm of Black Power, where chapter members organized lectures about history and politics by renowned scholars, and highlighted the pageantry of Blackness and Black artistic expression by featuring Samba dancers and an art show by Beta members Marvin Kelly and Bobby O'Neil. However, the showpiece of the conference came when heavyweight boxer and social justice champion Muhammad Ali delivered the keynote address.[136] In one memorable line, Ali told the crowd: "I don't need to ask you how you are—if you're Black . . . , I know you're catching hell. I'm the champion of the world and I'm still catching hell."[137] Further evidence of Beta chapter's investment with the Black Art Movement include its sponsored activities, such as hosting Gil-Scott Heron, who was a journalist for the school newspaper "The Lincolnian."[138]

Ali was a lightning rod for American controversy by 1968. Born Cassius Marcellus Clay Jr. at Louisville, Kentucky, in 1942, he secretly converted to the Nation of Islam in 1963. Ali, however, did not announce his conversion until 1964, whereupon he demanded people call him Ali and revealed his close affiliations with ministers Elijah Muhammad (né Elijah Robert Poole) and Malcolm X. In 1967, two years after Malcolm X's assassination, Ali refused to allow federal military officials to draft him into the US Army during the Vietnam conflict. Ali petitioned the officials for a conscientious objector status, but they rejected his petition. Ali stood firm and consequently dealt with being stripped of his heavyweight championship, sentenced to prison, and fined $100,000 by the US Selective Service. The US Supreme Court intervened, so Ali did not have to serve prison time, but his stance on the draft and American military involvement in Vietnam made him a pariah to millions of mainstream American citizens, especially White citizens, and an even larger hero for millions more Black, mixed race, and humanitarian White citizens.[139]

College-age Black men were particularly supportive of Ali. Their respect helped make him one of the most sought-after speakers in the United States. At the Black Identity Conference, the Beta chapter of Omega Psi Phi hosted on March 30, 1968, Ali spoke for nearly two hours before a capacity crowd of cheering students. The prize fighter-turned-Muslim minister called for more Black-related instruction at HBCUs and more unity and self-love for Black people and by Black people. Beta's hosting Ali ran counter to George Meares's rejection of Black Power as a strategy for achieving Black America's needs. As a subordinate chapter of the Second District and the national office, Beta had the autonomy needed to execute programs that held fast to the standards of the Fraternity's mandated programs. In inviting Ali, Beta's membership demonstrated that the winds of change were full blown to further redefine Black agency and activism, even within Omega Psi Phi.[140]

Turbulent Times

Five days after Ali's March 1968 speech at Lincoln University in Pennsylvania, a horrific incident occurred in Memphis, Tennessee, that lent force to Ali's contention about Black Americans catching hell. On April 4, a White assassin shot and killed Martin King Jr. People throughout the world mourned his death. In the United States, places such as Detroit, Michigan, Chicago, Illinois, Washington, DC, and Los Angeles, California, reeled and sweltered from literal and figurative heat caused by violent eruptions. Omega man Jesse L. Jackson Sr. was particularly affected by King's assassination: he was one of the final persons to see him alive. Jackson served as a pallbearer when Coretta Scott King laid her martyred husband to rest on April 9. King's assassination frustrated many Omega men, while angering many others, but the King tragedy also served to motivate Omegas to situate themselves more firmly as major forces in the quest for freedom and equality to which King committed himself. While specific Omega men such as Epsilon Phi's Memphis race man Benjamin Hooks were further motivated by the assassination, Grand Basileus Ellis F. Corbett, and other Omega men were at the fore of a campaign to expand adequate living accommodations for all citizens, answering the call to further King's efforts. Toward that end, Omega Psi Phi supported congressional passage of the Civil Rights, or Fair Housing, Act of 1968. Understanding the significance of King's martyrdom, US president Lyndon Johnson made a personal appeal to congressmen on April 5 to pass the act. They complied, and he signed the act into law on April 11, exactly one week after King took his final breath.[141]

The 1968 civil rights law was fewer than two months old when another politically motivated assassination rocked the country. On June 5, Palestinian immigrant Sirhan Bishara Sirhan shot and killed Democratic presidential candidate and former US attorney general Robert Francis Kennedy as Kennedy campaigned in Los Angeles, California. Sirhan opposed Israeli expansion into the Gaza Strip and the West Bank, among other neighboring localities, and targeted Kennedy because he supported Israel on the campaign trail. The fatal shooting was one of several happenings that made the Democratic National Convention from August 26 to 29 in Chicago, Illinois, a focal point of political unrest. Widespread disgust about American involvement in the Vietnam conflict worsened turmoil at the convention. Even though Omega men such as Xi Omicron's John L. Cashin were present and working to advance civil and human rights as chairman of the National Democratic Party of Alabama, the winter issue of *The Oracle,* the official organ of Omega Psi Phi, made no major public statement about the chaos. Instead, *The Oracle* broadcast news about the upcoming Fifty-Second Grand Conclave in Charlotte, North Carolina, from December 26 to 30, 1968, hosted by the Rho and Pi Phi chapters.[142]

"Re-evaluating Omega" was the theme of the Charlotte Conclave, which wound up making national news.[143] While delegates reelected Ellis F. Corbett as Grand Basileus, an emphasis on differing visions for the Fraternity conveyed by delegates advocating Black Power and their more traditionalist contemporaries, the *New York Amsterdam News* dubbed the two factions the "Young Turks" and the "Old Guard," respectively.[144] According to the *Amsterdam News*, "militant" delegates were relentless in their Black Power advocacy, igniting "fireworks" as early as the opening session on December 26.[145] A report submitted by the Internal Structures Committee that Omega Psi Phi founder Edgar A. Love chaired was one fiery topic.[146] He and others on the committee recommended revising the constitution, bylaws, and rituals of the Fraternity.[147] Delegates accepted the recommendation, but they disagreed about the particulars of the revision process and who should guide the process.[148] The *Amsterdam News* indicated delegates spent two days debating those matters before agreeing to a constitutional convention on October 23–24 1969, in Atlanta, Georgia, whose guidelines the Supreme Council developed on March 29, 1969.[149]

With that agreement and related fraternity business handled, Love and his fellow Omega Psi Phi founder Oscar J. Cooper delivered banquet speeches on December 30, 1968. When they took their seats, presiding national officers rose from theirs to bestow awards. Jesse Jackson Sr. was one recipient. The Fraternity recognized him for his civil rights efforts. Finally, "the curtain came down on the 52nd Grand Conclave of the Omega Psi Fraternity," the *Amsterdam News* declared.[150] Before the newspaper concluded its coverage of the Charlotte Conclave, however, the paper declared the election or the reelection of

Old Guard, or traditionalist, officers such as Grand Basileus Ellis Corbett was a clear indication the Young Turks, or militants, were not going to change the general direction of the Fraternity too easily or too fast.[151]

Amid holding conclaves, revising governing documents, questioning policies and practices, debating competing fraternal and sociopolitical ideologies, recognizing civil rights activists or building new coalitions in the wake of new civil rights legislations, and maintaining high standards for admission into Omega Psi Phi, its existing members, as microcosms of other Black Americans, weathered storms and suffered losses during the late 1960s. For instance, past Grand Basileus Isham Gregory Newton died on October 3, 1965. Founder Frank Coleman passed away on February 24, 1967. Poet Langston Hughes transitioned on May 22, 1967. Their deaths and many recent others impacted Omega Psi Phi greatly by 1969 but, on June 13, 1969, local officials in New York City, softened the blow surviving Omega men felt by dedicating the Langston Hughes Apartments in Brooklyn. Those who attended the dedication remembered the apartments' namesake as a champion of Black people, holding aloft vistas of better days to come, especially regarding race relations. Ellis B. Weatherless, Basileus of the local Xi Phi graduate chapter, of which Hughes was a member, gave a speech at the apartments' dedication. Weatherless described Hughes as a "humanitarian [who] expressed concern for the well-being of all people. He inspired them to become great Americans, dedicating themselves to the betterment of our society in which all ethnic groups, regardless of race or creed, must learn to live together in an atmosphere of brotherly love."[152]

The group of Omega men responsible for organizing the constitutional convention scheduled for Atlanta, Georgia, on October 23 and 24, 1969, were optimistic about a spirit of brotherly love pervading every conventioneer. Revising the Omega Psi Phi constitution, bylaws, and ritual was a central purpose of the convention, which the Charlotte Conclave of December 26-29, 1968, mandated. Regrettably, a paucity of registered delegates in the first half of 1969 caused convention organizers to place a reminder and a warning in the summer issue of *The Oracle*: "Unless one more than one third of the total chapters register their delegates on or before September 24 . . . the convention will necessarily be cancelled."[153]

Ultimately, 300 delegates from 207 chapters attended the Atlanta convention in October 1969.[154] Of those 300 conventioneers, approximately one hundred were undergraduates.[155] In an editorial that seemed to approve the Black Power movement that older and more sociopolitical traditional Omega men such as former Grand Basileus George Meares despised, Robert Gregory of the Epsilon Alpha chapter remarked: "These young militants possessed all the fire, zeal and enthusiasm which typifies today's youth."[156]

Unlike Meares and comparably minded stalwarts, Omega men who represented "many of the elite and erudite college campuses across the nation" and who were content with simply being seen during their neophyte, prophyte, and subsequent undergraduate years, Gregory explained, "Today's undergraduate brothers must now be 'heard and seen,' and ... at Atlanta this was a living demonstration."[157] But, attempting to ensure no one misinterpreted his remarks to suggest that undergraduates were disruptive, Gregory declared that Executive Secretary H. Carl Moultrie "made it quite evident ... the convention was highly successful."[158] Among other agenda items, delegates completed revisions to the Omega Psi Phi constitution, bylaws, and ritual mandated by delegates to the Charlotte Conclave from December 26 to 30, 1968. Delegates to the Atlanta convention voted to make the revisions effective immediately after officer elections concluded during the Fifty-Third Grand Conclave in Pittsburgh, Pennsylvania, from August 1 to 6, 1970.[159]

While the Fraternity celebrated its golden anniversary, it suffered loss in the passing of founder Frank Coleman, Grand Basileus I. Gregory Newton, and famed poet Langston Hughes among countless others. The conditions outlined in this chapter present Omega Psi Phi's role in navigating the modern civil rights movement and Black Power. The diversity of Black experiences in the United States—whether college educated or not—gave purview to the issues tackled by the Fraternity, as Omega Psi Phi did its best to help mankind through its cardinal principle of uplift. Through these episodes, the Fraternity showed its might and versatility and the will to fight for all of humanity—whether political issues, education, employment, economics, or housing. However and unbeknownst, the Fraternity was gearing up for an even bigger fight—the rolling back of civil rights gains where White southern conservatives targeted voting. This served as the backdrop to the oncoming decade full of promise and pitfalls.

Chapter 6

Keeping Our Lamps Trimmed and Burning

Critical Crossroads in Omega Psi Phi Fraternity, 1970–1989

In 1970, the Fraternity had just passed one of its most transformative decades—the 1960s. For Omega men and the broader Black America, the lingering tension and symmetry between traditional civil rights approaches and the more assertive Black Power ethos carried over in the 1970s. In the traditional sense, new Omega men were prompted to continue leadership roles in the NAACP and the National Urban League. But as a byproduct of civil rights advances and urban unrest, some other Omega men were presented opportunities to become the first Black people to be hired into corporate America executive roles. Those notable milestones occurred just as the Fraternity's last two living founders—Oscar James Cooper and Edgar Amos Love—died in the early 1970s. Their deaths prompted deliberations among Omega men about how best to honor the founders' legacy and how to carry it forward.

The answer to those questions emerged in the latter half of the 1970s. In a rapidly evolving society, particularly for Black Americans, Omega men sought to memorialize key Black historical figures as an anchor to guide its National Social Action program into a new era. There was a call among Omega men to honor the past as a guide to the future. The Founders' Memorial was established, and several Omega men and notable Black women were recognized with historical markers across the United States. But nothing captured Omega men's dedication to Black advancement more than the federal government formally recognizing Black History Month—a testament to Omega man Carter G. Woodson and the Fraternity's efforts in the 1920s to study Black history and literature.

The 1980s, however, brought an urgency to old pressures. Societal issues related to drug abuse, the HIV and AIDS epidemic, and racial profiling by law enforcement warranted that Omega men step into new territory regarding their role in aiding American society. In turn, the Fraternity ramped up its efforts to register Black Americans to vote. That effort coincided with Omega man Jesse L. Jackson Sr.'s campaign to run for president of the United States. His presidential campaign embodied a changing of the guard: whereas some young activists of the 1960s, like Jackson, became involved in politics, some undergraduate Omega men in the 1980s called for greater unity in the Fraternity's quest to uplift its members and Black Americans writ large.

Therefore, this two-decade era set the stage for the modern Omega Psi Phi and its expanding roles in corporate leadership, the study of Black history, voting rights, and politics.

Beyond this Place of Wrath and Tears: Omega Psi Phi and the 1970s

Omega Psi Phi entered the 1970s with an enthusiasm brought on by political, judicial, educational, and related civil rights victories of the 1960s and preceding decades. At the outset of 1970, the Alpha Omega chapter in Washington, DC, provided the Fraternity with a great reason to be optimistic about the rest of the year on the local level. The spring issue of *The Oracle* featured photographs of Alpha Omega members breaking ground on a $10 million development project in the southeastern quadrant of the city. Members of the chapter cosponsored the project, called Capital City, with the US Department of Housing and Urban Development. When completed, the plaza would include mixed-income housing units, a shopping center, and a space for teaching facilities. In assisting with the development of Capital City, Omega Psi Phi put resources back into an area of the nation's capital where disinvestment impacted Black Americans severely, and the area's residents received the Fraternity's noble gesture warmly. Elsewhere in the country, national leaders of the Fraternity announced the continuation of a scholarship program that Omega Psi Phi began cosponsoring with Coca-Cola USA in 1968. The program assisted Black youth who earned solid marks on college board examinations, had good leadership qualities, and wanted to attend colleges or universities but who lacked the financial resources to do so.[1]

Omega Psi Phi's national leaders applauded local and national successes like the development project and the Coca-Cola USA partnership. Nonetheless, the leaders believed the Fraternity needed to do more work for Omega to reach its maximum potential. As of summer 1970, James S. Avery Sr. of Scotch Plains, New Jersey, was responsible for guiding that process: delegates to the Fifty-Third Grand Conclave held in Pittsburgh, Pennsylvania, from August 1 through 6 elected him Grand Basileus. Originally from Cranford, about four miles northeast of Scotch Plains, Avery attended Cranford High School where his classmates elected him as the first Black student council president in Cranford history. Avery finished the high school in 1941 and, after one year as a scholarship student at Columbia University in New York City, decided to enlist in the US Marine Corps. Officials rejected him because he had pes planus (fallen arches, flat feet). Still wanting to serve the country during wartime, Avery entered the US Army Reserve in 1942, a move that allowed him to continue matriculating through Columbia. His matriculation stopped, however, when military officials placed his reserve unit on active duty. After serving in the Judge Advocate General's Department, a time during which he faced overt discrimination for the first time, motivating him to support the Double V (Double Victory) campaign, Avery earned an honorable discharge and returned to Columbia.[2]

Avery completed an undergraduate degree and a graduate degree in education from Columbia University. He then began teaching and coaching in Cranford. His professionalism, concern for students, and allegiance to the community drew attention from a parent employed as an assistant manager with the Esso Standard Oil Company (later Exxon). The parent informed Avery the company needed an employee to work in education and race relations, and Avery's background made him an excellent candidate to fill the position. Avery began at Esso Standard Oil in 1956 and was productive immediately, forging business relationships with local and national entities. As cochairman and later vice chairman of the United Negro College Fund from 1965 to 1967, Avery helped generate more than $12 million in donations for historically Black colleges and universities (HBCUs). His employer, Esso Standard Oil, established one grant that increased from $50,000 to $150,000. Those endeavors were meritorious; however, Avery's ancillary dealings with various Omega men in Scotch Plains during his early years at Esso Standard Oil caused him to become interested in the Fraternity.[3]

Avery's meeting of founders Edgar Amos Love and Oscar James Cooper was particularly impactful. Their and other Omegas' devotion to the Fraternity's four cardinal principles—manhood, scholarship, perseverance, and uplift—were simpatico. Thus, Avery joined the Omicron Chi chapter on May 29, 1957. Omega's national officials granted a charter to Omicron Chi on April 7, 1955, and Avery was the chapter's first initiated member. Asked decades later how he won election as Grand Basileus to Omega Psi Phi in fewer than thirteen years in the Fraternity, Avery responded:

> I took my entrance into Omega Psi Phi . . . very seriously and solemnly. I have always had the greatest respect for the fraternal vision of our Founders and for the Four Cardinal Principles of our organization. I have committed my entire life to emulating those principles. I have constantly spoken of the sacred vows we took and of a love of Omega as a symbol of the best one could be. I am sure that my love, my concern and my respect for Omega's ideals along with my vision for Omega were the factors that propelled me onward in the Fraternity. I can proudly say I have never seen my participation as one based upon political motives, I just wanted to do all I could to advance the true cause of Omega. It was

the Brothers around me who saw the depth of my fraternal devotion and my intense desire to serve.[4]

Avery delivered his first official address as Grand Basileus in the summer of 1971.[5] In the address, he articulated his belief that Omega Psi Phi and other Greek-letter fraternities had lost their grounding: "Until a few years ago, fraternity men seemed to live on pedestals, endowed with an aura of exclusivity and specialness, envied by those not selected to wear the symbols of Greekdom. Today," Avery lamented, "the crashing of pedestals can be heard 'round the fraternal world."[6] Omega Psi Phi, he declared, had to recalibrate itself firmly and usefully into a Black American community whose members were determined to enjoy the inalienable rights and privileges of first-class citizenship. Omega men, Avery went on, "have condemned almost every institution in America for lacking relevance to the needs of our time, yet, we have failed to put sufficient relevancy into our own organizational efforts. . . . The bell tolls for us in Omega."[7] Urging the Fraternity to readjust its priorities by putting standard patterns of social togetherness in its proper relationship to social awareness, he called for new strategies and new tactics for "social revolution":

> The men of Omega helped to lead the Black revolution that brought about many of the legal gains that exist today. We are even better equipped to help remove the roadblocks that stymie the future progress and development of our people.
>
> Where[,] then, do we put our emphasis? As I see it, the emphasis must now be on our purposeful educational development, building self-dignity, and race pride, motivating our young people, parent counseling, providing housing for the needy, solving community health problems, helping the indigent and less fortunate—activities that provide a powerful line of offense in the war against frustration, poverty, and inequity. We in Omega must be in the front line in this critical phase of our human history.[8]

When Avery penned his address in 1971, an illicit drug crisis fueled in part by the inequality about which he wrote lingered in the shadows of many American communities. In deprived areas where social minorities comprised numerical majorities, drug use was particularly acute. Besides destitute or underemployed civilians trying to cope with their hardships, combat veterans returning from Vietnam used narcotics in an attempt to forget, however temporarily, the tragic scenes they witnessed on the battlefield. As a World War II combat veteran, Avery knew about the ghosts of war and the lengths to which many servicepersons would go to rid themselves of those ghosts. That a large number of youths seemed to be using potentially deadly narcotics to prepare them to fight domestic battles (e.g., abject poverty, inadequate education, parental abuse) or simply used drugs recreationally deepened Avery's concern.[9]

At a two-day fraternal conference held in October 1971 at the University of Maryland, College Park, Avery and other members of the Omega Psi Phi Supreme Council launched a new social action program that specifically targeted a countrywide antidrug initiative called Project Uplift. Via the initiative, which Avery and other council members envisioned reaching every college, university, and neighborhood in the country, the Fraternity would lead the way in national awareness. Because drug addiction, poverty, and related maladies were prevalent in many Black communities, especially in major cities and towns, Avery heavily prioritized Black locales. Avery knew curtailing the sometimes-intergenerational afflictions that Project Uplift targeted was a daunting task, but he was confident that, with 300 active chapters and 30,000 members, Omega Psi Phi had the manpower, expertise, and drive to be successful.[10]

Lloyd Bell and Samuel Clarence Coleman Jr. cochaired the Omega Psi Phi National Social Action Committee as well as Project Uplift. Bell was a Duquesne University-trained psychologist and assistant vice chancellor at the University of Pittsburgh. Coleman, a University of Michigan graduate, was the first Black member of the housing authority in Newburgh, New York. Aware of the vital need to address narcotics abuse, Bell and Coleman urged their fellow Omega men to be social activists, dedicating both time and energy to combating the oppressive effects of drug addiction. In an article featured in the winter 1972 issue of *The Oracle*, Bell, a Black Power advocate, discussed the power of narcotics. According to him, making narcotics difficult to access was the best practice against addiction.[11]

Amid ongoing racial and drug crises in 1972, Omega man Vernon Jordan Jr. served in his second year as executive director of the National Urban League. Born and reared in Atlanta, Georgia, Jordan completed David T. Howard High School with honors in 1953. He then enrolled in DePauw University in Greencastle, Indiana, where he was enrolled when he became a 1956 initiate of the Zeta Phi chapter in Indianapolis. After earning a law degree from Howard University in 1960, Jordan returned to his hometown, Atlanta, and clerked for renowned civil rights lawyer Donald Lee Hollowell. In 1961, the National Association for the Advancement of Colored People (NAACP) named Jordan field secretary for Georgia, a position he held until 1963. During the next year, Jordan joined the Southern Regional Council for the Voter Education Project as its director. In 1966, Jordan demonstrated his rising political renown by attending a national civil rights conference organized by US president Lyndon Johnson. Jordan continued to ascend after departing the Southern Regional Council for the Voter Education Project in 1968 and becoming president of the United Negro College Fund in 1970. He remained in that role until succeeding longtime National Urban League executive director Whitney Moore Young Jr. after his death in 1971.[12]

As executive director of the National Urban League, Jordan sought to expand the mission of his predecessor, Young, by placing more emphasis on politics than Young. According to Jordan, the National Urban League would execute a threefold plan to assist Black Americans attain equality. Jordan explained his plan in the winter 1972 issue of *The Oracle*: he and others in the National Urban League would continue to be "forceful advocates for the cause of black people and other minorities."[13] With one of Omega Psi Phi's most powerful sons at the helm, the National Urban League itself would continue being a "result-oriented, issue-oriented organization dedicated to serving the people [and a] bridge between the races, forging unity and harmony in a land torn by strife and division," Jordan concluded, and Omega Psi Phi would be one of the organization's most integral partners.[14]

As Jordan laid out his plan for the future of the National Urban League, Omega Psi Phi flew its flag at half-staff when Fraternity founder Oscar Cooper died on October 11, 1972, in Philadelphia, Pennsylvania. Besides founding the Fraternity, Cooper was one of the country's most notable and one of the country's longest licensed Black physicians. After graduating from the Howard University School of Medicine on June 5, 1918, he practiced in North Philadelphia for forty-eight years, which included residency service at the Mudgett Hospital in Center City, Philadelphia, and then operated a private practice in the city. Cooper was a member of the National Medical Association, an organization of Black and multiracial physicians founded on November 26, 1895, because the American Medical Association (AMA) was segregated. More than a half century later, US president Lyndon Johnson signed the Civil Rights Act of 1964 into law on July 2. In so doing, he legislated the AMA and similarly constituted organizations to desegregate. Eventually, Cooper joined the AMA. He also belonged to the Philadelphia County Medical Association and to the Medical Society of Eastern Pennsylvania. At his funeral service, which took place on Saturday, October 14, 1972, at the First African Baptist Church in South Philadelphia, attendees mourned his death but celebrated the full life he led and helped countless others lead.[15]

The fall 1972 issue of *The Oracle* featured a tribute to Cooper and Edgar Love, the only living founder of Omega Psi Phi. Morehouse College president emeritus, civil rights stalwart, Ninety-Six, South Carolina native, and beloved Omega man Benjamin Elijah Mays fashioned the tribute, and he was an ideal person to do so. For decades, Mays, not unlike Cooper and Love, used Judeo-Christian teachings to apprise people of their divine responsibility to challenge injustice. For example, as dean of the Howard University School of Religion from 1935 to 1940 and later as president of Morehouse from 1940 to 1967, Mays mentored some of the most influential leaders of the civil rights movement. Martin Luther King, Jr. was one of his most well-known mentees. Because of Mays's influence on prominent and unknown educators, students, ministers, laypersons, policy makers, and scores of other individuals who took part in the twentieth-century freedom struggle, some persons referred to Mays as the "schoolmaster to the Negro leaders," others the "schoolmaster of the movement."[16]

"In Honor of Brothers Cooper and Love," the Mays tribute featured in the winter 1972 *Oracle* and was a reprint of a keynote address he delivered at a testimonial banquet the Mu Omega chapter held in Philadelphia, Pennsylvania, on June 10, four months before Cooper's death.[17] Mays began his speech by discussing Omega Psi Phi's birth and record of achievement during its sixty years of existence. He revisited statements Cooper and Love made during the Golden Anniversary Conclave, starting with Love: "We, the Founders, gave [the Fraternity] life and down across the years great leaders among us have given it love and devotion. The listing of any without the naming of all would be unfair," according to Love. But, in Omega Psi Phi's first fifty years, he continued, "we have weathered practically every adversity that could come upon us—two World Wars, recessions, depressions and adverse criticism by non-Greeks and non-sympathetic college administrations. We are stronger today because of these and more determined to keep our standards high and our reputation unsullied. May heaven smile upon us and a kind Providence continue to guide us."[18] Cooper beseeched Golden Anniversary Conclave delegates: "Let's all together . . . approach the coming years with determination to keep Omega in the foreground of fraternal circles and granting that we have made some mistakes, let us profit by those mistakes, for one is worthy or not in that he does or does not profit by his mistakes. However, perfection is something we strive for," Cooper declared, "and like a variable we never reach, . . . we get profound gratification in the striving and feel justified in any forward move to the desired pinnacle."[19]

Mays respected Cooper's and Love's opinions, and he celebrated Omega Psi Phi's strides from 1911 to 1961; nevertheless, Mays thought the Fraternity did more for American society from 1961 to 1971 than during the Fraternity's first half century. He referenced watershed moments in US history during which Omega Psi Phi performed central roles. Examples included the May 17, 1954, *Brown* decision; the Montgomery, Alabama, bus boycott from December 5, 1955, to December 20, 1956; the Freedom Rides through Alabama and Mississippi from May 4 to December 10, 1961; and the King-led marches in Birmingham, Selma, and Washington, DC, before his assassination on

April 4, 1968. Mays praised "our young men and women," whom he claimed "did what those of us who are older could not have done. They sat [in], picketed, boycotted, went to jail, some dying, in order that we could live in dignity and respect. In the last decade, we got the 1964 Civil Rights Act, the 1965 Voting Rights Act and the 1968 Housing Act. Blacks are holding positions never held before and working where they have never worked before."[20]

Mays believed Omega Psi Phi's existence itself was prophetic. That prophesy, a vision of three college students and their trusted adviser, Mays declared in June 1972, was unfolding to deliver Black communities to a society free of the rife of anti-Black racism. Mays asserted that Omega's four cardinal principles—manhood, scholarship, perseverance, and uplift—went from God's lips to the founders' ears.[21] He stressed the founders chose scholarship because they knew the importance of well-developed minds. "How wise they were," Mays pronounced, stating manhood entailed qualities such as "courage, bravery, virility," and maturity.[22] A "real man," Mays went on, "is not for sale. He has convictions to what is right and wrong, what is moral and immoral. . . . He is not a perfect man but what he stands for makes him respected [by] those who know him."[23] In relation to perseverance, a third Omega cardinal principle, Mays said "no one gets anywhere without [it. Perseverance was] that quality in man to continue steadfastness in an undertaking or aim until the object is accomplished. Perseverance included hard work, faith, and hope."[24] And, finally, uplift demonstrated the goodwill in humankind—for example, doing work to benefit people. Mays discussed "Jesus curing the sick and raising the dead, giving sight to the blind, and hearing to the deaf, giving speaking to the dumb and walking to the lame."[25] Uplift, Mays elaborated, was Cooper's "ministering to the sick and dying often without pay. This is Omega Psi Phi Fraternity," Mays concluded.[26]

Whereas Mays's tribute to Cooper and Love was a highlight of the winter 1972 issue of *The Oracle*, future issues of Omega Psi Phi's official organ contained tributes to deceased Omega men such as Zephaniah Alexander Looby, who died on March 24, 1972, and explored Black liberation, a goal to which Looby devoted most of his life to achieving.[27] The summer 1973 issue of *The Oracle* celebrated the National Urban League's executive director, Vernon E. Jordan Jr., whom national leaders named Citizen of the Year, and H. Carl Moultrie on his judicial appointment to the Superior Court for the District of Columbia.[28] Similar to Looby, Jordan and Moultrie committed the majority of their lives to fighting inequality. Jordan was a civil rights titan on the national scene who graced the cover of the February 19, 1973, issue of *Newsweek* magazine, asking a timely question: "What Ever Happened to Black America?"[29] In the *Newsweek* article of the same title, he discussed his commitment to assisting Black poor people and to fighting for other marginalized citizens.[30] As regards Moultrie, his judicial record was sterling. He also was Omega Psi Phi's national Executive Secretary emeritus, formerly served as president of the Washington, DC, branch of the NAACP, and was the recipient of numberless accolades. Upon his superior court appointment, members of Alpha Omega chapter told him they knew "the judicial process of our courts are in good hands with men of your stature sitting on the benches."[31]

In addition to discussing Looby, Jordan, and Moultrie, the summer 1973 *Oracle* focused on Black involvement in business and in social problems.[32] *Essence* magazine founder, publisher, treasurer and Omega man Edward T. Lewis discussed the status of Black-owned businesses in the United States as well as ways for Black Americans of all classes to improve their financial conditions.[33] Taking a few lines from a speech Jordan made at the annual meeting of the Cleveland, Ohio, Urban League on January 28, 1972, Lewis proclaimed: "The drive for political empowerment goes hand in hand with the drive for economic empowerment. It is not enough to point with pride at Black income figures creeping slowly point by point to levels still less than two-thirds of White income. Economic empowerment means putting green dollars into Black pockets and filling jobs at all levels with skilled Black workers."[34] Reiterating a crucial point, Lewis stated: "Black awareness alone is not enough. Black pride is not enough. Slogans of Black capitalism on the part of Government is not enough . . . many other things must happen before Black businesses are a true reality in this country."[35]

Along the same lines, chemist, civil rights activist, and National Welfare Rights Organization founding executive director George Alvin Wiley discussed problems associated with welfare recipients in the United States. According to Wiley, who earned a bachelor of science degree from the University of Rhode Island in 1953 and a PhD degree from Cornell University in 1957 but who was not a member of Omega Psi Phi, children and elderly people were the main victims of social and economic repression in 1973.[36] As the Movement for Economic Justice's national coordinator, Wiley said his associates and he were "going beyond poor people. We're interested in all people with a stake in economic reforms."[37] Lewis and Wiley understood the dismantling of discrimination was just the beginning—if Black America was going to be free, it would need economic empowerment and to be self-determined, strategic, and accountable in its path forward.

The Memorial Stones

In 1974, the United States Postal Service honored Omega man Langston Hughes by issuing a commemorative stamp with his likeness as part of the service's Black Heritage series. That stamp was an honor for which Samuel C.

Coleman Jr. and others on the Omega Psi Phi National Social Action Committee had called for since 1970. Sadly, a tragedy overshadowed the Postal Service's unveiling of the stamp: the Fraternity's final living founder, Edgar Love, died on May 1. Until he took his final breath, Love bound himself to the ideals of the Fraternity, living up to the motto *friendship is essential to the soul*. Throughout his sixty-three years of service in Omega, Love served as Grand Basileus twice and was a tireless mentor to thousands of Omega men. He witnessed the Fraternity grow from a single chapter at Howard University in Washington, DC, to more than 300 chapters in the United States, Africa, Germany, and the West Indies.[38]

Love's career as a minister of the gospel in the Methodist Church was one of his most lasting legacies. Being a thirty-third degree Mason, an NAACP life member, a husband to Virginia Louise Love (née Ross), a father to Jon Edgar Love, a grandfather to John Nathan and Virginia Love, and a founder of Omega Psi Phi were comparably important parts of his legacy. He epitomized an Omega man, as well as a race man, holding fast to the words of "Omega Dear."

According to the spring 1974 issue of *The Oracle*, a large delegation of Omega men performed the last rites for Love "as a service of triumph" on May 8 at the Sharp Street Memorial United Methodist Church in Baltimore, Maryland.[39] One person, writing decades later, recounted:

> Ailing and nearing the end of her own life, the tiny, fair-skinned widow of Edgar Amos Love, Virginia Louise Ross silently wept from the front pew of the massive Sharp Street Memorial United Methodist Church. Her only son, [Jonathan, or] Jon Edgar, sat nearby with his wife, [Virginia Lottier, or] Bunny, and their two children, John Nathan and Virginia [Elizabeth]. The renowned Morgan State College Chorale filled the quire while the Rev. Richard L. Clifford [who presided over the last rites] sat pensively at the cathedral. Members of the Omega Psi Phi Fraternity surrounded the casket, holding hands and singing their fraternal hymn as an ode to their fallen founder. Seated to capacity, some twelve-hundred United Methodist Church ministers and Civil Rights leaders, friends, parishioners, well-wishers and colleagues filed slowly through the nave and crammed into the Mother Church of Black Methodism in Baltimore, Maryland, paying their final respects to the venerable minister, civil and human rights activist and reformer, Bishop Edgar Love. The granite and brick Gothic Revival church, with its sharply pitched tympanum, austere lancet windows and lavish chancel overlooking the casket draped with the American flag and surrounded by flowers provided a most apropos backdrop for the somber occasion.[40]

Grand Basileus Marion W. Garnett, First Vice Grand Basileus Edward Braynon Jr., Grand Keeper of Finance John Moore, Grand Counselor James Felder, *The Oracle* editor Otto McLarrin, and national Executive Secretary Harold J. Cook attended the May 1974 service.[41] Attendees who formerly held national offices included past Grand Basileis Grant Reynolds, George E. Meares, and James Avery, and Executive Secretary emeritus H. Carl Moultrie.[42] Several leading Masonic and Sigma Pi Phi officers, Morgan Christian Center trustees, and well-known officials in the United Methodist Church, where Love was a bishop, attended the funeral service as well.[43]

Garnett—a Jeffersonville, Indiana, native, World War II naval veteran, University of Chicago graduate, licensed attorney, circuit judge, and 1947 initiate of Iota chapter—spoke during Love's last rites in 1974.[44] Repeating an adage regarding great people never dying because their legacies lived on, Garnett declared "as long as there is an Omega brother on earth, our founder Bishop Love shall never die."[45] In reality, for the first time in Omega's history, the Fraternity existed without a founder's guidance. Nonetheless, members were determined to carry on the legacies of all founders.

Because Love was a humanitarian interested in the international community, undergraduate Omega men across the United States expanded the global focus of their social action program. Among other acts, they developed "Africare—Omega Psi Phi Cares," a fundraising project designed to assist 6 to 13 million West Africans who faced disease, malnutrition, and starvation.[46] The financial goal of the project was reasonable: $30,000 from 300 undergraduate chapters, or one hundred dollars from each chapter.[47] Project chairman Cleotha Payne Lucas was a Spring Hope, North Carolina, native who after enduring poverty as a youth spent time in the US Air Force before earning an undergraduate degree from the University of Maryland, Eastern Shore, and a graduate degree from American University in Washington, DC.[48] He urged all members of the Fraternity, not simply undergraduates, to "show you care! Act now!"[49]

The Omega Psi Phi Supreme Council authorized the continuation of another worthy project in early 1974: a founders' memorial at Howard University in Washington, DC. The council sanctioned the project in late 1972, but Howard officials had to approve it. They took approximately sixteen months to grant their approval. According to a description of the memorial's design in the fall issue of *The Oracle*, the memorial, when completed, would be seven feet one inch in height, would weigh 18,000 pounds, would rest on a round base six feet in diameter, and would cost at least $15,000 to assemble and erect.[50] *The Oracle* described further: the "four lower sides [of the memorial] shall bear a raised gold metallic bust of the Founders with sandblasted, gold-frosted, sunken letters. The middle sand stoned portion shall bear on each of the four sides one of the cardinal principles. The top portion on the east and west sides shall bear [an] inscription. On the north and south sides shall be the motto of the Fraternity."⁵¹

Founders' Memorial was a fine gesture but, as skilled crafts persons worked to construct the memorial honoring Omega Psi Phi's four most revered members, some Omega men, such as Alfred S. Carter, Jr., believed the Fraternity had not done enough to recognize women who made fine contributions to Black agency and uplift in the United States. Such beliefs were reasonable. Omega Psi Phi, as a Fraternity, rarely acknowledged leading women or the issues they faced as leaders. A noticeable exclusion to that general rule occurred from July 10 to 12, 1974, when Omega's national leadership took advantage of an opportunity to participate in the federal government's memorializing Mary McLeod Bethune by unveiling a bronze statue of her in Lincoln Park. A distinguished church leader, educator, humanitarian, organizer, suffragette, and writer born in Mayesville, South Carolina, Bethune was a long-time delegate to the General Conference of the Methodist Episcopal Church; however, founding the Educational and Industrial Training School for Negro Girls (now called Bethune-Cookman University) in Daytona, Florida, was her most notable accomplishment. She likewise advised four American presidents including Franklin Delano Roosevelt, with whom she helped lead the Federal Council of Negro Affairs (the Black Brain Trust, Black Cabinet); she directed the Division of Negro Affairs in the National Youth Administration; and she founded the National Council of Negro Women. Because Bethune's statue was the first permanent monument to celebrate a woman of any ethnicity in a public park in the nation's capital, the social action committee for the local Delta Theta chapter of Omega Psi Phi enthusiastically supported the federal government erecting the statue. Acting as a microcosm of the Fraternity, the committee touted Bethune as a pioneering woman in American history generally and in African American history specifically.⁵²

Not long after the Fraternity celebrated the unveiling of the Bethune statue in Washington, DC, *The Oracle*'s Otto McLarrin discussed matters that were unworthy of celebration, such as the lack of access to health care, food deserts, and related problems in African American communities.⁵³ McLarrin, who in the summer of 1974 began writing a weekly column for the National Newspaper Publishers Association called "Happiness through Health,"⁵⁴ exhorted readers of the fall issue of *The Oracle* to come to grips with the growing problem of hypertension, or high blood pressure.⁵⁵ For years, Omega Psi Phi had raised funds to combat sickle cell anemia. McLarrin lauded that effort, but he believed hypertension was the "real killer among America's Black population."⁵⁶ For each person whose life sickle cell disease took, McLarrin noted, hypertension took one hundred persons' lives.[57] Not only was hypertension the leading cause of death among Black people in the United States, but hypertension also caused Black people in the country to have shorter life expectancies than White people.[58] According to McLarrin, Black people were twice as likely than White people to suffer from hypertension due to diet and stress brought on by anti-Black racism, which many health-care professionals referred to as a silent killer because there are no noticeable symptoms for heart attack.[59] While other Omega men continued to serve on the front lines of battles for human and civil rights, McLarrin soldiered in the medical theater for such rights. His writing columns, articles, and performing other activities to promote good physical and mental health served as a call to action to get regular screenings, checkups, and similar preventative measures. McLarrin was one of many Omega men who, together with members of other predominantly Black organizations, led major campaigns against hypertension.

Omega Psi Phi and the Second Reconstruction

Omega Psi Phi held its Fifty-Sixth Grand Conclave in Phoenix, Arizona, from December 26 to 30, 1974. A panel session called "The Law, Economics, and You" was the first installment in a series to engage Omega men who were judges, legislators, mayors, or other elected public officials.[60] Omega men Sherman Smith, Clarence Lightner, and Corneal Davis were panelists. Smith was a superior court judge in Los Angeles, California. Lightner was mayor of Raleigh, North Carolina. Davis was an Illinois state representative.[61] The panelists discussed some of the freedoms that Black Americans and other social minorities gained through the enactment of civil rights laws during the second Reconstruction. They also discussed attempts by conservatives to push Black Americans back into second-class citizenship.[62]

Omega Psi Phi's recognizing Earl Gilbert Graves Sr., a 1954 initiate of the Pi chapter at Morgan State College in Baltimore, Maryland, as the Fraternity's 1974 Citizen of the Year was another highlight of the Phoenix Conclave.[63] In his reception speech, titled "Leaning on the Shield," Graves declared "there is nothing minority or Black about trying to do business on Main Street U.S.A. There is only one set of rules in terms of how you survive in business, and that is to run the business . . . as business people, not as Black businesspeople [but] as businesspeople who happen to be Black."[64] Graves discussed three successful entities in Chicago, Illinois: the Johnson Publishing Company, the Johnson Hair Products Company, and Parker House Sausage Company.[65] He attributed their success to Black patronage, "political climates that encouraged and supported Black economic development," and political movements such as Jesse Jackson Sr.'s efforts with Operation People United to Save Humanity, or PUSH.[66] Graves also discussed Motown Records, a Black-owned company headquartered in Detroit, Michigan, that netted approximately $46 million in gross sales in 1974.[67] Graves predicted Motown would exceed that amount in 1975 once the company "brings in the receipts from" *Lady Sings the Blues*, a blockbuster film whose rights Motown owned.[68] Graves maintained his life's work in business and commerce was meant to lead Black communities to economic stability, a primary component of the larger Black freedom struggle.

Much of Graves's sentiments were set in motion and gained traction by watching Black spiritual leaders, businessmen, and political figures who asserted that Black freedom was steeped in finance and economics. How closely Graves watched Nation of Islam leader Elijah Muhammad was unknown when Graves accepted the Citizen of the Year award from Omega Psi Phi during the Phoenix Conclave, but many Omega men continued to mourn Muhammad's death on February 25, 1975. Many Americans deemed Muhammad controversial, but many Omegas respected his attempts to ameliorate problems besetting Black people through economic empowerment and financial freedom. Muhammad ascended to the stage of Black leadership through his religious and business efforts, which represented aspects of Black liberation theology. As Omega man and *Birmingham World* editor Emory Jackson noted, Muhammad taught "clean living, self-discipline, self-help and self-confidence."[69] Another Omega man, John Stevenson Marshall Kilimanjaro, publisher of the *Carolina Peacemaker*, said Muhammad "has done his work on this earth. But his teachings and admonitions are yet with us as during his testimony that truly, what is with us and will continue to be—goals worth pursuing and a way of life worth investigating."[70] Here, Kilimanjaro asserts that the aforementioned teachings of Muhammad and several other freedom fighters were invaluable to Black forward advancement.

Furthering notions of Black freedom, *The Oracle* reprinted Vernon Jordan Jr.'s speech discussing best practices for an integrated society. Criticizing the shamefully racist presidency of Richard Milhous Nixon, Jordan claimed the Nixon administration's "policy of 'benign neglect' . . . whittled away . . . progress made during the Second Reconstruction of the 1960s [via] the political manipulation of highly charged, emotionally symbolic 'social issues.'"[71] In so doing, Jordan explained, the same administration furthered a concerted effort by those desirous of creating two distinct "Americas, one rich and white, one poor and black," even though the fundamental interests of the country's Black and White communities were the same or similar.[72] For example, they all needed basic social, political, economic, and cultural assurances; good, stable jobs; fair wages; and decent housing.[73] Nearly all were victims of racist symbols, code words, and smokescreens that obscured such essential shared interests.[74]

To combat such dastardly maneuvers, Jordan suggested new leadership groups whose members owed their existences to the Civil Rights Act of 1964, the Voting Rights Act of 1965, the Civil Rights Act of 1968, and the 1968 War on Poverty needed to wage full-scale warfare by participating in the Leadership Conference on Civil Rights that A. Philip Randolph and Roy Wilkins, an Omega man, helped found in 1950.[75] To quote Jordan, "Much of the Second Reconstruction was concerned with winning for Black people and other minorities rights that had long been denied us—the right to vote, to sit in desegregated schoolrooms, to use public accommodations, and to compete on an equal basis for jobs. Through the vehicles of executive orders, court decisions and Congressional actions, most of these rights have been secured."[76]

As Jordan shed light on significant matters affecting the social, political, and economic plight of the Black American community, other Omega men celebrated. Also celebrated was American jazz pianist, civil rights advocate, and Omega life member, William "Count" Basie. The founder of the Count Basie Orchestra was honored in Washington, DC, before Omega brothers and Quettes—their wives or women partners—as he headlined for the Shady Grove Music Fair. During this celebration, famed jazz singer and first lady of song Ella Fitzgerald and Oscar Peterson accompanied Basie.[77] Other Omega men celebrated were Hughlyn F. Fierce, who was elected as the president of the Freedom National Bank of New York, William Toles selected to head the Jamaica Chamber of Commerce, and Herbert Bell Shaw, the presiding prelate to the African Methodist Episcopal Zion Church.[78]

During the early months of 1975, Omega Psi Phi recognized Simon H. Scott Jr. He was an active member in the Theta Rho chapter in Germany who hailed from Charleston, South Carolina, where he completed the Avery Institute.[79] Scott then matriculated through Johnson C. Smith University in Charlotte, North Carolina, and the McCormick Theological Seminary at Chicago, Illinois, earning degrees in 1948 and 1950, respectively. Though notable, Scott's involvement in Theta Rho and his educational background were not the reasons for the 1975 recognition, however. He was a decorated colonel and chaplain in the US Air Force whom high-ranking military officials at the European headquarters promoted to command chaplain. In that capacity, Scott supervised 110 Catholic, Jewish, and Protestant chaplains in all North Atlantic Treaty Organization countries—videlicet, England, Germany, Greece, Holland, Italy, and Turkey. As yet another testament to the respect Scott commanded, his own supervisors chose him to represent the Office of the Chief of Chaplains during the 1974 World Congress on Evangelism in Lausanne, Switzerland.[80]

Recognizing the individual accomplishments of Omega men was a commonality in the first half of 1975, but one of the greatest recognitions of any group of Omegas occurred during the latter half of the year. On November 16, members of the Fraternity dedicated Founders' Memorial. Omega men from around the country made the pilgrimage to Washington, DC, to attend the dedication, which took place on the eve of the Fraternity's sixty-fourth anniversary. At the dedication, thousands of attendees basked in the glow of Omega Psi Phi's importance as the first Black Greek-letter collegiate fraternity founded at an HBCU. Omega men and Washington's larger Black community, to include several high-ranking public officials and other dignitaries, gathered to celebrate the permanent memorial to Omega Psi Phi founders Frank Coleman, Oscar Cooper, Ernest Just, and Edgar Love. Of especial significance, many family members and other loved ones of Coleman, Cooper, Just, and Love were on hand to see Founders' Memorial "forever consecrated and dedicated in granite," to quote Grand Basileus Marion W. Garnett.[81]

Coleman, Cooper, Just, and Love were not the only Omega men whom appreciative individuals and groups memorialized in late 1975. On December 19, the Association for the Study of Afro-American Life and History (ASALH) and the Amoco Foundation unveiled a bronze marker commemorating the lifework of Carter Godwin Woodson. The association unveiled the marker near New Canton, Virginia, an unincorporated town in Buckingham County not far from where Woodson was born on December 19, 1875. In an address delivered to several hundred individuals who attended the unveiling of Woodson's historical marker in 1975, ASALH president and Virginia State College history professor and non-Omega Edgar Allan Toppin Sr. said, "few people ever emerged from such obscure beginnings . . . and made such a lasting imprint."[82]

On January 1, 1976, thirteen days after ASALH commemorated Woodson, the US government began commemorating its 200th year since declaring independence from Britain. The bicentennial ushered in new moments of uncertainty because while the United States celebrated its emancipation from British rule, the nation worked toward tightening the grip of tyranny toward Black Americans. Not every American citizen enjoyed the ideals of life, liberty, and the pursuit of happiness about which Thomas Jefferson wrote in the declaration that he and other colonial leaders signed on July 4, 1776; however, as Omega man Roy O. Wilkins made plain in a 1976 speech at the Omega Psi Phi Leadership Conference, American citizens had witnessed several major civil rights victories since circa 1950.[83] Wilkins told listeners that social minorities had achieved basic political rights such as franchise protection. They also could "enjoy public accommodations without facing insults" and take advantage of "all public programs financed by federal funds."[84] Wilkins likewise spoke about the Fair Employment Practice Committee and the 1968 civil rights law that prohibited "racial, ethnic, and religious discrimination in the purchase and sale of housing," among other rights and privileges.[85]

In counterpoints, Wilkins argued the abovementioned victories were not enough to guarantee future equality. He stated, "Civil rights must include the social and economic conditions which will permit their fulfillment. Those conditions are not yet secured."[86] Elaborating, Wilkins contended that freedom seekers had to "elect to office men and women who will rally us, again, to noble purposes[,] who can move us forward once more to a worthy goal—toward becoming a nation that lives up to the promise of 200 years ago: a true and shining society of equals."[87] The most notable legislative achievements in 1975, Wilkins went on, resulted from the 1965 federal voting rights law, which he described as "one of the most effective pieces of civil rights legislation ever enacted. Thanks to its passage[,] enforcement," and 1970 congressional extension, Wilkins declared, suffrage protections included social minorities besides Black Americans.[88] Excluding the voting rights law, he concluded, "accomplishments in 1975 were few and far between; much of our energy was expended in defense of earlier gains."[89]

Though unrelated to national politics, the Fifty-Seventh Conclave of Omega Psi Phi in Atlanta, Georgia, from August 15 to 20, 1976, was a victory for the Fraternity. The conclave marked the fourth time Atlanta served as host to Omega's biggest annual event. By 1976, Washington, DC, Philadelphia, and St. Louis had the same distinction. Some members of the Fraternity labeled Atlanta "Omega-town" because it had four undergraduate chapters, Psi (1922) at Morehouse College, Beta Psi at Clark College (1923), Alpha Sigma at Morris Brown College (1935), and Zeta Theta at Georgia State University (1969); one intermediate chapter, Tau (1922) at Atlanta University; and one graduate chapter, Eta Omega (1919), under whose umbrella the undergraduate chapters functioned.[90] It was during this time that plans were underway for the chartering of the Delta Kappa chapter at the Georgia Institute of Technology, which would be done so in the fall of 1976. Nicknamed the "grandfather of all graduate chapters," Eta Omega had active, informed, and vocal members who helped lead a city that was fast becoming the social, political, economic, and cultural capital of the South: Atlanta.[91]

Atlanta's ascendance in the mid- to late 1970s occurred as socially and politically conservative White Americans attempted to roll back civil rights gains. Southern conservatives led the attempt, and voting was a primary target. Their disenfranchisement campaign gave rise to serious concerns among Black Americans, who composed the primary group White conservatives sought to disenfranchise. To combat the conservatives, Omega man Eddie Williams, president of the Joint Center for Political and Economic Studies, encouraged his fellow Omega men to lead voter mobilization efforts.[92]

Despite a rise in Black elected officials subsequent to the 1965 federal voting rights law, which facilitated the development of a Black New South vis-à-vis politics and government, according to some observers, Williams estimated Black officials still accounted for less than 1 percent of elected public officeholders in the region.[93]

People had sufficient reason to believe Williams's estimations because he was a nationally recognized political analyst. Williams also was a highly sought-after speaker and US Army officer who earned a bachelor of arts degree in journalism from the University of Illinois at Urbana-Champaign in 1956. With degree in hand, he wrote for the *Memphis Star-Times* and later for the *Atlanta Daily World*, among other newspapers. Eventually, Williams launched a career in punditry and statecraft. In 1976, writing quantitatively about what he considered to be major threats to Black political life, he stated:

1. Only 55 percent of the 14 million eligible Black voters are registered. The [US] Census Bureau reports that "among the 5.2 million Blacks who were not registered in 1974, nearly one-half reported that they were not interested or disliked politics."
2. Between 1970 and 1974, Black registration declined about six percentage points, thus giving Blacks the lowest registration rate reported for any of the last five general elections.
3. In 1974 the turnout rate was an alarmingly low [at] 34 per cent, and only one of every six Blacks in the 18–24 age group went to the polls.
4. Of the 2.6 million registered voters who did not vote in 1974, 45 per cent said they were not interested.[94]

If Omega Psi Phi led a massive voter registration drive and members of the Fraternity themselves cast ballots in large numbers, Williams suggested, they could help make the United States more democratic and inclusive. He understood that Black Americans made up "ten percent of the national electorate, and their unique geographic distribution and concentrations give them a powerful political advantage, especially in close Presidential elections."[95] Furthermore, there were 120 congressional districts in which Black voters had the potential to influence elections, Williams declared.[96] On the state level, Williams continued, Black people were "grossly misrepresented" in government.[97] In the South, where Black people comprised 18.4 percent of the population—the highest of any region in the country—Black lawmakers held only 5 percent of the seats in state legislatures.[98] In sixty-seven counties, primarily in the South, where Black people composed at least 50 percent of the counties' total populations, there was not a single Black person on a county governing board.[99] In the same region (the South), Black people made up no less than 6,000 of the 25,000 residents in twenty-eight cities, but no Black person held a position in a municipal governing body.[100] Based on Williams's data, within eleven years after enactment of the Voting Rights Act of 1965, Black Americans seemed to have begun to experience voter fatigue or lacked faith in a political process that made it difficult to account for the political consensus for Black Americans.

Despite pressing issues and outright problems among Black citizens in the United States in 1976, organizers of bicentennial celebrations encouraged them to acknowledge their contributions to the country. On July 6, in Wilberforce, Ohio, ASALH unveiled a historical marker on the campus of Central State University commemorating US Army colonel and honorary member Omega Charles D. Young. He was one of the first Black graduates of the US Military Academy at West Point and the highest-ranking Black military officer during World War I. The July 6, 1976, celebration was the second time in a single year ASALH erected a marker for an honorary member of Omega Psi Phi. As stated earlier in this chapter, the association commemorated Carter G. Woodson in the same manner on December 19, 1975. Fewer than two months later, US president Gerald Rudolph Ford Jr. formally recognized Black History Month, an outgrowth of the Negro History Week celebration Woodson began on February 7, 1926. Ford, speaking during an address he made on February 10, 1976, encouraged his fellow citizens to join with him in seizing "the opportunity to honor the too-often neglected accomplishments of Black Americans in every area of endeavor throughout our history."[101]

The ASALH connected with Omega Psi Phi again on November 21, 1976. Amid a bicentennial celebration at South Carolina State College (now University) in Orangeburg, ASALH executive director J. Rupert Picott Sr. presented college administrators with a bronze plaque honoring Omega Psi Phi founder and renowned biologist Ernest E. Just. Just was one of thirteen esteemed citizens whom Picott and other ASALH national officers selected for the special bicentennial honor.[102] Not to be outdone, Omega Psi Phi presented "a special salute to those ebony fighting men who, for so many years, have been excluded from the pages of this nation's history books."[103]

Charles Young was the quintessential fighting man whose bravery, honor, and leadership were worthy of being saluted. As per the fall 1976 issue of *The Oracle*, Young "probably would have become our nation's first black general but was forced into a medical retirement."[104] Omega men likewise recognized the Fifth-fourth Massachusetts Infantry, a predominantly Black Union regiment whose troops fought in several battles during the American Civil War; the 367th Infantry, one of several Buffalo Soldier regiments during World War I; and the 369th Infantry, a New York National Guard regiment known commonly as the Harlem Hell Fighters during World War I and World War II.[105] Omega Psi Phi also emphasized founders Frank

Coleman and Edgar Love being two of several members of the Fraternity who "trained to become military officers at the Fort Des Moines Army Base in Iowa for which influential Black citizens called and a small but equally as influential set of their White peers supported." Senior military officers assigned both Coleman and Love to Buffalo Soldier regiments. "Other brothers, commissioned as officers," the fall 1967 issue of *The Oracle* noted, "were either members of Alpha (Howard University), Beta (Lincoln University, Pa.) and Gamma (Boston) or initiated into the War Chapter through special dispensation granted by Grand Basileus James O. McMorries (1916–17)."[106] *The Oracle* continued: "Twenty-one Brothers were commissioned at Fort Des Moines and given assignments overseas or at home serving as instructors in camps or units at Black colleges."[107]

Besides recognizing the manhood and patriotism of combat veterans in 1976, Omega Psi Phi acknowledged Black educator and feminist, early Delta Sigma Theta Sorority member, and civil rights icon Mary Eliza Church Terrell with an article in the summer 1976 *Oracle*. One of the first Black women to attend Oberlin College in Ohio, Terrell earned an undergraduate degree in 1884 and a graduate degree in 1888 before teaching at Wilberforce College in Xenia, about four miles southwest of Wilberforce. In 1887, Terrell moved to Washington, DC, where she taught and served as superintendent at the academically rigorous M Street (later Paul Laurence Dunbar) High School. In the nation's capital, Terrell also performed groundwork for NAACP and became an eminence in the Black women's club movement. Her several movement activities included organizing and serving as inaugural president of the College Alumnae Club in 1910. The fundamental goal of the club was twofold; to raise curricular standards at HBCUs and to secure female suffrage countrywide, a privilege the Nineteenth Amendment to the US Constitution granted in 1920. Three years later, Terrell and her associates renamed their club the National Association of Colored Women. In addition to those endeavors, Terrell, in 1935, helped Mary McLeod Bethune develop the National Council of Negro Women and, as discussed in chapter 3 of this book, served as founder and inaugural president of the National Association of Colored Women. In her 1940 autobiography, *A Colored Woman in a White World*, Terrell closed by pronouncing boldly: "While I am grateful for the blessings which have been bestowed upon me and for the opportunities which have been offered, I cannot help wondering sometimes what I might have become and might have done if I had lived in a country which had not circumscribed and handicapped me on account of my race, but had allowed me to reach any height I was able to attain."[108]

Countless members of Omega Psi Phi continued to ask questions similar to Terrell's query through the bicentennial and into the next year, 1977.

Indeed, civil rights comprised the order of the day in the Fraternity during those two years. Omega men also made safeguarding existing civil rights victories and designing the types of strategies and tactics needed to help achieve new victories central elements in other organizations to which they belonged. Heading such organizations was yet another part of that civil rights effort. For instance, when Omega man Roy Wilkins retired and became the NAACP's executive director emeritus in July 1977, a second Omega man, Benjamin Lawson Hooks, succeeded him.[109] Hooks was a Memphis, Tennessee, civil rights leader, minister, lawyer, and criminal court judge whom members of the Epsilon Phi chapter of Omega Psi Phi initiated in November 1942 while he attended LeMoyne-Owen College in his hometown.[110] After enrolling in the US Army, Hooks relocated from Memphis to Washington, DC, where he completed Howard University in June 1944 and then earned a law degree from DePaul University in Chicago in 1948 because Tennessee law prevented him from performing legal study in the state.[111]

According to several 1976 and 1977 reports, "Hooks was the best choice in a large field of distinguished civil rights leaders and professionals who desired to guide the sixty-seven-year-old NAACP forward after Wilkins's retirement." Hooks understood that for the NAACP to survive and, moreover, expand from 1977 onward, he and other executives had to handle internal and external problems smoothly. In 1977, as Wilkins neared retirement, several people labeled the NAACP dormant and claimed its financial problems were rampant. Hooks was aware of such beliefs; nevertheless, in a *Washington Post* newspaper interview, he stated "Wilkins is a hard act to follow."[112] The statement was heartfelt, but Hooks believed the NAACP needed a new image. He fit the bill because he had much experience litigating discrimination cases and, among other characteristics and traits, related easily with sundry types of people. Hooks was gregarious, popular on the lecture circuit, and understood the media. Even so, heading the NAACP was not a simple task, as he had to strike a balance between changing popular perception about the NAACP, creating a new look for the organization via modern strategies and tactics, while preserving its traditional programs and means of fighting injustice through the courts.[113]

Omega Psi Phi's national leaders realized Hooks's success as executive director of the NAACP was of paramount importance to maintaining the Fraternity's place at the fore of the civil rights movement. Therefore, the leaders partnered with Hooks to develop and execute a unified agenda for Black liberation. Because their liberatory quest was worldwide, they looked for opportunities to impact both foreign and domestic communities. Pursuant to achieving that goal, Omega leaders chartered the Pi Xi chapter in Nassau, Bahamas, on August 22, 1977.[114] The chartering ceremony took place at

GranVilla at Hibiscus Estates on West Bay Street, the home of Granville Bain, and made Pi Xi the fifth international chapter chartered in the Fraternity at that time after Tau Chi in Monrovia, Liberia, Theta Rho in Frankfurt, Germany, Zeta Xi in St. Thomas, Virgin Islands, and Lambda Xi in Youngsan, South Korea.[115]

Progress and Perils—The Late 1970s

Omega Psi Phi's national leadership chose "Pursuit of Excellence as a Means to Black Survival" as the theme for the Fraternity's Fifty-Eighth Grand Conclave at the Hyatt Regency in New Orleans, Louisiana, from December 26 to 30, 1977 where delegates reelected Edward J. Braynon Jr. as Grand Basileus.[116] Leading up to the New Orleans Conclave, Fraternity founder Ernest Everett Just was honored as one of the noted Black biologists in his home state of South Carolina with a bronze plaque at South Carolina State College (now University). Through expansion and public history, the Fraternity's emphasis on advancing a better quality of life for Black people was demonstrated.

The late 1970s bore witness to similar conditions endured by Black Americans at the turn of the century prior to the modern civil rights movement. Among those conditions, poverty was a constant problem in both periods. In the winter 1977 issue of *The Oracle*, one of its first editors, John P. Murchison Sr., discussed the need for a "larger share of the capitalistic leverage stemming from social forces and acquired community civilities" along the Georgia Avenue corridor in Washington, DC.[117] According to Murchison, civil rights legislation did not assuage "pockets of poverty," and "upgrading . . . economic potentials and skills" was the only solution to ensure "constructive growth and community stability."[118] Andrew Bell, in a separate winter 1977 *Oracle* article, declared the improving conditions of Black Americans centered on cities and where social programs focused on the implementation of skills and nostalgia for place would create vested interests in community vitalization.[119] Bell wrote, "The name of [the] game is [the] revitalization of neighborhoods, the preservation of vital areas of our urban geography and the targeting of efforts" to conjoin the interests of affected residents.[120] Bell suggested the US Department of Housing and Urban Development needed to follow the example of certain African leaders by marrying the "concerns of the vested interest with the hopes of the disenfranchised."[121]

As members of Omega Psi Phi fought injustice on multiple fronts, the US Supreme Court dealt them and other justice-seeking Americans a deafening blow via a 1978 ruling in a case styled *Regents of the University of California v. Bakke*.[122] As per the Cornell Law School Legal Information Institute, the court ruled any college or university that used race or ethnicity as "a definite and exclusive basis for an admission decision violated the Equal Protection Clause of the Fourteenth Amendment and Title VI of the Civil Rights Act of 1964."[123] The *Bakke* decision furthered an already uneven playing field in higher education by privileging White citizens in general, and White male students in particular, who did not have a history of segregation, underfunded and hence often shabby facilities, and related consequences of legal educational Jim Crowism. The court ruling proved there continued to be institutional forces working to systemically flatten full-scale human and civil rights curves bending toward justice and equality. Omega man Harold Lee (Doc) Holliday Jr. of Kansas City, Missouri, addressed such issues while receiving an award recognizing him as the Fraternity's Outstanding Citizen of the Year in 1977.[124] According to Holliday, a 1965 Howard University alumnus who in 1968 became the first Black graduate of the University of Missouri School of Law, the *Bakke* decision was part and parcel of a plan by the Supreme Court's conservative judges to dismantle affirmative action:

> In 1968 a madman named Richard Milhous Nixon, was elected President of this country. . . . And he was reelected in 1972, and one of the primary reasons that he was elected and reelected is a result of apathy of Black people to merely take a walk, pull a lever, punch a card, and determine the destiny of this country.
>
> As a result of those seeds that were not sown, he was allowed to appoint persons to the Supreme Court of this country, who, it was known, are clearly and totally unsympathetic with the circumstance of Black people in America. As a result of not sowing the proper seeds, we now sit and wait and hope that the rhetoric and the influence and the prestige of persons such as Thurgood Marshall will save the day as far as affirmative action is concerned.[125]

Holliday made a valid point: suffrage reforms brought on by the 1965 Selma, Alabama, campaign and buttressed by the same year's federal voting rights law had grown the number of Black Americans eligible to cast ballots, as well as the actual number of Black public officeholders. However, political gains did not always result in lasting social or educational gains because White conservative lawmakers and judges, among conservatives in other professions, devised legal means to nullify the gains. Richard Nixon's presidency foreshadowed the coming of a full-scale assault on American democracy, which took place from the late 1970s through the mid-1980s, attempting to stymie political gains secured by Black Americans due to the legislation of the 1960s.

Whereas Omega Psi Phi recognized Holliday in 1977 for his decades of outstanding work, *Ebony* magazine editors ranked seventeen other Omega men among the one hundred most influential Black Americans in 1978. *The Oracle* explained selection criteria "affects, in a decisive way, the lives, thinking and actions of large segments of the nation's Black population. The individual commands widespread national influence among Black, and/or is unusually influential with those Whites whose policies and practices significantly affect a large number of Blacks."[126] The seventeen Omega men who made the list were: Clifford Alexander Jr., secretary, Department of the Army; Edward J. Braynon Jr., Omega Psi Phi Grand Basileus and dentist; Christopher Fairfield Edley Sr., United Negro College Fund president; Earl G. Graves Sr., business mogul and *Black Enterprise* magazine publisher; Ernest Gideon Green, Little Rock Nine civil rights pioneer and US Department of Labor assistant secretary; Aloysius Leon Higginbotham Jr., US Court of Appeals, Third Circuit, judge; Jesse Hill Jr., Atlanta Life Insurance Company president and chief executive officer; Benjamin L. Hooks, NAACP executive director; Jesse L. Jackson Sr., Operation PUSH national president; Robert Earl James Sr., National Bankers Association president; Vernon Jordan Jr., National Urban League executive director; William Jesse Kennedy III, North Carolina Mutual Life Insurance Company president; Clarence Maurice Mitchell Jr., NAACP Washington Bureau director; Robert Nelson Cornelius Nix Sr., US congressman representing Pennsylvania; Spottswood William Robinson III, US Court of Appeals, District of Columbia, judge; Herbert Bell Shaw, African Methodist Episcopal Church senior bishop; and Walter Edward Washington, Washington, DC, mayor.[127] Those men were microcosms of other Omegas who in 1978 led efforts to promote Black manhood, scholarship, perseverance, and uplift in all fields of human endeavor. They made clear that, as a whole, the Fraternity continued to embody those four cardinal principles founders Frank Coleman, Oscar Cooper, Ernest Just, and Edgar Love established in 1911.

Omega's accolades were not singularly bound to earthly issues: Omega men left their imprint in space as well. Ronald Erwin McNair and Frederick Drew Gregory were fine embodiments of those facts. McNair was born in Lake City, South Carolina, in 1950. In his early life, he attended a local high school called George Washington Carver as a teenager. McNair, a physically fit and extremely cerebral student, was captain of the football and track teams and president of the band, the Better Speech Club, Future Teachers of America, the French club, and the senior class. After earning valedictory honors in 1967, he studied mathematics and physics during a summer program at Duke University in Durham, North Carolina. Nuclear decay was his primary research area. In 1968, McNair enrolled at North Carolina Agricultural and Technical (A&T) in Greensboro. He majored in physics, studying infrared layers and performing computer analyses, among other curricular activities. Being initiated by the Mu Psi chapter in 1969 was one notable extracurricular activity

McNair undertook prior to being graduated magna cum laude in 1971. For the next five years, he studied in the United States and abroad including work in theoretical laser physics in 1975 at l'École d'Été de Physique Théorique (the Summer School of Theoretical Physics) in Les Houche, France. Experts from Canada, England, Finland, France, the United States, and its Cold War foe, the Union of Soviet Socialist Republics, instructed, mentored, and worked alongside McNair. In 1976, he earned a PhD degree in physics from the Massachusetts Institute of Technology.[128]

McNair's fellow Omega man, Frederick D. Gregory, was a Washington, DC, native and nephew of Omega eminence Charles Richard Drew (Gregory's mother, Nora Rosella Gregory [née Drew] and Charles were siblings). Early in his life, Gregory completed Anacostia High School. New York City congressman Adam Clayton Powell Jr. nominated him for admittance to the US Air Force Academy in Colorado Springs, Colorado. Its administrators accepted Gregory, the only Black cadet in his freshman class. Enduring periodic discrimination, he completed a degree in military engineering in 1964. Gregory then undertook flight helicopter training at the Stead Air Force Base in Reno, Nevada, earning his wings in 1965. Next, Gregory served as a helicopter rescue pilot at the Vance Air Force Base in Enid, Oklahoma, before his deployment to Vietnam. In 1967, while under heavy fire, he rescued four marines and earned the Distinguished Flying Cross for his gallantry. After acquiring skills and flight hours for fixed-wing airplanes and helicopters, Gregory in 1970 trained as a test pilot in the US Navy before accepting an assignment with the 4950th Test Wing the federal government established in 1971 at the Wright Patterson Air Force Base near Dayton, Ohio. At the time, the air force conducted test flights in helicopters as well as in fixed-wing airplanes, and Gregory had experience in both aircraft. Assigned to the Langley Research Center in Hampton, Virginia, in 1974, Gregory logged more than 3,800 hours of flight experience in helicopters, fixed-wing airplanes, and thirty-eight other flying vehicles.[129]

In 1977, as McNair researched and wrote about physics, Gregory earned a master of science degree in information systems technology from George Washington University in Washington, DC. Gregory, a Washington native, underwent initiation into the Alpha Omega chapter of Omega Psi Phi in his hometown in 1959. In 1978, while holding the rank of major in the air force, Gregory became one of thirty-five new candidates whom National Aeronautics Space Administration (NASA) officials selected to participate in the space shuttle program that NASA officials launched in 1958. McNair joined Gregory as a candidate in the 1978 class. They trained at the Johnson Space Center in Houston, Texas. Though historical, their participation in the space shuttle program did not constitute a first in Omega Psi Phi or American history;

1952 Xi Epsilon chapter initiate Robert Henry Lawrence Jr. preceded them. He was a Chicago, Illinois, native who finished Englewood High School on his way to earning a chemistry degree from Bradley University in Peoria, about 170 miles southwest of Chicago, in 1956. Having participated in the Reserve Officers' Training Corps while an undergraduate, Lawrence earned a commission in the US Air Force during the same year he finished Bradley. After completing a PhD degree in physical chemistry from the Ohio State University in Columbus in 1965, Lawrence not only became the first Black astronaut in American history, but he also was the only astronaut in the Manned Orbiting Laboratory spaceflight program with a doctorate. While undergoing flight training aboard an F-104 *Starfighter* supersonic jet at the Edwards Air Force Base in California in 1967, the main landing gear of the jet collapsed during landing. *Starfighter* ejected Lawrence and his training supervisor, Harvey John Royer, the Philadelphia, Pennsylvania-born air force major who piloted the jet. Royer, then chief of operations at the Aerospace Research Pilots School, survived the accident, but Lawrence died.[130]

As McNair and Gregory worked in 1978 to extend the positive legacy of Omega spacemen affiliated with NASA, other Omegas questioned the need of the Fraternity to remain in the National Pan-Hellenic Council (NPHC). Omega Psi Phi's national Executive Secretary and chief administrative officer, Willie Joseph Wright—a Pompano Beach, Florida, native who earned a bachelor of science degree from Bethune-Cookman College (now university), a master of science degree from the University in Wisconsin, and a doctor of education degree from the University of Florida—provided an answer to that question in the summer issue of *The Oracle*. Wright posed this question, "Within the threads of the fabric of the world, where stands the National Pan-Hellenic Council (NPHC)? Where stands Omega? Where stand other fraternities and sororities in our concerns and efforts of the part of all peoples meager and non-existent accessibility to the total freedom, the goods, and services of the Universe?"[131]

Whereas Omega Psi Phi Executive Secretary Willie Wright possibly gestured toward a new crisis on the horizon, the dearth of Black Leadership, Omega man and 1936 Nu Omega initiate Charles Wright addressed the subject directly in "Our Most Endangered Species: The Black Leader," a speech he gave in November 1978 at the Founders' Day banquet of the Nu Omega chapter in Detroit, Michigan.[132] Charles Wright offered a timely critique that while acknowledging political and related societal strides Black leaders helped engender during the 1960s suggested that leadership arc had flattened by the late 1970s. Wright wrote, "Conservationists have drawn up lists of the most seriously threatened plants and animals. Among the rarest mammals are the Red Wolf, the Great Panda and the Javan Rhinoceros. The list of birds [en route] to extinction include the Puerto Rican Parrot, the Ivory-Billed Woodpecker and the Whooping Crane."[133] But an "even rarer bird than any of these and one who has been threatened with extinction for a far longer period of time," Wright contended, "is the Black leader."[134]

According to Charles Wright, a Black leader was "free—free of any feeling of racial inferiority, free of the compulsion to strive for material wealth or social status, free of hatred, and free of fear."[135] Wright continued, "Although a series of amendments have been adopted to correct the folly of the Founding Fathers, the Constitution, still, does not guarantee the growth and development of Black Leaders. This Society has made no provisions for the uncompromising Black Leader who cannot be made to feel inferior, frightened, bought, or co-opted. It is, therefore, understandable that all Blacks, who qualify under this definition, encounter serious difficulty with the Establishment, often ending tragically."[136] Wright invoked the names of Medgar W. Evers, Malcolm X, Martin King Jr., and Paul Robeson to support his claims. Assassins' bullets silenced Evers, Malcolm X, and King; the American government silenced Robeson.[137]

Wright, in "Our Most Endangered Species," named lesser known individuals who paid the ultimate price (death) or who escaped death but suffered tremendously for taking stands against injustice. Even though their sacrifices did not garner much, if any, notice or fanfare among most American citizens, Wright believed those freedom fighters deserved recognition. Among other persons, he mentioned Thomas Hency Brewer Sr., a Saco, Alabama, native who after earning a degree from the Meharry College of Medicine in Nashville, Tennessee, in 1920 moved to Columbus, Georgia, and practiced medicine. A tireless civil rights activist who cofounded the Columbus branch of the NAACP in 1939 and who eventually developed a close friendship with NAACP executive director and Omega man Roy Wilkins, Brewer tried to help bring democracy to Black masses in Columbus by challenging Georgia's all-White primary system and the state's long history of ethnic segregation.[138]

Lucio Flowers, a White department store owner, shot and killed Brewer in 1956 following an argument they had about a White police officer who beat and then arrested a separate Black man outside the building that housed Brewer's office and Flowers's store. After killing Brewer, who owned the building, Flowers, a renter, claimed self-defense in a subsequent trial. The jury found Flowers innocent of a legally punishable crime, but some citizens suspected Flowers killed Brewer because of Brewer's fervent political activism. Whatever the case, Wright and Wilkins' fellow Omega man, William Montague Cobb, memorialized Brewer in a 1956 issue of the *Journal of the National Medical Association*: "Dr. Brewer was a natural leader and always a champion of the 'little man' and a fighter for equal rights for his people," Cobb wrote, adding that Brewer, a recipient of the Omega Award for Outstanding Community Service by the Lambda Iota chapter, "died, as he had lived, in behalf of others. He has passed us the torch, and we may not break faith, lest he not sleep."[139]

US president James (Jimmy) Earl Carter Jr. was another individual whom Wright discussed in his 1978 *Oracle* article, "Our Most Endangered Species."[140] Many Americans believed Carter was a conscientious individual, a real humanitarian, but Wright thought Carter seemed indifferent toward the human rights of Black "dissidents."[141] To demonstrate his point, Wright discussed well-known activists such as Benjamin Franklin Chavis Jr. of Oxford, North Carolina. Born in 1948, Chavis as a teenager joined the Southern Christian Leadership Conference (SCLC) and worked directly alongside its first president, Martin Luther King Jr. Among other activities, Chavis served as SCLC youth coordinator for North Carolina. In 1968, following several more civil rights activities, Chavis enrolled in St. Augustine College (now University), an HBCU in Raleigh. Eventually, Chavis transferred to the University of North Carolina at Charlotte where he became the first Black student to earn an undergraduate degree in chemistry.[142]

In 1972, ten White and two Black jurors found Chavis and eight other Black young men—Reginald Epps, Jerry Jacobs, James McKoy, Wayne Moore, Marvin Patrick, Connie Tindall, Willie Vereen, and William (Joe) Wright—guilty of malicious burning, or arson, and of conspiring to commit assault against emergency personnel during a riot in Wilmington, North Carolina, on February 6 and 7, 1971. Violent White supremacists initiated the riot. During an originally peaceful demonstration at the Gregory Congregational United Church of Christ to protest the unfair treatment of Black and multiracial students attending New Hanover High School, a predominantly White institution they had to attend subsequent to the closing of a local all-Black high school, the White supremacists fired gunshots into Gregory Congregational. Ultimately, two men lay dead, a grocery store went up in flames, and multiple persons atop the roof of Gregory Congregational allegedly shot at White firemen who attempted to control the blaze. The ten White and two Black jurors who delivered the verdict in October 1972 found Chavis, Epps, Jacobs, McKoy, Moore, Patrick, Tindall, Vereen, and Wright guilty of torching the store and shooting at the firemen. Jurors found a tenth codefendant—White social worker, poverty opponent, and community leader Ann Shepard, who acquired separate counsel—guilty of accessory. The jurors' bogus verdict, which followed much prosecutorial misconduct, resulted in the trial's White judge, Robert Martin, sentencing Chavis, Epps, Jacobs, McKoy, Moore, Patrick, Tindall, Vereen, and Wright to prison sentences totaling 282 years.

Chavis's sentence was the longest, thirty-four years. Martin sentenced Shepard to between seven and fifteen years in prison.[143]

As soon as Martin sentenced the Wilmington Ten, individual citizens and groups such as the Congress of Racial Equality, the NAACP, the SCLC, the Student Nonviolent Coordinating Committee, and Omega Psi Phi, among other Black Greek-letter organizations, began lobbying North Carolina's White governor, James Baxter Hunt Jr., for commutations. Hunt commuted Shepard's sentence first. Hunt followed with commutations for Epps, Jacobs, McKoy, Moore, Patrick, Tindall, Vereen, and Wright in January 1978. They exited prison later during the same year. Hunt decided he would consider a commutation for Chavis in January 1980. That decision, which Omega man Charles Wright believed US president James E. Carter Jr. could pressure Hunt to reverse and commute Chavis's sentence before January 1980, was a principal reason Wright in his winter 1979 *Oracle* article, "Our Most Endangered Species," essentially characterized the humanitarianism for which Carter was known for as bogus.[144] According to Charles Wright, the hardships Chavis endured owing to the Wilmington, North Carolina, riot and his consequent imprisonment served notice that the "respectability politics" of the Carter administration did not include Black people and hence illustrated a "continuing hypocrisy that all non-White minorities have had to face from this government."[145]

Wright's 1979 article, which appeared in print shortly before Hunt commuted Chavis's sentence in December rather than January 1980, suggested that Black Americans had failed to groom enough leaders to meet the needs of the Black masses.[146] Persons such as Chavis, in Wright's opinion, were notable exceptions to that general rule. Continuing to explore the past and present societal conditions that made or destroyed leaders, Wright suggested the founders of Omega Psi Phi faced similar manifestations of White supremacy (e.g., White primaries, poll taxes, lynching parties) in November 1911. By the time his article appeared in the winter 1979 issue of *The Oracle*, however, Wright believed *Bakke* and *Bakke*-like court decisions, a rapidly expanding drug culture, and related vices were destroying Black America. "Unless we give added support to the existing of organizations and help create new ones that speak to our specific needs," Wright declared, the "unfortunate history" of Black second-class citizenship "may repeat itself. To what extent," he asked his fellow Omega men, "is our Fraternity making sure that history does not repeat itself?"[147] Wright was prophetic: the 1980s constituted a decade in which Black Americans witnessed the shift from the industrial age to the information age—resulting in the loss of jobs, the war of drugs due to the rise of crack cocaine and the subsequent over policing of Black communities, which resulted in the school-to-prison nexus, and an AIDS epidemic, which overwhelmingly plagued Black communities. In short, Black Americans felt "'buked and scorned" as the Tuskegee Institute Singers lamented in a gospel tune the group recorded decades earlier, in February 1916, as the founders and other members of Omega Psi Phi worked diligently to uplift Black Americans.[148]

The Eighties—A Second Nadir

Many Omega men entered the year 1980 with hopes of progress. Unfortunately, equally as many, if not more, Black Americans witnessed destitute conditions in the next nine years. In the early 1980s, the United States experienced increased unemployment, and poor Black Americans suffered the most, according to the Department of Commerce.[149] Job shortages disproportionately affected Black men, who composed the primary selection pool of Omega Psi Phi's recruitment, but shortages also impacted Black women and teenagers aged sixteen years or older. For example, in 1980, Black overall unemployment was 13.4 percent, more than double the percentage of White overall unemployment, at 6 percent.[150] By 1985, those percentages increased to 15.6 and 6.6 percent, respectively.[151] Simultaneously, companies increasingly looked internationally to complete manufacturing tasks, leaving limited opportunities for domestic workers, especially in the Northeast and the Midwest, two fertile areas of employment for millions of Black Americans since the great migrations of the early twentieth century. With changes in transportation, technology, and Cold War posturing by the United States and Soviets, numerous manufacturing jobs moved from urban to suburban places by 1980. Between 1980 and 1990, the median income for White families rose from $34,481 to $36,915, a 7 percent increase, while the median income for Black family income changed marginally from $21,151 to $21,454, or 1.4 percent.[152]

Notwithstanding, Black America awaited an attack that would try to flatten all political games made from the legislation of the 1960s. When Ronald Reagan, a "B-movie actor turned California Governor"[153] kicked off his 1980 presidential campaign, the then governor made an appearance at the Neshoba County Fair where he gave a speech on August 3, 1980. The speech drew attention for his use of the phrase "states' rights." Onlookers sensitive to social justice maintained that Reagan's choice of location for the event—the fairgrounds were just a few miles from Philadelphia, Mississippi—was vitriolic. The town was associated with the 1964 murders of civil rights workers James Chaney, Andrew Goodman, and Michael Schwerner, who sought to bring democracy and racial justice to Mississippi through the Student Nonviolent Coordinating Committee's Mississippi Freedom Summer. Reagan promised to "restore to states and local governments the power that properly belongs to them." Here Reagan dog whistled toward southern White voters and an extension of Richard Nixon's southern strategy.[154]

American citizens elected Ronald Wilson Reagan as president on November 4, 1980. The continued expansion of the Black electorate in the South and in other places affected most directly by the August 6, 1965, Voting Rights Act resulted in hundreds of additional Black elected local, state, and national officials by the time Reagan entered office on January 21, 1981. Despite those electoral successes, many Black Americans felt isolated because Reagan worked openly to purportedly "make America great again" by pushing Black communities back to second-class citizenship as witnessed in the 1940s, 50s, and 60s. But not every occurrence of the early 1980s dismayed Black Americans. For example, on April 12, 1983, voters in Chicago, Illinois, elected Black native Chicagoan Harold Washington as mayor. His victory quickened Omega man Jesse Jackson Sr., president of Operation PUSH, a Chicago-based organization, to consider vying for political office. Jackson's desire sped even faster as he watched voters in southern cities such as Charlotte, North Carolina, Birmingham, Alabama, and New Orleans, Louisiana, elect or reelect Black mayors. Their triumphs convinced Jackson he could galvanize enough social-minority voters to influence the Democratic national primary and win the party nomination for president of the United States. Thus, he organized the Rainbow Coalition, a grassroots organization made up of Blacks, Latinos, peace activists, women, and other people who believed mainstream politicians in the country forgot or never cared about them.[155]

On May 30, 1983, as Jackson developed his Rainbow Coalition, Omega Psi Phi was one of several Black fraternities with a noticeable presence at the first Greek Leadership Conference on Civil Rights and Economics in Chicago, Illinois. Among other decisions, the 217 conferees who represented more than 600,000 members of Black fraternities and sororities agreed to endorse a march on Washington, DC, on August 27, almost exactly twenty years after the historic August 28, 1963, March on Washington at which Alpha Phi Alpha member and civil rights leader Martin Luther King Jr. delivered his famous "I Have a Dream" speech. In addition to supporting the 1983 march, conference goers vowed to foster Black voter registration efforts countrywide, broaden opportunities for wealth acquisition for residents in their respective communities, and improve K-12 educational facilities. Omega Psi Phi Grand Basileus L. Benjamin Livingston Jr. and National Executive Secretary emeritus H. Carl Moultrie along with Walter G. Amprey, Mark A. Iles, Moses Conrad Norman Sr. (a future Grand Basileus), Kenneth Taylor, and Elbert A. Walton were official representatives of the Fraternity at the Greek Leadership Conference on Civil Rights and Economics.[156]

Omegas such as Livingston, Moultrie, Amprey, Iles, Norman, Taylor, and Walton enjoyed the high levels of comradery and unity of purpose in Chicago, but they were ecstatic about the Sixty-Second Grand Conclave of Omega Psi Phi in Kansas City, Missouri, from August 13 to 20, 1983. Like the leadership conference in Chicago on May 13, civil rights constituted a major topic at the conclave. Fittingly, several national leaders who delivered keynote addresses were civil rights icons. They included three Omega men: Benjamin Hooks, executive director of the NAACP; Michael Milburn, assistant pastor at the St. John Missionary Baptist Church in Oklahoma City, Oklahoma; and Jesse L. Jackson Sr., founder and director of Operation PUSH. A notable non-Omega member who also spoke was Walter Edward Fauntroy, a US congressman representing Washington, DC. After touting a successful NAACP membership campaign, Livingston presented Hooks with a $8,952.38 check for the NAACP's civil rights fund and a second check, in the amount of $7,000, to Fauntroy for the August 27, 1983, March on Washington. Immediate past Grand Basileus Burnel E. Coulon Sr. made a similar presentation to Jackson, who received $8,000 from the Fraternity to assist with a seemingly imminent presidential bid by Jackson.[157]

Coulon was a New Orleans, Louisiana, native who after completing Booker T. Washington High School fought during World War II and then enrolled at Tuskegee Institute (now University). While a student at Tuskegee, Coulon joined the Lambda Epsilon chapter of Omega Psi Phi in 1950. In 1953, after his student days were over, Coulon accepted a position as public relations director at Mississippi Vocational College (now called Mississippi Valley State University) near Itta Bena. In 1956, Coulon became public relations director of the South-Central Athletic, which was a sports league of some Black colleges located in Mississippi, Arkansas, Louisiana, and Texas. In 1965, he made Indianapolis, Indiana, his home, where, he distinguished himself as an educator, newspaper publisher, high school administrator, and member of the Zeta Phi chapter of Omega Psi Phi. He and many others who attended the Kansas City Conclave in 1983 were confident Jackson would run for the American presidency even though Jackson had not made a formal announcement about his intention. Jackson, however, did urge every conclave attendee to register to vote. Seeming to harken back to the traditional periods of the first and second Reconstructions of the 1860s through the 1870s and the 1950s through the 1960s, respectively, Jackson told one group of attendees: "there's a freedom train coming, but if you aren't registered, you can't ride."[158]

Jackson's anticipated presidential bid quickened the Omega spirit when *The Oracle* editor Samuel R. Shepard made Jackson one of the persons featured on the cover of the fall 1983 issue of Omega Psi Phi's official organ. Jackson graced the cover of *The Oracle*, standing next to Felmon Devoner Motley, the Fraternity's national public relations chairman and photographer. Motley held a *Time* magazine on whose cover Jackson was featured. Regarding the fall 1983 *Oracle*'s own cover, Lawrence Douglas Wilder was another Omega man on it. A Richmond, Virginia, native and 1950 initiate of the Zeta chapter at Virginia Union University, Wilder was a state senator (whom Virginians later elected governor) in the fall of 1983. Besides Jackson, Motley, and him, the "Father of Black History," Carter Woodson, and a trio of recently deceased Omegas who once served on the Woodson Home Project Committee of the ASALH—namely, Wiley E. Daniels Sr., Robert L. Gill, and Daniel B. Neusom—were the remaining Omegas on the cover of the fall 1983 *Oracle*.[159]

Editor Shepard, business and professional editor Emerson E. Brown, photographer John W. Williams, and other Omega men who assisted with *The Oracle* believed Jackson, a former Second Vice Grand Basileus, well-known civil rights activist, and Baptist minister, was a man who bridged gaps between old Omegas, especially in or from the South, and young Omegas all across the country. Before the second Reconstruction of the mid-twentieth century, many of the former men spent much of their lives in a segregated society, whereas most of the latter men were born or came of age as the 1954 and 1955 *Brown* decisions; the 1957, 1960, 1964, and 1968 federal civil rights laws; the 1965 federal voting rights law; and related court decisions and laws furthered the desegregating of society that older Omegas help initiate before the second Reconstruction. That some younger Omegas enjoyed the benefits of desegregated schools, first-class citizenship, uninhibited voting, and fair housing during the early 1980s but did not know or appreciate fully the hard-fought battles that produced those victories was a major concern for Shepard and members of his editorial team. Because of such ignorance or indifference, they and several other Omegas believed Black Americans faced the flattening of human and civil rights during the Reagan years.[160]

Jackson discussed voting and other civil rights matters during a weeklong trip he took to Europe in September 1983, almost two months before the formal launch of his presidential campaign in November and the release of the winter edition of *The Oracle*. The US Army sponsored the tour, during which members of the Theta Rho chapter headquartered in Frankfurt, Germany, hosted Jackson. At one event, held September 17 at the International Hotel, that drew approximately fifty attendees, Jackson spoke about possibly entering the field of Democratic presidential candidates as well as his duties as national president of Operation PUSH. In relation to the former topic, Jackson predicted large voter turnout would be key to whichever candidate won the 1984 election on November 6. He therefore charged members of Theta Rho with educating their compatriots about the significance of becoming registered voters.[161]

By September 17, 1983, the date Jackson encouraged Theta Rho's membership to press civilian and military officials to champion voter registration, President Ronald Reagan's actions were felt as racist economic and social policies, and Jackson rose as a serious contender for Black Americans and some White progressives as a Democratic presidential candidate. Reagan, in an attempt to win over Black, mixed-race, minority, and broad-minded White voters, signed legislation on November 2 authorizing Martin Luther King Jr.'s birthday to become a national holiday—an annual commemoration to which Reagan had objected frequently since entering office on January 20, 1981. Among the many vocal Omega men who supported the King holiday before Reagan's authorization in 1983, Virginia state senator and respected politician L. Douglas Wilder was one of the loudest. Wilder led a nine-year campaign in favor of the holiday. According to Wilder, commemorating King annually would remind people of the late civil rights icon's unwavering devotion to nonviolence, servant leadership, fair business practices, world peace, and helping poor people.[162]

Historically, Black organizations like Omega Psi Phi formed networks with other businesses, civil rights organizations, and religious groups, among other entities, to aid Black middle-class and lower-class (e.g., working poor) citizens. By November 2, 1983, the date Reagan authorized the King holiday, some politicians and journalists believed those networks became more difficult to sustain owing to rising numbers of single-parent, female-headed households; marginally educated, chronically unemployed, welfare-dependent, and criminal recidivists; and other factors that produced a larger Black underclass than preceding decades. Against those assessments, and likely because of Reagan's authorization, Jackson on November 3 announced his candidacy for the American presidency.[163]

Not long after Jackson officially launched his presidential campaign in November 1983, the Theta Rho chapter he visited in September hosted another Omega man, Grand Basileus L. Benjamin Livingston Jr., midway through November. Livingston spent several days touring and discussing the state of the Fraternity in Frankfurt, Darmstadt, Heidelberg, Stuttgart, and Karlsruhe. While in Frankfurt on November 9, Livingston enjoyed a banquet in his honor and fielded many questions about the Supreme Council. Visiting Frankenstein Castle in the Odenwald mountain range was a joyous occasion during the Darmstadt tour on November 9. His hosts, though, were familiar with the area, so learning about the general condition of the Fraternity was important to them. Livingston indicated Omega Psi Phi was in excellent shape owing to the leadership of the immediate past Grand Basileus, Burnel E. Coulon Sr., on whose momentum Livingston was determined to build. Members of Theta Rho treated Livingston to a full day of events in Heidelberg on November 10. They began with a tour of the city and ended with a banquet for Omegas and their wives or significant others. In Stuttgart, which Livingston visited on the fourth day of his visit, he toured a Mercedes-Benz factory and dined at a Chinese restaurant, among other fraternal activities. Karlsruhe was a bit nostalgic for Livingston: as an army private during the 1950s, he stayed in the town. A November 12, 1983, a disco in Kaiserslautern was the penultimate event for Livingston. The next day, he delivered the keynote address for the Achievement Week banquet and dance at which Theta Rho contributed $5,000 to local high school seniors and recognized the man of the year for Theta Rho chapter, Charles Banks III, Basileus of the chapter.[164]

Livingston's German visit took place as Black Americans in the United States grappled with several issues. Unfair standardized testing for admittance to college or universities or to compete in competitive athletics at those institutions; homelessness; converted powder cocaine, or crack; HIV and AIDS; police militarization; a school-to-prison nexus; and Black brain drain were foremost. With regard to standardized testing, Proposition 48 was a major cause of concern for some Black Americans. Adopted by more than 1,200 delegates to the National Collegiate Athletic Association's seventy-seventh annual convention in San Diego, California, on January 10–12, 1983, Proposition 48 mandated that, as of January 13, 1986, any individual who desired to play Division I sports competitively had to maintain a 2.0 overall grade point average on a 4.0 scale in eleven core high school courses.[165] The same individual had to earn at least 700 of 1,600 points on the Scholastic Aptitude Test or at least fifteen of thirty-six points on the American College Test to qualify as a Division I freshman student-athlete.[166]

Hundreds of well-known and influential coaches, athletic directors, and other decision makers at Division I institutions were present during the tumultuous debate in San Diego in January 1983. Georgetown University head basketball coach John Robert Thompson, a non-Omega member and one of the most prominent coaches in collegiate basketball, staged a walkout as a protest in a contest against Boston College. "I've done this because, out of frustration, you're limited in your options of what you can do in response to something I felt was very wrong," Thompson said two hours before the game. "This is my way of bringing attention to a rule a lot of people were not aware of—one which will affect a great many individuals. I did it to bring attention to the issue in hopes of getting [NCAA members] to take another look at what they've done, and if they feel it unjust, change the rule."[167] Many more of his coaching peers and administrators at HBCUs, as well numerous Omega men, both in and out of academe, favored maintaining or increasing academic standards; however, they did not favor Proposition 48 because, excepting mathematics and science, the standardized tests whose scores the proposition mandated for a freshman to participate in Division I athletics were culturally, economically, politically, and socially biased.[168]

Apalachicola, Florida, native and Tennessee State University in Nashville president Frederick S. Humphries was a microcosm of HBCU decision makers who opposed Proposition 48 in 1983. Conveying the shared opinions of other HBCUs presidents in an article the *New York Times* printed on January 17, 1983, Humphries opposed Proposition 48 because the ad hoc committee whose members drafted the proposal did not contain adequate representation from HBCUs and implemented unfair standardized test requirements:

> Thus, Proposition 48 would have minimum impact on the major institutions who generated it to clean up athletics and who have produced academic credibility problems, and maximum impact on those institutions in Division I and especially the historically Black colleges, who have a distinguished record of educating marginal students in higher education. It is interesting to note that the major universities of Division 1 . . . could have established more rigorous academic requirements via their own conference affiliations to meet their specific needs, rather than impose academic criteria which we believe to be unfair to student-athletes and to a large segment of Division I institutions. Standardized testing and the use of standardized test scores have been the subject of much research in higher education, especially as they impact on opportunities for higher education. There is an impressive body of knowledge that points to the insufficiency of standardized test scores in predicting the success of Blacks in higher education.[169]

Omega man (and future presidential candidate) Jesse Jackson Sr. echoed the sentiments of Humphries and the HBCU presidents for whom Humphries wrote in January 1983. During a speech Jackson delivered at Southern University in Baton Rouge, Louisiana, the then-most populous HBCU in the country, Jackson said Proposition 48 was "short-sighted and mean-spirited."[170] Tying the National Collegiate Athletic Association's enactment of the proposition with the legal chains White lawmakers, judges, and other officials utilized to impede or to prevent voting by non-White citizens in times of yore, Jackson barked: "They used literacy tests to deny us the right to vote. Then they want us to use standardized tests because White boys are inferior athletes to Blacks."[171] Not mincing a single word, Jackson "held out the threat of social, political and legal pressure" to undo Proposition 48, the Phoenix, Arizona, *Republic* newspaper reported.[172] As per the paper, he chanted: "NC-double-A, the preachers are coming.... NC-double-A, Black lawyers are coming. NC-double-A, the Black caucus is coming. NC-double-A, Black students are coming. And we don't like what we see."[173]

Run, Jesse, Run—A Glimmer of Hope in Reagan's America

Omega Psi Phi Grand Basileus L. Benjamin Livingston Sr. liked what he saw in his fellow Omega man, Jackson, in January 1983.[174] Livingston's high regard for Jackson had not diminished by the time he competed in his first national Democratic Party primary debate a year later, on January 15, a day before the inaugural King holiday.[175] The televised debate was bittersweet to Jackson, a foot soldier to King during the 1960s civil rights movement. Assisting with voter registration was one of Jackson's fortes and, during the television debate on January 15, 1983, he emphasized the need to continue registering citizens so they could vote on November 6, 1984.[176] Many viewers responded well to Jackson's policy emphases and his oratorical abilities: "He's a better extemporaneous spokesman" than his Democratic opponents, one New York voter remarked amid the debate.[177] Jackson, the *New Yorker* elaborated, "is in a similar situation to Reagan, who comes from an acting background. [Jackson, though, is a Baptist] preacher, and he comes from a talking background."[178]

Despite Jackson's proposed domestic platform and his charisma, he never became the Democratic Party's presidential nominee in 1984.[179] While his biggest issue was that he was Black in America, media outlets focused on his public relations nightmare having called a Jewish person "Hymie" and New York City "Hymietown."[180] To make matters worse for Jackson, his campaign never reached the level of financial support it needed to compete across the country for the duration of the primary contest. When delegates to the Democratic National Convention assembled in San Francisco, California, from July 16 to 19, they selected US vice-president Walter F. Mondale of Ceylon, Minnesota, as their party's presidential nominee.[181]

President Ronald Reagan defeated Mondale to win reelection on November 6, 1984. With the general election in the rearview, members of Omega Psi Phi recalibrated and refocused, cognizant the human and civil rights of Black Americans likely would remain under attack for the next four years. Parenthetically, "The Importance of Political Action Now," the Fraternity's theme for National Achievement Week from November 11 to 17, was appropriate.[182] Omega men continued to stress the importance of being active on the political front during their Sixty-Third Grand Conclave in Louisville, Kentucky, from December 26 to 30, 1984. Delegates elected Moses C. Norman Sr., assistant superintendent of public schools in Atlanta, Georgia, as Grand Basileus. He was born and reared near Macon, Georgia, and earned a bachelor of arts degree in English from Clark College (now called Clark-Atlanta University) in 1957.[183] Norman completed a master of arts degree in English language and literature from the University of Michigan in Ann Arbor, and he held a PhD degree in educational leadership and management from Georgia State University in Atlanta.[184] Norman sat in Omega's top seat during the Fraternity's seventy-fifth anniversary. In the early days of his administration, he presented a ten-point plan to improve operations through centralization. Specifically, Norman sought to forge stronger fraternal connections between the national headquarters in Washington, DC, and the international, district, state, and local chapters. Executing that plan included "raising and enhancing the image and the esteem of Omega [and] impacting the social, political, academic, economic, moral, and cultural order at the local, state, national, and international levels through aggressive and responsible programs."[185]

In 1985, Norman and his leadership team focused their attentions on the rise of alcohol and drug abuse, which increased homelessness resulting from the domestic policies of the Reagan administration.[186] Sponsors of the 1968 civil rights, or fair housing, act President Lyndon Johnson signed into law on April 11 intended that piece of legislation to help solve homelessness problems by "prohibiting discrimination concerning the sale, rental, and financing of housing based on race, religion, national origin, sex, (and as amended) handicap and family status."[187] Benjamin Foster Jr., a Raleigh, North Carolina, native and a member of the Tau Iota chapter in Hartford, Connecticut, wrote an article for the summer–fall issue of *The Oracle* titled "No Place for the Homeless."[188] In the article, he cited a 1984 study by the Department of Housing and Urban Development that concluded the number of "Blacks, women and young people among the 'street residents' had increased" at an alarming rate.[189] As per the same US Department of Housing and Urban Development report, Black men ranging in age from the late twenties to the mid-thirties comprised 40 percent of homeless people in the country, and women comprised 16 percent.[190] "To effectively deal with this national catastrophe," meaning homelessness, Foster asserted, "the government will have to recognize its role and rearrange its priorities accordingly. It will, for instance, have to consider the fact that politics, economics and the social environment have a tremendous effect on mental health. With the disintegration of the extended family system, appropriate measures must be adopted to help ease the depression, anger, stress, and the low self-esteem that threaten the lives of poverty-stricken people."[191]

Homelessness was not the only catastrophe, to quote Foster, that caused Omega men to take holistic views of problems besetting American society. Crack cocaine was another serious problem—and not simply for crack users. The epidemic also hurt their families and other loved ones, crack sellers, and innocent victims of the violence, theft, and other bad consequences of the epidemic. Users' relatives and close associates including youth often had to shoulder financial, emotional, and myriad other burdens of witnessing people about whom they cared addicted to crack. Violence associated with crack use and distribution showcased a disregard for respect and dignity. For street dealers, a considerable number of whom were uneducated or undereducated Black men, teenagers, or, in some cases, boys, crack brought fast money, and the thirst for such money frequently created hostile temperaments and dangerous situations. Crack hit populous urban communities particularly hard due in part to the typically close proximity of residents, and many of those communities were predominantly Black. Indeed, the rise of crack during the early to mid-1980s gripped Black America. Several scholarly and popular publications of those years noted crack was the country's biggest problem and, according to the *Atlanta Journal-Constitution*, Black people were more concerned about crack than any other ethnic group.[192] As crack flooded heavily Black communities, some observers contended that crack's proliferation in those communities typified the ruthless reality of the Reagan presidency.[193]

In many American localities, crack dependency in the 1980s reflected socioeconomic class differences. While drug use in general was down among those in Black upper and middle classes in comparison to the 1970s, poor Black people's dependency to crack and other debilitating drugs was high.[194] In truth, crack was detrimental wherever the drug was present in large quantity and available. Crack left people reeling, pushing some users to petty crimes and others to serious offenses. With Black Americans witnessing the shift from the industrial age to the information age, a recession, the war on drugs due to the rise of crack cocaine and the subsequent overpolicing of Black communities, which resulted in the school-to-prison nexus, along with "Voodoo economics," or "Reaganomics"—as presidential candidate (and eventual vice president) George Herbert Walker Bush and conservative radio host Paul Harvey Aurandt, respectively, termed Reagan's neoliberal, trickle-down, supply-side, monetary policies—exacerbated crack and other drug problems in the country.[195]

Responses to the crack epidemic differed greatly among American citizens. Louis Abdul-Haleem Farrakhan Muhammad Sr., a Nation of Islam minister born Louis Eugene Walcott in New York City, who long admired Omega Psi Phi, regarded crack's sudden emergence as evidence of a genocidal plot by a cabal of sinister White American leaders.[196] According to Muhammad, who usually went by Farrakhan, members of that cabal wanted Black and other social minorities, especially youth, to "sell death to each other."[197] Before the deliberate introduction of crack into social-minority communities, Farrakhan asserted further, the same White American leaders allowed poverty to operate as a "subtle form of genocide."[198] In stark contrast to Farrakhan, Black conservatives such as Philadelphia, Pennsylvania, native Robert Leon Woodson Sr. argued the crack epidemic represented the failure of government-sponsored welfare programs to uplift social minorities. Instead of those programs, Woodson believed neighborhood empowerment via self-help was the primary elixir for nearly every societal ill facing the Black community.[199]

The Diamond Jubilee

As Farrakhan, Woodson, and many other American citizens debated the genesis, symbolism, and other facets of the crack epidemic in the United States, some members of Omega Psi Phi prepared for a new civil rights movement they deemed imminent. Others prepared for the diamond anniversary of the Fraternity in 1986. When that year arrived, sons of Omega from across the globe celebrated seventy-five years of embodying manhood, scholarship, perseverance, and uplift—the four cardinal principles that founding fathers Edgar Amos Love, Oscar James Cooper, Frank Coleman, and Ernest Everett Just wrote into the Fraternity's keystone on November 17, 1911. The Tau Omega chapter in Greensboro, North Carolina, was responsible for one celebratory occasion in 1986. Together with the Alamance County Historic Properties Commission, the chapter dedicated a historical marker recognizing the lifework of Omega man, acclaimed physician, pioneering researcher, and beloved professor Charles Drew. The dedication took place in Burlington, a town in Alamance, on April 5; and his widow, Minnie Lenore Drew (née Robbins), and several additional family members were able to attend.[200]

Unfortunately, Omega man and astronaut Ronald E. McNair was unable to celebrate the dedicating of Drew's marker, whether in person or remotely. McNair died from an explosion during takeoff for the US space shuttle *Challenger* in Cape Canaveral, Florida, on January 28, 1986. McNair, a mission specialist on the crew, was thirty-five years old and, similar to Drew, represented the best and brightest young minds in the Fraternity at the time of his death. Another Omega man, H. Carl Moultrie, doubtless celebrated Drew's marker, but he did not attend its dedication ceremony. Moultrie was battling cancer when the ceremony took place on April 5; therefore, he was too sick to make the trip from Washington, DC, to Burlington, North Carolina. Moultrie's inability to make the ceremony was unfortunate considering that, during the preceding three years, the Fraternity that all three men—McNair, Drew, and Moultrie—loved dearly experienced some of the most significant growth in its history. After Moultrie joined McNair and Drew in Omega chapter on April 9, 1986, Grand Basileus Norman led Moultrie's memorial on April 13.

According to a commemoratory article in the winter 1986–87 issue of *The Oracle*, a large contingency of Omega men from both nigh and far honored the life and the legacy of the man who, because of his lengthy service to the Fraternity, historical memory, and relationship with thousands of regular to eminent members, befitted the sobriquet "Mr. Omega."[201]

Hundreds, maybe thousands, of delegates to the "Diamond Jubilee 75th Anniversary Conclave" shared precious memories of McNair, Drew, Moultrie, and other deceased Omega men whom they revered when the delegates met in Washington, DC, from July 26 to August 1, 1986.[202] During business sessions, Grand Basileus Norman laid a foundation for the Fraternity's next twenty-five years leading up to its Centennial on November 17, 2011. In the winter 1986–87 issue of *The Oracle*, Norman reaffirmed his administration's commitment to Omega's four cardinal principles: manhood, scholarship, perseverance, and uplift. He insisted the Fraternity's membership had to demonstrate its commitment to those principles "in more concrete ways than singing, stomping, meeting and declaring greatness"; rather, each member and chapter should work to achieve a set of purposeful, reasonable, and well-defined outcomes.[203] Norman explained:

> The real measure of a man is the quality of his contribution to the betterment of his fellow man. Certainly, this is true of Men of Omega Psi Phi Fraternity, Inc. . . . We have many outstanding and worthy programs, projects, and initiatives within our arsenal of services to our communities. I am highlighting as our centerpiece for the next year or more the following as imperatives for each of us:
> 1. Project Manhood
> 2. The Assault on Illiteracy
> 3. Voter Education, Registration, and Participation
> 4. Support of Black Colleges and Universities
> 5. Leadership Training
> 6. Omega Says No to Drugs.[204]

Norman closed by proclaiming the "world does not yet have as full an appreciation for our history and worth as we desire and deserve. These vehicles of service can do much to place these perceptions and understandings in the proper perspective."[205]

As Norman challenged his fellow Omegas to prioritize constructive social-service programs and reputable deeds more than stomping and declaring greatness, among other less important acts and actions, a new civil rights movement seemed to be on the horizon. As with the earlier movement of the 1950s and 1960s, members of Omega Psi Phi were prepared for frontline service. Frustrated that universal equality still did not exist in the country by the mid- to late 1980s, a sense of forcefulness and urgency reminiscent of the Black Power movement of the late 1960s emerged. Similar to the late 1960s, the views of more traditionalist freedom fighters during the mid- to late 1980s sometimes differed from the views of their more militant compatriots. Ideological divides even pervaded Omega Psi Phi, whose members simultaneously experienced rifts owing to fraternal matters. In many instances, age helped determine one's stance on such matters. Darryl Robinson, a member of the Chi Zeta chapter at Clemson University, explored basic generational differences among Omegas in an article he wrote for the summer 1986 issue of *The Oracle* titled "Omega: A House Divided."[206] "I bring pen to paper," Robinson declared, "because Omega now finds her house in dour disarray, with undergraduates all too untrusting of graduates and graduates often insincere to undergraduate needs and wants."[207]

To undergraduates, Robinson conveyed:

1. Though we neglect to realize it, we sometimes conflict with Omega's intent and tarnish her image.
2. We usually do not give our older brothers the esteem they deserve—not because they "out rank" us but because they are older and should be wiser. I do not suggest that we blindly take orders but use wisely their advice.
3. We must remain financially secure. No great organization can thrive without good leadership, which requires money. And, the unfortunate lawsuits we have pending (among other things) necessitate our need for money.
4. We must accentuate our fraternal lives politically. We all too frequently complain of the rules yet will not place ourselves in a position to change them.[208]

Robinson believed the acts he enumerated "and more are necessary if we are to fully participate in Omega. The burden of offering the olive branch does not fall entirely on us as undergraduates. Our graduate brothers must extend their glove as well."[209] Among those acts graduates needed to take, Robinson proposed they:

1. Work with and not dictate to us [undergraduates]. Brothers such as Wallace Keese, Tyrone Gilmore, and Lonnie Holeman, all of the Sixth District, have proven that it is possible. When coerced to do something against one's will, humans often rebel or alienate. Brothers are human! Realize that young men today are of similar distinction as those who founded this great brotherhood. Give us a chance.

2. Continue some old Omega practices. I appeal to my brothers to abandon the mission of abolishing some legacies such as "hopping" ... which remain dear to us undergraduates. If we are forced to abrogate these essential parts of Omega life, we will feel disoriented with our heritage. "Stepping" is not the only tradition facing expatriation; the threat is as imminent in other vitally important customs. If you are truly interested in a unified Omega, you will respect this plea.
3. Graduates should also try to understand and respect our way of showing Omega enthusiasm. If at times we seem far removed from and callous towards your view of Omega, understand that in their most virgin form our actions earnestly symbolize our pride in Omega and desire to perpetuate her most sacred tenet FRIENDSHIP. After all[,] most of what you object to was plagiarized ... from you. We simply "Feel the Fire."[210]

A bright and gregarious engineering student, Robinson represented the long tradition of Omega men expressing themselves intellectually in the pages of *The Oracle*. His essay brought to light the generational tensions within Omega as well as in the Black freedom struggle of the time and for years to come.

Several of Robinson's statements characterized Que Dogs, meaning Omega men with rowdy dispositions who lived in the present. Que Dogs emphasized pledging, and they enjoyed hopping. Often referred to as stepping or marching, hopping was a choreographed and synchronized maneuver long associated with Black Greek-letter step shows by the mid-1980s. Of equal significance as those acts, Que Dogs had affinity for canine images, particularly bulldogs. After George Clinton released his now-classic song "Atomic Dog" on the album *Computer Games* in 1982, the song became the unofficial rallying cry for Ques, both undergraduates and graduates.[211] Though there were aspects of the Que Dog culture that promoted fraternity, friendship, and fellowship, there also was an abrasiveness and hostility toward that aspect of Fraternity culture. As Robinson made clear in "Omega: A House Divided," tensions had reached fever pitch by the summer of 1986, when his article appeared in *The Oracle*, and it was clear to many Omegas the Fraternity was at a critical crossroad.[212]

The 1970s and 1980s presented old problems in new ways where Omega Psi Phi responded both nationally and internationally. However, the prowess of the Fraternity's work had more impact at the local levels. In this one of the Fraternity's responses to the pitfalls that beset society was the establishment of the Youth Leadership Council, which focused on issues faced by Black male youth around self-esteem, social and personal responsibility, family unity, academic growth and development, and conflict resolution engaging young men and their parents.²¹³ With the sickle cell crisis and the rise of the AIDS epidemic, Omega responded with local blood drives, which registered blood donors and encouraged citizens to donate blood in support of the American Red Cross.²¹⁴ Local chapters held food and clothing drives as seen through Achievement Week programs, where they donated to the Salvation Army and gave Thanksgiving baskets to those in need.²¹⁵ Omega Psi Phi uplifted members who strived to push for equity and equality in the midst of civil and human rights rollbacks. Of these, Omega man Jesse Jackson's campaigns for US president in 1984 and 1988 galvanized not only Omega's search for a better nation, through his Rainbow Coalition platform he brought a colorful constituency together in search of American democracy. The Fraternity enjoyed international growth with new international chapters chartered. Thus, Omega Psi Phi weathered the storms and looked forward to new horizons.

Chapter 7

Holding Aloft Vistas of Purple and Gold

Omega Psi Phi Fraternity, 1990 to the Present

By 1990, Omega leadership looked to the past as a model to guide the Fraternity toward its Centennial Celebration. The worsening social conditions that Black Americans faced during the 1980s warranted an appraisal of the best way for the Fraternity to help communities move forward. In many ways, however, the challenges of the 1990s were not completely different from longstanding issues in the United States. Education and learning remained crucial to Black advancement. But to address those issues, the Fraternity first had a meeting of the minds among Omega men. From there, the Supreme Council took serious study of previous Omega's men work and, in turn, took an aggressive stance on literacy in the early 1990s. Meanwhile, individual Omega men continued to accomplish new firsts—including one becoming the nation's first Black governor since the Reconstruction era. By the late 1990s, with an eye toward the future, the Fraternity tweaked some of its internal mechanisms. Omega men also relocated its international headquarters away from Washington, DC, to Atlanta, Georgia, and sent a delegation abroad to maintain its commitment to aiding African nations, particularly in post-apartheid South Africa.

The Fraternity, however, did not neglect domestic issues. In the early 2000s, Omega men revamped its Public Policy Forum—well timed with a growing conservative political leadership and national moments that highlighted federal neglect of Black Americans. Omega men, therefore, stepped to the forefront of advising US presidents no different than previous generations had done. The Barack Obama Administration benefitted from such counsel. In the most recent decade, Omega men elevated national dialogue around the killings of unarmed Black people and have led conversations before the Congressional Black Caucus. In total, while the broader national and international landscape has changed dramatically, Omega Psi Phi and its members remain involved in some of the most pressing issues facing Black people today.

Delegates to the Sixty-sixth Grand Conclave held in Detroit from late July to early August 1990 sanctioned the moratorium; however, consistent lobbying by Omega men caused Norman's successor, C. Tyrone Gilmore, to address such matters in the fall-winter 1990–91 issue of *The Oracle*. Gilmore recognized his administrative team faced many challenges but was confident its members were capable of meeting each challenge. He therefore highlighted six imperatives for the team:

1. The Membership Intake Program
2. Project Manhood—A reinvestment in the development of our undergraduate brothers and the Black male youth of America
3. Leadership Training
4. Regular dissemination of the *Oracle* and *Omega Bulletin* to inform the membership
5. Develop long range planning of not less than five years that includes fiscal feasibility, programmatic objectives, and program performance...
6. Strive to increase corporate sponsorship for continual enhancement of Undergraduate affairs, Talent Hunt, Youth Leadership Programs and to depreciate conclave registration fees.[1]

Of the six imperatives Gilmore listed, the membership intake program was the toughest to carry out. Many Omegas not only disliked the program, but they also disagreed with the way national leadership decided the program. According to some disapproving Omegas, the leadership voted to approve membership intake clandestinely rather than holding open meetings to discuss the program.[2] Therefore, many such Omegas refused to comply with the new membership intake program and continued to carry out traditional pledge processes. What's more, they articulated their points of contention with membership intake wherever and whenever possible, to include on occasion public spaces where nonmembers were present.

As Omegas expressed their dissatisfaction with the membership intake program through deeds as well as through words, Gilmore worked to guide the positive reemergence of the Fraternity publicly. To do so, he introduced a strong platform that emphasized three Rs: reclamation, retention, and recruitment. His platform mirrored the relief, reform, and recovery scheme former American president Franklin Delano Roosevelt developed as part of his New Deal during the Great Depression. Gilmore unveiled his platform in the summer–fall 1991 issue of *The Oracle*. Increasing the Fraternity's membership and launching a letter-writing campaign to the US Stamp Advisory Committee advocating a commemorative stamp honoring Omega Psi Phi founder Ernest E. Just were two aspects of the platform. Besides discussing those proposed acts, Gilmore in *The Oracle* gave special thanks to Omega men and astronauts Charles Frank Bolden Jr. and Frederick D. Gregory for upholding the ideals on which Just, Coleman, Cooper, and Love founded the Fraternity. Bolden and Gregory graced the cover of *The Oracle* issue in which Gilmore described his platform to remind the splintering membership of its noble past and to recenter the Fraternity on honor, academic achievement, human and civil rights, mentorship, and related indices of manhood, scholarship, perseverance, and uplift.³

As Grand Basileus, Gilmore knew his administration was crucial to Omega's future. Thus, his method was similar to the African concept *Sankofa*, which essentially meant one should recall the past to progress positively in the future.⁴ As Black America witnessed a new resurgence of African art and culture as seen through a boom of movies, music, and culture depicting Black life, Omega men, while identifying as Black, employed the notion of Africans in the Americas demonstrating the larger connection to the African diaspora.⁵ Demonstrating that resurgence, the summer–fall 1991 *Oracle* contained an article by the publication's editor, Charles H. Turner II, titled "History and Its Effect on Race Relations."⁶ Turner, a 1968 graduate of North Carolina Agricultural and Technical State University where he earned a bachelor of arts in history, explored ways many history textbooks and instructors failed students by continuing to exclude Black people, issues, and accomplishments—a regrettable matter about which Omega Psi Phi honorary member, scholar, and Association for the Study of Negro Life and History founder Carter G. Woodson thought, spoke, and wrote ad infinitum.⁷ "Due to the manner in which History has been written and taught to the American White and Black children from the past to the present," Turner declared in 1991, such writings and teachings have "played no small part in more firmly imbedding race prejudice, and in giving foundation for the belief that the Caucasian is superior to Blacks. It has succeeded in doing just this by giving a biased account of the Blacks' past, if an account is given at all."⁸ To facilitate civility and to help ensure scholarly fairness, Turner said the "approach of history of the past and early present must be altered. It must be altered because as a pure science it must give actual unbiased fact of thorough research of all groups within the area it is studying. It is not serving as a true science when it attempts to play up one group and humiliate another in the eye of the world."⁹

In "What Is Our Call?," another article in the summer–fall 1991 *Oracle*, Omega Psi Phi Grand Counselor, former undergraduate Supreme Council member (and future Grand Basileus) Lloyd J. Jordan recounted how just before the United States entered World War I, an intrepid group of Omega men demanded US president Thomas Woodrow Wilson give Black Americans the opportunity to train as officers.¹⁰ Jordan, a 1975 Omicron Sigma initiate from Chicago, Illinois, also recounted how Woodson inspired millions of American citizens to study and disseminate facts about Black life, history, and culture.¹¹ Jordan likewise provided insight into Omega Psi Phi's impact on the

New Negro movement and its expressive arm, the Harlem Renaissance. New Deal limitations vis-à-vis Black Americans and various Omegas' civil rights battles were additional subjects Jordan broached in his 1991 article.[12] Because the "New Deal was no deal for African Americans," Jordan contended, "the Fraternity gave both physical and financial support to many organizations like the International Brotherhood of Red Caps and . . . the NAACP."[13]

Moving his attention to the post-World War II years, Jordan referenced Omegas leading numerous human and civil rights campaigns. Their efforts in cultural relations, employment, health, housing, law, public education, and social security were particularly noteworthy, Jordan declared. He spotlighted lawyers George L. Vaughn, Francis Morse Dent, James Madison Nabrit Jr., Spottswood William Robinson III, and Wiley Austin Branton as well as plaintiff and activist Charles Goode Gomillion. Together, Jordan wrote, they in 1960 helped successfully challenge gerrymandering in Tuskegee, Alabama, the county seat of Macon, which sweltered with antidemocratic practices at the time. While Jordan did not mention Omega man Fred David Gray, it is important to do so. Gray argued *Gomillion v. Lightfoot*, whose November 14 decision by the US Supreme Court established the one person, one vote principle.[14]

As spelled out throughout this book, members of Omega Psi Phi were active on all civil rights fronts from the founding of the Fraternity in 1911 through the civil rights movement during the 1950s and 1960s. Jordan in his 1991 article criticized what he viewed as contentment among Omegas during the 1970 and 1980s. Similar to members of other predominantly Black organizations, Jordan wrote, Omegas believed they "had arrived and . . . became complacent and lulled into a false sense of security."[15] Jordan, evoking the spirit of Martin Luther King Jr., among other freedom fighters of yore, stated: "It is now more than ever that we as a Fraternity and as individuals must rededicate ourselves to our Cardinal Principles of Manhood, Scholarship, Perseverance and Uplift. We must become the drum majors for the existence of African-American people."[16]

Generational Differences

One of Omega Psi Phi's primary challenges during the early 1990s regarded older members who had led the Fraternity while King was alive or during the years immediately following his death. In general, their wisdom was undisputable by 1990, but they often were unwilling to spread wisdom or to share power, especially with younger Omegas whom they considered less prepared or simply unwilling to uphold the high standards set by founders

Oscar Cooper, Frank Coleman, Ernest Just, and Edgar Love. Many older Omegas of the early 1990s were baby boomers, meaning they were born between 1946 and 1964, and hence came of age during the segregationist 1950s, 1960s, or 1970s.[17] Accordingly, their life experiences tended to be different from the typical experiences of Generation Xers born between 1965 and 1980.[18]

Michael Anthony Jefferson, a 1984 Chi Omicron initiate, explored generational differences among Omegas in an article titled "A Changing of the Guard" that also appeared in the summer–fall 1991 issue of *The Oracle*.[19] An attorney and charter member of the recently established Epsilon Iota Iota chapter of Omega Psi Phi in New Haven, Connecticut, Jefferson reminded *The Oracle* readers that young men could have great ideas; hence, older leaders should not hesitate to pass the torch when their prospective successors were ready to take charge.[20] According to Jefferson, American society was moving fast toward a period as explosive as the 1960s.[21] In his judgment, the 1990s had the potential to surpass the 1960s in terms of explosiveness.[22] Among other combustible matters, the 1990s economic system was beginning to collapse because of widespread greed and corruption, and muddleheaded public officeholders were uttering catchphrases and slogans instead of devising and implementing real domestic and foreign policies to assist present and future citizens.[23] Writing about Black leaders, in particular, Jefferson opined:

> Today, many Black leaders in America . . . seem to lack vison which will rescue the masses of our people from dismal plight that characterizes our present-day reality. Many "old guard," specifically, civil rights leaders of the past, readily admit that they have "run out" of new ideas needed to combat the ills confronting our people today. This clearly indicates that the time has come for a changing of the guard.
>
> We must not forget that two of our greatest leaders—Malcolm X and Dr. King—were relatively young men when they assumed leadership roles in our struggle. They provided our people with new ideas, new methods of struggle and a renewed sense of hope that Black people needed so desperately at that time. They served as the vanguard of a generation which brought our people one step closer to liberation.
>
> Those who make up the "old guard" today must not become so blinded by their own quest for power and glory that they refuse to pass on the mantle of leadership. This will only delay our march toward liberation. They must realize that new ideas and new methods of struggle must be employed in the struggle today just as they were in their day. This is not to suggest that the "old guard" is no longer needed in our

struggle, for their wisdom based on years of experience can be an invaluable resource for those who must now take hold of the reins of leadership.

Our struggle is one that is far more from over. Each generation must play its part. For if it were not [for] the effort put forth by generations that preceded our own[,] we would not have made it this far. Today, it is our turn. Those who were born during the turbulent tears of sixties and early seventies must carry on where our parents and grandparents left off. The time has come for a changing of the guard.[24]

Such matters of leadership had linear progressions, commencing with the late nineteenth century and into the early twentieth century. For instance, Omega man Carter G. Woodson, along with Alexander Crummell, William Edward Burghardt Du Bois, James Weldon Johnson, and other members of the American Negro Academy, established in 1897 after *Plessy v. Ferguson*, challenged leading Black Americans born or reared during post-Civil War Reconstruction to alter their strategies and tactics to meet changes of the late 1890s. Rather than acquiescing to White supremacy, Crummell, Du Bois, Johnson, and their like-minded contemporaries believed and organized from within and took a stand against Jim Crow. During the 1920s, younger New Negro and Harlem Renaissance advocates such as Omega man Langston Hughes began to challenge Johnson, Woodson, Du Bois, and comparably well-known leaders of preceding generations (Crummell died in 1898). While Hughes and many other New Negroes and Harlem Renaissance proponents extended the arts-and-letters emphases of the American Negro Academy, several older Black American leaders—particularly Du Bois, whom Hughes revered—initially thought the Harlem Renaissance component of the New Negro movement was folly. In a similar generation gap, Woodson and Hughes's fellow Omega man, Bayard Rustin, and those of his generation who helped lead the second Reconstruction including its Black Power phase challenged strategies and tactics of New Negroes. Rustin and his contemporaries organized the masses—including working folk who were not afforded a college education—while demonstrating the perennial necessity of architecture, literature, music, painting, poetry, sculpture, and cognate disciplines and fields. Minister and scholar Charles Eric Lincoln in 1969 cofounded the Black Academy of Arts and Letters, an ideological descendant of the American Negro Academy. Future Omega men born immediately before, during, or after Lincoln and forty-nine other highbrows founded the academy, later challenged notions of leadership that emerged during the second Reconstruction. Instead of sitting high and looking low, Generation Xers believed leaders should lead from the field.[25]

The Dawning of a New Omega

In 1980, the final year of Generation X births according to the Pew Research Center, among other sources, the US Department of Education issued a national report indicating the reading and comprehension abilities of 44 percent of Black citizens was at a fourth-grade level. By departmental metrics, that category of citizen was not well suited intellectually to be a full-time member of the mainstream workforce. A set of Black publishers affiliated with Black Media, a corporation headquartered in New York City, read the report and initiated a national program called the Assault on Illiteracy. At the second annual Hall of Fame Community-Building Awards dinner held in 1983 at Howard University in Washington, DC, where four young and industrious Black men founded Omega Psi Phi in 1911, *National Black Monitor* magazine honored Grand Basileus Moses C. Norman Sr. for his leadership in promoting the Assault on Illiteracy program, among other worthy initiatives. Norman continued to lead the national efforts of the Fraternity until his retirement as Grand Basileus in 1990. His successor, C. Tyrone Gilmore, extended the relation the Fraternity had with the program.[26]

The summer–fall 1991 issue of *The Oracle* contained an article written by Omega man Leonard Douglas, a forty-year member of the Fraternity. He discussed Assault on Illiteracy leaders, staffers, and volunteers creating a plan they labeled Goals for the Year 2000 and Beyond. National officials for Omega Psi Phi and more than ninety additional organizations including the NPHC, the Improved Benevolent and Protective Order of Elks of the World, and the Prince Hall Masons agreed to help execute the plan. A second article in the summer–fall 1991 *Oracle* reported Omega Psi Phi Grand Basileus Gilmore was a national chairman for the Long Range Planning and Resource Committee of the Assault on Illiteracy program. He and chairs for the nine other standing committees—Black Business and Professional Support and Involvement, Black Church Support and Involvement, Interorganizational Liaison, Parental Support and Involvement, Professional Education, Public Education, Public Information, Service and Rehabilitation, and War Chest—developed twelve shared goals to combat illiteracy and uplift Black communities by strengthening Black businesses and historically Black colleges and universities (HBCUs), lowering unemployment rates, and decreasing crime and teen pregnancy. As was the case for decades, Gilmore and other Omegas who participated in the Assault on Illiteracy program understood that social action was an effective vehicle to make a positive impact on Black America.[27]

As made clear by the commitment to the Assault on Illiteracy program, Grand Basileus Gilmore believed refocusing Omega Psi Phi on the four cardinal principles of the Fraternity—manhood, scholarship, perseverance, and uplift—was the best way to revitalize the true Omega spirit. He also desired to continue revitalizing *The Oracle*. With exception to a brief period from the fall of 1988 through the spring of 1991, *The Oracle* had been the most comprehensive and consistent reservoir of information about the Fraternity since the first issue of *The Oracle* appeared in June of 1919. As stated previously, when *The Oracle* ended its two-year hiatus in 1991, many Black Americans and Black-led organizations needed to reestablish themselves to catch up with the changing times. *The Oracle* explored a few crises but also broadcast information about Omega men and other people who served as ambassadors for Black communities within the country and elsewhere in the world.

Omega man Lawrence Douglas Wilder Jr. was an exemplar of Black ambassadorship in the United States. In the fall of 1989, he won a general election to become the first known Black governor in the country since Pinckney Benton Stewart Pinchback who served as acting governor of Louisiana in the winter of 1872–73. As stated in chapter 6, Wilder was a 1950 initiate of the Zeta chapter at Virginia Union University in Richmond, his hometown. He earned an undergraduate degree in chemistry from Virginia Union in 1951 before federal military officials conscripted him into the army during the Korean War. Wilder volunteered for combat, earning a Bronze Star for valor and attaining the rank of sergeant. After the war, he worked in the medical field and commenced graduate work in chemistry but eventually decided to study law at Howard University, which he began in 1956 and finished in 1959. In 1969, after operating a private practice in Richmond, Wilder entered politics and became the first Black person to serve in the Virginia Senate since the first Reconstruction. Sixteen years later, in 1985, voters elected him the first Black lieutenant governor and the first Black person elected to a statewide office in Virginia.[28]

On July 12, 1990, the National Association for the Advancement of Colored People (NAACP) bestowed its coveted Spingarn Medal on Wilder, who sat in Virginia's governor's chair from January 13, 1990, until January 15, 1994.[29] As he occupied that coveted seat, other Omegas also celebrated Black history, made history, or were the subjects of historical commemorations. Riding high on the momentum galvanized by the Sixty-Seventh Grand Conclave held in Atlanta, Georgia, from July 30 to August 6, 1992, Omega Psi Phi and South Carolina Educational Television cosponsored a Black history telethon that networks broadcast across the United States as well as in multiple Asian and European countries in February 1993.[30] On June 5, the Black South Carolina Hall of Fame inducted founder Ernest Just posthumously.[31] From July 10 to 18, the South Carolina State Museum featured Just in an exhibition titled "A Spark of Genius: Medicine, Science, and Creative Thought in South Carolina," a companion to a traveling exhibit by the Smithsonian called "The

Real McCoy: African-American Invention and Innovation, 1619–1930."[32] "A Spark of Genius" also featured Omega men and astronauts Charles F. Bolden and Ronald E. McNair.[33] Omega Psi Phi Grand Basileus Gilmore was pleased to announce a $20,000 contribution the Fraternity made to the Carter G. Woodson Educational Center, which earmarked funds to house the Carter G. Woodson Leadership Institute, the Woodson Adopt-A-School Program, the Association for the Study of African American Life and History Speakers Bureau, and the Carter G. Woodson Scholars Medallion.[34] Besides that contribution, he mentioned the Omega World Headquarters Building Fund Committee that former Grand Basileus Moses Norman authorized during the Detroit Conclave from July 28 to August 2, 1990.[35] Gilmore sat on the committee, which met in Charlotte, North Carolina, from August 20 to 22, 1993.[36] "We were able to spend valuable time charting a course and plan of action that will eventually lead to a new World Headquarters Building," Gilmore recollected in the summer–fall 1993 *Oracle*.[37] Believing the Fraternity had "a unique opportunity to make this dream a reality," he declared enthusiastically: "Let us challenge ourselves to approach this task with gusto!"[38]

Charles Turner II, editor of *The Oracle*, agreed wholeheartedly with Gilmore. Both men, as microcosms of other national leaders in Omega Psi Phi, envisioned the headquarters (complete with a museum) extending the Fraternity's long record of achievement, and they made no apology for being ambitious. With several mandated programs governed by men with high ideals who desired to make additional worthy contributions to both American and global society, Turner noted, Omega Psi Phi was in a good position to continue making its mark on domestic and foreign social orders.[39]

In September 1993, Johnson Publishing Company's *Ebony* magazine featured an article chronicling Omega Psi Phi's contribution to global society.[40] The article indicated the Fraternity had 662 chapters worldwide and a membership that exceeded 100,000. The article mentioned numerous "well-known personalities" being Omegas, and listed Jesse Louis Jackson Sr., Michael Jeffrey Jordan, and Lawrence Douglas Wilder Jr. as representatives.[41] Deceased Omegas named in the same *Ebony* article included Charles Richard Drew, Langston Hughes, Percy Lavon Julian, Benjamin Elijah Mays, and Carter Godwin Woodson. Highlighting the leading roles Omegas had performed for decades in the pursuit of equality, Grand Basileus C. Tyrone Gilmore Sr. declared: "We feel that we're way out front in the area of civil rights, going back to the days when Roy Wilkins and Wiley Branton were first initiated as brothers."[42] Wilkins was a charter member of the Xi chapter at the University of Minnesota in Minneapolis in 1921, and Branton joined Alpha Omega chapter in Washington, DC, in 1953. Considering their contributions to the civil rights movement as well as the more recent contributions of Omegas such as Jackson, Wilder, Benjamin Lawson Hooks, and Vernon Eulion Jordan Jr., Gilmore elaborated, "we feel that we're definitely ahead of the game."[43]

In addition to discussing prominent members of Omega Psi Phi, the 1993 *Ebony* article discussed innovative financial, economic, sociopolitical, and educational initiatives the Fraternity sponsored or cosponsored. The Omega Psi Phi Fraternity Federal Credit Union, established in 1986, was the first business venture of its type led by a Black Greek-letter organization. By 1993, the credit union had 700 members and loaned more than $225,000 to creditworthy clients. Among other sources of pride and achievement, Omega Psi Phi raised or contributed hundreds of thousands of dollars to help sponsor grants, scholarships, and related forms of assistance in partnership with organizations such as the NAACP and the United Negro College Fund. In 1990, Omega Psi Phi created a program whereby the Fraternity donated $50,000 per year to the United Negro College Fund. In 1992, Omega's national leadership tripled that amount, which excluded donations from individual chapters throughout the country. Besides those endeavors, Omega Psi Phi developed endowed chairs at two HBCUs—namely, Rust College in Holly Springs, Mississippi, and Wiley College in Marshall, Texas—and was in the process of developing two additional endowed chairs at other HBCUs.[44]

Restoring and preserving Youngsholm, the 150-year-old Wilberforce, Ohio, home of Omega man and US army colonel Charles D. Young, was another Omega Psi Phi initiative *Ebony* showcased in its September 1993 article about the Fraternity.[45] Constructed in 1832, purchased by Young in 1907, and located approximately one mile from Wilberforce University, the house served as an Underground Railroad way station according to some reports.[46] By 1993, Omega's general membership had spent $500,000 on the restoration and preservation project, which Omega's national leadership intended to complement the African American Museum in Wilberforce. Other examples of the Fraternity's commitment to aiding Black historical figures and spaces included its sponsorship of a Library of Congress exhibition titled "Moving Back Barriers: The Legacy of Carter G. Woodson" and a cosponsored teleconference program about Black history.[47] Omega Psi Phi collaborated with the Public Broadcasting Service and with South Carolina Education Television to produce the teleconference program.[48]

As the September 1993 *Ebony* article made clear, Project Manhood—the revamped national leadership tutorial and leadership development program for Black male youth in general and Black male preteens and teens in particular—was yet another important undertaking of Omega Psi Phi. Members selected Black male youth to join in leadership conferences during Grand Conclaves. Omega's long-standing Talent Hunt program and essay-writing contest were additional major initiatives into which the Fraternity's national membership devoted time, money, and energy. Local chapters created their own initiatives to mentor Black youth including adopting schools, collaborating with boys' and girls' clubs, organizing summer camps, and tutoring at-risk students. Camp Long near Aiken, South Carolina, was an exemplary summer initiative, according to the *Ebony* article.[49]

Toward a New Millennium

Grand Basileus Gilmore, Grand Keeper of Records and Seal Adam E. McKee, Jr., and other national officials presented a program called Omega 2000 as part of their general plan to help create or maintain positive change for Omega Psi Phi. McKee indicated the Supreme Council approved Omega 2000 in December 1992. Since that time, he went on, the program had become one of the most significant initiatives in the history of the Fraternity. According to McKee and Gilmore, the visionary agenda of Omega 2000 included completing the new international headquarters about which Gilmore wrote in the summer–fall 1993 issue of *The Oracle*, creating a position for a full-time public relations director at the headquarters, and establishing a benefits program for members and multiple foundations to address academics, criminal activities, and boys' camps. Together with adhering to the revised Fraternity manual, adhering to the membership intake process, and practicing "caring and sharing of fraternity and friendship, key ingredients of a true brotherhood," among other constructive acts, Gilmore proclaimed in the winter–spring 1994 issue of *The Oracle* that Omega 2000 was a guiding principle for future success.[50]

Determined to chart a smooth path forward for Omega Psi Phi, Grand Basileus C. Tyrone Gilmore commissioned a comprehensive review committee during the fiscal year 1993–94. Former Grand Basileis Edward Joseph Braynon Jr., Burnel Elton Coulon Sr., Marion Winston Garnett, Loveless Benjamin Livingston Jr., Moses Norman Sr., and Tucker composed the committee. Readying the revised Fraternity ritual for Gilmore's review and the Supreme Council's possible approval was Braynon, Coulon, Garnett, Livingston, Norman, and Tucker's primary task. As per the winter–spring 1994 issue of *The Oracle*, Norman oversaw the ritual's revision and thus served as the comprehensive review committee's initial chair during the self-discovery meeting. Norman eventually surrendered the chair to Tucker, who presided over the rest of the meeting.[51]

Braynon, Coulon, Garnett, Livingston, Norman, and Tucker acknowledged multiple problems Omega Psi Phi faced recently. Increasing membership, improving administrative and financial operations, enhancing conclave programing, and shoring up *The Oracle* and the *Omega Bulletin* were paramount. Braynon, Coulon, Garnett, Livingston, Norman, and Tucker committed themselves to devising solutions to those problems and to all others in apolitical manners. Regarding membership, they believed the Fraternity needed to pursue international prospects aggressively—a belief that ran counter to traditional Omega stances on recruitment. Braynon, Coulon, Garnett, Livingston, Norman, and Tucker also believed the Fraternity should provide insurance for each national officer but, as conscientious fiduciary stewards, said the day-to-day operations of every officer required mandatory auditing. If Gilmore's administrative team did not agree to an audit, Tucker and his peers on the comprehensive review committee recommended the Supreme Council utilize its constitutional power to intervene to ensure the audits. The committee likewise recommended creating a national position called director of undergraduate activities to help ensure all undergraduates had ample leadership development opportunities and to fashion a program that defined clearly fraternal expectations for undergraduates in relation to their character. The committee suggested updating the Omega Psi Phi constitution to match changes approved at Grand Conclaves, which committee members agreed needed revitalizing to include more development activities for delegates and their families. Additionally, the comprehensive review committee Tucker chaired endorsed a stronger membership reclamation project. As part of its endorsement, the committee recommended national headquarters offer financial incentives to local chapters to spur interest in the project.[52]

Some of the final major recommendations Braynon, Coulon, Garnett, Livingston, Norman, and Tucker made in 1994 regarded the geographical districts in Omega Psi Phi, *The Oracle*, the *Omega Bulletin*, and the monetary condition of the Fraternity. To be specific, restructuring certain districts might achieve greater parity and hence increase stability among all districts. Aware of the power of *The Oracle* and the dexterity of the *Omega Bulletin*, Braynon, Coulon, Garnett, Livingston, Norman, and Tucker sought to increase feature articles on life skills and issue the *Omega Bulletin* on a quarterly, if not a monthly, basis. Furthermore, the six past Grand Basileis advised the Fraternity's present leadership to reconsider the executive director's role and to provide money for a director of development to broaden Omega's "scope and influence through fundraising, [both] internally and externally."[53]

As Braynon, Coulon, Garnett, Livingston, Norman, and Tucker made recommendations to Gilmore in 1994, other members of the Fraternity addressed issues regarding human and civil rights in the United States and elsewhere in the world as part of the Omega 2000 platform. For example, local chapters created programs to quell violence in blighted neighborhoods due to postindustrial conditions, a lack of access to health care, jobs, and a quality education, and the arrival of crack cocaine. After Cleveland, Ohio, served as the host of the Sixty-Eighth Grand Conclave held from July 22 to July 29, 1994, where Dorsey Columbus Miller Jr., a 1962 Psi chapter initiate was elected as Grand Basileus, Omegas in the country and abroad also looked forward to christening a new international headquarters. They achieved that goal on December 30, 1994, when national officials completed all necessary paperwork for the Fraternity to become the proprietor of the Omega Psi Phi World Center, a building at 3951 Snapfinger Parkway in Decatur, Georgia, a suburb east of Atlanta. For some members of the Fraternity, relocating the headquarters from 2714 Georgia Avenue Northwest in Washington, DC, presented a tenuous situation that simmered just beneath Omega's surface. In particular, certain members in the Third District comprising Washington and Virginia said relocating the headquarters was questionable at best and irresponsible at worst because property value in the Washington metro area skyrocketed as urban renewal and gentrification prompted a massive land grab by real estate moguls seizing on the reversal of White flight. If the Fraternity held on to the Georgia Avenue headquarters, Third District critics predicted, the Fraternity would improve its financial portfolio because property value along Georgia Avenue doubtless would increase in the immediate future. All the same, more than 1,000 individuals attended the December 9, 1995, ribbon-cutting ceremony in Decatur.[54]

Omega man William Henry (Bill) Cosby Jr., one of the most celebrated actors in the world, and Earl Gilbert Graves Sr., publisher of *Black Enterprise* magazine, were featured personalities at the ribbon-cutting ceremony in December 1995. Cosby, an April 1988 initiate of the Beta Alpha Alpha chapter in White Plains, New York, was master of ceremony. Graves delivered the keynote address. In addition to the main event at which Cosby and Graves appeared, the Fraternity hosted a broad range of activities for members and their families. There was a luncheon for Quettes and Omega men when the Grand chapter inducted National Basketball Association star Shaquille Rashaun O'Neal of the Orlando Magic. During one interview, Fort Lauderdale, Florida, businessman, educator, and Omega Psi Phi Grand Basileus Dorsey Miller—a Morehouse College graduate from Ocala, Florida, who earned a master's degree from the University of Florida in Gainesville and a doctorate from Florida Atlantic University in Boca Raton—confirmed "Omegas are on the move."[55] Despite skeptics, Miller declared, the Fraternity had "tremendous success" relocating the headquarters from Washington, DC, to Decatur, Georgia, and hoped to "pay off the building" by January 1997.[56]

As regards the 1994 decision to relocate the headquarters of Omega Psi Phi from Washington to Decatur, part of that decision might have resulted from the myth and the maxim of nearby Atlanta as a Black mecca, an enclave of

Black prosperity.[57] In a 1994 article, the allure of Atlanta (which Washington had possessed since the Civil War), the *Atlanta Voice*, the largest Black-owned newspaper in Georgia, declared: "There is a drug that has been around for over 20 years that had been making African Americans pack up all of their meager belongings and move, sometimes across country, often with little or no planning or savings, seeking a better life. That drug is called—Atlanta."[58] Despite federal census data indicating Washington being a more progressive city for Black Americans than Atlanta in categories such as education, home ownership, income, and poverty, that Atlanta provided immense opportunities for Black Americans and organizations such as Omega Psi Phi was undeniable.[59] Black political empowerment, the Atlanta University Center, and "Sweet" Auburn Avenue were three of many reasons the Atlanta metro area, including Decatur, represented the quintessence of the Black New South.[60] Whereas some Atlantans once deemed Auburn Avenue a Black Wall Street similar to more familiar places such as Durham, North Carolina, and the Greenwood community in Tulsa, Oklahoma,[61] *Ebony* magazine, the Atlanta Convention Bureau, and city boosters characterized Auburn Avenue as the richest single predominantly Black-occupied thoroughfare in the world.[62]

Many scholars agreed that Atlanta's Black two-time mayor, Maynard Holbrook Jackson Jr., was responsible for much of the city's late twentieth-century rise. Jackson's gold-standard affirmative action initiatives and his tax breaks, spawned by the Sunbelt boom—the shift from industrialism to the information age creating technical jobs and a Black return migration—were particularly effective at stimulating growth in Georgia's predominantly Black state capital.[63]

As a testament to the global prowess of Atlanta by the year 1990, on September 18, the International Olympic Committee chose Atlanta instead of Athens, Greece, to host the Centennial Olympic Games from July 19 to August 4, 1996, based on a representation of Atlanta's civil rights lore centered on the iconic remembrance of the city's most beloved son, the late Martin Luther King Jr., Mayor Jackson, Atlanta's first Black mayor, and United Nations ambassador and mayor Andrew Young—elected by Black communities, a progressive White community, and a White business elite—stood at the world's stage.[64] While Jackson and Young get the credit for this development, it was Omega man LeRoy Walker, a 1942 initiate into the Beta Phi chapter, who orchestrated this feat. Walker was not only the first Black coach for any US Olympic team, he was also the first Black president to serve on the US Olympic Committee, serving as president of the Athletics congress (now known as USA Track and Field) and treasurer of the United States Olympic Committee from 1988 to 1992 and leading the committee from 1992 to 1996, shepherding the games.[65]

Though Decatur was the second most affluent area for Black property owners in the United States, it was not Atlanta.[66] The games were more than a year away when Omega Psi Phi moved into their international headquarters in Decatur on December 9, 1995; but, as some Omega officials suspected before that date, the decision to relocate the headquarters from Washington, DC, continued to spawn debate in the Fraternity when the Olympics commenced on July 19, 1996.[67] Some Omegas contended the relocation basically reflected a coup by leading members of the Fraternity in the Fifth, Sixth, Seventh, and Ninth Districts—all located in the southern corridor, known familiarly as the heartland of Black America because of large Black populations and numerous well-known civil rights campaigns—who wielded their political will within the Fraternity to bring the highest administrative offices to the South. In reality, Mayor Jackson; former mayor and United Nations ambassador Andrew Jackson Young Jr., who succeeded Jackson as mayor in 1982 and thereupon served through the reelection of Jackson in 1990; and other influential Black citizens in and around the Atlanta metro area made effective sales pitches to Omega national officials to relocate the international headquarters in Decatur. Hefty tax incentives that municipal officials in Washington did not offer were especially appealing to Omega officials. Additionally, as one of the biggest and busiest airports in the world, William B. Hartsfield International in Atlanta made that city and nearby Decatur accessible to travelers from around the globe on a daily basis.[68]

Building Bridges across the Black World

As Omega Psi Phi enjoyed its newest headquarters in December 1995 and into January 1996, the Fraternity continued to implement the first phase of its African Project. In March 1995, First Vice Grand Basileus Adam McKee Jr. headed a four-member fraternal delegation who flew to South Africa to discuss plans to construct an Omega village, a health clinic, and a March 1996 visit by physicians in the Fraternity to help implement those and related plans. Omega men Charles Christopher, Walter Johnson, and Walter Wrenn accompanied McKee on the initial trip to South Africa in 1995. They enjoyed their conversations with local community leaders. Conversing with human rights icon and Anglican bishop Desmond Mpilo Tutu also was very special to McKee, Christopher, Johnson, and Wrenn.

In addition to the South African project, Omega Psi Phi's "aggressive social agenda" for 1996 included "projects for the Perpetuation of the Black Male, Senior Citizens, and Habitat for Humanity."[69] The Fraternity's membership also worked on agenda items that, though not aggressive, were equally as significant to its long history of service as the foregoing projects. A commemorative stamp honoring Omega Psi Phi founder and renowned biologist Ernest Just was foremost.[70] According to the spring 1996 issue of *The Oracle*, officials with the United States Postal Service dedicated the stamp as part of the Black Heritage series on February 1.[71] The dedication ceremony took place inside the ambulatory care building of the Howard University Hospital in Washington, DC, a stone's throw away from Thirkield Hall where Just, Frank Coleman, Oscar Cooper, and Edgar Love founded Omega Psi Phi.[72]

George Kimbrough McKinney, a 1954 initiate into Pi chapter and the first Black person to serve as a US marshal in Maryland, was another Omega man the spring 1996 *Oracle* highlighted. McKinney was a Providence, Rhode Island, native who spent his childhood in Boston, Massachusetts, as well as in Petersburg and Richmond, Virginia. A 1956 graduate of Morgan State College, on whose faculty his father once served, McKinney joined the US Army and became an Eighty-Second Airborne Division paratrooper. He earned the title of jump master, completed jungle training, and eventually became a jungle expert. McKinney was a decorated captain by the time of his honorable discharge in 1965, whereupon he accepted a position as deputy marshal in Maryland. Summarizing future activities, *The Oracle* indicated he was a member of numerous special details. Though unmentioned by the publication, several details were responsible for civil rights matters. For example, McKinney was present in Houston, Texas, when Muhammad Ali refused induction into the US Army in 1967. McKinney was also present during the Pentagon protests in Washington, DC, later during the same year. In 1968, he was part of a detail in Memphis, Tennessee, when an assassin gunned down Martin King Jr. In 1973, an appointment by US president Richard Milhous Nixon made McKinney the third Black marshal in the history of the District of Columbia. During the next year, McKinney was the marshal who subpoenaed Nixon for his role in the Watergate scandal. In 1995, after two more decades of honorable service in various government capacities since the Nixon subpoena, McKinney became a marshal in Maryland. President William Jefferson (Bill) Clinton appointed him.[73]

Nathaniel Glover Jr., the first Black person elected sheriff in Duval County, Florida, was yet another Omega man whose story the spring 1996 issue of *The Oracle* recounted. Born and reared in Jacksonville, the county seat of Duval, Glover as a seventeen-year-old in 1960 unknowingly wandered into a mob of Klanspersons and other White supremacists. They were bent on viciously suppressing Black youth activists who were staging a sit-in at a racially segregated lunch counter in a downtown store. Witnessing such cruelty motivated Glover to pursue a career in law enforcement. First, however, he finished a segregated high school called New Stanton in 1961 and then played football on scholarship at Edward Waters College, an HBCU in Jacksonville. At Edwards

Waters (of which he later served as president), Glover pledged the Chi chapter of Omega Psi Phi. Once graduated from the college, he joined the local police department. For eighteen months, starting in 1966, Glover was a patrolman. He then became a detective and, after a brief stay in that role, was a sergeant. By 1986, Glover was chief detective, rose to deputy director of services in 1988, director of services in 1991, and was elected county sheriff in 1995. Glover, a member of the Theta Phi chapter of Omega Psi Phi at the time of his election, was the first Black sheriff in Florida since post-Civil War Reconstruction.[74]

A piece of legislation drafted in 1996 by state lawmakers in California, site of the Sixty-Ninth Grand Conclave of Omega Psi Phi, held in Los Angeles, California, from July 25 to July 29, 1996, was less praiseworthy than the accomplishments of Glover. Titled the California Civil Rights Initiative but known commonly as Proposition 209, its sponsors designed the legislation to allow voters to amend the state constitution to prohibit governmental entities from considering ethnicity, race, or sex when hiring, entering contracts, making decisions affecting education, and in certain other scenarios involving the use of public funds. Despite the colorblind language of Proposition 209, the legislation tilted an already uneven playing field further in favorable of White Californians, especially males. Local, state, and national officials in Omega Psi Phi challenged the transparent attempt by sponsors and other supporters of Proposition 209 to roll back affirmative action and various other unnamed human and civil rights advances. In a clear denouncement of Proposition 209 and its backers, conclave organizers selected the theme "On to California—Battlefield for Affirmative Action," with the intention of making the conclave "a forum for discussion, debate and exchange of ideas on the most important public policy issue in the nation today," Proposition 209.[75]

Continued Freedom Struggles and Successes

When Frank Coleman, Oscar Cooper, Ernest Just, and Edgar Love founded Omega Psi Phi Fraternity in 1911 during the Progressive period in American history, they created a brotherhood fostering friendship. They also created a vehicle and force against White supremacy. At the time, its bigoted proponents continued to display their quest for total control of American society through segregation, lynching, disenfranchisement, and similarly unjust acts. As preceding chapters in this book demonstrated, Coleman, Cooper, Just, Love, and other early members of Omega Psi Phi promoted universal equality as a general philosophy, but they were cognizant of the difficult challenges Black and other non-White citizens faced obtaining equality because of thick color lines across the United States. Such lines even persisted in the militaries from World War I through World War II. Consequently, brave and patriotic Omega men who fought abroad during wartime had to continue fighting for freedom and equality upon their return home. Concurrent with the Double V (Double Victory) campaign of the 1940s, Omega men who never donned military uniforms commanded or enlisted as nonviolent civil rights fighters to combat Jim Crow. Battles in the former Confederacy were most publicized, if not most frequent, as unreconstructed White people who longed for the status quo antebellum decades after the Civil War ended officially devised and executed a plethora of legal and extralegal schemes to maintain control of society. Combat zones in the former Confederate nation and elsewhere in the country expanded during the 1950s, causing some freedom fighters to embrace a more militant form of agency, protest, and self-help by the late 1960s and into the early 1970s: Black Power.

While some Omega men took part in every battle the preceding paragraph mentioned, others battled American injustice by promoting arts and letters, the sciences, and allied scholarly disciplines, fields, and subfields. Attempting to identify each member of the Fraternity who excelled in academe, music, painting, sculpting, writing, and cognate areas from Progressivism to Black Power would be as futile as trying to list the name of every Omega man who was a civil rights activist. Therefore, a sampling of endeavors must suffice. Omegas led the New Negro movement and its artistic component, the Harlem Renaissance, and they matriculated through or served as faculty members, administrators, and staffers at HBCUs throughout the country. Omega men also shone in athletics, politics, and other human endeavors. The 1980s presented serious internal and additional external issues to Omega Psi Phi but, as always, its members resolved those issues and continued to display manhood, scholarship, perseverance, and uplift from that decade through the 1990s.

The Seventieth Grand Conclave was hosted in New Orleans, Louisiana from July 10 to 16, 1998, and elected Lloyd Jordan, a 1975 Omicron Sigma chapter initiate, as the Grand Basileus to usher the Fraternity into the new millennium. He was reelected Grand Basileus at the Seventy-First Grand Conclave hosted in Indianapolis, Indiana, in July of 2000. For Black Americans, the dawning of the twenty first century created a quagmire for their communities. In January 2000, Florida state Senator and 1987 Upsilon Psi initiate Kendrick Meek, (D-Miami), along with Florida State Representative and 1999 Theta Phi initiate Anthony C. Hill, (D-Jacksonville), staged a day-long sit-in against the state's affirmative action policies in the offices of Florida Governor Jeb Bush. However, Florida's affirmative action would be the least of their worries. Ostensible civil rights violations came in the 2000 presidential election between US vice-president Albert Arnold Gore Jr., a Democrat, and George Walker Bush, a Republican. Here, the Supreme Court of the United

States reversed an order by the Florida Supreme Court for a selective manual recount of that state's US president election ballots.[76] As a result of that occurrence, the US Supreme Court and not the Electoral College decided the outcome of the presidential contest. In a five-to-four decision, the conservative majority of the court gave Bush the victory despite charges of Republican malfeasance during a recount in Florida, where Jeb Bush, brother of presidential candidate George Walker Bush and son of forty-first US president George Herbert Walker Bush, served as the state's governor. While 10 percent of Black voters in the state supported Bush, some Black Floridians believed election officials systematically disenfranchised them when 14.4 percent of their casted ballots were excluded in comparison to 1.6 percent of non-Black Floridians. Hill stated, "We have been disrespected as a group . . . we came out to vote for Al Gore, and our vote was supposed to be our equalizer. Now that has been taken away."[77] Other Black Americans had similar beliefs. To them, orchestrated attempts to suppress Black voting were not mere relics of the 1950s or 1960s. Omega Psi Phi responded to such beliefs by revamping the Omega Public Policy forum, where Jesse Jackson gave commentary at a 2003 Founders' Day ceremony at Howard University's Rankin Chapel, home of the Fraternity's founding. Jackson also gave similar comments to the NPHC representatives in Dallas, Texas, in December of 2003.[78]

In 2001, Bush won some goodwill with members of Omega Psi Phi by appointing Colin Luther Powell as the first Black secretary of state in the United States. While General Powell was not a member of Omega Psi Phi, his ascendency to chairing the Joint Chiefs of Staff and later becoming secretary of state rested on those Omega men and countless non-Omegas who had served before him, including Colonel Charles Young and Colonel George Spencer "Spanky" Roberts.

On September 11, 2001, Al-Qaeda terrorists hijacked and forced pilots to crash two domestic airplanes into the World Trade Center in the Manhattan borough of New York City. Al-Qaeda terrorists forced pilots to crash a third plane into the Pentagon in Arlington County, Virginia, about five miles southwest of Washington, DC. Another set of Al-Qaeda terrorists planned to crash a fourth plane into a federal building in Washington, but passengers fought the terrorists, causing the pilots to crash land the plane in a field close to the Indian Lake and Shanksville boroughs in Somerset County, Pennsylvania. Powell, as chairman of the Joint Chiefs of Staff, was one of the highest-ranking federal officials in the country when George W. Bush's administration decided to invade Iraq in 2003. Powell, Bush, and others in the administration claimed Iraqi president Saddam Hussein possessed weapons of mass destruction that he would use against the United States or that he would provide to Al-Qaeda, if not some other US foe. Omega Psi Phi contained numerous statesmen, politicians, military veterans, and other knowledgeable individuals in the United States and across the globe, and many did not think the US invasion of Iraq was legitimate. While international affairs drew ire from Omega men, George Grace, a 1973 initiate of the Pi Nu chapter, was elected as Grand Basileus at the Seventy-Second Grand Conclave held in Charlotte, North Carolina, from July 10 to 17, 2002.

At war in Iraq and Afghanistan, Omega men fought valiantly in Operation Iraqi Freedom. Yet, international issues did not take center stage. Hurricane Katrina pummeled New Orleans, Louisiana, and surrounding areas in August of 2005, causing an estimated $125 billion in damages and taking 1,392 lives, while US diplomats fumbled responsive aid or vacationed. Later in 2005, the Bush administration acknowledged conveying to Central Intelligence Agency personnel the decision of the US Department of Justice to permit enhanced interrogation techniques against suspected war criminals in American custody. Many Omegas believed this involvement in those techniques, which amounted to torture, was greater than the foregoing acknowledgment. That belief, together with the Hurricane Katrina debacle, worsened the shared opinions such Omegas had of the federal government. For them, the Bush administration seemed indifferent toward Black masses and had blind allegiance to neoconservative leaders in the Republican Party generally and to its standard-bearer, Bush, particularly.[79]

The Statehouse Convention Center in Little Rock, Arkansas, hosted the Seventy-Fourth Grand Conclave from July 20 to 23, 2006. Here, Omega delegates elected Warren G. Lee Jr., a 1971 initiate through the Eta Theta chapter, as the Grand Basileus. By 2006, many Black Americans, not simply members of Omega Psi Phi, were increasingly unpersuaded that the Bush administration prioritized universal equality. The consensus among Black Americans remained unchanged in 2007. Writing about a survey conducted that year by the Pew Research Center, historians John Hope Franklin and Evelyn Brooks Higginbotham indicated responses to two questions—"Are Blacks better or worse off now than five years ago?" and "Will life for Blacks be better or worse in the future?"—revealed "increased cynicism among" Black Americans.[80] Twenty-nine percent of respondents perceived conditions worsened for them from 2002 to 2007.[81] That percentage amounted to a 16 percent increase according to a Pew survey for the years 1994 to 1999.[82]

Despite significant dissatisfaction with domestic and foreign affairs during George W. Bush's two-term presidency from 2001 to 2009, Omega men continued to grow the Fraternity. Consistent with a 1994 recommendation from a comprehensive review committee comprising past Grand Basileis Edward J. Braynon Jr., Burnel E. Coulon Sr., Marion W. Garnett, Loveless B. Livingston Jr., Moses Norman Sr., and Hebert E. Tucker Jr., the Fraternity expanded further into countries outside the United States. In so doing, Omega Psi Phi helped create a new landscape for the Fraternity by increasing its diasporic membership. That pattern replicated demographic shifts in the United States in general. For example, Afro-Caribbean immigrants came from the Bahamas, Barbados, Haiti, Jamaica, or Trinidad and Tobago. Many Latinas and Latinos in Cuba, the Dominican Republic, and South America also immigrated to the United States. The greatest number of African immigrants came from sub-Saharan countries such as Ethiopia, Ghana, Nigeria, and Somalia. Though Omega Psi Phi worked on behalf of native and immigrant communities throughout the United States, the influx of Black people from different continents or countries who oftentimes had unique sets of ethnic identities or sociocultural values resulted in competing interests in the American localities to which they immigrated. However, Chicago, Illinois, community organizer-turned-state senator Barack Hussein Obama II forced native- and foreign-born Black people in the United States to have serious conversations about Black identity, further exposing differences within marginalized American communities.[83]

The President Is Black, Omega Psi Phi Is Too

Shortly after Birmingham, Alabama, hosted the Seventy-Fifth Grand Conclave from July 13 to July 17, 2008, the 2008 election of President Obama electrified the world. The sordid history of race relations in the United States provided context where Obama emerged as an abrupt departure from this nation's norms. Party politics aside, Obama served as a symbol to the potential of change, which was a buzzword during his historic campaign. Omega Psi Phi's excitement was on display when Obama not only graced the cover of the spring 2009 *Oracle* shortly after his election, but with a two-page spread showcasing the president and his family. In that edition of *The Oracle*, Obama's name appeared nineteen times. It seemed that there was a new day dawning in America.

Obama took his first meaningful step toward the national political stage on July 27, 2004. While campaigning to replace Peter Gosselin Fitzgerald, a Republican who represented Illinois in the US Senate, Obama delivered a masterful keynote address at the Democratic National Convention in Boston, Massachusetts. One of Obama's most rousing pronouncements during his 2004 address came toward its closing.[84]

Obama's July 2004 keynote address at the Democratic National Convention catapulted him beyond the US Senate. His address helped make him a frontrunner for the American presidency in 2008. When election day arrived on November 4, a plurality of American voters that included thousands of

Omega men provided Obama with 69,498,516 popular votes, 52.93 percent of the total count. His Republican competitor and fellow US senator, John Sidney McCain III, polled 59,948,323, which was 45.65 percent of the total. In the Electoral College, Obama triumphed 365 to 173. Consequently, on January 20, 2009, in a highly symbolic moment in American and world history, Obama took the oath of office to become the first Black president of the United States.[85]

Obama entered the presidency amid several crises within or involving the United States. The country was at war against terror and the American economy was suffering. In time, the Obama administration helped rescue the economy by revitalizing the automobile industry through a series of government-backed bailouts. The administration also reformed health care by providing affordable insurance coverage to millions of citizens via the Affordable Health Act. The administration likewise pushed the country toward a clean-energy future by reducing the nation's carbon blueprint through his Clean Power Plan. Upon his inauguration, President Obama seated Omega men in his administration. Charles Frank Bolden, Jr., a 1983 Gamma Nu initiate who retired as major general from the United States Marine Corps, was nominated and confirmed by the US Senate as the 12th administrator of the National Aeronautics and Space Administration (NASA), assuming duties on July 17, 2009. Later in 2014, President Obama appointed 1978 Kappa Lambda charter line member Gentry O. Smith as director of the Office of Foreign Missions with ambassadorial rank.[86]

During the Obama presidency and looking toward the Fraternity's Centennial Celebration, Omega Psi Phi held back-to-back Grand Conclaves. The seventy-fifth anniversary (Sixty-Fourth) Grand Conclave marked the move when the international meeting went from being held every eighteen months to every two years. The Seventy-Sixth Grand Conclave was held in Raleigh, North Carolina, in July 2010, where Andrew Ray, a 1965 Beta Sigma initiate, was elected Grand Basileus. Grand Basileus Ray was front and center when Omega Psi Phi turned one hundred years old at the Seventy-Seventh Grand Conclave, held inside the Walter Washington Convention Center in Washington, DC, from July 27 to 31, 2011, when 20,000 Omega men came together to usher the Fraternity into a new millennium and to rededicate themselves to its high ideals. During the Centennial Conclave, a surprise meeting with Obama was a highlight of the meeting according to the winter 2012–spring 2013 issue of *The Oracle*. Reminiscing about that meeting and other conclave activities, Grand Basileus Andrew A. Ray said the "Centennial was a glorious moment in time, when Omega Men from their respective stations in life met on the plane of friendship and fraternity... and parted on the square of Manhood, Scholarship, Perseverance and Uplift."[87]

Unfortunately for the Obama administration, Omega Psi Phi, and the United States as a whole, as Obama neared the end of four years in the White House and the Fraternity began one hundred more years internationally, prevalent racial tension and recurrent police brutality in the United States were constant reminders of the deferred dream of American equality about which Omega man Langston Hughes wrote decades earlier. Sanford, Florida, was the site of one of the most publicized ethnically motivated fatalities in 2012. During the evening hours of February 26, eight months before the next presidential election in the United States, George Michael Zimmerman shot and killed Trayvon Benjamin Martin. Zimmerman was a twenty-eight-year-old of Peruvian, Afro-Peruvian, and German descent who identified as Latino and White. Martin was a Black seventeen-year-old. Zimmerman profiled Martin as the teenager walked innocently through a gated community he was visiting with his father, Tracy Martin, whose fiancée resided in the community. Zimmerman, acting as a neighborhood watchman, exited the car he was driving and proceeded to chase and attack Trayvon, who wore jeans, a hooded sweatshirt, and sneakers. Trayvon defended himself and was besting Zimmerman in a fistfight. During the fight, Zimmerman pulled and fired a gun. A bullet struck Trayvon in the chest, killing him. In a nonemergency telephone call to local police before the killing, Zimmerman described Trayvon as "suspicious-looking" despite Trayvon having only a cellular telephone, "a bag of Skittles and a can of iced tea" in his hands.[88] Weeks later, Obama characterized Trayvon in a markedly different manner than Zimmerman's unarguably biased description: "If I had a son," Obama stated on March 23, "he'd look like Trayvon."[89]

Law enforcement personnel in Sanford eventually arrested Zimmerman and charged him with second-degree murder. His arrest was not immediate, however, because Florida had a law known commonly as Stand Your Ground that personnel said they had to consider in determining if Zimmerman should even be charged with a crime. Members of the Martin family hired Omega man Benjamin Lloyd Crump of Lumberton, North Carolina, as one of the lawyers to represent them in subsequent legal proceedings. Crump was a 1988 initiate of the Chi Theta chapter at Florida State University, where he also earned a law degree. By 2012, Crump had distinguished himself as one of the top civil rights lawyers in the country, but he knew securing justice for the Martin family would not be an easy task.[90]

On November 6, 2012, as Crump and his fellow lawyers gathered information for the Zimmerman trial, American voters elected Obama to a second presidential term. Obama won 65,915,795 popular votes and his Republican challenger, former Massachusetts governor Willard Mitt Romney, got 60,933,504. Those numbers reflected a closer presidential victory for Obama than in 2008. He triumphed by 4,982,291 popular votes in 2012 and 9,550,193 in

2008. In terms of percentages, Obama polled 51.06 of the popular vote in 2012 and Romney 47.20. That margin also was smaller than in 2008: 3.86 to 7.28 percentage points, respectively. The Electoral College outcome was similar: Obama won 332 votes and Romney 206, a difference of 129. In 2008, Obama won by 192 votes in the Electoral College.[91]

The reelection and subsequent inauguration of Obama on January 21, 2013, excited thousands of Omega men. Many tempered their remaining excitement, however, once jury selection for the trial of George Zimmerman concluded on June 20. Of the six women composing the jury, five were White and one was Black and Latino. Three of four alternate jurors were White. Two were female and one was male. The fourth alternate was White and Latino. According to Crump, the presiding judge in the Zimmerman trial allowed irrelevant testimony and, even though no lawyer cited Stand Your Ground during the trial, claimed precedent mandated the jury be instructed to consider Stand Your Ground as they deliberated. Crump recalled the judge specifically telling the jury that Zimmerman "had no duty to retreat and had the right to stand his ground and employ deadly force if he believed it was necessary to prevent great bodily harm or death."[92]

On July 13, 2013, the "all-female, mostly white" jury found Zimmerman not guilty of second-degree murder.[93] One White female juror, speaking during a televised interview days later, described Zimmerman as "a man whose heart was in the right place but just got displaced by the vandalism in the neighborhoods and, wanting to catch these people so badly, that he went above and beyond what he really should have done."[94] The woman, who planned to write a book about her time on the jury, said Zimmerman was "guilty of not using good judgment. When he was in the car, and he had called 911, he shouldn't have gotten out of that car."[95] Martin, the juror went on, "decided that he wasn't going to let [Zimmerman] scare him[,] got mad and attacked" Zimmerman.[96]

Such remarks and the acquittal vexed people worldwide. Many became angry and some furious. Though bothered by the acquittal, President Obama beseeched people to bridle their frustration and to be civil. In an official pronouncement issued on July 14, 2013, he declared: "The death of Trayvon Martin was a tragedy, not just for his family or for any one community, but for America. I know this case has elicited strong passions," Obama averred, and "in the wake of the verdict, I know those passions may be running even higher. But we are a nation of laws, and a jury has spoken. I now ask every American to respect the call for calm reflection from two parents who lost their young son."[97] Crump, the Omega man and lawyer who helped represent the Martin family, understood and respected Obama for encouraging civility.[98] At the same time, Crump thought the acquittal demonstrated how the American legal system often miscarried when Black lives were in the balance.[99]

Obama did not address any miscarriage of justice directly amid a press conference at which he spoke on July 19, 2013. Obama, however, did address the state law in Florida that certain jurors cited to justify acquitting Zimmerman six days earlier: "for those who resist that idea that we should think about something like these 'Stand Your Ground' laws, I'd just ask people to consider, if Trayvon Martin was of age and armed, could he have stood his ground on that sidewalk? And do we actually think that he would have justified in shooting Mr. Zimmerman, who had followed him in a car, because he felt threatened? And if the answer to that question is at least ambiguous," Obama reasoned, "then it seems to me that we might want to examine those kinds of laws."[100] During another part of the press conference, Obama revisited a comment he made in the wake of the senseless killing on February 26, 2012, regarding the possibility that Trayvon Martin would have looked similar to his own son if he had a son. Obama, though, added force to his original comment by saying "Martin could have been me 35 years ago. And when you think about why, in the African American community at least, there's a lot of pain around what happened [to Martin], I think it's important to recognize that the African American community is looking at the issue through a set of experiences and a history that doesn't go away."[101] Expounding, Obama inquired: "where do we take this [tragedy]? How do we learn some lessons from this and move in a positive direction? . . . Beyond protests or vigils," Obama concluded, "are there some concrete things that we might be able to do?"[102]

Continuing to assist with the White House Fatherhood and Mentoring Initiative was one way members of Omega Psi Phi answered the questions Obama posed on July 19, 2013. The initiative was an ongoing effort by the Obama administration to strengthen fathers and surrogate fathers (e.g., coaches), their families, and entire communities, and Omega Psi Phi was one of the first Black Greek-letter organizations to publicly support the initiative. As early as June 19, 2009, as Obama approached his fifth month in the presidency, Thabiti Bruce Boone, a 1987 Theta Omicron initiate, conversed with Obama during a White House meeting regarding fatherhood and mentorship. Boone was an acclaimed public speaker, musician, athlete, long-time youth organizer, and Rochester Institute of Technology alumnus reared in Brooklyn, New York. He also was an Omega man. The fatherhood-and-mentoring partnership among the Obama administration and Omega Psi Phi resulted from that 2009 conversation. Years later, while Boone served as the international representative of the Fraternity for the White House Fatherhood and Mentoring Initiative, he confirmed the Fraternity would "continue to be on the front line for President Obama, leveraging our Omega power, influence and 100 years of commitment to uplifting our people and communities."[103]

On September 20, 2013, the Congressional Black Caucus held a forum in Washington, DC. "Fatherhood in the African American Family: Saving Our Families in the Light of Trayvon Martin" was the theme.[104] Omega man, lawyer, and congressman Henry Calvin (Hank) Johnson Jr. of the Fourth District in Georgia delivered the keynote address, and a panel featuring members of all fraternities in the NPHC flanked him.[105] His fellow Omega man, Benjamin Crump, a member of the legal team for the Martin family, represented Omega Psi Phi.[106] A third Omega man, Grand Basileus Andrew Ray, and 1965 initiate of Beta Sigma chapter, gave remarks.[107] With the success of the 2013 event, President Obama's Fatherhood and Mentoring Initiative was hosted by Omega man and congressman James Clyburn III with a theme of "Fatherhood: Impacting the Lives of Fathers, Men, and Young Boys" and featuring Omega man Thabiti Boone of the President Obama White House Champion of Change in 2014. Remarks were given by Grand Basileus Antonio Knox, a 1978 initiate of Iota Iota chapter and charter member of Kappa Lambda chapter.[108]

As Johnson, Crump, Ray, fellow NPHC members, and their contemporaries in the Congressional Black Caucus discussed fatherhood, family, and judicial failure in the United States, conservative justices on the US Supreme Court gutted one of the most important pieces of legislation in American history: the 1965 Voting Rights Act President Lyndon Baines Johnson signed into law on August 6. In a June 25, 2013, ruling for a case styled *Shelby County v. Holder*, the justices eliminated certain protections against franchise discrimination. According to those justices, the use of Section 4 (b) of the Voting Rights Act to determine which jurisdictions were subject to preclearance requirement of Section 5 of the Voting Rights Act were unconstitutional, so the justices gave Congress power to update the law. In the wake of the *Shelby* ruling, Republicans who controlled local and state governments in places with long histories of discrimination ramped up ongoing efforts to suppress voters who tended to back Democratic candidates. Republicans in places with shorter histories of discrimination soon followed suit. Together, they ostensibly attempted to recreate political and government structures akin to White-dominated structures from the nadir to second Reconstruction periods. Consequently, Black, mixed-race, and humanitarian Americans of other ethnicities found themselves fighting for some of the same voting and related privileges of citizenship as their fore parents.[109]

Working for Omega . . . Still Got a Long Way to Go

The membership of Omega Psi Phi continues to be at the forefront of nearly every human endeavor imaginable: from politics to civil rights; to the arts, education, sports, and medicine; to championing the ills of social justice.

Indeed, the Fraternity is an exemplary organization. Case in point, members such as civil rights lawyer Benjamin Crump are leading the way in terms of the courts, seeking justice against police brutality and wrongful deaths. Congressman James Enos Clyburn, a longtime representative for the Sixth District in South Carolina and 1968 initiate into Charleston, South Carolina's Mu Alpha chapter, has led the fight for the democratic process where all voices of American citizens will be heard through voting. And today, as has been the case since the Fraternity's founding, many Omega men lead colleges and universities with an eye toward racial equality. The list includes North Carolina Central University's Johnson O. Akinleye, a 2000 Beta Phi initiate; Georgia State University's Malsworth Brian Blake, a 1990 initiate of the Delta Kappa chapter at the Georgia Institute of Technology; Alabama State University's Quinton T. Ross Jr., a 1990 initiate of the Gamma Sigma chapter at Alabama State University; South Carolina State University's Alexander Conyers, a 1987 initiate of the Xi Psi chapter at South Carolina State University; George Mason University's Gregory Washington, a 1986 initiate of the Kappa Lambda chapter at North Carolina State University; and Alabama Agricultural and Mechanical University's Daniel K. Williams, a 1983 initiate of the Upsilon Sigma chapter at Fort Valley State College.[110]

For the June 1919 issue of *The Oracle*, Omega Psi Phi founder Ernest Just wrote:

> Following the Great War, we are now in an era of universal reconstruction. This Nation, all nations, must play a part; we men of the Omega Psi Phi Fraternity, all men, must play a part. Earth, old traditions, hopes as old as man himself, ay, and prejudices too, our heritage from ages gone, part of the price we pay for our evolution, all of these are in the balance. Many of these must and shall go; we tremble lest others go. The world is well-nigh hysteria. Under the shock of these last four years, civilization, fresh from the rim of Hell is convulsive; orderly activity is difficult indeed in these hyper-excitable times. What shall we do? These times demand clean men, of clear vision, of straight thinking, of unselfish doing. And every Omega man must accept this challenge. Out of groups like ours, men who know and feel to the utmost. . . . Fidelity, Liberty and Fraternity, must come to the world's absolution. Only by the bonds of brotherhood, stronger than life or death, which shall grip harder and more securely as ever, greater numbers feel the tie, shall the world at last stand unfettered of evil, because chained in real Fraternity.[111]

Conclusion

With Faith in God and Heart and Mind demonstrates how the long struggle for Black freedom influenced, and was influenced by, the actions of the Omega Psi Phi Fraternity. Spanning more than a century, this history of Omega explains the spectra of social and economic struggles during the Black freedom movement. Through its analysis of the Fraternity, the book offers a detailed look at Black institution-building through one of the most prominent Black organizations of the twentieth and twenty-first centuries.

The contributions of Omega Psi Phi during the past century fit within the larger historiography of Black Americans' fight for racial equality. In examining Omega and its members, *With Faith in God and Heart and Mind* invites readers to consider or possibly reconsider how Black people sought solutions to their problems. The book goes beyond focusing on White people's violence toward Black people, as situated within the so-called Negro problem of the late nineteenth century. The book also demonstrates how Omega fits within the important work of early Black organizations—the Niagara Movement, the National Association for the Advancement of Colored People (NAACP), and other collegiate and professional associations—that emerged during the early 1900s. The way this book situates the Fraternity is important because Omega did not exist within a vacuum consumed or influenced only within itself. The founding of the Fraternity was in response to broad societal challenges and, frankly, to intraracial debates among Black Americans. The sheer existence of Howard University, as a Black institution of higher education, exemplifies some of those debates.

In 1911, when Edgar Amos Love, Oscar James Cooper, Frank Coleman, and Ernest Everett Just founded Omega Psi Phi, Howard's classical curriculum was a testament to which subjects university employees prioritized teaching Black youth. At the time, many Black Americans had limited access to educational resources, much less to the exclusivity of collegiate-level studies. Since Howard's 1867 founding as a federally chartered institution amid the country's first Reconstruction, the university had stood as an anchor on one distinctive end of a debate concerning Black education. The Fraternity's founding forty-four years later situated the organization within a debate over respectability in pursuit of racial equality. Omega quickly emerged through its membership selection as a premier organization whose roster included some of the most notable Black leaders of the early twentieth century. Concurrently, the Fraternity's founders and other Howard students, together with university employees and Washington, DC, wider Black community, took leadership in demanding a better society for Black Americans. Their combined efforts included Howard hosting the first collegiate chapter of the NAACP and the campus serving as a Black military training camp during World War I.

Following World War I, Omega men joined other Black Americans in debating how to achieve a just society in the United States. A foremost topic, academic education, had long been a focal point for the country's Black population. Historian James D. Anderson, a 1963 initiate of the Rho Gamma chapter, has written extensively about such matters. In *The Education of Blacks in the South* (1988), he noted that formerly enslaved Black people operated hundreds of common schools across the region during post-Civil War Reconstruction. More than fifty years later, while revanchist White educators and other leading citizens attempted to downplay Black contributions to American society, Omega's first national program focused on educating Black people about Black history and literature. This program reflected a tradition among Black people about the role and value of education at a time when White people who subscribed to the Dunning school of thought, named after a White Columbia University professor William A. Dunning, argued that Reconstruction was a failure and Black people were inferior.[1]

The Fraternity, which at first was too expansive in its efforts to efficiently operate its program for Black history and literature, had established itself at private Black colleges and many White colleges and universities outside of the South by 1921; however, Omega leaders eventually assessed the Fraternity's chapter expansion efforts alongside assessments of curricula at Black colleges and universities. Omega men addressed a decades-long debate about whether Black institutions of higher learning offered actual collegiate-level courses. This effort led to the formation of the National Association of Collegiate Deans and Registrars in Negro Schools in the 1920s. Soon, the association helped develop curricula that enabled more Black institutions, especially state-supported facilities, to achieve accreditation. That successful initiative, led by Omega men, demonstrated the benefit of Black leaders in Black education beyond the gaze of White officials who had long monitored and stifled Black formal learning.

During the Great Depression, Omega men contributed to the Black freedom movement in ways beyond higher education. Facing immense financial collapse and widespread poverty, Black banks, insurance companies, and related enterprises grew in prominence. Black Americans, not unlike many other non-White ethnic groups, long had been neglected by federal programs focused on economic development. This neglect prompted the emergence of

Black financial institutions focused on insuring Black people survived the Great Depression and its lingering effects. Fraternity members joined that effort by, among other acts, managing Black insurance companies, establishing local committees for Black affairs, and helping finance Black banks. The 1930s and the early 1940s also comprised an era of many Black firsts in the United States. Some Omega men served in the armed forces and became wartime heroes during World War II. Others advised US presidents. When the NAACP established a legal division, Omega men joined its ranks as some of the country's leading civil rights attorneys. Many of their legal victories helped shape laws or, alternatively, forced local-, state-, or federal-level accountability in the adherence of such laws.

Following World War II, Omega Psi Phi's involvement in civil rights expanded. From the late 1940s through the 1960s, the Fraternity and many other Black organizations adopted platforms that demanded elected officials address the hypocrisy between the country's touted ideals and the realities of its racial policies and practices. As Black veterans, including numerous Omega men, returned from World War II and the Korean War, the contradictions of romanticized and actual life for social minorities in the United States were evident. The Double V (Double Victory) campaign emerged during this period as Black people sought two victories: one abroad while fighting a war in the name of democracy and the other at home by defeating being treated like second-class citizens. That dichotomy spurred a series of legal battles over voting rights, with Omega men among the leading attorneys. In 1947, prominent civil rights organizer Bayard Rustin, a 1933 initiate of the Upsilon chapter, organized a Journey of Reconciliation, or Freedom Ride, by challenging segregation in public highway facilities. In 1963, following the more familiar Freedom Rides in 1961, he was a key participant in the March on Washington for Jobs and Freedom.[2]

The mid-twentieth-century activism of individual Omega men caused an internal debate among the brotherhood, a debate that captured how Black fraternities, sororities, and other organizations grappled with a changing national and indeed global society. By 1966, and despite passage of several notable pieces of federal civil rights legislation from 1957 to 1964, many young members of Omega Psi Phi deemed commonplace methods of challenging racist policies and practices through strategic legal battles and nonviolent protests *too slow* and steady to effect the revolutionary societal change they sought domestically and internationally. The Black Power ethos many young Omegas embraced created dissent within the Fraternity. They demanded members take a more assertive role in pressing for equal rights than the organization had taken hitherto. Generational tension became a byproduct of the Fraternity as some members rose to prominence within the White power structure. Unlike Omega's first decades, when members focused their organizing efforts on local levels, many leading members of the 1970s became careful not to threaten their increased influence on the national level.

By the 1980s, as new and evolving freedom struggles took root, Omega men confronted, and were confronted by, occurrences such as the war on drugs, a national housing crisis, police brutality, and attacks on affirmative action that all disproportionately impacted Black people. Aside from those external factors, internal tensions within the Fraternity emerged from philosophical differences (e.g., Black Power) among members. The social expansion of the Que Dog culture also emerged. Nonetheless, by 1986, Omega Psi Phi launched several programs for its chapters to implement. Paramount programs addressed illiteracy, voter registration, assistance to historically Black colleges and universities (HBCUs), and a say-no-to-drugs campaign. Such programs and similar others were rooted in the Fraternity's history of service with an eye toward the future.

This history of Omega Psi Phi is ripe for the present time. The Fraternity and its members prioritized Black advancement and equality throughout history, and each member has an obligation to uphold that tradition. Black organizations founded at the turn of the twentieth century expected their members to live personal and professional lives that exemplified a commitment to their communities. To do anything less was to neglect the organizations' missions. Many of the most prominent domestic and international racial issues that Omega Psi Phi historically addressed remain prevalent in society in the 2020s, albeit in different forms. In terms of education, the resegregation of public schools and the skewed distribution of academic funding often leaves Black children with fewer resources than their White contemporaries. Similarly, the question of racial justice, particularly by way of the disproportionate number of officer-initiated police stops and shootings against Black citizens, stirs parallels to when Omega and its member attorneys took on legal battles in the name of civil rights.

Today, Benjamin Crump, a 1988 initiate of the Chi Theta chapter, is a prominent attorney known for leading high-profile wrongful death lawsuits where Black people were killed by police. The litigations led by Crump are paired with Omega men who had led or joined local Black Lives Matter demonstrations. The activists who have demanded racial justice following the well-known, unfortunate, and preventable deaths of Breonna Taylor, George Floyd, and other private citizens at the hands of law enforcement officers stoke memories of the Black Power era. Such incidents fall alongside skyrocketing costs of living and housing discrimination, federal court cases challenging affirmative action, and unfair hiring practices.

Omega men are also continuing to forcefully support higher education, especially HBCUs. For instance, Harold M. Love Jr., a 1992 initiate of the Rho Psi chapter and member of the Tennessee House of Representatives, chaired the state's Joint Land-Grant Institution Committee. In 2021, that committee reported that the state owed Tennessee State University as much as $544 million in land-grant funding. Love and his fellow committee members found no record that the state of Tennessee had met its federal obligations in funding Tennessee State University compared to the predominately White University of Tennessee. Two years later, in 2023, the Joseph R. Biden administration released a report indicating that multiple other states had also underfunded its land-grant HBCUs.[3]

As the first official history of Omega Psi Phi since 1963, *With Faith in God and Heart and Mind* is a longer history of the contributions Omega and its members have made to the advancement of Black people in the United States. The book relates a story that demands critical reflection on how future generations will carry on the commitment to racial justice that has served as the foundation of Omega Psi Phi since 1911. The book also invites Omega men and the American populace alike to revisit and to rethink the long-standing roles that Black institutions and organizations have performed in the struggle for equality in the United States and abroad. Those histories, if interrogated carefully by scholars with intimate knowledge about such institutions and organizations, can serve as guideposts for making sense of society today. The book will also inform community activists who seek inspiration from previous generations' efforts to address the many enduring forms of discrimination. For as much as *With Faith in God and Heart and Mind* is about the Black past, the book also is about the future of Black advancement. With history as an indicator, we know past challenges have been confronted before as seen through the collective actions of the members of Omega Psi Phi, a collegiate fraternity, and those members of other Black organizations. It is time to move into a historical understanding that encourages building upon our predecessors' good works to construct a better future.

Acknowledgments

It is a difficult task to write a history of an organization that is more than one hundred years old. In our case, the life span of Omega Psi Phi—a historic Black collegiate fraternity—spans multiple generations, and members who were involved in its first decade are no longer living. This made writing this book both a challenge and a privilege. It was a unique opportunity to reconstruct a significant piece of Black history, but it was only possible due to a wide range of support.

We would like to begin by thanking Omega Psi Phi's 41st Grand Basileus David Marion for his unwavering and unfettered support in writing this book. Six years ago, in 2018 at the start of his four-year administration, Grand Basileus Marion charged us with writing a history of the Fraternity. He encouraged us as authors to lean on our respective professional expertise as scholars to write this book, and he wholeheartedly supported our approach to make this history of Black struggle, agency, and self-determination. We welcomed the opportunity to write a history of Omega Psi Phi that situated the Fraternity within the long Black Freedom Movement. Throughout the process, Grand Basileus Marion consulted with us and entrusted us, as Omega men and academics, to produce something that the Fraternity could be proud of and that would place Omega inside the Black body politic. We cannot thank him and the other members of the Supreme Council enough for their support.

Most notably, while writing this history of Omega Psi Phi, the COVID-19 pandemic altered many life schedules, including ours for writing this book. This environment created a sense of urgency, but also greater comradeship between the four of us. As the pandemic began to subside, the book began to take shape. As full-time academics, with research and administrative duties in our respective universities, we knew from the beginning the challenges of conducting archival work across the country and through online databases. Thus, we benefited tremendously from the diligent archival research of the Fraternity's International History & Archives Committee. The committee chairman, Keir Pemberton, served as an organized taskmaster who discussed the manuscript with us and, most importantly, provided us with the resources we needed throughout the process. Three other dedicated and knowledgeable Omega men—Jonathan Matthews, David Carl, and Sam Ryan—also met with us and provided primary sources they had spent years uncovering from the Fraternity's archives in Decatur, Georgia, and elsewhere across the United States. The Fraternity should be proud of these men who, without their work collecting primary sources, this book would not have been possible. We also extend our appreciation to the entire History & Archives Committee which, in addition to Brothers Pemberton, Matthews, Carl, and Ryan, included Alfonso Morrell, Donald Lucas, Don Lee (who entered Omega chapter while we wrote this book), and Chesley McNeil—with special thanks to former committee chairman Carl Blunt. Thanks, also, to Brother Kyle Yeldell for providing valuable information about Omega history.

Finally, in remembering Brother Lee, he was always a great source of support and encouraged us on many occasions. We know that this book will serve as an example of the lives that Lee and many other deceased Omega men lived. This book captures how the Fraternity brought together a collection of men who dedicated their lives to Black advancement. Their efforts happened in their neighborhoods as they molded their counties and states. In other cases, Omega men were national and global leaders. The Fraternity charged them all with a single duty: service. This history of Omega Psi Phi is not a litany of Fraternity who-what-when facts, but instead, it is a tribute to Omega men and how they have influenced the ongoing struggles for Black liberation in the United States and beyond.

Notes

Introduction

1. John Uri, "Honoring Black Astronauts during Black History Month," NASA, February 24, 2021, https://www.nasa.gov/history/honoring-african-american-astronauts/; Bob Granath, "Robert Lawrence Honored in 50th Anniversary Memorial Ceremony," NASA, December 18, 2017, www.nasa.gov/people-of-nasa/robert-lawrence-honored-in-50th-anniversary-memorial-ceremony/; Tonya Dixon, "N.C. A&T Honors Late Alumnus and Nasa Astronaut Ronald McNair in Annual Celebration," North Carolina Agricultural and Technical State University, January 25, 2022, www.ncat.edu/news/2022/01/2022-ronald-mcnair-legacy-celebration.php; and "Brother Major General Charles F. Bolden, Jr." *The Oracle* (Spring 2015): 15.

2. Herman Dreer, *The History of Omega Psi Phi Fraternity: A Brotherhood of Negro College Men, 1911 to 1939* (Washington, DC: Omega Psi Phi Fraternity, 1940), 22; Robert L. Gill, *The History of Omega Psi Phi and the Men Who Made Its History: A Concise History* (Washington, DC: Omega Psi Phi Fraternity, 1963), 88–89; John A. Garraty and Mark C. Carnes, *A Short History of the American Nation* (New York: Longman), 577–79. Also see the first issue of *The Oracle*, published in June 1919, 13–19.

3. Dreer, *History of Omega Psi Phi*; Gill, *Omega Psi Phi Fraternity*.

4. Kyle S. Yeldell, *The Soul of Omega: A History of Psi Chapter of Omega Psi Phi Fraternity, Inc. at Morehouse College* (Washington, DC: self-published, 2022).

5. Wendy Marie Laybourn and Gregory S. Parks, "Omega Psi Phi Fraternity and the Fight for Civil Rights," *Wake Forest Journal of Law and Policy* 6, no. 1 (February 2016): 213–301.

6. Judson L. Jeffries, "Malcolm X, the Omega Psi Phi Fraternity, Inc., and Morgan State College," *Spectrum: A Journal on Black Men* 8, no. 1 (Fall 2020): 127–50. Omega man Judson L. Jeffries has also published other Fraternity-related works: "The Two Gills: Enlightening and Empowering Others through Effective Use of Teaching and Scholarship," *Spectrum: A Journal on Black Men* 10, no. 1 (Autumn 2022): 103–24, and "Only the Ques Would Debate Malcolm X: The Civil Rights Movement's Big Six and the Safe Distance at Which They Kept America's Foremost Militant," *Journal of African American Studies* 26 (December 2022): 413–35.

7. Susan L. Smith, *Sick and Tired of Being Sick and Tired: Black Women's Health Activism in America, 1890–1950* (Philadelphia: University of Pennsylvania Press, 1995).

8. Treva B. Lindsey, *Colored No More: Reinventing Black Womanhood in Washington, D.C.* (Urbana: University of Illinois, 2017).

9. Please note that there are various original and updated editions of the following Black Greek-letter fraternity histories: Charles H. Wesley, *The History of Alpha Phi Alpha Fraternity: A Development in College Life* (Washington, DC: Foundation, 1953); William L. Crump, *The Story of Kappa Alpha Psi: A History of the Beginning and Development of a*

College Greek Letter Organization, 1911–1983, 3rd ed. (Philadelphia: Kappa Alpha Psi Fraternity, 1983). More recent additions of this book have Ralph J. Bryson as author. Anthony Asadullah Samad, *March On, March on Ye Mighty Host: The Comprehensive History of Phi Beta Sigma Fraternity, Inc. (1914–2013)* (Washington, DC: Phi Beta Sigma Fraternity, 2003). Also, see Maurice J. Hobson, "Tackling the Talented Tenth: Black Greek-Lettered Organizations and the Black New South," in *The Black Intellectual Tradition: African American Thought in the Twentieth Century*, ed. Derrick P. Alridge, Cornelius L. Bynum, and James B. Stewart (Urbana: University of Illinois Press, 2021), 176–203.

10. Paula J. Giddings, *In Search of Sisterhood: Delta Sigma Theta and the Challenge of the Black Sorority Movement* (New York: HarperCollins, [1988] 2009).

11. Vincent Harding, *There Is a River: The Black Struggle for Freedom in America* (New York: Harcourt, Brace, 1981), 50.

12. Omega men Keir Pemberton, Jonathan Matthews, David Carl, and Sam Ryan have, over the past decade, worked diligently to locate, collect, and digitize available primary sources about Omega and its members. Pemberton, Matthews, Carl, and Ryan have secured and preserved materials from official Omega sources as well as from unaffiliated sources such as newspapers.

13. M. Beaunorus Tolson, "Wanted: A New Negro Leadership," *The Oracle* 16, no. 2 (July 1937): 10.

14. Robert L. Gill to Cary D. Jacobs, November 20, 1962, Omega Psi Phi Archives Inc., History and Archives Committee, Decatur, GA.

Chapter 1

1. See Herman Dreer, *The History of Omega Psi Phi Fraternity: A Brotherhood of Negro College Men, 1911 to 1939* (Washington, DC: Omega Psi Phi Fraternity, 1940); Kenneth R. Manning, *Black Apollo of Science: The Life of Ernest Everett Just* (New York: Oxford University Press, 1984), 22; "The Government's Daily Weather Map," *Washington Post*, November 17, 1911; "The Government's Daily Weather Map," *Washington Post*, November 18, 1911.

2. George M. Fredrickson, *The Black Image in the White Mind: The Debate on Afro-American Character and Destiny, 1817-1914* (Middletown, CT: Wesleyan University Press, 1987), 198–255; Dreer, *History of Omega Psi Phi*, 22; "The Mother Pearl, The Alpha Chapter," accessed March 1, 2024, https://themotherpearl.org/the-beginning.

3. See Booker T. Washington, *The Negro Problem: A Series of Articles by Representative Negroes of To-Day* (Radford, VA: Wilder, [1903] 2008); W. Cabell Bruce, *The Negro Problem* (Baltimore: John Murphy, 1891); Fredrickson, *The Black Image in the White Mind*, 198–255; Rayford W. Logan, *The Betrayal of the Negro: From Rutherford B. Hayes to Woodrow Wilson* (New York: De Capo Press, 1997), 52–53.

4. See Henry Lyman Morehouse, "The Talented Tenth," *American Missionary* 50, no. 6 (June 1896): 182–83, published originally in *Independent* 48 (April 23, 1896): 1; and Maurice J. Hobson, "Tackling the Talented Tenth: Black Greek-Lettered Organizations and the Black New South," in *The Black Intellectual Tradition: African American Thought in the Twentieth Century*, ed. Derrick P. Alridge, Cornelius L. Bynum, and James B. Stewart (Urbana: University of Illinois Press, 2021), 176–203.

5. W. E. B. Du Bois, "The Talented Tenth," in Washington, *Negro Problem*, 13–30; Morehouse, "Talented Tenth."

6. "Dr. Booker T. Washington Speaks at Opening," *Howard University Journal* 7, no. 1 (October 10, 1909): 1–2; Booker T. Washington, "Need Negro Doctors: Room for More of Them, Says Booker T. Washington," *Evening Star* (Washington, DC), October 4, 1909.

7. W. E. B. Du Bois, "The College-Bred Community," in *The Education of Black People: Ten Critiques, 1916–1960*, ed. Herbert Aptheker (New York: Monthly Review, [1910] 2001), 49–59; W. E. B. Du Bois, *The Souls of Black Folk* (New York: Dover Publications, Inc., [1903] 1994), 55–67.

8. See James D. Anderson, *The Education of Blacks in the South, 1860–1935* (Chapel Hill: University of North Carolina Press, 1988), 244.

9. See Rayford Whittingham Logan, *Howard University: The First Hundred Years, 1867–1967* (New York: New York University Press, 1969), 69–247. For more on Howard and Black intellectuals, see Zachery R. Williams, *In Search of the Talented Tenth: Howard University Public Intellectuals and the Dilemmas of Race, 1926–1970* (Columbia: University of Missouri Press, 2010).

10. B. W. Thompson, "Howard University Crowded to Doors: Largest Number of Freshman Entries in the History of the University," *Afro-American* (Baltimore, MD), October 2, 1909; Paula J. Giddings, *In Search of Sisterhood: Delta Sigma Theta and the Challenge of the Black Sorority Movement* (New York: HarperCollins, [1988] 2009), 34, 46–60; *Catalogue Howard University 1909–10* (Washington DC: Howard University 1909), 187–188.

11. Chris Myers Asch and George Derek Musgrove, *Chocolate City: A History of Race and Democracy in the Nation's Capital* (Chapel Hill: University of North Carolina Press, 2017), 226. In 1910, White people made up 71.3 percent of Washington, DC's population and Black people 28.5 percent, according to Asch and Musgrove.

12. *Howard University Record* 5, no. 4 (1911): 4.

13. *Catalogue Howard University 1909–10* (Washington, DC: Howard University, 1909), 48. The opening ceremony for the incoming class was at Andrew Rankin Memorial Chapel on September 28, 1909. It should be noted that first-year students majoring in the arts or sciences received coursework in the liberal arts.

14. *Catalogue Howard University 1909–10*, 40.

15. *Catalogue Howard University 1909–10*, 51. Although Ernest E. Just was a biologist, his first position at Howard was as an instructor of English and rhetoric. Given the well-written and well-articulated speeches of him and other Omega founders, we submit Just's instruction was influential.

16. "News from the Capital City," *New York Age*, March 17, 1910, 3; Jonathan Matthews, "The Genesis of a Friendship," September 28, 2019, Omega Psi Phi Fraternity Inc., History and Archives Committee, Decatur, Georgia.

17. "News from the Capital City."

18. William C. Jason Jr., "Omega's Oscar James Cooper, M.D.," 3, n.d., Omega Psi Phi Fraternity Inc., History and Archives Committee, Decatur, GA. This document was postmarked November 4, 1959. Given the document's contents, Jason likely wrote it during the late 1950s. He addressed the item to Fraternity Grand historian Robert L. Gill.

19. Jason, "Omega's Oscar James Cooper," 3.

20. *Ancient History Encyclopedia*, s.v. "Gymnasium," by Mark Cartwright, May 9, 2016, www.worldhistory.org/Gymnasium/. For one nineteenth-century articulation of the intellectual aspects of the gymnasium expressed to the general public, see David William Cheever, "The Gymnasium," *Atlantic* (May 1859), www.theatlantic.com/magazine/archive/1859/05/the-gymnasium/305407/.

21. See, again, Cheever, "Gymnasium." For a discussion of racial uplift and physical activity, see J. Anthony Guillory, "The Physical Uplift of the Race: The Emergence of the African American Physical Culture Movement, 1900–1930" (PhD diss., University of Massachusetts-Amherst, 2015), https://scholarworks.umass.edu/cgi/viewcontent.cgi?article=1413&context=dissertations_2.

22. Dreer, *History of Omega Psi Phi*, 10.

23. Jason, "Omega's Oscar James Cooper," 4.

24. Oscar Cooper's later account differs slightly from the account in Herman Dreer's 1940 book, *The History of Omega Psi Phi*. See Jason, "Omega's Oscar James Cooper," 4.

25. "Love on Frank Coleman, 51st Grand Conclave Minutes (1967), Memorial Service," 32, Omega Psi Phi Fraternity Inc., History and Archives Committee, Decatur, GA.

26. Jason, "Omega's Oscar James Cooper," 3.

27. Charles H. Wesley, *The History of Alpha Phi Alpha Fraternity: A Development in College Life* (Washington, DC: Foundation, 1953), 40–43.

28. "The History of Omega Psi Phi by Founder, Bishop Edgar Amos Love," History and Archives Committee, Decatur, GA, 1.

29. Bettye Collier-Thomas and James Turner, "Race, Class and Color: The African American Discourse on Identity," *Journal of American Ethnic History* 1, no. 14 (Fall 1994): 5–31. Martin Kilson addressed colorism among early twentieth-century Black intellectuals extensively in *The Transformation of the African American Intelligentsia, 1880–2012* (Cambridge, MA: Harvard University Press, 2014), 9–43.

30. Edward H. Taylor, "Putting a Question Up to Howard Students," *Hilltop* 8, no. 10 (April 29, 1929): 1.

31. Omega Psi Phi Minutes, Thursday, November 15, 1911, as quoted in Dreer, *History of Omega Psi Phi*, 12.

32. Oscar J. Cooper to William C. Jason Jr., November 4, 1962, Omega Psi Phi Fraternity Inc., History and Archives Committee, Decatur, GA; Minutes, Thursday, November 17, 1911, as quoted in Dreer, *History of Omega Psi Phi*, 12–13.

33. Oscar J. Cooper to William Jason.

34. See Gail Bederman, *Manliness and Civilization: A Cultural History of Gender and Race in the United States, 1880–1917* (Chicago: University of Chicago Press, 1995).

35. Oscar J. Cooper to William Jason. Herman Dreer and Robert Gill listed the cardinal principles in different orders. Scholarship, manhood, perseverance, and uplift comprised Dreer's order, whereas Gill provided the following list: manhood, scholarship, perseverance, and uplift. Dreer, *History of Omega Psi Phi*, 13; Robert L. Gill, *The Omega Psi Phi Fraternity and the Men Who Made Its History: A Concise History* (Washington, DC: Omega Psi Phi Fraternity, 1963), 1.

36. Oscar J. Cooper to William Jason.

37. See Samuel Huber, *Efficiency and Uplift: Scientific Management in the Progressive Era, 1890–1920* (Chicago: University of Chicago Press, 1964).

38. Oscar J. Cooper to William Jason; Hobson, "Tackling the Talented Tenth," 178–79.

39. Anna Julia Cooper, *A Voice from the South* (New York: Oxford University Press, [1892] 1988).

40. W. E. B. Du Bois, *The Souls of Black Folk* (New York: Dover, [1903] 1994); C. G. Woodson, *The Education of the Negro Prior to 1861: A History of the Education of the Colored People in the United States from the Beginning of Slavery to the Civil War* (Washington, DC: Association for the Study of Negro Life and History, 1915).

41. Oscar J. Cooper to William Jason; Kevin K. Gaines, *Uplifting the Race: Black Leadership, Politics, and Culture in the Twentieth Century* (Chapel Hill: University of North Carolina Press, 1996).

42. Gill, *Omega Psi Phi Fraternity*, 1; Love lists the Greek order of the motto as *Philia Ophelema Psukis*. "The History of Omega Psi Phi by Founder, Bishop Edgar Amos Love," 3, n.d., Omega Psi Phi Fraternity Inc., History and Archives Committee, Decatur, GA.

43. "The History of Omega Psi Phi by Founder, Bishop Edgar Amos Love," 3.

44. "The History of Omega Psi Phi by Founder, Bishop Edgar Amos Love," 3. Edgar Love's training in divinity and all Omega founders' readings of Plato in Greek literature doubtless exposed them to conversations about the soul.

45. See Gloria Harper Dickinson, "Pledged to Remember: Africa in the Life and Lore of Black Greek-Letter Organizations," in *African American Fraternities and Sororities: The Legacy and the Vision*, ed. Tamara L. Brown, Gregory S. Parks, and Clarenda M. Phillips (Lexington: University Press of Kentucky, 2005), 1–35. Dickinson discussed tenets of the Egyptian mystery system as part of the rites and passages of Black Greek-letter organizations. Those tenets included control of thought, control of action, devotion of purpose, and faith in oneself to wield truth. Omega Psi Phi's four cardinal principles—manhood, scholarship, perseverance, and uplift—aligned with those tenets.

46. Dreer, *History of Omega Psi Phi*, 13–14.

47. Minutes, Thursday, November 23, 1911, in Dreer, *History of Omega Psi Phi*, 13.

48. Given Howard University's liberal arts curriculum when Edgar A. Love, Oscar J. Cooper, Frank Coleman, and Ernest E. Just founded Omega Psi Phi in 1911, they doubtless had thorough exposure to Greek mythology.

49. Dreer, *History of Omega Psi Phi*, 14.

50. Wm. Raimond Baird, *Baird's Manual of American College Fraternities: A Descriptive Analysis of the Society System in the Colleges of the United States, with a Detailed Account of Each Fraternity* (Philadelphia, PA: J. B. Lippincott, 1879); Wm. Raimond Baird, *Baird's Manual of American College Fraternities: A Descriptive Analysis of the Fraternity System in the Colleges of the United States*, 6th ed. (New York: Alcolm, 1905).

51. Edgar Love, interview by Mark Hyman, 1973, 2, Omega Psi Phi Fraternity Inc., History and Archives Committee, Decatur, GA. Love did not specify *Baird's Manual* was the book Ernest Just got before Frank Coleman, Oscar J. Cooper, and they chose a fraternity name for Omega Psi Phi; however, certain Omega practices, among other things, suggested that *Baird's Manual* was said book.

52. Baird, *Baird's Manual*, 3.

53. "The History of Omega Psi Phi by Founder, Bishop Edgar Amos Love," 1.

54. "The History of Omega Psi Phi by Founder, Bishop Edgar Amos Love," 2; Dreer, *History of Omega Psi Phi*, 19–20.

55. David Carl, a member of the Omega Psi Phi History and Archives committee, has pointed out that Reverend Garnett Russell Waller, who became a member of Gamma chapter in Boston, was a member of the Niagara group in 1905. See David L. Carl, "Rev. Garnett Russell Waller," Gamma Chapter/Omega Psi Phi Fraternity, Inc., accessed February 12, 2018, http://gamma1916.com/2018/02/rev-garnett-russell-waller/. Historian Chad Williams identifies Waller as a "cofounder" of the Niagara Movement. See Chad L. Williams, *The Wounded World: W.E.B. Du Bois and the First World War* (New York: Farrar, Straus and Giroux), 237.

56. See "The History of Omega Psi Phi by Founder, Bishop Edgar Amos Love," 2; Dreer, *History of Omega Psi Phi*, 19–20.

57. Dreer, *History of Omega Psi Phi*, 22.

58. Gill, *Omega Psi Phi Fraternity*, 2; "The History of Mother Pearl," accessed June 15, 2024, http://www.alphachapterques.com/index.cfm?e=inner4&itemcategory=82475.

59. "The History of Omega Psi Phi by Founder, Bishop Edgar Amos Love," 2.

60. "The History of Omega Psi Phi by Founder, Bishop Edgar Amos Love," 2.

61. "The History of Omega Psi Phi by Founder, Bishop Edgar Amos Love," 2–3.

62. "The History of Omega Psi Phi by Founder, Bishop Edgar Amos Love," 3.

63. See Dreer, *History of Omega Psi Phi*, 22–23; and Walter H. Mazyck, "Omega's Infancy," *The Oracle* 8, no. 3 (October 1929): 7–8; Gill, *Omega Psi Phi Fraternity*, 3–5.

64. E. A. Love, "Omega Psi Phi Banquet," *Howard University Journal* 9, no. 27 (May 17, 1912): 2.

65. See Gill, *Omega Psi Phi Fraternity*, 3; Mazyck, "Omega's Infancy," 8.

66. "Omega Psi Phi Holds Its House Warming," *Howard University Journal* 10, no. 9 (December 6, 1912): 1.

67. "Omega Psi Phi Holds Its House Warming," 1.

68. Jason, "Omega's Oscar James Cooper," 7.

69. "The Effect of Emancipation Upon the Physical Condition of the Afro-American," flyer, Omega Psi Phi Fraternity Inc., History and Archives Committee, Decatur, GA.

70. Kelly Miller, *Out of the House of Bondage: A Discussion of the Race Problem* (New York: Neale, 1914).

71. See Edgar A. Love to Kelly Miller, April 15, 1913; Frank H. Wimberley to Kelly Miller, April 15, 1913; and C. M. D. Harllee to Kelly Miller, April 15, 1913, Omega Psi Phi Fraternity Inc., History and Archives Committee, Decatur, GA.

72. T. B. D. Dyett, "Howard Again a Leader: First Student's Branch of N.A.A.C.P Formed Here," *Howard University Journal* 10, no. 23 (April 4, 1913): 3.

73. Dreer, *History of Omega Psi Phi*, 28.

74. See "Lincoln Pays Tribute to Mrs. Charlotte Wilson," *Lincolnian*, February 15, 1967, 3. Charlotte is listed in the 1910 Census as Lottie Gacher, wife of Nathaniel Gacher. *Thirteenth Census of the United States: 1910: Population* (Philadelphia, PA: US Census Bureau, April 19, 1910). When Lottie married Alphonso R. Wilson on June 1, 1924, her maiden name of Lottie French was listed on the marriage certificate. Omega Psi Phi Fraternity Inc., History and Archives Committee, Decatur, GA. Also, see Pennsylvania, US, Marriages, 1852–1868 for Charlotte N. French, Chester, vol. 18–19, 1920–1925, Omega Psi Phi Fraternity Inc., History and Archives Committee, Decatur, GA.

75. "Tribute Paid to 'Omega's Sister,'" *The Oracle* 46, no. 1 (March 1956): 13.

76. "Lincoln Pays Tribute to Mrs. Charlotte Wilson," 3.

77. A Beta chapter of the Omega Psi Phi website lists Herbert Forgys Anderson, Albert Sidney Beasley, William Edward Bush, Winston Stanley Douglas, Junius Edward Fowlkes, Leslie Elmore Ginn, George Abner Golightly, Howard Decker Gregg, Norman Alonzo Holmes, Emory Albert James, Harry Elmer James, Moses Lafyette Kiser, Henry McClellan Marlowe, Willis Gittens Price, Robert Allen Pritchett, Raymond George Robinson, Charles Reed Saulter, Fitz Patrick Stewart, Alonzo Merral Willis, and Andrew Lee Wallace as charterers. "Beta Lineage: The Charter Line," Beta Chapter, accessed November 27, 2023, www.beta1914.com/beta-lineage.

78. *Catalogue of Lincoln University Chester County, Penna: Sixty-Third Year 1917–1918* (Philadelphia, PA: Ferris & Leach, 1918), 72 (cited hereinafter as *1917–18 Lincoln University Catalogue*); Catalogue of Lincoln University Chester County, Penna: Sixty-Fourth Year 1918-1919 (Philadelphia, PA: Ferris & Leach, 1919), 73.

79. *Catalogue of Lincoln University Chester County, Penna: Sixty-First Year 1915–1916* (Philadelphia, PA: Ferris & Leach, 1916), 68 (cited hereinafter as *1915–16 Lincoln University Catalogue*).

80. *Catalogue of Lincoln University Chester County, Penna: Sixty-Second Year 1916–1917* (Philadelphia, PA: Ferris & Leach, 1917), 72 (cited hereinafter as *1916–17 Lincoln University Catalogue*); C. R. Saulter, "Beta Chapter," *The Oracle* (June 1919): 11. It should be noted that the first issues of *The Oracle* do not include volume numbers.

81. *1916–17 Lincoln University Catalogue*, 71, 72.

82. *1917–18 Lincoln University Catalogue*, 72.

83. *1915–16 Lincoln University Catalogue*, 71; *1916–17 Lincoln University Catalogue*, 10; *1917–18 Lincoln University Catalogue*, 70–71; *Catalogue of Lincoln University Chester County, Penna: Sixtieth Year 1914–1915* (Philadelphia, PA: Ferris & Leach, 1914), 69, 72.

84. For a discussion of respectability politics in the early twentieth century, see Evelyn Brooks Higginbotham, *Righteous Discontent: The Women's Movement in the Black Baptist Church, 1880–1920* (Cambridge, MA: Harvard University Press, 1993).

85. See Dreer, *History of Omega Psi Phi*, 25; and Gill, *Omega Psi Phi Fraternity*, 4.

86. G. E. Hall, "The College Branch of the N.A.A.C.P.," *Howard University Journal* 13, no. 1 (October 8, 1915): 5.

87. See Jonathan A. Matthews, "The Great War, Part I: Fort Des Moines & the War Chapter," *H&A: The History and Archives of Omega Psi Phi*, November 2018, 5–6; Dreer, *History of Omega Psi Phi*, 30; Gill, *Omega Psi Phi Fraternity*, 5; "Omega Psi Phi Inc., Gamma Chapter," accessed March 5, 2024, https://gamma1916.com.

88. "Omega Psi Phi," *Howard University Journal* 14, no. 5 (November 3, 1916): 2–3.

89. "The Sunday Lectures to the Omega Psi Phi Continued," *Howard University Journal* 14, no. 13 (January 19, 1917): 3; "The Omega Psi Phi Fraternity Sunday Lecture," *Howard University Journal* 14, no. 18 (March 12, 1917): 8.

90. "Sunday Lectures at the Omega Psi Phi," *Howard University Journal* 14, no. 15 (February 2, 1917): 3.

91. "Sunday Lectures at the Omega Psi Phi," 3; Anderson, *Education of Blacks in the South*, 23.

92. On Carter G. Woodson's election date into Omega Psi Phi, see Luther O. Baumgardner, "Alpha Chapter," *The Oracle* (June 1919): 10.

93. J. S. Heslip, "America: Her Attitude Toward the Negro," *Howard University Journal* 13, no. 2 (October 15, 1915): 1, 4–5.

94. Heslip, "America," 1, 4–5.

95. "Scholarship in School of Liberal Arts, Howard University 1914–1915," *Howard University Journal* 13, no. 14 (February 11, 1916): 2. It should be noted that scores reported were for the School of Liberal Arts.

96. Herman Dreer, "Omega Calls Her Sons of Light," Omega Psi Phi Fraternity Inc., History and Archives Committee, Decatur, GA.

97. Dreer, "Omega Calls Her Sons."

98. Dreer, "Omega Calls Her Sons."

99. Walter H. Mazyck, "Omega and Interfraternity Policy," *The Oracle* 9 (June 1930): 5.

100. Mazyck, "Omega and Interfraternity Policy," 5.

101. Mazyck, "Omega and Interfraternity Policy," 5; Dreer, *History of Omega Psi Phi*, 145–146.

102. Mazyck, "Omega and Interfraternity Policy," 5. National Pan-Hellenic Council, accessed December 13, 2023, www.nphchq.com/.

103. See Wilson Jeremiah Moses, *Black Messiahs and Uncle Toms: Social and Literary Manipulations of a Religious Myth* (University Park: Pennsylvania State University Press, 1993). Hazel Carby, in *Race Men* (Cambridge, MA: Harvard University Press, 2000), not only discussed patriarchal aspects of her primary subjects, Black race men, but she also challenged prevailing notions about Black men as natural leaders—indeed, saviors—of Black people. According to her, such ideas negated the significance of Black women. She analyzed twentieth-century language to support her basic contention.

104. J. Samuel Cook, "Of Vision and Power: The Life of Bishop Edgar Amos Love" (master's thesis, University of Toledo, 2009), 11–19.

105. Cook, "Of Vision and Power," 19.

106. Cook, "Of Vision and Power," 17–19.

107. Cook, "Of Vision and Power," 23.

108. Dreer, *History of Omega Psi Phi*, 4–5. Robert L. Gill, "The Wellsprings of Omega: The Founders," n.d., 9–13, Omega Psi Phi Fraternity, Inc., History and Archives Committee, Decatur, GA; a range of birth dates abound for Cooper in the historical record. Omega Psi Phi denotes the date as 1888, which is the date on Cooper's tombstone.

109. Gill, *Omega Psi Phi Fraternity*, 1; and Dreer, *History of Omega Psi Phi*, 4–5; Gill, "The Wellsprings of Omega," 9–13.

110. Dreer, *History of Omega Psi Phi*, 4; Jason, "Omega's Oscar J. Cooper," 2–3, 11.

111. "A Young 'Grad' Making Good," *Howard University Journal* 11, no. 10 (December 12, 1913): 7; Dreer, *History of the Omega Psi Phi*, 6; Otis Alexander, Frank Charles Coleman (1890–1967) July 26, 2023, https://www.blackpast.org/african-american-history/frank-charles-coleman-1890-1967/.

112. See Dreer, *History of Omega Psi Phi*, 6–7; and "Brother Coleman's Passing Leaves Void in Omega," *The Oracle* 56, no. 1 (Spring 1967): 5.

113. See *Annual Reports of the President and the Treasurer of Oberlin College for 1918–19* (Oberlin, OH: Oberlin College, 1919), 352; and "Negro Officer Takes Bride," *Washington Post*, May 26, 1918; Matthews, "The Great War," 22.

114. See Arthur P. Davis, "Ernest Everett Just," *Howard University Profiles* (May 1979): 1, in Omega Psi Phi Fraternity Inc., History and Archives Committee, Decatur, GA; Manning, *Black Apollo of Science*, 4–18.

115. Davis, "Ernest Everett Just," 1; Manning, *Black Apollo of Science*, 18–27.

116. See Shelby Grantham, "The Greatest Problem in American Biology," *Dartmouth Alumni Magazine*, November 1983, 25; and Manning, *Black Apollo of Science*, 22.

117. Davis, "Ernest Everett Just," 1.

118. Davis, "Ernest Everett Just," 1.

119. Manning, *Black Apollo of Science*, 26; Kimball Union Academy, *On the Hilltop: Two Hundred Years at Kimball Union Academy* (Meriden, NH: Nomad Press, 2012), 37.

120. Manning, *Black Apollo of Science*, 25–28; Davis, "Ernest Everett Just," 1.

121. Manning, *Black Apollo of Science*, 28–55.

122. Manning, *Black Apollo of Science*, 37–41.

123. Manning, *Black Apollo of Science*, 40.

124. S. Milton Nabrit, "Ernest E. Just," *Phylon* vol. 7, no. 2 (2nd quarter, 1946): 121; "Flashes from the Southeast," *The Oracle* 38, no. 1 (March 1948): 19.

125. Nabrit, "Ernest E. Just," 121.

126. See John A. Garraty and Mark C. Carnes, *A Short History of the American Nation* (New York: Longman, 2001), 561; History.com editors, "World War I," accessed August 11, 2023, https://www.history.com/topics/world-war-i/world-war-i-history.

127. See John Hope Franklin and Evelyn Brooks Higginbotham, *From Slavery to Freedom: A History of African Americans*, 10th ed. (New York: McGraw Hill, 2021), 370; Garraty and Carnes, *A Short History of the American Nation*, 561–64; Robert H. Zieger, *America's Great War: World War I and the American Experience* (Lanham, Maryland: Rowman & Littlefield, 2001).

128. See David Levering Lewis, *W. E. B. Du Bois: The Fight for Equality and the American Century, 1919-1963* (New York: Henry Holt, 2000), 37–50; William S. Nelson to W. E. B. Du Bois, April 6, 1921, in *W. E. B. Du Bois Papers*, MS 312, Special Collections and University Archives, University of Massachusetts Amherst Libraries (cited hereinafter as Du Bois Papers, UMass Amherst); see Jack B. Moore, *W. E. B. Du Bois* (Boston: Twayne Publishers, 1981), 53–55.

129. Dreer, *History of Omega Psi Phi*, 23; For Du Bois's use of the term "close ranks," see Joe William Trotter Jr., *The African American Experience* (Boston: Houghton Mifflin, 2000), 375.

130. Matthews, "Great War," 5–6.

131. Quoted in Matthews, "Great War," 6.

132. See Matthews, "Great War," 6–7, 18–22; Cook, "Of Vision and Power," 28–29, Logan, *Howard University*, 141.

133. See Matthews, "Great War," 7–8; Brian G. Shellum, *Black Cadet in a White Bastion: Charles Young at West Point* (Lincoln: University of Nebraska Press, 2006); Brian G. Shellum, *Black Officer in a Buffalo Soldier Regiment: The Military Career of Charles Young* (Lincoln: University of Nebraska Press, 2010), chap. 13, Kindle; and Charles Young, *Military Morale of Nations and Races* (Kansas City, MO: Franklin Hudson, 1912); see also Friedrich Katz, *The Life and Times of Pancho Villa* (Palo Alto, CA: Stanford University Press, 1998).

134. Charles Young to W. E. B. Du Bois, June 20, 1917, in Du Bois Papers, UMass Amherst.

135. See Shellum, *Black Officer*, chap. 13.

136. See "Howard University in the War," *Howard University Record* 13, no. 5 (May 1919): 38–44; and Matthews, "Great War," 7–8; 17–18.

137. See "Howard University in the War"; Matthews, "Great War," 12–13; and J. A. Thomas Jr., "The Camp Howard Chapter," *The Oracle* (June 1919): 19.

138. Thomas, "Camp Howard Chapter," 19–20; Matthews, "The Great War," 12.

139. "Calls Legion Best Friend of the Negro: Col. Young, U. S. A. Talks in Tremont Temple," *Boston Globe*, December 29, 1919, p. 4.

140. *Address of Booker T. Washington . . . Delivered at the Opening of the Cotton States and International Exposition, at Atlanta, Ga., September 18, 1895* (Atlanta, GA: n.p., 1895); "Calls Legion Best Friend."

141. See "Calls Legion Best Friend"; W. E. Burghardt Du Bois, *The Souls of Black Folk: Essays and Sketches* (Chicago: A. C. McClurg, 1903), vii; Shellum, *Black Officer*; and Charles Young to W. E. B. Du Bois, June 20, 1917, in Du Bois Papers, UMass Amherst.

142. "Calls Legion Best Friend."

143. "Calls Legion Best Friend."

144. Thomas, "Camp Howard Chapter," 20.

145. S. M. Douglass, "Introduction," *The Oracle* (June 1919): 3. Gill, *Omega Psi Phi Fraternity*, 7–8.

146. "Foreword," *The Oracle* (June 1919): 4, 5.

147. Lloyd H. Newman, "Grand Chapter," *The Oracle* (June 1919): 6–9.

148. Jonathan Matthews and Justin Valentine, "A Genesis of Growth: The War Chapter," August 4, 2016, Omega Psi Phi Fraternity Inc., History and Archives Committee, Decatur, GA; Dreer, *History of Omega Psi Phi*, 36, 38; H. H. Thomas, "Iota Chapter, Atlantic City, N. J.," *The Oracle* (August 1921): 22–23; Gill, *Omega Psi Phi Fraternity*, 88–93.

149. R. McCants Andrews, "Our Elder Brothers," *The Oracle* (June 1919): 20.

150. Andrews, "Our Elder Brothers," 20.

151. "Roll of Elected Active Members (Honorary)," *The Oracle* (June 1919): 26; Bobby Lovett, "James Carroll Napier (1845–1940): From Plantation to the City," in DeBlack, *Southern Elite*, 73–94; Sheena M. Morrison and Elizabeth Fee, "Charles V. Roman: Physician, Writer, Educator, Historian (1864–1934)," accessed March 11, 2024, https://www.ncbi.nlm.nih.gov/pmc/articles/PMC2837430/; Sheldon Avery, *Up from Washington: William Pickens and the Negro Struggle for Equality, 1900–1954* (Newark: University of Delaware Press, 1989); Tikia K. Hamilton, "The Cost of Integration: The Contentious Career of Garnet C. Wilkinson," *Washington History* 30, no. 1 (Spring 2018): 50–60.

152. Christopher A. Brooks and Robert Sims, *Roland Hayes: The Legacy of an American Tenor* (Bloomington: Indiana University Press, 2015), 5.

153. Brooks and Sims, *Roland Hayes*, 6–7.

154. F. W. Woolsey, "Conversation with . . . Roland Hayes," *Black Perspective in Music* 2, no. 2 (Autumn 1974): 179–85; "Roland Hayes of Gamma," *The Oracle* 3, no. 1 (March 1925): 20.

155. Howard P. Kennedy, "Roland Hayes: A Study in Achievement," *The Oracle* 2, no. 1 (December 1923): 18.

156. "Omega Psi Phi Annual Conclave," *Chicago Defender*, December 25, 1920.

157. "Omega Psi Phi Meet," *Chicago Defender*, December 4, 1920.

158. "Among the Clubs: Omega Psi Phi Fraternity Organizes Thirteenth Chapter in Philadelphia," *Philadelphia Tribune*, December 11, 1920.

159. "Omega Psi Phi Annual Conclave," *Chicago Defender*, December 25, 1920, 10.

160. "Omega Psi Phi Annual Conclave," 10.

161. C. G. Woodson "The Disruption of Virginia" (PhD diss., Harvard University, 1912).

162. Woodson, *Education of the Negro*.

163. We have not located a transcript of the actual speech Carter Woodson delivered at the Ninth Grand Conclave of Omega Psi Phi in Nashville, Tennessee, on December 27, 1920; however, Woodson gave a speech of the same title at Hampton Institute (now Hampton University) in Virginia, among other times later during the 1920s; "The Ninth Annual Convention," *The Oracle* (August 1921): 7.

164. Carter Godwin Woodson, *The Mis-Education of the Negro* (Washington, DC: Associated Publishers, 1933).

165. See Pero Gaglo Dagbovie, *The Early Black History Movement, Carter G. Woodson, and Lorenzo Johnston Greene* (Urbana: University of Illinois Press, 2007).

166. "Omega Psi Phi Fraternity Holds Conclave," *Atlanta Independent*, January 13, 1921, 5.

167. "The Ninth Annual Convention," *The Oracle* 2, no. 1 (August 1921): 7.

168. See Dagbovie, *Early Black History*, 229n12.

169. Dagbovie, *Early Black History*, 229n12; Carter G. Woodson, "Negro History Week," *Journal of Negro History* 11, no. 2 (April 1926): 238–42.

170. E. E. Just, "The Challenge," *The Oracle* (June 1919): 24.

171. Just, "Challenge," 24.

Chapter 2

1. On the number of members and chapters in 1920 and in 1930, see Harold H. Thomas, "Annual Message: The Grand Basileus," *The Oracle* (1921): 4 (the first issues of *The Oracle* do not include volume/issue numbers); Matthew W. Bullock, "A Letter from the Grand Basileus," *The Oracle* 9, no. 1 (April 1930): 1.

2. For more on the importance of Black history and education, see Carter G. Woodson, *The Negro in Our History* (n.p.: Associated Publishers, 1922). On Woodson's views of education, see Jarvis R. Givens, *Fugitive Pedagogy: Carter G. Woodson and the Art of Black Teaching* (Cambridge, MA: Harvard University Press, 2021).

3. "The Lynching Record," *Baltimore Afro-American*, January 7, 1921. For more on lynching, particularly the work on Ida B. Wells, see Ida B. Wells-Barnett, *On Lynchings* (New York: Dover Publications, [1892] 2014); Ida B. Wells-Barnett, *The Light of Truth: Writings of an Anti-Lynching Crusader* (New York: Penguin, 2014); Alfreda M. Duster, *Crusade for Justice: The Autobiography of Ida B. Wells* (Chicago: University of Chicago Press, 1970); Michele Duster, *Ida B. the Queen: The Extraordinary Life and Legacy of Ida B. Wells* (New York: Atria, 2021).

4. Darlene Clark Hine, "The Pursuit of Professional Equality: Meharry Medical College, 1921–1938, A Case Study," in *New Perspectives on Black Educational History*, ed. Vincent P. Franklin and James D. Anderson (Boston: G. K. Hall, 1978), 176; Mike Mitka, "The Flexner Report at the Century Mark: A Wake-Up Call for Reforming Medical Education," *Journal of the American Medical Association* 303, no. 15 (April 2010): 1466. For a brief overview of the report, see Andrew H. Beck, "The Flexner Report and the Standardization of American Medical Education," *Journal of the American Medical Association* 291, no. 17 (May 2004): 2139–40. On the Flexner Report's impact on Black medical education, see Todd Savitt, "Abraham Flexner and the Black Medical Schools," *Journal of the National Medical Association* 98, no. 9 (September 2006): 1415–24.

5. "Dr. C. V. Roman, Specialist," *Nashville Globe*, December 25, 1908. For two notable books Roman wrote, see his *American Civilization and the Negro: The Afro-American in Relation to National Progress* (Philadelphia: F. A. Davis, 1916) and *A Knowledge of History Is Conductive to Racial Solidarity . . . and Other Writings* (Nashville: Sunday School Union Print, 1911). See also "Charles V. Roman," National Medical Association, C. V. Roman Medical Society, Dallas Ft. Worth Chapter of the NMA, accessed December 26, 2020, https://nmadfw.org/cvroman/.

6. On the details of the 1920 conclave and speech topics, see "Omega Psi Phi Fraternity Holds Conclave," *Atlanta Independent*, January 13, 1921; also see Bobby Lovett, "James Carroll Napier (1845–1940): From Plantation to the City," in *Southern Elite and Social Change: Essays in Honor of Willard B. Gatewood Jr.*, ed. Thomas A. DeBlack (Fayetteville: University of Arkansas Press, 2002), 73–94.

7. "Omega Psi Phi Fraternity Holds Conclave."

8. "The Ninth Annual Convention," *The Oracle* 2, no. 1 (1921): 7.

9. Jonathan Matthews of the Fraternity's History and Archives Committee provided an unpublished manuscript titled "The Origin of Achievement Week." See page 3. A copy is in possession of the authors. Elements of the manuscript are available on the website of the Delta Mu Mu Chapter, "The Origin of Achievement Week: Omega's First Social Action Initiative," accessed May 1, 2024, https://www.dmmachievement.org/aw-history.

10. Regarding the Black population by state, see "Fourteenth Census of the United States Taken in the Year 1920: Population," US Census Bureau Records (1920), 3, 54, 86, 184, 202, 388, 528, 730, 984, 1056. For a detailed account of Black education prior to 1920, see Carter G. Woodson, *The Education of the Negro Prior to 1861: A History of the Colored People of the United States from the Beginning of Slavery to the Civil War* (Whitefish, MT: Kessinger, [1915] 2010), and Henry Allen Bullock, *A History of Negro Education in the South: From 1619 to the Present* (Cambridge, MA: Harvard University Press, 1967).

11. W. E. B. Du Bois and Augustus Granville Dill, *The College-Bred American Negro: A Social Study* (Atlanta, GA: Atlanta University Press, 1910), 13; Anderson, *Education of Blacks*, 238.

12. Regarding the Jones survey, see Anderson, *Education of Blacks*, 250. Also see W. E. B. Du Bois, *The College-Bred Negro* (Atlanta, GA: Atlanta University Press, 1900). For more on Thomas Jesse Jones, see Carter G. Woodson, "Personal: Thomas Jesse Jones," *Journal of Negro History* 35, no. 1 (January 1950): 107–9, and Donald Johnson, "W. E. B. DuBois, Thomas Jesse Jones and the Struggle for Social Education, 1900–1930," *Journal of Negro History* 85, no. 3 (Summer 2000): 71–95. On race during the Progressive Era, see David W. Southern, *The Progressive Era and Race: Reaction and Reform, 1900–1917* (Hoboken, NJ: Wiley, 2005).

13. Woodson, "Personal: Thomas Jesse Jones," 107–8.

14. For the "genuine sacrifice for Omega" quote, see "The Ninth Annual Convention," 7. Regarding William Stuart Nelson's status as a theology student, see "Grand Chapter Officers," *The Oracle* 2, no. 1 (1921): 8. The information about Raymond G. Robinson can be found in Herman Dreer, *The History of Omega Psi Phi Fraternity: A Brotherhood of Negro College Men, 1911 to 1939* (Washington, DC: Omega Psi Phi Fraternity, 1940), 28, 34, 37, 84. See p. 97 for more about Nelson as Director of Publicity.

15. "1,445 Women Register," *Commercial Appeal* (Memphis, TN), October 28, 1920. For further reading on the importance of the Nineteenth Amendment, particularly as it pertains to Black women, read Rosalyn Terborg-Penn, *African American Women in the*

Struggle for the Vote, 1850–1920 (Bloomington: Indiana University Press, 1998), and Martha S. Jones, *Vanguard: How Black Women Broke Barriers, Won the Vote, and Insisted on Equality for All* (New York: Basic Books, 2020).

16. Thomas, "Annual Message," 5. See also *Catalogue of Lincoln University Chester County, Penna: Sixty-Third Year 1917–1918* (Philadelphia, PA: Ferris & Leach, 1918), 77; and "Who's Who in Omega: Harold H. Thomas," *The Oracle* 7, no. 3 (October 1928): 21.

17. "The Lynching Record," *Atlanta Constitution*, January 1, 1921.

18. "The Lynching Record," *Atlanta Constitution*.

19. National Association for the Advancement of Colored People, "Lynchings in the United States," *Crisis* 23, no. 24 (February 1922): 165–69 (quotation on 166); "Texas Leads the Nation in Lynching for the Year of 1920: Total Lynchings Show Decrease of 22 Over the Year of 1919," *Dallas Express*, January 8, 1921.

20. Equal Justice Initiative, *Lynching in America: Confronting the Legacy of Racial Terror* (Montgomery, AL: Equal Justice Initiative, 2017), 40.

21. Equal Justice Initiative, *Lynching in America*, 40.

22. See Equal Justice Initiative, *Lynching in America*; National Association for the Advancement of Colored People, "Lynchings in the United States."

23. R. R. Moton, "The Lynching Record for the First Six Months, 1921," *Philadelphia Tribune*, July 16, 1921.

24. "The Lynching Record," *Atlanta Constitution*.

25. Carter Godwin Woodson, *The Mis-Education of the Negro* (Washington, DC: Associated Publishers, 1933), 3.

26. Thomas, "Annual Message," 5.

27. "Omega Psi Phi Fraternity Holds Conclave"; "Negro Fraternity to Meet in Atlanta," *Atlanta Constitution*, December 11, 1921.

28. "Negro History Facts," *Baltimore Afro-American*, May 20, 1921.

29. William Stuart Nelson, "The Campaign for the Study of Negro Literature and History," *The Oracle* (1921): 31. See also *Catalogue of Lincoln University 1921–1922* (Hampton, VA: Hampton University Press, 1922), 66; Thomas B. Hargrave Jr., *Coming of Age Behind the Magnolia Curtain: A Memoir of Thomas B. Hargrave, Jr.* (Bloomington, IN: AuthorHouse, 2013), 222.

30. All quotes are from Nelson, "The Campaign for the Study of Negro Literature and History," 31–32.

31. Frank Coleman, "The Negro Greek Letter Men's Opportunity for Service," *The Oracle* 2, no. 1 (1921): 29–30.

32. George E. Hall, "The Importance of the Study of Negro History and Literature," *Norfolk Journal and Guide*, May 7, 1921. On Hall and *The Oracle*, see Dreer, *History of Omega Psi Phi*, 87, 97. The emphasis on Black education also spoke to a larger debate over racial advancement. For further reading, see Thomas Aiello, *The Battle for the Souls of Black Folk: W. E. B. Du Bois, Booker T. Washington, and the Debate That Shaped the Course of Civil Rights* (Santa Barbara, CA: ABC-Clio, 2016).

33. "Pi Chapter," *The Oracle* 1, no. 2 (May 1922): 25–26; "Omega Psi Phi Chapter Here: Number of Prominent Citizens Taken into Graduate Chapter," *Baltimore Afro-American*, June 24, 1921. Pi Omega was initially designated as Pi chapter. The Fraternity soon thereafter renamed some chapters to mark a clearer distinction between undergraduate and graduate chapters. In 1923, the newly named Pi Omega in Baltimore helped established Pi chapter for undergraduates enrolled at Morgan College (present-day Morgan State University).

34. "Phi Chapter," *The Oracle* 1, no. 2 (May 1922): 28–29. As noted in the previous note, the Fraternity often redesignated chapters in its early decades. Therefore, Phi chapter was originally established at Talladega College in Alabama before being reassigned to the University of Michigan. "Xi Chapter," *The Oracle* 1, no. 2 (May 1922): 25.

35. "Omega Psi Phi Gives Reception in Atlanta," *Chicago Defender*, May 28, 1921.

36. Scott Ellsworth, *Death in a Promised Land: The Tulsa Race Riot of 1921* (Baton Rouge: Louisiana State University Press, 1992), 66; Roy Wilkins, foreword to *Anatomy of Four Race Riots: Racial Conflict in Knoxville, Elaine (Arkansas), Tulsa, and Chicago, 1919–1921*, by Lee E. Williams and Lee E. Williams III (Jackson: University Press of Mississippi, 1972), x, xiii. For the estimates on Tulsa deaths, we consulted numerous academic and popular sources. Historian Robin D. G. Kelley argued, "No matter what you might have seen on [the television series] Watchmen, in 1921, only six blocks of all of Greenwood were paved, and most Black working-class houses had outhouses, no underground sewage lines. But in the discourse surrounding the massacre, it seems like the fate of those few blocks in and around 'Black Wall Street' is all that matters." George Yancy, "Robin D. G. Kelley, "The Tulsa Race Massacre Went Way Beyond 'Black Wall Street,'" *Truthout*, June 1, 2021, https://truthout.org/articles/robin-kelley-business-interests-fomented-tulsa-massacre-as-pretext-to-take-land/.

37. "The Omega Psi Phi Holds Annual Banquet at Hotel Dale," *Philadelphia Tribune*, August 27, 1921.

38. "Omega Psi Phi Holds Annual Banquet at Hotel Dale."

39. For more on Marcus Garvey, Pan-Africanism, and the Universal Negro Improvement Association, see the following books: Hakim Adi, *Pan-Africanism and Communism: The Communist International, Africa and the Diaspora, 1919–1939* (Trenton, NJ: Africa World Press, 2013); Colin Grant, *Negro with a Hat: The Rise and Fall of Marcus Garvey and His Dream of Mother Africa* (Oxford: Oxford University Press, 2010); Judith Stein, *The World of Marcus Garvey: Race and Class in Modern Society* (Baton Rouge: Louisiana State University Press, 1985); Robert A. Hill, ed., *The Marcus Garvey and Universal Negro Improvement Association Papers*, vol. III, *September 1920–August 1921* (Oakland: University of California Press, 1984). For more on the Pan-African Congress in 1921, see M. W. Kodi, "The 1921 Pan-African Congress at Brussels: A Background to Belgian Pressures," *Transafrican Journal of History* 13, no. 1 (1984): 48–73.

40. "Urban League Weekly Bulletin," *Atlanta Constitution*, September 4 and 11, 1921.

41. "Society: Omega Psi Phi Banquet and Elect Officers," *Norfolk Journal and Guide*, November 12, 1921.

42. See "1922 Convention Program Planned," *Atlanta Constitution*, December 11, 1921; Maurice J. Hobson, *The Legend of the Black Mecca: Politics and Class in the Making of Modern Atlanta* (Chapel Hill: University of North Carolina Press, 2017), esp. 16–18; "Negro Fraternity to Meet in Atlanta"; and "Omega Psi Phi's in Conclave Dec. 27–31," *Chicago Defender*, December 3, 1921.

43. Hobson, *Legend of the Black Mecca*, 56.

44. "1922 Convention Program Planned."

45. William Gilbert, "The Tenth Annual Conclave," *The Oracle* 1, no. 1 (February 1922): 6; "Pickens to Address Negro Fraternity," *Atlanta Constitution*, December 27, 1921; "Urban League Weekly Bulletin," *Atlanta Constitution*, January 1, 1922.

46. Gilbert, "Tenth Annual Conclave," 7. On Pickens's election to the Fraternity, see Luther O. Baumgardner, "Alpha Chapter," *The Oracle* (June 1919): 10; William Pickens, *Bursting Bonds* (Boston: Jordan & More, 1923); "Urban League Weekly Bulletin," *Atlanta Constitution*, January 1, 1922; "Pickens to Address Negro Fraternity." Regarding the "leading orators" quote, see "Annual Convention of Omega Psi Phi," *Norfolk Journal and Guide*, January 7, 1922. For more on Pickens, see Sheldon Avery, *Up from Washington: William Pickens and the Negro Struggle for Equality, 1900–1954* (Newark: University of Delaware Press, 1989).

47. Gilbert, "Tenth Annual Conclave," 7. See also "Annual Convention of Omega Psi Phi"; S. J. Lloyd, "John Wesley Edward Bowen (1885)," A People History of the School of Theology, Boston University, accessed December 27, 2020, www.bu.edu/sth-history/prophets/john-wesley-edward-bowen-1885/; and "Negro Fraternity to Meet in Atlanta." In addition to being elected members of Omega Psi Phi, Bowen and William J. Trent Sr. were two of thirteen members of Sigma Pi Phi's Kappa member boule, organized on January 24, 1920. See, for example, Rodney J. Reed, *A Grand Journey: The History of Sigma Pi Phi Fraternity, 1904–2010* (New York: Fred Weidner & Daughter, 2015), 117.

48. Gilbert, "Tenth Annual Conclave," 7.

49. We consulted several primary sources to reconstruct J. Alston Atkins's frequent relocations. Key sources included Biographical/Historical Note, Finding Aid, Archives at Yale, accessed December 27, 2020, https://archives.yale.edu/repositories/12/resources/3544; "Chi Chapter and Its Members," *The Oracle* 1, no. 1 (February 1922): 22–24; "Gamma Chapter," *The Oracle* (1921): 13; "New Chapters: Delta Chapter," *The Oracle* (June 1919): 13; and J. A. Thomas Jr., "The War Chapter," *The Oracle* (June 1919): 19. Also see "Yale Law Student Win High Honors," *New York Age*, June 24, 1922. Atkins was not the only Black student enrolled at Yale Law School during the early 1920s. Three Black men—Charles A. Chandler, Mifflin Gibbs, and Leroy Pierce—were in the same class as Atkins. For more on Black lawyers generally, see J. Clay Smith Jr., *Emancipation: The Making of the Black Lawyer, 1844–1944* (Philadelphia: University of Pennsylvania Press, 1993).

50. Gilbert, "Tenth Annual Conclave," 8.

51. J. Alston Atkins, "National Offices: Office of the Grand Basileus," *The Oracle* 1, no. 1 (February 1922): 9.

52. Atkins, "Office of the Grand Basileus," 9.

53. Atkins, "Office of the Grand Basileus," 10.

54. Atkins, "Office of the Grand Basileus," 10.

55. George I. Lythcott, "National Offices: Office of the Grand Keeper of Seals," *The Oracle* 1, no. 1 (February 1922): 14.

56. "Campaign for the Study of Negro History and Literature," *The Oracle* 1, no. 1 (February 1922), 19.

57. "Campaign for the Study of Negro History and Literature," 18; Atkins, "Office of the Grand Basileus," 9.

58. "Plans Laid for Young Memorial March Twelfth: Communities and Colleges Prepare to Perpetuate Honor Day to Sir Galahad," *Chicago Defender*, March 10, 1923. For more on Charles Young, see Brian G. Shellum, *Black Cadet in a White Bastion: Charles Young at West Point* (Lincoln: University of Nebraska Press, 2006); Brian G. Shellum, *Black Officer in a Buffalo Soldier Regiment: The Military Career of Charles Young* (Lincoln: University of Nebraska Press, 2010); David P. Kilroy, *For Race and Country: The Life and Career of Colonel Charles Young* (Westport, CT: Praeger, 2003). On Black soldiers during World War I, in addition to

Charles Young, see Chad L. Williams, *Torchbearers of Democracy: African American Soldiers in the World War I Era* (Chapel Hill: University of North Carolina Press, 2010).

59. "Kappa Chapter, Syracuse University, New York," *The Oracle* 1, no. 2 (May 1922): 34; J. Alston Atkins, "Our National Officers: Office of the Grand Basileus," *The Oracle* 1, no. 2 (May 1922): 3.

60. W. E. Hill, "Rho Chapter," *The Oracle* 1, no. 2 (May 1922): 27. Omegas chartered the Rho chapter on December 5, 1921.

61. "Urban League Weekly Bulletin," *Atlanta Constitution*, March 12, 1922.

62. "Negroes Pay Tribute to Col. Charles Young," *Atlanta Constitution*, March 13, 1922.

63. "Among Our Chapters: Alpha Chapter," *The Oracle* 1, no. 2 (May 1922): 20; "Among Our Chapters: Psi Chapter," *The Oracle* 1, no. 2 (May 1922): 33; "Negro Postal Clerks Will Give Musicale," *Atlanta Constitution*, August 25, 1922.

64. See "Among Our Chapters: Alpha Chapter"; "Among Our Chapters: Beta Chapter," *The Oracle* 1, no. 2 (May 1922): 22. "Education," *Crisis* (March 1920): 278; William B. Hixson Jr., "Moorfield Storey and the Defense of the Dyer-Anti-Lynching Bill," *New England Quarterly* 42, no. 1 (March 1969): 65–81; "Lincoln University Athletic Council Re-Elects Williams," *New York Age*, December 25, 1920.

65. "College Frats Plan Anti-Lynching Day," *Norfolk Journal and Guide*, June 10, 1922.

66. "College Frats Plan Anti-Lynching Day."

67. See "Harding Gets Facts on Mobs thru Booklet," *Chicago Defender*, July 1, 1922; and "Lincoln University Athletic Council Re-Elects Williams." While many scholars have written about the significant efforts of Ida B. Wells-Barnett and a few other Black women to end lynching during the early twentieth century, women such as Lilla L. Martin—who completed Howard University in 1923 and then began teaching school—appear less frequently in such scholarship. About those and related matters, see Mary Jane Brown, *"Eradicating this Evil": Women in the American Anti-Lynching Movement* (Columbus: Ohio State University Press, 1998); Diana Ramey Berry and Kali N. Gross, *A Black Women's History of the United States* (Boston, MA: Beacon, 2020). Additionally, as demonstrated in the main text and more exhaustively by scholars like Mary Jane Brown, there was a clear connection between Black arts and the anti-lynching effort. Mary Jane Brown, "Advocates in the Age of Jazz: Women and the Campaign for the Dyer Anti-Lynching Bill," *Peace and Change* 28, no. 3 (July 2003): 378–419.

68. "Harding Gets Facts on Mobs thru Booklet."

69. "Harding Gets Facts on Mobs thru Booklet."

70. *The Oracle* 1, no. 3 (September 1922). The title "Education Number" appeared on the cover of the issue as scholarship achievement was the theme of said issue.

71. "Among Our Graduates," *The Oracle* 1, no. 3 (September 1922): 3–5.

72. "Brother Percy L. Julian," *The Oracle* 1, no. 3 (September 1922): 8.

73. See Caldwell Titcomb, "Earliest Black Members of Phi Beta Kappa," *Journal of Blacks in Higher Education*, no. 33 (Autumn 2001): 92.

74. "Brother Percy L. Julian," 8.

75. "Among Our Graduates," 4.

76. Alston Atkins, "National Offices: Our Fall Program," *The Oracle* 1, no. 3 (September 1922): 14; "Omega Psi Phi Frat Meets in Philadelphia," *Chicago Defender*, December 16, 1922. Not unlike Nashville, Tennessee, and Atlanta, Georgia, the location of the 1922 Grand Conclave in Philadelphia, Pennsylvania, was significant. The color line—

or race—was a paramount reason the conclaves were held in all three localities. For more about race and Philadelphia throughout much of American history, consider the following texts: W. E. B. Du Bois, *The Philadelphia Negro: A Social Study* (Philadelphia: University of Pennsylvania Press, 1899); Roger Lane, *Roots of Violence in Black Philadelphia, 1860–1900* (Cambridge, MA: Harvard University Press, 1986); Gary B. Nash, *Forging Freedom: The Formation of Philadelphia's Black Community, 1720–1840* (Cambridge, MA: Harvard University Press, 1991); and Julie Winch, *Philadelphia's Black Elite: Activism, Accommodation, and the Struggle for Autonomy, 1787–1848* (Philadelphia, PA: Temple University Press, 1988).

77. Du Bois, *Philadelphia Negro*.

78. "Omega Psi Phi Holds Conclave: Colored Fraternity to Foster Study of Negro History," *New York Amsterdam News*, January 10, 1923; Garnet C. Wilkinson was a notable principal speaker for the Philadelphia Conclave in December 1922. For more about him and his role in the public education system of Washington, DC, see Tikia K. Hamilton, "The Cost of Integration: The Contentious Career of Garnet C. Wilkinson," *Washington History* 30, no. 1 (Spring 2018): 50–60.

79. "Omega Psi Phi Holds Conclave"; "Dr. Pickens Made Strong Appeal for NAACP," *Norfolk Journal and Guide*, December 20, 1924.

80. "Omega Psi Phi Holds Conclave"; Simon J. Levien, "The Crimson Klan," *Harvard Crimson*, March 25, 2021.

81. "Omega Psi Phi Holds Conclave."

82. Previous histories of Omega Psi Phi have discussed reorganization under J. Alston Atkins's leadership. For more, see Dreer, *History of Omega Psi Phi*, 38–39, 51–54, 75, 104, 225; and Robert Gill, *The Omega Psi Phi Fraternity and the Men Who Made Its History* (Washington, DC: Omega Psi Phi Fraternity, 1963), 12–13.

83. Dreer, *History of Omega Psi Phi*, 37–38; Gill, *Omega Psi Phi Fraternity*, 12.

84. For the elected officers, see "The Supreme Council," *The Oracle* 2, no. 1 (December 1923): 4. Regarding the Grand Marshal position, see Dreer, *History of Omega Psi Phi*, 225–226; for the Fraternity's national offices between 1911 and 1961, see Gill, *Omega Psi Phi Fraternity*, 84–86.

85. John H. Purnell, "Outline of Plans for Fraternity Expansion," *The Oracle* 1, no. 4 (December 1922): 31; Thomas, "War Chapter," 16–17.

86. "Fraternities: Omega Psi Phi," *Baltimore Afro-American*, January 12, 1923.

87. "Omega Psi Phi Holds Conclave."

88. "Fraternity at Morgan," *Baltimore Afro-American*, May 25, 1923.

89. "Urban League Weekly Bulletin," *Atlanta Constitution*, May 13, 1923.

90. On Tau Omega, see "Chapter Notes: Tau Omega (Greensboro, N.C.)," *The Oracle* 2, no. 1 (December 1923): 27; Walter H. Mazyck, "Omega's Expansion Since the 11th Annual Conclave," *The Oracle* 2, no. 2 (May 1924): 15.

91. "Omega Psi Phi Fraternity Boasts Twenty-Four Chapters," *Pittsburgh Courier*, July 7, 1923. Andrew Buni's *Robert L. Vann of the Pittsburgh Courier: Politics and Black Journalism* (Pittsburgh, PA: University of Pittsburgh Press, 1974) is an informative book about Vann and the *Courier* as well as about the importance of Black newspapers generally.

92. "Celebrate Education Week," *Chicago Defender*, December 1, 1923.

93. J. Alston Atkins, "The Negro's Commercial Outlook," *The Oracle* 2, no. 1 (December 1923): 8.

94. Several historians have documented the covert and overt acts of resistance among Black teachers during the early twentieth century. A sampling of those historians includes Vanessa Siddle Walker, *The Lost Education of Horace Tate: Uncovering the Hidden Heroes Who Fought for Justice in Schools* (New York: New Press, 2018); Vanessa Siddle Walker, *Hello Professor: A Black Principal and Professional Leadership in the Segregated South* (Chapel Hill: University of North Carolina Press, 2009); and Givens, *Fugitive Pedagogy*.

95. Atkins, "Negro's Commercial Outlook," 8.

96. John H. Purnell, "Opportunities for Teaching Negro History," *The Oracle* 2, no. 1 (December 1923), 14.

97. Purnell, "Opportunities for Teaching," 12–13. On many White historians' strategic uses of history, see W. E. B. Du Bois, *Black Reconstruction in America: An Essay toward a History of the Part Which Black Folk Played in the Attempt to Reconstruct Democracy in America, 1860–1880* (New York: Harcourt, Brace, 1935), particularly the final chapter titled, "The Propaganda of History."

98. "Poro College," Annie Malone Historical Society, accessed June 6, 2021, www.anniemalonehistoricalsociety.org/poro-college.html.

99. For more on Poro College and middle-class Black St. Louis, as well as Herman Dreer's teaching at Poro, see Vanessa Garry, "The Ville: Jim Crow Schools as Defined by an African-American, Middle-Class Neighborhood," *Journal of Philosophy and History of Education* 69, no. 1 (2019): 15–26.

100. "Poro College." On St. Louis's racial history, see Walter Johnson, *The Broken Heart of America: St. Louis and the Violent History of the United States* (New York: Basic Books, 2020).

101. See Jelani M. Favors, "A Seedbed of Activism," in *Shelter in a Time of Storm: How Black Colleges Fostered Generations of Leadership and Activism* (Chapel Hill: University of North Carolina Press, 2019), 18–48 (regarding White abolitionism, particularly it is related to Black colleges' students); "Members of the Supreme Council," *The Oracle* 2, no. 2 (May 1924): 3; "Omega Psi Phi's in St. Louis," *Philadelphia Tribune*, January 5, 1924; "Omega Psi Phi Frat Select Washington," *Baltimore Afro-American*, January 11, 1924. The reorganizing of Fraternity offices in 1922 and 1923 resulted in many newspapers not accurately capturing Omega men's titles. For example, a January 1924 issue of the *Baltimore Afro-American* called William Gilbert the Grand Keeper of Seals instead of the Grand Keeper of Finance after the St. Louis Conclave in December 1923.

102. "J. Alston Atkins to Members of Omega Psi Phi, February 1924," in *Omega Bulletin*, Omega Psi Phi Fraternity Inc., History and Archives Committee, Decatur, GA, 1. For a later account of Atkins's resignation, see Dreer, *History of Omega Psi Phi*, 38–40, 75.

103. Ingram v. Wesley, 37 F.2d 201 (January 24, 1930), and Grovey v. Townsend, 295 U.S. 45 (April 1, 1935).

104. *Ingram v. Wesley*. For the quotation, see Gary M. Lavergne, *Before Brown: Heman Marion Sweatt, Thurgood Marshall, and the Long Road to Justice* (Austin: University of Texas Press, 2010), 24.

105. *Grovey v. Townsend*.

106. John W. Love to Members of Omega Psi Phi, February 1924, *Omega Bulletin*, Omega Psi Phi Fraternity Inc., History and Archives Committee, Decatur, GA, 2. Regarding the number of Fraternity chapters, see "Omega Psi Phi Frat Select Washington," *Baltimore*

Afro-American, January 11, 1924. For Sterling A. Brown as eventual Vice Grand Basileus, refer again to "Members of the Supreme Council."

107. Joanne V. Gabbin, *Sterling A. Brown: Building the Black Aesthetic Tradition* (Westport, CT: Greenwood Press, 1985).

108. Dreer, *History of Omega Psi Phi*, 40.

109. "Negroes at All-Race Congress Are Called to Join Foreign Born in Resisting Common Enemy, the Klan," *Daily Worker*, February 13, 1924. Numerous scholars have also written about the connection between anticommunist sentiment being intertwined with the critiques of the Black freedom movement. Gerald Horne, *Black Liberation/Red Scare: Ben Davis and the Communist Party* (Newark: University of Delaware Press, 1994); Jeff Woods, *Black Struggle Red Scare: Segregation and Anti-Communism in the South, 1948–1968* (Baton Rouge: Louisiana State University Press, 2004); and James Zeigler, *Red Scare Racism and Cold War Black Radicalism* (Jackson: University Press of Mississippi, 2015) represent those scholars. In 1952, William Z. Foster, the long-time general secretary of the Communist Party USA wrote the following: Foster, *History of the Communist Party of the United States* (New York: International Publishers, 1952). William M. Banks, in *Black Intellectuals: Race and Responsibility in American Life* (New York: W. W. Norton, 1996), 100–108, provided an overview of Black thinkers as Marxists or communists and their relationships to debates about race and class.

110. "Negroes at All-Race Congress."

111. "Omega Psi Phi Foreign Study Committee Meets," *Philadelphia Tribune*, March 8, 1924. Scholars have long chronicled the internationalism among Black activists and thinkers. Keisha N. Blain and Kevin K. Gaines are two twenty-first century representatives of those scholars. See Keisha N. Blain, *Set the World on Fire: Black Nationalist Women and the Global Struggle for Freedom* (Philadelphia: University of Pennsylvania Press, 2018), esp. 75–103; Kevin K. Gaines, *American Africans in Ghana: Black Expatriates and the Civil Rights Era* (Chapel Hill: University of North Carolina Press, 2006).

112. "Omega Psi Phi Foreign Study Committee Meets."

113. "Omega Psi Phi Foreign Study Committee Meets."

114. "Omega Psi Phi Fraternity Foreign Study Committee Meets"; William Stuart Nelson, "Apropos the International Scholarship," *The Oracle* 2, no. 2 (May 1924): 10.

115. "Union Wins Over Howard–Lincoln Triangle Debate," *Norfolk Journal and Guide*, May 10, 1924.

116. "Where to Go," *Pittsburgh Courier*, May 10, 1924; "Fraternities in Big Debate: Kappa Alpha Psi Wins Over Omega Psi Phi, Using Volstead Act as Basis for Argument," *Pittsburgh Courier*, May 24, 1924. On prohibition and Black Americans, see Lisa McGirr, *The War on Alcohol: Prohibition and the Rise of the American State* (New York: W. W. Norton, 2015).

117. Isaac C. Bannister, "Wash. News," *Baltimore Afro-American*, March 21, 1924. For samples of other chapters' memorial services held in March 1924, see "New York," *Baltimore Afro-American*, April 4, 1924; Albert W. Dent, "Student Compares Life of Col. Young to Great Martyr," *Chicago Defender*, April 12, 1924; "Fraternities Are Active Now," *Baltimore Afro-American*, March 18, 1924; and "Colonel Charles Young," *Pittsburgh Courier*, March 22, 1924.

118. J. P. Murchison, "The Negro and Civilization," *The Oracle* 2, no. 2 (May 1924): 12.

119. Herman Dreer, "Types of Negro Leadership," *The Oracle* 2, no. 2 (May 1924): 23.

120. On Black college leaders and the nuance of conservative leadership, see Crystal R. Sanders, "'We Very Much Prefer to Have a Colored Man in Charge': Booker T. Washington and Tuskegee's All-Black Faculty," *Alabama Review* 74, no. 2 (April 2021): 99–128; Eddie R. Cole, *The Campus Color Line: College Presidents and the Struggle for Black Freedom* (Princeton, NJ: Princeton University Press, 2020), 16–70; Favors, *Shelter*.

121. "Chapter Notes: Gamma Chapter," *The Oracle* 2, no. 2 (May 1924): 30.

122. "75 Students Register at Howard University: Names Entered for Spring Quarter as Winter Examinations Are Begun," *Washington Post*, March 16, 1924.

123. "Takes Up Law with Father," *Pittsburgh Courier*, March 22, 1924.

124. "Race Architect Named by California School Board to Design $84,000 Building: Advance of Paul R. Williams to Front Ranks Rapid After Winning Design Competitions," *Pittsburgh Courier*, September 20, 1924; and "California: Los Angeles," *Chicago Defender*, May 10, 1924.

125. For Eugene Ellis Alston personal background, see *Catalogue of Lincoln University Chester County, Penna: Sixty-Second Year 1916–1917* (Philadelphia, PA: Ferris & Leach, 1917), 80; *Catalogue of the University of Michigan 1920–1921* (Ann Arbor: University of Michigan, 1921), 729. Also see "University of Michigan 1924 Graduates Top 2,000 Mark," *Detroit Free Press*, June 14, 1924; and "Wilmington Boy Graduate of Michigan," *Pittsburgh Courier*, July 26, 1924.

126. "D.C. Lad Leads Class of 1924 at Williams College," *Baltimore Afro-American*, April 4, 1924; "2 Students Win High Honors," *Chicago Defender*, June 21, 1924; On the Williams–Dunbar agreement, see Alison Stewart, *First Class: The Legacy of Dunbar, America's First Black Public High School* (Chicago: Lawrence Hill Books, 2013), 99; Also see David A. Varel, *The Lost Black Scholar: Resurrecting Allison Davis in American Social Thought* (Chicago: University of Chicago Press, 2018).

127. See "2 Students Win High Honors"; and Bertis D. English, *Civil Wars, Civil Beings, and Civil Rights in Alabama's Black Belt: A History of Perry County* (Tuscaloosa: University of Alabama Press, 2020), 260–66.

128. Representative media coverage in advance of the Washington Conclave on December 27–31, 1924, included: "13th Annual Convention Omega Psi Phi Meets in Washington," *Philadelphia Tribune*, November 29, 1924; "Colored Fraternity to Meet in Capital: Omega Psi Phi Was Founded at Howard: Leaders Will be Honored," *Washington Post*, December 14, 1924; "Omega Psi Phi Fraternity to Meet at Howard: More Than 500 Delegates Are Scheduled for Fourteenth Annual Conclave," *Chicago Defender*, November 29, 1924; "Omega Psi Phi Meets in D.C.," *Baltimore Afro-American*, November 29, 1924; "Omega Psi Phi Meets in Washington D.C.," *Norfolk Journal and Guide*, December 6, 1924; "Omegas Plan Meeting in Washington," *Pittsburgh Courier*, December 6, 1924; and "Roland Hayes at First Dance," *Baltimore Afro-American*, December 13, 1924.

129. "Omega Psi Phi Fraternity to Meet at Howard."

130. "Colored Fraternity to Meet in Capital."

131. "Colored Fraternity to Meet in Capital."

132. "Omega Psi Phi Plans Business Conference," *Washington Post*, December 27, 1924.

133. For the Durkee quotation, see "Omegas Visit Grave of Col. Chas. Young," *Pittsburgh Courier*, January 3, 1925. On Durkee's personal background, see Rayford W. Logan, *Howard University: The First Hundred Years, 1867–1967* (New York: New York University Press, 1969), 187–88.

134. For more on Howard University, particularly its origins under White administrators, see Logan, *Howard University*.

135. "Fraternity Discusses Recognition of Negro," *Washington Post*, December 29, 1924.

136. "College Men Received at White House: 50 Delegates to Omega Psi Phi Meet, Greeted by Coolidge," *Baltimore Afro-American*, January 5, 1925.

137. "Fraternity Discusses Recognition of Negro."

138. "College Men Received at White House"; "Fraternity Discusses Recognition of Negro."

139. "College Men Received at White House."

140. "College Men Received at White House."

141. "Fraternity Discusses Recognition of Negro." Bowen's statements do resonate with the idea of—and some people's hope for—color blindness. For more, see Eduardo Bonilla-Silva, *Racism without Racists: Color-Blind Racism and the Persistence of Racial Inequality in the United States* (Lanham, MD: Rowman & Littlefield, 2006). Although Bonilla-Silva is not focused on the early years of the twentieth century, it provides a valuable perspective alongside Bowen's conclave address.

142. "Iota Omega Conclave Notes," January 5, 1925, Omega Psi Phi Fraternity Inc., History and Archives Committee, Decatur, GA, 1; "Coolidge to Receive Colored Fraternity," *Washington Post*, December 21, 1924; "College Men Received at White House."

143. On Coolidge's prior stances on Black education, see "Omega Psi Phi to Have an Audience with President," *Norfolk Journal and Guide*, December 20, 1924. Regarding Alpha Phi Alpha's education program being launched in 1922, see "Go to High School Go to College," Alpha Phi Alpha Fraternity, Inc., accessed February 16, 2023, https://apa1906.net/national-programs/go-to-high-school-go-to-college/. Also see, for example, "Bulletin Board: Alpha Phi Alpha," *Opportunity* 2, no. 14 (February 1924): 63; or "News of the Week in Colored Circles," *Lima Republican-Gazette* (Ohio), May 11, 1924, 22.

144. For the "program of higher education" quotation, see "Omega Psi Phi to Have an Audience with President." For more on the other Black fraternity and sorority programs, see Gregory S. Parks and Matthew W. Hughey, *A Pledge with Purpose: Black Sororities and Fraternities and the Fight for Equality* (New York: New York University Press, 2020), particularly chap. 3, "Finding Their Way: Black and Greek in the Midst of the Harlem Renaissance, the Roaring Twenties, and the Adolescence of Jim Crow (1923–1929)."

145. "Coolidge Will Greet Omegas," *Baltimore Afro-American*, December 20, 1924. See also "Iota Omega Conclave Notes," 1; and "Omegas Visit Grave of Col. Chas. Young."

146. "Iota Omega Conclave Notes," 2.

147. Dreer, *History of Omega Psi Phi*, 157, as quoting the *Omega Bulletin* of April 1927.

148. Dreer, *History of Omega Psi Phi*, 158–59.

149. See "Iota Omega Conclave Notes," 2.

150. "Iota Omega Conclave Notes," 2; Bobby L. Lovett, *A Touch of Greatness: A History of Tennessee State University* (Macon, GA: Mercer University Press, 2012).

151. For more on about White administrators' paternalism at Black colleges, see Anderson, *Education of Blacks*, 273–74, and Woodson, *Mis-Education of the Negro*, 27.

152. "Iota Omega Conclave Notes," 5.

153. See "Amherst College Honors Negro," *Kansas City Advocate*, January 25, 1918; Pete Daniel, "Black Power in the 1920s: The Case of Tuskegee Veterans Hospital," *Journal of Southern History* 36, no. 3 (August 1970): 368–88; Walter H. Mazyck, "Omega Psi Phi to

Meet at Tuskegee," *Baltimore Afro-American*, January 10, 1925; "Omegas Close 13th Conclave with Election," *Chicago Defender*, January 10, 1925; "Seven Whites at Tuskegee Hospital," *Montgomery Advertiser*, January 23, 1924; "John B. Garrett, 88: Was Bacteriologist," *Boston Globe*, October 6, 1980.

154. On the written invitations from Moton and Ward, see Mazyck, "Meet at Tuskegee." For more on Moton, Ward, and plans for the Tuskegee Conclave, see "The U. S. Veterans' Hospital, Tuskegee, Ala., Colonel Joseph Henry Ward," *Journal of the National Medical Association* 21, no. 2 (April–June 1929): 65–67; Oscar W. Adams, "What Negroes Are Doing," *Birmingham News*, January 6, 1924; Daniel, "Black Power"; "Dr. Ward to Tuskegee Hospital," *Birmingham Reporter*, January 5, 1924; "Comments by the Age Editors on Sayings of Other Editors," *New York Age*, April 12, 1930; "Omegas Close 13th Conclave with Election"; and "Seven Whites at Tuskegee Hospital."

155. "Omegas Psi Phi to Meet at Tuskegee," *New York Amsterdam News*, January 14, 1925.

156. Sanders, "We Very Much Prefer," 104.

157. "Omegas to Hold Convention at Tuskegee, Ala.: Frat Heads Arrange for Special Pullman Cars to Carry Visitors," *Chicago Defender*, October 24, 1925.

158. "Coolidge to Receive Colored Fraternity."

159. See "Roll of Members," *The Oracle* (June 1919): 26; "Editorial Notes," *The Oracle* 5, no. 3 (October 1926): 109.

160. For more about the Fisk Jubilee Singers, see Andrew Ward, *Dark Midnight When I Rise: The Story of the Fisk Jubilee Singers* (London: HarperCollins, 2001); and Arna Bontemps, *Chariot in the Sky: A Story of the Jubilee Singers* (Oxford: Oxford University Press, [1951] 2002).

161. John Wesley Work [Jr.], *Folk Song of the American Negro* (Nashville, TN: Fisk University, 1915). See also C. Michael Hawn, "History of Hymns: 'Go, Tell It on the Mountain,'" Discipleship Ministries, United Methodist Church, accessed December 29, 2020, www.umcdiscipleship.org/resources/history-of-hymns-go-tell-it-on-the-mountain-1.

162. See Eugene TeSelle, "The Nashville Institute and Roger Williams University: Benevolence, Paternalism, and Black Consciousness, 1867–1910," *Tennessee Historical Quarterly* 41, no. 4 (Winter 1982): 360–79; and R. Nathaniel Dett, "John W[.] Work," *Southern Workman* 54, no 10, (1925): 438.

163. "Who's Who in Omega: Lee M. McCoy," *The Oracle* 5, no. 4 (December 1926): 154.

164. "Who's Who in Omega: D. H. Sims," *The Oracle* 5, no. 3 (October 1926): 127.

165. For a reference to Omega presidents in the 1920s, see "Editorial Notes," 1. On the presidential tenures of Omega men, historically and contemporarily, see Jonathan Matthews, "Brothers Who Are/Were College Presidents," Omega Psi Phi Fraternity Inc., History and Archives Committee, Decatur, GA.

166. Anderson, *Education of Blacks*, 274.

167. Woodson, *Mis-Education of the Negro*, 27. On the racist behaviors of White presidents and faculty at Black colleges, specifically at Fisk and Hampton, see Anderson, *Education of Blacks*, 273–74. For an account of early Black college student protests, see Ibram X. Kendi (formerly Ibram H. Rogers), *The Black Campus Movement: Black Students and the Racial Reconstruction of Higher Education, 1965–1972* (New York: Palgrave Macmillan, 2012), 32–47, 49–62. For a lengthier account of these protests, see Raymond Wolters, *The New Negro on Campus: Black College Rebellions of the 1920s* (Princeton, NJ: Princeton University Press, 1975).

168. Alain Locke, ed., *The New Negro: An Interpretation* (New York: Albert & Charles Boni, 1925). See also Jeffrey C. Stewart, *The New Negro: The Life of Alain Locke* (Oxford: Oxford University Press, 2018), esp. 431, 436, 477–503 (regarding Locke at Howard University).

169. Robert C. White, "Chapter Notes: Beta," *The Oracle* 6, no. 1 (April 1927): 33.

170. Langston Hughes, "The Negro Artist and the Racial Mountain," *Nation*, June 23, 1926.

171. Throughout the 1920s, various entries in *The Oracle* included poems, essays, and other expressive writings celebrating New Negro movement artists who belonged to Omega Psi Phi. For an example of the reach of the New Negro attitude beyond Harlem, see Davarian L. Baldwin and Minkah Makalani, eds., *Escape from New York: The New Negro Renaissance beyond Harlem* (Minneapolis: University of Minnesota Press, 2013).

172. On the total number of chapters chartered in 1925, see Gill, *Omega Psi Phi Fraternity*, 17.

173. There are several accounts of the 1925 memorial services. For brevity, we reference two: "Frat Observes Young's Birthday: B'klyn Chapter of Omega Psi Phi Holds Memorial for Honored Solider," *New York Amsterdam News*, March 18, 1925; "Col. Charles D. Young Honored at Memorial," *Washington Post*, March 23, 1925. On the debate in New York City and Norfolk program, see "Local Chapters of Kappa Omega to Debate Child Labor Question," *New York Amsterdam News*, March 4, 1925; "Omega Psi Phi Holds Inspiring Meeting," *Norfolk Journal and Guide*, May 16, 1925.

174. "Cook to Get Phi Beta Kappa," *Baltimore Afro-American*, March 7, 1925; "Amherst Grad Takes Coveted Scholarship: William Mercer Cook Wins $1,500 Award to Study in Paris," *Baltimore Afro-American*, May 16, 1925.

175. "Race Student, Member of International Debating Team, Has Enviable Record: Is Editor of 'Bates Student,' a Dramatist of Note; Ranks Among First Eight as a Scholar and Belongs to Omega Psi Phi Fraternity," *Pittsburgh Courier*, May 16, 1925. The Alpha Psi was chartered in 1922 at Amherst College. It was later redesignated to Huston-Tillotson College in Austin, Texas, in 1953.

176. See Nettie George Speedy, "Dr. L. R. Hill, a Leading Citizen of His Home Town, Is Doing Much Good for His Race," *Chicago Defender*, September 26, 1925; and "Subordinate Chapters: Delta Chapter," *The Oracle* (1921): 14.

177. Matthews, "Brothers Who Are/Were"; "Testimonial Dinner for Doctor William Johnson Trent," official program, Livingstone College, Salisbury, North Carolina, February 12, 1952 (recognizing Trent for twenty-seven years of "unselfish service" as president); Judy Scales-Trent, *A Black Man's Journey from Sharecropper to College President: The Life and Work of William Johnson Trent* (Deadwood, OR: Monroe Street Press, 2016).

178. For more on McCoy, see also: "Chapter Notes: Epsilon Phi—Memphis, Tenn.," *The Oracle* 4, no. 2 (June 1925): 63; Guy Williams, "Chapter Notes: Epsilon Phi," *The Oracle* 4, no. 3 (November 1925): 105; "Chapter Notes: Epsilon Phi," *The Oracle* 5, no. 1 (February 1926): 32.

179. "Editorial Notes: History, Literature, Art," *The Oracle* 4, no. 2 (June 1925): 42; William Stuart Nelson, "The Negro and a World Vision," *The Oracle* 3, no. 1 (March 1925): 9.

180. For the quotation, see "Prevents Extradition of Negro to Georgia," *Weekly Press* (Mobile, AL), March 7, 1925; "Georgia Sheriff Forced to Return Home without Victim," *Philadelphia Tribune*, March 7, 1925.

181. For more on the Ku Klux Klan and on Bibb Graves, who won the 1926 governorship in Alabama, see Linda Gordon, *The Second Coming of the KKK: The Ku Klux Klan of the 1920s and the American Political Tradition* (New York: Liveright, 2017).

182. Regarding Bibb Graves, who won the 1926 governorship in Alabama, see Gordon, *Second Coming*.

183. "Omegas to Hold Convention at Tuskegee." See also Daniel, "Black Power."

184. "Chicago Gets 1926 Conclave of Omega Psi Phi Fraternity," *Chicago Defender*, January 9, 1926.

185. On Matthew W. Bullock helping charter Eta Phi in Boston, Massachusetts, see Dreer, *History of Omega Psi Phi*, 196. Bullock also appeared as a member of Eta Phi after its chartering in 1925. For reference to Bullock paying tribute to Booker T. Washington, see "Bullock Sees Triumph of Justice," *Philadelphia Tribune*, January 2, 1926.

186. "Bullock Sees Triumph of Justice."

187. "Chicago Gets 1926 Conclave."

188. "Bullock Sees Triumph of Justice."

189. "Bullock Sees Triumph of Justice." For more about southern resistance, particularly in Alabama, see Robin D. G. Kelly, *Hammer and Hoe: Alabama Communists during the Great Depression* (Chapel Hill: University of North Carolina Press, 1999).

190. J. Clyde Coates, "Chapter Notes: Gamma Chapter Boston, Mass.," *The Oracle* 3, no. 1 (March 1925): 23. On possibly being the first Black head coach at a predominately White school, see "Matthew Washington Bullock," Black Presence, University of Massachusetts Amherst, Office of Equity and Inclusion, accessed January 18, 2023, www.umass.edu/diversity/blackpresence/bullock.

191. "Chicago Gets 1926 Conclave."

192. "Chicago Gets 1926 Conclave."

193. "Chicago Gets 1926 Conclave." For more on the NAACP Legal Defense Fund in Alabama, see U. W. Clemon and Bryan K. Fair, "Making Bricks without Straw: The NAACP Legal Defense Fund and the Development of Civil Rights Law in Alabama 1940–1980," *Alabama Law Review* 52, no. 4 (Summer 2001): 1121–52.

194. "Chicago Gets 1926 Conclave."

195. "Chicago Gets 1926 Conclave."

196. U. S. Donaldson, "The Conclave at Tuskegee," *The Oracle* 5, no. 4 (December 1926), 145. On Achievement Week and its annual November date, see Dreer, *History of Omega Psi Phi*, 159.

197. On Earl Wilkins, see "Omega Begins at Howard University Nov. 17, 1911," *Chicago Defender*, December 19, 1925; E. O. Pearce, "Minnesota: St. Paul," *Chicago Defender*, February 13, 1926. Regarding Albert W. Dent, see "Who's Who in Omega: A. W. Dent," *The Oracle* 6, no. 1 (April 1927): 26. For more on Fuller and Williams, see Mary Kaplan and Alfred R. Henderson, "Solomon Carter Fuller, M.D. (1872–1953): American Pioneer in Alzheimer's Disease Research," *Journal of the History of the Neurosciences* 9, no. 3 (2000): 250–61; and Marc Appleton and Stephen Gee, *Paul R. Williams: Masters of Architects of Southern California* (Santa Monica, CA: Angel City, 2001), respectively.

198. "Registrars and Deans Organize an Association," *Norfolk Journal and Guide*, April 17, 1926.

199. "Registrars and Deans Organize an Association."

200. For the "Omega man of the highest" quotation and brief McKinney biographical overview, see "Chapter Notes: Gamma Chapter," *The Oracle* 2, no. 2 (May 1924): 31. Eta chapter was chartered on December 27, 1919. For more on the campuses it served, see Harold H. Thomas, "Subordinate Chapters: Eta Chapter," *The Oracle* (1921): 20. McKinney

appeared on the Eta chapter roster within the fraternity's official directory in 1921. For the complete chapter roster and his hometown, see "Official Directory: Eta Chapter," *The Oracle* (1921): 39; "Educator Mourned: Dr. T. E. McKinney Was Dean at Smith 33 Years," *Norfolk Journal and Guide*, July 14, 1962.

201. On the photograph of Gamma chapter, see "Athletics," *The Oracle* 2, no. 2 (May 1924): 48; J. Clyde Coates, "Chapter Notes: Gamma Rays," *The Oracle* 4, no. 3 (November 1925): 102.

202. Walter H. Mazyck, "A Suggested Program," *The Oracle* 5, no. 1 (February 1926): 1, 7–8.

203. "Registrars and Deans Organize an Association."

204. "Houston, of Dunbar, Named Principal of Armstrong High," *Washington Post*, January 30, 1926. On Eugene Clark, see "Who's Who in Omega," *The Oracle* 5, no. 3 (October 1926): 128.

205. On rumors of Mordecai W. Johnson's forthcoming hire, see Stewart, *New Negro*, 533.

206. For the quote on Mordecai W. Johnson, see Henry Lee Moon, "Aspects of Educational Achievement," *The Oracle* 6, no. 3 (November 1927): 85; "Who's Who in Omega: William Stuart Nelson," *The Oracle* 9, no. 3 (October 1930): 15.

207. For the "universal standard" quotation, see "Some Achievements of Omega Men," *The Oracle* 5, no. 3 (October 1926): 109. See also Anderson, *Education of Blacks*, 238 (providing the number of Black college students in 1926).

208. John H. Purnell, "Outstanding Achievements of the Negro," *The Oracle* 5, no. 3 (October 1926): 111. Several scholars have documented the support of White philanthropists for Black education. For broader historical surveys, see Anderson, *Education of Blacks*; Eric Anderson and Alfred A. Moss Jr, *Dangerous Donations: Northern Philanthropy and Southern Black Education, 1902–1930* (Columbia: University of Missouri Press, 1999); and Noliwe M. Rooks, *White Money/Black Power: The Surprising History of African American Studies and the Crisis of Race and Higher Education* (New York: Beacon, 2007). For an example of the amounts spent by White philanthropists, see James D. Anderson, "Philanthropy, the State and the Development of Historically Black Public Colleges: The Case of Mississippi," *Minerva* 35, no. 3 (Autumn 1997): 298.

209. See, as examples, of Black press coverage in advance of the Chicago Conclave: "Full Program Made for Omega Psi Phi Session," *Chicago Defender*, December 25, 1926; "Meet at Chicago," *New York Amsterdam News*, December 22, 1926; "Omegas Plan Big Meeting in Chicago," *Chicago Defender*, December 4, 1926; "Omega Psi Phi Announces Its Ann'l Conclave," *Norfolk Journal and Guide*, December 25, 1926; and "Omega Psi Phi to Meet at Chicago," *Philadelphia Tribune*, December 18, 1926.

210. "Meet at Chicago."

211. See the prior citation about Black press coverage in advance of the Chicago Conclave.

212. "Omega Closes 15th Annual Meeting Here," *Chicago Defender*, January 8, 1927.

213. "Omega Closes 15th Annual Meeting Here."

214. Aaron H. Payne, "The Fifteenth Annual Conclave: Observations," *The Oracle* 6, no. 1 (April 1927): 10.

215. James M. Nabrit Jr., "The Fifteenth Annual Conclave: Observations," *The Oracle* 6, no. 1 (April 1927): 11.

216. "Chicagoans Hosts to Omega Fraters," *Chicago Defender*, January 1, 1927.

217. "Omega Psi Phi Meets in Chicago," *Chicago Defender*, January 1, 1927.

218. "Omega Closes 15th Annual Meeting Here."

219. George L. Vaughn, "Report of Grand Basileus," 5, Fifteenth Annual Conclave, December 27–31, 1926, Omega Psi Phi Fraternity Inc., History and Archives Committee, Decatur, GA.

220. Walter H. Mazyck, "Report of Grand Keeper of Records and Seals," 10, Fifteenth Annual Conclave, December 27–31, 1926, Omega Psi Phi Fraternity Inc., History and Archives Committee, Decatur, GA.

221. Mazyck, "Report of Grand Keeper," 13 (first and second quotation) and 14 (third quotation).

222. "Reports of National Officers and Committees," 26, Fifteenth Annual Conclave, December 27–31, 1926, Omega Psi Phi Fraternity Inc., History and Archives Committee, Decatur, GA.

223. "Mazyck, "Report of Grand Keeper," 13; "Election of Officers," 32, Fifteenth Annual Conclave, December 27–31, 1926, Omega Psi Phi Fraternity Inc., History and Archives Committee, Decatur, GA.

224. "Chapter Notes: Tau Omega," *The Oracle* 6, no. 1 (April 1927): 30.

225. "Chapter Notes: Tau Omega," 30.

226. "Chapter Notes: Tau Omega," 30; "T. E. McKinney Heads Deans and Registrars," *Baltimore Afro-American*, March 19, 1927.

227. "Registrars and Deans in Negro Colleges to Meet," *Norfolk Journal and Guide*, February 4, 1928.

228. On the 1927 undergraduate chapters chartered, see Gill, *Omega Psi Phi Fraternity*, 90. On Wilkinson's support of Xi Psi, see "S. C. State College Plans for 1928," *Philadelphia Tribune*, January 12, 1928; "Orangeburg, S.C.," *Baltimore Afro-American*, January 14, 1928. Also see Matthews, "Brothers Who Are/Were."

229. Bernard Mueller, "Julius S. McClain," *The Oracle* 7, no. 1 (April 1928): 7.

230. On the 1928 and 1929 chapters, see Dreer, *History of Omega Psi Phi*, 41.

231. "Editorial Notes: The Expansion, How, Where, and Why," *The Oracle* 6, no. 2 (June 1927): 44.

232. "Editorial Notes: Brother Carter Godwin Woodson," *The Oracle* 6, no. 3 (November 1927): 78.

233. Woodson's letter to Dreer is quoted in "Editorial Notes: Brother Carter Godwin Woodson."

234. For chapter charter dates from 1911 to 1962, see Appendix IV in Gill, *Omega Psi Phi Fraternity*, 88–99.

Chapter 3

1. Mary Church Terrell, "What Role Is the Educated Negro Woman to Play in the Uplifting of Her Race?" in *Twentieth Century Negro Literature or a Cyclopedia of Thought on the Vital Topics Relating to the American Negro by One Hundred of America's Greatest Negroes*, ed. D. W. Culp (Atlanta, GA: J. L. Nichols, 1902), 172–77. Some contemporaneous sources referred to the National Association of Colored Women as the National Association of Afro-American Women, among other names. See, as an example, "National Association of Afro-American Women," *Appeal* (St. Paul and Minneapolis, MN), August 5, 1899.

2. "The Supreme Council," *The Oracle* 9, no. 1 (April 1930): 2. For more on Baltimore during this era, see Andor Skotnes, *A New Deal for All? Race and Class Struggles in Depression-Era Baltimore* (Durham, NC: Duke University Press, 2013).

3. "Record Session of Fraternity Closes: Omegas Elect Bullock Grand Basileus," *Baltimore Afro-American*, January 4, 1930.

4. "Record Session of Fraternity Closes"; Herman Dreer, *The History of Omega Psi Phi Fraternity: A Brotherhood of Negro College Men, 1911 to 1939* (Washington, DC: Omega Psi Phi Fraternity, 1940), 130.

5. "Record Session of Fraternity Closes."

6. "Letter from the Grand Basileus," *The Oracle* 9, no. 1 (April 1930): 1.

7. "Letter from the Grand Basileus," 1.

8. Dreer, *History of Omega Psi Phi*, 41. Also see chapter 2 on William Jasper Hale's earlier attempts to organize a chapter at Tennessee A&I (now named Tennessee State University).

9. "Letter from the Grand Basileus," 1.

10. "Letter from the Grand Basileus," 1.

11. "Letter from the Grand Basileus," 1.

12. "Editorials: The Importance of Conclave," *The Oracle* 9, no. 3 (October 1930): 4.

13. "Editorial Notes: Is the Oracle a Failure?" *The Oracle* 9, no. 1 (April 1930): 4.

14. Omega men were encouraged in June 1930 to start planning Achievement Week activities. For more, see "Achievement Week," *The Oracle* 9, no. 2 (June 1930): 1.

15. Linwood G. Koger, "Cash Prizes to Students: An Essay Contest," *The Oracle* 9, no. 3 (October 1930): inside cover.

16. A. F. Miller, "Being Historical-Minded," *The Oracle* 9, no. 4 (December 1930): 2.

17. Miller, "Being Historical-Minded."

18. "Letter from the Grand Basileus," *The Oracle* 9, no. 4 (December 1930): 1.

19. "Letter from the Grand Basileus," 1.

20. "Detroit Set to Receive Omega Horde," *Chicago Defender*, December 20, 1930. For more on Detroit, see Beth Tompkins Bates, *The Making of Black Detroit in the Age of Henry Ford* (Chapel Hill: University of North Carolina Press, 2012), particularly chaps. 3 and 5; and Richard Walter Thomas, *Life for Us Is What We Make It: Building Black Community in Detroit, 1915–1945* (Bloomington: Indiana University Press, 1992), particularly chaps. 2 and 3. Also see Herb Boyd, *Black Detroit: A People's History of Self-Determination* (New York: HarperCollins, 2017); Heather Ann Thompson, *Whose Detroit? Politics, Labor, and Race in a Modern American City* (Ithaca, NY: Cornell University Press, 2001).

21. "Omega Psi Phi Holds Conclave in Motor City," *Norfolk Journal and Guide*, January 10, 1931.

22. Robert G. McGuire Jr., "A Letter from the Advertising Manager," *The Oracle* 10, no. 1 (April 1931): 1. McGuire Jr. listed on the Alpha Psi committee as part of Alpha chapter's Summer chapter. For more, see Dutton Ferguson and L. Byron Hopkins Jr., "Chapter Notes: Alpha," *The Oracle* 8, no. 3 (October 1929): 23. McGuire Jr.'s father, Robert Grayson McGuire Sr., was a member of the Alpha Omega chapter in Washington. For more on McGuire Sr., see "Tentative Roster," *The Oracle* 7, no. 4 (December 1928): 17. Also see Sandra R. Gregg, "The McGuire Family Legacy," *Washington Post*, January 14, 1982.

23. "Editorials: Finishing the Work of the Conclave," *The Oracle* 10, no. 1 (April 1931): 3; William Moore, "Houston Conclave," *The Oracle* 10, no. 1 (April 1931): 4.

24. W. L. D. Johnson Jr., "Chapter Notes: Nu Phi," *The Oracle* 10, no. 1 (April 1931): 14.

25. Dewey R. Jones, "Chapter Notes: Sigma Omega," *The Oracle* 10, no. 1 (April 1931): 18.

26. James Dashiell, "Chapter Notes: Pi," *The Oracle* 10, no. 1 (April 1931): 19; Claude D. Black, "Chapter Notes: Xi," *The Oracle* 10, no. 1 (April 1931): 19.

27. Carlyle M. Tucker, "Our Economic Problem," *The Oracle* 10, no. 1 (April 1931): 3.

28. Tucker, "Our Economic Problem," 3.

29. See Dreer, *History of Omega Psi Phi*, 78; and Robert Gill, *The Omega Psi Phi Fraternity and the Men Who Made Its History* (Washington, DC: Omega Psi Phi Fraternity, 1963), 18, on the 1927 Employment Committee.

30. See Dreer, *History of Omega Psi Phi*, 79; and Gill, *Omega Psi Phi Fraternity*, 18.

31. "News Items: Brother Ira De A. Reid," *The Oracle* 9, no. 4 (December 1930): 5.

32. Ira De A. Reid, "After College What?" *The Oracle* 10, no. 2 (April 1931): 8.

33. Reid, "After College What?" 8.

34. Reid, "After College What?" 8.

35. Reid, "After College What?" 8.

36. Dreer, *History of Omega Psi Phi*, 143; and Gill, *Omega Psi Phi Fraternity*, 19.

37. The title of this chapter is pulled from this lyric in "Omega Dear."

38. Matthew W. Bullock, "The Grand Basileus," *The Oracle* 9, no. 3 (October 1930): 1.

39. Bullock, "Grand Basileus," 1.

40. Bullock, "Grand Basileus," 1.

41. On Rutherford as a member of the Fraternity's Employment Committee, see Dreer, *History of Omega Psi Phi*, 78; and Gill, *Omega Psi Phi Fraternity*, 18; "Alpha Omega Chapter: Chapter Lines," Omega Psi Phi Fraternity Inc., Alpha Omega Chapter, accessed March 6, 2023, https://alphaomegachapter.org/chapter-lines/#1666808019967-0fd57efa-82b3.

42. "Samuel Wilson Rutherford," *Journal of Negro History* 37, no. 2 (April 1952): 216.

43. "12 Negroes Honored for Achievements," *New York Times*, January 3, 1929.

44. "Two Harmon Prizes Are Won in Capital," *Washington Post*, January 3, 1929.

45. For more on Rutherford, see "Who's Who in Omega: S. W. Rutherford of Alpha Omega," *The Oracle* 4, no. 2 (June 1925): 59; and "Who's Who in Omega: Samuel Wilson Rutherford," *The Oracle* 9, no. 4 (December 1930): 28–29.

46. See "Who's Who in Omega: Lawrence A. Oxley," *The Oracle* 10, no. 1 (April 1931): 30; and "Civic Leader, Educator, Dies," *Washington Post*, July 5, 1973. Also see Thomas M. Camfield, "'Will to Win': The U.S. Army Troop Morale Program of World War I," *Military Affairs* 41, no. 3 (October 1977): 125–28.

47. "Who's Who in Omega: Lawrence A. Oxley," 30.

48. Lawrence A. Oxley, "North Carolina's Venture in Negro Welfare," *The Oracle* 10, no. 2 (June 1931): 7.

49. Jean R. Hailey, "William Nelson, Dean at Howard, Dies," *Washington Post*, March 30, 1977.

50. "Who's Who in Omega: Brother William Stuart Nelson," *The Oracle* 9, no. 3 (October 1930): 15.

51. Dutton Ferguson, "To an African Mask: A New Negro Litany," *The Oracle* 10, no. 2 (June 1931): 12.

52. "Houston Conclave," *The Oracle* 10, no. 2 (June 1931): 4.

53. Daniel B. Taylor, "Letter to the Supreme Council (Exclusively)," Omega Psi Phi Fraternity, July 19, 1931, Omega Psi Phi Fraternity Inc., History and Archives Committee, Decatur, GA.

54. Elmus Wicker, *The Banking Panics of the Great Depression* (Cambridge: Cambridge University Press, 1996), 22.

55. Matthew W. Bullock, "The Grand Basileus Speaks," *The Oracle* 11, no. 1 (April 1932): 4.

56. Taylor, "Letter to the Supreme Council."

57. Taylor, "Letter to the Supreme Council."

58. Bullock, "Grand Basileus Speaks," 4.

59. Bullock, "Grand Basileus Speaks," 4.

60. Bullock, "Grand Basileus Speaks," 4.

61. Dreer, *History of Omega Psi Phi*, 41; Gill, *Omega Psi Phi Fraternity*, 90. Gill noted that Tau Psi was chartered in 1932, but recently recovered documents reveal that chapter was chartered in November 1931. For more, see "Chapter History," The Mighty Tau Psi Chapter, accessed March 7, 2023, www.taupsi.com/chapter-history.

62. E. Roosevelt Page, "A Tribute to the Late Brother R. S. Wilkinson," *The Oracle* 11, no. 2 (June 1932): 27.

63. Bullock, "Grand Basileus Speaks," 4.

64. Richard York Nelson, "The Negro and the Depression," *The Oracle* 11, no. 1 (April 1932): 7, 9. For more on Nelson, see "Editorials: The Oracle," *The Oracle* 11, no. 1 (April 1932): 3; and "Who's Who in Omega: Richard York Nelson," *The Oracle* 11, no. 1 (April 1932): 19.

65. Langston Hughes, "Negro Ghetto," *The Oracle* 11, no. 1 (April 1932): 11.

66. "Who Who's in Omega: Percy Lavon Julian," *The Oracle* 11, no. 2 (June 1932): 26–27.

67. "Who Who's in Omega: Walter Nathaniel Ridley," *The Oracle* 11, no. 2 (June 1932): 27.

68. Matthew W. Bullock, "A Letter from the Grand Basileus," *The Oracle* 11, no. 3 (October 1932): 1. The letter was written in September 1932 but printed in this issue.

69. Bullock, "Letter from the Grand Basileus," 1.

70. Bullock, "Letter from the Grand Basileus," 1.

71. "On to Richmond," *The Oracle* 11, no. 3 (October 1932): 3.

72. "Richmond to Outdo Itself for Omega Frat," *Norfolk Journal and Guide*, December 24, 1932.

73. "Greek Letter Fraternities Hold Meetings: Omegas Convene in Richmond, Va., While Alphas Journey to Wash.," *Philadelphia Tribune*, December 22, 1932; "Omega Psi Phi Holds Annual Meet in Dixie," *Chicago Defender*, December 31, 1932.

74. "Stress Economy at Omega Psi Phi Conclave: Altruistic Activities Being Shelved during Depression," *Norfolk Journal and Guide*, December 31, 1932.

75. "Lieut. Oxley Heads Omegas; Durham Next Conclave," *Norfolk Journal and Guide*, January 7, 1933.

76. "Elections and Appointments," *The Oracle* 12, no. 1 (April 1933): 3.

77. Gill, *Omega Psi Phi Fraternity*, 19.

78. Dreer, *History of Omega Psi Phi*, 41–42.

79. "Lieut. Oxley Heads Omegas."

80. On Durham as a thriving Black city, see W. E. B. Du Bois, "The Upbuilding of Black Durham: The Success of the Negroes and Their Value to a Tolerant and Helpful Southern City," *World's Work* 23, no. 23 (January 1912): 334–38; Leslie Brown, *Upbuilding Black*

Durham: *Gender, Class, and Black Community Development in the Jim Crow South* (Chapel Hill: University of North Carolina Press, 2008).

81. "Elections and Appointments."

82. Booker T. Bradshaw, "Virginia Mutual Benefit Life Insurance Company," *The Oracle* 14, no. 3 (September 1935): 6.

83. For more, see James B. Mitchell, *The Collapse of the National Benefit Life Insurance Company* (Washington, DC: Graduate School for the Division of the Social Sciences, Howard University, 1939); Nannie H. Burroughs, "Rutherford, Lewis, Says Nannie Burroughs, Were Washington's Biggest Assets," *Baltimore Afro-American*, January 9, 1932.

84. Bradshaw, "Virginia Mutual," 5–6.

85. Lawrence A. Oxley, "A Letter from the Grand Basileus," *The Oracle* 12, no. 1 (April 1933): 1.

86. Oxley, "Letter from the Grand Basileus," 1.

87. Oxley, "Letter from the Grand Basileus," 1.

88. Oxley, "Letter from the Grand Basileus," 1.

89. Oxley, "Letter from the Grand Basileus," 1.

90. Oxley, "Letter from the Grand Basileus," 1.

91. James Haskins, *The Scottsboro Boys* (New York: Henry Holt, 1994).

92. Dan T. Carter, *Scottsboro: A Tragedy of the American South* (Baton Rouge: Louisiana State University Press, 1969).

93. "Defense Ahead in Decatur Trial Now," *Baltimore Afro-American*, April 8, 1933.

94. "Defense Ahead in Decatur Trial Now."

95. As quoted in Sheryll Cashin, *The Agitator's Daughter: A Memoir of Four Generations of One Extraordinary African-American Family* (New York: Public Affairs, 2008), 75. Also see Carter, *Scottsboro*, 201.

96. Bill Gibson, "Hear Me Talkin' to Ya," *Baltimore Afro-American*, August 5, 1933.

97. The "take care of" quote is from "Ku Klux on Rampage in Alabama: Try to Intimidate Those Who Testified in Scottsboro Trial," *Baltimore Afro-American*, April 29, 1933. On Sykes returning to Baltimore due to threats, see Liz Ryan, "90 Years On: Remembering the Scottsboro Boys," *Alabama Political Reporter*, December 29, 2021.

98. For one example, see Rita G. Koman, "Relief, Recovery, Reform: The New Deal Congressional Reaction to the Great Depression," *OAH Magazine of History* 12, no. 4 (Summer 1998): 39–48.

99. For more information on New Deal programs, refer to Harvard Sitkoff, *A New Deal for Blacks: The Emergence of Civil Rights as a National Issue* (New York: Oxford University Press, 1978); Raymond Wolters, *Negroes and the Great Depression: The Problem of Economic Recovery* (Westport, CT: Greenwood, 1974).

100. Jill Watts, *Black Cabinet: The Untold Story of African Americans and Politics during the Age of Roosevelt* (New York: Grove Atlantic, 2020); John B. Kirby, *Black Americans in the Roosevelt Era: Liberalism and Race* (Knoxville: University of Tennessee Press, 1980); Nancy J. Weiss, *Farewell to the Party of Lincoln: Black Politics in the Age of FDR* (Princeton, NJ: Princeton University Press, 1983).

101. Lawrence A. Oxley, "The Department of Labor and Occupational Adjustment of Negroes," *The Oracle* 15, no. 3 (September 1936): 8.

102. Frederick S. Weaver, "Omega Men in Washington, D.C.," *The Oracle* 15, no. 3 (September 1936): 7. Also see James Barron, "Robert C. Weaver, 89, First Black Cabinet Member, Dies," *New York Times*, July 19, 1997.

103. Lawrence A. Oxley, "A Tribute to the Late Brother Walter H. Mazyck," *The Oracle* 12, no. 3-4 (December 1933): 5.

104. Death certificate of Walter H. Mazyck, in possession of Omega Psi Phi Fraternity Inc., History and Archives Committee, Decatur, GA.

105. Page, "Tribute."

106. Campbell C. Johnson, "Captain Walter Herbert Mazyck," *The Oracle* 12, no. 3-4 (December 1933): 7.

107. Johnson, "Captain Walter Herbert Mazyck," 7.

108. Johnson, "Captain Walter Herbert Mazyck," 7; Dreer, *History of Omega Psi Phi*, 57.

109. Johnson, "Captain Walter Herbert Mazyck," 7.

110. Johnson, "Captain Walter Herbert Mazyck," 7.

111. Johnson, "Captain Walter Herbert Mazyck," 7.

112. "Review of George Washington and the Negro," *Journal of Negro History* 17, no. 2 (April 1932): 230.

113. Percy Scott Flippin, "Review of George Washington and the Negro," *Mississippi Valley Historical Review* 19, no. 2 (September 1932): 305. The journal is now named the *Journal of American History*.

114. Photo caption from: "The Latest Photograph of the Late Walter H. Mazyck Taken with His Bride of a Few Months," *The Oracle* 12, no. 3-4 (December 1933): 6.

115. "Latest Photograph of the Late Walter H. Mazyck," 6.

116. Oxley, "Tribute," 5.

117. Oxley, "Tribute," 5.

118. Oxley, "Tribute," 5.

119. Johnson, "Captain Walter Herbert Mazyck," 7.

120. Johnson, "Captain Walter Herbert Mazyck," 7.

121. Johnson, "Captain Walter Herbert Mazyck," 7.

122. "The Funeral Procession Leaving the Church," *The Oracle* 12, no. 3-4 (December 1933): 8.

123. "Poems by Walter H. Mazyck," *The Oracle* 12, no. 3-4 (December 1933): 10; S. Malcolm Dodson, "The Late Brother Walter H. Mazyck," *The Oracle* 12, no. 3-4 (December 1933): 2.

124. "Editorial: They Say He's Dead," *The Oracle* 12, no. 3-4 (December 1933): 11.

125. For one example of Omega men adopting "Members versus Men" as a slogan, see "Chapter Notes: Psi Chapter," *The Oracle* 6, no. 11 (June 1925): 72.

126. Lawrence A. Oxley, "Grand Basileus' Durham Conclave Letter," *The Oracle* 12, no. 3-4 (December 1933): 1.

127. Dreer, *History of Omega Psi Phi*, 79-80.

128. George W. Cox, "On to Durham," *The Oracle* 12, no. 1 (April 1933): 5.

129. Cox, "On to Durham," 5.

130. William S. Powell, "Spaulding, Asa Timothy," NCpedia, accessed March 13, 2023, www.ncpedia.org/biography/spaulding-asa-timothy; Oral History Interview with Asa T. Spaulding, April 13, 1979, Interview C-0013-1, Southern Oral History Program Collection

(#4007), Southern Oral History Program Collection, Southern Historical Collection, Wilson Library, University of North Carolina at Chapel Hill. See also North Carolina Mutual Life Insurance Company Archives, 1850, 1888–2000s, and undated, bulk 1920–2008, Duke University Archives and Manuscripts, Durham, NC.

131. Alexa Benson Henderson, *Atlanta Life Insurance Company: Guardian of Black Economic Dignity* (Tuscaloosa: University of Alabama Press, 1990); Brandon K. Winford, *John Hervey Wheeler, Black Banking, and the Economic Struggle for Civil Rights* (Lexington: University of Kentucky Press, 2019).

132. George W. Cox, "Charles Clinton Spaulding: President North Carolina Mutual Insurance Company," *The Oracle* 15, no. 2 (June 1936): 8–9.

133. James E. Shepherd, "North Carolina College for Negroes," *The Oracle* 12, no. 3–4 (December 1933): 1.

134. C. C. Spaulding, "North Carolina Mutual Life Insurance Company," *The Oracle* 12, no. 3–4 (December 1933): 32.

135. Spaulding, "North Carolina Mutual Life," 32.

136. Richard Earle Brown, "And So the Q's Met," *The Oracle* 13, no. 1 (April 1934): 10.

137. "Program," *The Oracle* 12, no. 3–4 (December 1933): 14.

138. "Omegas Close 21st Conclave at Durham, N.C.," *Baltimore Afro-American*, January 6, 1934; For the quote about the Joint Committee on National Recovery, see Lawrence S. Wittner, "The National Negro Congress: A Reassessment," *American Quarterly* 22, no. 4 (Winter 1970): 884. Also see John Preston Davis as a Bates College student, "Roster of Chapters: Alpha Psi Chapter," *The Oracle* 2, no. 2 (May 1924): 54.

139. John L. Gilmore, "The Economic Future of the Negro," *The Oracle* 13, no. 1 (April 1934): 6.

140. Donald D. Adams, "Chapter Notes: Epsilon, New York City," *The Oracle* 13, no. 1 (April 1934): 9.

141. Reprinted in *The Oracle* in June 1934, the original article is from Lucia Mae Pitts, "New Deal Personalities: A Series of Pen Sketches or Brief 'Human' Biographies of Men in the Government Service, Particularly Assigned to Promote the Welfare of the Negro," *Norfolk Journal and Guide*, April 28, 1934.

142. R. E. Cureton, "The Negro in the American Chaos," *The Oracle* 13, no. 3 (September 1934): 5.

143. Cureton, "American Chaos," 5.

144. The early conclaves are discussed in chapter 1, while the St. Louis Conclave in 1923 is discussed in chapter 2.

145. "Minutes of the Twenty-Second Annual Conclave," 1–2, December 27–30, 1934, Omega Psi Phi Fraternity Inc., History and Archives Committee, Decatur, GA.

146. "Minutes of the Twenty-Second Annual Conclave," 9, 11.

147. "Minutes of the Twenty-Second Annual Conclave," 25.

148. "Minutes of the Twenty-Second Annual Conclave," 71.

149. "Minutes of the Twenty-Second Annual Conclave," 77.

150. "Minutes of the Twenty-Second Annual Conclave." Delegates voted to use "innocent" instead of "condemned." The latter was used in the initial draft of the Scottsboro Boys resolution.

151. "Minutes of the Twenty-Second Annual Conclave," 62, 71.

152. "Minutes of the Twenty-Second Annual Conclave," 78.

153. "Minutes of the Twenty-Second Annual Conclave," 78.

154. "Minutes of the Twenty-Second Annual Conclave," 78–79.

155. "Minutes of the Twenty-Second Annual Conclave," 64–65, 79.

156. Sitkoff, *New Deal for Blacks*; Wolters, *Negroes and the Great Depression*.

157. Herman Dreer, "How the Negro Must Do Business," *The Oracle* 14, no. 3 (September 1935): 3.

158. Emmett J. Marshall, "Cuba and the Color Question: Is It Economic or Racial?" *The Oracle* 14, no. 3 (September 1935): 9–10.

159. Robert N. Owens, "The Negro Faces the Future," *The Oracle* 14, no. 3 (September 1935): 7.

160. Frederick S. Weaver, "Here and There with the Undergraduates," *The Oracle* 14, no. 2 (June 1935): 13.

161. Frederick Bradley, "Chapter Notes: Chi Psi Chapter," *The Oracle* 14, no. 2 (June 1935): 17.

162. "Omega Men in the Negro Press: Brother Albert W. Dent," *The Oracle* 16, no. 2 (July 1937): 5. For more on William Stuart Nelson, refer to chapter 2.

163. Powell, "Spaulding, Asa Timothy."

164. Frederick S. Weaver, "Sidelights on the 23rd Conclave," *The Oracle* 15, no. 1 (April 1936): 4.

165. Weaver, "Sidelights," 4.

166. "Elections and Appointments: Vice Grand Basileus William E. Baugh," *The Oracle* 12, no. 1 (April 1933): 3.

167. "Elections and Appointments."

168. Gill, *Omega Psi Phi Fraternity*, 23.

169. Fred B. Payton, "Mu and Mu Omega of Philadelphia Enter Final Stretch for the 1936 Silver Jubilee Conclave," *The Oracle* 15, no. 3 (September 1936): 12, 18.

170. "Omega Psi Phi Fraternity: Silver Anniversary—Philadelphia, PA Program," *The Oracle* 15, no. 4 (December 1936): 12.

171. "In Memoriam," *The Oracle* 15, no. 4 (December 1936): 13.

172. See Dreer, *History of Omega Psi Phi*, 42–43.

173. "Makers of Omega," *The Oracle* 15, no. 4 (December 1936): 19–20, 29–30.

174. "Makers of Omega," 19–20, 29–30.

175. W. C. Jason Jr., "What of the Challenge," *The Oracle* 16, no. 1 (March 1937): 3.

176. "Fraters Prepare for Philly Conclave," *Chicago Defender*, December 12, 1936.

177. "Omega Fraternity Endorses Fight on Lynching, Peonage," *Philadelphia Tribune*, December 31, 1936.

178. "Omega Fraternity Endorses Fight on Lynching, Peonage."

179. Gill, *Omega Psi Phi Fraternity*, 23.

180. "Minutes of the Twenty-Fifth Annual Conclave," 8, December 28–30, 1937, Omega Psi Phi Fraternity Inc., History and Archives Committee, Decatur, GA.

181. See Dreer, *History of Omega Psi Phi*, 43.

182. Regarding Dent's professional roles, see Gill, *Omega Psi Phi Fraternity*, 24. Regarding Nelson's presidency at Dillard, see "Omega Men in the Negro Press," *The Oracle* 16, no. 1 (March 1937): 5.

183. Gill, *Omega Psi Phi Fraternity*, 24–25.

184. Frederick S. Weaver, "'Mighty' Epsilon," *The Oracle* 18, no. 2 (June 1939): 50, 54.

185. Roger Moorhouse, *Poland 1939: The Outbreak of World War II* (New York: Basic Books, 2020).

186. On the publication month of the fraternity's first history book, see "Achievement Award Given Gen. B. O. Davis," *Chicago Defender*, January 4, 1941.

187. Louis R. Lautier, "Our Status in National Defense," *The Oracle* 19, no. 3 (October 1940): 62.

188. William B. Collier Jr., "Will Receive Citation at Meet Dec. 27: Former Head of Dillard Sociology Dept. Named for Honor Medal," *Chicago Defender*, December 7, 1940.

189. Collier, "Will Receive Citation."

190. Collier, "Will Receive Citation."

191. David A. Varel, *The Lost Black Scholar: Resurrecting Allison Davis in American Social Thought* (Chicago: University of Chicago, 2018), 30, 36, 43, 63.

192. Varel, *The Lost Black Scholar*, 110.

193. Collier Jr., "Will Receive Citation."

194. Gill, *Omega Psi Phi Fraternity*, 25.

195. W. Montague Cobb, "The Omega Fellowship and Scholarship Awards for 1940," *The Oracle* 21, no. 3 (October 1940): 82.

196. Gill, *Omega Psi Phi Fraternity*, 25.

197. "Omega Psi Phi Sets the Stage for '40 Conclave," *Chicago Defender*, December 14, 1940.

198. "Omega Psi Phi Sets the Stage for '40 Conclave."

199. "Omegas Hold Epoch-Making 29th Conclave at Nashville," *Norfolk Journal and Guide*, January 11, 1914.

200. "Grand Officers," *The Oracle* 20, no. 2 (June 1941): inside cover.

201. For Looby biographical information, see Will Sarvis, "Leaders in the Court and Community: Z. Alexander Looby, Avon N. Williams Jr., and the Legal Fight for Civil Rights in Tennessee, 1940–1970," *Journal of African American History* 88, no. 1 (Winter 2003): 47–48. For more on Looby, see J. Clay Smith Jr., *Emancipation: The Making of the Black Lawyer, 1844–1944* (Philadelphia: University of Pennsylvania Press, 1993), 62–63, 343–44.

202. "Ernest Everett Just: Founder and Scientist Passes," *The Oracle* 20, no. 4 (December 1941): 107. On the cause of death, see Kenneth R. Manning, *Black Apollo of Science: The Life of Ernest Everett Just* (New York: Oxford University Press, 1984), 328.

203. "Just: Founder and Scientist Passes."

204. "Who's Who in Omega: Ernest E. Just," *The Oracle* 9, no. 1 (April 1930): 17.

205. Ernest Everett Just, *Basic Methods for Experiments on Eggs of Marine Animals* (Philadelphia, PA: Blakiston's Sons, 1939); Ernest Everett Just, *The Biology of the Cell Surface* (Philadelphia, PA: Blakiston's Sons, 1939).

206. "Just: Founder and Scientist Passes."

207. "Just: Founder and Scientist Passes."

208. Kenneth R. Manning, *Black Apollo of Science: The Life of Ernest Everett Just* (New York: Oxford University Press, 1984), 207.

209. "Just: Founder and Scientist Passes."

210. Thurston Clarke, *Pearl Harbor Ghosts: The Legacy of December 7, 1941* (New York: Random House, 1991), 3.

211. Paul R. Williams, "We Change Our Architecture," *The Oracle* 21, no. 1 (March 1942): 3–7.

212. Don T. Nakanishi, "Surviving Democracy's 'Mistake': Japanese Americans & the Enduring Legacy of Executive Order 9066," *Amerasia Journal* 35, no. 3 (2009): 53–83.

213. Williams, "We Change Our Architecture," 7.

214. W. Montague Cobb, "Charles Richard Drew, M. D., 1904–1950," *Journal of the National Medical Association* 42, no. 4 (July 1950): 239, 242.

215. Charles R. Drew, "Banked Blood: A Study in Blood Preservation" (DMSc diss., National Library of Medicine, Columbia University, 1940), https://collections.nlm.nih.gov/catalog/nlm:nlmuid-101584649X142-doc.

216. Cobb, "Charles Richard Drew," 243.

217. Gill, *Omega Psi Phi Fraternity*, 45. Lane also served on the Fraternity's Scholarship Commission. For more, see Cobb, "Omega Fellowship," 82. For more on the Historical Division of the US Army, see "Finding Aid," Register of the United States Army European Command, Historical Division Typescript Studies, Hoover Institution Library and Archives, Stanford University, accessed on April 16, 2023, https://oac.cdlib.org/findaid/ark:/13030/tf696nb1jc/entire_text/.

218. Gill, *Omega Psi Phi Fraternity*, 45–46.

219. Gill, *Omega Psi Phi Fraternity*, 48.

220. "Brother John Thompson Receives Congressional Gold Medal," *The Oracle* 83, no. 2 (Summer 2013): 44; "Brother Hubert Poole Receives Congressional Gold Medal Posthumously," *The Oracle* 83, no. 2 (Summer 2013): 44; Robert S. Hammond, "First WWII Corpsmen, Montford Point Marine Camp," *The Oracle* 80, no. 2 (Summer 2010): 58; Melton A. McLaurin, *The Marines of Montford Point: America's First Black Marines* (Chapel Hill: University of North Carolina Press, 2007), 96.

221. Approximately number of Omega men at Tuskegee Army Air Field is tallied from the list of Omega men named in "Up in Arms: Tuskegee Army Air Field Ala.," *The Oracle* (December 1944): 4, 6, 10–11. No volume or issue number included. It is simply labeled as "Conclave Issue" and dated December 1944.

222. William B. Collier Jr., "Tuskegee Army Air Field," *The Oracle* (December 1944): 13. As stated in the previous noted, no volume or issue number included on this issue of *The Oracle*.

223. "Up in Arms," 6.

224. "Up in Arms," 10.

225. "Up in Arms," 4.

226. Christopher Paul Moore, *Fighting for America: Black Soldiers—The Unsung Heroes of World War II* (New York: Random House, 2005); Matthew F. Delmont, *Half American: The Epic Story of African Americans Fighting World War II at Home and Abroad* (New York: Viking, 2022).

227. "Up in Arms," 4.

228. James G. Thompson, "Should I Sacrifice to Live 'Half-American?'," *Pittsburgh Courier*, January 31, 1942, 3.

Chapter 4

1. Robert L. Gill, "Negro Americans Challenge Democracy," *The Oracle* 34, no. 2 (December 1945): 4.

2. "Other States Follow," *The Oracle* 39, no. 1 (March 1949): 21. Also see Anthony S. Chen, "'The Hitlerian Rule of Quotas': Racial Conservatism and the Politics of Fair Employment Legislation in New York State, 1941–1945," *Journal of American History* 92, no. 4 (March 2006): 1238–64.

3. Henry A. Wallace, "America for All Americans," *The Oracle* 35, no. 1 (March 1946): 4. "On Mordecai W. Johnson," see photo collage and caption in *The Oracle* 35, no. 1 (March 1946): 8.

4. Z. Alexander Looby, "Report of Past Grand Basileus," *The Oracle* 35, no. 1 (March 1946): 20–21, 25.

5. John H. Calhoun Jr., "Shall We Return the Fraternity to the Undergraduates?" *The Oracle* 34, no. 2 (December 1945): 13.

6. "Omega Psi Phi Balance Sheet, November 30, 1945," *Omega Bulletin* 27, no. 2 (February 1946): 3.

7. "New Chapters," *Omega Bulletin* 27, no. 1 (January 1946): 3.

8. Calhoun, "Shall We Return," 13.

9. Calhoun, "Shall We Return," 13.

10. "National Social Action Committee in Extensive Program: The Vice Grand Basileus Speaks," *Omega Bulletin* 27, no. 2 (February 1946): 1.

11. "National Social Action Committee in Extensive Program."

12. "The National Social Action Committee," *Omega Bulletin* 27, no. 2 (February 1946): 4.

13. "National Social Action Committee in Extensive Program," 1.

14. "National Officers of the Omega Psi Phi Fraternity: March 1946," *The Oracle* 35, no. 1 (March 1946): inside cover. The inside cover noted that Weiseger was Grand Keeper of Records and Seal by March 1946; however, that spring, he succeeded C. R. Alexander, who was elected in at the Washington Conclave. It was Weiseger's second stint in that office as Alexander was forced to resign due to professional obligations. For more, see Robert L. Gill, *The History of Omega Psi Phi Fraternity and the Men Who Made Its History: A Concise History* (Washington, DC: Omega Psi Phi Fraternity, 1963), 35–36.

15. "Presenting . . . the Grand Basileus," *The Oracle* 35, no. 1 (March 1946): 2, 27; "Johnson, Campbell Carrington," Biographical Sketch, 2015, Manuscript Division Finding Aids, Howard University, Washington, DC.

16. "National Social Action Committee in Extensive Program: Some Procedures That Should Be Followed by Chapters," *Omega Bulletin* 27, no. 2 (February 1946): 1.

17. Ira De A. Reid, "National Social Action Committee . . . ," *The Oracle* 35, no. 2 (May 1946): 7.

18. Reid, "National Social Action Committee," 7, 20.

19. Jessica Bliss, "How Thurgood Marshall Helped Bring Justice to a Tennessee Town and Was Nearly Jailed," *Tennessean*, October 13, 2017; Chris Lamb, "America's First Post-World War Race Riot Led to the Near-Lynching of Thurgood Marshall," *Washington Post*, February 25, 2021.

20. Lamb, "America's First."

21. "Meet William H. Hastie," *The Oracle* 35, no. 2 (May 1946): 26.

22. "Meet William H. Hastie," 27.

23. "Along the NAACP Battlefront: Victory Decisions," *Crisis* 53, no. 7 (July 1946): 210.

24. "Along the NAACP Battlefront," 211.

25. William T. Coleman Jr. and Donald T. Bliss, *Counsel for the Situation: Shaping the Law to Realize America's Promise* (Washington, DC: Brookings Institution Press, 2010), 24; Rawn James Jr., *Root and Branch: Charles Hamilton Houston, Thurgood Marshall, and the Struggle to End Segregation* (New York: Bloomsbury, 2010), 55.

26. *Morgan v. Virginia*, 328 U.S. 373 (June 3, 1946).

27. *Morgan v. Virginia*.

28. "Fares to Fort Worth Texas," *Omega Bulletin* 27, no. 4 (September 1946): 2.

29. Bliss, "How Thurgood Marshall"; Lamb, "America's First."

30. Ira De A. Reid, "Omega's Program of National Social Action," *The Oracle* 36, no. 4 (November 1946): 16.

31. Bliss, "How Thurgood Marshall"; Lamb, "America's First"; David Hudson, "Thurgood Marshall in Tennessee: His Defense of Accused Rioters, His Near-Miss with a Lynch Mob," *Tennessee Bar Journal* 56, no. 9 (September 2020), www.tba.org/?pg=Articles&blAction=showEntry&blogEntry=56556.

32. Ira De A. Reid, "Report of Achievement Week Director and Chairman of NSA Committee," Minutes of the Thirty-Second Annual Conclave [mislabeled as Thirty-Third Grand Conclave], 31a, December 27–30, 1946, Omega Psi Phi Fraternity Inc., History and Archives Committee, Decatur, GA.

33. Reid, "Report of Achievement Week," 32a.

34. John H. Calhoun Jr., "Report of the First Vice Grand Basileus," *The Oracle* 37, no. 1 (March 1947): 8.

35. Calhoun, "Report," 8.

36. Calhoun, "Report," 8.

37. Calhoun, "Report," 8.

38. Frank S. Horne, "A Long Way from Home," *The Oracle* 37, no. 1 (March 1947): 14.

39. "Dr. Frank S. Horne," *The Oracle* 38, no. 4 (December 1948): 5.

40. Horne, "Long Way from Home," 14.

41. W. Montague Cobb, "Strictly on Our Own," *The Oracle* 37, no. 3 (September 1947): 12.

42. Cobb, "Strictly on Our Own," 12.

43. Cobb, "Strictly on Our Own," 12.

44. Cobb, "Strictly on Our Own," 14.

45. George M. Houser and Bayard Rustin, "We Challenge Jim Crow," *The Oracle* 38, no. 1 (March 1948): 10–17.

46. Houser and Rustin, "We Challenge Jim Crow," 14.

47. Houser and Rustin, "We Challenge Jim Crow," 16.

48. J. Erroll Miller, "Safeguarding Civil Liberties," *The Oracle* 37, no. 3 (September 1947): 24.

49. Miller, "Safeguarding Civil Liberties," 26.

50. On biographical information, see Catherine Roth, "Grant Reynolds (1908–2004)," BlackPast, December 20, 2009, www.blackpast.org/african-american-history/reynolds-grant-1908-2004/. For the Reynolds–Powell election results, see Louis Lautier, "GOP Landslide in National Elections Gives Party Control Over House and Senate," *Black Dispatch* (Oklahoma City), November 16, 1946, 1. During the Great Depression, Reynolds left New York where he was a member of Epsilon chapter. He eventually settled in Missouri, where he completed his undergraduate studies in 1938.

51. *Committee Against Jim Crow in Military Service and Training* to W. E. B. Du Bois, November 17, 1947, W. E. B. Du Bois Papers (MS 312), Special Collections and University Archives, University of Massachusetts Amherst Libraries.

52. *Committee Against Jim Crow in Military Service and Training* to W. E. B. Du Bois.

53. Andrew William Ramsey, "The Achievement Program and Democracy," *The Oracle* 38, no. 1 (March 1948): 7.

54. Gill, *Omega Psi Phi Fraternity*, 91.

55. Chester Smith, "Application for an Undergraduate Chapter Charter: Indiana University," September 18, 1947, in possession of the authors.

56. Smith, "Application."

57. Ramsey, "Achievement Program and Democracy," 8.

58. Charles W. Collins, "Civil Rights," *The Oracle* 37, no. 4 (December 1947): 2–10.

59. Collins, "Civil Rights," 2.

60. Harry T. Penn, "A Challenge to Omega," *The Oracle* 37, no. 4 (December 1947), 11.

61. Minutes of the Thirty-Third Annual Conclave [mislabeled as Thirty-Fourth Grand Conclave], 1, December 27–30, 1947, Omega Psi Phi Fraternity Inc., History and Archives Committee, Decatur, GA. On the number of Omega men present, see "500 Gather in Detroit for 34th Omega Conclave," *Baltimore Afro-American*, January 10, 1948. Please note the national press repeated the Fraternity's error regarding the number of the conclave.

62. Campbell C. Johnson, "Report of the Grand Basileus," Minutes of the Thirty-Third Annual Conclave [mislabeled as Thirty-Fourth Grand Conclave], 8, December 27, 1947, Omega Psi Phi Fraternity Inc., History and Archives Committee, Decatur, GA.

63. Minutes of the Thirty-Third Annual Conclave, 46–48.

64. William H. Hastie, "Reacting to Racism," *The Oracle* 38, no. 1 (March 1948): 4.

65. "Robinson Honored," *The Oracle* 38, no. 2 (May 1948): 3, 27.

66. Lucius Jones, "Omega in Oklahoma," *The Oracle* 38, no. 1 (March 1948): 17; "The Victory of Greenwood: Amos T. Hall," The Victory of Greenwood, accessed May 17, 2023, https://thevictoryofgreenwood.com/2021/08/02/the-victory-of-greenwood-amos-t-hall/.

67. Ada Lois Sipuel Fisher, *A Matter of Black and White: The Autobiography of Ada Lois Sipuel Fisher* (Norman: University of Oklahoma Press, 1996).

68. Sipuel v. Board of Regents of the University of Oklahoma, 332 U.S. 631 (January 12, 1948).

69. Jones, "Omega in Oklahoma," 17.

70. *Sipuel v. Board of Regents*.

71. Missouri ex rel. Gaines v. Canada, 305 U.S. 337 (December 12, 1938).

72. Jones, "Omega in Oklahoma," 17.

73. Cheryl Elizabeth Brown Wattley, *A Step toward Brown v. Board of Education: Ada Lois Sipuel Fisher and Her Fight to End Segregation* (Norman: University of Oklahoma Press, 2014), 221–23.

74. "Omegas Picket Jim Crow Theater," *The Oracle* 38, no. 1 (March 1948): 19.

75. Regarding other Baltimore Ford's Theater picket participants, see Eddie R. Cole, *The Campus Color Line: College Presidents and the Struggle for Black Freedom* (Princeton, NJ: Princeton University Press, 2020), 57–58.

76. "Omegas Picket Jim Crow Theater," 19.

77. "Omegas Picket Jim Crow Theater," 19.

78. For more, see Cole, *Campus Color Line*, 34–36.

79. Ira De A. Reid, "Minerva's Southern Dilemma: Problem of Race & Regional Cooperation in Education," *Omega Bulletin* 29, no. 4 (April 1948), 7.

80. Reid, "Minerva's Southern Dilemma," 7.

81. Nedra Rhone, "Daughter Recalls John Wesley Dobbs' Part in Mission to Unmask Jim Crow," *Atlanta Journal-Constitution*, January 20, 2018, www.ajc.com/lifestyles/daughter-recalls-john-wesley-dobbs-part-mission-unmask-jim-crow/kUVZ6rPESdla3yWHkU2PRL/; Ray Sprigle, *In the Land of Jim Crow* (New York: Simon & Schuster, 1949); H. L. Mencken, *Minority Report* (New York: Alfred A. Knopf, 1956).

82. "Delta Omega Honors Race Leaders at Smoker," *Omega Bulletin* 29, no. 6 (September 1948): 6.

83. Kari Frederickson, *The Dixiecrat Revolt and the End of the Solid South, 1932–1968* (Chapel Hill: University of North Carolina Press, 2001); William D. Barnard, *Dixiecrats and Democrats: Alabama Politics, 1942–1950* (University of Alabama Press, 1974); Glenn Feldman, *The Great Melding: War, the Dixiecrat Rebellion, and the Southern Road to America's New Conservatism* (Tuscaloosa: University of Alabama Press, 2015).

84. "Our National Social Action Program," *Omega Bulletin* 29, no. 6 (September 1948): 4.

85. Executive Order 9981, July 26, 1948, General Records of the United States Government, Record Group 11, National Archives, Washington, DC.

86. "Executive Order 9981: Desegregation of the Armed Forces (1948)," National Archives, accessed on March 12, 2023, www.archives.gov/milestone-documents/executive-order-9981.

87. "Our National Social Action Program," 4.

88. "Programs: Chapters in Spotlight," *Omega Bulletin* 29, no. 9 (December 1948): 12.

89. Minutes of the Thirty-Fourth Annual Conclave [mislabeled as Thirty-Fifth Grand Conclave], 1, December 27, 1948, Omega Psi Phi Fraternity Inc., History and Archives Committee, Decatur, GA.

90. Minutes of the Thirty-Fourth Annual Conclave, 1.

91. Minutes of the Thirty-Fourth Annual Conclave, 16.

92. "Full-Time Executive Secretary Will Be Employed by Frat," *The Oracle* 39, no. 1 (March 1949): 2.

93. Minutes of the Thirty-Fourth Annual Conclave, 43.

94. "Brother William Stuart Nelson Back," *The Oracle* 38, no. 2 (May 1948): 26; "Omega Men in Liberia Guide Way to Progress," *The Oracle* 39, no. 1 (March 1949): 20.

95. Minutes of the Thirty-Fourth Annual Conclave, 44–46. Also see "Historic Decisions Made at Columbus," *The Oracle* 39, no. 1 (March 1949): 2.

96. Minutes of the Thirty-Fourth Annual Conclave, 58–60.

97. "Grand Basileus Penn Sends Greetings: A Challenge to Omega," *The Oracle* 39, no. 1 (March 1949): 2.

98. "Florida Law Graduates Don't Have to Pass Bar," *The Oracle* 39, no. 1 (March 1949): 22.

99. "Dr. R. C. Hatch Wins Alabama Appointment," *The Oracle* 39, no. 1 (March 1949): 18.

100. Minutes of the Thirty-Third Annual Conclave, 3.

101. "Truman Cites Negro Fund: Urges Support for $1,400,000 United College Drive," *New York Times*, April 12, 1949; "Suman Appeals for College Fund: Omega Men Asked to Support Drive," *The Oracle* 39, no. 1 (March 1949): 26.

102. Eric Anderson and Alfred A. Moss Jr., *Dangerous Donations: Northern Philanthropy and Southern Black Education, 1902–1930* (Columbia: University of Missouri Press, 1999).

103. "Truman Cites Negro Fund."

104. Jonathan Matthews, "Brothers Who Are/Were College Presidents," Omega Psi Phi Fraternity Inc., History and Archives Committee, Decatur, GA.

105. "New Executive Secretary Goes to Work for Omega," *The Oracle* 39, no. 3 (September 1949): 7.

106. "Is Hastie Headed for Supreme Court Bench?" *The Oracle* 39, no. 4 (December 1949): 8. The article was reprinted from the *Norfolk Journal and Guide*.

107. J. Cullen Fentress, "Hastie Banquet Guest List Reads Like 'Who's Who,'" *The Oracle* 39, no. 3 (September 1949): 9.

108. Charles J. Smith III, "William K. Payne: Acting President of Georgia State College," *The Oracle* 40, no. 1 (March 1950): 9.

109. Andrew Jackson, "WERD Is on the Air: J. B. Blayton, Omega's GKF, Open's First Negro Owned Radio Station," *The Oracle* 39, no. 4 (December 1949): 20–21.

110. Jackson, "WERD," 21.

111. Harry T. Penn, "Fraternity Leadership: A Pre-Conclave Message from the Grand Basileus," *The Oracle* 39, no. 4 (December 1949): 3.

112. "Little Politicians . . . ," *The Oracle* 39, no. 4 (December 1949): 1.

113. Minutes of the Thirty-Fifth Annual Conclave [mislabeled as Thirty-Sixth Grand Conclave], 1, December 28, 1949, Omega Psi Phi Fraternity Inc., History and Archives Committee, Decatur, GA.

114. Minutes of the Thirty-Fifth Annual Conclave, Report of the Housing Authority, 113.

115. Minutes of the Thirty-Fifth Annual Conclave, Report of the Housing Authority, 114.

116. "Zeta Epsilon Long Denied, 'Accepted' at Indiana U.," *The Oracle* 40, no. 4 (December 1950): 20.

117. "Zeta Epsilon Long Denied," 20.

118. Minutes of the Thirty-Fifth Annual Conclave, Report of the Housing Authority, 114.

119. "Omega Drops Color Bar: Enters Frat Council," *The Oracle* 40, no. 1 (March 1950): 8.

120. "First Inter-Racial Chapter in Omega Psi Phi Fraternity," *The Oracle* 39, no. 3 (September 1949): 3.

121. Norman Ledgin, "Inter-Racial Group at Rutgers Plans for Spring Initiation," *The Oracle* 40, no. 1 (March 1950): 27.

122. Minutes of the Thirty-Fifth Annual Conclave, Report of the Committee on Resolutions, Appendix III.

123. On election results, see Minutes of the Thirty-Fifth Annual Conclave, Report of the Time and Place Committee, 139.

124. W. Montague Cobb, "Charles Richard Drew, M. D., 1904–1950," *Journal of the National Medical Association* 42, no. 4 (July 1950): 239, 243.

125. Sterling Brown, "Omega's Tribute to a Distinguished Brother," *The Oracle* 40, no. 1 (March 1950): 8.

126. Brown, "Omega's Tribute," 8.

127. "Omega Dear" was sung at Charles R. Drew's funeral at the request of his wife, the former Minnie Lenore Robbins. "Alpha Chapter Assists at Drew Funeral," *The Oracle* 40, no. 2 (May 1950): 39.

128. "Dr. Carter G. Woodson Passes into 'Omega Chapter,'" *The Oracle* 40, no. 1 (March 1950): 10.

129. "Dr. Carter G. Woodson Passes into 'Omega Chapter.'"

130. "Dr. L. P. Jackson Succumbs Suddenly at Virginia State," *The Oracle* 40, no. 1 (March 1950): 5.

131. The elevated photograph of Jackson's funeral services indicates hundreds of guests. For more, see "Nu Psi and Delta Omega Chapters Pay Tribute to Brother Luther P. Jackson," *The Oracle* 40, no. 1 (March 1950): 5.

132. Robert L. Gill, "Brother Oscar J. Chapman Heads Delaware State," *The Oracle* 40, no. 2 (May 1950): 23.

133. "Tennessee A&I Head Is Loyal Omega Man," *The Oracle* 40, no. 2 (May 1950): 23.

134. A. A. Morisey, "Dr. F. L. Atkins Awarded 'Citizen of Year' Honor," *The Oracle* 40, no. 2 (May 1950): 11.

135. "Bio: Francis Atkins," Winston-Salem State University, accessed March 22, 2023, https://winstonsalem.prestosports.com/about/hall_of_fame/Hall_of_Fame_Bios/Francis_Atkins_Bio.

136. Morisey, "Dr. F. L. Atkins," 11.

137. Morisey, "Dr. F. L. Atkins," 11.

138. Sweatt v. Painter, 339 U.S. 629 (June 5, 1950); McLaurin v. Oklahoma State Regents, 339 U.S. 637 (June 5, 1950).

139. For an account of *Sweatt v. Painter* and the broader challenges to segregation at the University of Texas, see Dwonna Goldstone, *Integrating the 40 Acres: The Fifty-Year Struggle for Racial Equality at the University of Texas* (Athens: University of Georgia Press, 2006).

140. David W. Levy, *Breaking Down Barriers: George McLaurin and the Struggle to End Segregated Education* (Norman: University of Oklahoma Press, 2020). Also see George Lynn Cross, *Blacks in White Colleges: Oklahoma's Landmark Cases* (Norman: University of Oklahoma Press, 1975).

141. Samuel Coleman, "Omega Men at Front in Battle for Civil Rights," *The Oracle* 40, no. 4 (December 1950): 5.

142. Robert L. Gill, "Teaching in Mixed Schools No Novelty for Omega Men," *The Oracle* 40, no. 4 (December 1950): 8.

143. "Guide to the Allison Davis Papers 1932–1984," Biographical Note, Hanna Holborn Gray Special Collections Research Center, University of Chicago Library, accessed November 15, 2021, www.lib.uchicago.edu/e/scrc/findingaids/view.php?eadid=ICU.SPCL.DAVISA.

144. "Allison Davis Papers," 29.

145. Photo caption: "Omegas Give $500 to Negro College Fund," *The Oracle* 40, no. 3 (September 1950): 30.

146. "Brother Trent, Director of UNCF, is Typical 'Que,'" *The Oracle* 40, no. 4 (December 1950): 12.

147. "Omegas Re-Elect Entire Slate," *Chicago Defender*, January 13, 1951; Lawrence A. Hill, "Boston Memories Still Linger . . . ," *The Oracle* 41, no. 1 (March 1951): 24.

148. "Junior College Head Savannah Speaker," *The Oracle* 41, no. 1 (March 1951): 19; "Brother Seabrook Honored for 20 Years of Service," *The Oracle* 43, no. 3 (September 1953): 18.

149. "Omegas First on Campus at Fayetteville State," *The Oracle* 41, no. 3 (September 1951): 28.

150. "Omega Men 'Firsts' at University of North Carolina," *The Oracle* 41, no. 4 (December 1951): 27.

151. "Miami: The New South Readys for Conclave," *The Oracle* 41, no. 3 (September 1951): 9.

152. "Miami."

153. "Dr Benjamin E. Mays Addresses the NAACP National Convention," BlackPast, July 9, 2015, www.blackpast.org/african-american-history/1951-dr-benjamin-e-mays-addresses-naacp-national-convention/.

154. "Fraternity Urges Action in Florida Bomb Slaying," *Norfolk Journal and Guide*, January 5, 1952.

155. For longer accounts of the Moore bombing, see Ben Green, *Before His Time: The Untold Story of Harry T. Moore, America's First Civil Rights Martyr* (New York: Free Press, 1999). Regarding the Moores' work prior to the bombing, see Gilbert King, *Devil in the Grove: Thurgood Marshall, the Groveland Boys, and the Dawn of a New America* (New York: Harper, 2012).

156. "Fraternity Urges Action in Florida Bomb Slaying."

157. "Fraternity Urges Action in Florida Bomb Slaying."

158. "Omegas Elect Grant Reynolds; Honor Marshall and Townsend," *New York Amsterdam News*, January 12, 1952.

159. Gill, *Omega Psi Phi Fraternity*, 80.

160. Charles H. Thompson, "Introduction," *Journal of Negro Education* 21, no. 3 (Summer 1952): 231.

161. Thompson, "Introduction," 231.

162. See Missouri ex rel. Gaines v. Canada, 305 U.S. 337 (December 12, 1938) and previously cited cases: *Sipuel v. Board of Regents*; *Sweatt v. Painter*; *McLaurin v. Oklahoma State Regents*.

163. Mordecai Wyatt Johnson, "Welcome Address and Explanation of the General Purpose of the Conference," *Journal of Negro Education* 21, no. 3 (Summer 1952): 233.

164. Benjamin E. Mays, "The Present Status of and Outlook for Racial Integration in the Church Related White Colleges in the South," *Journal of Negro Education* 21, no. 3 (Summer 1952): 350.

165. "Bro. Mays Lecturer at Yale University," *The Oracle* 42, no. 2 (May 1952): 24.

166. Benjamin E. Mays, *Born to Rebel: An Autobiography* (Athens, GA: University of Georgia Press, [1971] 1987), 1.

167. Mays, *Born to Rebel*, 1; "Benjamin Elijah Mays: Dean of School of Religion, Howard University," *The Oracle* 15, no. 3 (September 1936): 10; "Benjamin Elijah Mays: College President," *The Oracle* 35, no. 2 (May 1946): 23.

168. Mays, *Born to Rebel*, 1.

169. "Mays: Dean of School of Religion," 10; "Mays: College President," 23.

170. "Mays: Dean of School of Religion," 10.

171. "Mays: College President," 23.

172. "Mays: Dean of School of Religion," 10.

173. "History: About Γ Chapter," Gamma Chapter, Omega Psi Phi Fraternity Inc., accessed November 24, 2022, http://gamma1916.com/about-γ-chapter/history/.

174. "Mays: College President," 24.

175. "Mays: College President," 24–25.

176. Mays, "Present Status," 352.

177. Mays, "Present Status," 352; "Brother Mays Named to Educational Council," *The Oracle* 40, no. 3 (September 1950): 24.

178. Richard Kluger, *Simple Justice: The History of* Brown v. Board of Education *and Black America's Struggle for Equality* (New York: Alfred A. Knopf, 1974), 261, 522.

179. James M. Nabrit Jr., "An Appraisal of Court Action as a Means of Achieving Racial Segregation in Education," *Journal of Negro Education* 21, no. 3 (Summer 1952): 422.

180. Nabrit, "Appraisal of Court Action," 425, 429.

181. "Grand Basileus Ends His Spring Speaking Tour," *The Oracle* 42, no. 2 (May 1952): 35.

182. Robert L. Gregory Jr., "Bro. Chase First Negro to Finish Univ. Texas," *The Oracle* 42, no. 3 (September 1952): 13.

183. "Brother Ray Gets Ph.D.," *The Oracle* 42, no. 3 (September 1952): 27.

184. "Xi Omega Has Social Action Plans," *The Oracle* 42, no. 3 (September 1952): 27.

185. "Brother Reynolds on National TV Program," *The Oracle* 42, no. 4 (December 1952): 4.

186. "'Democracy: Now or Never?': Theme of Achievement Week," *The Oracle* 42, no. 3 (September 1952): 11.

187. "President Truman Given Scroll for Civil Rights Stand," *The Oracle* 42, no. 4 (December 1952): 27.

188. "Fraternity Presents Scroll to Truman for Civil Rights," *The Oracle* 43, no. 1 (March 1953): 13.

189. Jack Saunders, "Omegas Call Out for UN's Support in 1953 Program," *Pittsburgh Courier*, January 10, 1953.

190. Saunders, "Omegas Call Out."

191. "7th District Pledges Aid in Segregation Battle," *The Oracle* 43, no. 3 (September 1953): 10.

192. "7th District Pledges Aid in Segregation Battle."

193. "6th District Cites Bishop for Segregation Stand," *The Oracle* 44, no. 2 (May 1954): 18.

194. "First to Get Ph.D. at University of Virginia," *The Oracle* 43, no. 3 (September 1953): 15; Robert Mcg. Thomas Jr., "Walter Ridley, 86, Who Broke Color Barrier to Get Ph.D., Dies," *New York Times*, November 3, 1996.

195. See Aldon D. Morris, *The Origins of the Civil Rights Movement: Black Communities Organizing for Change* (New York: Free Press, 1984), 17–25.

196. "Grant Reynolds 'Bows Out,' Leaves Big List of Achievements," *The Oracle* 44, no. 1 (March 1954): 9.

197. Gill, *Omega Psi Phi Fraternity*, 80.

198. "Grant Reynolds 'Bows Out,'" 9.

199. "Grant Reynolds 'Bows Out,'" 9.

200. "More Than 250 Delegates Attend 40th Grand Conclave," *The Oracle* 44, no. 1 (March 1954): 13, 49; "Howard Davis Is New 2nd Vice," *The Oracle* 44, no. 1 (March 1954): 12.

201. "More Than 250 Delegates Attend."

202. "More Than 250 Delegates Attend," 13, 49.

203. "Biographical Note," John F. Potts, Sr. Papers, College of Charleston, Charleston, SC, accessed November 17, 2023, https://findingaids.library.cofc.edu/repositories/3/resources/289.

204. "Scholarship Panel Probes into Reasons Why: At Conclave," *The Oracle* 44, no. 1 (March 1954): 6.

205. See Keith W. Olson, "The G. I. Bill and Higher Education: Success and Surprise," *American Quarterly* 25, no. 5 (December 1973): 596–610; Robert C. Serow, "Policy as Symbol: Title II of the 1944 G.I. Bill," *Review of Higher Education* 27, no. 4 (Summer 2004): 481–99.

206. Regarding the number of Fraternity chapters, see "Praise and Plans for Future from the Grand Basileus," *The Oracle* 45, no. 1 (March 1955): 4.

207. Brown v. Board of Education of Topeka, 347 U.S. 483 (May 17, 1954).

208. "Brown v. Board of Education: Meet the Legal Team," NAACP Legal Defense Fund, accessed October 1, 2022, www.naacpldf.org/brown-vs-board/meet-legal-minds-behind-brown-v-board-education/.

209. "Brother John F. Potts to Become Voorhees President on July 1st," *The Oracle* 44, no. 2 (May 1954): 5.

210. Edmund L. Drago, *Charleston's Avery Center: From Education and Civil Rights to Preserving the African American Experience*, rev. and ed. W. Marvin Dulaney (Charleston, SC: History Press, 2006).

211. "Bro. Jones Gets Ph.D Degree at Oklahoma Univ.," *The Oracle* 44, no. 3 (September 1954): 30.

212. "Iota Psi Ranks Fourth at OSU," *The Oracle* 44, no. 3 (September 1954): 29.

213. "Psi Psi Man Appointed to Naval Academy," *The Oracle* 44, no. 4 (December 1954): 32; "Psi Psi Chapter Reviews Prosperous School Year," *The Oracle* 45, no. 3 (September 1955): 10. Although *The Oracle* states Holland was appointed to the US Naval Academy, other Kentucky-specified sources note that Holland was nominated to the US Military Academy. See more from the Notable Kentucky African Americans database housed by the University of Kentucky, "Holland, James Phillip," accessed April 12, 2023, https://nkaa.uky.edu/nkaa/items/show/1268.

214. "Omegas Back Full Fight for Equality: Cite Dr. Mays," *Baltimore Afro-American*, January 8, 1955.

215. Minutes of the Forty-First Grand Conclave [mislabeled as Forty-Second Grand Conclave], 168, August 18–23, 1955, Omega Psi Phi Fraternity Inc., History and Archives Committee, Decatur, GA.

216. "Omega Vote 'Entire Resources' in Desegregation Battle Ahead," *The Oracle* 45, no. 3 (September 1955): 5.

217. Minutes of the Forty-First Grand Conclave, 350–51; "Omega Vote 'Entire Resources,'" 5.

218. Devery S. Anderson, *Emmett Till: The Murder That Shocked the World and Propelled the Civil Rights Movement* (Jackson: University Press of Mississippi, 2015); Clenora Hudson-Weems, "Resurrecting Emmett Till: The Catalyst of the Modern Civil Rights Movement," *Journal of Black Studies* 29, no. 2 (November 1998): 179–88.

219. "Nation Horrified by Murder of Kidnapped Chicago Youth," *Jet* 8, no. 19 (September 15, 1955): 9.

220. "50,000 Line Chicago Streets for Look at Lynch Victim," *New York Amsterdam News*, September 10, 1955.

221. "Brother Wheeler Makes Strong Plea for Integration," *The Oracle* 45, no. 3 (September 1955): 17.

222. Martin Luther King Jr., "2 Sept. 1957. 'A Look to the Future,' Address Delivered at Highlander Folk School's Twenty-Fifth Anniversary Meeting," in *The Papers of Martin*

Luther King, Jr., vol. 4, *Symbol of the Movement, January 1957–December 1958*, ed. Clayborne Carson (Berkeley: University of California Press, 2005), 269–76, 270 (one of multiple primary sources that contained the quotation by King). A sampling of books about the 1955–56 bus boycott in Montgomery, Alabama, includes Stewart Burns, *Daybreak of Freedom: The Montgomery Bus Boycott* (Chapel Hill: University of North Carolina Press, 1997); Fred Gray, *Bus Ride to Justice: The Life and Works of Fred D. Gray*, rev. ed. (Montgomery, AL: NewSouth Books, 2013); Jo Ann Robinson, *The Montgomery Bus Boycott and the Women Who Started It: The Memoir of Jo Ann Robinson*, ed. David J. Garrow (Knoxville: University of Tennessee Press, 1987). Also see Jeanne Theoharis, *The Rebellious Life of Mrs. Rosa Parks* (Boston, MA: Beacon, 2013).

223. Gray, *Bus Ride to Justice*, xi (the first of many pages on which Gray made the statement about destroying every segregated thing he found).

224. Mays, *Born to Rebel*, 265.

225. "Educators at Inauguration," *Baltimore Afro-American*, October 27, 1956.

226. "Willa Player, 94, Pioneer Black Educator," *New York Times*, April 30, 2003; Deidre B. Flowers, "The Launching of the Student Sit-in Movement: The Role of Black Women at Bennett College," *Journal of African American History* 90, no. 1 (Winter 2005): 56.

227. "Bro. W. T. Gibbs Is Acting A&T Prexy," *The Oracle* 46, no. 1 (March 1956): 7; "Brother Gibbs Is Inaugurated as President of A&T College," *The Oracle* 46, no. 4 (December 1956): 5.

228. "Brother Nabrit Is Inaugurated at Texas Southern University," *The Oracle* 46, no. 2 (May 1956): 7.

229. "Tallahassee Bus Boycott Leader Is 'Man of Year,'" *The Oracle* 46, no. 4 (December 1956): 30.

230. "Mississippi at Boiling Point Says Bro. T. R. M. Howard," *The Oracle* 46, no. 1 (March 1956): 22. For T. R. M. Howard's conclave remarks, see Minutes of the Forty-First Grand Conclave, 254–73.

231. "Miss Lucy Says Thanks Omegas for Donation," *The Oracle* 46, no. 2 (May 1956): 6.

232. Browder v. Gayle, 142 F. Supp. 707 (June 5, 1956).

233. "The Grand Basileus Speaks . . . ," *The Oracle* 46, no. 4 (December 1956): 4.

234. "Baltimore . . . Scene of 1956 Conclave," *The Oracle* 46, no. 4 (December 1956): 6. Regarding the weather, see "Conclave Sidelights," *The Oracle* 47, no. 1 (March 1957): 17.

235. "Famed Football Coach Now Building Track Champions: New Honors for Morgan College's Edward P. Hurt," *The Oracle* 40, no. 1 (March 1950): 10.

236. "Omegas Gird for Civil Rights Fight at Baltimore Conclave," *The Oracle* 47, no. 1 (March 1957): 6.

237. "Conclave Highlights," *The Oracle* 46, no. 4 (December 1956): 7; "Five Major Addresses Are Heard at Grand Conclave," *The Oracle* 47, no. 1 (March 1957): 10, 14–15, 29.

238. "Omegas Gird for Civil Rights Fight." On the origins of Talent Hunt, see J. Alston Atkins, "Permanent Talent Hunt Program," *The Oracle* 37, no. 4 (December 1947): 21; G. E. Matthews, "Sixth District Talent Hunt Developing Stars of Future," *The Oracle* 40, no. 1 (March 1950): 24; "Talent Hunt Program Scores in Its Grand Conclave Debut," *The Oracle* 44, no. 1 (March 1954): 11.

239. "Omegas Pay Near $11,000.00 in NAACP Life Memberships," *The Oracle* 47, no. 1 (March 1957): 5.

240. "Omegas Pay Near $11,000.00," 5.

241. "Omegas Pay Near $11,000.00," 5.

242. "Omegas Gird for Civil Rights Fight."

243. Adam Fairclough, *To Redeem the Soul of America: The Southern Christian Leadership Conference and Martin Luther King Jr.* (Athens: University of Georgia Press, 1987), 23.

244. "Theta Sigma Gives Up Dance for Civil Rights," *The Oracle* 47, no. 2 (May 1957): 30.

245. Wiley A. Branton, "Little Rock Revisited: Desegregation to Resegregation," *Journal of Negro Education* 52, no. 3 (Summer 1983): 250–69.

Chapter 5

1. See Maurice J. Hobson, "Tackling the Talented Tenth: Black Greek-Lettered Organizations and the Black New South," in *The Black Intellectual Tradition: African American Thought in the Twentieth Century*, ed. Derrick P. Alridge, Cornelius L. Bynum, and James B. Stewart (Urbana: University of Illinois Press, 2021), 176–204; Jacquelyn Dowd Hall, "The Long Civil Rights Movement and the Political Uses of the Past," *Journal of American History* 91, no. 4 (March 2005): 1233–63; Jeanne Theoharis, "Black Freedom Studies: Reimagining and Redefining Fundamentals," *History Compass* 4, no. 2 (March 2006): 348–67.

2. "Bro. W. T. Gibbs Is Acting A&T Prexy," *The Oracle* 46, no. 1 (March 1956): 7.

3. Eugene E. Pfaff Jr., *Keep on Walkin', Keep on Talkin': An Oral History of the Greensboro Civil Rights Movement* (Greensboro, NC: Tudor Publishers, 2011), 85.

4. William H. Chafe, *Civilities and Civil Rights: Greensboro, North Carolina, and the Black Struggle for Freedom* (Oxford: Oxford University Press, 1981), 60–61, 95.

5. For more on Ella Baker and her role in organizing students, see Barbara Ransby, *Ella Baker and the Black Freedom Movement: A Radical Democratic Vision* (Chapel Hill: University of North Carolina Press, 2003), 238–47; Howard Zinn, *SNCC: The New Abolitionists* (Boston, MA: Beacon, 1964), 32; Randal Maurice Jelks, *Benjamin Elijah Mays, Schoolmaster of the Movement: A Biography* (Chapel Hill: University of North Carolina Press, 2012), 210–11; Clayborne Carson, *In Struggle: SNCC and the Black Awakening of the 1960s* (Cambridge, MA: Harvard University Press, 1981), 19.

6. "Bombing Sets Off Nashville March: Negro Councilman's Home Wrecked—2,000 Protest," *New York Times*, April 20, 1960.

7. "The Price of Freedom," *The Oracle* 50, no. 2 (May 1960): 3.

8. "Some Observations on the Students Sit-Down Protests: The Basileus Speaks," *The Oracle* 50, no. 2 (May 1960): 34.

9. "Some Observations on the Students Sit-Down Protests," 34.

10. "Sixth District Gives $500 for Defense of Those Arrested in 'Sit-Down' Drive," *The Oracle* 50, no. 2 (May 1960): 9.

11. "Third District Endorses-Supports 'Sit-Down' Movement Now Underway," *The Oracle* 50, no. 2 (May 1960): 12.

12. Willie J. Pettis, "Two Zeta Brothers Sit-Down Leaders," *The Oracle* 50, no. 2 (May 1960): 16.

13. "4 College Presidents to Speak for Omegas," *Chicago Defender*, December 21, 1960.

14. "4 College Presidents to Speak for Omegas."

15. "Desegregation Family Honored by Fraternity," *Washington Post*, December 29, 1960.

16. "Omegas Expected to Stress Social Action at '61 Conclave," *Baltimore Afro-American*, January 14, 1961.

17. Maurice C. Daniels, *Horace T. Ward: Desegregation of the University of Georgia, Civil Rights Advocacy, and Jurisprudence* (Atlanta, GA: Clark Atlanta University Press, 2001), 150–52, 154–55.

18. For more, see Raymond Arsenault, *Freedom Rides: 1961 and the Struggle for Racial Justice* (Oxford: Oxford University Press, 2006).

19. Arsenault, *Freedom Rides*, 264.

20. "Statement by the Honorable Robert F. Kennedy Attorney General of the United States," May 24, 1961, www.justice.gov/sites/default/files/ag/legacy/2011/01/20/05-24-1961b.pdf.

21. Associated Press, "Cooling-Off Period Urged by Kennedy: Appeal Hailed by Patterson," *Montgomery Advertiser*, May 25, 1961.

22. Philip A. Goduth Jr., *Robert F. Kennedy and the Shaping of Civil Rights, 1960–1964* (Jefferson, NC: McFarland, 2013), 84.

23. "Men of Omega, 900 Strong, Pledge Continued Crusade for Equality," *The Oracle* 50, no. 3 (September 1961): 6.

24. "Bro. Robert Weaver Named to Highest U.S. Post in History," *The Oracle* 50, no. 1 (March 1961): 4.

25. "Attorney General Greets Omegas: Omegas Cite 2 Kennedy Appointees at Conclave," *Norfolk Journal and Guide*, August 26, 1961.

26. "Attorney General Greets Omegas."

27. "Men of Omega, 900 Strong," 6.

28. "Men of Omega, 900 Strong," 6.

29. "Men of Omega, 900 Strong," 6.

30. "Omegas Will Help Build African Research Center," *Norfolk Journal and Guide*, September 23, 1961.

31. "Brother Kermit Clifford King Heads University of Liberia," *The Oracle* 47, no. 2 (May 1957): 4.

32. "Your New Officers," *The Oracle* 50, no. 3 (September 1961): 6.

33. Judson L. Jeffries, "Malcolm X, the Omega Psi Phi Fraternity, Inc., and Morgan State College," *Spectrum: A Journal on Black Men* 8, no. 1 (Fall 2020).

34. "Men of Omega, 900 Strong," 6.

35. Peter Young, "'Black Muslim' Leader, Morgan Teacher Clash," *Baltimore Evening Sun*, March 29, 1962.

36. Jeffries, "Malcolm X," 137–38.

37. Jeffries, "Malcolm X," 146.

38. Jeffries, "Malcolm X," 134.

39. Jeffries, "Malcolm X," 128, 133–34, 138.

40. Jeffries, "Malcolm X," 131.

41. "Two Omega Scholars, Johnson and Robinson, First of Race to Be Admitted to Duke Univ." *The Oracle* 50, no. 1 (March 1962): 9.

42. "2 Die, 75 Hurt in Miss. Riot: Marshals Hurl Gas at Mob of Attackers," *Chicago Daily Tribune*, October 1, 1962; Eric Pace, "Tom Dent, 66, Civil Rights Campaigner and Poet," *New York Times*, June 11, 1998, www.nytimes.com/1998/06/11/arts/tom-dent-66-civil-rights-campaigner-and-poet.html.

43. Adam Fairclough, *To Redeem the Soul of America: The Southern Christian Leadership Conference and Martin Luther King, Jr.* (Athens: University of Georgia Press, 2001).

44. "Police Use Water, Dogs on Marchers," *Birmingham Post-Herald*, May 4, 1963.

45. See Eddie R, Cole, *The Campus Color Line: College Presidents and the Struggle for Black Freedom* (Princeton, NJ: Princeton University Press, 2020), particularly chap. 5; B. J. Hollars, *Opening the Doors: The Desegregation of the University of Alabama and the Fight for Civil Rights in Tuscaloosa* (Tuscaloosa: University of Alabama Press, 2013); Earl H. Tilford, *Turning the Tide: The University of Alabama in the 1960s* (Tuscaloosa: University of Alabama Press, 2014).

46. Michael Vinson Williams, *Medgar Evers: Mississippi Martyr* (Fayetteville: University of Arkansas Press, 2011); Minrose Gwin, *Remembering Medgar Evers: Writing the Long Civil Rights Movement* (Athens: University of Georgia Press, 2013).

47. Exec. Order No. 8802, 6 Fed. Reg. 3109 (June 25, 1941); A. Philip Randolph, "Let's March on Capital 10,000 Strong, Urges Leader of Porters," *Pittsburgh Courier*, January 25, 1941. Regarding organizers, see Wolfgang Saxon, "Thomas Kilgore, Jr., 84; Led 2 Baptist Groups," *New York Times*, February 10, 1998.

48. Martin Luther King Jr., "I Have a Dream," in *A Call to Conscience: The Landmark Speeches of Dr. Martin Luther King, Jr.*, ed. Clayborne Carson and Kris Shepard (New York: Warner Books, 2001), 75–88; Saxon, "Thomas Kilgore, Jr." (noting Kilgore completed divinity training at Union Theological Seminary).

49. "Omegas 'March' Too," *The Oracle* 52, no. 3 (September 1963): cover.

50. "Hundreds of Omegas Participate in 'March' Starting at Frat House," *The Oracle* 52, no. 3 (September 1963): 5; by 1963, the Fraternity house was owned by the Alpha and Alpha Omega chapters. In the mid-1950s, it was purchased in a collective effort of Alpha, Alpha Omega, and Tau Upsilon chapters. The Tau Upsilon chapter surrendered its charter as a second graduate chapter in Washington DC during the San Antonio Conclave in December 1960. For more, see "Tau Upsilon," Omega Psi Phi Fraternity Inc., Alpha Omega Chapter, accessed August 22, 2024, https://alphaomegachapter.org/tau-upsilon/.

51. V. P. Franklin, *Young Crusaders: The Untold Story of the Children and Teenagers Who Galvanized the Civil Rights Movement* (Boston, MA: Beacon Press, 2021).

52. Anna Hedgeman, *The Trumpet Sounds: A Memoir of Negro Leadership* (Chicago: Holt, Rinehart and Winston, 1964); Dorothy Height, *Open Wide the Freedom Gates: A Memoir* (New York: Public Affairs, 2003); "National Council Rights Aide," *New York Times*, April 4, 1964; Jennifer Scanlon, *Until There Is Justice: The Life of Anna Arnold Hedgeman* (New York: Oxford University Press, 2016).

53. "March on Washington for Jobs and Freedom Lincoln Memorial Program," August 28, 1963, in Bayard Rustin Papers, John F. Kennedy Library, National Archives and Records Administration, Washington, DC; Meghan Weaver, "'Freedom!': Black Women Speak at the March on Washington for Jobs and Freedom," *King Encyclopedia*, King Institute, accessed August 21, 2024, https://kinginstitute.stanford.edu/freedom-black-women-speak-march-washington-jobs-and-freedom.

54. Betty A. Dietz, "Woman Moving Force in March on Capital," *Dayton Daily News*, August 27, 1963, 20.

55. "March on Washington Commanded by Communist," *Heads Up* 2 (August–September 1963): 3.

56. Cary D. Jacobs, "The Grand Basileus Speaks: Endorses Mammoth Drive for Freedom and Jobs," *The Oracle* 52, no. 3 (September 1963): 4.

57. Jacobs, "Grand Basileus Speaks," 4.

58. Jacobs, "Grand Basileus Speaks," 4.

59. Coretta Scott King, *My Life with Martin Luther King, Jr.*, rev. ed. (New York: Henry Holt, 1993) 225; Frank Sikora, *Until Justice Rolls Down: The Birmingham Church Bombing Case* (Tuscaloosa: University of Alabama Press, 2005).

60. Glenn Eskew, "Bombingham," chap. 2 in *But for Birmingham: The Local and National Movements in the Civil Rights Struggle* (Chapel Hill: University of North Carolina Press, 1997), 53–83; "Protest Started in Philadelphia," *Montgomery Advertiser*, September 22, 1963.

61. Kimberley Mangun, *Editor Emory O. Jackson, the Birmingham World, and the Fight for Civil Rights in Alabama, 1940–1975* (New York: Peter Lang, 2019), 158; Mary Stanton, "Emory O. Jackson," Encyclopedia of Alabama, accessed November 25, 2022, http://encyclopediaofalabama.org/Article/h-1837.

62. See *Report of the President's Commission on the Assassination of President John F. Kennedy* (Washington, DC: United States Government Printing Office, 1964) (cited hereinafter as *Kennedy Report*).

63. *Kennedy Report*, xi, 112–117.

64. *Kennedy Report*, 112–117

65. *Kennedy Report*, xi.

66. Mangun, *Editor Emory O. Jackson*, 161.

67. Mangun, *Editor Emory O. Jackson*, 161.

68. Mangun, *Editor Emory O. Jackson*, 161.

69. "On the Passing of John Fitzgerald Kennedy," *The Oracle* 52, no. 4 (December 1963): 3.

70. Jesse L. Jackson, "Excellence: The Demand of the House," *The Oracle* (Summer 1964): 8–9, 19 (quotation on 9).

71. "On the Passing of John Fitzgerald Kennedy," 3.

72. "On the Passing of John Fitzgerald Kennedy," 3.

73. "On the Passing of John Fitzgerald Kennedy," 3.

74. See Atkins, "The Permanent Talent Hunt Program of the Sixth District," *The Oracle* 37, no. 4 (December 1947): 21–25.

75. Zoel S. Hargrove Jr., "Anatomy of a Talent Hunt," *The Oracle* 52, no. 4 (December 1963): 7.

76. Samuel Sharpp, "The Responsibility of the Negro College Man in [Today's] Civil Rights Struggle," *The Oracle* 54, no. 3 (September 1965): 7–9. *The Oracle* used *todays* instead of *today's* in the headline.

77. Sharpp, "Responsibility."

78. Hobson, "Tackling the Talented Tenth," 193–94; Maurice J. Hobson, "Ali and Atlanta: A Love Story in the Key of the Black New South," *Phylon* 54, no. 1 (Summer 2017): 81.

79. Hasan Kwame Jeffries, *Bloody Lowndes: Civil Rights and Black Power in Alabama's Black Belt* (New York: New York University Press, 2009), 181.

80. Edgar Amos Love, "Human Dignity, Ballots and Freedom," *The Oracle* 53, no. 3 (September 1964): 5.

81. Front matter, *The Oracle* 53, no. 3 (September 1964): 2.

82. Love, "Human Dignity."

83. John Hope Franklin and Evelyn Higginbotham, *From Slavery to Freedom: A History of African Americans*, 10th ed. (New York: McGraw-Hill, 2020), 524–26, 544–46.

84. David C. Colby, "The Voting Rights Act and Black Registration in Mississippi," *Publius* 16, no. 4 (Autumn 1986): 130 (noting the percentage of White registered voters in Mississippi increased from 69.9 to 92.4 from 1965 to 1968).

85. The cover of the March 1966 issue of *The Oracle* featured a photograph of Lawrence A. Oxley shaking a hand of Vice-President Hubert H. Humphrey Jr. as Humphrey congratulated Oxley on enactment of the Medicare bill. *The Oracle* obtained the photo from the *Pittsburgh Courier* newspaper, which included the photo on page two of its February 12, 1966, issue under the headline "Veep Meets Medicare Leader." The caption noted Oxley formerly served as special assistant to the US secretary of labor.

86. "Extension and Revision of Hill-Burton Hospital Construction Program," March 12, 1964, in *Hearings before a Subcommittee of the Committee on Interstate and Foreign Commerce, House of Representatives, Eighty-Eighth Congress, Second Session, on H.R. 10041* . . . (Washington, DC: Government Printing Office, 1964), 195–229 (quotation on 203, 204). See also Jean R. Hailey, "Lawrence A. Oxley, Civic Leader, Educator, Dies," *Washington Living New Deal Post*, July 5, 1973, 36; and "Lawrence Oxley (1887–1973)," Living New Deal, accessed February 19, 2023, https://livingnewdeal.org/glossary/lawrence-oxley-1887-1973/.

87. See Beatrix Hoffman, "The Challenge of Universal Health Care: Social Movements, Presidential Leadership and Private Power," in *Social Movements and the Transformation of American Health Care*, ed. Jane C. Banaszak-Holl, Sandra R. Levitsky, and Mayer N. Zald (New York: Oxford University Press, 2010), 23–38, esp. 44; "Lauds NMA Doctors on Medicare Stand," *Chicago Defender*, August 19, 1965, 10; "Signing of Medicare Bill Hailed by NMA Head," *Chicago Defender*, August 7, 1965, 31.

88. "Integration Battlefront: History of the Imhotep National Conference on Hospital Integration," *Journal of the National Medical Association* 54, no. 1 (January 1962): 116–119. The NMA, the Medico-Chirurgical Society of the District of Columbia, and the NAACP held the March 8–9, 1957, Imhotep National Conference on Hospital Integration at the Fifteenth Street Presbyterian Church in Washington, DC.

89. Hoffman, "Challenge," 44.

90. Hoffman, "Challenge," 44.

91. H. Carl Moultrie, "Just in Passing with the National Executive Secretary," *The Oracle* 55, no. 1 (Spring 1966): 5.

92. Social Security Amendments of 1965, Pub. L. 89–97, 79 Stat. 286 (July 30, 1965).

93. Aram Goudsouzian, *Down to the Crossroads: Civil Rights, Black Power, and the March against Fear* (New York: Farrar, Straus and Giroux, 2014). See also "15 Injured as Hundreds of Negroes Riot, Toss Rocks at Police, Smash Cars Here: Defy Allen, Repulsed by Tear Gas," *Atlanta Constitution*, September 7, 1966; Aram Goudsouzian, "Shot 55 Years Ago While Marching against Racism, James Meredith Reminds Us That Powerful Movements Can Include Those with Very Different Ideas," *Conversation*, June 2, 2021, https://theconversation.com/shot-55-years-ago-while-marching-against-racism-james-meredith-reminds-us-that-powerful-movements-can-include-those-with-very-different-ideas-161639; James Meredith, *Three Years in Mississippi* (Jackson: University Press of Mississippi, [1966] 2019), xix; James Meredith and William Doyle, *A Mission from God: A Memoir and Challenge for America* (New York: Atria Books, 2012).

94. George E. Meares, "From the Desk of the Grand Basileus," *The Oracle* 55, no. 3 (Fall 1966): 4, 6; "Last Rites for George E. Meares," *New York Amsterdam News*, February 15, 1975, A1; "Omegas Elect George E. Meares: Make Award to Mifflin Gibbs," *Baltimore Afro-*

American, May 6, 1950, 10. Chuck Cook, "Capturing History: Shooting of James Meredith," *Clarion-Ledger*, June 6, 2016.

95. Meares, "From the Desk," 4, 6; "George Meares, 65, Probation Officer," *New York Times*, February 9, 1975.

96. George E. Meares, "Reality, Reason, and Responsibility: Fundamentals for the Great Society," *The Oracle* 55, no. 4 (Winter 1966): 4.

97. Meares, "Reality, Reason, and Responsibility," 4.

98. Meares, "Reality, Reason, and Responsibility," 4. See also Associated Press, "Whites Win All Races in Lowndes County," *Birmingham Post-Herald*, November 9, 1966, 10.

99. Meares, "Reality, Reason, and Responsibility," 4.

100. Meares, "Reality, Reason, and Responsibility," 4.

101. Meares, "Reality, Reason, and Responsibility," 4.

102. Meares, "Reality, Reason, and Responsibility," 4. As introduced, one source noted, the Civil Rights Act of 1966 "barred racial discrimination in the selection of federal and state jurors, empowered the Attorney General to initiate desegregation suits and protected civil rights workers. The House added provisions empowering the Attorney General to enjoin actions depriving persons of their rights and prohibiting interstate travel for the purpose of inciting riot." *Revolution in Civil Rights* (Washington, DC: Congressional Quarterly, 1967), 85. "But in its Title IV—the open housing provision," the same source continued, "lay the seeds of its own destruction. As introduced, Title IV barred racial discrimination in the sale and rental of all housing." *Revolution in Civil Rights*, 85.

103. Langston Hughes, *Montage of a Dream Deferred* (New York: Henry Holt, 1951) (first quotation); Meares, "Reality, Reason, and Responsibility," 4 (second quotation).

104. Meares, "Reality, Reason, and Responsibility," 4.

105. Meares, "Reality, Reason, and Responsibility," 4.

106. Meares, "Reality, Reason, and Responsibility," 4 (including congressional defeat of the 1966 civil rights bill in phase two).

107. Meares, "Reality, Reason, and Responsibility," 4.

108. Meares, "Reality, Reason, and Responsibility," 4.

109. E. Franklin Frazier, *Black Bourgeoisie: The Book That Brought the Shock of Self-Revelation to Middle-Class Blacks in America* (New York: Free Press, 1957), 20. Here, Frazier noted the shift where education and behavior, features of the Black upper and middle classes, were usurped by a Black entrepreneur class, who did not seek the validation of White America. In this, tension between the Black upper and middle classes bolstered by the American Negro Academy held pejorative views toward the Black entrepreneurial class, who saw economic empowerment as their goal. Also, a full definition of racial uplift theory is the ethos of racial uplift comes from the notion of self-help or pulling oneself up by one's own bootstraps—a conservative ideology spawned during the time of the American Negro Academy. Though many proponents meant well, the idea that Black ethics and material gains sought White validation through a platform on which Black upper and middle classes acted as agents of civilization to the Black masses and that pejorative assumption was equally as damaging to Black agency and uplift as anti-Black racism bestowed on Blacks by racist Whites.

110. Meares, "Reality, Reason, and Responsibility," 4.

111. In 1947, William H. Gray Jr., president of the Florida Agricultural and Mechanical College, suggested the out-of-state scholarship program that White lawmakers and

administrators at public institutions of higher learning devised apparently originated in Missouri in 1921 to "provide a measure of educational quality for Negroes without violating the mores or racial relationships by admitting Negroes to white institutions or attempting the expensive and practically impossible task of establishing parallel and equal facilities for two races." Gray, "Recommendations of an Out-of-State Scholarship Fund for Negroes," *Journal of Negro Education* 16, no. 4 (Autumn 1947): 604.

112. Bernard W. Harleston, "Higher Education for the Negro," *Atlantic Monthly* 216, no. 5 (November 1965): 139–43.

113. Sweatt v. Painter, 339 U.S. 629 (June 5, 1950). See also "100 Years of African American Migration" (plenary session of the Association for the Study of African American Life and History, October 3, 2019, Charleston, South Carolina), C-Span, https://www.c-span.org/video/?464840-1/100-years-african-american-migrations; Derrick P. Alridge, "Teachers in the Movement: Pedagogy, Activism, and Freedom," *History of Education Quarterly* 60, no. 1 (February 2020): 1–23; Calvin Trillin, "An Education in Georgia: Charlayne Hunter, Hamilton Holmes, and the Integration of a State University," *New Yorker*, July 5, 1963.

114. George E. Meares, "From the Desk of the Grand Basileus: Northern Colleges Seek to Draw More Negroes from Southern Schools," *The Oracle* 54, no. 4 (December 1965): 7 (the *Wall Street Journal* newspaper cited the National Scholarship Service and the Fund for Negro Students for the 70 percent datum).

115. See "Black Brain Drain," *Billings Gazette* (Montana), December 29, 1968, 23, highlighting the importance of Black scholar Vincent Gordon Harding to the phrase "Black brain drain": "The same white academic institutions that helped to create the often tragic shortcomings of the Black colleges (by permitting them to languish as an academic ghetto) have entered into and are speedily intensifying what may be a deadly relationship to us," Harding wrote in a winter 1968 issue of *Columbia Forum*, continuing: "Now every Black PH.D. who has had his name mentioned twice, or who has published in the slightest review is besieged by northern, as well as southern white institutions." Vincent Harding, "Black Brain Drain," *Columbia Forum* 11, no. 3 (Fall 1968); Vincent G. Harding, "New Creation or Familiar Death: An Open Letter to Black Students in the North," *Negro Digest* XXVIII (March 1969): 5–14; "Toward the Black University," *Ebony* (August 1970): 156–59; Alex Poinsett, "The 'Brain Drain' at Negro Colleges," *Ebony* (October 1970): 74–82; "Blacks Return South," *Newsweek Atlanta*, February 20, 1974, in box 3, Newsweek Inc., Atlanta Collection, Stuart A. Rose Manuscript, Archives, and Rare Books Library, Emory University, Atlanta, GA; Fred M. Hechinger, "'Black Brain Drain' from Negro Colleges," *Kansas City Times* (Missouri), December 31, 1968, 21; and Maurice J. Hobson, *Legend of the Black Mecca: Politics and Class in the Making of Modern Atlanta* (Chapel Hill: University of North Carolina Press, 2017), 62.

116. Hobson, *Legend of the Black Mecca*, 62.

117. See John A. Hardin, *The Pursuit of Excellence: Kentucky State University, 1886–2020* (Charlotte, NC: Information Age, 2021), 120; Stephen Pickering, "Holland, James Phillip," in *The Kentucky African American Encyclopedia*, ed. Gerald L. Smith, Karen Cotton McDaniel, and John A. Hardin (Lexington: University Press of Kentucky, 2015), 249; and "Senator Names First Kentucky Negro to West Point," *Jet* 5 (March 25, 1954): 6.

118. "Edgar Amos Love to Brothers in Omega," April 5, 1966, in *The Oracle* 55, no. 2 (May 1966): 16.

119. "Edgar Amos Love to Brothers in Omega."

120. Harold D. Thompson, "Message from the Second Vice Grand Basileus," *The Oracle* 55, no. 2 (May 1966): 6.

121. Thompson, "Message," 6.

122. "Brother Coleman's Passing Leaves Void in Omega," *The Oracle* 56, no. 1 (Spring 1967): 5; H. Albion Ferrell, "Editorial," *The Oracle* 56, no. 1 (Spring 1967): 3; Omega Psi Phi Fraternity, Incorporated, International History and Archives Committee, "The History and Archives of Omega Psi Phi Fraternity 2018 Founders' Day/Centennial Armistice," November 2018, 17, Omega Psi Phi Archives (cited hereinafter as Omega History and Archives Committee, "2018 Founders' Day/Centennial Armistice").

123. "Brother Coleman's Passing Leaves Void in Omega"; Ferrell, "Editorial," 3; Omega History and Archives Committee, "2018 Founders' Day/Centennial Armistice," 17.

124. Mable R. Coleman, "Sincerest Gratitude to All," *The Oracle* 56, no. 1 (Spring 1967): 3.

125. Coleman, "Sincerest Gratitude to All."

126. "Conclave Program," *The Oracle* 56, no. 2 (Summer 1967): 4–5 (quotation on 4).

127. Ellis F. Corbett, "The Grand Basileus Speaks," *The Oracle* 56, no. 3 (Fall 1967): 4.

128. Robert L. Gill, *The Omega Psi Phi Fraternity and the Men Who Made Its History: A Concise History* (Washington, DC: Omega Psi Phi Fraternity, 1963).

129. Robert L. Gill, "What Do We Want Omega to Be?" *The Oracle* 56, no. 4 (Winter 1967): 4.

130. Corbett, "Grand Basileus Speaks"; Gill, "What Do We Want."

131. "Honors 40 Year Men," *The Oracle* 56, no. 4 (Winter 1967): 30–31 (one of several articles in the issue that referenced the National Achievement Week theme, "Wanted: Solutions to the Problems of America's Urban Society").

132. Meares, "Reality, Reason, and Responsibility," 4.

133. *The Kerner Report: The 1968 Report of the National Advisory Commission on Civil Disorders* (New York: Pantheon Books, [1968] 1988); Meares, "Reality, Reason, and Responsibility."

134. *Kerner Report*.

135. "Muhammad Ali Speaker for Beta," *The Oracle* 57, no. 2 (Summer 1968): 13–14.

136. "Muhammad Ali Speaker for Beta."; see also Hobson, *Legend of the Black Mecca*, 10, 204–205, 248, 250; Hobson, "All that Jazz: Forty Years of Influence Through the Atlanta Jazz Festival, A Brief and Concise History," in the official publication commemorating forty years of the Atlanta Jazz Festival: Forty Years. City of Atlanta, Mayor's Office of Cultural Affairs, Atlanta: Two Paths Press, 2017; Maynard Jackson Mayoral Administration Records, Robert W. Woodruff Library at the Atlanta University Center, Atlanta, box 45, folder 3.

137. "Muhammad Ali Speaker for Beta," 14.

138. "Gil Scott-Heron Receives first Omega Writing Award," *Lincolnian*, May 15, 1968, 3; Gil Scott-Herron, "WLIU Newsmen Need Help," *Lincolnian* 39, no. 6 (20 December 1968), 1.

139. Hobson, "Ali and Atlanta," 85.

140. "Muhammad Ali Speaker for Beta," 14.

141. Civil Rights Act of 1968, Pub. L. 90–284, 82 Stat. 73 (April 11, 1968).

142. Philip A. Goduti, Jr., *Robert F. Kennedy and the Shaping of Civil Rights, 1960–1964* (Jefferson, North Carolina: McFarland, 2013), 7, 224; Benjamin R. Milton, "Johnson Leads

Shocked Nation in Praying For Kennedy's Recovery," *Chicago Defender*, June 6, 1968; "RFK Suspect Identified as an Arab," *Chicago Tribune*, June 6, 1968; Dial Torgerson, "Kennedy Dies," *Los Angeles Times*, June 6, 1968; Alan L. Otten, "A Party Divided: Democrats' Rifts Post Problems for Candidates as Campaign Develops," *Wall Street Journal*, August 29, 1968; "Nixon Fishes as Chicago Burns," *Washington Post*, August 26, 1968; "Bro. Cashin Jr. Honored," *The Oracle* 58, no. 2 (Summer 1969), 24.

143. "Old Guard vs. Young Turks at Omega's Grand Conclave," *New York Amsterdam News*, January 11, 1969, 7.

144. "Old Guard vs. Young Turks."

145. "Old Guard vs. Young Turks."

146. Edgar Amos Love to Brothers in Omega; "Old Guard vs. Young Turks."

147. Edgar Amos Love to Brothers in Omega; H. Carl Moultrie, "Charlotte Grand Conclave Sets Up Constitutional Convention," *The Oracle* 53, no. 1 (Spring 1969): 6–7; "Old Guard vs. Young Turks."

148. Moultrie, "Charlotte Grand Conclave," 6; "Old Guard vs. Young Turks."

149. Moultrie, "Charlotte Grand Conclave," 6 (accidentally dating the Grand Supreme Council meeting March 29, 1969, instead of 1968); "Old Guard vs. Young Turks."

150. "Old Guard vs. Young Turks."

151. "Old Guard vs. Young Turks."

152. Ellis B. Weatherless, "Langston Hughes Dedication," *The Oracle* 58, no. 2 (Summer 1969): 6.

153. The Constitutional Convention was held October 23–24, 1969, at the Dinkler Plaza Hotel in Atlanta, Georgia. For more, see *The Oracle* 58, no. 3 (Fall 1969): 3. See the Spring 1969 issue of *The Oracle* for preview coverage of the Constitutional Convention.

154. Robert Gregory, "Editorial," *The Oracle* 58, no. 3 (Fall 1969): 3.

155. Gregory, "Editorial," 3.

156. Gregory, "Editorial," 3.

157. Gregory, "Editorial," 3.

158. Gregory, "Editorial," 3.

159. Gregory, "Editorial," 3; "Tentative Program 53rd Grand Conclave," *The Oracle* 58, no. 4 (Winter 1969): 17–19.

Chapter 6

1. "Omega Psi Phi–Coca Cola USA Announce 3rd Annual Scholarship Program," *The Oracle* 59, no. 1 (Spring 1970): 6; "Use U.S. Aid, Blacks Urged," *Pittsburgh Post-Gazette Black*, August 5, 1970, 24.

2. James S. Avery, Sr., *Others Thought I Could Lead: An Autobiography* (Tucson, AZ: Wheatmark, 2006); "Farewell Tribute to 28th Grand Basileus James S. Avery, Sr.," *The Oracle* 81, no. 24 (Summer 2011): 12–15; "Interest Mounting Over NAMD Dec 14th Meet," *Philadelphia Tribune*, December 11, 1965, 11; "Named PR Manager for Oil Company," *New York Amsterdam News*, December 7, 1968, 52; Glen E. Rice, "Interview with the Writer: 28th Grand Basileus, Brother James S. Avery, Sr.," *Omega's Clarion Call* 1, no. 2 (Summer 2007): 15–17.

3. Avery, *Others Thought I Could Lead*; "Chase Bank Official to Head UNCF's '67 Drive," *Chicago Defender*, January 21, 1967, 31; "Farewell Tribute to 28th Grand Basileus"; "Interest

Mounting Over NAMD" (one of several articles identifying Humble Oil and Refining Company, the parent company of Esso Standard Oil, as Avery's employer); "Named PR Manager for Oil Company"; Rice, "Interview with the Writer."

4. Rice, "Interview with the Writer," 16.

5. James S. Avery, "Message from the Grand Basileus," *The Oracle* 55, no. 1 (Summer 1971): 1 (cited hereinafter as Avery, "Summer 1971 Message"); "Farewell Tribute to 28th Grand Basileus"; "Named PR Manager for Oil Company."

6. Avery, "Summer 1971 Message."

7. Avery, "Summer 1971 Message."

8. Avery, "Summer 1971 Message."

9. See Avery, "Summer 1971 Message"; "National Fraternity Fights Drug Abuse," *Louisiana Weekly* (New Orleans), October 9, 1971, 12.

10. James S. Avery, "Message from the Grand Basileus," *The Oracle* 55, no. 2 (Winter 1972): 1; "National Fraternity Fights Drug Abuse."

11. See Lloyd H. Bell, "Drugs and the Black Community," *The Oracle* 55, no. 2 (Winter 1972): 5; "Dr. Bell Named to New Post at Univ. of Pittsburgh," *New Pittsburgh Courier*, May 3, 1969, 2; "Lloyd Bell," *Blue, Gold, and Black 2010*, A University of Pittsburgh Alumni Publication (Pittsburgh, PA: University of Pittsburgh, 2010), 129 (characterizing Bell as a man who "embodied the passion and defiance of the Black empowerment movement of the 1960s"); "National Fraternity Fights Drug Abuse"; "Newburgh, N. Y. Names a First," *Pittsburgh Courier*, March 14, 1964, 5; "Students Say Thanks," *New Pittsburgh Courier*, April 1, 1972, 6.

12. Vernon E. Jordan Jr. and Annette Gordon-Reed, *Vernon Can Read! A Memoir* (New York: Public Affairs, 2001); "Vernon Jordan Chosen to Head Urban League: Negro College Fund Chief to Take Post as Successor to Young before January," *Los Angeles Times*, June 16, 1971, 7.

13. Vernon E. Jordan Jr., "America at the Crossroads: Let Us, Mount Up with Wings as Eagles," *The Oracle* 55, no. 2 (Winter 1972): 25.

14. Jordan, "America at the Crossroads," 25.

15. Benjamin E. Mays, "In Honor of Brothers Cooper and Coleman," *The Oracle* 55, no. 3 (Fall 1972): 4 (vignette).

16. John Herbert Roper Sr., *The Magnificent Mays: A Biography of Benjamin Elijah Mays* (Columbia: University of South Carolina Press, 2021), 212 (first quotation), 262 (second quote). See also Randal Maurice Jelks, *Benjamin Elijah Mays, Schoolmaster of the Movement: A Biography* (Chapel Hill: University of North Carolina Press, 2014); Mays, "In Honor of Brothers Cooper and Coleman," 1–4; and Benjamin E. Mays, *Born to Rebel: An Autobiography* (Athens: University of Georgia Press, 2003). Mays instructed mathematics at Morehouse College from 1921 to 1924.

17. Otto McLarrin, "The Editor Speaks," *The Oracle* 55, no. 3 (Fall 1972): 42; Mays, "In Honor of Brothers Cooper and Coleman."

18. Mays, "In Honor of Brothers Cooper and Coleman," 2.

19. Mays, "In Honor of Brothers Cooper and Coleman," 2.

20. Mays, "In Honor of Brothers Cooper and Coleman," 1–2.

21. Mays, "In Honor of Brothers Cooper and Coleman," 2.

22. Mays, "In Honor of Brothers Cooper and Coleman," 3.

23. Mays, "In Honor of Brothers Cooper and Coleman," 3.

24. Mays, "In Honor of Brothers Cooper and Coleman," 3.

25. Mays, "In Honor of Brothers Cooper and Coleman," 3.

26. Mays, "In Honor of Brothers Cooper and Coleman," 3.

27. Otto McLarrin, "Omega Chapter! Alexander Looby," *The Oracle* 56, no. 2 (Summer 1973): 14.

28. Otto McLarrin, "The Editor Speaks," *The Oracle* 56, no. 2 (Summer 1973): 29; Frankie Patterson, "Alpha Omega Chapter Salutes 'Mr. Omega,'" *The Oracle* 56, no. 2 (Summer 1973): 16.

29. *Newsweek*, February 19, 1973, cover.

30. Vernon E. Jordan Jr., "What Ever Happened to Black America?" *Newsweek*, February 19, 1973, 29–34.

31. Patterson, "Alpha Omega Chapter Salutes," 16.

32. Edward Lewis, "The Involvement of Blacks in the Field of Business," *The Oracle* 56, no. 2 (Summer 1973): 1–3; George Wiley, "The Involvement of Blacks in the Social Problems," *The Oracle* 56, no. 2 (Summer 1973): 4–11.

33. Lewis, "Involvement of Blacks."

34. Lewis, "Involvement of Blacks," 3; Vernon E. Jordan Jr., "Survival," in *Representative American Speeches: 1971–1972*, ed. Waldo W. Braden (New York: H. W. Wilson, 1972), 49–58, stating: "The drive for political empowerment must go hand-in-hand with the drive for economic empowerment. It's not enough to point with pride at black income figures creeping slowly, point by point, to levels still less than two-thirds of white income. Economic empowerment means putting green dollars into black pockets and filling jobs at all levels with skilled black workers" (p. 56).

35. Lewis, "Involvement of Blacks," 3.

36. Nick Kotz and Mary Lynn Kotz, *A Passion for Equality: George Wiley and the Movement* (New York: W. W. Norton, [1977] 1979).

37. Wiley, "Involvement of Blacks," 8.

38. See "Fraternity Urges Stamp Honoring Langston Hughes," *Chicago Daily Defender*, September 19, 1970, 11; and "Omega Chapter, Brother and Founder Edgar Amos Love, September 10, 1891–May 1, 1974," *The Oracle* 57, no. 1 (Spring 1974): 36.

39. "Brother Bishop Edgar Love Is Dead! Omegas Pay Final Tribute to Last of Four Founders," *The Oracle* 57, no. 1 (Spring 1974): 33.

40. J. Samuel Cook, "Of Vison and Power: The Life of Bishop Edgar Amos Love" (master's thesis, University of Toledo, 2009), 1, 86 (noting Virginia Lattier-Love was the niece of the *Baltimore Afro-American*'s publisher, Carl J. Murphy Jr.; the great-great-granddaughter of its founder, John H. Murphy; and the daughter of George Lottier and Arnetta Murphy Lottier). See also "1,200 Attend Rites for Bishop Love," *Baltimore Afro-American*, May 18, 1974, 5; "Bishop Love, Last Founder of Omega, Dead at 82," *Baltimore Afro-American*, May 11, 1974, 3; and "Brother Bishop Edgar Love Is Dead!"

41. "Brother Bishop Edgar Love Is Dead!"

42. "Brother Bishop Edgar Love Is Dead!"

43. "Brother Bishop Edgar Love Is Dead!"

44. Kenan Heise, "Cook County Judge Marion W. Garnet, 76," *Chicago Tribune*, November 16, 1995, sec. 2, 14; "Name 13 New Circuit Judges," *Chicago Tribune*, March 13, 1974, 10.

45. "1,200 Attend Rites for Bishop Love."

46. "Omegas to Aid Starving West Africans: Africare Omega Psi Phi Cares Project to Raise for 10 Million Africans," *The Oracle* 57, no. 1 (Spring 1974): 50.

47. "Omegas to Aid Starving West Africans."

48. Emily Langer, "C. Payne Lucas, Leader of Relief Efforts across Africa, Dies at 85," *Washington Post*, September 20, 2018, www.washingtonpost.com/local/obituaries/c-payne-lucas-leader-of-relief-efforts-across-africa-dies-at-85/2018/09/20/78d97e92-bc4b-11e8-8792-78719177250f_story.html.

49. "Omegas to Aid Starving West Africans."

50. "Memorial to Our Founders," *The Oracle* 59, no. 3 (Fall 1974): 1.

51. "Memorial to Our Founders."

52. See Mary McLeod Bethune, *Building a Better World: Essays and Selected Documents*, ed. Audrey Thomas McKluskey and Elaine M. Smith (Bloomington: Indiana University Press, 1999); Nancy J. Giddens, "The Mary McLeod Bethune Week in Washington, D. C.," *Philadelphia Tribune*, July 16, 1974, 17; Evelyn Brooks Higginbotham, *Righteous Discontent: The Women's Movement in the Black Baptist Church, 1880–1920* (Cambridge, MA: Harvard University Press, 1994); Daina Ramey Berry and Kali Nicole Gross, *A Black Women's History of the United States* (New York: Beacon, 2021), 140, 146; Martha S. Jones, *Vanguard: How Black Women Broke Barriers, Won the Vote, and Insisted on Equality for All* (New York: Basic Books, 2020), xi, 207, 217–26, 254, 264, 310n16; "Mary McLeod Bethune," *Chicago Defender*, July 17, 1974, 15; Samuel R. Shepard, "Mary McLeod Bethune Memorial Dedication," *The Oracle* 59, no. 3 (Fall 1974): 12–13; Helene Southern Slater, "Washington Salutes Mrs. Bethune in Stirring Unveiling Ceremonies: The Legacy of Mary McLeod Bethune Is Unveiled and Enshrined," *New York Amsterdam News*, July 20, 1974, A1; and Jill Watts, *Black Cabinet: The Untold Story of African Americans and Politics during the Age of Roosevelt* (New York: Grove Atlantic, 2020). Brother Alfred S. Carter, Jr., spearheaded recognition of women's contributions through the Social Action Committee of Washington's Delta Theta chapter. While members of Omega Psi Phi worked on behalf of all Black people, a prevailing notion within the Fraternity regarding men knowing what was best for all people was patriarchal. The authors of this book recognize, without reservation, the need for Omega Psi Phi do better supporting women—on their terms—going forward.

53. Otto McLarrin, "High Blood Pressure, Rather than Sickle Cell Anemia Is the Real Killer among America's Black Population," *The Oracle* 59, no. 3 (Fall 1974): 16–17..

54. Otto McLarrin, "Happiness through Health," *Louisiana Weekly* (New Orleans), July 26, 1975, sec. 2, 5.

55. McLarrin, "High Blood Pressure."

56. McLarrin,"High Blood Pressure."

57. McLarrin, "High Blood Pressure," 152.

58. McLarrin, "High Blood Pressure."

59. Otto McLarrin, "Colonel Simon H. Scott, Jr., Command Chaplain of Air Force Chaplains in NATO Countries," *The Oracle* 60, no. 2 and 3 (Spring–Summer 1975): 1.

60. "The Law, Economics, and You," *The Oracle* 59, no. 3 (Spring–Summer 1975): 4–8, 28.

61. "The Law, Economics, and You."

62. "The Law, Economics, and You."

63. Earl G. Graves, "Leaning on the Shield," *The Oracle* 60, no. 1 (Winter 1975): 2–5, 52–55; "Omega Psi Phi Conclave in Arizona," *New Amsterdam News*, January 4, 1975, B6.

64. Graves, "Leaning on the Shield," 5 (full quotation), 53 (partial quote).

65. Graves, "Leaning on the Shield," 5.

66. Graves, "Leaning on the Shield," 5.
67. Graves, "Leaning on the Shield," 5.
68. Graves, "Leaning on the Shield," 5.
69. Emory Jackson, "Elijah Muhammad," *The Oracle* 60, no. 1 (Winter 1975): 23.
70. John Stevenson Marshall Kilimanjaro, "Elijah Muhammad's Success in the Plight of the Black Man: Elijah Muhammad as Salaam Aleikum," *The Oracle* 60, no. 1 (Winter 1975): 23.
71. Vernon Jordan, "Toward an Integrated Society," *The Oracle* 60, no. 1 (Winter 1975): 38.
72. Jordan, "Toward an Integrated Society," 38.
73. Jordan, "Toward an Integrated Society," 40.
74. Jordan, "Toward an Integrated Society," 40.
75. Jordan, "Toward an Integrated Society," 39.
76. Jordan, "Toward an Integrated Society," 39.
77. McLarrin, "High Blood Pressure."
78. McLarrin, "High Blood Pressure."
79. The Avery Institute was an American Missionary Association affiliated school founded as the Avery Normal Institute in 1865. It became the leading accredited institution in the South Carolina low country. In 1990, it joined the College of Charleston and now is known as the Avery Research Center for African American History and Culture.
80. "Chaplain Scott Is Distinguished Lecturer," *The Oracle* 60, no. 2 and 3 (Spring–Summer 1975): 1, 25; John E. Groh, *Air Force Chaplains 1971–1980* (Washington, DC: Department of the Air Force, 1986), 527; "Military Chaplaincy Means a Total Ministry: In Memory of Dr. Martin Luther King, Jr.," *The Oracle* 60, no. 2 and 3 (Spring–Summer 1975): 2; "Military Life as a Chaplain," *The Oracle* 60, no. 2 and 3 (Spring–Summer 1975): 3; Simon H. Scott Jr., "AF Command Chaplain Pleased with Article," *The Oracle* 60, no. 4 (Fall 1975): 60; Samuel Shepard, "Colonel Simon H. Scott, Jr.: Command Chaplain of Air Force Chaplains in NATO Countries," *The Oracle* 60, no. 2 and 3 (Spring–Summer 1975): 1. In 1961, Scott finished the Air Force Human Factors Course of the Hogg Foundation at the University of Texas in Austin. Along with his other training, the course served him well when he began supervising air force chaplains in England, Germany, Greece, Holland, Italy, and Turkey. Scott also supervised chaplains in Spain, which was not a member of the North Atlantic Treaty Organization in early 1975.
81. Marion W. Garnett, "Monument to Our Founders Forever Consecrated and Dedicated in Granite," *The Oracle* 61, no. 1 (Spring 1976): 2.
82. "Marker Unveiled to Dr. Carter G. Woodson in Va.," *New Pittsburgh Courier*, January 3, 1976. See also "Circle of Friends Honor Dr. Woodson," *New Journal and Guide* (Norfolk, VA), January 10, 1976, 6; J. Rupert Picott, "Editorial Comment: ASALH National Historical Marker Project," *Negro History Bulletin* 39, no. 4 (April 1, 1976): 561.
83. "Roy Wilkins Reports on 27 Years of Civil Rights Achievements," *The Oracle* 61, no. 1 (Spring 1976): 10, 22–23, 26, 31, 46–48.
84. "Roy Wilkins Reports," 10.
85. "Roy Wilkins Reports," 10.
86. "Roy Wilkins Reports," 10.
87. "Roy Wilkins Reports," 10.
88. "Roy Wilkins Reports," 10.
89. "Roy Wilkins Reports," 22.

90. Samuel R. Shepard, "Random Thoughts on Eve of the Grand Conclave," *The Oracle* 61, no. 2 (Summer 1976): 1.

91. Shepard, "Random Thoughts."

92. "Eddie Williams, Activist, 84; Pushed Black Advancement," *New York Times*, May 14, 2017, A24; Eddie N. Williams, "Wanted: Omega Men to Lead Voter Mobilization Effort," *The Oracle* 61, no. 2 (Summer 1976): 34–35, 51, 60.

93. See, among other sources, Ernest B. Ferguson, "Black People Returning South," *Atlanta Constitution*, August 12, 1971, 4A; Maurice J. Hobson, *Legend of the Black Mecca: Politics and Class in the Making of Modern Atlanta* (Chapel Hill: University of North Carolina Press, 2017); and Williams, "Wanted," 34–35.

94. Williams, "Wanted," 35.

95. Williams, "Wanted," 35.

96. Williams, "Wanted," 35.

97. Williams, "Wanted," 35.

98. Williams, "Wanted," 35.

99. Williams, "Wanted," 34.

100. Williams, "Wanted," 34.

101. "Ford Hails Observance of 'Black History Month,'" *Jet* 49, no. 23 (March 4, 1976): 27. See also "Afro-American History Association Dedicates Marker to Colonel Young," *The Oracle* 61, no. 3 (Fall 1976): 29; "Circle of Friends Honor Dr. Woodson"; "Marker Unveiled to Dr. Carter G. Woodson"; and Picott, "Editorial Comment."

102. "Afro-American History Association Dedicates Marker"; "Bicentennial Honors: Dr. E. E. Just Honored by Black History Association," *The Oracle* 61, no. 3 (Winter 1977): 10; "Memory of E. E. Just to Be Honored at State College," *Times and Democrat* (Orangeburg, SC), November 19, 1976, 3B; "On Campus," *Pittsburgh Courier*, December 25, 1976, 11.

103. "We Salute the Buffalo Soldier," *The Oracle* 61, no. 3 (Fall 1976): 4.

104. "We Salute the Buffalo Soldier."

105. See Hubert Jackson and Jackie Steele, "A Bicentennial Salute to the Black American Soldier," *The Oracle* 61, no. 3 (Fall 1976): 4–5, 42, 59–60; and Emmett J. Scott, *Scott's Official History of the American Negro in the World War* (Chicago: Homewood, 1919), 193, writing, "The 367th Infantry regiment was a part of the first contingent of the 92nd Division that sailed for overseas, leaving the port of embarkation at Hoboken, N. J., on June 19, 1918[; the] regiment made a notable record in France—the entire First Battalion of the 367th [Buffalo] Infantry being cited for bravery and awarded the Croix de Guerre, thus entitling every officer and man in the battalion to wear this distinguished French decoration."

106. Jackson and Steele, "Bicentennial Salute," 5, 42.

107. Jackson and Steele, "Bicentennial Salute," 42.

108. Mary Church Terrell, *A Colored Woman in a White World* (Salem, NH: Ayer, 1940 [1986]), 427. See also Patrick H. Walker Jr., "Mary Church Terrell: A Forgotten Black Feminist," *The Oracle* 61, no. 2 (Summer 1976): 32; and United States National Archives and Records Administration, "Mary Church Terrell (September 23, 1863–July 24, 1954)," January 5, 2021, www.archives.gov/research/african-americans/individuals/mary-church-terrell.

109. After much contention with members of the NAACP board of directors, Omega man Roy O. Wilkins retired from the executive directorship on July 1, 1977. A second Omega man, William M. Cobb, the NAACP's first Black president, headed the search

committee for Wilkins's successor. See, among other contemporaneous sources, "NAACP Board Is Unanimous: Benjamin Hooks Chosen Successor to Roy Wilkins," *The Oracle* 61, no. 3 (Fall 1976): 3; Jacqueline Trescott, "Benjamin L. Hooks: 'Wilkins Is a Hard Act to Follow,'" *Washington Post*, July 1, 1977; and United Press International, "Roy Wilkins Relinquishes NAACP Post," *Fort Lauderdale News*, July 1, 1977, 16A.

110. Benjamin L. Hooks, *The March for Civil Rights: The Benjamin Hooks Story* (Chicago: American Bar Association, 2003); documentation of Benjamin L. Hooks's initiation into Epsilon Phi chapter in Memphis on November 17, 1942, is in possession of authors.

111. Hooks, *March for Civil Rights*; Lucas Johnson II, "Civil Rights Leader Revived NAACP," *Miami Herald*, April 16, 2010, 5A.

112. Trescott, "Benjamin L. Hooks."

113. "NAACP Board Is Unanimous"; Trescott, "Benjamin L. Hooks."

114. "Charter Presentation Pi Xi Chapter Nassau," *The Oracle* 61, no. 3 (Winter 1977): 6–8, 58; Peter L. Mitchell, "History of Pi Xi Chapter: 1977–2018," Pi Xi Chapter, accessed June 6, 2021, https://pixichapter.com/history-of-pi-xi-chapter/.

115. The Theta Rho chapter of Omega Psi Phi was headquartered in Frankfurt, Germany, but served the entire European continent.

116. "Omega Psi Phi Fraternity, Incorporated, 58th Grand Conclave Program," *The Oracle* 61, no. 3 (Winter 1977): 5, 89.

117. John P. Murchison, "Bringing Our Mainstream Climate into Our Ghettos," *The Oracle* 61, no. 3 (Winter 1977): 19.

118. Murchison, "Bringing Our Mainstream," 19.

119. Andrew Bell, "Omega and Community Development," *The Oracle* 61, no. 3 (Winter 1977): 20, 44.

120. Bell, "Omega and Community Development," 44.

121. Bell, "Omega and Community Development," 44.

122. Regents of the University of California v. Bakke, 438 U.S. 265 (June 28, 1978).

123. Cornell Law School Legal Information Institute, "Regents of the University of California v. Bakke (1978)," last updated December 2020, www.law.cornell.edu/wex/regents_of_the_university_of_california_v_bakke_(1978)#:~:text=Primary%20tabs-,Regents%20of%20the%20University%20of%20California%20v.,Civil%20Rights%20Act%20of%201964.

124. James A. Fussell, "Advocate Harold Holliday Dies at 62," *Kansas City Star*, November 20, 2005, B1, B3, noting Harold Lee Holliday Sr. was the first Black person to be graduated from the Kansas City (later Missouri-Kansas) School of Law; Harold L. "Doc" Holliday Jr., "Response by Brother Holliday Stresses Role of Politics: Bakke Case Real Threat," *The Oracle* 62, no. 1 (Spring 1978): 9, 11, 73—"Bakke Case Another Product of Voter Apathy" was a secondary title; Holliday's speech commenced on p. 9; "Harold Lee Holliday, Jr.," *Kansas City Star*, November 22, 2005, B2; William W. Sutton, "Outstanding Citizen for 1977: Harold L. 'Doc' Holliday, Jr.," *The Oracle* 62, no. 1 (Spring 1978): 9–10.

125. Holliday, "Response by Brother Holliday," 11.

126. "17 Omega Brothers among Ebony Magazine's 100 Most Influential Black Americans," *The Oracle* 62, no. 2 (Summer 1978): 7.

127. "17 Omega Brothers," 7.

128. "Major Frederick Drew Gregory[,] Veteran Air Force Pilot," *The Oracle* 62, no. 2 (Summer 1978): 9; "Ronald Erwin McNair, Ph.D.[,] Civilian Physicist," *The Oracle* 62, no. 2

(Summer 1978): 9, 77; "Two Omega Brothers in Space Shuttle Program," *The Oracle* 62, no. 2 (Summer 1978): 8–9.

129. "Major Frederick Drew Gregory"; "The United States Navy Launches the USNS Charles R. Drew in Honor of a True American Pioneer," *The Oracle* 80, no. 21 (Spring 2010): 13.

130. William Drummond, "First Negro Astronaut Killed in Jet Fighter Crash at Edwards," *Los Angeles Times*, December 9, 1967, 1; Barbara C. Lawrence, "Maj. Robert H. Lawrence," *Ebony* 39, no. 4 (February 1984): 16—a letter to the editor requesting *Ebony* issue a corrective to a November 1983 article by Walter Leavy that claimed her husband, Robert H. Lawrence Jr., was piloting the F-104 Starfighter supersonic jet at the time of the fatal runway crash on December 8, 1967: *Ebony* complied with the request; Walter Leavy, "Lt. Colonel Guion S. Bluford Jr. Takes . . . A Historic Step into Outer Space," *Ebony* 39, no.1 (November 1983): 163–64, 166, 169, 170; "Two Omega Brothers in Space Shuttle Program," 8–9; United Press International, "Crash Kills Astronaut: Negro Spaceman Dies in Jet Accident," *South Bend Tribune* (Indiana), December 9, 1967, 1.

131. Willie J. Wright, "Has the National Pan-Hellenic Council Outlived Its Usefulness?" *The Oracle* 62, no. 2 (Summer 1978): 13–15.

132. Charles Wright, "Our Most Endangered Species: The Black Leader," *The Oracle* 63, no. 4 (Winter 1979): 9.

133. Wright, "Our Most Endangered Species," 9.

134. Wright, "Our Most Endangered Species," 9.

135. Wright, "Our Most Endangered Species," 9.

136. Wright, "Our Most Endangered Species," 9–10.

137. Wright, "Our Most Endangered Species," 9–10.

138. See "Black Doctor Killed Under 'Suspicious Circumstances,'" *Crisis* 90, no. 4 (April 1983): 23; William Montague Cobb, "Thomas Hency Brewer, Sr., M.D., 1894–1956," *Journal of the National Medical Association* 48, no. 3 (May 1956): 191–93; and Wright, "Our Most Endangered Species."

139. "Black Doctor Killed Under 'Suspicious Circumstances,'" 23; Cobb, "Thomas Hency Brewer, Sr."; Wright, "Our Most Endangered Species." An article in the April 1983 issue of *Crisis* discussed Thomas Hency Brewer Jr. asserting that a grand jury "refused to indict [Lucio] Flowers and the case was dropped." "Black Doctor Killed Under 'Suspicious Circumstances,'" 23. Brewer, in the same *Crisis* article, recounted a long-held suspicion among some Black people in Columbus, Georgia, that police officers killed Flowers to "suppress the truth" about the February 18, 1956, murder of Brewer Sr. "Black Doctor Killed Under 'Suspicious Circumstances,'" 23.

140. Wright, "Our Most Endangered Species," 10–11.

141. Wright, "Our Most Endangered Species," 10.

142. Kenneth R. Janken, "Vigilante Injustice," chap. 1 in *The Wilmington Ten: Violence, Injustice, and the Rise of Black Politics in the 1970s* (Chapel Hill: University of North Carolina Press, 2015), 11–42; Alex Kotlowitz, "Benjamin Chavis: A Bridge Too Far?" *New York Times*, June 12, 1994, sec. 6, 41.

143. See Associated Press, "Last Defendant in a Firebombing Is Released from Carolina Prison," *New York Times*, December 15, 1979, 10; Benjamin E. Chavis Jr., *Psalms from Prison* (New York: Pilgrim, 1983); John L. Godwin, *Black Wilmington and the North Carolina Way: Portrait of a Community in the Era of Civil Rights Protest* (Lanham, MD: University

Press of America, 2000); Janken, *Wilmington Ten*; Wayne King, "The Case against the Wilmington Ten," *New York Times*, December 3, 1978; Wayne Moore, *Triumphant Warrior: Memoir of Soul Survivor of the Wilmington Ten* (Ann Arbor, MI: Warrior, 2014); "Wilmington 10 Decision Draws Sharp Criticism," *Jet* 53, no. 21 (February 9, 1978): 9; and, among other sources, Wright, "Our Most Endangered Species," 10–11.

144. Wright, "Our Most Endangered Species," 10–11.

145. Hobson, *Legend of the Black Mecca*, 137 (first quotation); Wright, "Our Most Endangered Species," 10 (second quotation).

146. Associated Press, "Last Defendant"; Wright, "Our Most Endangered Species."

147. Wright, "Our Most Endangered Species," 12.

148. "I've Been 'Buked and I've Been Scorned," written and performed by the Tuskegee Institute Singers, Victor 18774-A, 10, 78 rpm, recorded on February 14, 1916, and released in 1918.

149. United States Department of Commerce, *Statistical Abstract of the United States 1992* (Washington, DC: US Department of Commerce, 1992), (cited hereinafter as US Commerce Dept., *1992 Statistical Abstract*); Hobson, *Legend of the Black Mecca*, 142–43; "Mattingly Urges Crackdown on All Cocaine Dealers," *Atlanta Daily World*, July 13, 1986. Here, US senator Mack Mattingly (R-GA) cosponsored legislation aimed at tightening the legal loopholes that protected cocaine dealers from prosecution.

150. US Commerce Dept., *1992 Statistical Abstract*.

151. US Commerce Dept., *1992 Statistical Abstract*.

152. US Commerce Dept., *1992 Statistical Abstract*.

153. Peniel Joseph, "From Ronald Reagan in Philadelphia, Miss., to Donald Trump in Tulsa: A Pattern of Racially Divisive Politics," *Washington Post*, June 19, 2020.

154. Maurice Hobson, "Behold the Black New South: How Black America Saved American Democracy through the Prism of the 2020 Election," Featured Editorial, *The Signal— the Office Organ of the Southeastern Region*, Sigma Pi Phi Fraternity (The Boulé), December 2020.

155. David Axelrod, "Washington Elected: City Has First Black Mayor," *Chicago Tribune*, April 13, 1983, 1, 4; Fred Barnes, "Jackson Aims at Other Election Challenges," April 15, 1983, *Baltimore Sun*, A12. Jesse Jackson's Rainbow Coalition of the 1980s was rooted in Chicago Black Panther Fred Hampton's conceptualization of the Rainbow Coalition in the 1960s. See Jakobi Williams, *From the Bullet to the Ballot: The Illinois Chapter of the Black Panther Party and Racial Coalition Politics in Chicago* (Chapel Hill: University of North Carolina Press, 2015).

156. Felmon D. Motley, "Omega Participates in Civil Rights Conference," *The Oracle* 67, no. 3 (Fall 1983): 4.

157. Felmon D. Motley, "62nd Grand Conclave in Kansas City, MO," *The Oracle* 67, no. 3 (Fall 1983): 5–6; "National Leaders Speak to Omega Brothers and Families at Conclave," *Philadelphia Tribune*, September 13, 1983, 18, reporting Omega Psi Phi contributed more than $25,000 to various causes during the Kansas City Conclave.

158. Lynn Beckwith Jr., "Omega: Striving for Excellence in Every Endeavor," *The Oracle* 67, no. 3 (Fall 1983): 120. See also "Burnel Elton Coulon," *Indianapolis Star*, September 2, 2018, 27A; Chollie Herndon, "It Says Here," *New York Age*, November 15, 1958, 22; *Jackson Advocate* (Mississippi), January 14, 1956, 7; Motley, "62nd Grand Conclave"; "Newsmakers of the Week: Roundup of the Week's Newsmakers," *Baltimore Afro-American*, November 22, 1957, 7; "Three Tuskegee Residents Given Student Honor," *Tuskegee Herald*, No-

vember 4, 1952, 1; Cynthia Jones Sadler, "Standing in the Shadows: African American Informants and Allies of the Mississippi State Sovereignty Commission" (PhD diss., University of Memphis, 2011), 67; Members of the Lambda Epsilon chapter of Omega Psi Phi at Tuskegee Institute initiated Burnel E. Coulon on November 15, 1950.

159. *The Oracle* 67, no. 3 (Fall 1983): cover; "Omegas Observe Black History Month during February," *The Oracle* 67, no. 3 (Fall 1983): 16.

160. *The Oracle* 67, no. 3 (Fall 1983): cover.

161. Darren Young, "Theta Rho Entertains Rev. Jesse Jackson on Army Sponsored Tour," *The Oracle* 67, no. 3 (Fall 1983): 1.

162. "Senator L. Douglas Wilder: Led Nine-Year Fight for Rev. Martin Luther King, Jr. Holiday in the State of Virginia," *The Oracle* 67, no. 3 (Fall 1983): cover; Maurice J. Hobson, "The King of Atlanta: Martin Luther King Jr. and Public Memory," Black Perspectives, April 3, 2018, www.aaihs.org/the-king-of-atlanta-martin-luther-king-jr-and-public-memory/.

163. For more on the myriad of opinions and studies on social issues in the 1980s, see Leon Dash, *Rosa Lee: A Mother and Her Family in Urban America* (New York: Basic Books, 1996); Daina Ramey Berry and Kali Nicole Gross, *A Black Women's History of the United States* (Boston: Beacon Press), 200–202; Milton Coleman, "Jackson Launches 1984 Candidacy," *Washington Post*, November 4, 1983, A1.

164. Freeman Holifield, "International Chapter Entertains the Grand Basileus in Germany," *The Oracle* 67, no. 3 (Fall 1983): 2–3 (quotation on 3).

165. National Collegiate Athletic Association, "Convention Agenda to Focus on Academics, Membership," *NCAA News* 19, no. 33 (January 5, 1983): 1, 12.

166. National Collegiate Athletic Association, "Convention Agenda," 1, 12.

167. Steve Berkowitz, "Thompson Stages Protest, Walks Out of Game," *Washington Post*, 15 January 1989, A1.

168. See, for example, Frederick S. Humphries, "Who Will Be Hit Hardest by Proposition 48?" *New York Times*, January 17, 1983, C4.

169. Humphries, "Who Will Be Hit." A 1988 article in the *New York Times* indicated Proposition 48 disqualified 213 of 274, or 77.7 percent, of recruits since 1986. Of those 213, according to the article, 185, or 86.8 percent, were Black. Those numbers seemed to corroborate the basic ideas Humphries presented in 1983—primarily, that standardized tests on which Proposition 48 depended were biased, often correlating with socioeconomic status or cultural exposure. Associated Press, "Blacks Hit Harder by Proposition 48, Survey Shows," *New York Times*, September 9, 1988, A25.

170. "Jesse Jackson Blasts NCAA," *Arizona Republic*, January 20, 1983, E4.

171. "Jesse Jackson Blasts NCAA."

172. "Jesse Jackson Blasts NCAA."

173. "Jesse Jackson Blasts NCAA."

174. L. Benjamin Livingston, "Grand Basileus Speaks," *The Oracle* 68, no. 1 (Summer-Fall 1984): 2.

175. Evans Witt, "Debate Helps Define Differences, Agreements among Candidates," *Durham Sun* (North Carolina), January 16, 1984, 3B.

176. "Witt, "Debate Helps Define Differences."

177. Dudley Clendinen, "Big Winner in Democrats' Debate: The Format," *Berkshire Eagle* (Pittsfield, MA), January 16, 1984, 10.

178. Clendinen, "Big Winner."

179. Maulana Karenga, "Jesse Jackson and the Presidential Campaign: The Invitation and Oppositions of History," *Black Scholar* 15, no. 5 (September–October 1984): 57–71.

180. Fay S. Joyce, "Jackson Admits Saying 'Hymie' and Apologizes at a Synagogue," *New York Times*, February 27, 1984, A16.

181. "Transcript of Mondale Address Accepting Party Nomination," *New York Times*, July 20, 1984, A12.

182. L. Benjamin Livingston, "The Grand Basileus Speaks," *The Oracle* 68, no. 2 (Winter 1985): 2.

183. "Moses C. Norman, 82: Pioneering Atlanta Educator was Influential, Inspirational," *Atlanta Journal-Constitution*, July 6, 2017, B2.

184. "Moses C. Norman, 82."

185. Moses C. Norman, "A Message from Our Grand," *The Oracle* 68, no. 3 and 4 (Summer–Fall 1985): 5.

186. Benjamin Foster, "No Place for the Homeless," *The Oracle* 68, no. 3 and 4 (Summer–Fall 1985): 19–20.

187. Civil Rights Act of 1968, Pub. L. No. 90–284, 82 Stat. 73 (April 11, 1968).

188. Foster, "No Place for the Homeless," *The Oracle* 68, no. 3 and 4 (Summer–Fall 1985): 19–20.

189. Foster, "No Place for the Homeless," 19.

190. Foster, "No Place for the Homeless," 19.

191. Foster, "No Place for the Homeless," 19.

192. "Mattingly Urges Crackdown on All Cocaine Dealers," *Atlanta Daily World*, July 13, 1986, 7. US senator Mack Francis Mattingly, a Republican from Georgia, cosponsored legislation to close legal loopholes protecting cocaine dealers from prosecution.

193. Hobson, *Legend of the Black Mecca*, 143; "Mattingly Urges Crackdown on All Cocaine Dealers," 7.

194. Hobson, *Legend of the Black Mecca*, 143.

195. Robert A. Bennett, "Economic Scene: Slump's Effect on the Banks," *New York Times*, October 22, 1982, D2; Robert Shogan, "Bush Ends His Waiting Game, Attacks Reagan," *Los Angeles Times*, April 14, 1980, 20, part 1.

196. Associated Press, "Farrakhan Closes African-American Summit," *Charlotte Observer* (North Carolina), April 24, 1989, 2A; Farrakhan became a member of the Fraternity in 2019.

197. Associated Press, "Farrakhan Closes."

198. Associated Press, "Farrakhan Closes."

199. Hobson, *Legend of the Black Mecca*, 143.

200. "Dedication and Unveiling of the Charles Richard Drew Memorial Marker," *The Oracle* 70, no. 1 (Winter 1986–1987): 4–5.

201. "A Farewell to Mr. Omega," *The Oracle* 70, no. 1 (Winter 1986–1987): 3; United Press International, "A Brother Remembered," *The Oracle* 69, no. 4 (Summer–Fall 1986): 52.

202. Moses C. Norman, "The Grand Basileus Speaks," *The Oracle* 70, no. 1 (Winter 1986–1987): 2.

203. Norman, "Grand Basileus Speaks."

204. Norman, "Grand Basileus Speaks."

205. Norman, "Grand Basileus Speaks."

206. Darryl Robinson, "Omega: A House Divided," *The Oracle* 69, no. 4 (Summer–Fall 1986): 7.
207. Robinson, "Omega."
208. Robinson, "Omega."
209. Robinson, "Omega."
210. Robinson, "Omega."
211. "Atomic Dog," written by George Clinton, Garry Shider, and David Spradley, and performed by Clinton, track two, side two, on *Computer Games*, Capitol ST-12246, 33⅓ rpm, released originally on November 5, 1982.
212. Robinson, "Omega."
213. "On the Youth Leadership Council," Omega Educational Foundation, accessed 26 November 2023, https://omegaeducationalfoundation.org/.
214. Bernard S. Little, "Omicron Gamma Sponsors Blood Drive," *The Oracle* 68, no. 2 (Winter 1985): 4.
215. "Upsilon Nu Welcomes Two: Awesome," *The Oracle* 71, no. 1 (Fall 1988): 34.

Chapter 7

1. C. Tyrone Gilmore, "The Grand Basileus Speaks...," *The Oracle* [72, no.] 1 (Fall–Winter 1990–91): 11.
2. Interview with several brothers conducted by Maurice Hobson, October 20, 2020. These interviews were conducted via Zoom and the names of the members are anonymous. The sentiments from the early 1990s echoed what the Fraternity's scholarship committee noted in 1954 (see page 159) when they wondered about why fewer Omega man earned Phi Beta Kappa membership than had been done in the 1920s. The tensions around membership were old, as the Fraternity had long focused on the best way to vet future Omega men.
3. C. Tyrone Gilmore, "Grand Basileus Speaks...," *The Oracle* 72, no. 3 (Summer–Fall 1991): 2.
4. "Go back and fetch it" is one common translation of *Sankofa*, a term for wisdom that many sources credit the Akan people of Ghana with coining, as in the proverb "Se wo were fi na wo Sankofa a yenkyi" ("It is not a taboo to go back and retrieve if you forget"). Clinton Crawford, *Recasting Ancient Egypt in the African Context: Toward a Model Curriculum Using Art and Language* (Trenton, NJ: Africa World, 1996), frontispiece.
5. Maurice J. Hobson, "Tackling the Talented Tenth: Black Greek-Lettered Organizations and the Black New South," in *The Black Intellectual Tradition: African American Thought in the Twentieth Century*, ed. Derrick P. Alridge, Cornelius L. Bynum, and James B. Stewart (Urbana: University of Illinois Press, 2021), 176.
6. Charles H. Turner II, "History and Its Effect on Race Relations," *The Oracle* 72, no. 3 (Summer–Fall 1991): 55.
7. Jacqueline Goggin, *Carter G. Woodson: A Life in Black History* (Baton Rouge: Louisiana State University Press, 1993); North Carolina Agricultural & Technical State University, *The 82nd Annual Commencement Sunday, May 13, 1973, 3:00 p.m.* (Greensboro, NC: North Carolina Agricultural & Technical State University, 1973), 12; Turner, "History and Its Effect," 55.
8. Turner, "History and Its Effect," 55.

9. Turner, "History and Its Effect," 55.

10. Lloyd J. Jordan, "Omega: What Is Our Call?" *The Oracle* 72, no. 3 (Summer–Fall 1991): 10. Jordan served as the thirty-sixth Grand Basileus from 1998 to 2002.

11. "Brief Resume on Supreme Council Members," *The Oracle* [72, no.] 1 (Fall–Winter 1990–91): 3; Jordan, "Omega," 10; "Meet the Members of the Supreme Council," *The Oracle* 73, no. 7 (Summer–Fall 1993): 7; "The Tenth District Welcomes Grand Basileus Lloyd Jordan to Founders Day and Achievement Week Celebration," *The Oracle* 76, no. 21 (Spring–Summer 1999): 48.

12. Jordan, "Omega," 10.

13. Jordan, "Omega," 10.

14. Jordan, "Omega," 10. See also Gomillion v. Lightfoot, 364 U.S. 339 (November 14, 1960); Fred Gray, *Bus Ride to Justice: The Life and Works of Fred D. Gray*, rev. ed. (Montgomery, AL: NewSouth Books, 2013), 4–5, 73, 111–21, 130, 144, 168, 248, 253, 287, 324, 332, 361, 391–93, 402, 408.

15. Jordan, "Omega," 10.

16. Jordan, "Omega," 10.

17. America Counts Staff, "By 2030, All Baby Boomers Will Be Age 65 or Older," United States Census Bureau, December 10, 2019, https://www.census.gov/library/stories/2019/12/by-2030-all-baby-boomers-will-be-age-65-or-older.html. Sociologist and cultural analyst Jonathan Pontell divided boomers into two groups, based on birth: I (1946–54) and II (1955–64), or the "Jones Generation," whose members were "weaned on Watergate," Pontell explained in 2000, adding: "we grew up expecting dishonest politicians.... We're Jonesin' for our brand of realistic idealism to be heard." Greg Seigle "Some Call It 'Jones,'" *Washington Post*, April 6, 2000, C4.

18. As per the Pew Research Center, someone in Generation X was born between 1965 and 1980. Michael Dimock, "Defining Generations: Where Millennials End and Generation Z Begins," Pew Research Center, January 1, 2019, https://www.pewresearch.org/short-reads/2019/01/17/where-millennials-end-and-generation-z-begins/. See also "Age Range by Generation," Beresford Research, accessed May 26, 2021, www.beresfordresearch.com/age-range-by-generation/.

19. Michael A. Jefferson, "A Changing of the Guard," *The Oracle* 72, no. 3 (Summer–Fall 1991): 13.

20. Jefferson, "Changing of the Guard." See also "Bro. Jefferson Reimagines Reconstruction," *The Oracle* 88, no. 32 (Summer 2017): 35. Omega Phi leaders chartered the Epsilon Iota Iota chapter in New Haven, Connecticut, on November 16, 1990.

21. Jefferson, "Changing of the Guard."

22. Jefferson, "Changing of the Guard."

23. Jefferson, "Changing of the Guard."

24. Jefferson, "Changing of the Guard."

25. "Black Academy of Arts and Letters Created," *Chicago Daily Defender*, April 3, 1969, 16; W. E. B. Du Bois, "Crisis of Negro Art," *Crisis* 32 (October 1926): 290–97; "'Generation Gap' a Part of the Black Revolution," *Los Angeles Sentinel*, May 22, 1969, A3; Alfred A. Moss Jr., *The American Negro Academy: Voice of the Talented Tenth* (Baton Rouge: Louisiana State University Press, 1981); *Plessy v. Ferguson*; Arnold Rampersad, *The Life of Langston Hughes*, vol. 1, *1902–1941, I, Too, Sing America*, 2nd ed. (New York: Oxford University Press, 2001), 19; Robert Reinhold, "Seeks to Recognize People Who Make 'Notable Im-

pact,'" *New York Times*, March 28, 1969, 42; "To Promote Arts and Letters: The American Negro Academy to Be Organized by Distinguished Educators," *Washington Post*, March 4, 1897, 12.

26. "AOIP Wins Praise," *Washington Informer* 22, no. 20 (March 5, 1986): 1; "Area Supt. Dr. Norman Cited in D.C.," *Atlanta Daily World*, July 2, 1989, 9; Lee A. Daniels, "The New Black Conservatives," *New York Times*, October 4, 1981, 20–23, 54, 58; Leonard Douglas, "The National Assault on Illiteracy Programs," *The Oracle* 72, no. 3 (Summer–Fall 1991); "OIC Announces Support for 'A-O-I-P' Program," *Washington Informer* 16, no. 34 (June 11, 1981): 12; "Omegas Convene during 12th District Meeting," *Los Angeles Sentinel*, May 10, 1990, C4; Calvin W. Rolark, "Let's Talk: An Excellent Program," *Washington Informer* 16, no. 34 (June 11, 1981): 3; "Let's Talk: Support for AOIP," *Washington Informer* 20, no. 2 (November 2, 1983): 18.

27. Edwin T. Johnson, "Omega Psi Phi Fraternity, Pi Chapter: African American Male Identity and Fraternity Culture 1923–2003" (PhD diss., Morgan State University, 2009), 71, 72n196; Leonard Douglas, "The Omega Experience: Forty Years of Fraternal Friendship and Service," *The Oracle* 72, no. 3 (Summer–Fall 1991): 36; Douglas, "National Assault"; "Goals for Year 2000 and Beyond," *The Oracle* 72, no. 3 (Summer–Fall 1991): 59; Kofi Owusu, "Importance of AOIP Addressed by NPHC," *Washington Informer* 20, no. 2 (November 2, 1983): 15; "Social Tidbits: Many Activities Planned for Fourth of July," *Washington Informer* 23, no. 39 (July 8, 1987): 15. "National Assault" and "Goals" are separate articles.

28. "L. Douglas Wilder, Governor, State of Virginia," *The Oracle* [72, no. 1] (Fall–Winter 1990–91): cover; Pinckney Benton Stewart Pinchback served as acting governor of Louisiana from December 9, 1872, to January 13, 1873. About his governorship and other subjects in the main text, see Walter Greaves Cowan and Jack B. McGuire, *Louisiana Governors: Rulers, Rascals, and Reformers* (Jackson: University Press of Mississippi, 2008), 102–9, esp. 107; P. B. S. Pinchback, "Rejection of Advice to Withdraw as a Candidate for Governor of Louisiana," undated letter, box 1, folder 16, Pinckney Benton Stewart Pinchback Papers, Howard University Libraries and the Spingarn Research Center Manuscripts Division, Washington, DC; Althea D. Pitre, "The Collapse of the Warmoth Regime, 1870–1872," *Louisiana History* 6, no. 2 (Spring 1965): 161–87; "Wilder Is Elected to State Senate," *Roanoke Times-Dispatch* (Virginia), December 3, 1969, A1, A6; and Dwayne Yancey, "Old-Fashioned Campaigning Gave Wilder Upset Win," *Roanoke Times and World-News* (Virginia), November 6, 1985, A7; Dwayne Yancey, "Win Shows Power Shift," *Roanoke Times and World-News* (Virginia), November 9, 1989, A1, A11. Only an image of Wilder appeared on the cover. The note had to provide at least one source of information for the statement in the main text.

29. George E. Curry, "High Hopes End Session of NAACP," *Chicago Tribune*, July 13, 1990; "Wilder Received Spingarn Award at Convention," *Atlanta Voice*, August 11–17, 1990, 8, noting Jesse L. Jackson Sr., a 1989 recipient of the Spingarn Medal was on hand to see his fellow Omega man, L. Douglas Wilder Jr., get the medal in 1990.

30. C. Tyrone Gilmore Sr., "Grand Basileus Speaks . . . ," *The Oracle* 73, no. 7 (Summer–Fall 1993): 2; see also "67th Omega Grand Conclave in City, July 30–August 6th," *Atlanta Daily World*, July 12, 1992; "The 67th Grand Conclave of Omega Psi Phi Fraternity Inc.," *Atlanta Voice*, July 18, 1992.

31. Gilmore, "Grand Basileus Speaks," *The Oracle* 73, no. 2 (Summer–Fall 1993): 2; "Webber, Gillespie, Frazier among S.C. Black Hall of Fame Inductees," *Times and Democrat* (Orangeburg, SC), April 29, 1993, 5B.

32. Gilmore, "Grand Basileus Speaks," *The Oracle* 73, no. 2 (Summer–Fall 1993): 2 (calling the exhibit "Blacks in Medicine, Science, and Creative Endeavors"); "Museum Aims to Get Blacks in Science, Medicine," *Times and State Weekend Democrat* (Orangeburg, SC), July 10, 1993, 14A; "Museum Offers Science Career Workshop," *Beaufort Gazette* (South Carolina), July 5, 1993, 7A; "South Carolinians Honored in Exhibit," *State Weekend* (Columbia, SC), July 2, 1993, 13.

33. Gilmore, "Grand Basileus Speaks," *The Oracle* 73, no. 2 (Summer–Fall 1993): 2; "Museum Aims to Get Blacks in Science, Medicine"; "Museum Offers Science Career Workshop"; "South Carolinians Honored in Exhibit."

34. Gilmore, "Grand Basileus Speaks," *The Oracle* 73, no. 2 (Summer–Fall 1993): 2.

35. Gilmore, "Grand Basileus Speaks," *The Oracle* 73, no. 2 (Summer–Fall 1993): 2; C. Tyrone Gilmore Sr., "The Grand Basileus Speaks . . . ," *The Oracle* 74, no. 8 (Winter–Spring 1994): 2 (cited hereinafter as Gilmore, "Grand Basileus Speaks," Winter–Spring 1994); "World Headquarters Building Fund Committee," *The Oracle* 73, no. 7 (Summer–Fall 1993): 51.

36. Gilmore, "Grand Basileus Speaks," Summer–Fall 1993.

37. Gilmore, "Grand Basileus Speaks," Summer–Fall 1993.

38. Gilmore, "Grand Basileus Speaks," Summer–Fall 1993.

39. Gilmore, "Grand Basileus Speaks," Summer–Fall 1993, 5; Charles H. Turner II, "From the Editor's Desk . . . Omega's Purpose," *The Oracle* 72, no. 3 (Summer–Fall 1991): 5.

40. "Omega Psi Phi: Organization, Founded at Howard, Stresses Leadership and Service," *Ebony* 48, no. 11 (September 1993): 112–14 (cited hereinafter as *Ebony*, "Omega Psi Phi").

41. *Ebony*, "Omega Psi Phi," 113.

42. *Ebony*, "Omega Psi Phi," 113.

43. *Ebony*, "Omega Psi Phi," 113.

44. *Ebony*, "Omega Psi Phi," 113. The endowed chairs at Rust College in Holly Springs, Mississippi, and Wiley College in Marshall, Texas, bore the names of Omega Psi Phi founders Frank Coleman, Oscar J. Cooper, Ernest E. Just, and Edgar A. Love. The *Ebony* article did not indicate if the two endowed chairs the Fraternity was developing in September 1993 also would bear the names of the founders.

45. *Ebony*, "Omega Psi Phi," 114; Brian G. Shellum, *Black Officer in a Buffalo Soldier Regiment: The Military Career of Charles Young* (Lincoln: University of Nebraska Press, 2010), 61, 185, 194, 255, 260, 280.

46. Shellum, *Black Officer*, 61.

47. *Ebony*, "Omega Psi Phi," 114.

48. *Ebony*, "Omega Psi Phi," 114.

49. *Ebony* "Omega Psi Phi," 114.

50. Gilmore, "Grand Basileus Speaks," Winter–Spring 1994, 2 (quote); Adam E. McKee, "Yesterday, Today and Tomorrow," *The Oracle* 74, no. 8 (Winter–Spring 1994): 14.

51. Burnel E. Coulon, "Omega's Grand Men of Leadership of Past Years Come Together and Hammer Out a Solid Document for Future Ceremonies for the Next Decade for Men of Omega," *The Oracle* 74, no. 8 (Winter–Spring 1994): 7.

52. Coulon, "Omega's Grand Men."

53. Coulon, "Omega's Grand Men."

54. See "A New Home for the Omegas," *New Journal and Guide* (Norfolk, VA), December 6, 1995, 1; John S. Epps, "Executive Director's Message: In Our Forefathers House, There Are Many Mansions," *The Oracle* 75, no. 10 (Spring 1995): 3; "Omega Psi Phi Headquarters Welcomed," *Atlanta Daily World*, December 10, 1995, 4; "Omega Psi Phi World Center," *The Oracle* 75, no. 10 (Spring 1995): 53; Portia A. Scott, "Omega Fraternity Opens New World Center: Thousands Attend Special Ribbon-Cutting in DeKalb," *Atlanta Daily World*, December 10, 1995, 1, 2; Portia A. Scott, "Omegas to Dedicate World Center Saturday," *Atlanta Daily World*, December 7, 1995, 1, 2; and Charles H. Turner II, "Manhood," *The Oracle* 75, no. 10 (Spring 1995): 4; Maurice Hobson, interview with several brothers conducted by Maurice Hobson, October 20, 2020. These interviews were conducted via Zoom and the names of the members will remain anonymous for fear of isolation and retribution.

55. Scott, "Omega Fraternity Opens," 2. See also "Dedication of Omega World Center: Bill Cosby Master of Ceremony," *The Oracle* 76, no. 12 (Fall 1995): 6; "Dedication of Omega World Center: Earl G. Graves Dedication Speaker," *The Oracle* 76, no. 12 (Fall 1995): 7; Chris Grimes, "Fraternity to Dedicate New Home," *Atlanta Journal-Constitution*, December 9, 1995, E1; and "News Makers: Frat Boy," *Charlotte Observer* (North Carolina), December 12, 1995, 2B. Members of the Beta Alpha Alpha chapter of Omega Psi Phi initiated William H. Cosby on April 18, 1988.

56. Scott, "Omega Fraternity Opens," 2.

57. Hobson, *Legend of the Black Mecca*.

58. "A Drug Called Atlanta," *Atlanta Voice*, July 30–August 5, 1994, 4.

59. Carrie Teegardin, "Despite Image, Atlanta Not Tops for Affluent Blacks," *Atlanta Constitution*, February 26, 1995, D3.

60. Gary M. Pomerantz, *Where Peachtree Meets Sweet Auburn: The Saga of Two Families and the Making of Atlanta* (New York: Scribner, [1996] 2021); Hobson, *Legend of the Black Mecca*; Add Seymour Jr., "Ex-Mayor Fondly Recalled on Street He Frequented: Grandfather Put 'Sweet' in Auburn Avenue Name," *Atlanta Journal-Constitution*, June 27, 2003, F3.

61. James Clingman, "Why Not Another Black Wall Street?" *Atlanta Daily World*, April 18, 1999, 3; Hannibal B. Johnson, *Black Wall Street 100: An American City Grapples with Its Historical Racial Trauma* (Forth Worth, TX: Eakin, 2020); Blake Hill-Saya, *Aaron Mcduffie Moore: An African American Physician, Educator, and Founder of Durham's Black Wall Street* (Chapel Hill: University of North Carolina Press, 2020); Seymour, "Ex-Mayor Fondly Recalled."

62. Emanuella Grinberg, "Life Returns—Slowly—to MLK's Old Neighborhood," CNN, January 17, 2016, www.cnn.com/2016/01/16/living/king-historic-district-auburn-avenue-feat/index.html.

63. Frederick Allen, *Atlanta Rising: The Invention of an International City 1946–1996* (Atlanta: Longstreet, 1996); Hobson, *Legend of the Black Mecca*.

64. Hobson, *Legend of the Black Mecca*, 178–79; Steven R. Weisman, "Atlanta Selected over Athens for 1996 Olympics," *New York Times*, September 19, 1990, A1, D29.

65. "Hall of Fame: LeRoy Walker," United States Olympic & Paralympic Museum, accessed January 24, 2024, https://usopm.org/leroy-walker/. "Leroy Walker, USOC's First Black Chairman, Dies," CBS News, 24 April 2012.

66. Emily Badger, "This Can't Happen by Accident: The Nation's Housing Recovery Is Leaving Blacks Behind," *Washington Post*, May 2, 2016.

67. Scott, "Omega Fraternity Opens."

68. Peter Applebome, "Scandal Casts Shadow over Atlanta Mayoral Race," *New York Times*, November 18, 1993, A16, ranking William B. Hartsfield International Airport as the fourth busiest in the United States; Tom Barry, Millard Grimes, and Bill Shipp, "The People, the Companies, the Images of Trend's Decade," *George Trend* 11, no. 1 (September 1, 1995): 24; Rick Brooks, "On Time? Not If You Take These Flights," *Wall Street Journal*, October 26, 1994; Mitchell Locin, "O'Hare to Lose Designation as Busiest Airport, FAA Says," *Chicago Tribune*, February 25, 1991, 4; Fred Muse, "Big Jobs Can Benefit from Owner-Controlled Insurance," *American City and Country* 110, no. 6 (May 1995): 50; Douglas W. Nelms, "Hartsfield: Big, Getting Bigger," *Air Transport World* 29, no. 9 (September 1992): 123–24; "O'Hare Soars Past Atlanta as Busiest Airport," *Chicago Tribune*, March 22, 1990, 3D.

69. Miller, "Grand Basileus Speaks," *The Oracle* 76, no. 14 (Spring 1996): 2.

70. "The Honorable Ernest Everett Just, One of the Omega Psi Phi Fraternity Founding Fathers Immortalized through the United States Postal Service Black Heritage Stamp Series," *The Oracle* 76, no. 14 (Spring 1996): 5.

71. "Honorable Ernest Everett Just."

72. "Honorable Ernest Everett Just."

73. "George K. McKinney," *Baltimore Sun*, June 24, 2012, 24; "George McKinney Confirmed as Maryland U.S. Marshal," *The Oracle* 76, no. 14 (Spring 1996): 7; Frederick N. Rasmussen, "First Black U.S. Marshal for Md. District," *Washington Post*, June 26, 2012, B6.

74. Tom Fiedler, "Popular Sheriff Disarms Racial Fear," *Miami Herald*, September 8, 1998, 9A; Nathaniel Glover, *Striving for Justice: A Memoir of a Black Sheriff in the Deep South* ([Brentwood, TN]: Forefront Books, 2023); "Omega Man Makes History Elected Florida's First Black Sheriff," *The Oracle* 76, no. 14 (Spring 1996): 7.

75. Miller, "Grand Basileus Speaks." See also Dave Lesher, "Battle over Proposition 209 Moves to the Courts," *Los Angeles Times*, November 7, 1996, A1, A22, reporting 54.3 percent of California voters supported Proposition 209 and 45.71 percent opposed it.

76. Brian Duignan, and the Editors of Encyclopedia, "Bush v. Gore," Encyclopedia Britannica, last updated August 29, 2023, www.britannica.com/event/Bush-v-Gore.

77. Gettleman, Jeffrey, "In Duval County, Views of Vote Process as Different as Black and White," *Los Angeles Times*, December 10, 2000.

78. Rev. Jesse Jackson, "Omega Public Policy," *The Oracle* 80, no. 5 (Winter 2004): 14; George W. Bush and Richard Cheney, Petitioners v. Albert Gore, Jr. and Joseph Lieberman, et al., 531 U.S. 98 (December 12, 2000); John Hope Franklin and Evelyn Brooks Higginbotham, *From Slavery to Freedom: A History of African Americans*, 10th ed. (New York: McGraw Hill, 2021).

79. For more details on the events of September 11, 2001, see National Commission on Terrorist Attacks upon the United States, *The 9/11 Commission Report: Final Report of the National Commission on Terrorist Attacks Upon the United States* (US Government Printing Office, 2004); Mitchell Zuckoff, *Fall and Rise: The Story of 9/11* (New York: HarperCollins, 2019); Lawrence Wright, *The Looming Tower: Al-Qaeda and the Road to 9/11* (New York: Alfred Knopf, 2006); Antonia Felix, *Condi: The Condoleeza Rice Story* (New York: Newmarket Press, 2002); Lara Jakes Jordan, "Rice Sticks by Bush Response," *Montgomery Advertiser*, September 5, 2005, 1A, quoting Condoleezza Rice who, while touring Mobile, Alabama, pronounced: "Nobody, especially the president, would have

left people unattended on the basis of race," 2A; Glenn Kessler, "Rice Defends Tactics Used against Suspects: Europe Aware of Operations, She Implies," *Washington Post*, December 6, 2005, A1, A26; Richard D. Knabb, Jamie R. Rhome, and Daniel P. Brown, "Tropical Cyclone Report: Hurricane Katrina, 23–30 August 2005" (published paper, National Hurricane Center, Miami, Florida, January 4, 2023), 11, 13; Scott Martelle, "Rice Memoir Casts an Eye at History: Exhaustive Account Includes Regrets Regarding Katrina," *South Florida Sun Sentinel*, November 13, 2011, 11G, restating Rice's regret vacationing in New York City, as Hurricane Katrina was destroying New Orleans, Louisiana; Rice, *Condoleezza Rice*; Rice, *No Higher Honor*; Eugene Robinson, "What Rice Can't See," *Washington Post*, October 25, 2005, A21.

80. Franklin and Higginbotham, *From Slavery to Freedom*, 679.
81. Franklin and Higginbotham, *From Slavery to Freedom*, 613–24.
82. Franklin and Higginbotham, *From Slavery to Freedom*, 613–24.
83. Franklin and Higginbotham, *From Slavery to Freedom*, 613–24.
84. "12 Years Later: Obama's DNC Speech Then and Now," *NBC News*, July 28, 2016; https://www.nbcnews.com/storyline/2016-conventions/12-years-later-obama-s-dnc-speeches-then-now-n618166.
85. Federal Election Committee, *Federal Elections 2008* . . . (Washington, DC: Federal Election Commission, 2009), 6.
86. "13 Years of the Affordable Care Act," Obama Foundation, accessed June 1, 2023, www.obama.org/13-years-aca/; "Climate Change and President Obama's Action Plan," White House, accessed June 1, 2023, https://obamawhitehouse.archives.gov/president-obama-climate-action-plan; Charles F. Bolden, Jr., National Aeronautics and Space Administration, https://www.nasa.gov/people/charles-f-bolden-jr/; accessed 28 January 2024; "President Obama Announces More Key Administration Post, "The White House Office of the Press Secretary, May 1, 2014; https://obamawhitehouse.archives.gov/the-press-office/2014/05/01/president-obama-announces-more-key-administration-posts, access 28 January 2024.
87. "Omega Psi Phi Celebrates 100th Year," *The Oracle* 83, no. 26 (Winter 2012–Spring 2013): 10.
88. Clarence Page, "An Invitation to Murder?" *Chicago Tribune*, March 21, 2012, 27 (first quotation: one of numerous contemporaneous publications reporting the assertion of George M. Zimmerman); Ben Crump, *Open Season: Legalized Genocide of Colored People* (New York: Amistad, 2019), 15, 17, 55–68 (second quotation on 57). See also Erin Aubry Kaplan, "Race: It's Gotten Personal for Obama; The Trayvon Martin Case Has Drawn the President Deeper into a Discussion of Being Black in America," *Los Angeles Times*, April 1, 2012, A25.
89. Barack Obama, "Remarks on the Nomination of Jim Yong Kim to be President of the World Bank and an Exchange with Reporters, March 23, 2012," in *Public Papers of the Presidents of the United States: Barack Obama* (cited hereinafter as *Obama Papers*), *2012*, book 1, *January 1 to June 30, 2012* (Washington, DC: United States Government Printing Office, 2016), 813, 345–46 (quotation on 346).
90. Crump, *Open Season*, 15, 17, 55–68.
91. Federal Election Committee, *2012 Election Results: Tables and Maps* (Washington, DC: Federal Election Committee, 2012), 2; "President Map," *New York Times*, November 29, 2012.

92. Crump, *Open Season*, 59; Rene Stutzman and Jeff Weiner, "All-Female, Mostly White Jury for Zimmerman Trial," *Hartford Courant* (Connecticut), June 21, 2013, A5.

93. Stutzman and Jeff Weiner, "All-Female, Mostly White." See also State of Florida v. George Zimmerman, 2012-CF-001083-A, Fla. Cir. Ct. (July 13, 2013).

94. "Juror: 'No Doubt' That George Zimmerman Feared for His Life," CNN, July 16, 2013, www.cnn.com/2013/07/15/justice/zimmerman-juror-book/index.html.

95. "Juror."

96. "Juror."

97. Barack Obama, "Statement on the Verdict in State of Florida v. George Zimmerman, July 14, 2013," in *Obama Papers, 2013*, book 2, *July 1 to December 31, 2013*, 813.

98. Crump, *Open Season*, 17, 55, 58.

99. Crump, *Open Season*.

100. Barack Obama, "Remarks on the Verdict in State of Florida v. George Zimmerman, July 19, 2013," in *Obama Papers, 2013*, book 2, 824–27 (quotation on 826).

101. Obama, "Remarks on the Verdict," 824.

102. Obama, "Remarks on the Verdict," 825.

103. On Thabiti Boone, see "Thabiti Boone," White House, accessed November 26, 2023 https://obamawhitehouse.archives.gov/champions/fatherhood/thabiti-boone; "Omega Psi Phi Fraternity, Incorporated, International Fatherhood Initiative," *The Oracle* 81, no. 23 (Winter 2011): 16–17 (quotation on 16). See also Thabiti Boone, "Down the Aisle, Walkin' the Walk," in *Be a Father to Your Child: Real Talk from Black Men on Family, Love, and Fatherhood*, ed. April R. Silver (New York: Soft Skull, 2008), 118–22; A. J. Dugger III, "Omegas Team Up with Project Go to Aid At-Risk Kids," *Murfreesboro Post* (Tennessee), October 27, 2013, 5; "Epsilon Rho and Xi Chapters Welcome Ques to Minneapolis for the Conclave," *The Oracle* 83, no. 26 (Winter 2012–Spring 2013): 26; Bakari Kitwana, *The Hip-Hop Generation: Young Blacks and the Crisis in African-American Culture* (New York: BasicCivitas Books, 2002), 157; Adrienne Leon, "'Proud Fathers' Rally Celebrates Men Who Serve," *Atlanta Voice*, June 24, 2011, 1, 3; Christi Parsons, "President Promises to Help Fathers," *Los Angeles Times*, June 22, 2010, A7; Andrew Ray, "From the Heart of the Grand Basileus," *Afro-American* (Baltimore, MD), July 23, 2011, B1–B2; Khrissah Thompson, "Obama to Unveil Fatherhood, Mentoring Program," *Arizona Republic*, June 21, 2010, A2.

104. CBC 2013 Forum Flyer, 2013 Annual Legislative Conference of the Congressional Black Caucus Foundation, September 20, 2013.

105. CBC 2013 Forum Flyer, 2013; Henry C. Johnson Jr. was born and reared in Washington, DC. He earned a bachelor of arts degree from Clark College in Atlanta, Georgia, in 1976 and a doctor of law degree from the Texas Southern Thurgood Marshall School of Law in Houston, Texas, in 1979. He practiced law in Decatur, eight miles northeast of Atlanta, until 1989. During that year, he accepted a position as an associate judge in the magistrate court of DeKalb County, where Decatur was the seat of government. Local voters elected him to the DeKalb County Commission in 2000. He served from 2001, the year he departed the court, to 2006, the year voters elected him to Congress.

106. CBC 2013 Forum Flyer, 2013; Crump, *Open Season*, 15, 17, 55–68.

107. CBC 2014 Forum Flyer, 2014 Annual Legislative Conference of the Congressional Black Caucus Foundation, September 25, 2014.

108. CBC 2013 Forum Flyer, 2013; CBC 2014 Forum Flyer, 2014.

109. Shelby County v. Holder, 570 U.S. 529 (June 25, 2013).

110. This information was corroborated by Brother Search provided by the official website of Omega Psi Phi Fraternity, Inc., accessed June 1, 2023, https://oppf.org/brother-site-map/.

111. Ernest Everett Just, "The Challenge," *The Oracle* 1, no. 1 (June 1919): 24.

Conclusion

1. James D. Anderson, *Education of Blacks in the South, 1860–1935* (Chapel Hill: University of North Carolina Press, 1988); John David Smith and J. Vincent Lowery, eds., *The Dunning School: Historians, Race, and the Meaning of Reconstruction* (Lexington: University Press of Kentucky, 2013). Refer to chapter 2 for more information.

2. Aside from the Double V campaign, as explained in Patrick S. Washburn, "The Pittsburgh *Courier's* Double V Campaign in 1942," *American Journalism* 3, no. 2 (1986): 73–86, the other information in this paragraph has been discussed throughout this book, particularly chapter 3.

3. Regarding Harold M. Love Jr., see Adam Friedman and Duane W. Gang, "Tennessee State University to Receive $250 Million in Gov. Bill Lee's Budget Proposal," *Tennessean*, January 31, 2022; and Katherine Mangan, "A Long-Neglected HBCU May Finally Get Its Money," *Chronicle of Higher Education*, February 1, 2022. For more on the Biden administration, see Danielle Douglas-Gabriel, "States Should Fix Underfunding of Land-Grant HBCUs, Biden Administration Says," *Washington Post*, September 18, 2023.

Index

Page numbers in *italics* refer to illustrations.

Achievement Week Project, 82–83, 91, 95, 102, 111, 157, 198
Adams, Donald D., 112
Adams, S. Herbert, 117
affirmative action, 226, 261, 264, 265, 278
African diaspora, 34, 250
AIDS/HIV epidemic, 204, 232
Akinleye, Johnson O., 274
Alexander, Clifford, Jr., 227
Alexander, C. R., 129, 318n14
Alexander, Raymond Pace, 136
Alexander, Sadie Tanner, 136
Ali, Muhammad, 189, 199–200, 263
Allen, Richard, 124
Allen, Samuel A., 24
Allen University, 77, 86, 118
Alpha Kappa Alpha Sorority, 5, 59, 138
Alpha Phi Alpha Fraternity, 5, 17, 21, 36, 59, 73, 140, 153, 155, 162
Alston, Eugene Ellis, 70–71
American Baptist Home Mission Society, 76
American Council on Human Rights, 142
American Negro Academy, 12, 253, 333n109
Amprey, Walter G., 234–35
Anderson, James D., 1, 47, 77, 276
Anderson, Marian, 185
Andrews, Robert McCants, 39
Annals of the American Academy of Political and Social Sciences, 97
Annie Malone Historical Society, 66
Arnall, Ellis G., 130
Assault on Illiteracy, 254–55
Associated Negro Press, 72
Association for the Study of Afro-American Life and History (ASALH), 2, 26, 42, 74, 82, 91, 138, 148, 219, 222

Ateman, Edward, 115
Atkins, Cyril F., 89
Atkins, Francis Loguen, 64, 149–50
Atkins, Jasper Alston, 37, 55–57, 58, 60–61, 65, 66, 74, 84; Grand Conclave address, Chicago, 86–87
Atlanta, Georgia, 54–56, 220, 260–61
Atlanta Constitution (newspaper), 49–50, 54
Atlanta Independent (newspaper), 42, 50
Atlanta University, 13
Atlanta Voice (newspaper), 261
Aurandt, Paul Harvey, 242
Avery, James S., Sr., 205–7, 214
Avery Institute, 160, 340n79

Baby Boomers, 252, 348n17
Baird, William Raimond, 20
Baird's Manual of American College Fraternities, 20
Baker, Ella, 176–77
Bakke Supreme Court decision, 225–26, 232
Baltimore Afro-American (newspaper), 50–51, 52, 69, 74, 105
Banks, Charles, III, 238
Barker, Prince A., 124
Barksdale, Richard Kenneth, 7
Basic Methods for Experiments on Eggs of Marine Animals (Just), 122
Basie, William "Count," 218
Baugh, William E., 102, 103, 110, 113–14, 116, 117–18
Baumgardner, Luther O., 28
Beech, Harvey, 152
Bell, Andrew, 225
Bell, Lloyd, 208
Bennett College, 162

Bethune, Mary McLeod, 106, 134, 215, 223
Biddle University, 37, 54, 58, 90. *See also* Johnson C. Smith University
Biden, Joseph R., 279
Biology of the Cell Surface, The (Just), 122
Birmingham World (newspaper), 186–87, 217
Black Academy of Arts and Letters, 253
Black Apollo of Science (Manning), 122
Black Art Movement, 199
Black Brain Drain, 194, 238, 334n115
Black Brain Trust, 92, 106, 112, 125, 215. *See also* Federal Council on Negro Affairs
Black Enterprise magazine, 4, 260
Black Greek-letter organizations: academic literature concerning, 4; anti-lynching campaigns, 59–60; and civil rights, 142; common goals, 86–87; history of, 5; National Pan-Hellenic Council, 29; step shows, 246; during World War I, 36
Black Heritage postage stamp series, 212–13
Black higher education: administrators, Black contrasted with White, 77–78, 85–86; curricula standards, 74–75, 83–85, 87–88, 89–90, 91; debate teams, 68–69, 115; Du Bois and Dill's rankings, 47–48; HBCUs (historically Black colleges and universities), 44, 47–48, 194–95, 206, 238–39, 276, 279; medical schools, 44; Omega Psi Phi college presidents, 77, 79, 85–86, 99, 118, 144, 149–150, 154, 163, 164, 176, 274; students' anti-lynching efforts, 59–60
Black History Month, 2, 204, 222
Black Identity Conference (1968), 199–200
Black Lives Matter movement, 278
Black National Medical Association (NMA), 190–91
Black Panther Party for Self-Defense, 189, 192
Black Power movement, 175–76, 188–89, 191–94, 202, 253, 265, 277
Black race uplift, 19, 33, 40, 144, 211
Blake, Malsworth Brian, 274
Blayton, Jesse B.: Grand Keeper of Finance, 102–3, 116, 120, 129, 139, 143, 147, 158, 181, 189, 191; WERD, Black-owned radio station, 145
Bolden, Charles Frank, Jr., 1, 249–50, 256, 269
Bonner, Murray, 80
Boone, Thabiti Bruce, 272, 273
Bowen, John Wesley Edward, 55, 58, 72, 73
Bradshaw, Tecumseh, 122
Branche, George C., 124
Brannon, William Griffith, 24
Branton, Wiley Austin, 166, 251, 256–57
Brascher, Nahum D., 72
Braynon, Edward Joseph, Jr., 214, 225, 227, 258–59, 267
Brewer, Thomas Hency, Sr., 230–31, 343n139
Brice, George Edward, 24, 28, 35
Brooks, George D., 51
Brouche, George C., 51
Browder v. Gayle, 163
Brown, Emerson E., 236
Brown, Grace Adelaide, 67
Brown, Lucius H., 28
Brown, Mary "Edna" (Coleman), 14, 31, 67
Brown, Sterling Allen, 1, 67, 122
Brown, Sterling Nelson, 13, 14, 31, 67
Brown v. Board of Education of Topeka, 160, 180, 193
Bruce, Roscoe Conkling, Sr., 26
Bruce, William Cabell, 12
Buffalo Soldier regiments, 222–23
Bullock, Matthew Washington, 81–82, 84, 93–95, 97–98, 99–100, 101, 102, 104
Bullock, Matthew Washington, Jr., 136
Bunche, Ralph J., 145
Burke, W. Spurgeon, 28
Bursting Bonds (Pickens), 54
Bush, George Herbert Walker, 242, 266
Bush, George Walker, 265–68
Bush, Jeb, 265–266

Cabrielle, James, 178
Cade, Fred C., 96
Calhoun, John H., Jr., 129, 133–34, 139
California Civil Rights Initiative, 264
Campaign for the Study of Negro History and Literature, 46, 50, 51, 55, 56–57, 58, 99; Black History movement, 42, 46–47, 50–51

Camp Howard, 37, 38, 55, 118
Capital City project, 205
Carmichael, Stokely, 192, 193
Carolina Peacemaker (newspaper), 217
Carr, William T., 52
Carter, Alfred S., Jr., 215
Carter, James "Jimmy" Earl, Jr., 231
Carter, Robert Lee, 136, 160
Carter, William Justin, Jr., 70
Carter G. Woodson Educational Center, 256
Carter G. Woodson Leadership Institute, 256
Cashin, John L., 201
Central Committee of Negro College Men (CCNCM), 35
Chaney, James, 187–88, 233
Chapman, Oscar James, 149
Chase, John S., 156
Chavis, Benjamin Franklin, Jr., 231
Chicago Defender (newspaper), 41–42, 54, 102
Children of Bondage (Davis & Dollard), 120
Chisholm, Isabel, 138
Christopher, Charles, 262
Civil Rights Act (1964), 209, 218, 226
Civil Rights Act (1968), 218
Civil Rights Bill (1966), 192, 333n102
civil rights movement: Freedom Rides, 178–79; and higher education, 194–200; mass demonstrations, 198–99; 1963 as pivotal year, 182–87; Omega Psi Phi leadership, 1950s, 153–65; Second Reconstruction (1970s), 216–25; sit-in demonstrations, 176–78; student involvement, 177; White backlash and violence, 178–79; women's roles in, 184–85, 290n103. *See also* racial issues
Claflin University, 118
Clark, Eugene, 85
Clayborne, Moses, 22
Clayton, Benjamin W., 56
Clemson College/University, 183, 245
Clinton, George, 246
Clinton, William Jefferson "Bill," 4, 263
Clyburn, James Enos, III, 273, 274

Coates, J. Clyde, 84
Cobb, James Adlai, 26
Cobb, William Montague, 134–35, 190, 191, 230–31
Coleman, Frank: as Alpha chapter Basileus, 2, 21–22; Campaign for the Study of Negro Literature and History, 51; Central Committee of Negro College Men (CCNCM), 35, 36; death of, 196, 202; family and education, 30–31; foundation of Omega Psi Phi, 1, 2, 11, 16–20; Founders' Memorial, 219; at Golden Anniversary Grand Conclave, 180; Howard University inter-fraternal committee, 28; Howard University lecture series, 70; at Just's funeral, 122; legacy and impact, 196–97, 252; lifelong Omega Psi Phi involvement, 165; memorial tributes, 222–23; National Social Action Committee, 130
Coleman, Mabel Raymond, 197
Coleman, Samuel Clarence, Jr., 208, 212–13
collectivism vs. individualism, 115
Collins, Addie Mae, 186
Collins, Charles W., 137, 139
Colored No More (Lindsey), 4
Colored Woman in a White World, A (Terrell), 223
colorism/color segregation, 17, 37, 67, 298n76. *See also* segregation
Commission on Civil Rights, 181
Committee Against Jim Crow, 136, 142, 183
Communist Party USA, 67; Scottsboro Boys, 105
Congressional Black Caucus, 248, 273
Congress of Racial Equality (CORE), 135, 178, 232
Conyers, Alexander, 274
Cooke, Christopher C., 22
Cook, Harold J., 214
Cook, William Mercer, 78, 89, 97
Coolidge, Calvin, 73, 82
Cooper, Anna Julia Haywood, 19
Cooper, James B., 30
Cooper, John Sherman, 161, 195

Index   359

Cooper, Mary M., 30
Cooper, Oscar James, 24, 116; Mu chapter banquet (1921), 53; death of, 209; family and education, 30; foundation of Omega Psi Phi, 1, 2, 11, 16–20; Founders' Memorial, 219; at Golden Anniversary Grand Conclave, 180; as Keeper of Seals, 21–22; legacy of, 252; lifelong Omega Psi Phi involvement, 165, 201; study habits/educational ideals, 15–16
Corbett, Ellis Franklin, 147, 158, 181, 183, 189, 191, 197, 200, 202
Corrin, Malcolm, 143, 147
Cosby, William Henry "Bill," Jr., 260
Cottin, John R., 52
Coulon, Burnel Elton, Sr., 235, 237–38, 258–59, 267
Cox, Courtland, 174
Cox, George W., 103, 110
Cox, Wendell F., 191
Cozart, Leland Stanford, 144
crack cocaine, 9, 232, 238, 241–43
Crisis (NAACP magazine), 6, 150
Crummell, Alexander, 19, 253
Crump, Benjamin Lloyd, 270–71, 273, 274, 278

Daily Worker (Communist Party newspaper), 67
Daniels, Wiley E., Sr., 236
Davis, Benjamin O., 169
Davis, Corneal, 216
Davis, Howard C., 158
Davis, John Preston, 79, 112
Davis, Lawrence A., 163
Davis, Walter Strother, 149, 178
Davis, William Boyd Allison, 70, 71, 119–20, 151
Deans, David Crockett, Jr., 111
Debrah, Ebenezer Moses, 180
Decatur, Georgia, 260–62
Delta Sigma Theta Sorority, 5, 14, 31, 59, 106, 165, 184, 223
Democratic National Convention (1948), 142
Democratic National Convention (1968), 201
Dempsey, Jack, 145

Dent, Albert Walter, 69, 83, 113, 115, 118–19, 130, 144, 163
Dent, Francis Morse, 36, 251
Dent, Thomas Covington, 182
Dent, Thomas Marshall, Jr., 36, 145
desegregation, 147–53; *Brown v. Board of Education,* 160; higher education, 155, 178; hospital integration, 190–91; Little Rock Central High School, 165–66; public schools, 153–54; public transportation, 162. *See also* segregation
Dickson, David Wilson Daly, 150
Dill, Augustus Granville, 47
Dillard University, 115, 118, 120, 165
Dingle, Alan Lowery, 28
Dingle, John Gordon, 28
Divine Nine, 5
Dobbs, John Wesley, 141
Dodson, S. Malcolm, 93, 102, 109, 114
Donaldson, Ulysses S., 82–83
Douglas, Leonard, 254
Douglas, Stanley Moreland, 2, 38
Douglas, Winston, 35
Douglass, Frederick, 6
Dreer, Herman, 3, 11, 16, 19–20, 27–28, 66, 67, 69–70, 74, 113–14; history book, 119; *Oracle* editorship, 114, 116
Drew, Charles Richard, 97, 123–24, 147–48, 228, 243, 256
Drew, Minnie Lenore, 243
drug crisis (1970s), 207–8. *See also* crack cocaine
Du Bois, William Edward Burghardt, 6, 12–13, 19; on Black higher education, 47; on color line, 37; legacy and impact, 253; Niagara Movement, 21; *The Philadelphia Negro,* 61–62; racial issues during World War I, 34, 36
Dunning, William A., 276
Durham, North Carolina, 103, 110
Durkee, James Stanley, 72
Dyer, Leonidas Carstarphen, 55
Dyer Anti-Lynching Bill, 59

Ebony magazine, 226–27, 256–57
Edley, Christopher Fairfield, Sr., 227

Edmonds, S. Randolph, 124
Education of Blacks in the South, The (Anderson), 47, 276
Education of the Negro Prior to 1861, The (Woodson), 19, 42
Edward Waters College, 263–64
Eisenhower, Dwight, 157
Ellah, Francis John, 180
Ellis, Roy, 106
Epps, Reginald, 231–32
Equal Justice Initiative, 49
Ernest Everett Just Organization in Biology, 195
Esso Standard Oil, 206
Eure, Dexter, 129
Evers, Medgar W., 183, 187–88, 230

Fair Housing Act (1968), 200
Farmer, James Leonard, Jr., 135, *174*, 178, 179, 182, 183, 184
Farrakhan Muhammad, Louis Abdul-Haleem, Sr., 242
Faubus, Orval, 165–66
Fauntroy, Walter Edward, 235
Federal Council of Negro Affairs, 92, 106, 215
Felder, James, 214
Fellowship of Reconciliation, 135
Ferguson, Dutton, 99
Ferrell, H. Albion, 197
Fierce, Hughlyn F., 218
Fifth-fourth Massachusetts Infantry, 222
Fisk University, 13, 37, 47, 55, 60, 61, 67, 74, 85, 87, 88, 120, 121, 125, 148, 304n167; Jubilee singers, 40, 76
Fitts, Howard M., Jr., *172*
Fitzgerald, Ella, 218
Fitzgerald, Peter Gosselin, 268
Fleming, William, 131
Flexner, Abraham, 45
Flexner Report, 45
Flint-Goodridge Hospital (Flint Medical College), 45, 120
Florida Agricultural and Mechanical (A&M) College, 47, 85, 333n111
Flowers, Lucio, 230–31, 333–34n111

Floyd, George, 278
Folk Song of the American Negro (Work), 76
Fontaine, William T., 151
Ford, Gerald Rudolph, Jr., 222
Ford's Theater (Baltimore), 140, 181
Fort Des Moines Army Base, 36, 107, 118, 130, 176, 223
Foster, Benjamin, Jr., 241
Franklin, John Hope, 267
Franklin, V. P., 184
Frederick Deming Industrial School, 31
Freedom Rides, 178–79, 277
Freedom Summer, 189–90, 233–34
Fuller, Solomon Carter, 83

Gaines, Lloyd, 140
Gans, Louis, 37
Garnett, Marion Winston, 189, 191, 214, 219, 258–59, 267
Garrett, John B., 75–76
Garrison, William Lloyd, 25
Garvey, Marcus Mosiah, Jr., 40, 53
Generation X, 252, 253–54, 348n18
George Washington and the Negro (Mazyck), 108
Gibbs, Mifflin T., 120
Gibbs, Warmoth Thomas, 89, 162, 164, 176
G.I. Bill (Servicemen's Readjustment Act, 1944), 127, 160
Giddings, Paula J., 5
Gilbert, William, 19, 22, 56, 63, 64, 66
Gill, Robert L., 3, 6, 128, 133, 151, 153, 164, 197–98, 236
Gilmore, C. Tyrone, Sr., 245, 248–50, 254, 256–57, 258
Glover, Nathaniel, Jr., 263–64
Gomillion, Charles Goode, 251
Gomillion v. Lightfoot, 251
Goodman, Andrew, 233
Goodwin, Reginald, 124
Gordon, Edmund Wyatt, 122
Gore, Albert Arnold, Jr., 265–66
Grace, George, 267
Grant, Naomi (Mazyck), 108
Graves, Bibb, 80

Graves, Earl Gilbert, Sr., 4, 216–17, 227, 260
Gray, Fred David, 162, 164, 251
Gray, Robert W., 143
Great War. *See* World War I
Greek Leadership Conference on Civil Rights and Economics, 234
Green, Ernest Gideon, 227
Greenberg, Jack, 160, *174*
Greene, Ervie W., 51
Greensboro, North Carolina, 64, 75, 83, 84, 88, 89, 162, 176–77, 227, 243
Greenup, Jeff, 181
Gregory, Frederick Drew, 1, 202, 227, 228, 249–50
Gregory, Nora Rosella, 228
Grovey v. Townsend, 66–67
gymnasiums, value of, 15–16

Hale, William Jasper, 46, 74, 77, 85, 86, 94, 149
Hall, Amos T., 139, 141
Hall, George E., 25, 51
Hall v. DeCuir, 132
Hampton Institute, 14, 48, 77, 119, 149, 156, 293n163
Harding, Vincent G., 5
Harding, Warren Gamaliel, 59–60, 68
Hargrave, Thomas B., 51
Harlem Hell Fighters, 222
Harlem Renaissance, 58–59, 77–78, 251
Harllee, Mitchell Depew, 23
Harris, Abram L., 122, 151
Harris, Charles, 22
Harris, Rencher N., 111
Harris, Richard H., 125
Hastie, Roberta Childs, 71
Hastie, William Henry, Jr., 70–71, 106, 120, 131, 133, 135, 138, 139, 145
Hatch, Robert Clinton, 143–44
Hawkins, Augustus F., 145
Hayes, Clarence A., 19, 22
Hayes, Fannie, 40
Hayes, Roland Wiltse, 40–41, 72
Hayes, William, 40
Hayes, Woody, 180
HBCUs (historically Black colleges and universities), 194–95, 206, 276, 279; opinions on Proposition 48, 238–39. *See also* Black higher education
Hedgeman, Anna Arnold, 184–85
Height, Dorothy I., 184
Heir of Slaves, The (Pickens), 54
Hendley, Charles Vergne, 28
Henry, Aaron Edd, 190
Heron, Gil-Scott, 199
Heslip, Jesse Solomon, 27, 35, 36
Higginbotham, Aloysius Leon, Jr., 227
Higginbotham, Evelyn Brooks, 267
Hill, Anthony C., 265–66
Hill, Jesse, Jr., 227
Hill, Leander Raymond, 79
Hill, Oliver, 160, 180
Hill, W. E., 58
Hill, William D., 111
History of Omega Psi Phi Fraternity, The (Dreer), 3, 67, 74
HIV/AIDS epidemic, 204, 232
Hobson, Maurice, 194
Hodges, Luther H., 161–62
Hoffman, Beatrix, 191
Holeman, Lonnie, 245
Holland, James Phillip, 161, 194–95, 326n213
Holliday, Harold Lee "Doc," Jr., 226
Hollowell, Donald Lee, 208
Holmes, Clarence F., Jr., 37, 39
Holmes, Hamilton, 178
Holmes, Norman Alonzo, 25
Hood, James, 183
Hooks, Benjamin Lawson, 200, 224, 227, 235, 257
Hope, John, 58
Hopkins, Thomas J., 58
Horne, Frank S., 120, 130, 131, 134
Houser, George M., 135
Houston, Charles Hamilton, 136, 155, 160
Houston, Gordon David, 26, 40, 85
Howard, Theodore Roosevelt Mason, 163
Howard University: administration's resistance to Omega Psi Phi, 21, 22; Beta chapter of Alpha Phi Alpha, 17; curriculum, 14–15, 275; history and overview, 11–16; interfraternal committee, 28–29; Mordecai Johnson's presidency, 85–86;

NAACP branch, 24; racial integration conference (1952), 153–54; Student Army Training Camp, World War I, 36–37
Howard University Journal, 23, 25, 27, 35
Howard University Medical Department, 45
Howard University Record, 14
Hughes, James Mercer Langston, 1, 78, 101, 193, 202, 212, 253, 256
Humphrey, Hubert Horatio, Jr., 190, 332n85
Humphries, Frederick S., 239
Hunt, James Baxter, Jr., 232
Hunter, Charlayne, 178
Hurricane Katrina, 267
Hurst, John, 52
Hurt, Edward P., 163–64
Hyman, Mark, 20

Ickes, Harold L., 106
Iles, Mark A., 234–35
Imhotep National Conference on Hospital Integration, 190–91
Immigration and Nationality Act (1952), 157
Inborden, T. S., 31
Indiana State Teachers College/State University, 136–137
Indiana University, 5, 13, 137, 146, 195
individualism vs. collectivism, 115
Ingram v. Wesley, 66
In Search of Sisterhood (Giddings), 5
Iota Phi Theta Fraternity, 5
Isabel, George A., 120
Ivey, James W., 150

Jackson, Emory Overton, 186–87, 217
Jackson, Jesse Louis, Sr.: awards and honors, 201, 235; Founders' Day ceremony, 266; as Second Vice Grand Basileus, 183, 185; Martin Luther King's assassination, 200; Operation PUSH, 217, 227; presidential campaign, 1, 4, 204, 234, 235–37, 240; on Proposition 48, 239–40
Jackson, Luther Porter, 1, 148–49
Jackson, Mahalia, 185
Jackson, Maynard Holbrook, Jr., 261
Jackson, Oliver, 181

Jacobs, Cary D., 6, 158, 181, 185–86
Jacobs, Jerry, 231–32
James, Emory A., 120
James, Robert Earl, Sr., 227
Jason, William Barrington, 22, 23, 30, 90
Jefferson, Michael Anthony, 252–53
Jeffries, Judson L., 4, 181
Jessye, Eva, 185
Jewell, Paul V., 89
Jim Crow laws, 27, 34, 48, 253; Committee Against Jim Crow, 136, 153
Johnson, Campbell Carrington, 63, 66, 107, 108, 109, 120, 129–30, 133, 138
Johnson, Fred D., 65, 69
Johnson, Henry Calvin "Hank," Jr., 273
Johnson, James R., 22
Johnson, James Weldon, 6, 253
Johnson, Lincoln, 80
Johnson, Lyndon Baines, 190, 198, 200, 208, 209, 273
Johnson, Mordecai Wyatt, 85, 99, 128, 153
Johnson, Walter, 262
Johnson, Walter Thaniel, Jr., 182
Johnson C. Smith University, 37, 54, 58, 84–85, 90, 139, 192, 218. *See also* Biddle University
Jones, Benjamin H., 19, 22
Jones, Dewey R., 106
Jones, Hiram F., 184
Jones, LeRoi, 188
Jones, Madison S., Jr., 150
Jones, Thomas B., 151
Jones, Thomas Jesse, 47–48
Jones, Woodrow H., 160–61
Jordan, Lloyd J., 250–51, 265
Jordan, Michael Jeffrey, 4, 256
Jordan, Vernon Eulion, Jr., 4, 208–9, 211–12, 217–18, 227, 257
Joseph Keasley Brick Agricultural, Industrial, and Normal School, 30–31, 196
Journal of Negro History, 2, 26, 42, 72, 108
Journey of Reconciliation, 135
Julian, Percy Lavon, 60–61, 101, 114, 122, 151, 256
Just, Charles Fraser, Jr., 31

Just, Ernest Everett: commemorative stamp, 263; death of, 121–23; family and education, 31–32; foundation of Omega Psi Phi, 1, 2, 11, 16–20; Founders' Memorial, 219; as honorary member, 40; honored at Washington Conclave (1924), 72; legacy of, 252; memorial tributes, 222, 255; on Omega Psi Phi's mission, 43; *The Oracle* (June 1919), 274; teaching career, 14–15, 285n15
Just, Inez, 121
Just, Mary Mathews Cooper, 31

Kappa Alpha Psi Fraternity, 5, 13–14, 36, 59, 69, 78, 137
Keese, Wallace, 245
Kelfa-Caulker, Richard Edmund, 180
Kelly, Marvin, 199
Kennedy, Howard, 41
Kennedy, J. A., 124
Kennedy, John Fitzgerald, 177–81, 185; assassination of, 187–88
Kennedy, Robert Francis, 178–80, 190; assassination of, 201
Kennedy, William Jesse, III, 227
Kent College of Law, 121
Kentucky State College/University, 113, 115, 224
Kerner, Otto, Jr., 198–99
Kerner Commission, 198–99
Kilgore, Thomas, Jr., 183
Kilimanjaro, John Stevenson Marshall, 217
Kimball Union Academy, 32
Kimbrough, Charles Talmage, 25, 57
King, Coretta Scott, 164, 200
King, Kermit Clifford, 181
King, Martin Luther, Jr., 162, 164, *174*, 176–177, 179, 182, 183, 230, 231; assassination of, 200, 263; "I Have a Dream" speech, 234; March on Washington, 184
Kittrell College, 85
Knight, Oscar E., 115
Knox, Antonio, 273
Knoxville Medical College, 45
Kornegay, Hobart, *173*
Ku Klux Klan, 26, 62, 80, 105, 186
Kyle, Earle F., 52

Lane, David A., 124
Lassiter, Thomas A., 139
Lawrence, Robert Henry, Jr., 1, 229, 343n130
Lawson, Bedford Vance, Jr., 136
Laybourn, Wendy M., 3
Leadership Conference on Civil Rights, 218
Lee, Warren G., Jr., 267
LeMoyne College/LeMoyne-Owen College, 113, 115, 224
Leonard Medical School, 45
"Letter from Birmingham Jail" (King), 182
Lewis, Clarence O., 19, 22
Lewis, Edward T., 212
Lewis, John, *174*, 183, 184
Lewis, Orville Maurice, 125
Lewis, Stephen J., 64
Lightner, Clarence, 216
Lillie, Frank Rattray, 32–33
Lincoln, Abraham, 25
Lincoln, Charles Eric, 253
Lincolnian, 24–25
Lincoln University (Missouri), 90
Lincoln University (Pennsylvania), 2, 24–25, 26, 39, 48, 49, 51, 53, 54, 59, 61, 64, 68, 70–71, 78, 88, 124, 149, 199, 200, 223
Lindsey, Treva B., 4
Little Rock Central High School, 165–66
Livingston, Loveless Benjamin, Jr., 234–35, 237–38, 258–59, 267
Livingston, Loveless Benjamin, Sr., 240
Livingstone College, 79, 86, 88, 90, 144, 151
Locke, Alain, 13, 77–78
Logan, Rayford Whittingham, 12, 145
Looby, Grafta Mosby, 177
Looby, Zephaniah Alexander, 59, 69, 120–21, 122, 128–29, 131, 133, 139, 177, 211; National Social Action Committee, 130
Love, Edgar Amos, 116, 162, 164; death, 213; family and education, 29–30; foundation of Omega Psi Phi, 1, 2, 11, 16–20, 22–23; Founders' Memorial, 219; at Golden Anniversary Grand Conclave, 180; as Alpha chapter Keeper of Records, 21–22; Kelly Miller's essay contest, 23; legacy of,

252; lifelong involvement in Omega Psi Phi, 165, 189, 191, 195, 201; memorial tributes, 213–14, 223; National Social Action Committee, 130; Pi Omega chapter, 52; speech at Philadelphia Conclave (1936), 117
Love, Harold M., Jr., 279
Love, John W., 63, 66, 67, 108; law practice, 130
Love, Jon Edgar, 213
Love, Julius C., 29
Love, Julius H., 19, 22
Love, Susie Carr, 29
Love, Virginia Louise, 213
Love, William A., 19, 22
Lovejoy, Elijah Parish, 66
Lowndes County Freedom Organization, 189, 193
Lucas, Cleotha Payne, 214
Lucas, John H., 173
Lucy, Autherine, 163
Lynching in America (Equal Justice Initiative), 49
Lythcott, George I., 56

Maddox, Lester Garfield, Sr., 192
Malcolm X, 181–82, 187–88, 199, 230
Malone, Annie Minerva, 66
Malone, Vivian, 183
Mangun, Kimberley, 186
manhood as principle, 18, 33, 180, 211
March on Washington (1963), 183, 184–86, 234
Marsh, William A., 152
Marshall, Charles Herbert, 66, 72
Marshall, Emmett J., 114
Marshall, Thurgood, 132–33, 139–40, 141, 153–54, 155, 160
Martin, Lilla L., 59
Martin, Robert, 231–32
Martin, Tracy, 270
Martin, Trayvon Benjamin, 270–72
Martin, William, 115
Mason, J. Quintin, 184
May, Cornelius, 125
Maynard, William R., 143, 147

Mays, Benjamin Elijah, 1, 119, 144, 152, 154–55, 162, 178, 182, 184, 256; tribute to Cooper and Love, 209–11
Mays, Hezekiah, 154
Mays, Louvenia Carter, 154
Mazyck, Naomi Grant, 108
Mazyck, Walter H., 22, 75, 84, 87–89, 93, 102, 103, 106–10, 117; law practice, 130
McCain, John Sidney, III, 269
McCarran-Walter Act, 157
McClain, Julius S., 53, 75, 88–89, 90, 94
McClenny, Earl Hampton, Sr., 144
McCoy, Frank L., 111
McCoy, Lee Marcus, 77, 79, 86, 144
McDougald, Richard Lewis, 111
McGuire, Robert Grayson, Jr., 96
McKee, Adam E., 258, 262
McKenzie, Fayette Avery, 61
McKinney, George Kimbrough, 263
McKinney, Theophilus E., 83–85, 88, 89, 91
McKoy, James, 231–32
McLarrin, Otto, 214, 215–16
McLaurin v. Oklahoma State Regents, 150
McLeod, Egbert Chappelle, 144
McMillian, Kay W., 129
McMorries, James Crawford, 25, 26
McMorries, James O., 223
McMorries, John H., 24
McNair, Carol Denise, 186
McNair, Ronald Erwin, 1, 227–28, 243, 256
McNeil, Samuel, 181
Meares, George E., 181, 183–84, 189, 191–93, 198, 214
medical education, 45–46
Medicare, 190–91, 332n85
Meek, Kendrick, 265
Meharry Medical College, 45, 141, 177
Meier, August A., 181
Meredith, James, 182, 191
Milburn, Michael, 235
Miller, Dorsey C., 189, 260
Miller, Kelly, 6, 13, 22; on conservative Blacks, 69–70; essay competition, 23; mathematics course, 15; Negro Sanhedrin, 67
Mink Slide, Tennessee, riot, 131, 132–33

Index 365

Mis-Education of the Negro, The (Woodson), 42, 77
Mississippi Health Project (Alpha Kappa Alpha), 4
Mississippi Valley Historical Review, 108
Missouri ex rel. Gaines v. Canada, 140
Mitchell, Clarence Maurice, Jr., 227
Mondale, Walter F., 240
Moon, Henry Lee, 150
Moore, Harriette, 152–53
Moore, Harry T., 152–53
Moore, John, 214
Moore, Wayne, 231–32
Morehouse, Henry Lyman, 12–13
Morehouse College, 13, 119, 152
Morgan, Irene, 132
Morgan State College/University, 5, 29, 40, 52, 54, 63, 64, 77, 88, 128, 163–64, 181–82
Morgan v. Virginia, 132, 135, 138, 145
Morrill Land Grant Act (1890), 47, 74
Motley, Constance Baker, 160
Motley, Felmon Devoner, 236
Moton, Robert Russa, 69–70, 76, 81
Motown Records, 217
Moultrie, H. Carl, 144, 181, 184, 202, 211, 214, 234–35, 243–44
Movement for Economic Justice, 212
Muhammad, Elijah, 199, 217
Murchison, John Prescott, 64, 69, 75, 106, 112, 225
Murray, Milo C., 143, 147, 151

Nabrit, James Madison, Jr., 1, 58, 86–87, 130, 136, 154–56, 160, 163–64, 180, 251
Nabrit, Samuel Milton, 33, 163, 178
Napier, James Carroll, 40, 46, 72
National Advisory Commission on Civil Disorders, 198
National Association for the Advancement of Colored People (NAACP), 12, 24, 183, 193, 208; fund-raising, 235; and racial uplift, 25; Scottsboro Boys, 105; Spingarn Medal, 86, 148, 255; Spingarn Medals, 121; Supreme Court cases, 150–51; Wilkins' leadership, 224

National Association of Collegiate Deans and Registrars in Negro Schools, 83–85, 89, 91
National Association of Colored Women, 223, 308n1; *lifting as we climb* motto, 93
National Black Monitor magazine, 254
National Business League, 12
National Council of Negro Women, 184, 215, 223
National Institute of Science, 33
National Labor Relations Act (1935), 114
National Medical Association, 209
National Medical College, Louisville, Kentucky, 45
National Pan-Hellenic Council (NPHC), 29, 93, 229, 254, 273
National Student Anti-Lynching League, 59
National Urban League, 138, 208, 209, 211
Nation of Islam, 181, 217
Neal, Alfred, 122
Negro History Week, 2, 43, 82–83, 222
Negro Literary Movement, 1; *See also* Harlem Renaissance
Negro Sanhedrin, 67, 74
Nelson, Dennis D., 124
Nelson, Richard York, 101
Nelson, William Stuart, 48, 50, 53, 68, 72–73, 79, 85, 99, 118, 143
Neshoba County, Mississippi, 233–34
Neusom, Daniel B., 236
Newman, Lloyd H., 39
Newman, Stephen Morrell, 35
New Negro, The (Locke), 77–78
New Negro movement, 78, 251, 265, 305n171
New Orleans Improvement Association, 165
Newsome, Clarence, 177
New South, 152, 221, 261
Newton, Isham Gregory, 177, 178, 202
New York Amsterdam News (newspaper), 62, 86, 97, 161, 201
Niagara Movement, 12, 21, 54
Nix, Robert Nelson Cornelius, Sr., 227
Nixon, Richard Milhous, 178, 217, 226, 263
Norfolk Journal and Guide (newspaper), 59, 84, 89, 102

Norman, Moses Conrad, Sr., 234–35, 240–41, 244, 258–59, 267
North Carolina A&T State University/ Negro Agricultural and Technical College, 83, 84, 88, 89, 90, 162, 164, 176, 227, 250
North Carolina Mutual Life Insurance Company, 110, 111, 115, 168, 227
Northwestern Trust Company, 99–100, 112
Norvell, Aubrey James, 191

Obama, Barack Hussein, II, 248, 268–73
Omega Bulletin, 119
"Omega Calls Her Sons of Light" (Dreer), 11, 27–28
"Omega Dear" (official hymn), 97, 148, 213
Omega Psi Phi and social action: African Project (1996), 262; Africare project (1974), 214; alcohol and drug abuse, 241; anti-lynching campaign, 114; Black Americans, educational opportunities for, 44–45; Black Brain Trust, 106; Black education reform, 65–66, 69–70; Black History movement, 56–57, 64; Black Identity Conference (1968), 199–200; campaign for Black history and Campaign for the Study of Negro Literature and History, 50, 74, 99; civil rights movement, 153–65, 185; Committee Against Jim Crow, 153; Credit Union, 257; desegregation efforts, 147–53; employment issues/assistance, 96–97, 98, 113–14, 120, 233; global Black community, 262–64; health issues, 215–16; homelessness, 241; housing assistance, 93, 146; illiteracy and educational standards, 254–55; National Social Action Committee, 130–31, 133–34, 137, 138, 141–43, 146, 157, 165; post–World War II civil rights activism, 127–39; Project Manhood, 244, 249, 257–58; Project Uplift, 208; Public Policy Forum, 248; scholarship funds, 205, 206; Social Action Committee, 213; social revolution (1970s), 206–12; Youth Leadership Council, 246–47

Omega Psi Phi chapters: Alpha, 2, 19, 21–22, 25, 26, 27, 28, 36, 37, 39, 48, 51, 53, 58, 59, 63, 64, 69, 85, 88, 99, 104, 107, 108, 113, 121, 122, 125, 130, 157, 158, 223; Alpha Alpha, 102; Alpha Omega, 184, 205, 228, 256; Alpha Psi, 79, 112; Alpha Sigma, 220; Beta, 2, 3, 6, 24–26, 39, 48, 49, 51, 53, 57, 59, 61, 64, 78, 88, 113, 199, 200, 223, 289n77; Beta Alpha Alpha, 260; Beta Phi, 111, 274; Beta Psi, 69, 220; Beta Sigma, 158; Chi, 55, 56, 264; Chi Alpha, 118; Chi Phi, 90; Chi Psi, 113; Chi Sigma, 136, 137; Chi Theta, 270, 278; Chi Zeta, 245; Delta, 39, 45–46, 48, 55, 56, 74, 79, 94, 119, 141; Delta Alpha, 110, 113; Delta Gamma, 152; Delta Kappa, 220, 274; Delta Omega, 141; Delta Psi, 99; Epsilon, 2, 39, 53, 65, 69, 78, 112, 118, 135, 181, 183, 191, 319n50; Epsilon Alpha, 113; Epsilon Iota, 156; Epsilon Iota Iota, 252; Epsilon Omega, 77; Epsilon Phi, 79, 224; Epsilon Psi, 78; Eta, 39, 52, 53, 63, 64; Eta Alpha, 113; Eta Omega, 69, 220; Eta Phi, 81; Eta Psi, 87, 125; Gamma, 2, 3, 26, 40, 51, 55, 56, 62, 70, 81, 84, 89, 154, 176, 197, 223, 288n55; Gamma Nu, 269; Gamma Sigma, 117, 144, 162, 274; Iota, 39, 53, 63, 110; Iota Iota, 269; Iota Omega, 76; Iota Psi, 87, 147, 160; Kappa, 39, 57, 69; Kappa Lambda, 269, 274; Kappa Omega, 70; Kappa Psi, 87; Lambda, 39, 53, 63, 70, 123; Lambda Alpha, 158; Lambda Epsilon, 235; Lambda Iota, 231; Lambda Omega, 78; Lambda Phi, 87; Lambda Psi, 90; Lambda Sigma, 118; Mu, 41, 53; Mu Alpha, 274; Mu Omega, 210; Mu Phi, 87, 145; Mu Psi, 90, 227; Mu Sigma, 118; Nu, 53; Nu Omega, 110, 229; Nu Phi, 87, 96; Nu Psi, 90; Nu Sigma, 118; Omicron, 69; Omicron Chi, 206; Omicron Phi, 87; Phi, 52; Phi Phi, 102; Phi Psi, 160; Pi, 52, 63, 64, 140, 295n33; Pi Alpha, 118; Pi Psi, 90, 110, 115; Pi Xi, 224–25; Psi, 3, 58, 69, 83, 115, 143, 147, 220, 260; Psi Phi, 102–3; Psi Psi, 113, 161; Rho, 58; Rho Alpha, 118; Rho Phi, 113, 118; Rho Psi, 94, 119, 120, 279; Rho Sigma, 136, 137; Sigma Alpha, 118,

Omega Psi Phi chapters (cont.) 152; Sigma Omega, 110; Sigma Phi, 143, 163; Sigma Psi, 100; Tau, 69, 220; Tau Alpha, 118; Tau Chi, 181; Tau Iota, 241; Tau Omega, 64, 89, 243; Tau Psi, 100; Theta, 107, 135, 178; Theta Omicron, 272; Theta Phi, 264; Theta Psi, 39, 87–88, 129, 134; Theta Rho, 218, 236–38; Theta Sigma, 165; Upsilon, 63, 110 135, 277; Upsilon Alpha, 118; Upsilon Omega, 86, 110; Upsilon Phi, 147; Upsilon Psi, 102; Upsilon Sigma, 274; Xi, 53, 64–65, 79, 256; Xi Alpha, 134; Xi Epsilon, 229; Xi Omega, 140, 156; Xi Phi, 87; Xi Psi, 90, 274; Xi Sigma, 118; Zeta, 32, 39, 51, 68–69, 102, 177, 236, 255; Zeta Alpha, 113; Zeta Epsilon, 137, 146; Zeta Phi, 116, 136, 137, 208, 235; Zeta Theta, 220

Omega Psi Phi Fraternity: academic literature concerning, 3; bookkeeping practices, 56; cardinal principles, 18–19, 27, 42, 46, 180, 206, 211, 227, 243, 251, 254–55; Committee on Recommendations, 75, 88; constitutional convention (1969), 202–3; current impact, 273–74, 278; dues and financial stability, 95–96, 102, 104, 129, 195–96; educational standards, 64, 80, 83–90; escutcheon design, 19–20; executive secretary position, 144; expansion/new chapters, 45–57, 75, 87–89; fiftieth anniversary, 176–82; foreign study committee, 68; foundation/creation, 16–20; Founders' Memorial, 214–15, 219; generational differences, 236, 245, 251–53, 277–78; global outreach, 268; during Great Depression, 92–118; growth and expansion post–World War I, 38–41; honorary members, 27, 39–41; inactive chapters, 104; internal reorganization (1922–24), 62–63; international chapters, 181, 224–25; legacy and impact, 1–2, 210–11; Membership Intake Program, 249–50; mission and goals, 1; motto, 19; Omega 2000, 258, 259–60; Omega Psi Phi World Center, 260; public debate on current issues, 68–69; resistance to, 20–25; structure and administration, 19, 74; "Sweetheart Song," 120; 21st-century challenges, 258–62; undergraduate vs. graduate chapters, 63; World War I, 33–38, 73–74; World War II, 118–25; Youth Leadership Council, 246–47

Omega Psi Phi Fraternity and the Men Who Made Its History, The (Gill), 3, 6, 197

Omega Psi Phi Grand Conclaves: First, Washington, DC (1912), 2; Fourth, Oxford, Pennsylvania (1915), 39; Fifth, Washington, DC (1916), 39; Sixth, Oxford, Pennsylvania (1917), 39; Seventh, Washington, DC (1917), 39; Eighth, Boston, Massachusetts (1919), 37–38; Ninth, Nashville, Tennessee (1920), 41–43, 45–46; Tenth, Atlanta, Georgia (1921), 54–56; Eleventh, Philadelphia, Pennsylvania (1922), 61–62; Twelfth, St. Louis, Missouri (1923), 65–66; Thirteenth, Washington, DC (1924),71–76, 106; Fourteenth, Tuskegee (1925), 80–83; Fifteenth, Chicago (1926), 86–89; Eighteenth, Baltimore, Maryland (1929), 93; Nineteenth, Detroit, Michigan (1930), 94–96; Twentieth, Richmond, Virginia (1932), 101–3, 106; Twenty-First, Durham, North Carolina (1933), 110–12; Twenty-Second, St. Louis, Missouri (1934), 113–14; Twenty-Third, Atlanta, Georgia (1935), 115; Twenty-Fourth, Philadelphia (1936), 115, 116–17; Twenty-Fifth, Cleveland, Ohio (1937), 115; Twenty-Sixth, Chicago (1938), 115, 118; Twenty-Seventh, New York City (1939), 118–19; Twenty-Eighth, Nashville, Tennessee (1940), 119–21; Twenty-Ninth, Indianapolis, Indiana (1941), 120, 121; Thirty-First, Washington, DC (1945), 128; Thirty-Second, Fort Worth (1946), 133–34; Thirty-Third, Detroit (1947), 137–39; Thirty-Fourth, Columbus, Ohio (1948), 142–43; Thirty-Fifth, Chicago (1949), 146–47; Thirty-Sixth, Boston, (1950), 151–52; Thirty-Seventh, Miami (1951), 152–53; Thirty-Eighth, Philadelphia (1952), 157; Thirty-Ninth, Cincinnati,

Ohio (1953), 158; Fortieth, Atlanta, Georgia (1954), 161; Forty-Second, Baltimore (1956), 163–65; Forty-Sixth, San Antonio, Texas (1960), 178; Forty-Seventh, Washington, DC (1961), 179–81; Forty-Ninth, Denver, Colorado (1964), 189; Fiftieth, Detroit, Michigan (1965), 191; Fifty-First, Boston (1967), 197–98; Fifty-Second, Charlotte, North Carolina (1968), 201–2; Fifty-Third, Pittsburgh, Pennsylvania, (1970), 202, 205; Fifty-Sixth, Phoenix, Arizona, (1974), 216–17; Fifty-Seventh, Atlanta, Georgia (1976), 220; Fifty-Eighth, New Orleans (1977), 225; Sixty-Second, Kansas City, Missouri (1983), 235; Sixty-Third, Louisville, Kentucky (1984), 240–42; Sixty-Fourth, Washington, DC (1986), 244; Sixty-sixth, Detroit, Michigan (1990), 256; Sixty-Seventh, Atlanta, Georgia (1992), 255–56; Sixty-Eighth, Cleveland, Ohio (1994), 260; Sixty-Ninth, Los Angeles (1996), 264; Seventieth, New Orleans, Louisiana (1998), 265–66; Seventy-First, Indianapolis, Indiana (2000), 265; Seventy-Second, Charlotte, North Carolina (2002), 267; Seventy-Fourth, Little Rock, Arkansas (2006), 267; Seventy-Fifth, Birmingham, Alabama (2008), 268; Seventy-Sixth, Raleigh, North Carolina (2010), 269; Seventy-Seventh, Washington, DC (2011), 269; Houston (1931) cancellation, 99–100; World War II hiatus, 123
O'Neal, Shaquille Rashaun, 260
O'Neil, Bobby, 199
Operation People United to Save Humanity (PUSH), 217, 234
Oracle, The, 2, 6, 22; on Black education, 65, 80; on Black History movement, 56–57; civil rights movement coverage, 135, 177, 183–84; on economic recovery, 114–15; "Economic Status of the Negro," 112; establishment of, 38–39; on expansion at majority-White campuses, 91; Great Depression issue (April 1932), 101; on impact of Grand Conclaves, 94–95; Jesse Jackson's presidential bid, 235–36; mission and function, 254–55; on Nashville Conclave (1920), 42–43, 48, 49; "The Negro in the American Chaos," 112–13; scholarship, emphasis on, 60–61; "To an African Mask" (Ferguson), 99; Walter Herbert Mazyck tribute issue, 109
Oswald, Lee Harvey, 187
Out of the House of Bondage (Miller), 23
Owens, Robert N., 115
Oxley, Lawrence August: advocacy for social welfare programs, 190–91; on Black advancement/justice, 98–99, 104; on economic difficulties (1930s), 110, 112–13; as Grand Basileus, 102–4, 106, 108–9, 115, 117; on national defense, World War II, 120

Paine College, 85, 88
Pan-African Congresses, 34, 53, 68, 118–19
Parker, Don Carlos, 117
Parks, Gregory S., 3
Parks, Rosa Louise, 162
Parrish, Charles Henry, Sr., 77, 86
Patrick, Marvin, 231–32
Patterson, John M., 179
Paul, William C., 116
Payne, Aaron H., 86
Payne, William K., 145
Penn, Harry T., 137–38, 139, 142, 143, 146, 147
Penn, William Fletcher, 55
perseverance as principle, 18–19, 33, 211
Pershing, John Joseph, 35
Peterson, Oscar, 218
Phi Beta Kappa (academic honor society), 60–61, 71, 160
Phi Beta Sigma Fraternity, 5, 59, 183
Philadelphia, Pennsylvania, 61–62
Philadelphia Negro, The (Du Bois), 61–62
Philadelphia Tribune (newspaper), 102, 117
Pickens, William, 40, 54–55, 62, 64
Picott, J. Rupert, Sr., 222
Pietro, Alonzo, 81
Pinchback, Pinckney Benton Stewart, 255
Pinkston, Frank G., 177
Player, Willa Beatrice, 162
Pleasants, William H., 19, 22

Plessy v. Ferguson, 253
Poro College, 66
Potts, John Foster, Sr., 158–59, 160, 161, 178
poverty, 34, 199, 208, 218, 225, 243
Powell, Adam Clayton, Jr., 136, 228
Powell, Colin Luther, 266–67
Pratt, Harry F., 52
Princip, Gavrilo, 33
Prohibition (Volstead Act), 69
Project Uplift, 208
Proposition 48, 238–39
Proposition 209, 264
Pruitt, Audrey, 189, 191
Pullen, Don Q., 120
Purdue University, 136–137
Purnell, John H., 63, 64, 65–66, 86, 113, 117

Que Dog culture, 246, 278

racial issues: abolitionism, 61–62; anti-lynching campaigns, 55, 58, 59–60, 111, 114; armed forces during World War II, 119–20, 123–24; Black leadership, need for, 229–30; Black pride/White resistance, 80; desegregation, 147–53; economic inequality, 233, 278, 338n34; housing discrimination, 134; international perspectives on, 114–15, 143; lynching, 45–46, 49–50, 131; Northern states contrasted with Southern, 26–27; pleas for peace and non-violence, 37–38; racial profiling by law enforcement, 204; school desegregation, 153–54; Scottsboro Boys court case, 104–5; segregation, 143, 146–47; stereotypes and misinformation concerning Black Americans, 73; Veterans Administration and discrimination, 138; White academic leadership, dangers of, 77–78; White atonement, 62; White backlash/resistance, 139–47, 165, 220–21. *See also* civil rights movement; White supremacy
racial uplift, 19, 33, 40, 144, 211
Rainbow Coalition, 234
Randolph, A. Philip, 136, *174*, 183, 184, 218
Ray, Andrew A., 269, 273

Ray, Charles A., 156
Rayford, Lee, 124
Reagan, Ronald Wilson, 233–34, 237, 240
Reed, George, 69
Regents of the University of California v. Bakke, 225–26, 232
Reid, Ira De Augustine, 93, 96–97, 130–31, 133, 141
Reynolds, Grant, 135–36, 138, 142, 147, 153, 156, 158–59, 183, 214
Richardson, Cordell, 199
Riddick, Walter H., 158, 181, 189, 191
Ridley, Walter Nathaniel, 1, 101, 158, 164, 180
Roberts, George Spencer "Spanky," 124, *169, 171,* 266
Robertson, Carole Rosamond, 186
Robeson, Paul, 230
Robinson, Darryl, 245–46
Robinson, David, 182
Robinson, Jackie, 138–39
Robinson, Raymond G., 48, 52
Robinson, Spottswood William, III, 160, 180, 227, 251
Rockefeller, John D., Jr., 144
Roger Williams University, 76, 86
Roman, Charles Victor, 40, 46, 64
Romney, Willard Mitt, 270–71
Roosevelt, Eleanor, 106
Roosevelt, Franklin Delano, 92, 105–6, 123, 130, 183, 215
Ross, Quinton T., Jr., 274
Rowan, Carl T., 156
Royer, Harvey John, 229
Rust College, 77, 86, 88, 139, 257
Rustin, Bayard, 135, 165, *174*, 176–77, 182, 183, 253, 277
Rutherford, Samuel Wilson, 98, 103

sacrifice, ideal of, 74
Sanders, Crystal R., 76
Sanford, Florida, 270–71
Sankofa, 250, 347n4
Saulter, Charles Reed, 25
scholarship as principle, 18, 33, 60–61, 180, 211

Schwerner, Michael, 233
Scott, Simon H., Jr., 218
Scottsboro Boys, 104–5, 114
Seabrook, James Ward, 151
segregation: on college campuses, 146–47, 182–83; in Florida, 143; Ford's Theater (Baltimore), 140, 181; Omega members' experiences of, 236
Servicemen's Readjustment Act (1944), 127, 160
Seventeenth Provisional Training Regiment, 35, 36
Sharpp, Samuel, 188
Shaw, Herbert Bell, 218, 227
Shaw University, 99
Shelby County v. Holder, 273
Shepard, Ann, 231–32
Shepard, Samuel R., 235–36
Shepherd, James E., 111
Sheridan, Richard Brinsley, 15
Sherrod, Charles, 177
Sick and Tired of Being Sick and Tired (Smith), 4
Sidat-Singh, Wilmeth W., 125
Sigma Gamma Rho Sorority, 5
Sigma Pi Phi Fraternity, 5, 214, 297n47
Simmons College, 77, 86, 100
Sims, David Henry, 77, 86
Sipuel, Ada Lois, 139
Sipuel v. Board of Regents of the University of Oklahoma, 139–40, 150
Sirhan, Sirhan Bishara, 201
Sixteenth Street Baptist Church, Birmingham, Alabama, 186
slavery, impact of, 23, 46–47
Smith, Alfred E., 106
Smith, Chester, 137
Smith, Gentry O., 269
Smith, Marcellus G., *169*
Smith, Sherman, 216
Smith, Susan L., 4
social gospel theology, 29–30
Social Security Act (1935), 114
Soul of Omega, The (Yeldell), 3
Souls of Black Folk, The (Du Bois), 19

Southern Christian Leadership Conference (SCLC), 165, 176–77, 182, 231, 232
Southern University, 158, 239
South to Freedom (Rowan), 156
Spaulding, Asa Timothy, 110, 115, 146, *168*
Spaulding, Charles Clinton, 111
Spaulding, George H., 164
Spectrum: A Journal on Black Men, 4
Spingarn, Joel Elias, 24, 34–35
Stephenson, Gladys, 131
Stephenson, James, 131
Sterrett, Paris V., 116
Stewart, J. D., 88–89
Stewart, John S., 111
Student Nonviolent Coordinating Committee (SNCC), 192, 193, 232, 233
Suman, John R., 144
Sumner, Charles, 25
Sumner Normal School, 63, 69
Sweatt, Heman Marion, 150
Sweatt v. Painter, 150, 156
Sykes, Frank "Doc" Jehoy, 104–5, 114

"talented tenth," 12–13, 29, 38–39
Taylor, Breonna, 278
Taylor, Daniel B., 75, 88–89, 93, 99
Taylor, Kenneth, 234–35
Taylor, Robert Robinson, 81
Tennessee A&I State Normal School for Negroes / Tennessee State University, 74–75, 77, 86, 94, 149, 279
Terrell, Mary Eliza Church, 19, 93, 223
Thirkield, Wilbur Patterson, 21, 22, 32
Thomas, Harold Hillyer, 49, 50, 51, 52, 58, 111
Thomas, Jesse O., 114, 116
Thomas, Julius A., 37, 38
Thompson, Harold D., 191, 195–96
Thompson, John Robert, 238
Thorpe, Earl E., 1
Till, Emmett, 161
Till-Mobley, Mamie Elizabeth, 161
Tindall, Connie, 231–32
"To an African Mask: A New Negro Litany" (Ferguson), 99
Toles, William, 218
Tolson, Melvin Beaunorus, 6

Index 371

Toppin, Edgar Allan, Sr., 219
Townsend, Jackson "Jack," 115
Trent, William Johnson, Jr., 120, 151
Trent, William Johnson, Sr., 55, 79, 85, 86, 90, 144
Truman, Harry S., 142, 144, 157, 190, 191
Tucker, Carlyle M., 96
Tucker, Herbert E., Jr., 147, 158, 161, 163, 177, 180, 184, 258–59, 267
Tucker, Robert H., 181
Tulsa, Oklahoma, race massacre (1921), 52–53, 60, 150, 296n36
Turner, Charles H., II, 250, 256
Tuskegee, Alabama: Omega Psi Phi Conclave (1925), 80–83; Tuskegee Airmen, *171*; Tuskegee Army Air Field, 124–25; Tuskegee Institute, 13, 69, 76; Tuskegee Institute Singers, 233
Tutu, Desmond Mpilo, 262

United Negro College Fund, 144, 151, 206, 209, 257
Universal Negro Improvement Association, 53
University of West Tennessee, 45
uplift, racial, as principle, 19, 33, 144, 211
Urban League, 212

Vaughn, George L., 75, 81, 87, 90, 251
Vereen, Willie, 231–32
Villa, Francisco "Pancho," 35
Virginia Mutual Benefit Life Insurance Company, 103
Virginia Theological Seminary and College, 77, 86
Voice from the South, A (Cooper), 19
Volstead Act, 69
Voorhees School and Junior College, 160
Voter Education Project, 208–9
voting rights, 48–49, 92, 102, 220–22; Freedom Summer, 189–90; Voting Rights Act (1965), 190, 193, 218, 222, 234, 273

Waddell, William H., 124
Wake Forest Journal of Law and Policy, 3
Walcott, Louis Eugene, 242

Walker, James A., *169*
Walker, LeRoy, 261
Wallace, George, 182–83
Wallace, Henry A., 128
Waller, Garnett Russell, 21
Walton, Elbert A., 234–35
Ward, Joseph H., 76, 81
War on Poverty, 218
Washington, Booker Taliaferro, 13, 69–70, 76
Washington, Charles B., 19, 22
Washington, DC, 14
Washington, Gregory, 274
Washington, Harold, 234
Washington, Walter Edward, 227
Wayne State University, 118
Weatherless, Ellis B., 202
Weaver, Frederick S., 120
Weaver, Mortimer G., 89
Weaver, Robert Clifton, 106, 120, 134, 179–80
Weiseger, James Arthur, 111, 115–16, 139, 318n14
Wesley, Carter Walker, 60, 66
Wesley, Charles H., 122
Wesley, Cynthia Dionne, 186
West, James O., 197
Westmoreland, Edgar P., 19, 22
West Virginia Collegiate Institute / West Virginia State University, 87–88, 124, 134–35
Wheeler, John Hervey, 111, 161–62, *168*
White, Charles W., 64
White House Fatherhood and Mentoring Initiative, 272, 273
White supremacy, 12, 133–34, 263, 264–65; in 21st century, 250; Birmingham, Alabama, targeting of, 186; in science fields, 33; Wilmington, North Carolina riot (1971), 231–32. *See also* civil rights movement; racial issues
Wilberforce University, 135, 257
Wilder, Lawrence Douglas, Jr., 236, 237, 255–56, 349n29
Wiley, George Alvin, 212
Wiley College, 135, 257
Wilkins, Earl, 83

Wilkins, Roy O., 53, 150, 161, 164–65, *174*, 183–85, 218, 219–20; NAACP leadership, 224
Wilkinson, Garnet C., 40, 62, 64, 85
Wilkinson, Robert Shaw, 90, 100–101, 107, 159
Williams, Arthur Daniel, 59–60
Williams, Daniel K., 274
Williams, Eddie, 220–21
Williams, John W., 236
Williams, Millard Curtis, 163
Williams, Nathaniel D., 129
Williams, Paul Revere, 70, 83, 123, 145
Wilmington Ten, 231–32
Wilson, Charlotte "Lottie," 24–25, 288n74
Wilson, Thomas Woodrow, 34, 250
Wimberley, Frank H., 19, 22, 23, 28, 53
Woods, Robert Clisson, 77, 86
Woodson, Carter Godwin: Association for the Study of Negro Life and History, 74, 91, 250; background and overview, 2, 26–27; Black History and culture, 7, 9, 53; Black issues during World War I, 34; death and legacy, 148–49; as honorary member, 40; honored at Washington Conclave (1924), 72; *Journal of Negro History*, 108; legacy and impact, 253, 256; memorial tributes, 219, 222, 236; Negro History Week, 82–83; Ninth Grand Conclave, 41–43, 46, 64, 293n163; photo, *167*; on White academic leaders, 77
Woodson, Robert Leon, Sr., 243
Woodson Adopt-A-School Program, 256
Work, John Wesley, Jr., 76, 86
World War I, 33–38
World War II, 118–25; Double V campaign, 126, 206, 265, 277
Wrenn, Walter, 262
Wright, Charles, 229–30, 232
Wright, William "Joe," 229, 231–32

Xavier University (Louisiana), 118

Yale Law Journal, 55
Yeldell, Kyle, 3
Young, Andrew, 261
Young, Charles D.: Charles Young Memorial Sunday, 104; death, 57; Eighth Grand Conclave speech (1919), 37; as honorary member, 34, 40, 57; memorial tributes, 58, 69, 73, 78, 107, 134–35, 222; US Army service, 2, 35–36, 222; Youngsholm, 257; Young Scholarship for Foreign Study, 68
Young, Whitney Moore, Jr., *174*, 183, 184, 209

Zeta Phi Beta Sorority, 5, 59